The Creation of States
in International Law

The Creation
of States in
International Law

James Crawford

Clarendon Press · Oxford
1979

Oxford University Press, Walton Street, Oxford OX2 6DP

OXFORD LONDON GLASGOW
NEW YORK TORONTO MELBOURNE WELLINGTON
NAIROBI DAR ES SALAAM CAPE TOWN
KUALA LUMPUR SINGAPORE JAKARTA HONG KONG TOKYO
DELHI BOMBAY CALCUTTA MADRAS KARACHI

Published in the United States by
Oxford University Press, New York

© *James Crawford 1979*

British Library Cataloguing in Publication Data
  Crawford, James
    The creation of states in international law.
    1. State succession
    2. States, New
    I. Title
    341.26   JX4053   78-40308

  ISBN 0-19-825347-8

Typset by CCC at William Clowes & Sons Limited
Beccles and London

Foreword

A MAJOR study of the creation of States has long been wanted. Scholars are commonly diverted from areas of the first importance by the lure of the more conspicuously up-to-date, and by a concern to avoid the more extensive zones of inquiry. Another factor is a reserve in the face of material which is said to be 'political' and, therefore, not a proper subject of legal analysis. Dr. Crawford has had the nerve and the energy to tackle a set of problems central to the workings of state relations. In doing so he has not only teased out a range of difficult questions of principle but has also provided a most useful handbook of information on the formation and extinction of states and the related phenomena of mandates, trusteeships, non-self-governing territories, international dispositive powers, and collective recognition.

It is a pleasant task to introduce a work which will make a considerable contribution to the literature both of international law and of international relations in the broader context. The book is a fairly reduced version of a very substantial text submitted for the degree of Doctor of Philosophy at Oxford. Since I acted as supervisor, I can claim a certain credit in the manner of an impresario. By the same token, the performance was Dr. Crawford's.

IAN BROWNLIE

31 January 1977

Preface

SINCE THE development of the modern international system, statehood has been regarded as the paramount type of international personality; indeed, in doctrine if not in practice, States were for a time regarded as the only international persons. This is no longer so; but the political paramountcy of States over other international actors, with whatever qualifications, continues, and statehood remains the central type of legal personality. Problems of definition, and of application of the definition, of statehood thus occupy an important place in the structure of international law. None the less, the topic of statehood has been rather neglected by writers. There is an abundance of practice, a surprising volume of case law, and a large number of studies of particular instances or problems of territorial status. The general treatises all contain the mandatory section on statehood and legal personality, and some of these treatments are of a high order. But, apart from Marek's study on identity and continuity of States (published in 1954 and reissued in 1968), and various accounts of recognition of States in books on recognition generally, there is, to the writer's knowledge, no monograph dealing with the topic of statehood as such, in the light of the substantial modern practice in that field. This observation is not of course original: the writer's interest in the topic was engaged by observations in two leading works to this effect.[1] This study attempts to deal with the representative modern doctrine and practice in relation to the public international law of statehood and territorial status; and thus, however inadequately, to contribute to filling the void mentioned by Professors Jennings and Brownlie.

Perhaps the most controversial issue in this area is the relationship between statehood and recognition. The view that recognition is constitutive of State personality derives historically from the positive theory of international obligation. However, this view does not correspond with State practice; nor is it adopted by most modern writers. On the other hand, in this as in

[1] Jennings, *Acquisition of Territory*, 11–12; Brownlie, *Principles*, 74.

other areas, relevant State practice—including recognition practice, especially where recognition is granted or withheld on grounds of the status of the entity in question—is of considerable importance. Against this background, this study examines the criteria for statehood in international law, and the various ways in which new States have been created in the period since 1815.

Traditionally, the criteria for statehood have been regarded as resting solely on considerations of effectiveness. Entities with a reasonably defined territory, a permanent population, a more or less stable government and a substantial degree of independence of other States have been treated as States. Other factors, such as permanence, willingness to obey international law, and recognition, have usually been regarded as of rather peripheral importance. To some extent this represents the modern position. However, several qualifications are necessary.

In the first place, this standard view is too simple. Much depends on the claims made by the entities in question, and on the context in which such claims are made. In some circumstances, criteria such as independence or stable government may be treated as flexible or even quite nominal; in other cases they will be strictly applied. Apart however from the necessary elaboration of the criteria for statehood based on effectiveness, a serious question arises whether new criteria have not become established, conditioning claims based on effectiveness by reference to fundamental considerations of legality. Practice in the field of self-determination territories is the more developed, but the same problem arises in relation to entities created by illegal use of force. These criteria, taken together, are on the whole reflected in United Nations practice; they also provide a flexible but generally applicable standard against which to consider the status of the numerous unusual or 'anomalous' territorial entities (Taiwan, the Holy See, Andorra, and so on).

Problems of the creation of States have commonly been regarded as matters 'of fact and not of law'. This view was again simplistic, since it assumed the automatic identification of States, whether by recognition or the application of criteria based on effectiveness. In practice, identification and application of the criteria to specific cases or problems raise interesting and difficult problems, some of which are dealt with in Part II of this study. These problems do not of course occur in isolation; they are classifications, rather than exclusive mandatory 'modes' of the creation of States. However, the problems discussed in each context (dependent States, devolution, secession, and so on) have common features which justify such separate classification.

Superimposed on these classifications of the methods of the creation of States are the various more overtly international competences or authorities affecting the creation of States: these are dealt with in Part III. The problem of international powers of disposition has attracted a good deal of practice since 1815. More specifically, the development of self-government of colonial territories under the Mandate and Trusteeship systems, and pursuant to Chapter XI of the Charter (non-self-governing territories) has attracted a substantial body of practice.

Finally, certain incidents of the creation of States, such as commencement or acquisition of territory by new States, and certain related problems (identity, continuity, reversion, and extinction) are discussed in a concluding section.

So far as is possible, the text is correct to 31 December 1977.

NOTE

In this study, the word 'State' in the sense of the political unit will be capitalized. This practice avoids confusion with other meanings of the word, and is as recommended in Fowler's *Modern English Usage*. The State is not however allocated a sex: where necessary the pronouns 'it' and 'its' are used.

See also Dowdall, 'The Word "State"' (1923), 39 *LQR* 98–125, 98.

Acknowledgements

THIS STUDY is a revised and condensed version of a thesis submitted in 1976 for the degree of Doctor of Philosophy in the University of Oxford. Part of the research was done while I was at University College, Oxford, under an Australian Shell Scholarship: the remainder, and the bulk of the writing, was completed in Adelaide. During this time, I was fortunate in having as supervisor Professor Ian Brownlie. Professor Brownlie's rigorous but sympathetic guidance and advice have been invaluable. I wish to thank my examiners, Professor James Fawcett of King's College, London, and Dr. Maurice Mendelson of St. John's College, Oxford, for their valuable criticism and for the tolerance shown towards an over-large thesis. Professor D. P. O'Connell, Chichele Professor of Public International Law in the University of Oxford and formerly Professor of International Law in the University of Adelaide; Dr. J. M. Finnis, of University College, Oxford; Mr. E. Lauterpacht Q.C., Legal Adviser to the Australian Government; Professor Arthur Rogerson, Bonython Professor of Law in the University of Adelaide, and Dr. D. J. Devine, also made helpful comments or offers of assistance. I must also thank the following for their support and assistance: the Librarian and staff of the Law Library, the University of Adelaide; the Librarians and staff of the Bodleian Law and Codrington Libraries, Oxford; the Shell Company of Australia, and in particular Mr. R. L. Dahlenburg; the Chairman, Professor H. K. Lücke and members of the Department of Law in the University of Adelaide; Professor A. C. Castles; Mr. David St. L. Kelly, A.L.R.C.; Dr. Julius Varsanyi; Dr. R. S. White of the University of Newcastle-upon-Tyne; Mrs. J. Johnson and Mrs. J. Smith, who patiently deciphered the manuscript.

Finally, my deepest thanks are owed to my wife, Marisa Luigina, to whom this work is also dedicated, for her support and encouragement.

Adelaide
28 February 1977

Whereas the States of the world form a community
governed by international law . . .

*Draft Declaration on Rights and Duties
of States*, Preambular Paragraph 1, annexed
to G. A. Resolution 375(IV), 6 December 1949

Contents

Select Table of Abbreviations   *xxiii*

PART I: THE CONCEPT OF
STATEHOOD IN INTERNATIONAL LAW

1. STATEHOOD, RECOGNITION, AND INTERNATIONAL LAW   3

   1.1 Introductory   3

   1.2 Statehood in early international law   5

       (1) Doctrine   5

       (2) Some aspects of State practice   9

   1.3 Recognition and Statehood   10

       (1) The early view of recognition   10

       (2) Positivism and recognition   12

       (3) Statehood in nineteenth-century international law   12

   1.4 Recognition of States in modern international law   15

       (1) Introductory   15

       (2) Recognition: the great debate   16
           (i) The constitutive theory   17
           (ii) The declaratory theory   20

       (3) Conclusions   23

   1.5 Certain basic concepts   25

       (1) International legal personality   25

       (2) 'Sovereignty'   26

       (3) The distinction between 'State' and 'government'   27

       (4) The distinction between 'State personality' and 'State succession'   29

2. THE CRITERIA FOR STATEHOOD   31

   2.1 Introductory   31

   2.2 Classical criteria for Statehood   36

       (1) Defined territory   36

       (2) Permanent population   40

(3) Government 42

(4) Capacity to enter into relations with other States 47

(5) Independence 48

    (i) Separate existence within reasonably coherent frontiers 52

    (ii) Absence of subjection to the authority of another State or States 52

        (a) Formal independence 52

        (b) Actual independence 56

        (c) The relation between formal and actual independence 69

(6) Sovereignty 71

(7) Other criteria 71

    (i) Permanence 71

    (ii) Willingness and ability to obey international law 72

    (iii) A certain degree of civilization 73

    (iv) Recognition 74

    (v) Legal order 74

3. CRITERIA FOR STATEHOOD SUGGESTED AS A RESULT OF MODERN DEVELOPMENTS IN INTERNATIONAL LAW 77

3.1 Legality and Statehood 77

(1) *Jus cogens* in modern international law 79

    (i) Legal effects of *jus cogens* on acts or situations other than treaties 81

    (ii) Status of entities created by illegal treaties 82

(2) Illegality and Statehood: some tentative conclusions 83

3.2 Statehood and self-determination 84

(1) Self-determination in modern international law 85

    (i) Self-determination before 1945 85

    (ii) The principle of self-determination in the United Nations Charter 89

    (iii) Identifying the unit of self-determination: the problem of criteria 91

        (a) The mandate and trusteeship systems 92

        (b) Non-self-governing territories: Chapter XI of the Charter 92

        (c) Other cases of application of the principle to particular territorial disputes or situations 93

    (iv) The consequences of self-determination 94

(v) Conclusions   95

(2) Statehood and the operation of the principle of self-determination   102

(3) Self-determination and effectiveness: the case of Rhodesia   103

3.3 Entities created by the illegal use of force   106

(1) The relation between self-determination and the rules relating to the use of force   108

   (i) Assistance to established local insurgents   113

   (ii) Military intervention in aid of self-determination   114

3.4 Other cases   119

(1) Entities not claiming to be States   119

(2) Puppet States and the 1949 Geneva Conventions   119

(3) Apartheid and the Bantustan policy   120

(4) Violation of conventional stipulations providing for independence   120

3.5 Non-recognition in modern international law   120

(1) Non-recognition and territorial status   121

(2) The consequences of non-recognition   124

4. ISSUES OF STATEHOOD BEFORE UNITED NATIONS ORGANS   129

4.1 General considerations   129

4.2 League and United Nations membership   131

(1) Membership practice under the League of Nations   131

(2) The United Nations: original membership   132

(3) The United Nations: admission to membership   133

4.3 Statehood for other United Nations purposes   137

(1) Statehood and dispute settlement: Articles 32 and 35 (2)   137

(2) Claims to be parties to the Statute of the International Court of Justice   138

(3) Other cases   139

4.4 The micro-State problem   139

5. THE CRITERIA FOR STATEHOOD APPLIED: SOME SPECIAL CASES   142

5.1 General considerations   142

5.2   Entities unrecognized as separate States: Taiwan (Formosa)   143

(1)   Historical background   143

(2)   The present legal status of Taiwan   146

(3)   Conclusions   151

5.3   Entities recognized as States 'for special reasons': The Vatican
City and the Holy See   152

(1)   The international status of the Vatican City   154

(2)   The international status of the Holy See   156

(3)   The relation between the Holy See and the State of the
City of the Vatican   157

5.4   'Internationalized territories': The Free City of Danzig   160

(1)   The concept of 'Internationalized territories'   160

(2)   The legal status of the Free City of Danzig   163

(3)   Recent trends in internationalization: Cyprus   166

PART II: THE CREATION OF
STATES IN INTERNATIONAL LAW

6.   ORIGINAL ACQUISITION AND PROBLEMS OF STATEHOOD   173

6.1   General considerations   173

6.2   International status of native communities   176

(1)   Statehood of native communities   176

(2)   Legal personality of native communities not regarded as
States   177

6.3   Acquisition of territory from native communities   182

(1)   Status of native treaties of cession   182

(2)   Legal effects of native treaties   183

(3)   Grants of territory to private persons   184

6.4   Original occupation of territory by a new State   184

7.   THE CREATION AND STATUS OF DEPENDENT STATES AND OTHER
DEPENDENT ENTITIES   186

7.1   General principles   186

7.2   Protectorates and protected States   187

(1)   Protected States   188

(2)   International protectorates   194

(3) Colonial protectorates 198

(4) Legal effects of protectorates 201

   (i) Relations *inter se* of protected and protecting State 201

   (ii) Protectorates and State succession 203

   (iii) Termination of protected status 205

   (iv) Other legal effects 207

7.3 Other cases 209

  (1) Special treaty relations 209

  (2) Vassal States and suzerainty 209

  (3) Autonomy and residual sovereignty 211

  (4) Spheres of influence 214

8. DEVOLUTION 215

8.1 Introductory 215

8.2 Explicit grants of independence 216

  (1) Purported but illusory grants of independence 218

  (2) Partial or incomplete grants of independence 218

  (3) Grants in violation of self-determination 219

   (i) Grants to unrepresentative governments within self-determination units 219

   (ii) Grants disruptive of the 'territorial integrity' of a self-determination unit 220

  (4) Grants of independence in furtherance of illegal policies: the Transkei? 222

   (i) Origins of the Transkei: the Bantustan policy 222

   (ii) The status of the Transkei 225

  (5) Colonial enclaves and other rights of pre-emption 227

  (6) Derogations from grants of independence 228

8.3 Relinquishment of sovereignty without grant 228

8.4 The gradual devolution of governmental power: general principles 229

  (1) Preliminary considerations 229

  (2) The 'unitary State' theory 230

  (3) General principles of the status of devolving entities 232

8.5 The principles applied: The devolution of States within the British Commonwealth 238

9. SECESSION   247

9.1 Secession as a method of the creation of States   247

9.2 The criteria for Statehood in secessionary situations   248

  (1) The relevance of recognition   248

    (i) Metropolitan recognition   248

    (ii) Recognition by third States   252

    (iii) Recognition of belligerency   252

  (2) The traditional test of independence in a secessionary
situation   255

  (3) Independence and secession in modern international law   257

    (i) The secession of a self-determination unit   258

      (a) Secession in furtherance of self-determination   258

      (b) Secession in violation of self-determination   263

      (c) The relevance of the illegal use of force   263

    (ii) Secession within a metropolitan State   263

    (iii) Secession fomented by external illegal force 266

9.3 Certain incidents of secession in modern international law   266

  (1) The legality of secession in modern international law   266

  (2) Belligerency and insurgency in modern civil war   268

  (3) The application of the laws of war to civil conflicts   269

  (4) The problem of intervention: aid to seceding regimes   270

  (5) Problems of continuity and commencement   270

10. THE DIVIDED STATES   271

10.1 General principles: the category 'divided States'   271

10.2 The 'two Germanies'   273

  (1) Quadripartite control and its effects on Germany   274

  (2) The creation of the Federal Republic of Germany   275

  (3) The creation of the German Democratic Republic   276

  (4) Residual quadripartite competences over 'Germany as a
whole'   277

  (5) The status of Berlin   278

  (6) Issues of identity and continuity   280

10.3 Other cases of 'divided States'   281

  (1) Korea after 1947   281

(2) Vietnam after 1945   284

(3) China after 1948   286

10.4 Conclusions   286

11. UNIONS AND FEDERATIONS OF STATES   288

11.1 The classification of political unions   288

11.2 Federation, confederation, and other forms of political union   290

(1) Real and personal unions   290

(2) Federations and confederations   291

(3) Unusual formations   294

(4) Associated States   295

11.3 Unions of States in international organizations   295

PART III: THE CREATION OF
STATES IN INTERNATIONAL ORGANIZATIONS

12. INTERNATIONAL DISPOSITIVE POWERS   301

12.1 Introductory   301

12.2 Territorial dispositions by multilateral treaty   302

(1) Dispositions in treaties of peace   302

   (i) The nineteenth-century practice   302

   (ii) The First World War settlements   308

   (iii) The Second World War settlements   309

      (a) The re-establishment of annexed or conquered States   310

      (b) Poland 1939–1946   311

(2) Dispositions anticipatory of peace treaties   312

(3) Dispositions delegated to groups of States   313

(4) International status of dispositions pursuant to multilateral treaties   315

12.3 Problems of collective recognition   319

(1) The concept of 'collective recognition'   319

(2) Collective recognition in international organizations   322

(3) Collective conditional recognition   322

12.4 Territorial dispositions by international organizations   323

(1) General principles   323

(2)   The Concert of Europe   324

(3)   The League of Nations   325

(4)   The United Nations and territorial dispositions   325

    (i) General principles: delegated and inherent authority   325

      (a)   General Assembly   328

      (b)   The Security Council   328

    (ii)   Functions pursuant to the peace treaties   329

      (a)   Trieste   329

      (b)   Disposition of Italian Colonies in Africa   330

    (iii)   Functions pursuant to the Mandate and Trusteeship
Systems   332

    (iv) Other cases   332

      (a)   West Irian   332

      (b)   Jerusalem   333

    (v)   Conclusion   333

12.5   The notion of 'international dispositive powers'   333

13.   MANDATES AND TRUST TERRITORIES   335

13.1   General   335

13.2   Termination of Mandates and Trusteeships   337

  (1)   Termination of Mandates   337

    (i)   During the period of the League   337

    (ii)   After the dissolution of the League   340

    (iii)   By transfer to Trusteeship   341

  (2)   Termination of Trusteeships   341

  (3)   Legal effects of termination   342

13.3   Revocation of Mandates and Trusteeships   344

  (1)   Revocation of Mandates during the period of the League   344

  (2)   Revocation of Trusteeships   348

  (3)   Revocation of Mandates by United Nations organs   350

14.   NON-SELF-GOVERNING TERRITORIES: THE LAW AND PRACTICE
OF DECOLONIZATION   356

14.1   Introductory   356

14.2   The development in practice of Chapter XI of the Charter   358

  (1)   The definition of 'non-self-governing territories'   358

  (2)   The ambit of Chapter XI in practice   360

  (3)   Application of Chapter XI to non-colonial territories   362

14.3 The international status of non-self-governing territories 363

   (1) 'Sovereignty' and non-self-governing territories 363

   (2) The use of force and non-self-governing territories 364

   (3) The legal personality of dependent peoples 366

14.4 Termination of non-self-governing status: the forms of self-government 367

   (1) Termination of non-self-governing status 367

      (i) Criteria of self-government 367

      (ii) Determination of cessation of non-self-governing status 368

   (2) The forms of self-government 369

      (i) Independence 369

      (ii) Incorporation in another State 369

      (iii) Association 370

         (a) Association arrangements in practice since 1952 371

         (b) The international legal status of Associated States 375

      (iv) Colonial enclaves and rights of revindication 377

PART IV: PROBLEMS OF COMMENCEMENT, CONTINUITY, AND TERMINATION

15. THE COMMENCEMENT OF STATES 387

15.1 The problem of commencement 387

   (1) Problems of commencement in municipal courts 387

   (2) Problems of commencement in international *fora* 389

   (3) 'Illegal entities' and problems of commencement 391

15.2 States '*in statu nascendi*' 391

15.3 New States and the acquisition of territorial sovereignty 396

   (1) The acquisition of statehood as a 'mode of acquisition' of territory 397

   (2) Claims to the entire territory of a new State 398

16. PROBLEMS OF IDENTITY, CONTINUITY, AND REVERSION 400

16.1 The problem of identity and continuity: general considerations 400

16.2 Some applications of the concept of continuity   403

    (1) Territorial changes   404

      (i) In general   404

      (ii) 'Imperial States'   404

    (2) Changes in population   405

    (3) Changes in government   405

    (4) Changes in international status   406

    (5) Belligerent occupation   407

    (6) Continuity and illegal annexation   407

    (7) Identity without continuity   407

    (8) Multiple changes and State continuity   408

16.3 Reversion to sovereignty   412

    (1) Rights of reversion by treaty   412

    (2) Reversion of territorial enclaves   412

    (3) *Postliminium*   412

    (4) Reversion to sovereignty   414

17. THE EXTINCTION OF STATES   417

17.1 General principles   417

17.2 Extinction and illegal annexation   418

17.3 Extinction and prescription   419

CONCLUSION   421

Appendices:
1. *List of States and Territorial Entities Proximate to States*   424
2. *League Mandates and United Nations Trusteeships*   426
3. *The United Nations and Non-Self-Governing Territories, 1946–1977*   429

Bibliography   437

Table of Cases   481

Index   489

Select Table of Abbreviations

AD	*Annual Digest of Public International Law Cases*
AFDI	*Annuaire Français de Droit International*
AJ	*American Journal of International Law*
AJ Supp.	*American Journal of International Law, Supplement*
Akehurst, *Modern Introduction*	M. Akehurst, *A Modern Introduction to International Law* (London, 3rd edn., 1977)
Al-Baharna	H. Al-Baharna, *The Legal Status of the Arabian Gulf States* (1968)
ALJ	*Australian Law Journal*
ALR	Australian Law Reports
Am. Pol. Sc. R.	*American Political Science Review*
Annuaire	*Annuaire de l'Institut de Droit International*
Arangio-Ruiz	G. Arangio-Ruiz, *L'État dans le sens de droit des gens et la notion du droit international* (Bologna, 1975; and in (1975) 26 *OZfOR* 3–63, 265–406)
ASCL	*Annual Survey of Commonwealth Law*
BFSP	*British and Foreign State Papers*
Bibl. Viss.	*Bibliotheca Visseriana, Dissertationum Ius Internationale Illustrantium*
BPIL	*British Practice in International Law*
Brierly, *Collected Papers*	J. L. Brierly, *The Basis of Obligation in International Law and Other Papers* (ed. H. Lauterpacht and C. H. M. Waldock, Oxford, 1958)
Brierly, *Law of Nations*	J. L. Brierly, *The Law of Nations* (6th edn., ed. Waldock, Oxford, 1963)
Briggs, *Law of Nations*	H. W. Briggs, *The Law of Nations. Cases, Documents and Notes* (2nd edn., N.Y., 1952)
Brownlie, *Principles*	I. Brownlie, *Principles of Public International Law* (Oxford, 2nd edn., 1973)
Brownlie, *Use of Force*	I. Brownlie, *International Law and the Use of Force by States* (Oxford, 1963)
BY	*British Yearbook of International Law*
Can. B.R.	*Canadian Bar Review*
Can. YIL	*Canadian Yearbook of International Law*

Charpentier, *Reconnaissance*	J. Charpentier, *La Reconnaissance internationale et l'évolution du droit des gens* (Paris, 1956)
Chen, *Recognition*	T. C. Chen, *The International Law of Recognition* (ed. L. C. Green, London, 1951)
CILSA	*Comparative and International Law Journal of Southern Africa*
CMLR	Common Market Law Reports
CMLR	*Common Market Law Review*
Col. JTL	*Columbia Journal of Transnational Law*
CTS	*Consolidated Treaty Series*
Dir. Int.	*Diritto Internazionale*
DSB	*Department of State Bulletin*
ECJ Rep.	European Court of Justice, *Reports of the Jurisprudence of the Court*
Fawcett, *British Commonwealth*	J. E. S. Fawcett, *The British Commonwealth in International Law* (London, 1963)
For. Aff.	*Foreign Affairs* (Washington)
GAOR	*General Assembly Official Records*
Grotius ST	*Transactions of the Grotius Society*
Grotius SP	C. H. Alexandrowicz, ed., *Grotius Society Papers 1968 Studies in the history of the law of nations* (The Hague, 1970); *id. 1972* (The Hague, 1972)
Hackworth, *Digest*	G. H. Hackworth, *Digest of International Law* (15 vols., Washington, 1940–44)
HR	Académie de Droit International, *Recueil des cours*
H.C. Deb.	*House of Commons Debates* (5th series unless otherwise stated)
H.L. Deb.	*House of Lords Debates*
Higgins, *Development*	R. Higgins, *The Development of International Law through the Political Organs of the United Nations* (London, 1963)
I.C.J. Rep.	International Court of Justice, *Reports of Judgements, Advisory Opinions and Orders*
ICJ Rev.	*Review of the International Commission of Jurists*
ICLQ	*International and Comparative Law Quarterly*
ILC Ybk.	*Yearbook of the International Law Commission*
ILM	*International Legal Materials*
ILQ	*International Law Quarterly*

ILR	International Law Reports
Indian JIL	*Indian Journal of International Law*
Indian YIA	*Indian Yearbook of International Affairs*
Int. Aff.	*International Affairs* (London)
Int. Conc.	*International Conciliation*
Int. Org.	*International Organization*
IR	Irish Reports
Is. Yb. HR	*Israeli Yearbook of Human Rights*
JDI	*Journal du Droit International (Clunet)*
Jennings, *Acquisition of Territory*	R. Y. Jennings, *The Acquisition of Territory in International Law* (Manchester, 1963)
Kamanda, *Legal Status of Protectorates*	A. M. Kamanda, *A Study of the legal status of protectorates in public international law* (Geneva, 1961)
Keesing's	*Keesing's Contemporary Archives*
Kelsen, *Principles*	Hans Kelsen, *Principles of International Law* (2nd edn., rev. R. W. Tucker, N.Y., 1966)
Kiss, *Pratique Française*	A. C. Kiss, *Répertoire de la pratique française en matière de droit international public* (7 vols., Paris, 1962–72)
Lauterpacht, *Collected papers*	E. Lauterpacht, ed., *International Law. Being the Collected Papers of Hersch Lauterpacht* (Cambridge, vols. 1–3, 1970 77)
Lauterpacht, *Recognition*	H. Lauterpacht, *Recognition in International Law* (Cambridge, 1948)
Lauterpacht, *Development*	H. Lauterpacht, *Development of International Law by the International Court* (London, 1958)
LNOJ	League of Nations *Official Journal*
LNTS	League of Nations *Treaty Series*
LQR	*Law Quarterly Review*
Marek, *Identity and Continuity*	K. Marek, *Identity and Continuity of States in Public International Law* (Geneva, 1954)
Mendelson	M. H. Mendelson, 'Acquisition of Membership in Selected International Organizations' (Oxford, MS.D. Phil. d. 5229, 1971)
MLR	*Modern Law Review*
Moore, *Digest*	J. B. Moore, *A Digest of International Law* (Washington, 8 vols., 1906)
Moore, *IA*	J. B. Moore, *International Arbitrations*

Moore, *Int. Adj.* *(M.S.)*	J. B. Moore, *International Adjudications (Modern Series)*
NILR	*Nederlands International Law Review*
NRG	G. F. de Martens, *Nouveau Recueil Général de Traités*
NYIL	*Netherlands Yearbook of International Law*
NYUJILP	*New York University Journal of International Law and Politics*
NZULR	*New Zealand Universities Law Review*
O'Brien, *New Nations*	W. V. O'Brien, ed., *The New Nations in International Law and Diplomacy* (N.Y., 1965)
O'Brien & Goebel, 'U.S. Recognition Policy'	W. V. O'Brien & J. Goebel, 'United States Recognition Policy and the New Nations', in O'Brien, ed., op. cit. 98–228
O'Connell, *State Succession*	D. P. O'Connell, *State Succession in Municipal Law and International Law* (Cambridge, 2 vols., 1967)
Oppenheim	L. Oppenheim, *International Law—A Treatise* (1st edn., London, 1905; Vol. 1, 8th edn. (ed. Lauterpacht), 1955; Vol. II, 7th edn., 1952)
OZfOR	*Osterreichische Zeitschrift fur öffentliches Recht*
PAS	*Proceedings of the American Society of International Law*
RDI	*Revue de Droit International (de la Pradelle)*
Rdi	*Rivista di Diritto Internazionale*
RDILC	*Revue de Droit International et de Legislation Comparée*
RDISDP	*Revue de Droit International, de Sciences Diplomatiques et Politiques*
Répertoire suisse	P. Guggenheim, ed., *Répertoire suisse de droit international public (1914–1939)*, I–IV (Basle, 1975)
Rep. MAT	*Reports of Decisions of Mixed Arbitral Tribunals*
Rest. 2nd	American Law Institute, *Restatement, Second. Foreign Relations Law of the United States* (1965)
RGDIP	*Revue Général de Droit International Public*
RIAA	*Reports of International Arbitral Awards*
RJPIC	*Revue Juridique et Politique Indépendance et Cooperation*
Rollet	H. Rollet, *Liste des engagements bilatéraux et multilatéraux au 30 juin 1972 ; accords et traités souscrits par la France . . .* (Paris, 1973)

Rousseau, *DIP* II	Charles Rousseau, *Droit international public*, Tome II *Les sujets de droit* (Paris, 1974)
Schwarzenberger, *International Law*	G. Schwarzenberger, *International Law as applied by International Courts and Tribunals* (3 vols., London, 1957–1976)
Schwarzenberger, *Manual*	G. Schwarzenberger, *A Manual of International Law* (6th edn., London, 1976)
SCOR	*Security Council Official Records*
Smith, *GB & LN*	H. A. Smith, *Great Britain and the Law of Nations* (2 vols., London, 1932)
Sørensen, *Manual*	M. Sørensen, ed., *Manual of Public International Law* (London, 1968)
UNCIO	*United Nations Conference on International Organization, San Francisco, 1945*
UN *Jur. Ybk.*	United Nations *Juridical Yearbook*
UNMC	*United Nations Monthly Chronicle*
Repertory	United Nations, *Repertory of Practice of United Nations Organs*
UNTS	*United Nations Treaty Series*
U.S. Digest	*Digest of United States Practice in International Law* (1973–76)
USFR	*Papers Relating to the Foreign Relations of the United States*
Verhoeven, *Reconnaissance*	J. Verhoeven, *La Reconnaissance internationale dans la pratique contemporaine: les relations publiques internationales* (Paris, 1975)
Whiteman, *Digest*	M. M. Whiteman, *Digest of International Law* (Washington, 15 vols., 1963–1973)
Ybk. AAA	*Association des Auditeurs et Anciens Auditeurs de l'Académie de Droit International de la Haye, Annuaire*
YBWA	*Yearbook of World Affairs*
ZfV	*Zeitschrift fur Ausländisches Offentliches Recht und Volkerrecht*

PART I: THE CONCEPT OF STATEHOOD IN INTERNATIONAL LAW

1. Statehood, Recognition, and International Law

> The formation of a new State is ... a matter of fact,
> and not of law. (Oppenheim (1st edn., 1905) Vol. I,
> 624; (8th edn., 1955) Vol. I, 544.)

> ... (T)he existence of a State is a question of fact and
> not of law. The criterion of statehood is not legitimacy
> but effectiveness... (A. Eban (Israel), arguing
> against a request for an advisory opinion of the
> International Court on the international status of
> Palestine: *SCOR* 340th mtg., 27 July 1948, 29–30.)

1.1 INTRODUCTORY

AT THE turn of the century some fifty acknowledged States
constituted the world community. Immediately before World
War II there were about seventy-five States. Today there are
well over 150.[1] The emergence of so many new States represents
one of the major political developments of this century. It has
changed the character of international law and the practice of
international organizations to a considerable extent. It has been
one of the most important sources of international conflict.

However, that a problem is of great, even very great,
importance in international relations does not entail that it is
regulated by international law. And it is still commonly asserted
that 'the formation of a new State ... is a matter of fact, and not
of law.'[2] This position is supported by a wide spectrum of legal
opinion. For example, one of the most common arguments of the
declaratory theory—that is, the theory that statehood is a legal
status independent of recognition—is that, where a State actually
exists, the legality of its creation or existence must be purely
abstract: the law must take account of the new situation, despite

---

[1] See Appendix I for a complete list.
[2] Oppenheim, § 209(1); cf. Erich (1926), 13 *HR* 427–507, 442; Jones (1935), 16 *BY* 5–
19, 15–16; Marston (1969), 18 *ICLQ* 1–40, 33; Arangio-Ruiz, 8–9 *et passim*.

its illegality.[3] Equally, so it is said, where a State does not exist, rules requiring it to exist can only be pointless, a denial of reality. The criterion must be effectiveness, not legitimacy. On the other hand, according to the constitutive theory—that is, the theory that the rights and duties pertaining to statehood derive from recognition only—the proposition that the existence of a State is a matter of fact only seems axiomatic. If 'a State is, and becomes, an International Person through recognition only and exclusively . . .'[4] then rules granting to a community any 'right to statehood' are *a priori* impossible.

It will be argued that neither theory of recognition satisfactorily explains modern State practice in this area. The declaratory theory assumes that territorial entities can be—by virtue of their mere existence—readily classified as having the one particular legal status, and thus, in a way, confuses 'fact' with 'law'.[5] For, accepting that effectiveness is the dominant principle in this area, it must none the less be a *legal* principle. A State is not a fact in the sense that a chair is a fact; it is a fact in the sense in which it may be said a treaty is a fact: that is, a legal status attaching to a certain state of affairs by virtue of certain rules.[6] And the declaratist's equation of fact with law also obscures the possibility that the creation of States might be regulated by rules predicated on other fundamental principles—a possibility which, as we shall see, is borne out to some extent in modern practice. On the other hand, the constitutive theory, although it draws attention to the need for cognition, or identification, of the subjects of interna-

---

[3] Cf. Chen, *Recognition*, 38 ('a State, if it exists in fact must exist in law'). This proposition is of course a tautology, and the problem of separate non-State entities was not in issue in the passage cited. Elsewhere Chen accepts the view that statehood is a legal concept not a 'physical existence' (63), as well as the possibility of the illegality of the creation or existence of a 'State' (8–9). Cf. Charpentier, *Reconnaissance*, 160–7. Lauterpacht's formulation is preferable: 'The guiding juridical principle applicable to all categories of recognition is that international law, like any other legal system, cannot disregard facts and that it must be based on them provided they are not in themselves contrary to international law' (*Recognition*, 91). But in view of the gnomic character of this proposition, it can hardly be regarded as a 'guiding juridical principle'. For Lauterpacht's interpretation of the formula that the existence of a State is a matter of fact only see ibid. 23–4.

[4] Oppenheim (1st edn.), 108; (8th edn.), 125.

[5] Cf. Lauterpacht, *Recognition*, 45–50 for an effective critique of the 'State as fact' dogma. His dismissal of the declaratory theory results in large part from his identification of the declaratory theory with this dogma.

[6] Cf. Kelsen (1929), 4 *RDI* 613–41, 613. Waldock (1962), 106 *HR* 5–250, 146 correctly describes the problem as a 'mixed question of law and fact'.

tional law, and leaves open the possibility of taking into account relevant legal principles not based on 'fact', incorrectly identifies that cognition with diplomatic recognition, and fails to consider the possibility that identification of new subjects may be achieved by way of general rules, rather than on an *ad hoc*, discretionary, basis.

Fundamentally, the question is whether international law is itself, in one of its more important aspects, formally a coherent or complete system of law.[7] According to predominant nineteenth-century doctrine, there were no rules determining what were 'States' for the purposes of other international law rules; the matter was within the discretion of existing recognized States.[8] The international law of that period thus exhibited a formal incoherence which was an expression of its radical decentralization.[9]

But if international law is still, more or less, organizationally decentralized, it is generally assumed that it is a formally complete system of law. Certainly this is the case with respect to nationality, and the use of force. This then is an investigation of the question whether, and to what extent, the formation and existence of States is regulated by international law, and is not simply a 'matter of fact'.

1.2 STATEHOOD IN EARLY INTERNATIONAL LAW

(1) *Doctrine*[10]

It will first of all be useful to look briefly at the changing opinions on the topic since the seventeenth century. Grotius, for example, defined the State as 'a complete association of free men, joined together for the enjoyment of rights and for their common interest'.[11] His definition is philosophical rather than legal. The existence of States was taken for granted; the State, like the men who compose it, was automatically bound by the law of nations (*jus gentium*), which was practically identical with the law of

---

[7] Cf. Chen, *Recognition*, 18–19.
[8] Cf. Oppenheim (1st edn.), 108; *contra* (8th edn.), 126.
[9] The same incoherence has been noted in respect of the legality of war: Lauterpacht, *Recognition*, v-vi, 4–5; and the discretionary character of nationality: Brownlie (1963), 39 *BY* 284–364, 284; *Principles*, 73. Cf. Briggs (1950), 44 *PAS* 169–81, 172.
[10] Cf. Guggenheim (1971), 3 *U. Tol. LR* 203–13.
[11] *De Iure Belli ac Pacis* (1646) I, Ch. 1, § xiv.

nature: 'outside of the sphere of the law of nature, which is also frequently called the law of nations, there is hardly any law common to all nations.'[12] So the existence of States as distinct subjects of that law posed no problem. Much the same may be said of Pufendorf, who, in a work most of which is moral philosophy rather than legal inquiry, defined the State as 'a compound moral person, whose will, intertwined and united by the pacts of a number of men, is considered the will of all, so that it is able to make use of the strength and faculties of the individual members for the common peace and security.'[13] Pufendorf agreed both with Grotius and Hobbes[14] that natural law and the law of nations were the same: 'Nor do we feel that there is any other voluntary or positive law of nations which has the force of law, properly so-called, such as binds nations as if it proceeded from a superior . . . [Convergences of State behaviour] belong either to the law of nature or to the civil law of different nations . . .'[15] Victoria, on the other hand, although writing much earlier, gave a definition of the State much more legal in expression and implication than either Grotius or Pufendorf, though one still based on scholastic argument: 'A perfect State or community . . . is one which is complete in itself, that is, which is not a part of another community, but has its own laws and its own council and its own magistrates, such as is the Kingdom of Castile and Aragon and the Republic of Venice and the like . . . Such a state, then, or the prince thereof, has authority to declare war, and no one else.'[16] Here we can detect the requirements of government and independence. Moreover, Victoria is writing not a general moral-theological treatise but one with a specific purpose; his definition is also for a purpose, that is, to determine which entities may declare war. Nevertheless, it is fair to say that the writers of the naturalist school were not concerned with the problem of statehood, because any ruler, whether or not independent, was bound by the law of nations, which was merely the application of the natural law to problems of government.

---

[12] Loc. cit. Grotius excepts certain regional customs. For a discussion of State sovereignty in Grotius see Dickinson, *The Equality of States in International Law* (1920), 55–60.

[13] *De Iure Naturae et Gentium Libri Octo* (1672) VII, Ch. 11, § 13, para. 672.

[14] *De Cive* Ch. 14, paras. 4–5 (1642).

[15] II, Ch. 3, § 156.

[16] *De Indis et de Iure Belli Relectiones* (publ. 1696): *De Iure Belli*, para. 7, §§ 425–6.

The same may be said, although with some reservations and for different reasons, of the writers of the early positivist period, of which Vattel was the most influential. His *Le Droit des gens, ou principles de la loi naturelle, appliqués à la conduite et aux affaires des nations et des souverains* is an extraordinary amalgam of the earlier views with deductions from the sovereignty and equality of States tending to overturn those views. For Vattel, 'Nations or States are political bodies, societies of men who have united together and combined their forces, in order to procure their mutual welfare and security . . .'[17] The basic criterion then is that such nations be 'free and independent of one another'.[18] But a distinction is now drawn between States as defined, and 'sovereign States', though the difference is still one of terminology.

Every Nation which governs itself, under whatever form, and which does not depend on any other Nation, is a *sovereign State*. Its rights are, in the natural order, the same as those of every other State. Such is the character of the moral persons who live together in a society established by nature and subject to the law of Nations. To give a Nation the right to a definite position in this great society, it need only be truly sovereign and independent; it must govern itself by its own authority and its own laws.[19]

The novel elements in this definition are the wide-reaching implications Vattel draws from the notion of the equality of States, the effect of which is to make States the sole judge of their rights and obligations under the Law of Nations. Thus, 'the *Law of Nations* is in its origin merely the *Law of Nature applied to Nations* . . . We use the term *necessary Law of Nations* for that law which results from applying the natural law to Nations . . .'[20] Although the positive law of nations may not, in principle, conflict with this necessary law, yet the latter is 'internal' to the State, and the positive law 'external', and other sovereigns are only entitled and able to judge the actions of other independent States by this

---

[17] *Le Droit des Gens* (1758) I, introduction, § 1; Ch. 1, § 1. For an illuminating account see Ruddy, *International Law in the Enlightenment. The Background of Emmerich de Vattel's 'Le Droit des Gens'* (N.Y., 1975), esp. 119–44.

[18] Introduction, § 15.

[19] Ibid. I, Ch. 1, § 4. But he subsequently states that authority and laws are not enough for sovereignty where there is no control over foreign affairs (treaties, making war, alliances): ibid. § 11.

[20] Introduction, §§ 6–7 (itals. his). The 'necessary Law of Nations' was thus a form of *jus cogens*—permanent and imprescriptible (§ 9).

external standard: 'A Nation is . . . free to act as it pleases, so far as its acts do not affect the perfect rights of another Nation, and so far as the Nation is under merely *internal* obligations without any *perfect external* obligation. If it abuse its liberty it acts wrongfully; but other Nations can not complain, since they have no right to dictate to it.'[21] Here a deduction from 'sovereignty' overturns what has previously been held to be the basis of the law of nations. But, as yet, no further deduction is drawn from this independence or sovereignty to deny the juridical existence of new States; sovereignty is inherent in a community and thus independent of the consent of other States: 'To give a Nation the right to a definite position in this great society, it need *only* be truly sovereign and independent . . .'[22]

The link between these earlier views and the nineteenth century positivist view of statehood may be illustrated from Wheaton's classic *Elements of International Law.* Under the influence, apparently, of Hegel[23] he came to regard statehood for the purposes of international law as something different from actual independence:

Sovereignty is acquired by a State, either at the origin of the civil society of which it is composed, or when it separates itself from the community of which it previously formed a part, and on which it was dependent. This principle applies as well to internal as to external sovereignty. But an important distinction is to be noticed . . . between these two species of sovereignty. The internal sovereignty of a State does not, in any degree, depend upon its recognition by other States. A new State, springing into existence, does not require the recognition of other States to confirm its internal sovereignty . . . The external sovereignty of any State, on the other hand, may require recognition by other States in order to render it perfect and complete . . . [I]f it desires to enter into that great society of nations . . . such recognition becomes essentially necessary to the complete participation of the new State in all the advantages of this society. Every other State is at liberty to grant, or refuse, this recognition . . .[24]

As was to be expected, this view was combined with a denial of

---

[21] Ibid. § 20.
[22] Ibid. I, Ch. 1, § 4 (my itals.).
[23] *Werke* (1854) VIII, pt. 3, para. 331; cited by Alexander (1958), 34 *BY* 176–98, 195.
[24] *Elements* (3rd edn., 1846), 55–7. For his earlier hestitations see ibid. (1st edn., 1836), 192–4.

the law of nature as the foundation of international law,[25] and of the universality of the latter.[26]

It will be noticed that, although Wheaton here reproduces Vattel's 'internal/external' terminology, he puts it to a different use. For Vattel the 'internal' law was the law of nature, the necessary, though imperfect, element of the law of nations. Wheaton, having dispensed with the law of nature, means by 'internal' those aspects of the government of a State confined to its own territory, and distinguished from 'foreign affairs'.[27] By Wheaton's time the positive law of nations was concerned only with the latter; nor could there be any *necessary* obligations owed to States by virtue of their mere 'political existence'. The law of nations was becoming an artificial system studied in the consensual areas of inter-State relations (treaties, diplomatic relations, etc.). The area of basic relations between States *qua* States (in particular, war) was excluded from its scope.

(2) *Some aspects of State practice*

Despite its claims to universality, the early law of nations had its origins in the European State-system. Within that system, and despite certain divergences, writers of both naturalist and positivist schools had at first little difficulty with the creation of States. New States could be formed by the union of two existing States: more common was the union of States in a personal union under one Crown (for example, Aragon and Castile in 1479; England and Scotland in 1603)—a union which frequently became permanent. Equally, it was agreed that princes or rulers could create new States by division of existing ones.[28] New States could also be formed by revolution, as when Portugal (1640–68) and the Netherlands (1559–1648) broke away from Spain. What was unclear was whether the revolutionary entity could be treated as an independent State before its recognition by the mother-State. Pufendorf thought not, on the grounds that '. . . if a man who, at the time, recognized the sovereignty of another as his superior, is to be able to become a king, he must secure the consent of that superior who will both free him and his dominions

[25] Ibid. Ch. 1, § 5.

[26] Ibid. § 11.

[27] As we have seen (p. 7, n. 19), Vattel made the same distinction, although it is not developed and is in fact inconsistent with other elements of his work.

[28] Cf. Pufendorf, *De jure Naturae et Gentium* VII, Ch. 3, para. 690.

from the bond by which they were tied to him.'[29] Vattel was less categorical: subjects remained bound to a sovereign 'without other conditions than his observance of the fundamental laws', and thus, in most cases, secession was contrary to the basic compact which was the foundation of the State. However, if a sovereign refused to come to the aid of part of the Nation, it might provide for its own safety by other means.[30] In practice other States tended to conduct relations on an international plane with the entity in revolt before its recognition by the mother State. The point was clearly established in this sense, if it was not already so, by the revolution of the South American provinces from Spain in the nineteenth century.[31]

The impression given by this brief review is that, despite the relatively small amount of State practice, nothing in early international law precluded the proper solution of the legal problems raised by the creation and existence of States. That impediment, as we shall see, arose later with the application by nineteenth-century writers of a thoroughgoing positivism to the concept of statehood and the theory of recognition.

1.3   RECOGNITION AND STATEHOOD

(1) *The early view of recognition*

Although the early writers occasionally dealt with problems of recognition, it had no separate place in the law of nations before the middle of the eighteenth century. The reason for this was clear: sovereignty, in its origin merely the location of supreme power within a particular territorial unit, necessarily came from within and therefore did not require the recognition of other States or princes. As Pufendorf stated: '. . . just as a king owes his sovereignty and majesty to no one outside his realm, so he need not obtain the consent and approval of other kings or states, before he may carry himself like a king and be regarded as such . . . [I]t would be an injury for the sovereignty of such a

---

[29] Loc. cit.

[30] *Le Droit des Gens* I, Ch. 17, § 202; cf. Gentili, *On the Law of War* I, §§ 185–7.

[31] See Frowein (1971), 65 *AJ* 568–71; Smith, *GB & LN* I, 115–70; de Martens, *Nouvelles Causes célèbres du droit des gens* (Paris, 1843) I, 113–209, 370–498 (American War of Independence). Cf. Wheaton, *Principles* I, Ch. 2, § 26; and *infra*, Ch. 9.

king to be called in question by a foreigner.'[32] The only doubtful point was whether recognition by the parent State of a new State formed by revolution from it was necessary, as we have seen, and that doubt related to the obligation of loyalty to a superior, which, it was thought, might require release: the problem bore no relation to constitutive theory in general. The position of recognition then towards the end of the eighteenth century was as stated by Alexandrowicz: 'In the absence of any precise and formulated theory, recognition had not found a separate place in the works of the classic writers whether of the naturalist or early positivist period, and this is the reason why Ompteda (1785) observes that nothing special has been written on the subject.'[33] When recognition did begin to attract more detailed consideration, about the middle of the century, it was in the context of recognition of monarchs, especially elective monarchs: that is, in the context of recognition of governments. von Steck[34] and later Martens[35] discussed the problem, reaching similar conclusions. Recognition, at least by third States in the case of secession from a metropolitan State, was either illegal intervention or it was unnecessary.[36] As one writer put it, '. . . in order to consider the sovereignty of a State as complete in the law of Nations, there is no need for its recognition by foreign powers; though the latter may appear useful, the *de facto* existence of sovereignty is sufficient.'[37] Thus, even after the concept of recognition had become a separate part of the law, the position was still consistent with the views held by the early writers.

The writers of the early period of eighteenth century positivism, whenever faced with the eventuality of recognition as a medium of fitting the new political reality into the law, on the whole rejected such a solution, choosing the solution more consistent with the natural law tradition. Even if the law of nations was conceived as based on the consent of States, this anti-naturalist trend was not yet allowed to extend to the field of recognition.[38]

---

[32] *De Iure Naturae et Gentium* VII, Ch. 3, para. 690.

[33] (1958) 34 *BY* 176–98, 176.

[34] *Versuche über verschiedene Materien politischer und rechtlicher Kenntnisse* (1783).

[35] *A Compendium of the Law of Nations* (1789), 18 ff.

[36] Alexandrowicz, op. cit. 180 ff. and authorities there cited.

[37] Saalfeld, *Handbuch des positiven Völkerrechts* (1833), 26; cited by Alexandrowicz, op. cit. 189.

[38] Ibid. 191. Cf. also (1961) 37 *BY* 506–15.

(2) *Positivism and recognition*

But this was, it is clear, a temporary accommodation. According to positivist theory, the obligation to obey international law derived from the consent of individual States. If a new State subject to international law came into existence, new legal obligations would be created for existing States. The positivist premiss therefore required consent—either to the creation of the State itself, or to its being subject to international law with respect to the States affected. It would be interesting to trace the evolution of international law doctrine from the essentially declaratory views of Martens and von Steck to the essentially constitutive ones of Hall and Oppenheim.[39] The important point is, however, that the shift in doctrine did happen, although it was a gradual one, in particular because, while States commonly endorsed the positivist view of international law, their practice was not always consistent with this profession. Thus unrecognized States and native peoples with some form of regular government were in practice given the benefit of, and thought to be obliged by, the whole *corpus* of international law.[40] The problem was thus largely theoretical, but it was none the less influential. For if one starts from the premiss that 'Le droit des gens est un droit contractuel entre des Etats'[41] the conclusion as to recognition and statehood seems to be inevitable:

'. . . le droit international, qui est contractuel et qui a par conséquent la liberté immanente de s'étendre aux partenaires de son choix, comprend tels États dans sa communauté et n'y acceuille pas tels autres . . . [L]a reconnaissance est un accord. Elle signifie l'extension de la communauté de droit international à un nouvel État.'[42]

(3) *Statehood in nineteenth-century international law*

It would seem useful here to attempt a summary of the position

---

[39] Wheaton's view (*supra*, p. 8, n. 24) that the 'external' sovereignty of a State is, but its 'internal' sovereignty is not dependent upon recognition may be taken as an intermediate point.

[40] Smith, *GB & LN* I, 14–18; *post*, Chapter 6.

[41] Redslob (1934), 13 *RDI* 429–83, 430–1.

[42] Loc. cit. It should be noted that the essential theoretical problem related to the duties of the new State rather than its rights. Existing States could consent to the rules of law in respect of yet-to-be-created States, but those States could not for their part so consent: e.g. Anzilotti, *Corso di Diritto Internazionale* (3rd edn., 1929) I, 163–6, cited Jaffé, *Judicial Aspects of Foreign Relations*, 90n. Cf. however Lauterpacht, *Recognition*, 2.

with regard to statehood and recognition in the nineteenth century. There was of course no complete unanimity among text-writers: nevertheless what we find is an interrelated series of doctrines, based on the premiss of positivism, the effect of which was that the formation, and even the existence of States was a matter outside the then accepted scope of international law. Oppenheim's *International Law* provides the clearest as well as probably the most influential expression of these interrelated doctrines. The main positions relevant here were as follows:

(1) International law was regarded as the law existing between civilized nations. In 1859 the British Law Officers spoke of international law 'as it has been hitherto recognized and now subsists by the common consent of Christian nations'.[43] Members of the society whose law was international law were the European States between whom it evolved from the fifteenth century onwards, and those other States accepted expressly or tacitly by the original members into the society of Nations; for example the United States of America and Turkey.[44]

(2) States as such were not therefore necessarily members of the Society of Nations. Recognition, express or implied, solely created their membership and bound them to obey international law.[45] States not so accepted were not (at least in theory) bound by international law, nor were the 'Civilized Nations' bound by it in their behaviour towards them, as was evidenced by their behaviour with regard to Africa and (in part) to China.[46]

(3) Only States, then, or rather only those entities recognized and accepted as States into international society, were bound by international law and were international persons. Individuals and groups were not subjects of international law. 'Since the Law of Nations is based on the common consent of individual States,

---

[43] Cited Smith, *GB & LN* I, 12, 14.

[44] Oppenheim (1st edn.), 17; (8th edn.), 18. On Turkey's 'membership' see Smith, *GB & LN* I, 16–17; Hall, *International Law* (2nd edn., 1884), 40; Wood (1943), 37 *AJ* 262–74; 46 *BFSP* 12. In the *European Commission of the Danube*, Ser B. No. 14 (1927), 40, Art. VII of the Treaty of Paris was referred to as bringing about 'the elevation of the position of Turkey in Europe'. But cf. *Barcelona Traction (Second Phase)* I.C.J. Rep. 1970 p. 3, 308–9 (Judge Ammoun).

[45] Oppenheim (1st edn.), 17; (8th edn.), 18.

[46] Ibid. (1st edn.), 34; (8th edn.), 50. Lauterpacht omits the sentence 'It is discretion, and not International Law, according to which the members of the Family of Nations deal with such States as still remain outside that family.'

and not of individual human beings, States solely and exclusively are the subjects of International Law.'[47]

(4) The binding force of international law derived from this process of seeking to be recognized and acceptance.

New States which came into existence and were through express or tacit recognition accepted into the Family of Nations thereby consented to the body of rules for international conduct in existence at the time of their admittance.[48]

International Law does not say that a State is not in existence as long as it is not recognized, but it takes no notice of it before its recognition. Through recognition only and exclusively a State becomes an International Person and a subject of International Law.[49]

This satisfied the positivist canon that could discover the obligation to obey international law only in the consent of States.

(5) Accordingly how a State *became* a State was a matter of no importance to traditional international law, which concentrated on recognition as the agency of admission into 'civilized society'—a sort of juristic baptism, entailing the rights and duties of international law. 'Pre-states' had not consented to be bound by international law, nor had other States accepted them. States *in statu nascendi* were in no sense international persons. How they acquired territory, what rights and duties they had or owed to others as a result of activities before they were recognized as States, these were irrelevant to international law:

The formation of a new State is, as will be remembered from former statements, a matter of fact and not of law. It is through recognition, which is a matter of law, that such new State become subject to International Law. As soon as recognition is given, the new State's territory is recognized as the territory of a subject of International Law, and it matters not how this territory is acquired before the recognition.[50]

Hence also, the acquisition of territory by a new State was not regarded as a mode of acquisition of territory in international law, though revolt was a method of losing territory. 'Revolt

---

[47] Oppenheim (1st edn.), 18. By 'States' Oppenheim presumably meant 'recognized States'.

[48] (1st edn.), 17; (8th edn.), 18.

[49] Ibid. (1st edn.), 108. The second sentence only is in the 8th edn., 125. Cf. to the same effect Webster in Moore, 1 *Digest* 5–6.

[50] Oppenheim (1st edn.), 264; (8th edn.), 544. Cf. Phillimore, *Commentaries upon International Law* (2nd edn., 1871) I, 79.

followed by secession is a mode of losing territory to which no mode of acquisition corresponds.'[51]

1.4 RECOGNITION OF STATES IN MODERN INTERNATIONAL LAW

(1) *Introductory*

It is against this background that the modern law of statehood, and its relation with recognition, must be examined. The effect of the positivist doctrine was to place all the emphasis, in matters of statehood, on the question of recognition.[52] And this is still so as far as the municipal law of many States is concerned; for example English courts will not determine for themselves any questions of statehood at issue before them, even where the matter is between private citizens.[53] They will sometimes be able to avoid the unnecessary and sometimes harmful effects on private rights of the commonly political act of recognition by means of construction.[54] The executive will on occasions leave the matter, in substance, for the courts to decide.[55] But where the international status of any entity is squarely in issue, executive certification is binding.[56] Of course, the rule might also be waived by statute: the nearest approach is the extended definition of 'foreign state' in the Foreign Enlistment Act, 1870 (U.K.), s. 30.

---

[51] Oppenheim (1st edn.), 297; (8th edn.), 579.

[52] As both Verhoeven and Charpentier have pointed out, the rubric 'recognition' covers a very wide variety of situations. The term here is used to indicate the relatively formal diplomatic recognition of States and governments.

[53] This was not always so: *Yrisarri v. Clement* (1825) 2 C. & P. 223, 225 *per* Best C.J. For an illuminating discussion of the cases in which Lord Eldon laid down the modern rule see Bushe-Foxe, (1931) 12 *BY* 63–75; (1932) 13 *BY* 39–48. See also Jaffé, *Judicial Aspects of Foreign Relations*, 79.

[54] *Luigi Monta of Genoa v. Cechofracht Co. Ltd.* [1956] 2 Q.B. 522 (term 'government' in a charterparty); *Kawasaki Kisen Kabashiki Kaisha of Kobe v. Bantham Steamship Co. Ltd.* [1939] 2 K.B. 544 (C.A.) ('war'). For an extreme case of 'construction' see *The Arantzazu Mendi* [1939] A.C. 256, criticized by Lauterpacht, *Recognition*, 288–94.

[55] *Duff Development Co. v. Kelantan Government* [1924] A.C. 797, 825 *per* Lord Sumner; and cf. the certificate in *Salimoff v. Standard Oil Co.* 262 N.Y. 220 (1933) just before U.S. recognition of the Soviet government.

[56] *Luther v. Sagor* [1921] 3 K.B. 532; but cf. *Carl Zeiss Stiftung v. Rayner and Keeler Ltd. (No. 2)* [1971] 1 A.C. 853, esp. 953–4 *per* Lord Wilberforce. The modern American position is less rigid: *Wulfsohn v. R.S.F.S.R.* 234 N.Y. 372 (1923); *Solokoff v. National City Bank* 239 N.Y. 158 (1924); *Bank of China v. Wells Fargo Bank & Union Trust Co.* 209 F. 2d. 467 (1953), and for discussion see O'Connell, *International Law* I, 172–81.

However necessary or desirable it may be that the courts of a State should speak on matters of statehood with the same voice as the government of that State, in the international sphere the intimate connection established by nineteenth-century doctrine between recognition and statehood has done considerable harm. For a tension is thereby created between the conviction of lawyers, over a wide philosophical spectrum, that recognition is, despite its political overtones, essentially a legal act in the international sphere,[57] and that of politicians that they are, or should be, free to determine (once an entity possesses the requisite qualifications) the question of recognition on political grounds. This has led to some curious attempts at reconciliation.[58] The United Kingdom alone seems to have accepted a duty to recognize;[59] and even its statement is by no means an assertion of the constitutive theory of recognition.[60]

(2) *Recognition: the great debate*

Before examining State practice, however, it is necessary again to refer to the theoretical conflict over the nature of recognition. For a further effect of nineteenth-century practice has been to focus attention more or less exclusively on the act of recognition itself, and its legal effects, rather than on the problem of the elaboration of rules determining the status, competence, and so on of the various territorial governmental units.[61] To some

---

[57] Kelsen (1941), 35 *AJ* 605–17; Schwarzenberger, *International Law* I, 127–36, 134; Lauterpacht, *Recognition*, 6 and *passim*.

[58] Alexander (1957), 46 *AJ* 631–40. The same tension exists over the relation between U.N. Membership and recognition.

[59] Cf. (1951) 4 *ILQ* 387–8; Akehurst, *Modern Introduction*, 65.

[60] In 1948, the British position, while supporting a duty to recognize, was that: 'the existence of a State should not be regarded as depending upon its recognition but on whether in fact it fulfils the conditions which create a duty for recognition' (A/CN. 4/2 (1948), 53). It is significant that Lauterpacht relies heavily on the practice of U.K. and U.S. courts in recognition cases: e.g. *Recognition*, 44, 70–3. He regards this practice as consistently constitutive, and hence tends to minimize the importance of the exceptions to the non-recognition rule accepted in U.S. courts (146–7). However, the difference between modern British and American practice is better explained by the differences in the operation of the principle of non-justiciability of 'political' disputes. British judicial practice is not, therefore, based on a particular view of the international law of recognition: but cf. ibid. 154–5. For discussion of the changing U.S. practice in recognition cases see *Bank of China* v. *Wells Fargo Bank & Union Trust Co.* 104 F. Supp. 59 (1952), 63–6.

[61] Cf. Bot, *Non-Recognition and Treaty Relations* (1968), 1.

extent this was inevitable, as long as the constitutive position retained its influence, for a corollary of that position was, as we have seen, that there could be no such rules. Examination of the constitutive theory is, therefore, first of all necessary.

(i) The constitutive theory[62]

The tenets of the strict constitutive position, as adopted by Oppenheim and others, have been referred to already.[63] Many, if not most, of the adherents of the constitutive position are also positivist in outlook.[64] On the other hand, it may well be possible to reconcile the declaratory theory with positivism, and it is certainly true that many writers have been both declaratory and positivist.[65] Moreover Lauterpacht, who was not a positivist, was one of the more subtle and persuasive proponents of a form of the constitutive position.[66] Apart from the general tenets of positivism, the most persuasive argument for the constitutive position is a distinct one. Lauterpacht formulates it in the following way:

[T]he full international personality of rising communities . . . cannot be automatic . . . [A]s its ascertainment requires the prior determination

---

[62] Constitutive writers include the following: Kelsen (1941), 35 *AJ* 605–17; Schwarzenberger, *International Law* I, 134; Anzilotti, op. cit.; Redslob, op. cit.; Lauterpacht, *Recognition*; Jellinek, *Allgemeine Staatslehre* (5th ed., 1928), 273; Le Normand, *La Reconnaissance Internationale et ses Diverses Applications* (1899); Patel, *Recognition in the Law of Nations* (1959), 119–22; Jennings (1967), 121 *HR* 327–605, 350; Devine, [1973] *Acta Juridica* 1, 90–145; Verzijl, *International Law* II, 587–90 (with reservations). Hall's position is of interest: 'although the right to be treated as a state is independent of recognition, recognition is the necessary evidence that the right has been acquired': *International Law* (8th edn., 1924, Higgins ed.), 103. Cf. also the German argument in the *Customs Union Case*, Ser. C. No. 53, 52–3. It is argued that the Permanent Court adopted a constitutive position in *Certain German Interests in Polish Upper Silesia*, Ser. A. No. 7 (1926), 27–9, but this was in the context of the belligerency of the Polish National Committee, not the existence of Poland as a State.

[63] *Supra*, pp. 13–15.

[64] Lauterpacht, *Recognition*, 38–9; but cf. Jaffé, op. cit. 80–1.

[65] Cf. Chen, *Recognition*, 18n.41.

[66] Lauterpacht, *Recognition*, 2 distinguishes two major assertions of orthodox constitutive theory: viz. 'that, prior to recognition, the community in question possesses neither the rights nor the obligations which international law associates with full Statehood; [and] . . . that recognition is a matter of absolute political discretion as distinguished from a legal duty owed to the community concerned'. Lauterpacht adopts the first but not the second of these proportions. It can be seen that neither is distinctly positivist: what is so is their combination. Cf. Kunz (1950), 44 *AJ* 713–19; Higgins, *Development*, 136.

of difficult circumstances of fact and law, there must be *someone* to perform that task. In the absence of a preferable solution, such as the setting up of an impartial international organ to perform that function, the latter must be fulfilled by States already existing. The valid objection is not against the fact of their discharging it, but against their carrying it out as a matter of arbitrary policy as distinguished from legal duty.[67]

In other words, it is said that, in every legal system, some organ must be competent to determine with finality and certainty the subjects of the system. In the present international system, that organ can only be the States, acting severally or collectively. Since they act as organs of the system, their determinations must have definitive legal effect.

It is first of all clear that this argument is not generally applicable in modern international law. Determination of the legality of the use of force, or of the violation or termination of a treaty, may involve 'difficult circumstances of fact and law', but it could not be contended that the views of particular States as to such matters are 'constitutive' or conclusive. Were that so, international law would be merely a system of imperfect communications: every rule of international law would be the subject of, in effect, an 'automatic reservation' with respect to every State (in the absence of the compulsory jurisdiction of some court or tribunal).

If it is argued that the problem of determining the subjects of international law is so important that, exceptionally, there must exist some method of conclusive determination, yet it is difficult to see that equating the individual States with the centralized organ of the 'normal' legal system has this effect. There would be nothing conclusive or certain (as far as other States were concerned) about a conflict between different States as to the status of a particular entity. Moreover, it is not necessarily the case that problems of status are peculiarly important, either in theory or practice. International law has relatively few subjects, and the status of a great majority of them is not open to serious doubt. On the other hand, problems relating, for example, to the legality of the use of force occur with unfortunate frequency, and are often of very great difficulty. Fortunately, it is not argued

---

[67] *Recognition*, 55 (itals. his); cf. Kelsen, op. cit. 606–7.

that individual State pronouncements should therefore be definitive.[68]

Two further arguments add decisive support to the rejection of the constitutive position. In the first place, if State recognition is, *pro tanto*, determining, then it is difficult to conceive of an illegal recognition, and quite impossible to conceive of a recognition which is invalid or void. Yet the invalidity of certain acts of recognition has been accepted in practice, and rightly so.[69] Otherwise recognition would constitute an alternative form of intervention. It is of interest that Lauterpacht himself, in at least one place, allowed the possibility of an *invalid* act of recognition.[70] If that is possible, then the test for recognition must be extrinsic to the act of recognition; that is, established by general international law. And that is a denial of the constitutive position.

A second difficulty with the constitutive position is its relativism. As Kelsen points out, it follows from constitutivist theory that '. . . the legal existence of a state . . . has a relative character. A state exists legally only in its relations to other states. There is no such thing as absolute existence.'[71] To those who do not share Kelsen's philosophical premisses, this seems a violation of common sense.[72] Lauterpacht, who accepts the relativity of recognition as inherent in the constitutive position, nevertheless refers to it as a 'glaring anomaly'[73] and a 'grotesque spectacle' casting 'grave reflection upon international law'.[74] Moreover, in his opinion 'It cannot be explained away, amidst some complacency, by questionable analogies to private law or to philosophical relativism.'[75] But if a central feature of the

---

[68] Lauterpacht accepts that the decentralized function of recognition is quite unsatisfactory: *Recognition*, 67. He thus has to rely on an unsatisfactory situation as the chief support for his position.

[69] Cf. for example the German and Soviet 'recognition' of the 'extinction' of the Polish State in 1939: *infra*, pp. 311–12.

[70] He regarded Italian and German recognition of the Franco regime as 'illegal *ab initio*': *Recognition*, 234n.3; cf. 95n.2.

[71] Kelsen, op. cit. 609. But cf. Green, *International Law* (1973), 34.

[72] Cf. Verhoeven, *Reconnaissance*, 714–15. Kelsen himself was previously declaratist: (1929) 4 *RDI* 613–41, 617–18: 'en présence des règles positives incontestables du droit international, [on] ne peut nier que l'État nouveau ait des droits et des obligations internationales avant même d'être reconnu par les anciens États.'

[73] *Recognition*, 67.

[74] Ibid. 78.

[75] Loc. cit.

constitutive position is open to such criticism, the position itself must be regarded as questionable. Moreover, aside from the various logical objections,[76] Lauterpacht's position is dependent on a straightforward assertion about State practice: '. . . much of the available evidence points to what has here been described as the legal view of recognition. Only that view of recognition, coupled with a clear realization of its constitutive effect, permits us to introduce a stabilizing principle into what would otherwise be a pure exhibition of power and negation of order . . .'[77] But State practice demonstrates neither acceptance of a duty to recognize,[78] nor a consistent constitutive view of recognition. Moreover, Lauterpacht's argument, which is the passage cited was almost avowedly *de lege ferenda*,[79] assumes the insufficiency of the declaratory view of recognition.

(*ii*) *The declaratory theory*

According to the declaratory theory, recognition of a new State is a political act which is in principle independent of the existence of the new State as a full subject of international law.[80] In Charpentier's terminology, statehood is opposable to non-recognizing States.[81] This position has the merit of avoiding the logical and practical difficulties involved in constitutive theory, while still accepting a role for recognition in modern practice. It has the further, essential, merit of consistency with that practice, and it is supported by a substantial body of opinion, both judicial and academic. What is regarded as the *locus classicus* is a passage of Taft C.J.'s in the *Tinoco Arbitration*:

The non-recognition by other nations of a government claiming to be a national personality, is usually appropriate evidence that it has not attained the independence and control entitling it by international law

[76] A further logical objection relates to the difficulty of a duty to recognize an entity which has, prior to recognition, *ex hypothesi* no rights: see *Recognition*, 74–5, 191–2. None the less, the community is 'entitled to claim recognition', but this is an unenforceable or imperfect right. Even so, if it is a legal right then *cadit quaestio*. Cf. Chen, *Recognition*, 52–54.

[77] *Recognition*, 77–8.

[78] Cf. Verhoeven, *Reconnaissance*, 576–86.

[79] Cf. *Recognition*, 78.

[80] See Chen, *Recognition*, for a full discussion of this position. It is of interest that L. C. Green's annotations to the published edition are consistently constitutivist: in this respect Green follows Schwarzenberger rather than Chen.

[81] Charpentier, *Reconnaissance*, 15–68, 160–7.

to be classed as such. But when recognition *vel non* of a government is by such nations determined by enquiry, not into its *de facto* sovereignty and complete governmental control, but into its illegitimacy or irregularity of origin, their non-recognition loses something of evidential weight on the issue with which those applying the rules of international law are alone concerned ... Such non-recognition for any reason ... cannot outweigh the evidence disclosed ... as to the *de facto* character of Tinoco's government, according to the standard set by international law.[82]

But this was a case of recognition of governments, and it is arguable that, whilst recognition of governments might be declaratory in effect, recognition of new States is not. Where an authority in fact exercises governmental functions within an area accepted as being already a 'State-area', there might seem to be nothing for recognition to constitute, at least at the level of international personality. On the other hand, recognition of a new State involves the demarcation of a certain area as a 'State-area' for the purposes of international relations, with consequent effect upon the rights and duties of other States. In such a case, it might be argued that recognition, at least in the non-formal sense of 'treating like a State', is central rather than peripheral to the issue of international capacity.[83]

But legal opinion in the context of recognition of States also seems to contradict this view.[84] As a German-Polish Mixed Arbitral Tribunal stated in reference to the existence of the new State of Poland: '... the recognition of a State is not constitutive but merely declaratory. The State exists by itself and the recognition is nothing else than a declaration of this existence, recognized by the States from which it emanates.'[85] Less well

---

[82] (1924) 18 *AJ* 147–74, 154; cf. also *Hopkins Claim* (1927) 21 *AJ* 160–7, 166; *Cuculla* v. *Mexico*, Moore *IA* III, 2873, 2876–7; *Wulfsohn* v. *R.F.S.F.R.* 138 N.E. 24 (1923) *per* Andrews J., 25; app. diss. 266 U.S. 580 (1924).

[83] This was Le Normand's view: op. cit., 268; cited Chen, *Recognition*, 14n.1.

[84] It is of interest to note that even *de facto* recognition (which in any case is declining as an institution intermediate between non-recognition and full recognition) has come to be granted or withheld for political reasons: a situation that would be intolerable on any other than declaratist principles. Cf. Jennings, *Report of International Law Conference, London 1962* (1963), 21–31. The U.S. since 1943 has used the terms '*de facto*' and '*de jure*' only in relation to governments: O'Brien & Goebel, 'U.S. Recognition Policy', 205–7. On *de facto* recognition in general see Lauterpacht, *Recognition*, 329–48; Chen, *Recognition*, 270–300; Charpentier, *Reconnaissance*, 294–302.

[85] *Deutsche Continental Gas Gesellschaft* v. *Polish State* (1929) 5 AD No. 5.

known in this context is the Report of the Commission of Jurists on the Aaland Islands. The passage of the Report dealing with the independence of Finland enumerated the various recognitions given to Finland, but went on to say that:

these facts by themselves do not suffice to prove that Finland, from this time onwards, became a sovereign State ... [T]he same legal value cannot be attached to recognition of new States in war-time, especially to that accorded by belligerent powers, as in normal times ... In addition to these facts which bear upon the external relations of Finland, the very abnormal character of her internal situation must be brought out. This situation was such that, for a considerable time, the conditions required for the formation of a sovereign State did not exist.[86]

It will be seen that the Jurists, while accepting the legal value of recognition as evidence, were not prepared to accept it as conclusive, but instead referred to the 'conditions required for the formation of a sovereign State' apart from recognition.[87]

Among writers the declaratory doctrine, with differences in emphasis, is now predominant. Brownlie states the position succinctly: 'Recognition, *as a public act of state*, is an optional and political act and there is no legal duty in this regard. However, in a deeper sense, if an entity bears the marks of statehood, other states put themselves at risk legally, if they ignore the basic obligations of state relations.'[88]

[86] *LNOJ*, Sp. Supp. No. 4 (1920), 8.

[87] The Report of the Commission of Rapporteurs is less explicit. Certain passages are at least capable of a constitutivist interpretation: e.g. *LN* Council doct. B7: 21/68/106 (1921), 23. But the crucial element in the Rapporteurs' argument was the continuity between the independent State of Finland after 1917, and the autonomous State of Finland before 1917. This continuity was regarded as a continuity of legal personality, despite absence of recognition of pre-1917 Finland: cf. the reference to 'an autonomous Finland which ... on the 6th December 1917, proclaimed her full and entire independence of Russia, detached herself from the latter by an act of her own free will, and became thereafter herself a sovereign State instead of a dependent State' (ibid. 22).

[88] *Principles*, 94 (his itals.); cf. 90–3. Other declaratist writers include: O'Connell, *International Law* I, 123–34; Chen, *Recognition*; Brierly, *Law of Nations*, 139; Charpentier, *Reconnaissance*, 196–200; Starke, *Studies in International Law*, 91–100; Marek, *Identity and Continuity*, 130–61; Fawcett, *The Law of Nations* (2nd edn., 1971), 49, 55; Higgins, *Development*, 135–6; Akehurst, *Modern Introduction*, 60–3; Jaffé, *Judicial Aspects of Foreign Relations*, 97–8; Erich (1926), 13 *HR* 427–500, 457–68; Kunz (1950), 44 *AJ* 713–19; Borchard (1942), 36 *AJ* 108–11; Brown, ibid. 106–8; Waldock (1962), 106 *HR* 147–51. See also the Resolutions of the *Institut du Droit International* (1936): 'La reconnaissance a un effet déclaratif. L'existence de l'État nouveau avec tous les effets juridiques qui s'attachent à cette existence n'est pas affectée par le refus de reconnaissance d'un ou

Moreover, States do not in practice regard unrecognized States as exempt from international law,[89] and they do in fact carry on a certain, often quite considerable amount of informal intercourse, extending even to joint membership of the various inter-State organizations.[90] Recognition is increasingly intended and taken as an act, if not of political approval, at least of political accommodation.[91]

(3) *Conclusions*

It is sometimes suggested that the 'great debate' over the legal nature of recognition has been beside the point, and that it is mistaken to categorize recognition as either declaratory or constitutive.[92] French writers, following de Visscher, have tended to regard recognition as combining both elements.[93] To some extent one can sympathize with these views: none the less, the proper position is that in principle the denial of recognition to an entity which otherwise qualifies as a State cannot entitle the non-recognizing States to act as if the entity in question was not a State. The categorical constitutive position, which implies the

plusieurs États': Wehberg, ed., *Institut de Droit International, Table Général des Résolutions 1873–1956* (1957), 11; and cf. Brown, [1934] *Annuaire* 302–57. See also *Temple Case* I.C.J. Rep. 1962 p. 6, 130–1 (Judge Spender, diss.).

[89] Brownlie, *Principles*, 92n.; Briggs (1949), 43 *AJ* 113–21, 117–20; Charpentier, *Reconnaissance*, 45–8, 56–68; Whiteman, 2 *Digest* 604–65. Cf. the Protocol of the London Conference, 19 Feb. 1831: 18 *BFSP* 779, 781 (Belgium); Marek, *Identity and Continuity*, 140. Non-recognition of North Korea and of Israel was not regarded as precluding the application of international law rules to the Korean and Middle East wars: Brownlie, *Use of Force*, 380 and n.

[90] Bot, *Non-Recognition and Treaty Relations* (1968); and see Whiteman, 2 *Digest*, 524–604; Moore, 1 *Digest* 206–35; Hackworth, 1 *Digest* 327–63, for details of these informal contacts. Failure to comply with international law is often cited as a justification for non-recognition.

[91] Cf. Lachs (1959) 35 *BY* 252–9, 259; Higgins, *Development*, 164–5. Verhoeven goes so far as to conclude that recognition is 'un acte purement politique, dépourvu comme acte de volonté d'effets de droit': *Reconnaissance*, 721. This follows from his basic thesis of the diversity of 'recognitions', and of the relations or situations being recognized. But it does not follow that recognition may not have legal effects in a particular case or type of case. What does follow is the need to study the particular types of case, rather than 'recognition' simply.

[92] Akehurst, *Modern Introduction* (2nd edn.), 78; cf. (3rd edn.), 62–3.

[93] De Visscher, *Problèmes d'interpretation judiciaire en droit international public* (Paris, 1963), 191; cited by Salmon, *La Reconnaissance d'État* (Paris, 1971), 19 ff. Cf. Charpentier, *Reconnaissance, passim*; de Visscher, *Théories et Réalités* (4th rev. edn., 1970), 258. Verhoeven, *Reconnaissance*, 548 refers in the same vein to a 'dialectical relationship' between recognition and the criteria for statehood, although his basic position remains declaratist: ibid. 545, 714–15, 720.

contrary view, is unacceptable. But it would be equally unacceptable to deny that, in practice, recognition can have important legal and political effects. For example, where an entity is widely recognized as a State, especially where such recognition has been accorded on non-political grounds, that is strong evidence of the statehood of that entity—though it is not conclusive.[94] Equally, where the status of a particular entity is doubtful, or where some necessary element is lacking, recognition, apart from its evidential importance, may oblige the recognizing State to treat the recognized entity as a State, and may thus contribute towards the consolidation of its status. In Charpentier's terms, recognition may render opposable a situation otherwise not opposable.[95]

In some situations, too, States may without acting unlawfully recognize an entity as a State even though it clearly does not qualify as such: in these circumstances bilateral legal obligations may be created, but the personality of the entity in question remains particular and non-opposable. Similarly, the term 'recognition' is sometimes used to describe acts which are properly speaking constitutive of a particular State or legal person: for example, a multilateral treaty establishing a new State will extend the signatories' recognition of that State. This situation is to be distinguished from that where the State or entity existed before the treaty, which merely confirms the status as recognized.[96]

The tentative conclusion is that the international status of a State 'subject to international law' is, in principle, independent of recognition, although the qualifications already made suggest that the differences between declaratory and constitutive schools are less in practice than might have been expected. This conclusion is tentative only, in that it assumes that there exist in international law and practice workable criteria for statehood. If there are no such criteria, or if they are so imprecise as to be practically useless, then recognition must be in practice discretionary, as well as determinative, and the constitutive position will have returned, as it were, by the back door.[97] The

---

[94] Cf. Taft C.J., *Tinoco Arbitration*; cited *supra* p. 20–1.
[95] Charpentier, *Reconnaissance*, 217–25.
[96] But cf. Wright (1954), 48 *PAS* 23–37.
[97] Cf. Anzilotti, *Corso di Diritto Internazionale* (3rd edn., 1929) I, 163–6.

question whether such criteria do exist will be discussed in the next Chapter.

1.5 CERTAIN BASIC CONCEPTS

Throughout this work, reference will be made to certain basic concepts. A brief examination of some of these is thus desirable.

(1) *International legal personality*

The term 'international legal personality' has been defined as 'the capacity to be bearer of rights and duties under international law'.[98] The term 'capacity' in this context is perhaps unfortunate: any person or aggregate of persons presumably has capacity to be given rights and duties by States.[99] The question is not 'capacity' but the extent to which the entity in question actually has such rights and duties. To say that a particular entity is an international legal person is to say only that the entity is in fact accorded particular rights, or subjected to particular duties, under international law. Thus the International Court, in determining whether the United Nations had 'such a nature as involves the capacity to bring an international claim' asked itself the question:

... whether the Charter has given the Organization such a position that it possesses, in regard to its Members, rights which it is entitled to ask them to respect. *In other words*, does the Organization possess international personality? This is no doubt a doctrinal expression, which has sometimes given rise to controversy. But it will be used here to mean that if the Organization is recognized as having that personality, it is an entity capable of availing itself of obligations incumbent upon its Members.[100]

An important distinction in this area is to be noted. In the *Reparations Case* one question was whether the United Nations might claim reparations for injury to its agents committed by nationals of a non-Member State. The Court gave an affirmative answer, stating that '... fifty States, representing the vast majority of the members of the international community, had

---

[98] Schwarzenberger, *Manual*, 53.
[99] Cf. *Danzig Railway Officials*, Ser. B. No. 15 (1928), 17–18.
[100] *Reparations Case* I.C.J. Rep. 1949 p. 174, 178 (my itals.).

the power, in conformity with international law, to bring into being an entity possessing objective international personality, and not merely personality recognized by them alone, together with capacity to bring international claims.'[101] A distinction is thus drawn between 'objective international personality' and personality recognized by particular States only. It would appear that the former exists wherever the rights and obligations of an entity are conferred by general international law, and the latter where an entity is established by particular States for special purposes. States clearly are included in the former category: the Order of St. John of Jerusalem, Rhodes and Malta is a good example of the latter.[102] The Court held that, by virtue of the importance of its functions and the extent of its membership, the United Nations was also in the former category, an 'objective' legal person.[103]

There is thus a distinction between 'general' (or 'objective') and 'special' (or 'particular') legal personality. General legal personality binds *erga omnes*: particular legal personality binds only consenting States. But no further implications may be drawn from the fact of legal personality: the extent of the powers, rights and responsibilities of any entity is to be determined only by examination of its actual position.[104]

(2) *'Sovereignty'*

The term 'sovereignty' has a long and troubled history, and a variety of meanings. In its most common modern usage, sovereignty is the term for the 'totality of international rights and duties recognized by international law' as residing in an independent territorial unit—the State.[105] It is not itself a right,

---

[101] I.C.J. Rep. 1949 p. 174, 185.

[102] *Infra*, p. 160, n. 101.

[103] For criticism see Schwarzenberger, *International Law* I, 128–9, 469–71, 523, 596. Brownlie describes the passage cited as 'an assertion of political and constitutional fact rather than a reasoned conclusion', but regards it as 'appropriate and necessary' in the special circumstances: *Principles*, 670. Cf. also Oppenheim (8th edn), 407, 880, 928–9.

[104] See further O'Connell (1963), 67 *RGDIP* 5–43; Lauterpacht (1947), 63 *LQR* 438–460, (1948) 64 *LQR* 97–119; Siotto-Pintor (1932), 41 *HR* 245–361; Aufricht (1943), 37 *Am. Pol. Sc. R.* 217–43; Scelle, in Lipsky, ed., *Law and Politics in the World Community* (1953), 49–58.

[105] Cf. *Reparations Case* I.C.J. Rep. 1949 p. 174, 180. See generally Whiteman, 1 *Digest* 233–82; Korowicz, *Organisations internationales et souveraineté des États membres* (1961); Sukiennicki, *La Souveraineté des États en droit international moderne* (1927); Kamal Hossain,

nor is it a criterion for statehood.[106] It is a somewhat unhelpful, but firmly established, description of statehood; a brief term for the State's attribute of more-or-less plenary competence. No further legal consequences attach to sovereignty than attach to statehood itself. It is not to be confused with the constitutional lawyer's problem of supreme competence within a particular State: thus the 'sovereignty of Parliament' could coexist with the effective abandonment of the sovereignty of the United Kindom.[107] Nor is it to be confused with the exercise of 'sovereign rights': a State may continue to be sovereign even though important governmental functions are carried out, by treaty or otherwise, by another State. In such a case it is said that, provided the local unit in all the circumstances remains 'independent', it retains its sovereignty but that in certain respects the exercise of that sovereignty has been entrusted to another entity.[108] And, finally, 'sovereignty' does not mean actual equality of rights or competences: the actual competence of a State may be restricted by its constitution, or by treaty or custom. The term 'sovereignty' accurately refers not to the totality of powers which all States have, but to the totality of powers which States may, under international law, have. The danger of drawing implications from the term is thus evident.[109]

(3) *The distinction between 'State' and 'Government'*

The distinction between 'State' and 'Government' has received little attention, although it is a problem of considerable intrinsic difficulty.[110] One of the prerequisites for statehood is the existence

'State Sovereignty and the U.N. Charter' (Oxford, MS. D. Phil. d. 3227, 1964). Hossain distinguishes three meanings of sovereignty:

(1) State sovereignty as a distinctive characteristic of States as constituent units of the international legal system;

(2) Sovereignty as freedom of action in respect of all matters with regard to which a State is not under any legal obligation; and

(3) Sovereignty as the minimum amount of autonomy which a State must possess before it can be accorded the status of a 'sovereign state'. A fourth—sovereignty as plenary international authority to administer territory—may be added.

[106] *Infra*, p. 71.

[107] Cf. *Harris* v. *The Minister of the Interior* [1952] 2 S.A. (AD) 428.

[108] *Infra*, p. 190.

[109] Cf. Westlake, *International Law* (1904) I, 237; Hart, *The Concept of Law* (1961), 217–8.

[110] Cf. the paucity of authority cited in Whiteman, 1 *Digest* 911–16. See also Jennings (1967), 121 *HR* 350–2; Arangio-Ruiz, 260–303; Verhoeven, 66–71.

of an effective government; and the main, indeed, for most purposes the only, organ by which the State acts in international relations is its (central) government. There would thus seem to be a close relation between the two concepts. According to O'Connell: 'Until the middle of the nineteenth century, both types of change [change of State and change of government] were assimilated; and the problems they raised were uniformly solved. With the abstraction of the concept of sovereignty, however, a conceptual chasm was opened between change of sovereignty and change of government ...'[111] This 'post-Hegelian'[112] development O'Connell criticizes as 'dogmatic' and 'arbitrary'.[113] In the context of succession to obligations—that is, in the context of the legal effects of changes in State or government—it is more useful and more cogent in his view to pay regard not to any such distinction but to the real changes or continuities in political, social and administrative structure.[114] He thus advocates, in effect, a return to the eighteenth-century position of practical assimilation of changes of State and government.[115]

It can readily be admitted that some changes of government have greater and more traumatic effects than many changes of State personality.[116] None the less it seems a fair assumption that changes in State personality are more likely to be of greater social and structural importance than changes in government. In any case international law does distinguish between change of State personality and change of government.[117] Thus, *prima facie*, the State continues to exist, with concomitant rights and obligations, despite revolutionary changes in government, or despite a period in which there is no, or no effective, government.[118] Belligerent occupation, it is established, does not affect the continuity of the State, even where there exists no government claiming to represent the occupied State.[119] The

---

[111] *State Succession* I, 5–6.

[112] Ibid. vi.

[113] Ibid. I, 7; II, vi.

[114] Ibid. II, vi.

[115] Ibid. I, 7.

[116] Cf. the debate as to whether the U.S.S.R. was a new State or simply a new government after 1917: *infra*, p. 405.

[117] Wright (1952), 46 *AJ* 299–308, 307; cf. Jessup, *Modern Law of Nations*, 43.

[118] *Infra*, p. 405

[119] *Infra*, p. 407.

legal position of governments-in-exile is thus dependent on the distinction between government and State.[120] So also is the characterization of a lengthy conflict such as the Spanish Civil War as a 'civil' rather than as 'international' war.[121] The concept of representation of States in international organizations also depends upon the distinction.

Moreover, in the context of State succession, it is important to note that, in arguing for a closer identification of 'State' and 'government', O'Connell is seeking to maximize the extent to which treaty obligations and the like are legally transmitted from one State to its successor.[122] However, the law of State succession has developed otherwise: it is now generally accepted that successor States, in particular newly independent States, have substantial freedom as to the succession of treaty rights and obligations. To obliterate the distinction between 'change of State' and 'change of government' would now only decrease the stability of legal relations between governments, and would thus have precisely the opposite effect from that for which O'Connell was arguing.

(4) *The distinction between 'State personality' and 'State succession'*

There is then a clear distinction in principle between the legal personality of the State, and the government for the time being of the State.[123] This serves to distinguish in turn the field of State personality (which includes the topics of identity and continuity of States) and that of State succession.[124] State succession depends upon the conclusion reached as to State personality.[125] This is not to say, however, that the topic of State succession is entirely irrelevant to this study. Views taken of particular State succession

[120] Whiteman, 1 *Digest* 921–30; Oppenheimer (1942), 26 *AJ* 568–95; Verhoeven, *Reconnaissance*, 76–83.

[121] For the distinction between government and State in the Spanish Civil War, see *Government of Spain* v. *Chancery Lane Safe Deposit Ltd.*; *State of Spain* v. *Chancery Lane Safe Deposit Ltd.*, *The Times*, 26 May 1939; noted (1944) 21 *BY* 195–6.

[122] Cf. *State Succession* I, 30–5. The argument, for opposite reasons, was advanced by La Forest (1966), 60 *PAS* 103–11; cf. the reactions of Briggs (ibid. 125), Aufricht (126).

[123] Cf. O'Connell, *State Succession* I, 3; and in 1972 *Grotius SP*, 23–75, 26–8; Charpentier, *Reconnaissance*, 15–16.

[124] Marek, *Identity and Continuity*, 9–14, 9 describes the two as 'mutually exclusive'; cf. Pereira, *La Succession d'États en Matière de Traité* (1969), 7–11. The I.L.C. has also resisted attempts at eroding the distinction in its work on State succession: see e.g. *ILC Ybk*, 1974/II (1), 14–16, 30–1.

[125] Hall, op. cit. 114, cited O'Connell, *State Succession* I, 3.

situations may illuminate related problems of personality. In some areas, at least, the principles and policy considerations involved are the same. In particular the problem of 'State succession' in the case of devolving territories (for example, the British Dominions) is in part a matter of succession and in part a matter of personality.[126] None the less the two areas remain formally distinct.

[126] *Infra*, p. 240.

2. The Criteria for Statehood

2.1 INTRODUCTORY

IF THE effect of positivist doctrine in international law was to place the emphasis, in matters of statehood, on the question of recognition, then the effect of modern doctrine and practice has been to return the attention to issues of statehood and status, independent of recognition. Nevertheless there is no generally accepted and satisfactory modern legal definition of statehood.[1] This may well be because the question normally arises only in the borderline cases, where a new entity has emerged bearing some but not all of the characteristics of undoubted States. International lawyers are thus confronted with difficult problems of characterization; and, as has been suggested, such problems do not occur, and cannot be solved, except in relation to the particular issues and circumstances.[2] But, it may be asked, are there any legal consequences which attach to statehood as such, but which are not legal incidents of other forms of international personality? To put it another way, is there a legal concept of statehood, or does the meaning of the term vary infinitely depending on the context?[3] We have discussed the attempt to

---

[1] Both the League's Committee of Experts for the Progressive Codification of International Law (see their *Minutes* (ed. Rosenne, 1972) I, 38–9), and the I.L.C. have consistently rejected proposals to codify rules relating to recognition and statehood. Cf. Lauterpacht, *Collected Papers* I, 477–9. For debates on the issue in the I.L.C., see e.g. *ILC Ybk.* 1949, 64–8, 81–8, 150–2, 171–4, 178; ibid., 1956/II, 107; ibid., 1966/II, 178, 192; ibid., 1970/II, 178, 306. The rather delicate balance between reluctance and need to deal with the issue is demonstrated in the Draft Articles on State Succession in respect of Treaties; Art. 2 para. 1 (e) defines the 'succession of States' by reference to the 'fact of succession'; but Art. 6 provides that only successions of States occurring consistently with international law are governed by the Articles. Cf. however Vallat, *ILC Ybk* 1974/II (1), 18–19 for a reassertion of the long-standing position.

The topic of recognition of States and governments has remained on the I.L.C. work programme since 1949, but little interest has been shown in pursuing the matter. At the 1973 Session, during a discussion of the future work programme, the consensus was that: 'The question of recognition of States and governments should be set aside for the time being, for although it had legal consequences, it raised many political problems which did not lend themselves to regulation by law' (*ILC Ybk.* 1973/I, 175 (Bilge); also 164 (Castañeda); but cf. 165, 170 (Tsuruoka)).

[2] *Supra*, p. 15.

[3] Cf. Weissberg, *International Status of the United Nations* (1961), 193–4.

dispense with criteria for statehood by way of recognition.[4] On the other hand some modern writers come close to denying the existence of statehood as a legal concept in the interests of a thoroughgoing functionalism. Such views are of value as a reaction against absolutist notions of statehood and sovereignty,[5] but statehood does appear to be a term of art in international law; though of course, like all legal, and especially international legal, concepts it is one of open texture. The following exclusive and general legal characteristics of States may be instanced.

(1) In principle, States have plenary competence to perform acts, make treaties, and so on, in the international sphere: this is one meaning of the term 'sovereign' as applied to States.

(2) In principle States are exclusively competent with respect to their internal affairs, a principle reflected by Article 2(7) of the United Nations Charter. This does not of course mean that they are omnicompetent, in international law, with respect to those affairs: it does mean that their jurisdiction is *prima facie* both plenary and not subject to the control of other States.

(3) In principle States are not subject to compulsory international process, jurisdiction, or settlement, unless they consent, either in specific cases or generally, to such exercise.[6]

(4) States are regarded in international law as 'equal', a principle also recognized by the Charter (Article 2(1)). This is in part a restatement of the foregoing principles, but it may have certain other corollaries.[7] It is a formal, not a moral or political, principle. It does not mean, for example, that all States are entitled to an equal vote in international organizations;[8] merely that, in any international organization not based on equality, the consent of all the Members to the derogation from equality is required.

(5) Finally, any derogations from these principles must be clearly established: in case of doubt an international court or tribunal will decide in favour of the freedom of action of States,

---

[4] *Supra*, pp. 17–20.

[5] Cf. Higgins, *Development*, 11–17, 42–5, 54–7; Riphagen (1975), 6 *NYIL* 121–65.

[6] *Monetary Gold removed from Rome in 1943* I.C.J. Rep. 1954 p. 19; *Western Sahara Case* I.C.J. Rep. 1975 p. 12, 33.

[7] See Dickinson, *The Equality of States in Public International Law* (1920): the notion of equality of States is not historically a deduction from sovereignty, however: ibid. 56, 334–6.

[8] Cf. Brierly, *The Law of Nations*, 130–3.

whether with respect to external[9] or internal affairs,[10] or as not having consented to a specific exercise of international jurisdiction,[11] or to a particular derogation from equality.[12] This presumption—which is of course rebuttable in any case—is important in practice, as well as providing a useful indication of the status of the entity in whose favour it is invoked. It will be referred to throughout this study as the *Lotus* presumption—its classic formulation being the judgment of the Permanent Court in *The Lotus*.[13]

These five principles, it is submitted, constitute in legal terms the hard core of the concept of statehood, the essence of the special position in customary international law of States. It follows from this, as a rule of interpretation, that the term 'State' in any document *prima facie* refers to States having these attributes; but this is of course subject to the context. Courts will tend towards strictness of interpretation of the term 'State' as the context predicates plenitude of functions—as for example in Article 4(1) of the United Nations Charter.[14] Conversely, if a treaty or other document is concerned with a specific issue, the word 'State' may be construed liberally—that is, to mean 'State for the specific purpose' of the treaty or document.

The list of five principles thus enunciated appears nominal,

---

[9] *The Lotus*, Ser. A No. 10 (1927), 18; though, of course, in external affairs the strength of the presumption is less, since it must be weighed against the equal rights of other States.

[10] *Polish War Vessels in the Port of Danzig*, Ser. A/B No. 43 (1931), 142.

[11] *Eastern Carelia Opinion*, Ser. B. No. 5 (1923), 27-9.

[12] *Interpretation of Peace Treaties (Second Phase)* I.C.J. Rep. 1950 p. 221, 228-9.

[13] Ser. A No. 10 (1927), 18. The cogency of the *Lotus* presumption in modern law has been doubted: see e.g. Brownlie, *Principles*, 609. It was referred to with approval by the Permanent Court in its Order of 6 Dec. 1930 in the *Free Zones Case*, Ser. A No. 24, 11-12. But it was not applied by the Court in cases involving the constitution of international organizations, when a relatively extensive interpretation was adopted: see *Competence of the I.L.O. with respect to Agricultural Labour*, Ser. B. Nos. 2-3 (1922), 23-6; *Competence of the I.L.O. to regulate, incidentally, the work of the Employer*, Ser. B. No. 13 (1926), 21-3; *Jurisdiction of the European Commission of the Danube*, Ser. B. No. 14 (1927), 36, 63-4; *contra* Judge Negulesco diss., 104-5. And cf. *Territorial Jurisdiction of the Oder Commission*, Ser. A. No. 23 (1929), 26. Like most of the so-called 'rules of interpretation' the *Lotus* presumption found no place in the Vienna Convention on the Law of Treaties, Arts. 31-3. It was not applied by the majority in the *Admissions Case* I.C.J. Rep. 1948 p. 63; cf. diss. op. (Judges Basdevant, Winiarski, McNair, Read), 86, referring to it as 'a rule of interpretation frequently applied by the Permanent Court'. It was applied by the Majority in the *Asylum Case* I.C.J. Rep. 1950 p. 266, 275. See also Lauterpacht (1949), 26 *BY* 48-85; Delupis, *International Law and the Independent State* (1974), 23-5.

[14] *Infra*, p. 133.

but it would seem difficult to add more substantive candidates. Thus the possession of a nationality is not conclusive for statehood.[15] Nor is the fact that an entity is governed by international law conclusive: international organizations with separate legal personality,[16] devolving governments,[17] in fact all subjects of international law are so governed. The rule embodied in article 2(4) of the Charter, enjoining the use of force by States except in certain cases, applies also to certain non-State entities.[18] That an entity is responsible for its external affairs (even if it does not itself conduct them) is not conclusive, since non-States may also be responsible for international wrongs.[19] On the other hand, the fact that an entity is not internationally responsible for its acts is probably conclusive against its being a State,[20] though which of two entities is responsible in a situation of divided competences is often a question of great difficulty. And it is sometimes said that States only are competent to develop or change customary international law.[21] Even if true, this is unhelpful as a criterion because it is not equally (or at all) true of all States. Many other examples could be given.

If there is then a legal concept of statehood, it follows that the law must find some means of determining which entities are 'States', with the above attributes; in other words, of determining the criteria for statehood. It is with this that we are here concerned.

Two preliminary points should however be made. First, upon examination the exclusive attributes of States listed above are found not to prescribe specific rights, powers or capacities which all States must, to be States, possess: rather they are presumptions

[15] Andorra, which is probably not a State, none the less has its own nationality: Bélinguier, *La Condition juridique des vallées d'Andorra* (1970), 206–21, 221; Ourliac, in *Mélanges Maury* I, 403–15.

[16] *Supra*, p. 26.

[17] *Infra*, p. 232.

[18] Brownlie, *Use of Force*, 380–1; Higgins, *Development*, 221–2.

[19] This is probably the case with the U.N.: Weissberg, *International Status of the United Nations*, 209; cf. 1975 U.N. *Jur. Ybk.* 153–5.

[20] Cf. Waldock: 'a distinction must be made between the conduct of international relations, and responsibility for international relations. The latter phrase has always been used in connection with dependent territories in the past, and was the best short definition possible.' *ILC Ybk.* 1972/I, 271; and for discussion of this formula, ibid. 1974/II (1), 26–8.

[21] *Nanni* v. *Pace and the Sovereign Order of Malta* (1935) 8 AD No. 2.

as to the existence of such rights, powers, or liberties, rules that these exist unless otherwise provided for. This must be so, since the actual powers, rights, and liberties of particular States vary considerably. The legal consequences of statehood are thus seen to be—paradoxically—matters of evidence, or rather of presumption. Predicated on a basic or 'structural' independence,[22] statehood does not involve any necessary substantive rights. Equally the law recognizes no general duty on a State to maintain that independence: independence is protected while it exists, but there is no prohibition on its partial or permanent alienation.[23] The legal concept of statehood provides a measure for determining whether in a given case rights have or have not been lost.

Secondly, the criteria for statehood are rather special rules, in that their application conditions the application of most other international law rules. As a result, existing States have sometimes tended to assert more or less complete freedom of action with regard to new States. This may explain the reluctance of the International Law Commission to frame comprehensive definitions of statehood when engaged on other work—albeit work which assumed that the category 'States' is ascertained or ascertainable.[24] It follows that, at the empirical level, the question must again be asked: whether, given the existence of international law rules determining what are 'States', those rules are sufficiently certain to be applied in specific cases, or else have been kept so uncertain or open to interpretation as not to constitute rules at all. And this question is independent of the point—which is accepted—that States may on occasions treat as a State an entity which does not come within the accepted definition of the term.[25] The question is rather—can States legitimately refuse, under cover of the 'open texture' of rules, to treat entities as States which do in fact qualify? To prevent that is the point of having— if in fact we do have—'objective' criteria for statehood.

---

[22] For the concept of independence see *infra*, pp. 48–71.

[23] Cf. Judge Anzilotti, sep. op., *Austro-German Customs Union Case*, Ser. A/B No. 41 (1931), 59.

[24] *Supra*, p. 31, n. 1.

[25] Thus the Holy See (1870–1929) and British India (1919–47), were treated as States for at least some purposes. Cf. also *supra*, p. 24. But cf. Higgins, *Development*, 41n.69; Marek, *Identity and Continuity*, 145, both of whom are too unqualified in their support of the 'declaratory theory'.

2.2   CLASSICAL CRITERIA FOR STATEHOOD

The best known formulation of the basic criteria for statehood is that laid down in Article 1 of the Montevideo Convention, 1933:

The State as a person of international law should possess the following qualifications: (a) a permanent population; (b) a defined territory; (c) government; and (d) capacity to enter into relations with other States.[26]

It is a characteristic of these criteria—and of the others to be examined in this section—that they are based on the principle of effectiveness among territorial units. By contrast, recent suggested criteria to be examined in the next Chapter either supplement or in certain cases contradict this principle. But they operate only in rather exceptional cases: the accepted criteria must first be dealt with.[27]

(1)   *Defined territory*

It is evident that States are territorial entities. 'Territorial sovereignty . . . involves the exclusive right to display the activities of a State.'[28] Conversely, the right to be a State is dependent at least in the first instance upon the exercise of full governmental powers with respect to some area of territory. But, although a State must 'possess' some territory, there appears to be no rule prescribing the minimum area of that territory. States may thus occupy an extremely small area, provided they are independent in the sense to be explained. Monaco and Nauru, for example, are respectively only 1·5 and 21 square kilometres in area.[29] The relation between statehood and territorial sovereignty thus appears to be of a special kind—a point which the traditional law failed to emphasize, since it concentrated on

---

[26] 165 *LNTS* 19. Cf. Crane, *The State in Constitutional and International Law* (Baltimore, 1907), 65; Kelsen (1929) 4 *RDI* 613–41, 614.

[27] The literature is rather sparse. See however Brownlie, *Principles*, 74–82; Rousseau, *DIP* II, 13–44; Higgins, *Development*, 11–57; Lauterpacht, *Recognition*, 26–32; Marek, *Identity and Continuity*, 161–90; Chen, *Recognition*, 54–62; Kamanda, *Legal Status of Protectorates*, 175–87; Antonowicz (1966–7), 1 *Pol. YIL* 195–207; Whiteman, 1 *Digest* 221–33, 2 *Digest* 68–119 (mostly recognition of governments); Devine (1971), 34 *MLR* 410–17; Mendelson, 82–169.

[28] *Island of Palmas Case* (1928) 1 *RIAA* 829, 839 *per* Judge Huber.

[29] For the Vatican (0·4 km.) see *infra*, p. 154; generally see Mendelson (1972), 21 *ICLQ* 609–30, 610–17; Verhoeven, *Reconnaissance*, 54.

problems of acquisition of territory by already existing States, on the view that territorial sovereignty was analogous to the ownership of land by natural persons. That analogy was of limited value even in those situations, and in the case of acquisition of territory by new States it was positively misleading.[30] The relation will be examined in a later Chapter: it is enough to say here that the category 'statehood' probably takes priority over the category 'acquisition of territory'; in other words, that the establishment of a new State on certain territory defeats claims by other States which relate to the whole of the territory so occupied; and where the claims relate to part only of the territory, makes them dependent for settlement on the consent of the new State.

It is suggested then that a new State may exist despite claims to its territory, just as an existing State continues despite such claims.[31] Two different situations may be distinguished: first, where the claim relates to the entire territory of a new State; secondly, where it relates to the boundaries of the State. In particular cases the two types of claim may coexist. This was so with Israel in 1948: it was argued that G.A. Resolution 181 (II) of 29 November 1947 in some way conferred territory on the new State, so that the case was merely one of undefined frontiers, but the other view is tenable. In any case Israel was admitted to the United Nations on 11 May 1949.[32] Jessup, arguing for Israel's admission on behalf of the United States, discussed the requirement of territory in the following terms:

One does not find in the general classic treatment of this subject any insistence that the territory of a State must be exactly fixed by definite frontiers ... The formulae in the classic treatises somewhat vary, ... but both reason and history demonstrate that the concept of territory does not necessarily include precise delimitation of the boundaries of that territory. The reason for the rule that one of the necessary attributes of a State is that it shall possess territory is that one cannot contemplate a State as a kind of disembodied spirit ... (T)here must be

---

[30] Cf. Jennings, *Acquisition of Territory*, 7–11.
[31] The point was assumed by the Permanent Court in two cases: *Monastery at St. Naoum (Albanian Frontier)*, Ser. B. No. 9 (1924); *Polish-Czechoslovakian Frontier (Question of Jaworzina)*, Ser. B No. 8 (1923). But cf. the stricter view proposed in the British Memorial: *Interpretation of the Treaty of Lausanne*, Ser. C. No. 10, 202–3. There is no reference to the matter in the judgment: Ser. B. No. 12 (1925). See further, *infra*, pp. 396–9.
[32] G.A. Res. 273 (III) (37–12:9); S.C. Res. 70, 4 Mar. 1949 (9–1 (Egypt): 1 (U.K.)).

some portion of the earth's surface which its people inhabit and over which its Government exercises authority. No one can deny that the State of Israel responds to this requirement . . .[33]

Claims to the entire territory of a State have commonly been raised in the context of admission to the United Nations: this was the case with Israel, and also with Kuwait and Mauritania.[34] The proposition that a State exists despite claims to the whole of its territory was not challenged in these cases. In any event, customary international law prohibits the settlement of territorial disputes between States by the threat or use of force, and a State for the purpose of this rule means any entity established as a State in a given territory, whether or not that territory formerly belonged to, or is claimed by, another State.[35]

It is only to be expected then that claims to less than the entire territory of a new State and, in particular, boundary disputes, do not affect statehood. A German-Polish Mixed Arbitral Tribunal stated the rule succinctly:

Whatever may be the importance of the delimitation of boundaries, one cannot go so far as to maintain that as long as this delimitation has not been legally effected the State in question cannot be considered as having any territory whatever . . . In order to say that a State exists . . . it is enough that this territory has a sufficient consistency, even though its boundaries have not yet been accurately delimited, and that the State actually exercises independent public authority over that territory.[36]

And the International Court in the *North Sea Continental Shelf Cases* confirmed the rule as it were *en passant*:

The appurtenance of a given area, considered as an entity, in no way governs the precise delimitation of its boundaries, any more than uncertainty as to boundaries can affect territorial rights. There is for instance no rule that the land frontiers of a State must be fully delimited and defined, and often in various places and for long periods they are

---

[33] *SCOR* 383rd. mtg., 2 Dec. 1948, 41.

[34] On Kuwait see Al Baharna, *The Legal Status of the Arabian Gulf States* (1968), 250–8; Hassouna, *The League of Arab States and Regional Disputes* (1975), 91–140. On Mauritania see Higgins, *Development*, 18–19, 307. For Bahrein see *infra*, p. 191. Cf. also Mendelson, 100–8.

[35] *Infra*, p. 398.

[36] *Deutsche Continental Gas-Gesellschaft* v. *Polish State* (1929) 5 A.D. No. 5, 14–15.

not, as is shown by the case of the entry of Albania into the League of Nations.[37]

The question is whether there are any exceptions to this rule which are not better referred to defects of government or independence. Higgins states that 'when the doubts as to the future frontiers [are] of a serious nature, statehood [becomes] in doubt. Thus when in 1919 Estonia and Latvia were recognized by the Allied Powers, no recognition was granted to Lithuania on the express ground, that owing to the Vilna dispute, its frontiers were not yet fixed.'[38] In view of what has been said, this may be doubted: in any event the specific example given, that of Lithuania, is not such a case. It is true that *de jure* recognition of Lithuania by the Allies was refused because of the Vilna dispute,[39] but this action appears to have been politically motivated; it was not an expression of an Allied view that Lithuania was not a State. The British Under-Secretary of State for Foreign Affairs had previously admitted that the Polish occupation of Vilna (Wilno) was an occupation 'of Lithuanian territory',[40] and as late as 1920 the Prime Minister agreed that the same considerations applied to the *de jure* recognition of Lithuania as to Latvia and Estonia.[41] The merits of the Vilna dispute appear to have been very decidedly in favour of Lithuania,[42] and the Allied actions to have been based more on the desire for a strong Poland than an appreciation of those merits.[43] However that may be, it is clear that Lithuania and the other so-called 'Border States' were independent States by mid-1919, despite then-existent or subsequent territorial claims. Arbitrator Reichmann in *Germany* v. *Reparations Commission* stated that: 'Le Gouvernement lithuanien a été reconnu *de facto* en septembre 1919, mais il existait comme Gouvernement indépendent déjà lors de la signature du Traité de Versailles . . .'[44]

[37] I.C.J. Rep. 1969 p. 3, 32.

[38] Higgins, *Development*, 20n.

[39] *H.C. Deb.* Vol. 139, col. 2207, 21 Mar. 1921.

[40] Ibid. Vol. 116 (1919), col. 1201, 28 May 1919.

[41] Ibid. Vol. 129 (1920), col. 240, 11 May 1920.

[42] Lapradelle, le Fur, Mandelstam, *The Vilna Question* (1929); Langer, *Seizure of Territory*, 22–5; Scelle (1928), 35 *RGDIP* 730–80; *LNOJ* Sp. Supp. No. 4 (1920); Brockelbank (1926), 20 *AJ* 483–501.

[43] Cf. Judge Anzilotti, *Railway Traffic Between Lithuania and Poland*, Ser. A/B No. 42 (1931), 123.

[44] (1924) 1 *RIAA* 524, 525 (13th Question).

Lithuania was thus not included in the territory of 'Russia' within the meaning of Article 260 of the Treaty at the time it was signed (28 June 1919). And the same opinion was evidently held, though it was not directly in point in either case, by the Permanent Court in two cases concerning Lithuania.[45]

It appears then that even a substantial boundary or territorial dispute with a new State is not enough to bring statehood into question. The only requirement is that the State must consist of a certain coherent territory effectively governed—a formula which demonstrates that the requirement of territory is rather a constituent of government and independence than a separate criterion of its own.

(2) *Permanent population*

If States are territorial entities, they are also aggregates of individuals. A permanent population is thus necessary for statehood, though, as in the case of territory, no minimum limit is apparently prescribed. For example in 1973 the estimated population of Nauru was only 6,500; that of San Marino was 20,000. Of putative States with very small populations, only the Vatican City may be challengeable on this ground, and this as much because of the professional and non-permanent nature of its population as its size.[46]

The rule under discussion requires States to have a permanent population: it is not a rule relating to the nationality of that population. It appears that the grant of nationality is a matter which only States by their municipal law (or by way of treaty) can perform.[47] Nationality is thus dependent upon statehood, not the reverse. Whether the creation of a new State on the territory of another results in statelessness of the nationals of the previous State there resident,[48] or an automatic change in nationality,[49] or in retention of the previous nationality until

---

[45] In the *Railway Traffic Case*, Ser. A/B No. 42 (1931), 112, the Court thought the establishment of Lithuania antedated the seizure of Vilna on 9 Oct. 1920. See also *Panavezys–Saldutiskis Ry. Case*, Ser. A/B No. 76 (1939), 10. To the same effect *Répertoire suisse* I, 439–41.

[46] *Infra*, p. 154.

[47] *Nottebohm Case (Second Phase)* I.C.J. Rep. 1955 p. 4, 23.

[48] Cf. the Israeli cases in the period (1948–52) when there was no Israeli nationality law: 17 ILR 110–12. See also *Naqara* v. *Minister of the Interior* (1953) 20 ILR 49.

[49] *A.B.* v. *M.B.* (1951) 17 ILR 110, referring to the 'absurd result of a State without nationals'; Draft Convention of Harvard Law Research, Art.18(2); *Wildermann* v. *Stinnes* 2 AD No. 120 (1924); *Poznanski* v. *Lentz & Hirschfeld* (1925) 4 *Rep. MAT* 353.

provision is otherwise made by treaty or the law of the new State[50] is a matter of some doubt. The problem is made more difficult because of the confusion prevalent between 'international nationality' (i.e. nationality under the 'effective link' doctrine) and municipal nationality. Persons could very well be regarded as nationals of a particular State for international purposes before the State concerned had established rules for granting or determining its (municipal) nationality. On the other hand, apart from treaty a new State is not obliged to extend its nationality to *all* persons resident on its territory. Two views of the matter may be contrasted:

... in view of the rule that every State must have a determinate population (as an element of its statehood), and therefore nationality always has an international aspect, there is no very fundamental distinction between the issue of statehood and that of transfer of territory ... [T]he evidence is overwhelmingly in support of the view that the population follows the change of sovereignty in matters of nationality.[51]

Although inhabitants of territory ceded by or seceding from the Crown lose their British nationality, it does not follow that they acquire either automatically or by submission that of the successor State. The latter may withhold the granting of its nationality to all or portions of the persons concerned ... Undesirable as it may be that any persons become stateless as a result of a change of sovereignty, it cannot be asserted with any measure of confidence that international law, at least in its present stage of development, imposes any duty on the successor State to grant nationality.[52]

A tentative reconciliation may be suggested: in the absence of provision to the contrary, persons habitually resident in the territory of the new State automatically acquire the nationality of that State, for all international purposes, and lose their former nationality, but this is subject to a right in the new State to delimit more particularly which persons it will regard as its nationals. This view is at least consistent with the judgment of the Permanent Court in the *Case Concerning Acquisition of Polish Nationality*:

[50] *Date of Entry into Force of Versailles Treaty (Germany) Case* 32 ILR 339 (1961); Weis, *Nationality and Statelessness in International Law* (1956), 151 ff.
[51] Brownlie (1963), 39 *BY* 284–364, 320.
[52] O'Connell, *State Succession* I, 497–528, 503.

the Minorities Treaties in general, and the Polish Treaty in particular, have been concluded with new States, or with States which, as a result of the war, have had their territories considerably enlarged, and whose population was not therefore clearly defined from the standpoint of political allegiance. One of the first problems which presented itself in connection with the protection of the minorities was that of preventing these States from refusing their nationality, on racial, religious or linguistic grounds, to certain categories of persons, in spite of the link which effectively attached them to the territory allocated to one or other of these States.[53]

(3) *Government*

The requirement that a putative State have an effective government might be regarded as central to its claim to statehood. 'Government' or 'effective Government' is obviously a basis for the other central requirement of independence.[54] Moreover, international law defines 'territory' not by adopting private law analogies of real property, but by reference to the extent of governmental power exercised, or capable of being exercised, with respect to some area and population. Territorial sovereignty is not ownership of, but governing power with respect to, territory. There is thus a strong case for regarding government as the most important single criterion of statehood, since all the others depend upon it. The difficulty is, however, that the legal criteria for statehood are of necessity nominal and exclusionary: that is to say, their concern is not with the central, clear cases but with the borderline ones. Hence the application of the criterion of government in practice is much less simple than this analysis might suggest.

A striking modern illustration is that of the former Belgian Congo, granted a hurried independence in 1960 as the Republic of the Congo (now Zaire). The situation in the Congo after

---

[53] Ser. B No. 7 (1923), 15. Cf. also *Nationality (Secession of Austria) Case* 21 ILR 175 (1954); *Murray* v. *Parkes* [1942] 2 K.B. 123; Graupner (1946), 32 *Grotius ST* 87–120.

[54] It is clear that 'government' and 'independence' are closely related as criteria—in fact they may be regarded as different aspects of the requirement of effective separate control. For present purposes, government is treated as the exercise of authority with respect to persons and property within the territory claimed; whereas independence is treated as the exercise, or the right to exercise, such authority with respect to other international persons, whether within or outside the territory claimed. Other writers draw a similar distinction but in different terms: for example Wheaton ('internal' and 'external' sovereignty); Kamanda, *Legal Status of Protectorates*, 175–82 ('sovereignty' (internal) and 'independence' (external)).

independence has been described elsewhere.[55] No effective preparations had been made; the new government was bankrupt, divided, and in practice hardly able to control even the capital. Belgian and other troops intervened, shortly after independence, under claim of humanitarian intervention; and extensive United Nations financial and military assistance became necessary almost immediately.[56] Among the tasks of the United Nations force was, or came to be, the suppression of secession in Katanga, the richest Congolese province.[57] Anything less like effective government it would be hard to imagine.

Yet despite this there can be little doubt that the Congo was in 1960 a State in the full sense of the term. It was widely recognized. Its application for United Nations membership was approved without dissent.[58] United Nations action subsequent to admission was of course based on the 'sovereign rights of the Republic of the Congo'.[59] On no other basis could the attempted secession of the Katanga province have been condemned as 'illegal'.[60]

What then is to be made of the criterion of 'effective government'? Three views can be taken of the Congo situation in that regard. It may be that international recognition of the Congo was simply premature or wrongful, because, not posssessing an effective government, the Congo was not a State.[61] It may be that the recognition of the Congo was a case where an entity not properly qualified as a State is treated as such by other States, for whatever reason; that is, a case of constitutive recognition. Alternatively, it may be that the requirement of 'government' is less stringent than has been thought, at least in

[55] Kanza, *Conflict in the Congo* (1972), 192; Barraclough, ed., *Survey of International Affairs 1959–60*, 396–436; Hoskyns, *The Congo since Independence* (1965); Higgins, *Development*, 162–4.

[56] See e.g. the U.N.–Congolese Agreement on Financial Assistance, 23 Aug. 1960, 373 *UNTS* 327, providing $5,000,000 to finance normal imports (Art. 4) and 'to meet its current budgetary needs, preference being given to the government pay-roll and emergency relief expenditure' (Art. 7). Cf. Saïd, *De Léopoldville à Kinshasa. Le situation économique au Congo ex-Belge au jour de L'indépendence* (Neuchâtel, 1969).

[57] *Infra*, pp. 263–5.

[58] S.C. Res. 142, 7 July 1960; G.A. Res. 1480 (XV), 20 Sept. 1960.

[59] Cf. G.A. Res. 1974 (ES-IV), 20 Sept. 1960 (70–0:11), para. 6.

[60] S.C.Res. 169, 24 Nov. 1961 (9–0: 2).

[61] This was, it seems, the older view: Baty (1934), 28 *AJ* 444–55. Higgins describes the Congo's U.N. admission as a derogation from 'the fairly distinct pattern of consistent adherence to the requirement of a stable and effective government': *Development*, 21–2.

particular contexts. The last view, it will be argued, is to be preferred.[62]

The point about 'government' is that it has two aspects: the actual exercise of authority, and the right or title to exercise that authority. Prior to 1960 Belgium had that right, which it transferred to the new entity. Of course the Congo could thereafter have disintegrated; none the less, by granting independence, Belgium estopped itself from denying the consequences of that independence. There was thus no international person as against whom recognition of the Congo could be illegal. *Prima facie* a new State granted full formal independence by a former sovereign has the international right to govern its territory:[63] hence the United Nations action in support of that right. On the other hand, in the revolutionary situation no such estoppel exists and (apart from the principle of self-determination)[64] statehood can only be obtained by effective and stable exercise of governmental powers.[65] Although acquisition of territory does not provide an exact analogy, the difference is the same as between cession and prescription.

The position of Finland in 1917–18 provides a good example of the latter situation. Finland has been an autonomous part of the Russian Empire from 1807; it declared its independence after the November revolution. Its territory was thereafter subject to a series of military actions and interventions, and it was not until after the defeat of Germany by the Entente and the removal of Russian troops from Finnish territory by Sweden, that some degree of order was restored. In those circumstances it was not surprising that the Commission of Jurists appointed by the League to report on certain aspects of the Aaland Islands dispute were of opinion that:

for a considerable time, the conditions required for the formation of a sovereign State did not exist. In the midst of revolution and anarchy, certain elements essential to the existence of a State, even some elements of fact, were lacking for a fairly considerable period. Political and social life was disorganized; the authorities were not strong enough to

---

[62] Cf. the position in Cyprus at various stages after 1960: *A.G.* v. *Ibrahim* 48 ILR 6 (1964).

[63] *Infra*, Chapter 8.

[64] *Infra*, pp. 102–3, 258–63.

[65] *Infra*, Chapter 9.

assert themselves; civil war was rife; further, the Diet, the legality of which had been disputed by a large section of the people, had been dispersed by the revolutionary party, and the Government had been chased from the capital and forcibly prevented from carrying out its duties; the armed camps and the police were divided into two opposing forces, and Russian troops, and after a time Germans also, took part in the civil war . . . It is therefore difficult to say at what exact date the Finnish Republic, in the legal sense of the term, actually became a definitely constituted sovereign State. This certainly did not take place until a stable political organization had been created, and until the public authorities had become strong enough to assert themselves throughout the territories of the State without the assistance of foreign troops. It would appear that it was in May 1918, that the civil war was ended and that the foreign troops began to leave the country, so that from that time onwards it was possible to re-establish order and normal political and social life, little by little.[66]

The test applied, with comparative strictness, by the Jurists may be taken accurately to state the requirement of government in a secessionary situation where the principle of self-determination is inoperative. The Commission of Rapporteurs, on the other hand, disagreed with the Jurists on this point, because of the importance they attached to Soviet recognition of Finland,[67] and, more particularly, because of Finland's continuity of personality before and after 1917. They therefore applied rules relating to the restoration of law and order in Finnish territory, and to the legality of foreign assistance for that purpose,[68] rather than the stricter rules relating to the creation *ab initio* of stable government in a new State.[69]

The following conclusions suggest themselves. First, to be a State, an entity must possess a government or a system of government in general control of its territory, to the exclusion of other entities not claiming through or under it.[70]

Second, international law lays down no specific requirements

---

[66] *LNOJ* Sp. Supp. No. 4 (1920), 8–9.

[67] *LN* Council Doct. B7: 21/68/106 (1921), 22.

[68] Ibid. 23.

[69] Larnaude and Struycken, two of the Commission of Jurists, later reaffirmed their view before the Council: *LNOJ* Sept. 1921, 697. Huber was absent and could not give an opinion.

[70] This meets the common case where some of the functions of government are exercised by other States or entities on a basis of agency.

as to the nature and extent of this control, except, it seems, that it include some degree of maintenance of law and order.[71]

Third, in applying the general principle to specific cases, the following must be considered: (i) whether the statehood of the entity is opposed under title of international law: if so, the requirement of effectiveness is likely to be more strictly applied. (ii) Whether the government claiming authority in the putative State, if it does not effectively control it, has obtained authority by consent of the previous sovereign and exercises a certain degree of control.[72] (iii) In the latter case at least, the requirement of government may be liberally construed. (iv) Finally, there is a distinction between the creation of a new State on the one hand and the subsistence or extinction of an established State on the other.[73] There is normally no presumption in favour of the status of the former, and the criterion of effective government therefore tends to be applied more strictly.

It is thought that these considerations are borne out by established practice. Thus the factors favouring the statehood of the Congo apply *a fortiori* to the cases of Ruanda and Burundi,[74] as well as to other cases of 'premature independence'. On the other hand, where attempts at secession are not supported by self-determination principles, the requirement of effectiveness is strictly construed: this was so with Biafra, for example.[75]

The requirement of government thus has the following legal effects. Negatively, the lack of a coherent form of government in a given territory militates against that territory being a State, in the absence of other factors, such as the grant of independence to that territory by a former sovereign. The continued absence of a government will tend to the dissolution of any State in that area. Certain, particularly nomadic, tribes may not have government in the sense required and so may not be States, though they may have a more limited legal personality.[76] Positively, the existence of a system of government in, and

---

[71] This leaves the possibility of international claims for failure to maintain a degree of order (e.g. *Mexican Union Railway Case* (1930) 5 *RIAA* 115), but these are predicated on, and within wide limits do not negate the personality of the State.

[72] Cf. Higgins, *Development*, 24; *infra*, p. 218.

[73] *Infra*, pp. 403–12.

[74] Cf. Higgins, *Development*, 22–3.

[75] *Infra*, p. 265.

[76] *Infra*, pp. 177–81.

referable to, a specific territory indicates without more a certain legal status, and is in general a pre-condition for statehood. Continuity of government in a territory is one important factor determining continuity of the State concerned, as well as continuity between different forms of legal personality.[77] And, although the law distinguishes States from their governments, normally only the government of a State can bind that State, for example by treaty. The existence of a government in a territory is thus a pre-condition for the normal conduct of international relations.

To summarize, statehood is not 'simply' a factual situation but a legally defined claim of right, specifically to the competence to govern a certain territory. Whether that claim of right exists depends both on the facts and on whether it is disputed. Like other territorial rights, government as a pre-condition for statehood is thus, after a certain point, relative. But it is not entirely so: each State is an original foundation predicated on a certain basic independence. This was represented in the Montevideo formula by 'capacity to enter into relations with other States'.

(4) *Capacity to enter into relations with other States*

Capacity to enter into relations with States is no longer, if it ever was, the exclusive prerogative of States.[78] On the other hand, States preeminently possess that capacity; but this is not a criterion, but rather a consequence, of statehood, and one which is not constant but depends on the status and situation of particular States.[79] It might still be said that *capacity* to enter into the full range of international relations is a useful criterion.[80] But capacity or competence in this sense depends partly on the power of internal government of a territory, without which international obligations may not be carried into effect, and partly on the entity concerned being separate for the purpose of such relations so that no other entity both carries out and accepts responsibility for them. In other words, capacity to enter into

---

[77] *Infra*, Chapter 16.
[78] *Supra*, p. 341.
[79] *Supra*, p. 351.
[80] Cf. Montevideo Convention, Art. 1 (d); *Restatement 2nd, Foreign Relations Law of the U.S.*, §§ 4, 100(c).

relations with other States, in the sense in which it might be a useful criterion, is a conflation of the requirements of government and independence. To the latter we must now turn.

(5) *Independence*

Independence is the central criterion of statehood.[81] As Judge Huber stated in the *Island of Palmas Case*:

Sovereignty in the relations between States signifies independence. Independence in regard to a portion of the globe is the right to exercise therein, to the exclusion of any other State, the functions of a State. The development of the national organization of States during the last few centuries, and, as a corollary, the development of international law, have established this principle of the exclusive competence of the State in regard to its own territory in such a way as to make it the point of departure in settling most questions that concern international relations.[82]

It must first be said that different legal consequences may be attached to lack of independence in specific cases. Lack of independence can be so complete that the entity concerned is not a State but an internationally indistinguishable part of another dominant State.[83] A grant of 'independence' may, in certain circumstances, be a legal nullity, or even an act engaging the responsibility of the grantor, as with so-called 'puppet States'.[84] Or an entity may be independent in some basic sense but act in a specific matter under the control of another State so that the relation becomes one of agency, and the responsibility of the latter State is attracted for illegal acts of the former.

Moreover, although our concern is with independence as the basic element of statehood in international law, in other contexts the term can have other meanings. In paricular, it is important to distinguish independence as an initial qualification for statehood, and as a criterion for its continued existence. For example, the presumption of continuity of existing legal rights, which may be regarded as a general principle of law, may operate in different directions in the two cases. A new State

---

[81] See Higgins, *Development*, 25–42; Kamanda, *Legal Status of Protectorates*, 188–91; Verzijl, *International Law* II, 455–90; Mendelson, 114–67, and works cited *infra*.

[82] (1928) 2 *RIAA* 829, 838.

[83] e.g. colonial protectorates: *infra*, p. 199.

[84] *Infra*, pp. 62–5.

formed by secession from a metropolitan State will have to demonstrate substantial independence, both formal and real, before it will be regarded as definitively created.[85] On the other hand, the independence of an existing State is protected by international law rules against illegal invasion and annexation, so that the State may, even for a considerable time, continue to exist as a legal entity despite lack of effectiveness.[86] Throughout the following discussion therefore, the context in which the claim to independence or to loss of independence is made is of considerable significance.

There is a further, related, distinction to be drawn between independence as a criterion for statehood, and independence as a right of States.[87] These distinctions are relevant to an examination of the 'leading case' on independence, the *Austro-German Customs Union Case*,[88] which involved the meaning of the term 'independence' in a treaty designed to guarantee the continuance of Austria and its separation from Germany; and the question of the putative loss of independence of an existing State. The Court was asked to advise whether the proposed customs union between Germany and Austria was consistent with obligations of Austria under the Treaty of Saint-Germain and the Protocol of Geneva.[89] The judges were unanimous in holding that the proposed regime, based as it was on the equality of the two parties and with provision for withdrawal at twelve months notice,[90] was not an 'alienation' of independence. Indeed, that proposition could 'scarcely be denied'.[91] But, by eight votes to seven, the Court held the proposed union illegal. The Majority

---

[85] *Supra*, p. 45; *infra*, p. 266.

[86] *Infra*, Chapters 16, 17.

[87] Cf. Whiteman, 5 *Digest* 88–124.

[88] Ser. A/B No. 41 (1931).

[89] By Art. 88 of the Treaty of St.-Germain, 1919, Austria's independence was inalienable except with the consent of the League Council: Austria undertook 'to abstain from any act which might directly or indirectly or by any means whatever compromise her independence . . . by participation in the affairs of another Power': 112 *BFSP* 317, 360. By Protocol No. 1 of 1922, Austria again undertook not to alienate its independence, to abstain from all 'negotiation and from any economic or financial undertaking calculated directly or indirectly to compromise this independence', and not to grant 'to any State whatever a *special régime or exclusive advantages* calculated to threaten this independence': 116 *BFSP* 851 (my itals.).

[90] Protocol of Vienna, Arts. XI(3), XII: 134 *BFSP* 991. The proposal was in fact abandoned before the Court's judgment.

[91] Majority Opinion, Ser. A/B No. 41, 52; Judge Anzilotti, ibid. 66–7.

Opinion, while agreeing that Austria's independence was not 'strictly speaking' endangered within the meaning of Article 88, held that the proposed union was a 'special regime or exclusive advantages calculated to threaten [*sc.* economic] independence' within the meaning of the Protocol.[92] Judge Anzilotti doubted whether the Protocol could, in any case, legally extend the Treaty, but held the union inconsistent with both Treaty and Protocol.[93] A strong minority held it inconsistent with neither.[94] The case has been subject to the most stringent criticism:[95] moreover it is one of those instances where a majority can be found against each possible *ratio decidendi*. Nevertheless, its importance in our context is much less than has been made out, for several reasons.

For it seems clear that the Protocol, with its emphasis on 'economic independence', asserted an extensive interpretation of Article 88. The Protocol seems to suggest that 'a special regime or exclusive advantages' threatening merely 'economic independence' was prohibited by Article 88, a point the Majority expressly denied.[96] Moreover, the various agreements were not concerned with the criteria for statehood but with the preservation of full independence as a (possibly unwelcome) duty incumbent upon Austria for the benefit of general European peace.[97] This point was emphasized in the French submission, and in the oral argument of M. Basdevant,[98] and was implicitly accepted in the Majority Opinion:

> *irrespective of the definition of the independence of States which may be given by legal doctrine or may be adopted in particular instances in the practice of States*, the independence of Austria, according to Article 88 of the Treaty of Saint-Germain, must be understood to mean the continued existence of Austria within her present frontiers as a separate State with the sole

[92] Ibid. 52.

[93] Ibid. 64, 73.

[94] Ibid. 81–7.

[95] Brierly, in *Collected Papers*, 242–9 (1933); Morgenthau, *Politics among Nations* (5th edn., 1973), 426; Lauterpacht, *Development*, 47–9.

[96] Ser. A/B No. 41, 52.

[97] Ibid. 57 (Judge Anzilotti).

[98] Cf. French submission, Ser. C No. 53, 128: 'le Traité de Saint-Germain et le protocole de 1922 ... ont envisagé non la conception théorique de l'indépendance des États, mais l'indépendance de l'Autriche ... telle qu'elle se comportait en 1919.' Emphasized in oral argument of Basdevant: ibid. 400, 404, 417. Cf. the remark of M. Kaufmann, ibid. 508–9; Basdevant's reply, 566–7.

right of decision in all matters economic, political, financial or other with the result that that independence is violated, as soon as there is any violation thereof, either in the economic, political, or any other field, these different aspects of independence being in practice one and indivisible.[99]

This passage is often cited as a definition of independence, but it must be referred to its specific context. As a general definition of independence as the criterion of statehood it is much too absolute.

The Minority Opinion differed not so much over the definition of 'independence' for the relevant purposes as over the disputed questions of fact.[100] On the other hand, the definition of independence given by Judge Anzilotti has become the *locus classicus* and deserves quotation at length:

... the independence of Austria within the meaning of Article 88 is nothing else but the existence of Austria, within the frontiers laid down by the Treaty of Saint-Germain, as a separate state and not subject to the authority of any other State or group of States. Independence as thus understood is really no more than the normal condition of States according to international law; it may also be described as sovereignty (*suprema potestas*), or external sovereignty, by which is meant that the State has over it no other authority than that of international law ...

It follows that the legal conception of independence has nothing to do with a State's subordination to international law or with the numerous and constantly increasing states of *de facto* dependence which characterise the relation of one country to other countries. It also follows that the restrictions upon a State's liberty, whether arising out of ordinary international law or contractual engagements, do not as such in the least affect its independence. As long as these restrictions do not place the State under the legal authority of another State, the former remains an independent State however extensive and burdensome those obligations may be.[101]

Two main elements are involved here: the separate existence of an entity within reasonably coherent frontiers; and the fact

[99] Ser. A/B No. 41, 45 (my itals.). Cf. the significantly wider terms of Art. 4 of the Austrian State Treaty, 1955: 217 *UNTS* 225, 229.

[100] They thus gave a purely formal, and unhelpful, definition of independence: 'A State would not be independent in the legal sense if it was placed in a condition of dependence on another Power, if it ceased itself to exercise within its own territory the *summa potestas* or sovereignty, i.e. if it lost the right to exercise its own judgment in coming to the decisions which the government of its territory entails.' Ibid. 77.

[101] Ibid. 57–8. But cf. Anzilotti's view (a denial of any objective rules defining statehood) in his *Corso di Diritto Internazionale* (3rd edn. 1929) I, 163–6.

that the entity is 'not subject to the authority of any other State or group of States', which is to say, that it has over it 'no other authority than that of international law'.[102]

(*i*) *Separate existence within reasonably coherent frontiers*

'Separate existence' in this sense would seem to be dependent upon the criteria discussed already; that is, upon the exercise of substantial governmental authority with respect to some territory and people. Where this exists, the area concerned is potentially a 'State-area', but as Judge Anzilotti made clear, some further element is necessary.

(*ii*) *Absence of subjection to the authority of another State or States*

In this context, two different situations are possible. It may be that an entity, while not formally independent, operates in fact with substantial freedom in both internal and external affairs. This situation arises where formal or nominal claims are made to 'suzerainty' or 'residual sovereignty', or alternatively where the gradual grant of power from a metropolitan State to a former colony masks the emerging statehood of the latter. And, secondly, it may be that an entity formally independent is in fact under the direction of another State to the extent that its formal independence is nugatory or meaningless. The two situations correspond with an ambiguity in the word 'authority' or (in Vattel's formulation) 'rule', which may mean a claim of right, or the actual exercise of power in derogation from such a claim. It is thus necessary to distinguish 'formal' from 'actual' independence, and to determine their relation.[103]

(*a*) *Formal independence*   Formal independence exists where the powers of government of a territory (both in internal and external affairs) are vested in the separate authorities of the putative State. The vesting of power, in this sense, may be the result of the municipal law in force in the territory concerned, or it may be the result of a grant of full power from the previous sovereign; it may be established, or recognized, by bilateral or multilateral treaty. Formal independence thus involves, in

---

[102] Cf. Vattel, *Droit des gens* I, Ch. 1, §§ 5–11; Sovereignty is 'the right to self-government', so that a people 'under the rule of another' is not a State.
[103] Marek, *Identity and Continuity*, 162–89; Higgins, *Development*, 26.

Rousseau's terminology, *'l'exclusivité de la compétence'*.[104] This aspect is best illustrated by examining the factors which have been regarded as relevant to formal independence.

(i) *Situations not derogating from formal independence*

The following types of situation are not regarded, in international practice, as derogating from formal independence, although if extended far enough, they may derogate from actual independence.[105]

(1) *Constitutional restrictions upon freedom of action.* The written constitutions of many States contain legally enforceable restrictions on governmental action: these are, of course, entirely consistent with independence. An extreme case was the 1960 Constitution of the Republic of Cyprus.[106] Provided no other State possesses discretionary authority to alter the constitution of the State concerned,[107] the fact that the latter has no power even to change its Constitution is not a derogation from formal independence. Canada only acquired that power (and then with certain exceptions) in 1949, after more than twenty years of independence.[108] The power referred to is of course municipal legal authority: the people of a State normally have the international competence to change their constitution in violation of previous municipal law,[109] though here again Cyprus is an apparent exception.

(2) *Municipal illegality of the actual government of a State.* It is a further corollary of the rule that revolutions do not affect the continuity of the State, that the municipal illegality of its actual government is not a derogation from formal independence.[110]

(3) *Treaty obligations.* The International Court has frequently confirmed the principle that treaty obligations do not derogate from the formal independence of the States parties. In *The Wimbledon*, which concerned the effects on Germany of the Treaty of Versailles, the Court

decline[d] to see in the conclusion of any treaty by which a State

---

[104] Rousseau (1948), 73 *HR* 171–253, 220; and his DIP II, 55–93 (to the same effect).

[105] *Infra*, p. 56. Cf. Verzijl, *International Law* II, 455–90.

[106] *Infra*, p. 167.

[107] This seems to have been an objection to Cracow's independence: Ydit, *Internationalized Territories*, 95–108, 107; *infra*, p. 161.

[108] By the British North America Act (No. 2) 1949, s. 1.

[109] That is, revolutions do not affect the continuity of the State: *infra*, p. 405.

[110] See the cases cited by Marek, *Identity and Continuity*, 38–42.

undertakes to perform or refrain from performing a particular act an abandonment of its sovereignty. No doubt any convention creating an obligation of this kind places a restriction upon the exercise of the sovereign rights of the State, in the sense that it requires them to be exercised in a certain way. But the right to enter into international engagements is an attribute of State sovereignty.[111]

And this principle was confirmed in a number of other decisions of the Permanent Court.[112]

(4) *The existence of military bases or other territorial concessions (whether under treaty or by reservation in a grant of independence).* Military or other territory concessions do not, of themselves, constitute a derogation from formal independence. The sometimes extensive territorial concessions granted by the North African States and China nevertheless preserved the formal 'territorial integrity and political independence' of those States.[113] One consequence of continued statehood in such situations seems to be the ability to cancel or avoid such arrangements, whether or not legally.[114]

(5) *The exercise of governmental competence on a basis of agency.* It is clear that the exercise of governmental competence by another international person or persons on behalf of and by delegation from a State is not inconsistent with formal independence. The foreign affairs and defence powers are quite often so delegated; as are certain economic or technical facilities. The important element is always that the competence is exercised not independently but in right of the State concerned.[115]

(6) *The possession of joint organs for certain purposes.* The creation of joint organs to carry out certain governmental functions is a quite common feature of international relations. Thus Austria-Hungary possessed joint organs for foreign affairs, defence, and currency, but Austria and Hungary arguably remained separate

---

[111] Ser. A. No. 1 (1920), 25. The same argument was raised by Germany, and rejected, before signature of the Treaty of Versailles: Temperley, *History of the Peace Conference at Paris* II, 397, 408.

[112] *Exchange of Greek and Turkish Populations*, Ser. B No. 10 (1925), 21; *Jurisdiction of the European Commission of the Danube*, Ser. B No. 14 (1927), 36; cf. Austrian Memorial in the *Customs Union Case*, Ser. C No. 53, 91–3.

[113] Verzijl, *International Law* II, 482–8.

[114] Higgins, *Development*, 32. On military 'servitudes' generally see ibid. 31–4; Esgain, in O'Brien, *New Nations*, 42–97; Delupis, *International Law and the Independent State*, 200–23.

[115] See further, Chapter 7.

international entities.[116] The operations of the European Communities are not regarded as inconsistent with the independence of the member States.[117]

(7) *Membership of international organizations, even those possessing a degree of coercive authority.* Despite the extensive powers of the Security Council under the Charter, the United Nations 'is based on the principle of the sovereign equality of all its members'.[118] If United Nations membership preserves independence, *a fortiori* this is true so far of other international organizations, possessing lesser powers.

(8) *The existence of special legal relations between two States as a result of devolution.* As will be seen, where a State comes into existence by gradual devolution, special relations may well continue to exist between the new and the old State. These may include common citizenship, special provision for immigration, extradition, and such matters, and special defence arrangements. Within certain limits such relations do not prejudice formal independence.[119]

(2) *Situations regarded as derogating from formal independence*

Two basic situations may be regarded as derogating from what would otherwise be formal independence, as defined above.[120]

(1) *The existence, as a matter of international law, of a special claim of right, irrespective of consent, to the exercise of governmental powers.* Where a State claims the right to exercise governmental authority over a territory, the formal independence of that territory is in issue. This is another expression of Rousseau's requirement of *l'exclusivité de la compétence.*[121] Excluded from the category of 'special claims of right' are rights under general international law: for example, the rights of a belligerent occupant. Included in the category 'special claim of right' for example would be the claim of the Government of Great Britain

---

[116] See generally, *infra*, pp. 290–1, 404–5.

[117] *Infra*, pp. 295–7.

[118] Charter Art. 2(1). On the relationship between State sovereignty and the Charter see also Bourquin, *L'État souverain et l'organisation internationale* (1959); Ninčić, *The Problem of Sovereignty in the Charter and in the Practice of the United Nations* (1970); Korowicz, *Organisations internationales et souveraineté des États membres* (1961), 185–257.

[119] *Infra*, pp. 229, 232, 237–8.

[120] *Supra*, p. 52.

[121] (1948) 73 *HR* 171–253, 220.

to bind the Dominions, without their separate consent, to the Treaty of Lausanne, 1924;[122] or the claim of the Porte to conclude concessions for lighthouses in Crete and Samos.[123] The acceptance by the Nationalist authorities of the proposition that Taiwan is part of a single China is perhaps a further example.[124] In this context it is crucial that the governmental authority is claimed as of right, and not on the basis of consent by the local unit.

(2) *Discretionary authority to determine upon and effect intervention in the internal affairs of the putative State.* Such authority, whether or not the result of a treaty or other consensual arrangement, would appear to be inconsistent with formal independence. A most striking example was the British claim to 'paramountcy' over the Indian Native States.[125] What is crucial here is *la compétence de la compétence*: the undetermined powers of intervention possessed by France in respect of Monaco, for example, have led to doubts concerning the latter's independence.[126] The point is that, in the absence of machinery for adjudication, a broad discretionary power of intervention could always be used with colour of right to deny local independence. Monaco would thus appear not to have formal independence.[127]

(b) *Actual independence* Apart from formal independence, it may be necessary to enquire further as to the actual or effective independence of the putative State: this element corresponds to Rousseau's 'plénitude de la compétence'.[128] Actual independence is essentially relative, or in Rousseau's terms 'quantitative': the difficulty of applying it arises because it is a matter of degree.[129]

Actual independence, for our purposes, may be defined as the minimum degree of real governmental power at the disposal of

[122] *Infra*, pp. 244–5.

[123] *Infra*, pp. 232–6.

[124] *Infra*, pp. 151–2.

[125] *Infra*, p. 210.

[126] *Infra*, p. 194. Another example was Cuba under the Treaty of Future Relations of 22 May 1903, incorporating the Platt Amendment in the Act of Congress of 2 Mar. 1901: 96 *BFSP* 548, esp. Art. 3. The debate among international lawyers is summarized by Fitzgibbon, *Cuba and the United States 1900–1935* (1935), 89–93. The 1903 Treaty was abrogated by a much less draconic Treaty of 29 May 1934: 6 *Bevans* 1163.

[127] To the same effect, Mendelson, 160, 249–51. For the relation between formal and actual independence see *infra*, p. 69.

[128] (1948) 73 *HR* 171–253, 248.

[129] Cf. *Duff Development Co.* v. *Government of Kelantan* [1924] A.C. 797, 814 *per* Viscount Finlay.

the authorities of the putative State, necessary for it to qualify as 'independent'. It is thus a matter of political fact, and its evaluation in specific cases will tend to raise, whether in an international or a municipal forum, particularly acute problems. Nevertheless, it need not be said that the problem 'escape[s] all definition'.[130] The way in which a rule is applied to the sorts of factual situations that arise is hardly less of a legal problem than the enunciation of the rule itself: this is especially so when the rule is of a general, and to that extent unhelpful, character. An examination of the practice reveals, first, that the degree of actual independence necessary to satisfy this branch of the rule may be minimal, but that in cases of conflict of legal rights the rule is of considerable importance; and, secondly, that there are several presumptions as to the existence or otherwise of actual independence, which aid in application, and indeed condition the application, of the rule. Again the rule may be illustrated by an examination of factors which have been regarded as relevant.

(1) *Situations not derogating from actual independence*

(1) *Diminutive size and resources.* Diminutive size and resources are consistent with both formal and actual independence, as has been seen.[131]

(2) *Political alliances: Policy orientation between States.* The existence of close political and ideological links between States is a feature of modern (indeed of any) international relations. Such links do not of themselves derogate from actual independence.[132]

(3) *Belligerent occupation.* Pending a final settlement of the

---

[130] Marek, *Identity and Continuity*, 112.

[131] *Supra*, p. 36.

[132] This issue was raised by the Anglo-Iraqi Treaty of Alliance of 30 June 1930, 132 *BFSP* 280, intended to regulate relations after the termination of the Mandate. The treaty provided for 'co-ordination' of foreign policies (Art. 1), mutual assistance in war (Art. 4), and granted to the U.K. extensive facilities in time of war, including two permanent air bases (Art. 5). The 'sovereign rights of Iraq' were reserved, and the treaty was to be renegotiated after 25 years; the new treaty must still preserve Britain's essential communications (Art. 11). The Permanent Mandates Commission, while expressing certain reservations, nevertheless concluded that 'although certain of the provisions of the Treaty . . . were somewhat unusual in treaties of this kind, the obligations entered into by Iraq towards Great Britain did not explicitly infringe the independence of the new State'. Main, *Iraq from Mandate to Independence* (1955), 104–12, 110. The Treaty of Alliance came into force upon Iraq's admission to the League on 3 Oct. 1932. It was replaced by a Special Agreement of 4 Apr. 1955: 162 *BFSP* 112, when the British bases were closed down.

conflict, belligerent occupation does not affect the continuity of the State.[133] The governmental authorities may be driven into exile or silenced, and the exercise of the powers of the State thereby affected. But it is settled that the powers themselves continue to exist. This is strictly not an application of the 'actual independence' rule but a legal exception to it, based on the maxim *ex factis ius non oritur.*

(4) *Illegal intervention.* Equally, illegal intervention, in the absence of *debellatio,* does not extinguish either the formal or (up to a point) the actual independence of the State. The Soviet invasion of Czechoslovakia, and subsequent events there, were not regarded by other States as putting an end to the existence of Czechoslovakia as a State. The same was true of the earlier intervention in Hungary, although the credentials of the Hungarian delegation were not approved in the period 1956–63, as a gesture of disapproval of the Kadar government.[134] No equivalent action has been taken in the Czechoslovak case. On the other hand, the continuance of even an illegal occupation for a sufficiently long time after the cessation of hostilities will lead to the extinction of the occupied State by *debellatio*:[135] this must be taken to have been the case with Hyderabad.[136]

(2) *Situations derogating from actual independence*

Three factors are relevant here:

(1) *Substantial illegality of origin.* Where an entity comes into existence in violation of certain basic rules of international law, its title to be a 'State' is in issue. Traditional international law in matters of statehood based itself almost exclusively on the principle of effectiveness: in matters of statehood it was not the case that *ex injuria jus non oritur,*[137] although illegality of origin might be considered as a ground for non-recognition. The question whether, and to what extent, the modern law has developed criteria of statehood not based on effectiveness is examined in the next Chapter.

---

[133] *Infra,* p. 407. For Iran (1941–6), see *infra,* p. 69.

[134] Higgins, *Development,* 158–9; other cases of allied and belligerent occupation are discussed *infra,* pp. 68–9.

[135] *Infra,* p. 419.

[136] *Infra,* p. 211.

[137] See Kelsen, *Principles of International Law* (2nd edn., 1966), 420–33; Touscoz, *Le Principe d'effectivité dans l'ordre international* (1964), 125–8, and *infra,* pp. 74–84 for further discussion.

(2) *Entities formed under belligerent occupation.* However in at least one case pre-1939 international law appeared to condition effectiveness by considerations of legality. As has been said, it was, and remains, clear law that belligerent occupation does not deprive the occupied State of its independence, though it might suspend the exercise of the powers of the State.[138] As a result, even before 1939, any new 'State' established during belligerent occupation was presumed not to be independent.[139] But it is important to note that this was rather a presumption than a substantive rule. The independence of the illegal entity was probably not precluded, although of course its formation might attract the responsibility of the occupying State.[140]

This distinction between illegality of origin and effectiveness was however blurred during the Manchurian crisis. There, as the Lytton Commission found, Japanese action contrary both to the Covenant and the Kellogg-Briand Pact had resulted in the establishment of the 'State of Manchukuo', a puppet State under Japanese control.[141] This inspired the well-known 'Stimson doctrine': the refusal of the United States, and of the large majority of the League, to 'admit the legality of any situation *de facto* . . . which may impair . . . the sovereignty, the independence, or of the territorial and administrative integrity of the Republic of China . . .' or to recognize 'any situation . . . brought about by means contrary to the covenants and obligations of the Pact of Paris of August 27, 1928' [or, in the case of League Members, of the Covenant].[142] In its reply to the Stimson note, the Japanese Government, while denying responsibility, doubted whether 'the impropriety of means necessarily and always avoids the end

---

[138] *Supra*, p. 58.

[139] Marek, *Identity and Continuity*, 111–26: the same rule applies to puppet governments.

[140] See also *infra*, p. 118.

[141] Manchukuo's independence was proclaimed on 18 Feb. 1932, under the former Chinese Emperor Henry Pu-yi. The regime was eventually recognized by or had relations with Japan (see the Protocol of Good Neighbourship, 1932: 135 *BFSP* 637), San Salvador, Germany, Italy, and Poland.

[142] Secretary of State to Chinese and Japanese Govts., 7 Jan. 1932: *USFR* 1932/III, 7; endorsed by Assembly Resolution of 24 Feb. 1933: *LNOJ* Sp. Supp. No. 101/I, 87. Japanese action in Manchuria was in violation of Art. 12 of the Covenant, but in view of the fact that the hostilities were not part of a declared 'war', there was doubt whether Japan was technically in breach of Art. 16 ('resort to war'): Lauterpacht (1934), 28 *AJ* 43–60. There was however a clear breach of Art. 2 of the Pact of Paris: 128 *BSFP* 447. See also Jessup, *Birth of Nations*, 305–34.

secured';[143] a point the 'academic validity' of which was conceded by some commentators.[144] Since Manchukuo was both illegally created and not independent, the need in practice to distinguish the two points did not arise. But extensive enquiry by the League and its Committees into the reality or otherwise of its independence would have been unnecessary if the illegality of its creation operated as a permanent bar on statehood.[145]

For present purposes then, the following rules were established by 1945. (1) Where a putative State (or government) was created in territory under belligerent occupation, there was a strong presumption against its actual independence. (2) A non-independent 'State' (or 'government') so established was regarded as no more than the agent of the belligerent occupant, with no more competence to bind the occupied State than its principal. The status of these rules in the modern law will be discussed in the next Chapter.[146]

(3) *Substantial external control of the State.* It is established that an entity which, while possessing the formal marks of independence, is in substance subject to foreign domination and control is not 'independent' for the purposes of statehood in international law. In applying this principle, two difficulties arise. First, in certain cases at least, external interference may not be regarded as 'foreign', and may not therefore derogate from the statehood of the entity concerned. For example, the fact that a foreign citizen is head of State does not necessarily mean that the State concerned is subject to foreign control, if the head of State operates as the local government or upon the advice of such a government.[147] But these examples are exceptional, and limited in scope. What is necessary in this type of case is a relatively precise and binding understanding as to the capacity in which the various powers are exercised.[148]

Secondly, and more generally, the problem is to determine at what point foreign influence becomes 'control' or 'domination'.

---

[143] (1932) 26 *AJ* 343.

[144] Wright, ibid. 342–8, 345.

[145] See also *infra*, p. 62.

[146] *Infra*, pp. 106–18.

[147] This is the case with those Commonwealth Members which have retained the Crown as Head of State. For the curious case of Rajah Brooke, see Smith, *GB & LN* II, 83–96. For personal unions see *infra*, p. 290.

[148] This is the crucial problem with Andorra: *infra*, p. 142.

This is notoriously difficult. However, examination of some of the cases of 'non-independent States' may help to indicate certain basic criteria.

(i) *Protected States*. The problem of protectorates and other dependent States will be discussed in Chapter 7. An illustration of the problem of lack of actual independence is provided by the case of Kelantan. Under an Agreement of 1910 the Sultan agreed to have no political relations with any foreign power except through the British Government and to follow in all matters of administration (save those touching the Mohammedan religion and Malay custom) the advice of a British adviser.[149] The House of Lords was subsequently faced with the issue of the sovereign immunity of the Sultan in British courts, which was settled in the Sultan's favour by a Foreign Office certificate. The substantive point was however raised in an interesting way: it was said that the certificate (which incorporated the text of the 1910 Agreement) was self-contradictory, and that the matter was thus effectively still open. Counsel for the Company argued that

The distinguishing mark of an independent sovereign power is that it has reserved to itself the right to manage its own internal affairs, but by the terms of the agreement ... the King of England has the right to appoint a resident official to tell the Sultan ... how he is to manage the internal affairs of his country. That is wholly inconsistent with the idea of an independent sovereignty as that term is understood by jurists of repute...[150]

For the Sultan it was argued merely that 'some dependence on the protecting power is not inconsistent with sovereignty'.[151] The majority of their Lordships held the certificate not to be contradictory, since the Foreign Office must be taken to have considered the Agreement before determining the question: its determination was in any case conclusive, irrespective of conflict. However, Viscount Finlay and Lord Carson (who dissented on a different point) disagreed on the question of actual independence. Viscount Finlay thought that '[w]hile there are extensive limitations upon its independence, the enclosed documents do not negative the view that there is quite enough left to support

---

[149] 103 *BFSP* 518, Arts. 1–2.
[150] *Duff Development Co.* v. *Government of Kelantan* [1942] A.C. 797, 800.
[151] Ibid. 803.

the claim to sovereignty'.[152] Lord Carson, on the other hand, thought it 'difficult to find in these documents the essential attributes of independence and sovereignty in accordance with the tests laid down by the exponents of international law'.[153] The case was perhaps borderline, but it is difficult to see that the Government of Kelantan had much, if any, real power at all. Lord Carson was thus correct on the general issue, but as Fawcett has pointed out, British practice has favoured the immunity of even merely formal sovereigns or princes.[154]

(ii) *So-called Puppet States.* The term 'puppet State' is used to describe nominal sovereigns under effective foreign control, especially in cases where the establishment of the puppet State is intended as a cloak for manifest illegality. The creation of Manchukuo has already been mentioned: in that case the Lytton Commission's Report of October 1932 found as a fact that 'The independence movement, which had never been heard of in Manchuria before September 1931, was only made possible by the presence of Japanese troops and for this reason the present regime cannot be considered to have been called into existence by a genuine and spontaneous independence movement'[155]—a conclusion endorsed by the League Assembly.[156] On this basis Manchuria was held to be still Chinese territory, although it remained in Japanese control until 1945. The Yalta Agreement provided merely that China would 'retain full sovereignty in Manchuria'.[157] No formal action was deemed necessary for the reacquisition by China of the Three Provinces, and there was no reference to Manchuria in the Peace Treaty of 1951. In particular there was no retrocession or renunciation of title by Japan.[158] This provides strong confirmation of the view that Manchuria remained under Chinese sovereignty in the period 1932–45.

---

[152] Ibid. 816.

[153] Ibid. 830.

[154] *British Commonwealth*, 126–9.

[155] *LN* Publ. 1932 VII A.12, 71; in Wright *et. al.*, *Legal Problems in the Far Eastern Conflict* (1941), 57–8.

[156] Resolution of 24 Feb. 1933: *LNOJ* Sp. Supp. No. 101/I, 87; Wright, op. cit. *Contra* Cavaré, (1935) 42 *RGDIP* 5–99.

[157] Whiteman, 3 *Digest* 600–26, 600.

[158] But by Art. 8(a) Japan recognized *inter alia* 'any other arrangements by the Allied Powers for or in connection with the restoration of peace': 136 *UNTS* 45. Cf. *In re Nepogodin's Estate* (1955) 22 ILR 90 (Manchuria part of China in 1945).

The same conclusion must be reached with regard to two European 'States' established in German occupied territories. Slovakia was a nominally independent part of Czechoslovakia under German protection from 18 March 1939 to April 1945. It was accorded a certain degree of recognition at least *de facto* prior to September 1939,[159] but there can be little doubt as to its puppet character.[160] Croatia was also established on occupied (Yugoslavian) territory, between 1941 and 1945. A United States International Claims Commission held that Yugoslavia was not a successor State to Croatia, and that damage to property caused by the puppet State was not action 'by Yugoslavia'.

Croatia embraced approximately one-third of the total area of Yugoslavia and approximately one-third of its population. At all times during the period of its existence as a so-called independent State, forces headed by Mihalovic and Tito conducted organized resistance within it. At no time ... was Croatia's control of its territory and population complete. It was created by German and Italian forces and was maintained by force and the threat of force, and as soon as the threat subsided Croatia ceased to exist ... [I]t appears well established that ... Croatia was ... during its entire 4-year life, ... subject to the will of Germany or Italy or both, in varying degrees, except as to civil administration matters ... It was unwanted by, and never became a part of, the permanent Government of Yugoslavia. It was not established through any dereliction on the part of the Government of Yugoslavia and that Government had no control over the acts of Croatia. It further seems clear that neither the Government of Yugoslavia nor its peoples received benefits from the takings alleged ... Croatia is defined by contemporary writers as a 'puppet state' or 'puppet government', terms which appear to be of comparatively recent adoption in the field of international law ... A 'puppet state' or local *de facto* government such as Croatia also possesses characteristics of 'unsuccessful revolutionists' and 'belligerent occupants'. It is ... settled that a State has no international legal responsibility to compensate for damage to or confiscation of property by either ...

---

[159] Marek, *Identity and Continuity*, 287–91, 290. The U.S. did not recognize it: *USFR* 1941/III, 32–3. The Czechoslovak Government-in-exile was recognized by the Allies during the War: e.g. *H.C. Debs.* Vol. 356, col. 552, 20 Dec. 1939; ibid. Vol. 373, col. 861, 18 July 1941. This must have involved withdrawal of the previous *de facto* recognition accorded to Slovakia. See also Lemkin, *Axis Rule in Occupied Europe* (1944), 139–44; Langer, *Seizure of Territory*, 207–44.

[160] Marek, op. cit.; *USFR* 1948/IV, 434; *contra* Mikus, *La Slovaquie dans le drame de l'Europe* (1955), 97–204.

[F]or the reasons ... given ... the Government of Yugoslavia is not factually or legally a successor to the Government of Croatia.[161]

Although the findings of fact, and the actual decision reached by the Tribunal, were undoubtedly correct, it is doubtful whether comparison of a puppet entity with a local *de facto* government is of much value. Puppet entities—whether 'States' or 'governments'—bind the existing State only so far as the Geneva Conventions allow:[162] different tests apply to genuine *de facto* governments. Moreover, even if a puppet entity extended over the entire State, its status would be the same—that is not true of *de facto* governments. Finally, it is clear that Croatia was a 'puppet State', not a 'puppet government' of an existing State. The distinction may have consequences for the extinction or continuity of the previous State.[163]

In the absence of general recognition or other special factors, the status of a puppet entity, and its international capacity, are therefore minimal. Thus a request for annexation or intervention made by the puppet government of an admitted State is without international validity: the Baltic States annexed in 1940 by the Soviet Union provide the best example.[164] Neither can a cession of territory by such a government bind the State.[165] It is established, in both types of case, that the existence of a puppet entity does not *per se* lead to the extinction of the previously existing State.[166]

The question remains how the puppet character of a given entity is to be determined. In practice this raises less difficulty than might have been thought. The presumption of puppet character of regimes constituted under belligerent occupation,[167] or subsequent to illegal intervention or to the threat or use of force, is frequently of assistance. Apart from that, it is of course a question of fact. In the cases mentioned, the factors taken into account have included the following: that the entity concerned

---

[161] *Socony Vacuum Oil Co. Claim* (1954) 21 ILR 55, 58–62. Cf. the useful analysis by Sereni (1940), 35 *Am. Pol. Sc. R.* 1144–51.

[162] *Supra*, p. 59.

[163] *Infra*, p. 411.

[164] Marek, *Identity and Continuity*, 375–416; *infra*, p. 419.

[165] On the Lublin Government of Poland, see *infra*, pp. 408–12.

[166] *Infra*, pp. 410–12.

[167] *Supra*, p. 60.

was established illegally, by the threat or use of external armed force; that it did not have the support of the vast majority of the population it claimed to govern; that in important matters it was subject to foreign direction or control;[168] that it was staffed, especially in more important positions, by nationals of the dominant State. It was not regarded as relevant that certain individuals or groups (including minority groups) in the territory concerned carried out normal administrative functions, or constituted the formal government, if the elements mentioned above were present.[169] In such circumstances, any acts of puppet entity must be regarded as void *ab initio*, as far as binding the previously effective State, except to the extent that they can be regarded as acts of the belligerent occupant itself,[170] or unless and until ratified by an effective government of the State concerned. Thus by Article 31 of the Peace Treaty of 1947, Italy recognized 'that all agreements and arrangements made between Italy and the authorities installed in Albania by Italy from April 7, 1939 to September 3, 1943, are null and void'.[171]

With the reservations already made, this would seem to be declaratory of the general law.[172]

(iii) *Purported grants of colonial independence.* There appears to be a presumption in favour of the actual independence of ex-colonies granted formal independence by their metropolitan State, as has been pointed out.[173] Nevertheless where the grant is only partial,[174] or where there is evidence that real control has

---

[168] But the influence of a belligerent occupant on a pre-existing government in the occupied State may not be enough: the Vichy regime was regarded as the genuine government of France until 1944. As a result de Gaulle's Free French were not accorded recognition as the French government-in-exile: see e.g. *H.C. Deb.* Vol. 371, col. 1713, 27 May 1941; Flory, *Le Statut international des gouvernements réfugiés* (1952).

[169] Other cases of puppet entities include Napoleonic Holland (Marek, *Identity and Continuity*, 170–3); the Kuusinnen Government of Finland, 1939–40 (ibid. 66–8); and Albania, 1939–44 (ibid. 331–7). On the puppet government set up by the Japanese in the Philippines, see *USFR* 1943/III, 1105–7; U.N.L.S., *Materials on Succession of States* (1967), 143–6.

[170] Cf. *In re G.* (1945) 12 AD No. 151 (on the puppet governments in Greece during World War II); Ténékides (1947), 51 *RGDIP* 113–33.

[171] 49 *UNTS* 3.

[172] Cf. Marek, *Identity and Continuity*, 336; and see generally Verhoeven, *Reconnaissance*, 54–64, 93–9.

[173] *Supra*, p. 44.

[174] As with the Associated States in Vietnam: O'Brien & Goebel, 'U.S. Recognition Policy', 147–51.

not been transferred, other States are justified in withholding recognition, and may well be bound to do so.[175]

In this context the cases of Syria and Lebanon (1942–6) are of considerable interest. These two 'A' Mandates had been 'provisionally recognized' as independent in 1919, but had remained under effective French control until 1940.[176] In 1941, Allied Forces evicted the Vichy French administration and installed a Free French administration under General Catroux. By proclamation of 27 September 1941 the French Delegate General purported to transfer to Syria 'all rights and prerogatives of an independent and sovereign State, limited only by the exigencies of the war and the security of its territory'.[177] The United Kingdom shortly accorded recognition to Syria and Lebanon,[178] but the United States declined to do so,[179] agreeing only to accredit a 'diplomatic agent'.[180] In March 1943, when General Catroux replaced the existing Syrian regime with a new provisional government,[181] Secretary of State Hull described the change as 'essentially only a replacement of one French-appointed regime for another'.[182] While accepting the need for control of certain aspects of government by the military authorities, the State Department required 'a considerable degree of independence' with respect to civilian activities.[183] Specifically, Acting Secretary of State Willis on 22 August 1943 described his Government's

established policy to defer recognition of another executive until:

[175] For the case where recognition of colonial independence is justified despite a lack of full independence see *infra*, p. 261.

[176] Cf. Whiteman, 2 *Digest* 188–9. For 'A' Mandates generally see *infra*, pp. 339, 426.

[177] *USFR* 1941/III, 786. Cf. Whiteman, 2 *Digest* 189 (Lebanon). However, a French *aide-mémoire* at the same time argued that, because the Mandate required termination by the League, 'the regime ... set up in Syria during the war cannot be anything but provisional': *USFR* 1941/III, 791.

[178] Cf. *H.C. Deb.* Vol. 393, col. 157, 27 Oct. 1943.

[179] Memorandum of 16 Dec. 1941: *USFR* 1941/III, 813.

[180] '[T]he Department contemplates the extension only of limited recognition to Syria and Lebanon, at least for the present. Since diplomatic agents are accredited by the U.S. to areas such as Morocco which are less than fully independent, the establishment of such a rank in Beirut would be in accord with the existing situation there.' Ibid. 1942/IV, 656; cf. 663, 665. Other reasons for the U.S. refusal were the uncertainty over the future French position in the area, and the maintenance of U.S. rights under the treaty of 1924: 120 *BFSP* 399.

[181] It was argued that 'non-recognition by most foreign States justified in itself a continuing exercise of the mandatory power': *USFR* 1943/IV, 956.

[182] Ibid. 966.   [183] Ibid. 970.

1) It is in possession of the machinery of State, administering the government with the assent of the people thereof

2) It is in a position to fulfil the international obligations and responsibilities incumbent upon a sovereign State under treaties and international law. We welcome the successful re-establishment of constitutional government in Syria as an important step toward the fulfilment of these conditions, but believe that there must be an effective transfer of substantial authority and power to the new government before serious consideration can be given to the extension of full recognition.[184]

In November 1943, after elections had been held, the French Delegate General once again removed a local (in this case Lebanese) government—an action reversed only after strong Allied protests.[185] There followed an 'accelerated transfer of governmental powers': on 5 September 1944 the United States concluded that 'the local Governments may now be considered representative, effectively independent and in a position satisfactorily to fulfil their international obligations and responsibilities'.[186] 'Full and unconditional' recognition followed, despite the continued presence of French troops in the Levant and the failure of the French and local governments to agree on a treaty of future relations. In the American view 'the war powers exercised by the French and British authorities . . . could not be considered inconsistent with or derogatory to the independence of the States, since these powers have been freely and willingly granted and have been repeatedly confirmed by the local governments'.[187] The presence of French troops gave rise to further difficulty in May 1945, when force was used in an attempt to secure agreement on a treaty of future relations. A British ultimatum, accompanied by military intervention, ensued; but on this occasion, the illegality of French action was a corollary of the independence of Syria and Lebanon, and of their original membership of the United Nations.[188] The Syrian

---

[184] Ibid. 987; repeated in a Memorandum of 25 Oct: ibid. 1000–1 and cf. also 1007–1008.

[185] Ibid. 1022 et seq.; Khadduri (1944), 38 *AJ* 601–20.

[186] *USFR* 1944/V, 774.

[187] Ibid. 796 (5 Oct. 1944).

[188] *USFR* 1945/VIII, 1093, 1124, 1130–1, 1179. For a full account see Longrigg, *Syria and Lebanon under French Mandate* (1958), esp. 317–18. Also Whiteman, 2 *Digest* 188–98, 218–26; O'Brien and Goebel, 'U.S. Recognition Policy', 190–4. For termination of the Mandates see *infra*, pp. 337–40.

and Lebanese cases demonstrate well the requirement of independence as a criterion for statehood. Substantial local control exercised by a government with popular support was, properly, regarded as sufficient to override continuing French claims. Once independence had been acquired, it provided a basis for regulating remaining restrictions upon independence, actual or asserted.

(iv) *Other cases of absence or loss of actual independence.*[189] The category of non-independent entities is not, of course, closed: nor would much purpose be served by further detailed description. The basic contention is that the degree of actual independence necessary, as a matter of general international law, and apart from special requirements that may exist in particular cases, is slight.[190] To prove lack of real independence, one must show 'foreign *control* overbearing the decision-making of the entity concerned on a wide range of matters and doing so systematically and on a permanent basis'.[191] To establish such lack of independence, in the absence of foreign occupation or illegal military intervention, is thus to overcome a formidable burden of proof, though it may be said that in practice puppet or non-independent entities are often self-evident.[192] Perhaps the most difficult case is where an existing government remains in power during a period of foreign occupation in time of war: a situation which occurs both with respect to allied and enemy forces. The case of Vichy France has been mentioned already.[193]

The extent to which statehood may coexist with substantial lack of independence is demonstrated by the case of Iran under

---

[189] Cf. the distinction between acquisition and loss of independence: *supra*, p. 48.

[190] Cf. the interesting discussion in Hart, *The Concept of Law*, 216–17, where the requirement of independence is described as variable and essentially 'negative in force'. Kamanda, *Legal Status of Protectorates*, 188–91 goes so far as to describe it as a fiction. As a legal concept, however, although its operation is variable, it will often be far from 'fictional' in effect. The most important 'particular case' is secession in a non-colonial context, where substantial and continued independence is required: *infra*, pp. 263–6.

[191] Brownlie, *Principles*, 76 (his itals.); Eagleton, *International Government* (3rd edn., 1957), 82–3 has 'regular control or direction by another State'.

[192] The lengthy opposition to Mongolia's U.N. admission was, ostensibly at least, based on lack of effective independence. After ten rejections in the Security Council (1946–57) the Mongolian People's Republic was eventually admitted by S.C. Res. 166 (1960) (9–0: 1, 1 n.p.); G.A. Res. 1630 (XVI), 27 Oct. 1961 (accl.). Cf. the pertinent comments of Higgins, *Development*, 28–30, 40; and see generally Friters, *Outer Mongolia and its International Position* (1951); Nemzer (1939), 33 *AJ* 452–64; Hackworth, 1 *Digest*, 75–6; Whiteman, 3 *Digest*, 600–16.

[193] *Supra*, p. 65, n. 168. Cf. the Italian Social Republic, *infra*, p. 72.

Allied occupation from 1941 to 1946. In August of 1941 Soviet and British forces occupied Iran to forestall fears of impending German control. Both parties emphasized that they had 'no designs on Iranian sovereignty or territorial integrity'[194] and that the occupation of the country would be temporary.[195] The occupation was followed by a change in government, Reza Shah Pahlevi replacing his father. The former was not treated as a puppet government, and the change in government was widely recognized.[196] The American view was that the British and Russian occupation was necessary and justified, although fears were expressed as to the future independence of Iran.[197] At the Teheran Conference, the three Allies reaffirmed 'their desire for the maintenance of the independence, sovereignty and territorial integrity of Iran.[198] Under these circumstances, there was never any possibility of, or, it is believed, justification for, the view that Iran had in some way ceased to exist, despite the inability of the Iranian government effectively to control events in parts of its territory during the war.[199]

(c) *The relation between formal and actual independence* The two concepts of formal and actual independence analysed here are closely linked: their exact relation is however complex. Where formal independence and actual independence, as defined coexist, then there is no problem. Equally, where formal independence masks the lack of any actual independence the entity is to be regarded as not independent for the purposes of statehood.[200] Much more difficult is the intermediate case: that is, where a certain lack of formal independence coexists with substantial *de facto* independence—as with the Dominions in

---

[194] *USFR* 1941/III, 439. See also the Tripartite Treaty of Alliance of 29 Jan. 1942: 144 *BSFP* 1017, Arts. 1, 4, 6.

[195] Loc. cit., and cf. *USFR*1941/III, 443.

[196] Ibid. 462.

[197] Memorandum of 23 Jan. 1943: ibid. 1943/IV, 331–3; cf. 378–9.

[198] Declaration regarding Iran, 1 Dec. 1943: ibid. 413.

[199] For the Soviet refusal to evacuate northern Iran, and the Azerbaijan secession movement, see *USFR* 1945/VIII, 359–522: ibid. 1946/VII, 289–567; Hamzavi, *Persia and the Powers, An Account of Diplomatic Relations 1941–1946* (1946). For a strong application of the same presumption in favour of continued independence, cf. *Restitution of Household Effects belonging to Jews departed from Hungary* (1965) 44 ILR 301 (Hungary under German control, 1938–44). The decision might well have been different if an occupied *enemy* State's legislation had been in point.

[200] Subject to recognition, *infra*, p. 74, or substantial illegality, *infra*, p. 84.

1924. The problem is examined in Chapter 8. It must be emphasized that specific issues, and the specific legal consequences sought to be drawn from alleged lack of independence, are of great importance: so too, in borderline cases, are such factors as recognition (especially if the practice is consistent), and permanence, which may provide valuable confirmatory evidence.[201] Finally, in applying the flexible and in some situations minimal requirements of the independence rule, certain presumptions are of value.[202]

(1) As a matter of general principle, any territorial entity formally separate and possessing a certain degree of actual power is capable of being, and *caeteris paribus*, should be regarded as, a State for general international law purposes. The denomination *sui generis* often applied to entities which, for some reason, it is desired not to characterize as States is of little help. On the one hand the regime of rules concerning States provides a flexible and readily applicable standard; on the other, the induction of the multitude of necessary (and usually unexpressed) rules regarding a '*sui generis* entity' is both laborious and, usually, unnecessary. The assumption that for example 'internationalized territories' are *a priori* excluded from statehood in the legal sense is unwarranted, since it exaggerates the importance and rigidity of the international legal regime of statehood.[203] Significantly the International Court has never made that assumption.

(2) More specifically, it is submitted that independence for the present purposes may be presumed where: (i) an entity is formally independent, and (ii) its creation was not attended by serious illegality. On the other hand the presumption is against independence where either: (i) the entity in question is not formally independent, or (ii) though formally independent, its creation was attended by serious illegalities, or where (iii) in the case of territory under belligerent occupation, a new regime is created with the express or tacit consent of the occupant.[204]

(3) There is also, as we have seen, a strong presumption in favour of the continued statehood of existing States, despite sometimes very extensive loss of actual authority.

(4) Finally, as has been suggested, the presumption is in

201 *Infra*, p. 72.   203 *Infra*, p. 165.
202 *Supra*, p. 60.   204 *Supra*, p. 59.

favour of the independence of a territorial unit as a whole, when it has been granted full formal independence by its former metropolitan State.[205]

It has been assumed here that an entity may become a State despite serious illegalities in the method or process of creation. In traditional international law that assumption was unchallenged, and the only problems were problems of application. The question will be examined in the next Chapter.

(6) *Sovereignty*

The term 'sovereignty' is sometimes used in place of 'independence' as a basic criterion for statehood. However it has, as has been seen, another more satisfactory meaning as an incident or consequence of statehood, namely, the plenary competence that States *prima facie* possess.[206] Since the two meanings are distinct, it seems preferable to restrict 'independence' to the prerequisite for statehood, and 'sovereignty' to the legal incident.

The term 'sovereign' is also, it may be noted, used in other senses, for example, to indicate actual omnicompetence with respect to internal or external affairs. Thus it can be said that, while Cyprus is an 'independent State' it is not 'sovereign', because a rigid constitution places certain acts beyond its power.[207] This meaning of the term 'sovereign' is perhaps the most common in political discourse. Nevertheless as a matter of international law a State or other entity has in general no entitlement to 'sovereignty' in this wider sense.

(7) *Other criteria*

Certain other criteria are sometimes suggested as necessary for statehood.

(*i*) *Permanence*

The American Law Institute's Draft Restatement provides as a precondition for recognition, *inter alia*, that an entity 'shows

---

[205] *Supra*, p. 44.

[206] *Supra*, p. 27. See especially Rousseau (1948), 73 *HR* 171–253, for a forceful argument in favour of the distinction and terminology adopted in the text—though his essay concerns rather the consequences of than the preconditions for statehood.

[207] *Infra*, p. 167.

reasonable indications that the[se] requirements . . . will continue to be satisfied'.[208] But no such requirement is contained in its definition of 'State'[209] and in fact States may have a very brief existence, provided only that they have an effective independent government with respect to a certain area and population. Thus the Mali Federation lasted only from 20 June to 20 August 1960, when it divided into two separate States. And British Somaliland was a State for five days, from 26 to 30 June 1960,[210] when it united with the former Italian Trust Territory of Somaliland to form the Somali Republic.[211]

This is not to say that permanence is not relevant to issues of statehood in some cases. In particular where another State's rights are involved (for example in a secessionary situation), or where certain criteria for statehood are said to be missing, continuance of an entity over a period of time is of considerable evidential value.[212] In the divided State situations, whatever the original legality of the establishment of certain of those regimes, long continuance has forced effective recognition of their position.[213] Permanence is thus not strictly a criterion of statehood in the sense of an indispensable attribute: it is a sometimes important piece of evidence as to the possession of those attributes.

(ii) *Willingness and ability to observe international law*

It is sometimes said that 'willingness to observe international law' is a criterion for statehood.[214] But it is particularly necessary to distinguish recognition from statehood in this context. Unwillingness or refusal to observe international law may well

---

[208] *Rest. 2nd, Foreign Relations Law of the U.S.* (1965), § 100.

[209] Ibid. § 4.

[210] It was informally accorded separate recognition by the U.S.: (1960) 43 *DSB* 87; Whiteman, 1 *Digest* 216–17. See also Waldock, *ILC Ybk* 1972/II, 34–5; Contini (1966), 60 *PAS* 127.

[211] An earlier and less well known case was that of Yugoslavia, independent on 31 Oct. 1918, which united with Serbia to form the Serb-Croat-Slovene State on 1 Dec. 1918: Marek, *Identity and Continuity*, 239–44; *contra*, *Peinitsch* v. *Germany* (1923) 2 *Rep. MAT* 621.

[212] Cf. the U.S. position with regard to Yemen: Whiteman, 2 *Digest* 240–1.

[213] *Infra*, Chapter 10; and cf. *Carl Zeiss Stiftung* v. *Rayner & Keeler Ltd.* (*No. 2*) [1967] 1 A.C. 853, 907 *per* Lord Reid. On the shortlived Italian Republic of Salò, see *Levi Claim* (1957) 24 ILR 303; *Trèves Claim*, ibid. 313; and 43 AD No. 4; 29 ILR 21, 34, 51.

[214] Moore, 1 *Digest* 6; Hackworth, 1 *Digest* 176–9; Whiteman, 2 *Digest* 72–3, 78–82; and *supra*, p. 67 (Syria and Lebanon).

constitute grounds for refusal of recognition,[215] or for such other sanctions as the law allows, just as unwillingness to observe Charter obligations is a ground for non-admission to the United Nations. Both are however distinct from statehood.[216]

A different, though connected, point is whether inability to observe international law may be grounds for refusal to treat the entity concerned as a State. H. A. Smith puts the point thus: 'a State which has fallen into anarchy ceases to be a State to which the normal rules of international intercourse can be applied.'[217] But again one must distinguish between permitted sanctions for breach of international obligations (which used to extend to armed reprisals and war), and a lack of responsibility for public order or government such that the territory concerned ceases to be part of the defaulting State or (if the whole State territory is concerned) such that it ceases to be a State. The former circumstance is clearly distinguishable from the latter and much more common. The latter case concerns not 'ability to obey international law' but a failure to maintain any State authority at all. As such it is referable to the criterion of government; reference to international law is unnecessary and confusing.

(iii) A certain degree of civilization

United States practice, in particular, has on occasions supported the view that, to be a 'State of International Law the inhabitants of the territory must have attained a degree of civilization such as to enable them to observe with respect to the outside world those principles of law which are deemed to govern the members of the international society in their relations with each other.'[218] But once again this requirement is better formulated as one of government: 'international law presupposes, not any common faith or culture, but a certain minimum of order and stability.'[219]

[215] Cf. *Rest. 2nd.*, § 103. For U.S. practice see O'Brien and Goebel, 'U.S. Recognition Policy', 106 ff.

[216] Chen, *Recognition*, 61–2; Lauterpacht, *Recognition*, 109–14; Charpentier, *Reconnaissance*, 289–90; Brownlie, *Principles*, 80.

[217] *GB & LN* I, 18–19, citing an Opinion of Harding on anarchy in Mexico: FO. 83/2305, 20 Mar. 1857.

[218] Hyde, *International Law* (2nd edn., 1947) I, 23; cf. 127–9; cited in relation to Indonesia, Whiteman, 1 *Digest* 223–4.

[219] Smith, *GB & LN* I, 18; cf. Brownlie, *Principles*, 80; Chen, *Recognition*, 60. In *Hunt* v. *Gordon* (1883) 2 N.Z.L.R. 160, 186 Richmond J. declined to recognize a Samoan

(iv) Recognition

As we have seen, recognition is not strictly a condition for statehood in international law. 'An entity not recognized as a State but meeting the requirements for recognition has the rights of a State under international law in relation to a non-recognizing State . . .'[220] On the other hand, in some cases at least,[221] States are not prohibited from recognizing or treating as a State an entity which for some reason does not qualify as a State under the general criteria discussed in this Chapter. Such recognition may well be constitutive of legal obligation for the recognizing or acquiescing State; but it may also tend to consolidate a general legal status at that time precarious or *in statu nascendi*. Recognition, while in principle declaratory, may thus be of great importance in particular cases.[222] In any event, at least where the recognizing government is addressing itself to legal rather than purely political considerations, it is important evidence of legal status.[223] Particular problems of the relation between recognition and status are dealt with elsewhere in this study.

(v) Legal order

Since the modern State is the territorial basis for a legal order,[224] it might be thought that the existence of a 'legal order', or at least its basic rules, is a useful criterion for the existence of the State.

As a political organization, the state is a legal order. But not every legal order in a state . . . The state is a relatively centralized legal order . . . The legal order of primitive society and the general international law order are entirely decentralized coercive orders and therefore not states . . . In traditional theory the state is composed of three elements, the

nationality on the ground that, although Samoa was recognized as independent, it was not recognized as a civilized Power 'capable of accepting a transfer of allegiance'. The Court of Appeal, affirming, relied rather on the absence of British recognition and of orderly government: ibid. 198–202, 267–8. To the same effect, *Hunt* v. *R.* (*No. 2*) (1882) 1 Fiji L.R. 59, 63 *per* Gorrie C.J. (Samoa); *The Helena* (1701) 4 C. Rob. 3, 5–7 *per* Sir Wm. Scott (the Barbary States).

[220] *Rest. 2nd.*, § 107; *supra*, p. 23.

[221] For non-recognition see *infra*, p. 120. For the test of prematurity of recognition of secession see *infra*, p. 257.

[222] See e.g. the discussion *infra*, on Formosa (pp. 143–52), Monaco (pp. 193–4), Austria after 1938 (pp. 310–11), seceding States generally (pp. 248–66), and the non-extinction of 'Germany' after 1945 (pp. 274–5).

[223] *Supra*, p. 24.   [224] D'Entrèves, *The Notion of the State* (1967), 96.

people of the state, the territory of the state, and the so-called power of the state, exercised by an independent government. All three elements can be determined only juridically, that is, they can be comprehended only as the validity and the spheres of validity of a legal order.[225]

It is of course clear that 'legal order' is an important element of government, hence an indication of statehood; but its status as a distinct criterion is open to doubt. Thus a revolutionary (that is, illegal) change of constitution does not necessarily affect the identity or continuity of the State.[226] Entities which, by all other criteria, are States, at the time they come into existence may have only rudimentary or fragmentary legal systems. In extreme cases, there may be no more than a diffused willingness to accept the system to be established by a Constituent Assembly.[227] Moreover a single State may well compose several interlocking legal systems, having a complex interrelation and without the subordination of one to the other—this is the case with federations. As a criterion, 'legal system' seems to be least helpful in just those cases for which the criteria exist.

Alternatively, it can be argued that, although 'legal system' as a whole may not be a useful criterion, the existence of a 'basic norm' within a State is both necessary and sufficient. Thus Marek finds it . . .

both necessary and possible to define the 'separateness' of the State in strictly legal terms: and in these terms it simply means that every State is determined by the basic norm of its legal order, which it does not share with any other State. This basic norm is its own; it is not, and cannot be, derived from any other State order. In other words, *the legal source, the reason of validity* of the legal order of a State cannot be found in the legal order of one or several other States . . . for if it were, the entity in question would not be an independent State, but a component legal order of that State or group of States by whom it would be delegated.[228]

Nevertheless, as a separate criterion the 'basic norm' is no better. It is, as Marek points out, a purely formal notion, and as such, it fails in two distinct ways. First, it fails to explain the independence

---

[225] Kelsen, *The Pure Theory of Law* (2nd edn., trans. Knight, 1964), 286–7.

[226] *Infra*, p. 405.

[227] Austria in 1918 seems to be an example: Marek, *Identity and Continuity*, 202. The common phenomenon of continuity of law is not in point here.

[228] Ibid. 168 (my itals.). She none the less accepts that change in the basic norm *per se* does not change the State: ibid. 188.

of a State whose basic norm was given it by the legal system of another State. In such a case, formal and sometimes even municipal legal dependence may coexist with international independence.[229] Equally, Marek is driven to reject, *a priori*, the statehood of 'internationalized territories' such as the Free City of Danzig; a position both too rigid and inconsistent with practice.[230] Secondly, the basic norm can only explain the case of puppet States, with full formal but no actual validity, by an equivocation on the term 'reason for validity.' In such circumstances, the 'reason' appealed to is not formal but material, a conclusion of political fact in all the circumstances.

It follows that one can only know the basic norm of a State when the State itself is identified as such. Like international responsibility,[231] the basic norm is a conclusion to the problems of existence, identity, and continuity, not the means of their solution. Nor can there be such a thing as an 'independent' basic norm;[232] merely a basic norm of a State that is independent. Again, this is not to deny that the legal system of an entity is a part of its general system of government, and as such relevant to questions of existence, identity, and continuity of statehood.[233]

---

[229] Cf. *infra*, p. 229.
[230] Marek, *Identity and Continuity*, 168n.2; *infra*, p. 165.
[231] With which Marek compares it: ibid. 189.
[232] Ibid. 188.
[233] For similar criticism see Kamanda, *Legal Status of Protectorates*, 181–2.

3. Criteria for Statehood Suggested as a Result of Modern Developments in International Law

3.1 LEGALITY AND STATEHOOD

IT has been seen that the traditional criteria for statehood were based almost entirely on the principle of effectiveness. The proposition that statehood is a question of fact derives strong support from this equation of effectiveness and statehood. In other words, although it is admitted that effectiveness in this context is a legal requirement, it is denied that there can exist legal criteria for statehood not based on effectiveness. In Charpentier's view: 'les tentatives de développement de régles de légalité objective détachées de l'effectivité jointes à l'absence de sanctions capables de les faire respecter entraînent fatalement un *conflit entre le droit et le fait* dans lequel celui-là risque de l'emporter, constituant ainsi à lui seul un critère de validation de l'extension illégale des compétences.'[1] We must first distinguish two possible positions: that there can *a priori* exist no criteria for statehood independent of effectiveness, and that no such criteria exist as a matter of positive law. Clearly, if the former position be correct, there can be no inquiry into the effect of particular rules on status. That position thus requires examination.

The first point to be made is that, in recent practice, effective separate entities have existed which have, universally, been agreed not to be States—in particular, Rhodesia and Formosa. Moreover, non-effective entities have also been generally regarded as being, or continuing to be, States: for example, Guinea-Bissau before Portuguese recognition,[2] and the various entities illegally annexed in the period 1936–40. The proposition that statehood must always be equated with effectiveness is not supported by modern practice. None the less, various arguments have been adduced in support of that view.

---

[1] Charpentier, *Reconnaissance*, 127–8 (italics his). Cf. Mouskhély (1962), 66 *RGDIP* 469–85, 475, referring to 'les tentatives de réglementation juridique de la naissance des États'; Verhoeven, *Reconnaissance*, 548–9, 589–91.

[2] *Infra*, p. 260.

In the first place, it is argued that to apply rules of this type in the absence of an authoritative system of determination of status is quite impracticable. Since there will be no certainty as to the application of peremptory rules in this situation, in the absence of some form of collective recognition,[3] no such rules can be accepted. This is, of course, a variant of an argument which is central to the constitutive position in general:[4] the arguments which were adduced in that context are equally relevant here. No such compulsory procedure for determining disputed questions exists elsewhere in the law, and the view that statehood is, exceptionally, a matter requiring such certification has already been rejected. 'Collectivization of recognition' is no doubt desirable,[5] but since 1945 there has developed in United Nations practice and elsewhere a system of certification which has in substance fulfilled the function of collective recognition, without the attribute of complete and binding certainty.[6]

A second argument is that international law risks being ineffective and creating a 'fatal conflict between law and fact', if it challenges the validity of effective situations, especially situations of power such as the existence of States. But the question is exactly whether the term 'State' should be regarded as for all purposes and in all cases equivalent to certain situations of power. It could be said that international law risks being ineffective precisely if it does not challenge effective but illegal situations. For example, the Rhodesian situation is probably, because of the general non-recognition of an effective situation, closer to solution than it would otherwise have been. That non-recognition is, as we shall see, both obligatory and a result of lack of status of the entity in question.[7] Of course, effectiveness remains the dominant *general* principle, but it is quite consistent with this that there should exist specific, limited, exceptions based on other fundamental principles.

A further, more persuasive, argument relates to the difficulty of applying the rule of extinctive prescription to a situation where law and fact conflict for a long period of time. None the less this difficulty arises most acutely in the area where the

---

[3] Cf. Charpentier, *Reconnaissance*, 318.
[4] *Supra*, p. 18.
[5] Cf. Lauterpacht, *Recognition*, 78.
[6] Briggs (1950), 44 *PAS* 169–81. See also Chapter 4.
[7] *Infra*, pp. 103–6.

continued acceptance of non-effective legal entities is most clearly demonstrated: that is, in the area of the non-extinction of States by illegal annexation. The application of the doctrine of extinctive prescription in this area is discussed in Chapter 17. It is sufficient to say here that the same problems of application occur in other contexts (for example, acquisition and loss of territory), and that this difficulty ought not to prevent a proper study of established practice.

It may also be argued that, if international law withholds legal status from effective legal entities, the result is a legal vacuum undesirable both in practice and principle. But this assumes that international law does not apply to *de facto* illegal entities; this is simply not so. Relevant international legal rules can apply to *de facto* situations here as elsewhere. For example, Formosa, though not a State, is not free to act contrary to international law, nor does it claim such a liberty. The process of analogy from legal rules applicable to States is quite capable of providing a body of rules applicable to non-State entities. The argument that no such rules apply smacks of the old view that international law can only apply to States.

Fundamentally, the argument that international law cannot regulate or control effective territorial entities is an expression of the view that international law cannot regulate power politics at all; that it is, essentially, non-peremptory. But, on its own terms and with whatever results, international law is undoubtedly in a stage of development towards greater coherence. In the present context, an important recent development has been the acceptance of the notion of *jus cogens*; that is, of relatively imprescriptible and peremptory international legal rules. This development, and its possible relevance to questions of statehood, must now be considered.

(1) Jus cogens *in modern international law*

The existence of a hierarchy of international law rules has long been posited; but to avoid confusion certain preliminary distinctions must be made. There are rules which are preconditions for effective international activity—for example, *pacta sunt servanda*. To abrogate that rule is not possible: a treaty providing that *pacta sunt servanda* is mere reaffirmation; a treaty denying it is an absurdity. The point is that the very activity of treaty-making assumes the general rule. Equally, a treaty abolishing States (without providing for their replacement by other governmental forms) would be meaningless, because the activity of international relations as at present carried on assumes States as the basic international units. It follows that, in discussing the problem of *jus cogens*, we are concerned only with what may be called substantive, not with structural, rules.[8] It also follows that the problem of *jus cogens* is the problem of restrictions upon the possible freedom of action of States, not of limitations upon some absolute liberty that States have never had. Thus the proposition that States are in principle free to make whatever treaties they like is too absolute: rather, States are in principle free to make whatever provision they like concerning their own rights (or, in general, concerning the rights of their nationals). The *pacta tertiis* rule has nothing to do with *jus cogens*: States simply do not have, in the absence of consent, the competence to deprive other States of their legal rights by way of treaty. A treaty attempting to impose duties on third States is not void—as is a treaty in violation of a *jus cogens* norm. It merely provides a possible set of rules which are, in the absence of the consent of the State or States affected, non-opposable.[9] So the principle of consent is a further, structural, principle of international law, distinct from *jus cogens*.

The problem is whether the principle of State autonomy as enunciated admits of exceptions. Modern opinion, though not quite unanimous,[10] is substantially in favour of *jus cogens*, which may be said to have received its *imprimatur* in the text of the Vienna Convention. Article 53 provides that:

A treaty is void, if, at the time of its conclusion, it conflicts with a peremptory norm of general international law. For the purposes of the present Convention, a peremptory norm of general international law is a norm accepted and recognized by the international community of States as a whole as a norm from which no derogation is permitted and

---

[8] Cf. (to the same effect) Verdross (1966), 60 *AJ* 55–63, 58–9; Scheuner (1967), 27 *ZfV* 520–32, 525.

[9] Vienna Convention of the Law of Treaties (1969), Art. 34.

[10] At the Vienna Conference only Liechtenstein opposed the notion outright. Among writers Schwarzenberger is notable for his opposition: (1965) 43 *Texas LR* 455–78; but cf. *International Law* I, 425–7. Cf. also Sztucki, *Jus Cogens and the Vienna Convention on the Law of Treaties* (1974), for a full account.

which can be modified only by a subsequent norm of general international law having the same character.[11]

Jus cogens is thus well established, but the content of the category is less well settled, and despite last minute redrafting, Article 53 is of little help, being quite circular.[12] Nevertheless the extent of disagreement over the content of *jus cogens* can be exaggerated, and it may well be that in practice courts will have less difficulty in applying the rule than might have been thought.[13] Scheuner suggests three categories of *jus cogens*: rules protecting the foundations of international order, such as the prohibition of genocide or of the use of force in international relations except in self-defence; rules concerning peaceful co-operation in the protection of common interests, such as freedom of the seas, and rules protecting the most fundamental and basic human rights, and, one might add, the basic rules for the protection of civilians in time of war. At least the first and third of these would appear to be genuine *jus cogens* norms. On the other hand, some suggested candidates are much less certain: the invalidity of unequal treaties,[14] and self-determination,[15] are both controversial even as *jus dispositivum*: the suggestion that they constitute *jus cogens* rules is difficult to accept.[16]

These few rules then have a special character in modern international law. Treaties in conflict with them are void,[17] and pre-existing treaties are annulled when *jus cogens* norms inconsistent with them come into existence.[18] But the question arises whether *jus cogens* norms invalidate situations other than treaties.

(*i*) *Legal effects of* jus cogens *on acts or situations other than treaties*

It may be suggested that *jus cogens* norms must invalidate not just treaties but all legal acts and situations inconsistent with

---

[11] Arts. 65–6 provide for judicial settlement of disputes concerning, *inter alia*, Art. 53. The Convention is not yet in force. For the *travaux préparatoires* see Rosenne, *The Law of Treaties* (1970), 290–3.

[12] Rousseau, *DIP* I, 149–51; de Visscher (1971), 75 *RGDIP* 5–11, 7.

[13] Cf. Schwelb (1967), 61 *AJ* 946–75; Reisenfeld (1966), 60 *AJ* 511–15.

[14] Judge Ammoun, *Barcelona Traction (Second Phase)* I.C.J. Rep. 1970 p. 3, 304.

[15] Loc. cit. and Scheuner (1967), 27 *ZfV* 520, 525, both referring (erroneously) to Brownlie, *Principles* (1st edn.), 75, 412; cf. ibid (2nd edn.), 500n.4. See also Bedjaoui, *ILC Ybk.* 1975/I, 48.

[16] Self-determination may however be protected by the *pacta tertiis* rule: *infra*, p. 366.

[17] Vienna Convention, Art. 53; cf. *USFR* 1946/VIII, 1082–3 (France).

[18] Vienna Convention, Art. 69. There is no severability: Art. 44(5).

them. This goes beyond the terms of the Vienna Convention itself, although as a codification of treaty law it was arguably outside its province to go further. But Article 53 does state that 'no derogation is permitted' from *jus cogens* norms, and this language seems to be sufficiently wide to include acts other than treaties. It is difficult to accept that a rule should be sacrosanct in one context and freely prescriptible in another. But it must be admitted that *jus cogens*, which was designed to deal with problems of the validity of treaties, is acutely difficult to apply to problems of territorial status.[19] In these latter cases, the question must be whether the illegality is so central to the existence or extinction of the entity in question that international law may justifiably, and exceptionally, treat an effective entity as not a State (or a non-effective entity as continuing to be a State). Arguably a rule which was *jus dispositivum* in the context of treaties might yet be sufficiently relevant and important to be regarded as a criterion for statehood. However, *jus cogens* would still be relevant here in two ways. That a particular rule is one of *jus cogens* must be relevant in determining whether illegality under that rule is such as to warrant refusing to accept the statehood of the entity created in breach of the rule. And that the rule violated is one of *jus cogens* would be relevant in applying the principle of extinctive prescription.

(ii) *Status of entities created by illegal treaties*

One further specific situation requires consideration. States, and internationalized territories proximate to States, are quite often created pursuant to treaty provisions. Article 71 of the Vienna Convention provides:

1. In the case of a treaty which is void under article 53 the parties shall:
   (a) eliminate as far as possible the consequences of any act performed in reliance on any provision which conflicts with the peremptory norm of general international law; and
   (b) bring their mutual relations into conformity with the peremptory norm of general international law.

2. In the case of a treaty which becomes void and terminates under article 64, the termination of the treaty:

---

[19] Scheuner (1967), 27 *ZfV* 520, 525n. On different grounds, Marek, *Guggenheim Festschrift* (1968), 426–59, 439–41.

(a) releases the parties from any obligation further to perform the treaty;

(b) does not affect any right, obligation or legal situation of the parties created through the execution of the treaty prior to its termination;

provided that those rights, obligations or situations may thereafter be maintained only to the extent that their maintenance is not in itself in conflict with the new peremptory norm of general international law.

It would seem to follow that, where a State is created under a treaty not at the time illegal, the State's legal existence is not affected by subsequent invalidity of the treaty. This is particularly so in that the new State may not be a party to the treaty under which it is created, so that whilst the 'rights obligations or situations' of the parties may be inconsistent with the new peremptory norm, this will not be the case with the 'rights obligations or situations' of the new State created under the treaty. On the other hand, there is nothing illogical about a State being a party to the treaty which constitutes it, so that different legal consequences could result from an essentially fortuitous circumstance. However, it is hard to imagine a situation actually arising in which a treaty creating a State (as distinct from one providing for its termination) could be a breach of a *jus cogens* norm. The same arguments apply to article 71(1), which requires only that the *parties* 'bring their mutual relations into conformity with the peremptory norm', and eliminate 'as far as possible' the consequences of acts performed in execution of the treaty. A State granted independence under a treaty to which it was not a party would thus usually be immune from the effects of Article 71.

(2) *Illegality and Statehood: some tentative conclusions*

It has been argued that there is nothing *a priori* incoherent about the legal regulation of statehood on a basis other than that of effectiveness. And, although this has been denied,[20] there is a considerable amount of practice supporting regulations of this type. This position was foreshadowed by Lauterpacht in 1948:

International law acknowledges as a source of rights and obligations such facts and situations as are not the result of acts which it prohibits

[20] Charpentier, *Reconnaissance*, 127–8; Chen, *Recognition*, 54. Cf. Verhoeven, *Reconnaissance*, 607–17.

and stigmatizes as unlawful . . . It follows from the same principle that facts, however undisputed, which are the result of conduct violative of international law cannot claim the same right to be incorporated automatically as part of the law of nations . . .[21]

Thirty years later, it can be argued that other conditions unrelated to effectiveness may be relevant.[22] No doubt the principle of effectiveness remains the dominant criterion, but practice does not support the view that it is the only one. On the other hand, although international law has developed the formal concept of *jus cogens*, that concept, at least as elaborated in the Vienna Convention, is not the key to the inquiry. The provisions of the Convention relating to *jus cogens* do not have and were not intended to have direct application to situations involving the creation of States. Their importance is rather indirect, as has been said: the emphasis on the centrality and permanence of certain basic rules. In the context of statehood, what is necessary is not reliance upon the provisions of the Vienna Convention,[23] but an examination of rules specifically adapted to the context.

Finally, three different problems must be distinguished: illegality affecting the creation of a State; illegality affecting the title of its government to represent it, and illegality affecting its termination. Different considerations may apply in each case, and only the first problem will be dealt with here.[24]

3.2   STATEHOOD AND SELF-DETERMINATION

The relation between statehood and self-determination is an important, and to some extent a neglected, problem. A significant body of practice attests the reality of the link; but it remains to be seen whether self-determination as such has become a criterion of statehood; and if so, with what effects. It will be argued here that self-determination, to the limited extent to which it operates as a legal right in modern international law, is a criterion of

---

[21] Lauterpacht, *Recognition*, 409–10; cf. ibid. 285, 340–1.

[22] Cf. Eekelaar, in Simpson ed., *Oxford Essays in Jurisprudence* (2nd. ser., 1973), 22–43, 39–40; Mendelson, 114; Brownlie, *Principles*, 823; Reuter, *ILC Ybk.* 1975/I, 45.

[23] But see Bokor-Szegö, *New States in International Law* (1970), 66–75.

[24] For illegality and extinction of States see *infra*, Chapter 17. Illegality and governmental representation is a topic on which practice is, to say the least, scanty. It is outside the scope of this study.

statehood. The first point to be established is the legal status of self-determination.

(1) *Self-determination in modern international law*

There has been since 1945 perhaps no more divisive issue among writers (at least in the Western tradition of international law) than the question whether there exists a legal right or principle of self-determination of peoples. Self-determination as a legal right or principle would represent a significant erosion of the principle of sovereignty. It is a dynamic principle which, if consistently applied, could bring about significant changes in the political geography of the world. It is an overtly political principle, which raises important questions about the nature of international law and the justiciability of political disputes. And, for our purposes, it would be a most significant exception to the traditional notion that the creation of States is a matter of fact and not of law.

(i) *Self-determination before 1945*

The concept of self-determination has obvious antecedents, but its appearance as an operative political principle dates from the Bolshevik revolution and the peace settlements at the end of the First World War.[25] It was an issue in the *Aaland Islands case* before the first session of the League. The population of the islands claimed the right to attach themselves to Sweden rather than Finland, at the time when Finland itself was establishing its independence from the Russian Empire.[26] The League appointed two Commissions to investigate different aspects of the dispute. An International Commission of Jurists reported that the matter was not one within Finland's domestic jurisdiction under Article 15 paragraph 8 of the Covenant, because Finland at the time was not definitively established, and because the principle of self-determination had a role to play in the case of *de facto* revolutionary entities such as Finland in 1919. Thus, although the Commission of Jurists rejected the principle of self-determi-

[25] For Soviet practice in this period see Carr, *The Bolshevik Revolution 1917–1923* (1950), 414–35. The term was also given currency by President Wilson: see Hackworth, 1 *Digest* 422–5. It is implicit in the Fourteen Points, and was included in the first American draft for the Covenant, though it was subsequently deleted.

[26] *Supra*, p. 44. See also Barros, *The Aaland Islands Question* (1968); Delavoix, *Essai historique sur la séparation de la Finlande et de la Russie* (1932).

nation, it did so only in the context of entities definitively established as States.[27] The Committee of Rapporteurs on the other hand particularly disagreed with the view that Finland was a new State: rather, in their opinion, it was a continuation of an autonomous State of Finland which had always included the Aaland Islands.[28] There was thus no question of Finland in 1917 not being definitively constituted, and the principle of self-determination was therefore inapplicable. About self-determination, the Rapporteurs had this to say:

This principle is not, properly speaking a rule of international law and the League of Nations has not entered it in its Covenant. This is also the opinion of the International Commission of Jurists . . . It is a principle of justice and of liberty, expressed by a vague and general formula which has given rise to most varied interpretations and differences of opinion . . . To concede to minorities, either of language or religion, or to any fraction of a population the right of withdrawing from the community to which they belong, because it is their wish or their good pleasure, would be to destroy order and stability within States and to inaugurate anarchy in international life; it would be to uphold a theory incompatible with the very idea of the State as a territorial and political unity . . . The separation of a minority from the State of which it forms a part and its incorporation in another State can only be considered as an altogether exceptional solution, a last resort when the State lacks either the will or the power to enact and apply just and effective guarantees.[29]

Although the Reports on the Aaland Islands are thus authority for the proposition that self-determination was not a legal principle in 1920, that proposition requires some elaboration. In the first place, it is most doubtful whether modern international law would accept the application of self-determination to a situation such as the Aaland Islands. Moreover the second Report seems to admit the possibility that the principle will apply to territories which are so badly misgoverned that they are in effect alienated from the metropolitan State. This situation may be described as that of *carence de souveraineté*, and, although

---

[27] Report of Commission of Jurists (Larnaude, Huber, Struycken), *LNOJ* Sp. Supp. No. 3 (Oct. 1920), 5–6. For Fisher's proposal accepting the report (adopted without dissent), see *LNOJ* Oct. 1920, 395.

[28] Report of the Committee of Rapporteurs (Beyens, Calonder, Elkens), 16 Apr. 1921: *LN* Council Doct. B7/21/68/106 [VII], 22–3.

[29] Ibid. 27–8.

the modern law remains undeveloped, it is, it will be suggested, one way in which the principle can apply in particular cases. Finally, the Rapporteurs expressly stated that Finland was a 'people' in a way in which the population of the Aaland Islands was not; so that, on the assumption that Finland had not been a separate entity before 1917, its secession from the Russian Empire would have been fully justified.[30] It is also of interest to note that United States' recognition of Finland was accorded after elections regarded as demonstrating the representative nature of its government.[31] This may not be the principle of self-determination, but it is certainly rather like it. The Council accepted the Report of the Committee of Rapporteurs, recognized Finnish sovereignty over the Islands, but recommended certain minority guarantees.[32] This and other cases of minority guarantees, as well as conventional arrangements such as plebiscites and the Mandate system, demonstrate the political force of the principle of self-determination in the inter-war period.[33] None the less there was little general development of the principle before 1945.[34]

Thirty years later a vast literature and several advisory opinions of the International Court have failed to settle the matter: indeed the intensity of the dispute might lead one to suppose a failure on each side to analyse with sufficient care the opposing positions. In this respect two preliminary distinctions may be of assistance.

In the first place it is necessary to distinguish clearly the political principle or value of self-determination from the putative legal right or principle. The former, as a principle of general application, has had a place in democratic thought since at least 1789, and has at particular periods (most notably 1917–20) assumed great prominence in international affairs.[35] The latter is of much more recent origin, and applies as of right (if at

---

[30] Loc. cit.

[31] *USFR* 1919/II, 211, 213.

[32] *LNOJ* Sp. Supp. No. 5, 24. Cf. de Visscher (1921), 2 *RDILC* 35–56, 243–84; Padelford and Andersson (1939), 33 *AJ* 465–87; 9 *LNTS* 212.

[33] Calogeropoulos-Stratis, *Le Droit des peuples à disposer d'eux-mêmes* (1973), 62–86.

[34] Cf. the quite favourable discussion, *de lege ferenda*, by Bisschop (1921–2), 2 *BY* 122–132, 129–30; and see the important early study of Redslob, *Le Principe des nationalités* (1930).

[35] See e.g. Cobban, *The Nation State and National Self-Determination* (rev. edn., 1969).

all) only to a restricted category of cases. The weight sometimes accorded the political principle of self-determination had no doubt contributed, at least to some degree, to the body of practice to be examined here; but this general ideal is too vague and ill-defined to constitute a legal principle, much less a positive legal rule applying of its own force to particular 'peoples' or to 'peoples' in general. Yet it is sometimes assumed that proponents of a legal right or principle of self-determination are committed to just this view of the ambit of the right or principle. The distinction is the same as that between the general political value of 'sovereignty' which is often claimed to inhere in a particular group or polity, and the legal notion or principle of sovereignty, which has, as we have seen,[36] a considerably more restricted scope.

This comparison leads to the second point: there is a clear but not always articulated distinction between the identification of territories to which the legal principle of sovereignty applies, and the legal consequences of that principle in its application to territories already determined. In the present stage of development of international law, 'sovereignty' applies as a legal right (or more properly, a legal presumption) only to territories constituted or accepted as States under the criteria discussed here. This is one reason why we speak of a *principle* of sovereignty; since the notion of a right presupposes identification of the subject of the right, and that identification must be made *aliunde* the principle of sovereignty.[37] Moreover it might be the case that the territories to be regarded as 'sovereign' would be determined in practice by political rather than legal considerations; and yet the consequences of the principle in its application to the territories so determined would be legal. This was Oppenheim's view of the sovereignty of States: sovereignty was a legal principle applying to entities identified by the purely political act of recognition.[38] A legal principle of self-determination would present an almost exact analogy. In practice since 1945 there has been a considerable elaboration of the legal consequences of the principle of self-determination for particular territories; but the question of the ambit of self-determination,

[36] *Supra*, p. 27.

[37] The problem of determining the territories to which self-determination applies is thus very similar to the problem of determining the criteria for statehood.

[38] *Supra*, p. 13.

the territories to which it applies, has at least arguably remained as much a matter of politics as law. In any discussion of the problem this distinction must be carefully observed.

(ii) The principle of self-determination in the United Nations Charter

The Charter twice mentions self-determination expressly: in Article 1(2) where one of the 'purposes of the United Nations' is stated to be the development of 'friendly relations among nations based on respect for the principle of equal rights and self-determination of peoples', and in Article 55, where the same formula is used to express the general aims of the United Nations in the fields of social and economic development and respect for human rights. By elaborating these rather cryptic references, the General Assembly has attempted in a very large number of resolutions to define more precisely the content of the principle. Thus, the Colonial Declaration (clause 2) stated that 'All peoples have the right to self-determination; by virtue of that right they freely determine their political status and freely pursue their economic, social and cultural development.'[39] The principle has also been reaffirmed by the Security Council, for example by Resolution 183 of 11 December 1963, by ten votes to none with one abstention.[40] The status of self-determination as a 'fundamental obligation' was further emphasized by its being linked with the 'prohibition of the threat or use of force in international relations' in Resolution 2160 (XXI), which affirmed that

(b) Any forcible action, direct or indirect, which deprives peoples under foreign domination of their right to self-determination and freedom and independence and of their right to determine freely their political status and pursue their economic, social and cultural development constitutes a violation of the Charter of the United Nations. Accordingly, the use of force to deprive peoples of their national identity, as prohibited by the Declaration on the Inadmissibility of Intervention in the Domestic Affairs of States and the Protection of Their Independence and Sovereignty contained in

---

[39] G.A. Res. 1514 (XV), 14 Dec. 1960 (89–0:9), 'Declaration on the Granting of Independence to Colonial Countries and Peoples'. For the status of the 'Colonial Declaration' see Asamoah, *The Legal Significance of the Declaration of the General Assembly* (1966), pp. 164–73. See also G.A. Resns. 1541 (XV); 2105 (XX); 2200A (XXI); 2625 (XXV), Annex.

[40] Other more recent examples include S.C. Resns. 301 (1971) (Namibia); 377 (1975) (Western Sahara); 384 (1975) (Portuguese Timor).

General Assembly Resolution 2131 (XX), constitutes a violation of their inalienable rights and of the principle of non-intervention.[41]

And in its Declaration of Principles annexed to Resolution 2625 (XXV), the Assembly dealt in the following terms with 'The principle of equal rights and self-determination of peoples'.

By virtue of the principle of equal rights and self-determination of peoples enshrined in the Charter . . . all peoples have the right freely to determine, without external interference, their political status and to pursue their economic, social and cultural development, and every State has the duty to respect this right in accordance with the provisions of the Charter . . .

The territory of a colony or other non-self-governing territory has, under the Charter, a status separate and distinct from the territory of the State administering it; and such separate and distinct status under the Charter shall exist until the people of the colony or non-self-governing territory have exercised their right of self-determination in accordance with the Charter . . . Every State shall refrain from any action aimed at the partial or total disruption of the national unity or territorial integrity of any other State or country.[42]

However, one difficulty that arises here is that the General Assembly has no general law-making capacity. Resolutions, with certain limited exceptions, have only recommendatory force, and the Assembly has no capacity to impose new customary legal obligations on States.[43] Of course, the Assembly undoubtedly has some measure of discretion as to the way in which it carries out its interpretative functions. But the resolutions cited do not seem to be interpretations of the Charter as such (or if they are so, are so only to a limited degree). The Charter mentions self-determination only twice, and in both cases it seems to mean something rather different from the usual understanding of 'self-determination'. That term has in fact two quite distinct meanings. It can mean the sovereign equality of existing States, and in particular the right of a State to choose its own form of government without intervention. It can also mean the right of a specific territory ('people') to choose its own form of government irrespective of the wishes of the rest of the State of which that territory is a part. Traditional international law recognized the

[41] 30 Nov. 1966 (98–2:8).
[42] 24 Oct. 1970 (adopted without vote); see McWhinney (1966), 60 *AJ* 1–33.
[43] See the authorities cited *infra*, p. 91, n. 47.

first but not the second of these, from which it is said that it did not recognize the right of self-determination.[44] The Charter, in referring as it does to 'equal rights and self-determination' in Articles 1(2) and 55, seems at least primarily to be referring to self-determination also in this first and uncontroversial sense.[45] Self-determination in the second sense is not mentioned, though it is implicit in Articles 73(b) and 76(b). In proclaiming a general right of self-determination, and in particular of immediate self-determination, the resolutions cited go beyond the terms of the Charter however liberally construed.

This does not however foreclose the status of self-determination as a matter of customary international law. State practice is just as much State practice when it occurs in the 'parliamentary' context of the General Assembly as in more traditional diplomatic forms. The practice of States in assenting to and acting upon law-declaring resolutions may be of considerable probative importance, in particular where that practice achieves reasonable consistency over a period of time. Where a resolution is passed by 'a large majority of States with the intention of creating a new binding rule of law'[46] and is acted upon as such by States generally, then that action will have what can properly be called a quasi-legislative effect. The problem, as always, is one of evidence and assessment.[47] But, as we have seen, such an assessment requires two distinct inquiries: whether there exists any criteria for the determination of territories to which a 'right of self-determination' is to be accorded; and whether, in its application to those territories, self-determination can properly be regarded as a legal right, and if so, to what effect. To these questions we must now turn.

(iii) Identifying the unit of self-determination: the problem of criteria

It is a peculiarity of this area of practice that it is possible to be

---

[44] Parry, in Sørensen, ed., *Manual*, 1–54, 19–20.

[45] Cf. 6 *UNCIO* 955; Kaur (1970) 10 *Indian JIL* 479–502.

[46] *Fisheries Jurisdiction Case (Second Phase)* I.C.J. Rep. 1974 p. 3, 162 (Judge Petrèn).

[47] See further Asamoah, *The Legal Significance of the Declarations of the General Assembly* (1966), 169–73; Castañeda, *The Legal Significance of Resolutions of United Nations Organs* (1969), 120–1; Higgins, *Development*, 1–10; Falk (1966), 60 *AJ* 782–91; Onuf (1970), 64 *AJ* 349–55; Johnson (1955–6), 32 *BY* 97–122; Sloan (1948), 25 *BY* 1–33; Judge Tanaka, diss., *South West Africa Cases (Second Phase)* I.C.J. Rep. 1966 p. 6, 291–3. For a stricter view see Judge Fitzmaurice, diss., *Namibia Opinion* I.C.J. Rep. 1971 p. 6, 280–1, and in *Institut de Droit International. Livre du Centenaire* (1973), 268–71. Cf. Judge Lauterpacht, sep. op., *Voting Procedure Case* I.C.J. Rep. 1955 p. 67, 116.

more certain about the 'consequences' of self-determination than about the criteria for the territories to which the principle is regarded as applying. Much of the emphasis, in practice, has been on the application of the principle to territories to which it had come to apply either by a form of recognition or by agreement pursuant to conventional arrangements. The effect of this practice has been to elaborate sometimes cryptic references to the principle in the constituent documents, acting in some ways as a form of administrative law of the institutions in question. These institutions are dealt with in more detail elsewhere in this study, but may be briefly mentioned here.

(a) *The mandate and trusteeship systems*   Established respectively under Article 22 of the League of Nations Covenant and Chapters XII and XIII of the Charter, these two systems provided both for the enlightened administration of the territories in question (the notion of a 'sacred trust'), and for their 'progressive development towards self-government or independence'.[48] Formal 'securities for performance' of these obligations were established. In particular, the principle of self-determination, as the International Court has twice expressly affirmed,[49] was made applicable to mandated and trust territories, which are, as it were, the primary type of self-determination territory.[50]

(b) *Non-self-governing territories: Chapter XI of the Charter*   A more significant extension of the principle, certainly in retrospect, was brought about in Chapter XI of the Charter, which applies to 'territories whose peoples have not yet attained a full measure of self-government'. Chapter XI was the result of a compromise between those seeking an extension of the Trusteeship system to all 'colonial' territories, and those resisting such change.[51] The result was an acceptance, in more or less the same terms, of the substantive obligations of the Mandate and Trusteeship systems—acceptance in particular of 'the principle that the interests of the inhabitants of these territories are paramount', and of an obligation 'to develop self-government'[52] but with a much more

---

[48] Charter, Art. 76b.

[49] *Infra*, p. 96.

[50] For further discussion see *infra*, Chapter 13.

[51] Cf. Russell and Muther, *A History of the United Nations Charter* (1954), pp. 813–24.

[52] Charter, Art. 73. Reference is also made to the 'sacred trust', in language borrowed from Article 22 of the Covenant.

attenuated form of international accountability.[53] In practice Chapter XI of the Charter has been subjected to a pronounced form of 'progressive interpretation', a process which has received the imprimatur of the International Court,[54] and the approval of a large majority of States.[55]

(c) *Other cases of application of the principle to particular territorial disputes or situations* Finally, in quite a number of cases the principle of self-determination has been adopted by the parties as a criterion for settlement of a particular dispute or issue; for example, the use of plebiscites in determining boundaries.[56]

It will be seen that in each of these cases the problem of identification has been solved in practice by processes of express agreement or, at least, acquiescence. Indeed for the first and third categories this was necessarily so.[57] Early practice pursuant to Chapter XI of the Charter, which appears to apply to defined territories irrespective of the consent of the States administering them, was also quasi-conventional in nature: member States were asked to list territories to which, in their own assessment, Chapter XI applied, and no general examination has been made of the appropriateness or otherwise of their responses.[58] However practice since 1946, though predicated on a narrow interpretation of the term 'territories whose peoples have not yet attained a full measure of self-government',[59] has been rather more searching; it is to this practice that one must look to find even rudimentary criteria for self-determination territories.

Thus the General Assembly listed, after some years of study, 'Principles which should guide Members in determining whether or not an obligation exists to transmit information called for

---

[53] *Infra*, p. 356.

[54] *Namibia Opinion* I.C.J. Rep. 1971, p. 16, 31, cited *infra*, p. 96; *Western Sahara Opinion* I.C.J. Rep. 1975, p. 12, 32–3, cited *infra*, p. 358.

[55] See further *infra*, Chapter 14.

[56] Cf. Bowett (1966), 60 *PAS* 129, 130–1. See further the works cited *infra*, p. 98, n. 80.

[57] Thus Charter Art. 77(2) made it clear that there was no automatic transfer of territories from mandate to trusteeship, and the International Court held that there was no obligation to negotiate trusteeship agreements: *Status of South West Africa Opinion*, I.C.J. Rep. 1950 p. 128, 139–40; cf. Judge de Visscher at 187–90. Art. 77(1)(c) provided for other territories to be 'voluntarily placed' under the system by states responsible for their administration: There have been no such territories.

[58] *Infra*, p. 360.

[59] *Infra*, p. 359.

under Article 73(e) of the Charter'.[60] Pursuant to those principles, the Assembly has on several occasions 'determined' that particular territories did qualify as territories to which Chapter XI applied, whether with or without the approval of the member State administering the territory in question.[61] Other suggestions to the same effect have been made.[62]

These excursions would seem to have been amply justified by the terms of Chapter XI, which is not expressed to depend on the consent of particular administering powers; but the absence of any more peremptory[63] or thorough delimitation of non-self-governing territories remains significant. Although there may be room for criticism of the General Assembly's record in this area, it may also be that the criticism should be directed at the relatively restrictive definition of 'non-self-governing territories' which has been adopted: that definition (at least as elaborated in Resolution 1541 (XV)) refers exclusively to the notion of 'colonial territories' *in 1945*, despite the fact that Ch. XI itself expressly includes territories acquired after 1945. But, given that definition, it is the case that (small islands apart) virtually all the territories which would, under the twin criteria of geographical separateness and political subordination, have qualified as non-self-governing have been treated as such, at least for a time. It is also significant that the principle of self-determination has continued to be regarded as relevant to those territories even when they were no longer reported on under Article 73(e).[64]

(iv) *The consequences of self-determination*

Where a territory is subjected to a particular regime predicated upon the principle of self-determination, the consequences of that subjection have of course been defined in the first place in the instruments themselves. The effect of subsequent practice has none the less been marked: the principle of self-determination has been regarded as having a number of significant legal effects

---

[60] G.A. Res. 1541 (XV), Annex, 15 Dec. 1960 (69–2:21); *infra*, p. 360.

[61] *Infra*, p. 361.

[62] For Bangladesh see *infra*, p. 116. In the *Namibia Opinion*, Judge Fitzmaurice stated that 'on any view S.W. Africa is a non-self-governing territory' under Chapter XI of the Charter: I.C.J. Rep. 1971 p. 6, 296.

[63] The Annex to G.A. Res. 1541 (XV) refers to 'Principles which should guide *Members* . . .' The Assembly's role is treated, at best, as secondary.

[64] *Infra*, p. 361 for further discussion.

on the institutions or territories in question. Only a brief and summary statement is possible here, but the following examples may be given.

It is arguable that traditional rules relating to the use of force and to neutrality in armed conflicts between a metropolitan or administering State and indigenous forces in a non-self-governing territory have been modified, even modified substantially.[65] Despite significant qualifications in the original instruments, the principle of self-determination has come to be regarded as dominant.[66] A most striking example is the case of 'C' Mandates, such as South West Africa: the 'C' Mandate was regarded by some as a form of disguised annexation,[67] but that view did not prevail.[68] Institutions based on self-determination have also been regarded as having a relatively permanent, or 'dispositive', status; for example, the Mandate regime survived the extinction of the League of Nations in 1946, with the result, *semble*, that United Nations membership effected a form of novation of reporting responsibilities from the League Council to the General Assembly.[69] The principle has also been regarded as justifying the revocation or termination of rights to administer territory conferred by international agreement in the event of fundamental violation of the humanitarian interests sought to be protected by those agreements.[70] These matters are discussed further elsewhere.[71]

(v) Conclusions

The issue then is whether there is sufficient State practice, carried out with a conviction that the activity is obligatory, to establish self-determination—at least as a principle capable of generating these types of consequences—as part of customary international law. Although this view has been denied by some writers,[72] it was adopted by the International Court in two recent

---

[65] *Infra*, p. 117.

[66] Cf. *Namibia Opinion*, I.C.J. Rep. 1971 p. 6, 31; *infra*, p. 96.

[67] Cf. the dispute on the point between South Africa and the Permanent Mandates Commission; noted (1931) 12 *BY* 151.

[68] Cf. Wright, *Mandates under the League*, 324–7; *infra*, p. 336.

[69] *Status of South West Africa Case*, I.C.J. Rep. 1950 p. 128.

[70] *Infra*, pp. 344–55.

[71] See generally Chapters 13, 14.

[72] Fitzmaurice, for example, calls it juridical nonsense: *Institut de Droit International, Livre du Centenaire* (1973), 196, 233. See also Verzijl, *International Law* I, 324; Blum (1975),

cases. In the *Namibia Opinion* a majority of the Court stated that

... the subsequent development of international law in regard to non-self-governing territories, as enshrined in the Charter of the United Nations, made the principle of self-determination applicable to all of them. The concept of the sacred trust was confirmed and expanded to all 'territories whose peoples have not attained a full measure of self-government' (Art. 73). Thus it clearly embraced territories under a colonial regime. Obviously the sacred trust continued to apply to League of Nations mandated territories on which the international status had been conferred earlier. A further important stage in this development was the Declaration on the Granting of Independence to Colonial Countries and Peoples ... which embraces all peoples and territories which 'have not yet attained independence'. Nor is it possible to leave out of account the political history of mandated territories in general. All those which did not acquire independence, excluding Namibia, were placed under trusteeship. Today, only two out of fifteen, excluding Namibia, remain under United Nations tutelage. This is but a manifestation of the general development which has led to the birth of so many new States.[73]

This important passage was cited with approval by the Court in the *Western Sahara Case*, in an Opinion which strongly affirmed the right of the people of the territory to determine their future political status, notwithstanding claims to revindication on the part of Morocco and Mauritania.[74] Self-determination was also reaffirmed as the relevant juridical principle in several of the separate opinions:[75] the most interesting of these, for our purposes, were those of Judges Dillard and Petrèn.

Judge Dillard, after referring briefly to the contrasting opinions on the point, went on:

... to call attention to the fact that the present Opinion is forthright in proclaiming the existence of the 'right' in so far as the present proceedings are concerned. This is made explicit in paragraph 56 and is fortified by calling into play two dicta in the *Namibia* case to which are added an analysis of the numerous resolutions of the General

---

10 *Israel L.R.* 509–14; Emerson (1971), 65 *AJ* 459–75, and *Self-Determination Revisited in the Era of Decolonization* (1964); Devine, [1974] *Acta Juridica* 183–209; Jenks, in *Law in the World Community* (1967), 134–49, 141; Guilhaudis, *Le Droit des peuples à disposer d'eux-mêmes* (1976).

[73] I.C.J. Rep. 1971 p. 6, 31; cf. Judge Ammoun, 73–5; Judge Padilla Nervo, 115.

[74] I.C.J. Rep. 1975 p. 12, 31–3. For discussion see *infra*, p. 384.

[75] Cf. Judge Ammoun, ibid. 99–100; Judge Nagendra Singh, 30–1; Judge de Castro, 170–1.

Assembly dealing in general with its decolonization policy and in particular with those resolutions centering on the Western Sahara (Opinion, paras. 60–65). The pronouncements of the Court thus indicate, in my view, that a norm of international law has emerged applicable to the decolonization of those non-self-governing territories which are under the aegis of the United Nations. It should be added that the force of these pronouncements is in no way diminished by virtue of the theoretically non-binding character of an advisory opinion.[76]

Later Judge Dillard referred to:

the cardinal restraint which the legal right of self-determination imposes. That restraint may be captured in a single sentence. It is for the people to determine the destiny of the territory and not the territory the destiny of the people. Viewed in this perspective it becomes almost self-evident that the existence of ancient 'legal ties' of the kind described in the Opinion, while they may influence some of the projected procedures for decolonization, can have only a tangential effect in the ultimate choices available to the people.[77]

This forthright view may be compared with the nuances of Judge Petrèn's separate opinion. He pointed out that:

a veritable law of decolonization is in the course of taking shape. It derives essentially from the principle of self-determination of peoples proclaimed in the Charter of the United Nations and confirmed by a large number of resolutions of the General Assembly. But, in certain specific cases, one must equally take into account the principle of the national unity and integrity of States, a principle which has also been the subject of resolutions of the General Assembly. It is thus by a combination of different elements of international law evolving under the inspiration of the United Nations that the process of decolonization is being pursued ... [H]owever ... the wide variety of geographical and other data which must be taken into account in questions of decolonization have not yet allowed of the establishment of a sufficiently developed body of rules and practice to cover all the situations which may give rise to problems. In other words, although its guiding principles have emerged, the law of decolonization does not yet constitute a complete body of doctrine and practice. It is thus natural that political forces should be constantly at work rendering more precise and complete the content of that law in specific cases like that of Western Sahara.[78]

[76] I.C.J. Rep. 1975 p. 12, 121–2.
[77] Ibid. 122.
[78] Ibid. 110.

There is here a certain studied ambiguity. The passage may simply mean that, although the guiding principles (and in particular the principle of self-determination) of the 'law of decolonization' have emerged, certain aspects of the application of those legal principles remain unclear and thus *de lege ferenda*. This, as we shall see,[79] is the case; although the area of uncertainty can be exaggerated, and the Court did in fact, with a considerable degree of unanimity, provide an answer to a Request concerning just such an area of doubt. On the other hand, the passage might be interpreted as meaning that, since the application of the guiding principles remains in some cases unclear or uncertain, the principles themselves, and thus the whole 'law of decolonization' remain essentially *de lege ferenda*. This latter interpretation implies a somewhat cataclysmic view of the growth and creation of international law rules: until a suggested rule has become entirely clear in principle and application, it is not a rule at all. That view would constitute a powerful solvent in many areas of customary law, but it is of doubtful validity, and it is equally doubtful that Judge Petrèn in fact adopted it. 'Guiding juridical principles' can coexist with uncertainties as to their application in specific cases: so long as there exists a 'hard core' of reasonably clear cases, the status of the principle in question need not be doubted. On the other view, the emergence of a 'law of decolonization' must await the completion of the process of decolonization, since only then would no doubts or difficulties exist. The principle of self-determination as a general principle of international law also commands substantial academic support.[80] In the absence of any compelling considerations of principle there would be little justification for rejecting it as a part of the substantive law. In

---

[79] *Infra*, Chapter 14.

[80] Cf. Scelle, in *Spiropoulos Festschrift* (1957), 385–92; Brownlie, *Principles*, 575–8; Delupis, *International Law and the Independent State* (1974), 13–18; Calogeropoulos-Stratis, op. cit.; Rigo Sureda, *The Evolution of the Right of Self-Determination* (1973) (the best monograph); Umozurike, *Self-Determination in International Law* (1972); Lachs (1960–1), 1 *Indian JIL* 429–42; Higgins, *Development*, 90–106; Bokor-Szegö, *New States and International Law* (1970), 11–51; Nawaz, [1965] *Duke LJ* 82–101; Tunkin, *Theory of International Law* (1974), 60–9 (and refs. to Soviet literature); Wright (1954), 48 *PAS* 23–37; Mustafa (1971), 5 *Int. L.* 479–87; Akehurst, *Modern Introduction*, 281–4; Šukoviċ in Šahoviċ, ed., *Principles of International Law concerning Friendly Relations and Cooperation* (1972), 323–74; and the bibliography, *infra*. *Contra*, see the works cited *supra*, p. 95 n. 72. Much of the dissent is based on the assumption that self-determination is asserted as a general right of 'peoples'. See *Supra*, pp. 91–4 for discussion of the problem of application.

fact, three main arguments of principle are adduced to the contrary.

First, it is argued that the notion of self-determination involves in some way a logical contradiction:

> The initial difficulty is that it is scarcely possible to refer to an entity as an entity unless it already is one, so that it makes little juridical sense to speak of a claim to *become* one, for in whom or what would the claim reside? By definition, 'entities' seeking self-determination are not yet determined internationally ... Alternatively, if they do possess such rights, they are entities which are already determined internationally ...[81]

With respect, this argument involves an equivocation on the terms 'entity' and 'determination'. The identification of a self-determination unit is a different thing from the determination by that unit in accordance with appropriate procedures of its future status. Equally, there is nothing self-contradictory in an entity having a limited status, consisting primarily in the right at some future time to choose some more permanent status.

A second, more plausible, argument is that it is impossible to delineate with sufficient or indeed with any precision the unit to which the right of self-determination is to be attributed. This point is made, somewhat caustically, by Ivor Jennings: 'On the surface it seem[s] reasonable: let the people decide. It [is] in fact ridiculous because the people cannot decide until somebody decides who are the people.'[82] The short answer is that, in fact, certain rules, and a fairly extensive body of practice relating to those rules, enable us to identify with reasonable precision the units to which self-determination applies as of right (in this study referred to as self-determination units).[83] Specifically, the principle of self-determination applies, or may apply, in four categories of cases. First, it applies to entities whose right to self-determination is established under or pursuant to international agreements, and in particular to mandated, trust and non-self-governing territories.[84] Secondly, it applies to existing States, exluding for the purposes of the self-determination rule those parts of the State which are themselves self-determination units

---

[81] Fitzmaurice, in Institut de Droit International, *Livre du Centenaire* (1973), 233n.

[82] *The Approach to Self-Government* (1956), 56.

[83] To the same effect, Higgins, *Development*, 104.

[84] See *infra*, Chapters 13, 14.

as defined. In this case, the principle of self-determination takes the well-known form of the rule preventing intervention in the internal affairs of a State: this includes the right of the people of the State to choose for themselves their own form of government. In this sense self-determination is a continuing, and not a once-for-all right. Since it appears that self-determination units are coming increasingly to be States (subject to the second rather than the first meaning of self-determination) it may be suggested that self-determination in the future will be a more conservative principle than has sometimes been thought, or feared. However, there is a third possible category of self-determination units: that is, entities part of a metropolitan State but which have been governed in such a way as to make them in effect non-self-governing territories, or, in other terms, territories subject to *carence de souveraineté*.[85] This third category is acutely controversial: there is only one, and that a disputed, modern example—Bangladesh.[86]

Consideration of this third, debatable, category brings us back to the third and final objection to the principle of self-determination. 'The "right of self-determination" has . . . always been the sport of national or international politics and has never been recognized as a genuine positive right of "peoples" of universal and impartial application, and it never will, nor can be so recognized in the future . . .'[87] This is of course a variant of the 'double standards' argument which is used in other areas of international law and relations. It must be admitted that the principle of self-determination could well apply to territories and peoples to which it does not, *de lege lata*, apply. However it is rather late in the day to contest the application of self-determination to dependent peoples and colonial territories. The impact of the double-standards argument, if accepted, must therefore be substantially in that third area of misgovernment

---

[85] Cf. *supra*, p. 86.

[86] *Infra*, p. 116. For the sake of completeness a fourth category of application should be referred to: *sc.* the case in which the principle of self-determination is adopted by the parties as a criterion for settlement of a particular dispute or issue: e.g. the use of plebiscites in determining boundaries. On this application see in particular Bowett (1966), 60 *PAS* 129–35, 130–1. But cf. Calogeropoulos-Stratis, op. cit., for a more extensive view: noted (1974–5) 47 *BY* 450–1.

[87] Verzijl, *International Law* I, 324; cf. Fitzmaurice, op. cit. 232–3; Blum (1975), 10 *Israel L.R.* 509–14.

and denial of fundamental human rights. But the extension of self-determination to that type of case would appear to be precisely the point of the double-standards argument. It would seem then that the following conclusions are supported by current practice.

(1) International law recognizes the principle of self-determination.

(2) It is however not a right applicable directly to any group of people desiring political independence or self-government. Like sovereignty, it is a legal principle: Fawcett calls it a 'directive principle of legislation'.[88] It applies as a matter of right only after the unit of self-determination has been determined by the application of appropriate rules.

(3) The units to which the principle applies are in general those territories established and recognized as separate political units; in particular it applies to the following:

(a) Trust and mandated territories, and territories treated as non-self-governing under Chapter XI of the Charter;

(b) States, excluding for the purposes of the self-determination rule those parts of States which are themselves self-determination units as defined;

(c) (Possibly) other territories forming distinct political-geographical areas, whose inhabitants do not share in the government either of the region or of the State to which the region belongs, with the result that the territory becomes in effect, with respect to the remainder of the State, non-self-governing;[89]
and

(d) All other territories or situations to which self-determination is applied by the parties as an appropriate solution or criterion.

(4) Where a self-determination unit is not already a State, it has a right of self-determination: that is, a right to choose its own political organization. Such a right, in view of its close connection

---

[88] Fawcett (1971), 132 *HR* 386–91, 387.
[89] In determining the territories in this category, G.A. Resolution 1541 (XV), *Annex* ('Principles which should guide Members in determining whether or not an obligation exists to transmit the information called for in Article 73e of the Charter of the United Nations') will provide useful, if not authoritative, guidance.

with fundamental human rights, is to be exercised by the people of the relevant unit without coercion and on a basis of equality ('one man, one vote').[90]

(5) Self-determination can result either in the independence of the self-determining unit as a separate State, or in its incorporation into or association with another State on a basis of political equality for the people of the unit.[91]

(6) Matters of self-determination cannot be within the domestic jurisdiction of the metropolitan State.[92]

(7) Where a self-determination unit is a State, the principle of self-determination is represented by the rule against intervention in the internal affairs of that State, and in particular in the choice of the form of government of the State.

(2) *Statehood and the operation of the principle of self-determination*

The relation between the legal principle of self-determination and statehood must now be considered. It has been seen already, in situations such as the Congo, that the principle of self-determination will operate to reinforce the effectiveness of territorial units created with the consent of the former sovereign.[93] However, this only holds good where the new unit is itself created consistently with the principle of self-determination. Where, as with the *bantustans* in South-West Africa (Namibia), a local unit is created in an effort to prevent the operation of the principle to the larger unit, different considerations apply.[94] The same principle holds good in cases of secession. The secession of a self-determination unit, where self-determination is forcibly prevented by the metropolitan State, will be reinforced by the principle of self-determination, so that the degree of effectiveness required as a precondition to recognition may be substantially less than in the case of secession within a metropolitan unit. The contrast between the cases of Guinea-Bissau and Biafra is marked, and can be explained along

---

[90] See Johnson, *Self-determination with the Community of Nations* (1967), and the early classic studies by Wambaugh, *A Monograph on Plebiscites* (1920); *Plebiscites since the World War* (1933).

[91] See further Chapters 13 and 14.

[92] Higgins, *Development*, 90–106; Brownlie, *Principles*, 577; and cf. *Aaland Island Case, supra*, p. 85.

[93] *Supra*, pp. 44–7.

[94] *Infra*, p. 221.

these lines. As a consequence, the rules relating to intervention in the two cases are, it seems, different. These problems will be elaborated later in this study.[95]

These are, perhaps, ancillary or peripheral applications of the principle. The question remains whether the principle of self-determination is capable of preventing an effective territorial unit, the creation of which was a violation of self-determination, from becoming a State. Practice in this area is not well developed, but in one case—Rhodesia—the problem has been raised squarely.

(3) *Self-determination and effectiveness: the case of Rhodesia*[96]

Since its unilateral declaration of independence on 11 November 1965, the minority government has exercised effective control within the territory of Southern Rhodesia, and it is the only government which has exercised such control, despite British claims to do so under the Southern Rhodesia Act 1965 and generally. There can be no doubt that, if the traditional tests for independence of a seceding colony were applied, Rhodesia would be an independent State.[97] However, Southern Rhodesia is not recognized by any State as independent, nor has it been regarded as a State by the United Nations.[98] The unilateral declaration of independence was immediately condemned by the General Assembly,[99] and the Security Council, which decided 'to call upon all States not to recognize this illegal racist minority regime in Southern Rhodesia and to refrain from rendering any assistance to this illegal regime'.[100] A further Council Resolution of 20 November 1965 stated that the declaration of independence had 'no legal validity' and referred to the Smith government as

[95] *Infra*, p. 257. For self-determination and the use of force see *infra*, pp. 108–18.

[96] See also *infra*, p. 220.

[97] Fawcett (1971), 34 *MLR* 417; Coetzee, *The Sovereignty of Rhodesia and the Law of Nations* (1970).

[98] In 1966 the minority government forwarded communications to the Secretary-General and affirmed a right, as a 'state which is not a Member of the United Nations' to participate in proceedings under Article 32 of the Charter. The Secretary-General stated that 'the legal status of Southern Rhodesia is that of a Non-Self-Governing Territory under resolution 1747 ... and Article 32 of the Charter does not apply ...' There was no dissent from this view, and the minority government was not invited to participate under Article 32 or otherwise: *SCOR* 1280th mtg., 18 May 1966, 23. For criticism, Stephen (1973), 67 *AJ* 479–90.

[99] G.A. Res. 2024 (XX), 11 Nov. 1965 (107–2:1).

[100] S.C. Res. 216 (1965), 12 Nov. 1965 (10–0:1), para. 2.

an 'illegal authority'.[101] Partly, at least, on this basis various types of sanction have been authorized against Southern Rhodesia. The present position is that, despite the effectiveness of the government in Southern Rhodesia, the United Kingdom is regarded as the administering authority of the territory which is still a non-self-governing territory under Chapter XI of the Charter.

Against this background, only three positions seem possible: that Rhodesia is in fact a State, and that action against it, so far as it is based on the contrary proposition, is illegal; that recognition is constitutive, and in view of its non-recognition Rhodesia is not a State; or that the principle of self-determination in this situation prevents an otherwise effective entity from being regarded as a State. In view of the consistent practice referred to, the first position is difficult to accept.[102] Moreover, it would appear that the Southern Rhodesian government does not itself dissent from the view that the United Kingdom retains authority with respect to its affairs, since it apparently accepts that any settlement of the situation must be approved and implemented by the United Kingdom. The question of recognition has been discussed already, and the conclusion reached that recognition is in principle declaratory.[103] It may therefore be the case that Southern Rhodesia is not a State because the minority government's declaration of independence was and is internationally a nullity, as a violation of the principle of self-determination. In Fawcett's words:

... to the traditional criteria for the recognition of a regime as a new State must now be added the requirement that it shall not be based upon a systematic denial in its territory of certain civil and political rights, including in particular the right of every citizen to participate in the government of his country, directly or through representatives elected by regular, equal and secret suffrage. This principle was affirmed in the case of Rhodesia by the virtually unanimous condemnation of the unilateral declaration of independence by the world community, and by the universal withholding of recognition of the new regime which was a consequence.

[101] S.C. Res. 217 (1965) (10–0:1), para. 3.
[102] To the same effect Brownlie, *Principles*, 101; Higgins (1967), 23 *The World Today* 94–106, 98; it is also the view of Harold Wilson, *The Labour Government 1964–1970* (1971), 966. *Contra* Marston (1969), 18 *ICLQ* 1–40, 33; Verhoeven, *Reconnaissance*, 548.
[103] *Supra*, p. 23.

It would follow then that the illegality of the rebellion was not an obstacle to the establishment of Rhodesia as an independent State, but that the political basis and objectives of the regime were, and that the declaration of independence was without international effect.[104]

This view has been contested by Devine, who, significantly, was forced from a quasi-declaratory[105] to a firmly constitutive view[106] of recognition by his consideration of the Rhodesian affair. Devine's position is to some extent vitiated by his misreading of Fawcett's criterion as one of 'good government'.[107] It is quite clear that good government is not a criterion for statehood, but the contrary is not contended.[108] The position is a more limited one: that where a particular territory is a self-determination unit as defined, no government will be recognized which comes into existence and seeks to control the territory as a State in violation of self-determination.[109] This principle does not—at this stage of the development of international law and relations—constitute a principle of law with respect to existing States.[110] But the evidence in favour of this principle as it applies to self-determination units, and in particular to non-self-governing territories, though it may be restricted to the one case of

---

[104] (1965–6) 41 *BY* 103–21, 112–13, citing the Universal Declaration, the Colonial Declaration and G.A. Res. 648 (VI). Brownlie regards the status of Rhodesia as flowing from 'particular matters of fact and law' without further elaboration: op. cit. Marshall argues that, because Rhodesia remained a monarchy but the Queen refused to act, there was 'no legal entity which can be recognized': (1968) 17 *ICLQ* 1022–34, 1033. But the proclamation of a Republic in 1970 has not been regarded as altering Rhodesia's international status—and certainly has not increased that status. Okeke, *Controversial Subjects of Contemporary International Law* (1974), 88 refers to Fawcett's position with apparent approval, but none the less concludes that 'Rhodesia ranks among the entities which are endowed with statehood under international law' (104–5).

[105] [1967] *Acta Juridica* 39–47.

[106] [1973] *Acta Juridica* 1–171, 142–5; also McDougal and Reisman (1968), 62 *AJ* 1–19, 17. Cf. Devine (1969), 2 *CILSA* 454 66.

[107] (1971) 34 *MLR* 410; cf. [1973] *Acta Juridica* 83–6.

[108] Cf. Fawcett's reply (1971), 34 *MLR* 417.

[109] Devine accepts the proposition that the Smith government came into existence in violation of self-determination in a political sense: [1973] *Acta Juridica* 67. But he regards self-determination as 'too controversial, unaccepted and vague to be used by the Rhodesians as a shield or by anyone else as a sword against them': ibid. 77.

[110] That is to say, it does not invalidate the position of unrepresentative governments in existing States. The analogue of self-determination in the case of existing States is the duty of non-intervention in internal affairs. The incidents of that duty are somewhat controversial: they are in any event essentially negative. But for the Transkei see *infra*, p. 222.

Rhodesia,[111] is consistent and uniform. It appears then that a new rule has come into existence, prohibiting entities from claiming statehood if their creation is in violation of an applicable right to self-determination.[112] That this principle is capable of having very substantial effects if generally applied may be conceded. However the relatively limited extent of the right of self-determination has been noted. Moreover it can hardly be regretted that a rule which merely ratifies the international position of effective but totally unrepresentative regimes is open to change.[113]

3.3   ENTITIES CREATED BY THE ILLEGAL USE OF FORCE[114]

Article 2 paragraph 4 of the Charter prohibits the threat or use of force against the territorial integrity or political independence of any State or in any other manner inconsistent with the purposes of the United Nations. This prohibition does not affect the right of self defence against armed attack under Article 51.[115] These rules concerning illegal use of force are the clearest case of *jus cogens* norms, although separate provision was made for them in the Vienna Convention.[116] Moreover the principle that territory may not be validly acquired by the illegal

[111] Cf. Devine (1971), 34 *MLR* 415, and Fawcett's reply, ibid. 417. Rhodesia is undoubtedly the plainest instance, but the situation has analogues: e.g. the Bantustans in South West Africa, as to which see *infra*, pp. 220–1. The situation in Guinea-Bissau was an instance for the operation of the rule in the reverse situation: *infra*, pp. 260–2. Moreover it is quite possible for a rule to consolidate by virtue of consistent practice in one central, even if isolated, case: e.g. the development of neutrality in the American Civil War.

[112] The Privy Council in *Madzimabamuto* v. *Lardner-Burke* [1968] 3 W.L.R. 1229, 1250 did not consider this position, arguing instead that Southern Rhodesia was not a State because the legitimate government was still trying to reassert itself. Cf. *In re James* [1977] 2 W.L.R. 1 (C.A.). For recent developments see (1977), 81 *RGDIP* 1189–98; 17 *ILM* 261, 492; S.C. Res. 423 (1978).

[113] See further, *infra*, p. 220.

[114] The literature on statehood and the use of force is, to say the least, sparse. Hunnings (1962–3), 32 *Ybk. AAA* 58–65 does not consider the problem. There is a useful and characteristic contribution by Baty (1926–7), 36 *Yale LJ* 966–84 (based of course on the old regime of rules relating to the use of force). The relation between State extinction and the use of force has been considered extensively: *infra*, p. 418.

[115] See generally Brownlie, *Use of Force*; Higgins, *Development*, Pt. IV; Bowett, *Self Defence in International Law* (1958).

[116] Vienna Convention on the Law of Treaties, Arts. 52, 53. Art. 52 was reaffirmed in the *Icelandic Fisheries Case (First Phase)* I.C.J. Rep. 1973 p. 3, 19.

use of force is well established.[117] The principles of State succession do not, it seems, apply to cases involving the violation of the Charter, and in particular of Article 2 paragraph 4.[118] The protection accorded States by Article 2 paragraph 4 extends to continuity of legal personality in the face of illegal invasion and annexation: there is a substantial body of practice protecting the legal personality of the State against extinction, despite prolonged lack of effectiveness.[119] In summary, the prohibition of the threat or use of force in international relations is one of the most fundamental of international law rules: the international community has with considerable consistency refused to accept the legal validity of acts done or situations achieved by the illegal use of force. If ever effective territorial entities were to have their status regulated by international law, it would, one would think, be so regulated by the rules relating to the use of force.

Of course, quite apart from Article 2 paragraph 4, there is a presumption against the independence of entities created by the use of force or during a period of belligerent occupation.[120] The question is whether the modern law regulates the creation of States to any greater degree than this, in a situation involving illegal use of force. The difficulty of the problem is increased because, in most of the relatively few cases in which it has arisen, other factors have been determining.

For example, in the Manchurian crisis the question whether Manchukuo could have become an independent State notwithstanding the illegal Japanese intervention was never really in issue, since the puppet nature of the Manchukuo regime was and remained evident. It is true that the League of Nations resolutions which proclaimed the duty of non-recognition referred not to lack of independence but to violation of the Covenant and the Pact of Paris.[121] Recognition was stated to be 'incompatible with the fundamental principles of existing international obligations'.[122] Despite these fairly categorical statements, League

---

[117] Whiteman, 5 *Digest* 874–965 and authorities there cited.
[118] I.L.C. Draft Articles on State Succession in respect of Treaties, A/8710/Rev. 1, Art. 6. Cf. *ILC Ybk.* 1972/II, 60.
[119] *Infra*, p. 418.
[120] *Supra*, p. 60.
[121] Assembly Resolution, 11 Mar. 1932: *LNOJ* Sp. Supp. No. 101/I, 87.
[122] Assembly Resolution, 24 Feb. 1933: ibid., *Sp. Supp.* No. 112/II, 14. The language of the resolution is taken directly from the Lytton Commission's Report: C.663.M.320.1932

action was predicated on the Lytton Commission's finding that Manchukuo was not 'a genuine and spontaneous independence movement'. Given its total lack of independence the question whether, had it been effectively independent, it would have been deprived of statehood because of Japanese violations of the Covenant and the Pact of Paris did not really arise. The various entities created during the war by illegal use of force were also regarded as puppets and thus not independent.[123] And the status of Taiwan has been determined, not by any illegality by which it has been enabled to survive as a separate entity, but by the insistence of both governments involved that Taiwan remains part of China—a view acquiesced in by all other States.[124]

The puppet-State situation illustrates the difficulty, almost the dilemma, involved in any consideration of the relation between statehood and the illegal use of force. Either the entity owes its existence directly and substantially to the illegal intervention—in which case it is unlikely to be, and will be presumed not to be, independent—or it does not, in which case the normal criteria for statehood would presumably apply. This is not a true dilemma however, since it is conceivable that an entity created by external illegal force could be genuinely independent in fact. The situation most clearly relevant is that of Bangladesh. However that case involved also a problem of self-determination, so that we must first consider the relation between self-determination and the rules relating to the use of force.

(1) *The relation between self-determination and the rules relating to the use of force*

The question of the relation between self-determination and

[VII], 128. The Chinese position was that 'in pursuant of the obligations created by the Covenant . . . it is incumbent upon the League to use, to the fullest extent necessary, its authority to prevent such a changed political situation from being created, or, if created *de facto*, from being recognized by the League or by its members as of a *de jure* character. Indeed, if brought into a *de facto* existence, in violation of the Covenant . . . it is the contention of the Chinese Government that the League should use its authority to break down that *de facto* situation in order that the political order existing prior to September . . . may be re-established' (*L.N. Doc.* A. (extr.) 105.1932[VII] (23 Apr. 1932), 8).

[123] *Supra*, pp. 62–5. Another interesting example, which bears close comparison with Manchuria, was the Azerbaijan independence movement in 1945–6 in northern Iran under Soviet occupation: cf. *USFR* 1945/VIII, 512.

[124] *Infra*, pp. 150–2.

the rules relating to the use of force has been neglected:[125] this discussion is therefore a tentative one. That there is, in all probability, a significant connection between the two legal principles is apparent from the Charter itself. Article 2 paragraph 4 includes an undertaking not to use force 'in any other manner inconsistent with the Purposes of the United Nations', and 'respect for the principle of equal rights and self-determination of peoples' is one of those purposes. It might however be argued that the use of force contrary to the Purposes of the United Nations is only a subordinate aim of Article 2 paragraph 4 (cf. the word 'other'); that is, that the prevention of the use of force against the territorial integrity or political independence of States is the primary aim of the paragraph, and that the protection or advancement of the other purposes is legal only where it does not involve the use or threat of force against the territorial integrity or political independence of any State. To put in at its lowest, this is a plausible interpretation of Article 2 paragraph 4: moreover the development of Article 2 paragraph 4 in practice has tended to emphasize the prevention of overt aggression rather than, for example, the use of force by an incumbent against insurgents claiming for a territory a right of self-determination.[126] In view of these uncertainties, the problem of the relationship between self-determination and the use of force must be considered not under some general rubric but in relation to the various types of situation that may arise. In some areas practice is reasonably well developed: in others we are reduced to speculation on the basis of general principles.

The following situations may be envisaged:

(1) A self-determination unit (other than a State) is prevented from exercising its right to self-determination by the use of force.

(2) A self-determination unit is invaded and annexed by force without being allowed to opt for annexation or any alternative status.

---

[125] See however Rigo Sureda, 346–51; Žourek, *L'Interdiction de l'emploi de la force en droit international* (1974), 108–11; Bennouna, *Le Consentement à l'ingérence militaire dans les conflits internes* (1974), 159–70; Dugard (1967), 16 *ICLQ* 157–90; Šukoviè, op. cit. (*supra*, p. 98, n. 80), 363–8.

[126] In the *Corfu Channel Case* I.C.J. Rep. 1949 p. 4, the International Court condemned the threat of force in a self-help operation where the other party's behaviour was hardly consistent with Article 1 of the Charter.

(3) An effective self-governing entity is created in violation of an applicable right to self-determination by external illegal force.

(4) An effective self-governing entity is created in accordance with an applicable right to self-determination by external illegal force.

It should be noted that the much debated problem of the legitimacy of rebellion, or of a local insurgent's 'right to self-defence against colonial domination' is not really in point here. Debate on the lawfulness or otherwise of the use of force by a non-State entity presupposes at least some degree of legal personality of that entity. Assuming that the legal personality derives from the legal right of the entity in question to self-determination, it seems most unlikely that the use of force to assert that right should be illegal. On that view, the existence of a right would be precisely what made its exercise illegal.[127] It is probably the case that the use of force by a non-State entity in exercise of a right of self-determination is legally neutral, that is, not regulated by law at all (although the *jus in bello* may well apply).[128] *A fortiori*, the question of a legal right to self-defence is not in point either. What is relevant is the legality or otherwise of action by other States in assisting or opposing the self-determination unit.

Before discussing the particular situations enumerated above, it is necessary to refer to the most important statement of principles in this area, the Declaration on Principles of International Law approved by Resolution 2625 (XXV). In its elaboration of Article 2 paragraph 4, the Declaration states that 'Every State has the duty to refrain from any forcible action which deprives peoples referred to in the elaboration of the principle of equal rights and self-determination of their right to self-determination and freedom and independence.' The elaboration of the principle of equal rights and self-determination repeats this formulation, and goes on to state that 'In their actions against, and resistance to, such forcible action in pursuit of the exercise of their right to self-determination, such peoples are

[127] Cf. Devine, [1973] *Acta Juridica* 1, 72–8; Okeke, *Controversial Subjects of International Law* (1974), 86.
[128] On the applicability of the laws of war to self-determination conflicts see *infra*, p. 270.

entitled to seek and receive support in accordance with the purposes and principles of the Charter.'[129] Taken literally, these propositions establish a close relationship between the two relevant principles, with the principle of self-determination taking priority over the prohibition of the use of force against the territorial integrity of a State. That primacy can perhaps best be expressed in the proposition that the phrase 'territorial integrity of any State' in Article 2 paragraph 4 excludes, so far as action in furtherance of self-determination is concerned, the territory of any self-determination unit as defined. The question is whether this, rather formidable, proposition, which has a certain amount of doctrinal support,[130] is also supported by relevant State practice.

Perhaps the most straightforward situation to be looked at is that where a self-determination unit (other than a State) is prevented from exercising its right to self-determination by the use of force. Examples of such a situation were the Portuguese African colonies before 1974. Military action taken by an administering power to suppress widespread popular insurrection in a self-determination unit is quite clearly capable of being a denial of self-determination and therefore illegal on that ground. Both the General Assembly and the Security Council[131] have repeatedly condemned what they have described as 'colonial wars' and 'acts of repression' in the Portuguese territories, but they have refrained from characterizing the situations as aggressive war for the purposes of Article 2 paragraph 4. The contrast is demonstrated, more or less conclusively, by General Assembly Resolution 3061 (XXVIII) which, pursuant to the thesis of the independence of Guinea-Bissau,[132] condemned Portugal for 'illegal occupation . . . of certain sectors of the Republic . . . and acts of aggression committed against the people of the Republic'.[133] The difference between this language and that used in the case of Angola and Mozambique is significant. It is also consistent with the primary emphasis in Article 2

---

[129] Cf. Art. 7 of the Definition of Aggression, adopted without vote by G.A. Res. 3314 (XXIX), 14 Dec. 1974; G.A. Res. 3103 (XXVIII), 12 Dec. 1973 (83–13:19).

[130] *Supra*, p. 109, n. 125; Bedjaoui, *ILC Ybk.* 1975/I, 48–9. But neither Umozurike nor Calogeropoulos-Stratis refer to the problem at all.

[131] e.g. S.C. Res. 322 (1972); Anderson (1974), 4 *Denver JILP* 133–51.

[132] *Infra*, pp. 260–1.

[133] G.A. Res. 3061 (XXVIII), 2 Nov. 1973 (97–7:30).

paragraph 4 on prevention of direct military force against the territory of another State. It will be seen that the principle of self-determination does not deprive an administering State of its sovereignty with respect to a self-determination territory.[134] The use of force by a metropolitan power against a self-determination unit is not a use of force against the territorial integrity and political independence of a State, though it will of course be in another manner inconsistent with the purposes of the United Nations.

The second situation—that is, invasion and annexation of a self-determination unit by external force without according the people of the invaded territory any right to choose their future status—is also relatively straightforward. Invasion and annexation of territory is quite generally illegal, and the separate status of a territory for the purposes of self-determination rule would, if anything, reinforce the illegality. The only difficulty that could arise is in the case of annexation of a territory which is not, in the full sense, a self-determination unit but rather a 'colonial enclave'. The distinction between those two types of territory is an established part of United Nations practice, and is discussed in a later Chapter.[135] Assuming, for the moment, the validity of the distinction, it is none the less the case that forcible annexation by the surrounding ('enclaving') State is probably illegal, for the reasons stated above. When India invaded and annexed Goa in January 1961, a majority of the Security Council took the view— it is submitted correctly—that Indian action was illegal.[136] India claimed that Goa was historically and legally Indian territory and that Article 2 paragraph 4 did not, therefore, apply.[137] However, India had on several occasions expressly recognized Portuguese sovereignty over its Indian territories, whilst claiming their restitution. Bearing in mind the predominant Charter emphasis on peaceful change, the better opinion would appear to be that Article 2 paragraph 4 applies to any established *de facto* political boundary, and that, even in the rather special situation of a colonial enclave, the international interest in peaceful settlement of disputes takes priority over the specific claim of the

---

[134] *Infra*, p. 364.

[135] *Infra*, p. 377.

[136] S/5033; *SCOR* 988th mtg., 18 Dec. 1961, 26–7 (7–4:0).

[137] *SCOR* 987th mtg., 18 Dec. 1961, 89; ibid. 988th mtg., 18 Dec. 1961, 14–19.

enclaving State.[138] The significance of self-determination in this context is not so much that it cures illegality as that it may allow illegality to be more readily accommodated through the processes of recognition and prescription, whereas in other circumstances aggression partakes of the nature of a breach of *jus cogens* and is not, or not readily, curable by prescription, lapse of time or acquiescence. India therefore remained internationally responsible to Portugal for its illegal use of force,[139] though in view of the self-determination issue it may be that the measure of damages or other reparation would be different than in a case where self-determination was not involved.[140]

The third and fourth situations are considerably more difficult. The fourth situation is that in which an effective self-governing entity is created in pursuit of an applicable right to self-determination by external force which would, apart from any considerations arising from the principle of self-determination, be illegal under Article 2 paragraph 4. This type of case in practice involves two distinct problems: external aid to insurgents in a self-determination situation; and the large-scale use of force by another State aimed directly at 'liberating' a self-determination territory.

(i) *Assistance to established local insurgents*

On numerous occasions General Assembly resolutions have encouraged or enjoined assistance, civil or military, to local insurgents either in general terms or in relation to specific territories. For example, Resolution 2795 (XXVI) ('Question of Territories under Portuguese Administration'), by clause 13 '*Request*[ed] all States . . . in consultation with the Organization of African Unity, to render to the peoples of the Territories under Portuguese domination, in particular the population in the liberated areas of those Territories, all the moral and material assistance necessary to continue their struggle for the restoration of their inalienable right to self-determination and independence.'[141]

[138] On Goa see Brownlie, *Use of Force*, 349, 379–83; Higgins, *Development*, 187–8; Wright (1962), 56 *AJ* 617–32.

[139] By a treaty of 31 Dec. 1974, Portugal recognized Indian sovereignty over the former Portuguese territories in India: *Keesing's* 1975, 26922B.

[140] Had Portugal been successful in the *Right of Passage Case* I.C.J. Rep. 1960 p. 6, would the Court have awarded damages, *restitutio in integrum*, or merely a declaration?

[141] G.A. Res. 2795 (XXVI), 10 Dec. 1971 (105–8:5).

Resolutions in this form request what would seem to be illegal intervention against the established government in civil wars. Has the traditional rule of neutrality in civil wars ceased to apply in the case of colonial wars? Certainly that has been the contention of many of the newer States in the Assembly. For present purposes however, the question of the legality of aid to insurgents in non-self-governing or other self-determination territories is of peripheral importance. What is quite clear is that the receipt of such aid is not regarded as relevant where the local unit achieves effective self-government, whether by military or other means. For example, the fact that large amounts of aid were given to the PAIGC in Guinea-Bissau did not prevent general recognition of Guinea-Bissau as a State prior to Portuguese recognition.[142]

(ii) *Military intervention in aid of self-determination*

Where, on the other hand, the emergence of local self-government in a self-determination unit is the result not of insurgency but of external military intervention, the situation would appear to be quite different. With this situation must be considered the third case listed above; that is, the emergence of an effective self-governing entity as a result of military intervention in violation of self-determination. The two cases most closely relevant are Manchukuo and Bangladesh. Three possibilities exist. It may be that the effectiveness of the emergent entity is in all situations to be regarded as paramount, so that its illegality of origin—however serious—will not impede recognition as a State. It may be that, in both cases, the illegality of origin should be regarded as paramount in accordance with the maxim *ex injuria non oritur jus.* Or, thirdly, it may be that, in the self-determination situation, the status of the local entity and the legality of the use of force ought to be regarded as separate issues so that the illegality of the intervention should not prejudice the pre-existing right of the local unit to self-determination.

Any discussion of this problem will be of necessity tentative. Practice is undeveloped,[143] and the conflicts of political interest

---

[142] *Infra*, pp. 260–2.

[143] Manchukuo apart, there is no case where an effective entity illegally created by the use of external force has claimed statehood—that is, there is no analogue to the Rhodesian situation.

in situations of this type threaten to overwhelm considerations of principle and generality. On the other hand, very many areas of State practice which are in principle regulated by international law are also highly politicized. Moreover there do exist accepted principles of legality which regulate the legal effects of State conduct in areas closely related to the situation under discussion. For example, if State personality is preserved despite effective but illegal annexation by force, it is not *a priori* impossible that statehood should be denied an entity *created* by external illegal force. If the rule regulating the use of force in international relations is sufficiently important to outweigh the principle of effectiveness in the one situation, there seems to be no reason why it should not have a similar effect in the other situation. Equally, if a State cannot acquire territory by the use of force, it should not be able to achieve the same result in practice by fomenting, and then supporting, insurrection.[144] This latter consideration was an important one in the Manchurian crisis, although, as we have seen, the lack of independence of 'Manchukuo' enabled the situation to be dealt with, at least in form, within the structure of the legal rules deriving from the principles of effectiveness and *de facto* independence.

Any analysis of this problem must then centre on an assessment of the Bangladesh case.[145] It is clear that Indian intervention was decisive, in the events which occurred, in effecting the emergence of Bangladesh. There was substantial local support for autonomy, or, if that could not be obtained, for independence: there was also a reasonably substantial local insurgency. But there can be no doubt that Indian intervention was the dominant factor in the success of the independence movement. Yet Bangladesh, despite the Indian intervention, was rapidly and widely recognized as a State.[146] Indian intervention was criticized by many governments as a violation of the Charter,[147] but that illegality was not

---

[144] Baty (1926–7), 36 *Yale LJ* 966, 979–82; Hsu, *ILC Ybk.* 1949, 112–13.

[145] There is a useful, though hardly impartial, study by Chowdhury, *The Genesis of Bangladesh* (1972). The factual material presented by Chowdbury is corroborated, in large part, in *I.C.J. Review* No. 8 (June 1972), 23–62. The best analysis is that by Salmon, in *Multitudo legum, ius unum. Mélanges en honneur de Wilhelm Wengler* (1973) I, 467–90. See also Franck and Rodley (1972), 2 *Is. Ybk. HR* 142–75; Salzberg (1973), 27 *Int. Org.* 115–128.

[146] Salmon, op. cit. 478–9; (1974) 78 *RGDIP* 1172–4.

[147] Okeke, *Controversial subjects of international law* (1974), 142–57.

regarded as derogating from the status of East Bengal, or as affecting the propriety of recognition. Indeed, not even the fact that Indian troops remained in Bangladesh was regarded as detracting from independence, despite the presumption against independence in such circumstances which has been consistently applied elsewhere.[148]

The question whether East Bengal was, in 1971, a self-determination unit thus becomes important since, if it were not, or if recognition was given simply on the basis of effectiveness without regard to the legality of Indian intervention or to any denial of right to the people of East Bengal, then there would appear to be no criterion of legality regulating the creation of States by the use of external illegal force.

East Pakistan was not at any time after 1947 formally a non-self-governing territory. It would have been classified as 'metropolitan' and so outside the ambit both of Chapter XI of the Charter and (but for exceptional circumstances) the customary right of self-determination.[149] However, its status, at least in 1971, was not quite so clear, for several reasons. In the first place, East Bengal probably qualified as a Chapter XI territory in 1971, if one applies the principles accepted by the General Assembly in 1960 as relevant in determining the matter.[150] According to Principle IV of Resolution 1541 (XV), a territory is *prima facie* non-self-governing if it is both geographically separate and ethnically distinct from the 'country administering it'. East Pakistan was both geographically separate and ethnically distinct from West Pakistan: moreover the relation between West and East Pakistan, both economically and administratively, could fairly be described as one which 'arbitrarily place[d] the latter in a position or status of subordination'.[151] It is scarcely surprising then that the Indian representative described East Bengal as, in reality, a non-self-governing territory.[152] In any case, and this point is perhaps as cogent, it is hard to conceive of any non-colonial situation more apt for the description *'carence de souveraineté'* than East Bengal after 15 March 1971. Genocide is

---

[148] *Supra*, p. 60. Cf. [1974] *Rev. belge* 348–50.

[149] *Infra*, p. 360.

[150] G.A. Res. 1541 (XV), 15 Dec. 1960 (89–2:21). India and Pakistan both voted in favour. See further, *infra*, p. 362.

[151] Res. 1541 (XV), Annex, Principle V.

[152] *SCOR* 1606th mtg., 4 Dec. 1971, para. 185.

a clear case of abuse of sovereignty, and this factor, together with the territorial and political coherence of East Bengal in 1971 probably qualified East Bengal as a self-determination unit within the third, exceptional, category discussed above,[153] even if it was not, strictly speaking, a non-self-governing territory. The view that East Bengal had, in March 1971, a right to self-determination has received considerable juristic support,[154] and for the reasons given, seems justified. Moreover the particular, indeed the extraordinary, circumstances of East Bengal in 1971–1972 were undoubtedly important factors in the decisions of other governments to recognize, rather than oppose, the secession. The comparison with international opposition to secession in other cases is marked.[155]

Thus, Salmon, after a cautious and reasoned assessment, concludes:

La même idée qui si l'acte de force créant le Bangla-Desh fut illicite, le résultat ne l'est pas—car il fait suite à une autre violence qui empêchait ce peuple à disposer de lui-même—explique que n'ont point joué ici les règles qui interdisent de reconnaître une situation lorsque la reconnaissance constitue une intervention dans les affaires intérieures des autres États ou lorsqu'il s'agit d'une acquisition territoriale obtenue par la menace ou l'emploi de la force.[156]

The position which would appear to be most consistent with general principle as well as supported by such practice as there has been, seems then to be as follows.

(1) The use of force against a self-determination unit by a metropolitan State is a use of force against one of the purposes of the United Nations, and a violation of Article 2 paragraph 4 of the Charter. Such a violation cannot of course effect the extinction of the right.

(2) The annexation of a self-determination unit by external force in violation of self-determination will also not extinguish the right, except, possibly, in the controversial case of the

[153] *Supra*, p. 100.
[154] Chowdhury, op. cit. 188 ff.; Okeke, op. cit. 131–41; Mani (1972), 12 *Indian JIL* 83–99; Nawaz (1971), 11 *Indian JIL* 251–66; Nanda (1972), 66 *AJ* 321–36, cf. (1972) 49 *Denver LJ* 53–67. *Contra, I.C.J. Review* No. 8 (1972), 51–2.
[155] *Infra*, pp. 263–6. This is not to say that Indian intervention was necessarily legal: cf. Franck and Rodley (1973), 67 *AJ* 275–305.
[156] Salmon, op. cit. 490.

'colonial enclave', where the annexing State is the enclaving State and (probably) where the local population acquiesces in the annexation.

(3) Assistance by States to local insurgents in a self-determination unit may, possibly and exceptionally, be permissible. In any event, local independence will not, as a matter of law, be impaired by the receipt of such external assistance.

(4) An entity claiming statehood but created during a period of foreign military occupation will be presumed not to be independent. The presumption, where the military occupation is the result of illegal invasion, is particularly rigorous (but see paragraph 6, below).

(5) However, where the local unit is a self-determination unit, the presumption against independence in the case of foreign military intervention may well be dispelled. There is no prohibition against recognition of a new State which has emerged in such a situation. The normal criteria for statehood—predicated on a qualified effectiveness—apply.

(6) Illegality of intervention in aid of independence of a self-determination unit does not then, as a matter of law, impair the status of the local unit. On the other hand, *semble*, where a State illegally intervenes in and foments the secession of part of a metropolitan State, other States are under the same duty of non-recognition as in the case of illegal annexation of territory.[157] An entity created in violation of the rules relating to the use of force in such circumstances will not be regarded as a State. To this extent it is suggested that the presumption referred to in paragraph 4 above has become a rule of law.

(7) Finally, these conclusions are to some extent *de lege ferenda*. In particular situations, and especially those in which the application of self-determination to non-colonial territories is in issue, questions of acquiescence, consent and recognition remain important.

---

[157] The situation in Cyprus after the Turkish intervention in 1974 is illustrative. It is not thought that a 'Turkish State' on Cyprus created as a result of the intervention would have been recognized or accepted: indeed, despite their support of partition, the Turkish government appears to have accepted in practice the formal requirement of a unified Cypriot State. Cf. A.V.W. and A.J. Thomas (1975), 29 *Southwestern LJ* 513–46, 526–7, 543–5; (1975) 80 *RGDIP* 1109–11; Evriviades (1975), 10 *Texas ILJ* 227–64. See also *U.S. Digest* 1975, 6–7; but cf. *Hesperides Hotels Ltd.* v. *Aegean Turkish Holidays Ltd.* [1977] 3 W.L.R. 656, 661–7 *per* Lord Denning M.R.

3.4 OTHER CASES

(1) *Entities not claiming to be States*

Statehood can be described as a claim of right based on a certain factual and legal situation. The case of Formosa raises the interesting possibility that an entity which does not claim to be a State, even though it might otherwise qualify for statehood in accordance with the basic criteria, will not be regarded as a State.[158]

(2) *Puppet States and the 1949 Geneva Conventions*

Article 47 of the Third Convention relative to the Protection of Civilian Persons in Time of War (concluded to remedy evasion of the previous law through the use of puppet local authorites) provides that 'Protected Persons who are in occupied territory shall not be deprived . . . of the benefits of the present Convention by any change introduced, as a result of the occupation of a territory, into the institutions of government of the said territory, nor by any agreement concluded between the authorities of the occupied territories and the Occupying Power . . .'[159] Marek accordingly argues that 'the Geneva Convention has positively outlawed the creation of puppets as a means of indirectly violating the international occupation regime. It has branded them as illegal.'[160] This seems rather too categorical. Although such puppets (whether 'States' or 'governments') have no more governmental authority than the belligerent occupant itself, that does not mean that, within the limits of the Hague and Geneva Conventions, the action of such a regime as an organ or agent of the occupant will not be valid.

It is thus doubtful whether Article 47 establishes any categorical rule prohibiting puppet entities from being created, or from achieving real independence over a period of time. And this view is confirmed by the commentators on the Conventions.[161]

---

[158] On Formosa see *infra*, p. 151. Andorra is another possible case of an entity not claiming statehood: *infra*, p. 142.

[159] 75 *UNTS* 287.

[160] *Identity and Continuity*, 120.

[161] I.C.R.C., *Commentary* (1958) IV, 272–4; Draper, *The Red Cross Conventions* (1958), 38–9; U.S. Dept. of the Army, *Field Manual* FM 27–10 (1956), § 366.

(3) *Apartheid and the Bantustan policy*

The case of the Transkei has raised the possibility that an entity created by a State on its metropolitan territory pursuant to unlawful policies of racial discrimination against a majority of the people of the State in question may not be accepted as a new State. The question is discussed in a later Chapter.[162]

(4) *Violation of conventional stipulations providing for independence*

Multilateral treaties, whether peace or armistice agreements or international 'constitutional' treaties such as the Covenant and the Charter, frequently provide for the independence of certain territories either immediately or contingently. Where the territory concerned claims independence but the relevant treaty provisions are not complied with, complex problems arise. In general, a distinction must be made between formal or procedural violations, and violations of material provisions, and in particular of the purposes for or basic conditions upon which independence is to be granted. In the former case it seems that violations will not effect statehood provided genuine independence is attained.[163] In the latter the presumption may well be against statehood in the absence of compliance with the relevant provisions. Moreover, where the treaty is of such a kind that it creates a form of regime extending beyond the immediate parties, it may even be that no entity created in violation of material provisions of the treaty will be recognized as a State. For example, South Africa could not evade its responsibilities towards Namibia by the grant of independence to a minority regime there. However the matter depends to a considerable extent upon the relevant instruments, some of which are discussed elsewhere.

3.5 NON-RECOGNITION IN MODERN INTERNATIONAL LAW

The problem of non-recognition and its legal effects is a subject of some obscurity. Certain distinctions are, however, clearly fundamental. Most importantly there is a distinction between non-recognition for legal reasons and non-recognition for

---

[162] *Infra*, p. 222. Cf. Fawcett, cited *supra*, p. 104.
[163] Cf. the cases of Syria and Lebanon in 1944: *supra*, p. 66–8.

political reasons.[164] Political non-recognition, which has been a frequent occurrence since 1945, is of no direct interest here. It is discretionary, and its legal effects may be purely nominal, since they are largely whatever the States concerned intend them to be. Thus acts that might be thought to imply recognition will not constitute recognition if they are expressed not to do so.[165] What is of interest here is non-recognition on legal grounds. Such non-recognition is by no means a new phenomenon,[166] but, especially as 'collective non-recognition' it has achieved considerable prominence since 1932.[167] But two further distinctions may be noted. Recognition of an illegal situation is not necessarily forbidden by international law. A State directly affected may waive its rights in a particular matter, or other States may waive any interest they may have in the observance of the rule in question. Recognition is one form of waiver. Secondly, one may refuse to recognize the validity or the legality of a particular act and yet be bound to recognize or accept all or some of the consequences.

It must also be noted that we are here discussing two different concepts—nullity and illegality. An act which is void will, presumably, produce no direct legal consequences. An act which, while illegal, is still an 'act in law' may have direct legal effects. The relevance and extent of non-recognition in such cases may thus be different.

(1) *Non-recognition and territorial status*

The application of these principles to matters of territorial status involves the following considerations. Where an entity claims but does not qualify for statehood in accordance with the criteria discussed here, then recognition, although it may create legal effects on a bilateral basis, may well be illegal *vis-à-vis* the previous sovereign, and, in cases where the criterion relates to legality under general law, may also be illegal *erga omnes*. Non-recognition in such cases is enjoined by international law, as an

---

[164] Chen, *Recognition*, 411–15, and generally Brownlie, *Use of Force*, 413–23.

[165] Cf. Lauterpacht, *Recognition*, 369–408; Chen, *Recognition*, 189 ff.

[166] Sharp, *Duties of Non-Recognition in Practice 1775–1934* (1934); but cf. Lauterpacht, *Recognition*, 419.

[167] The practice is described in Brownlie, op. cit. See also Hill (1933), *Int. Conc.* No. 293, 355–477.

aspect of the substantive obligation of respect for the rules of international law. However, at least where the illegality is not of a fundamental nature, the question of recognition of an effective but illegal situation may well arise. The function of recognition in these circumstances is well expressed by Lauterpacht:

when the facts giving rise to the pretended new title are in violation of international law ... recognition fulfils a function altogether distinct from other aspects of recognition. It is no longer an act of administration of international law; it is a political function. While not intended to do away with the moral or legal opprobrium attaching to the original illegality, it validates its consequences. It is against recognition of this nature that the policy or the obligation of non-recognition is directed. The illegal act in question may be in violation of the individual right of another State. In that case recognition is in the nature of a waiver of a right affected by the attempted or consummated acquisition of the new title ... When the acts in question are in breach of general international law, such recognition ... assumes the character of a quasi-legislative measure in the general interest of international society and of international peace.[168]

In the context of statehood and territorial status, a specific technique which has thus been adopted in the case of 'illegal entities' is that of collective non-recognition. The duty of collective non-recognition made its appearance in the Stimson doctrine and the resolutions of the League in the Manchurian crisis.[169] It has also been invoked in the Rhodesian and Namibian cases. Non-recognition, in such cases, is in the first place enjoined by the status—or lack of it—of the entity in question. However the importance of a collective duty of non-recognition, as Lauterpacht pointed out, goes beyond this, in that it reinforces the legal position, and helps to prevent the consolidation of illegal situations. Its value in this respect is significant,[170] although non-recognition is not *per se* either a method of enforcement or, in any real way, a sanction.[171] It is a precondition

---

[168] Lauterpacht, *Recognition*, 412.

[169] *Supra*, p. 59. See also Langer, *Seizure of Territory* (1947).

[170] Cf. Chen, *Recognition*, 442–3; Bot, *Non-recognition and Treaty Relations*, 60–4.

[171] The principle of non-recognition in the Manchurian case was criticized, not without justification, as an evasion rather than an instance of enforcement action: McNair (1933), 14 *BY* 65–74; Williams (1933), 18 *Grotius ST* 109–29. See also Middlebush (1933), 27 *PAS* 40–55.

for other enforcement action, and a method of asserting the values involved in the relevant legal rules.[172]

A duty of non-recognition arises in two situations, which are to some extent co-extensive. When the illegality invoked is substantial, and in particular when it involves a norm of *jus cogens*, States have a duty under customary international law, individually and collectively, not to recognize the act as legal. The rule in question must either be one of the limited number of *jus cogens* norms, or, at any rate, a substantive rule of general international law, so that the illegality is one which involves the international community as a whole and not just particular States. As has been pointed out already, an obligation not to recognize the legality of an act does not necessarily involve an obligation not to recognize its effects. The extent of any further obligation depends upon the seriousness of the breach, and all the circumstances.

The uncertainty evident here has in practice been resolved by a more explicit process of collective non-recognition, in particular in international organizations. This is the second situation referred to. In the Rhodesian case, for example, non-recognition has been combined with economic sanctions under Chapter VII of the Charter, and the implications of non-recognition have been spelt out in considerable detail. Security Council Resolution 217 (1965) called upon States not to recognize or entertain 'any diplomatic or other relations with this illegal authority'.[173] Security Council Resolution 253 (1968) referred in addition to an obligation not to recognize passports issued by or on behalf of the 'illegal regime', and the need for withdrawal of consular and trade representation.[174] Security Council Resolution 277 (1970) called for non-recognition of governmental acts of the regime,

---

[172] Verhoeven is highly critical of the notion of a customary duty of non-recognition: *Reconnaissance*, 586–617. General international law in his view allows collective or individual non-recognition, but the duty of non-recognition in modern practice is conventional, not customary: ibid. 589. The notion of a general duty of non-recognition, in any event, involves a logical dilemma: non-recognition would lose 'tout raison d'être si la reconnaissance est impossible à défaut d'objet possible': ibid. 5; cf., 611. But the 'object' of non-recognition, in the cases we are considering, is not merely a state of affairs but an asserted legal status arising from that state of affairs. Illegality may preclude the attribution of that status initially: non-recognition is an attempt to prevent its attribution by the processes of recognition and consolidation. There is thus, it seems, no logical difficulty.

[173] 12 Nov. 1965 (10–0:1).

[174] 29 May 1968 (11–0:0).

and suspension from membership or association with specialized agencies and other organizations.[175]

(2) *The consequences of non-recognition*

Where non-recognition is obligatory (whether by resolution or treaty) the incidents of non-recognition will normally be spelt out in the instruments. However the question to what extent particular actions are prohibited as a result of the duty of non-recognition as a matter of customary international law in the absence of such an authoritative enumeration is an important one. It is of course clear that the duty of non-recognition of an illegal situation is considerably more onerous than the consequences of a policy of non-recognition in bilateral relations need be.

Since no Chapter VII action has been taken with respect to Namibia,[176] the obligations upon States in that situation have derived more or less exclusively from the principle of non-recognition. The matter was dealt with fully by the International Court in the *Namibia Opinion*. The Court held that the presence of South Africa in the mandated territory, following the revocation of the mandate, was illegal, and then went on to consider the legal effects for States of the illegality. The Majority Opinion stated, first, that United Nations members are 'under obligation to recognize the illegality and invalidity of South Africa's continued presence in Namibia' and to refrain 'from lending any support or any form of assistance to South Africa with reference to its occupation of Namibia', with certain exceptions.[177] The precise determination of matters inconsistent with this fundamental obligation the Opinion regarded as a matter for determination by 'the appropriate political organs of the United Nations acting within their authority under the Charter'.[178] However the Opinion did give some advice as to matters inconsistent with the declaration of illegality and which might imply recognition of the legality of South African administration. Non-recognition implied abstention from treaty

[175] 18 Mar. 1970 (14–0:1). Cf. Res. 288 (1970), para. 5 ('any form of recognition'); G.A. Res. 2946 (XXVII), para. 5 ('any action which might confer a semblance of legitimacy on the illegal . . . regime').
[176] Cf. (1975) 69 *AJ* 880–2.
[177] I.C.J. Rep. 1971 p. 3, 54.
[178] Ibid. 55.

relations concerning Namibia; cessation of 'active intergovern-
mental co-operation' under existing bilateral treaties relating to
Namibia; abstention from all diplomatic or consular activity in
Namibia, and, most notably, abstention from 'economic and
other forms of relationship or dealing with South Africa on
behalf of or concerning Namibia which may entrench its
authority over the Territory'. On the other hand, multilateral
treaties of a humanitarian nature should continue to be applied;
and invalidity did not extend to 'those acts, such as, for instance,
the registration of births, deaths and marriages, the effect of
which can be ignored only to the detriment of the inhabitants'.[179]
Non-member States, though not bound to any affirmative action,
were obliged not to recognize the legality of the South African
administration.[180] The Majority Opinion thus attributed substantial legal content to the duty of non-recognition, both with
respect to United Nations members and non-member States. On
this point, more than any other in the case, there was quite
substantial disagreement. Judges Petrèn, Onyeama, Fitzmaurice,
and Gros dissented, while Judge Ammoun on the other hand
seemed prepared to attribute even more extensive obligations to
the duty of non-recognition.[181] Judge Dillard, and to some extent
Judge de Castro, were prepared to support the majority opinion
only with reservations. Judge Dillard's opinion is representative.
After referring to Security Council Resolution 276 (1970) which,
in his view, invoked 'a negative duty of restraint, not a positive
duty of action', he continued:

The Opinion of the Court ... appears to be grounded at least in large
part on principles of non-recognition under international law, and is
thus in harmony with Security Council resolution 276. But a strong
caveat is needed to avoid any misunderstanding. I refer to the fact that
the references in operative clause 2 to '*any* facts' and '*any* dealings' are
to be read subject to the critically significant qualifying phrase '*implying
recognition of the legality*' of South Africa's presence in Namibia (emphasis
added). This announces, to repeat, the doctrine of non-recognition ...
But in my opinion the matter does not stop there. The legal
consequences flowing from a determination of the illegal occupation of
Namibia do not necessarily entail the automatic application of a
doctrine of nullity ... [T]he maxim *ex injuria jus non oritur* is not so

179 I.C.J. Rep. 1971 p. 6, 55–6. Judge Padilla Nervo (119–20) agreed.
180 Ibid. 56.
181 Ibid. 93–100.

severe as to deny that any source of right whatever can accrue to third persons acting in good faith. Were it otherwise the general interest in the security of transactions would be too greatly invaded and the cause of minimizing needless hardship and friction would be hindered rather than helped ... A detailed specification of the particular acts which may or may not be compatible with South Africa's illegal presence in Namibia cannot be determined in advance since they depend on numerous factors including not only the interests of contracting parties who acted in good faith but the immediate and future welfare of the inhabitants of Namibia.[182]

Judge Petrèn, on the other hand, dissented on the non-recognition point:

The very term *non-recognition* implies not positive action but abstention from acts signifying recognition. Non-recognition therefore excludes, above all else, diplomatic relations and those formal declarations and acts of courtesy through which recognition is normally expressed. Nevertheless, although the notion of non-recognition excludes official and ostentatious top-level contacts, customary usage does not seem to be the same at the administrative level, since necessities of a practical or humanitarian nature may justify certain contacts or certain forms of co-operation.

A similar approach seems to prevail in regard to international agreements. While non-recognition seems not to permit the formal conclusion of treaties between governments, agreements between administrations, for instance on postal or railway matters, are considered to be possible. In the same way, the legal effect to be attributed to the decisions of the judicial and administrative authorities of a non-recognized State or government depends on human considerations and practical needs ... [W]hat is important for the present Advisory Opinion is the fact that, in the international law of today, non-recognition has obligatory negative effects in only a very limited sector of governmental acts of a somewhat symbolic nature.'[183]

On the non-recognition issue, Judge Dillard thus takes a middle position between the dissentients on one hand and the extensive pronouncements of the Majority Opinion on the other. However there was at least a measure of agreement as to what the obligation of non-recognition involves. It was agreed that any diplomatic action implying the legality of South African

---

[182] Ibid. 166–7, citing Lauterpacht, *Recognition*, 420. Cf. Judge de Castro, 218–19.
[183] Ibid. 134–6. Cf. Judge Onyeama, 149; Judge Fitzmaurice, 295–8; Judge Gros, 339–41.

administration of Namibia was precluded, no less than outright recognition of legality. At the other end of the scale, it was agreed that acts unrelated to the political ends of the South African adminstration, or else such that non-recognition would harm rather than benefit the people of the territory could be recognized as valid. It was also agreed that the Security Council could particularize other acts inconsistent with recognition, although the legal status of such resolutions was controversial.[184] There is thus implicit in both majority and minority views a distinction between acts in pursuance of the illegal administration, and acts which, either by their nature ('ministerial acts') or because of the benefit involved to the inhabitants were to be regarded as untainted by the illegality of the administration. Recognition of the latter class of acts was not a breach of the duty of non-recognition. This distinction is of course familiar in other contexts as the distinction between personal and impersonal governmental acts.[185] The disagreement within the Court in the *Namibia Opinion* related not to the existence of such a distinction but to its application. It is significant that the Majority Opinion appears to have conflated the requirements under customary law and those under the Charter,[186] which the separate and dissenting opinions kept relatively distinct. On the other hand, comparison with the case of unrecognized States or governments was not entirely apt, in view of the distinction noted above between unrecognized but opposable situations, and illegal situations giving rise to a *duty* of non-recognition.[187] Having regard to that

---

[184] The Majority Opinion held that relevant Council resolutions were 'decisions' under Article 25 and thus binding, despite the absence of a determination under Article 39 of a threat to or breach of the peace: ibid. 54. Judge Ammoun (97–8) and Judge Padilla Nervo (118–19) agreed. Judge Petrèn disagreed: in his view the resolutions only constituted recommendations, although they might also be legal *authorizations* for action by particular States: 136–7. Judge Dillard expressed strong reservations: 150, 165–6. Judges Fitzmaurice (293), Gros (340), and *semble*, Onyeama (148–9) also disagreed.

[185] *Sc.* in the case of local *de facto* governments: Judge de Castro, 218–19. The older view was that *de facto* recognition was not inconsistent with the duty of non-recognition: see e.g. Lauterpacht, *Recognition*, 341, 347–8; cf. 285–7.

[186] Cf. I.C.J. Rep. 1971 p. 6, 55.

[187] The validity of this distinction is evident from the following example. It is established that a vote in favour of the admission of a State to the U.N. or the representation of a government does not imply recognition of the State or government: cf. Secretariat Memorandum on Representation, S/1466, Feb. 1950: *SCOR* 5th yr., Supp. for Jan–May 1950, 18–23. But such a vote would quite clearly be inconsistent with a duty of non-recognition of an illegal regime.

distinction, it seems possible to give the majority view, with Judge Dillard, qualified support.

In conclusion, the duty of non-recognition, despite its relatively recent origins, is now firmly entrenched as a specific technique for dealing with illegal regimes. So long as it is not mistaken for a sanction or for enforcement action, it would seem to be a valuable 'addition to the forces making for the reality of international law'.[188]

[188] Lauterpacht, *Recognition*, 435: cf. Chen, *Recognition*, 441.

4. Issues of Statehood before United Nations Organs

4.1 GENERAL CONSIDERATIONS

THE WORD 'State' occurs thirty-four times in the United Nations Charter. To be admitted to the United Nations an applicant must be *inter alia* a State.[1] To bring a question concerning international peace and security, or any other dispute, before the United Nations, it is necessary to be a 'State'.[2] To be entitled to participate without vote in the Security Council's consideration of any dispute, a party to the dispute must be a 'State'.[3] To become a party to the Statute of the International Court an applicant must be a 'State'.[4] There is thus much opportunity for disagreement about and development of the notion of statehood in United Nations organs.

On the other hand, the context of some of these uses of the term 'State' is different: different tests in practice may be required in each case. For example, the Security Council might be justified in allowing an entity to participate in its deliberations, although it might well hesitate to recommend admission of the same entity on the grounds that its legal status was transient or uncertain. Indonesia was invited to participate in 1947 over its dispute with the Netherlands, although its statehood was the very point at issue, and despite the fact that it probably did not then qualify as a 'State' for the purposes of Article 4.[5] A representative of Hyderabad was also heard by the Security Council under Article 35(2), in relation to a dispute about its status.[6]

Although the general criteria themselves permit some flexibility, and although contextual interpretation of the term 'State' is entirely justified,[7] care is necessary in determining which

---

[1] Art. 4(1); *Admissions Case* I.C.J. Rep. 1948 p. 57, 62.
[2] Art. 11(2), 35(2).
[3] Art. 32.
[4] Art. 93(2).
[5] *Infra*, p. 137.
[6] *Infra*, p. 211.
[7] Cf Higgins, *Development*, 11–14, 42–50; *supra*, p. 33.

contexts warrant a more extensive or attenuated meaning of the term. That Article 35(2) does so seems clear: the basic policy behind that Article, *audi alteram partem*, suggests that no nice distinctions should be drawn between States and entities with some status not equivalent to statehood. In particular this is so when the dispute concerns that status itself, since otherwise a preliminary decision would prejudice the merits of the case. On the other hand, Higgins suggests that 'entities which would not be considered states for the purposes of a claim for comprehensive participation in the United Nations might nevertheless satisfy the requirements of statehood where the claim is for limited participation.'[8] The proposition that an entity may be a 'State' for the purposes of admission to a regional or functional organization but not a 'State' for the purposes of admission to the United Nations has been vigorously disputed:

> not only is it *a priori* unlikely that the same concept—statehood—should be used in different senses by the same actors (the diplomatic representatives of States) in *fora* (intergovernmental organizations) for the same purposes (participation), but it is also a fact that the instances cited in support of the theory can, without exception, be better explained on other grounds, such as the presence of the veto in the U.N. and its absence in the Specialized Agencies.[9]

Moreover, it cannot be said that United Nations organs have consistently adhered to a contextual interpretation even in contexts such as Art. 35(2). Especially in the more recent practice, members have tended to emphasize the political or honorific element of statehood, and to treat all issues of status, however arising, in the same way. General unwillingness, where the status of an entity is controversial, to take sides in the political controversy[10] or, where an entity such as Rhodesia is concerned, to accord it any semblance of status,[11] must therefore be borne in mind. The following brief account none the less deals with the practice under the different rubrics.

---

[8] *Development*, 42–3.

[9] Mendelson (1972), 21 *ICLQ* 609–30, 614; to the same effect his 'Acquisition of Membership in Selected International Organizations' (Oxford, MS.D.Phil. d. 5229, 1971), 85–92, 167–70.

[10] Cf. Bangladesh, *supra*, p. 117.

[11] *Supra*, p. 103.

4.2 LEAGUE AND UNITED NATIONS MEMBERSHIP

(1) *Membership practice under the League of Nations*

Article 1(2) of the Covenant provided that:

Any fully self-governing State, Dominion or Colony not named in the Annex may become a Member of the League if its admission is agreed to by two-thirds of the Assembly, provided that it shall give effective guarantees of its sincere intention to observe its international obligations, and shall accept such regulations as may be prescribed ... in regard to its military, naval and air forces and armaments.[12]

The phrase 'fully self-governing State, Dominion or Colony' was used because, in Cecil's words 'some of the Members of the League, such as India and (at least in 1919) the British Dominions, were not "States"'.[13] Statehood was thus not a necessary prerequisite for admission to the League, although, in practice, only States were in fact admitted under Article 1(2). League practice in the matter of status for admission purposes was not extensive, although the requirements of statehood tended to be interpreted fairly strictly. Entities such as Armenia, Georgia and the Ukraine which had separated from the Russian Empire had their applications for membership rejected on the grounds of lack of stability or permanence.[14] Other States such as Latvia, Lithuania, and Estonia had their applications postponed until they could demonstrate some sort of permanence.[15] Liechtenstein was rejected on the grounds that, even though it was a State, it was too small to carry out its obligations under the Covenant.[16] League practice relating to the extinction of States on the other hand was not consistent, owing in large

---

[12] 119 *BFSP* 1. For exclusion from the Covenant of any reference to recognition see Graham, *The League of Nations and the Recognition of States* (1933), 43–4.

[13] Hunter Miller, *The drafting of the Covenant* I, 284; for the position of the Dominions in 1919 see *infra*, p. 243. Cecil conceded that, even on this formulation, India did not qualify since (like the Philippines) it was not a 'self-governing' Colony (ibid. 164; cf. Wilson, 165–6). Smuts however pointed out that India qualified as an original member under Article 1(1), and that Article 1(2) was accordingly irrelevant (loc. cit.). Further on India see *infra*, p. 406.

[14] Graham, op. cit. 26–32; Scelle (1921), 28 *RGDIP* 132–6.

[15] *Supra*, p. 39; and Piip (1920), 6 *Grotius ST* 35–43. The Baltic States were admitted by the Second Assembly on 22 Sept. 1921: *LNOJ* Oct. 1921, 863–8.

[16] *Infra*, p. 140.

part to the political vicissitudes of the period, 1935–40, during which the various issues arose.[17]

(2) *The United Nations: original membership*

Like the League Covenant, and for the same reasons, the United Nations Charter distinguished between original and admitted members. The distinction was pointed out by the Rapporteur (Membership) of the Committee I/2 to Commission I at the San Francisco Conference:

As regards original members their participation in the Organization is considered as acquired by right, while that of future members is dependent on the fulfilment of certain conditions . . . [T]he definition adopted would serve to calm the fears of certain nations participating in our deliberations which, properly speaking, are not *States* and for this reason might be denied the right of membership in the Organization.[18]

As the Report delicately puts it, 'certain nations' which became original members of the United Nations were not States: viz. India, which had been a League member but the status of which was unchanged from 1919; the Philippines, which was in much the same position as India; and two of the Union Republics of the Soviet Union, Byelorussia and the Ukraine. The membership of these two constituent Republics of the U.S.S.R. deserves brief comment. Stalin had originally proposed that, pursuant to a 1944 amendment to the Soviet Constitution, all sixteen federal Republics should be admitted. At the Yalta Conference it was agreed that the United Kingdom and the United States would support the original membership of the two Republics,[19] and they were accordingly unanimously admitted as participants at the San Francisco Conference.[20] However, as a United States' memorandum pointed out, the Soviet constitution did not permit the Soviet Republics 'to control their own foreign policy or affairs' and they were accordingly 'not Sovereign States under

---

[17] Cf. Green, in Schwarzenberger, ed., *Law Justice and Equity* (1967), 152–67, 157–8. On League membership practice in general see Graham, op. cit.; Scelle (1921), 28 *RGDIP* 122–38; Hudson (1924), 18 *AJ* 436–58; Feinberg (1952), 80 *HR* 297–393; and Schwarzenberger, *The League of Nations and World Order* (1936).

[18] (1945) 7 *UNCIO* 324, Doc. 1178; Whiteman, 13 *Digest* 191–2. But Art. 3 of the Charter, referring to original Members, does use the term 'State'.

[19] *USFR* 1945, *The Conferences at Malta and Yalta*, 975–6.

[20] (1945) 1 *UNCIO* 165, 168.

International Practice'.[21] Stetinnius and Eden supported the
membership proposal at San Francisco on the basis of the
contribution of the two Republics to the war effort, rather than
on grounds of status.[22]

(3) *The United Nations: admission to membership*

Article 4 of the Charter states:

1. Membership in the United Nations is open to all other peace-loving
States which accept the obligations contained in the present Charter
and, in the judgement of the Organization, are able and willing to
carry out these obligations.
2. The admission of any such State to membership in the United
Nations will be affected by a decision of the General Assembly upon the
recommendation of the Security Council.

The 'requisite conditions' for admission are thus five in number:

to be admitted to membership in the United Nations, an applicant
must (1) be a State; (2) be peace-loving; (3) accept the obligations of
the Charter; (4) be able to carry out these obligations; and (5) be
willing to do so.[23]

In United Nations practice, it appears that the same meaning
has been attributed to the term 'State' in Article 4(1) as it has in
the customary law. This is what one would expect, given that full
membership of the United Nations involves a fairly wide range
of rights, duties, and powers: the context confirms, rather than
rebuts, the presumption that the term 'State' in a legal document
means 'State for the purposes of international law'.[24] The

---

[21] *USFR* 1945, *The Conferences at Malta and Yalta*, 746–7. The analogy with India was
rejected on the grounds that 'India has for some period past been gradually developing
international relations, and is generally regarded as having more of the attributes of
separate nationhood than the Soviet Republics.' See also Dolan (1955), 4 *ICLQ* 629–36;
Timasheff (1945), 14 *Fordham LR* 180–90; Uibopuu (1975), 24 *ICLQ* 211–45.

[22] *Supra*, n. 20. There were in all 51 Original Members. 46 States (including the
Dominions and India) were invited to San Francisco. Byelorussia, the Ukraine,
Argentina, and Denmark were admitted to the Conference. The Polish Provisional
Government was only admitted later in the proceedings, after 'reconstitution' of the
Polish Government in accordance with the Yalta Decision: see Whiteman, 13 *Digest* 190–
191. The Vatican tentatively inquired about original membership in 1944 and was
discouraged by the Secretary of State from applying: *infra*, p. 156.

[23] *Admissions Case* I.C.J. Rep. 1948 p. 57, 62.

[24] *Supra*, p. 33. For a more extensive view of Art. 4, cf. Reisman, *Puerto Rico and the
International Process: New Roles in Association* (1974), 53–62 ('broadest range of territorial
communities').

question arises to what extent United Nations organs have conformed to the criteria of statehood in examining and approving applications for membership. In a comprehensive review of the practice to 1962, Higgins concluded that:

> variations in United Nations practice concerning claims of statehood are a result not of an abandonment of traditional legal criteria . . . but of the proper use of flexibility in interpreting these criteria in relation to the claim in which they are presented. Concomitantly, the basic criteria of population, fixed territory, stable and effective government and sovereign independence have been—and should be—followed quite closely.[25]

But it has also been pointed out that purely political considerations often intrude in decisions concerning admission: the terms of Article 4 itself would seem to invite this.[26] This is not to say that legal considerations are irrelevant; merely that, in considering claims to admission under Article 4, legal and political factors may be difficult to separate. Moreover, if the Charter permits certain political considerations to be taken into account, it remains difficult to tell in specific cases whether the real political factors at issue have been permissible ones. There have been cases of what can only be considered premature recommendations for admission—for example, the case of the Republic of Vietnam, which, in 1950, was probably neither formally independent of France nor had a stable and effective government in the territory it claimed to govern.[27] Other cases where the legality or propriety of United Nations action on admissions have been doubted are dealt with elsewhere in this study.

A major factor in the last decade, as before, affecting United Nations admission policy has been the emphasis on the principle of universality of membership, a principle which has been all but achieved, as can be seen from Table 1.

[25] Higgins, *Development*, 11–57, 54; to the same effect, Mendelson, 84. See also Whiteman, 13 *Digest* 188–263; Aufricht (1949), 43 *AJ* 679–704; Rudzinski, *Int. Conc.* No. 480 (1952); Gross (1954), 48 *PAS* 37–59; Verhoeven, *Reconnaissance*, 470–3; and Schermers, *International Institutional Law* (1972) I, 26–81, for a more general survey.

[26] Cf. *Admissions Case* I.C.J. Rep. 1948 p. 57, 63 (Majority Opinion); 85–6 (Joint Dissenting Opinion).

[27] *Infra*, p. 284.

TABLE I

U.N. Membership 1945–1977

		% increase per 5-year period
Original Members (1945)	51	—
December 1950	60	17·6
December 1955	76	26·7
December 1960	99	30·3
December 1965	117	18·1
December 1970	127	8·5
December 1975	144	13·5
December 1977	149	—

An examination of practice over the last fourteen years reveals that most of the applications for membership were, at least at the time they were approved, relatively uncontroversial. Of the thirty-eight successful applications since January 1963, no fewer than thirty-three[28] were approved without any objection in both the Security Council and the General Assembly. A further application, that of the United Arab Emirates, was approved with only one dissentient.[29] In several cases, however, some degree of opposition existed. The case of Oman is discussed elsewhere.[30] Kuwait's first application was vetoed by the Soviet Union, on grounds partly of lack of independence from Britain and partly of a territorial dispute with Iraq, mentioned already.[31] Kuwait was eventually admitted without opposition.[32] The first application of Bangladesh was vetoed by China: the grounds given were the alleged refusal of Bangladesh to comply with Assembly resolutions concerning repatriation of prisoners and withdrawal of foreign troops.[33] It was not contended that

[28] *Sc.* those of the Bahamas, Bahrain, Bangladesh, Barbados, Bhutan, Botswana, Cape Verde Islands, Comoro Archipelago, Djibouti, Equatorial Guinea, the Federal Republic of Germany, Fiji, Gambia, the German Democratic Republic, Grenada, Guinea-Bissau, Guyana, Lesotho, Malawi, Maldives, Malta, Mauritius, Mozambique, Papua New-Guinea, the People's Democratic Republic of Yemen, Qatar, São Tomé and Principe, Seychelles, Singapore, Surinam, Swaziland, Western Samoa, and Zambia.

[29] G.A. Res. 2794 (XXVI), 9 Dec. 1971 (93–1 (South Yemen): 0).

[30] *Infra*, p. 213. Oman's application was approved unanimously by S. C. Res. 299 (1971), 30 Sept. 1971; G.A. Res. 2754 (XXVI), 7 Oct. 1971 (117–1 (South Yemen): 2 (Cuba, Saudi Arabia)).

[31] *Supra*, p. 38; *SCOR* 985th mtg., 30 Nov. 1961, 9 (10–1:0).

[32] G.A. Res. 1872 (S–IV), 14 May 1963.

[33] *SCOR* 659th mtg., 26 Aug. 1972 (11–1 (China); 3 (Guinea, Somalia, Sudan)).

Bangladesh was not a State. General Assembly Resolution 2937 (XXVII), of 29 November 1972, adopted without vote, called for the admission of Bangladesh, which was achieved on 17 September 1974, *nemine dissentiente*.[34]

The question of the status of Guinea-Bissau also aroused controversy in both the General Assembly and the Security Council. However when, on 17 September 1974, Guinea-Bissau was admitted,[35] an agreement had already been reached for *de jure* recognition and withdrawal of forces.[36] The case of Guinea-Bissau is discussed in detail elsewhere.[37] More recently, the cases of the Republic of Korea, the two Vietnams (and after unification the Socialist Republic of Vietnam) and Angola have caused some division in the Security Council. In the former cases the disagreement related rather to the application of the principle of universality than to issues of status.[38] In the case of Angola, United States opposition to intervention in the civil war was at least tangentially related to statehood, but a large majority of members had no doubts on this score: in their view the dispute over governmental control did not affect the status of the former colony.[39] The case of the Congo, discussed already,[40] would seem to support this view.[41]

In retrospect, it can be seen that the period of greatest stress in terms of United Nations admission—the period during which the statehood of applicants was most commonly called in question—coincided both with the 'Cold War', and the time of most sweeping decolonization. This tends to confirm what has been said about the difficulty of separating extraneous political factors from the considerations permitted by Article 4. If practice

[34] S.C. Res. 351 (1974), 10 June 1974; G.A. Res. 3203 (XXIX), 17 Sept. 1974. See further *supra*, pp. 115–17.

[35] S.C. Res. 356 (1974), 12 Aug. 1974; G.A. Res. 3205 (XXIX), 17 Sept. 1974.

[36] 13 *ILM* 1244.

[37] *Supra*, p. 111; *infra*, p. 260.

[38] In August 1975, the Security Council refused (7–6:2) to consider an application for membership by the Republic of Korea. In consequence, the U.S. vetoed applications by the two Vietnams: 1836th mtg., 11 August 1975; 1846th mtg., 30 September 1975. Cf. Jacobs & Poirier (1976) 17 *Harvard ILJ* 581–607. After reunification the Socialist Republic of Vietnam was admitted by S.C. Res. of July, 1977 (consensus); G.A. Res. 32/2, 20 September 1977 (accl.).

[39] See *Keesing's* 1977, 28156.

[40] *Supra*, p. 43.

[41] Angola was admitted on 1 Dec. 1976: S.C. Res. 397 (1976) (13–0:1 U.S.A.)); G.A. Res. 31/104 (116–0:1(U.S.A.)). Cf. *U.S. Digest* 1976, 39–40.

since 1963 gives no grounds for doubting Higgins's general conclusion,[42] that conclusion with regard to the period 1948–62 might perhaps be thought too sanguine.

4.3 STATEHOOD FOR OTHER UNITED NATIONS PURPOSES

(1) *Statehood and dispute settlement: Articles 32 and 35(2)*

Article 32 of the Charter provides that States not United Nations members 'shall be invited to participate, without vote' in discussions in the Security Council relating to disputes to which they are parties. Article 35(2) provides that non-member States may bring disputes to which they are parties to the attention of the United Nations. The question of the status of entities parties to disputes under either of these Articles has been raised quite frequently, especially in the early years of the United Nations. As the United Nations has approached universality, the application of the term 'State' in these Articles has proved less troublesome. However, some brief reference is in order.[43]

In 1947 the Security Council issued invitations, on separate occasions, to Indonesia[44] and Hyderabad,[45] although the status of each was the very point in issue. In debate on the proposal to invite the Republic of Indonesia, it was argued that an entity could be a 'State' for the purposes of Article 32, or Chapter VII generally, even if it was not fully sovereign: 'while Article 32 referred to States, the plain intent of that Article . . . was that justice should be done to both parties to a dispute by requiring that both should have the chance to present their views.'[46] As we have seen, this view has much to recommend it, although the fact

---

[42] *Supra*, p. 134.

[43] Higgins, *Development*, 50–2; Bailey, *The Procedure of the UN Security Council* (1975), 145–52.

[44] *SCOR* 181st mtg., 12 Aug. 1947, 1940 (8–3:0).

[45] *Infra*, p. 211.

[46] *SCOR* 181st mtg., 12 Aug. 1947, 1924 (Sen, India). At a subsequent meeting the U.K. representative argued that the decision to invite Indonesia to participate was a violation of Art. 32: *SCOR* 184th mtg., 14 Aug. 1947, 1984–5. Representatives from East Indonesia and Borneo were however refused a hearing under Art. 32: ibid. 1992; 193rd mtg., 22 Aug. 1947, 2172. But the U.K. voted to hear representatives of Hyderabad, the status of which for Art. 32 purposes could hardly have been much better than that of Indonesia: *SCOR* 357th mtg., 16 Sept. 1948, 10–11.

that a particular group is a 'party' to a 'dispute' being considered by the Security Council is of itself insufficient, since the group may have no international status at all. Moreover this extensive view of Article 32 has not been consistently applied.[47] A Russian proposal to allow Bangladesh to participate in debates on the 1971 war met with little support: the Russian representative was driven to rely upon rule 39 of the Security Council's provisional Rules of Procedure.[48] On the other hand, the Soviet Union has on other occasions argued that Rule 39 was not an appropriate basis for invitations to governments, as distinct from individuals.[49]

It is submitted that the term 'State' in Articles 32 and 35(2) refers to territorial entities with some degree of international status, irrespective of the meaning of the term elsewhere in the Charter. However, in the light of the fairly variable practice outlined above, this view cannot be asserted with much confidence.

(2) Claims to be parties to the Statute of the International Court of Justice

Article 93(2) of the Charter provides that States not members of the United Nations may become parties to the Statute of the International Court 'on conditions to be determined in each case by the General Assembly upon the recommendation of the Security Council'. Once again, this paragraph will probably be of diminishing importance as the United Nations approaches universality of membership.[50] Only diminutive States, such as San Marino or Nauru, are likely to remain permanently outside the United Nations.[51]

---

[47] Cf. *supra*, p. 103. (Rhodesia).

[48] Rule 39 states: 'The Security Council may invite members of the Secretariat or other persons, whom it considers competent for the purpose, to supply it with information or to give other assistance in examining matters within its competence.'

[49] E.g. *SCOR* 193rd mtg., 22 Aug. 1947, 217 (East Indonesia and Borneo).

[50] Under Charter Art. 93(1), U.N. Members are automatically parties to the Statute of the Court. See also Higgins, *Development*, 48–50; Reisman, op. cit. 68–79; Gunter (1977), 71 *AJ* 110–24.

[51] 'Associated States', such as Nuie and the Cook Islands may well be in a different category: in practice it may be that the associating State could extend access to the Court to the associated State by a declaration under the Optional Clause, without the need for a separate admission procedure under Art. 93(2). The matter is however unclear. See further *infra*, p. 376.

Both Liechtenstein[52] and San Marino[53] have been admitted as parties to the Statute of the Court. Arguments that these entities were not States because of their lack of independence met with little support.[54]

(3) *Other cases*

United Nations organs have often been faced with issues of statehood in areas unrelated to applications for admission: indeed it can be argued that the contribution of the United Nations to the development of the customary law of statehood has been greater in such areas than in the context of Article 4.[55] Problems of identity, continuity and extinction are of particular interest, and are discussed later in this study.[56]

4.4 *The micro-State problem*

One problem that has arisen in recent practice, and given rise to considerable debate, is the matter of 'Micro-States'. The problem has implications with respect both to United Nations voting and finance. If the considerable number of small territories which are still dependent were to become independent and to seek membership, the present numerical and fiscal disparities within the United Nations, it is argued, would be exacerbated, perhaps to an intolerable degree. This prospect led certain States to advocate an intermediate form of United Nations membership, without voting rights or with only limited voting rights.[57] After some debate in the Security Council and elsewhere,[58] the Security

---

[52] *SCOR* 423rd mtg., 8 Apr. 1949, 16–17; 432nd mtg., 27 July 1949, 3, 5; S.C. Res. 71 (1949) (9–0:2); G.A. Res. 363 (IV), 1 Dec. 1949 (40–2:2). For Liechtenstein's participation in the Permanent Court, see Kohn (1967), 61 *AJ* 547–57, 555.

[53] *SCOR* 645th mtg., 3 Dec. 1953, 2–4; S.C. Res. 103 (1953) (10–0:1) (U.S.S.R.)); G.A. Res. 806 (VIII), 9 Dec. 1953 (61–0:5).

[54] See further *infra*, p. 190. Switzerland is also a party to the Court's Statute. For its position in relation to the U.N., see Wildhaber (1970), 12 *Malaya LR* 140–59.

[55] This is not to deny the effect of political certification which U.N. membership undoubtedly has: Claude (1966), 20 *Int. Org.* 367–79.

[56] *Infra*, Chapters 16, 17. For membership in specialized agencies see Higgins, *Development*, 42–8; Mendelson, *passim*; Gold, *Membership and Non Membership in the International Monetary Fund* (1974), 41–89.

[57] *SCOR* 1243rd mtg., 20 Sept. 1965, 12, 14–15 (France, U.S.A.).

[58] Secretary-General's Introduction to the Annual Report, 1965–6; *GAOR* 21st Sess., Suppl. 1A, 14; S/8296, 13 Dec. 1967 (U.S.A.); *SCOR* 1414th mtg., 18 Apr. 1968, 8–9; S/9327, 14 July 1969 (U.S.A.).

Council convened a Committee of Experts to consider the problem.[59] It held one public meeting on 9 October 1969,[60] and then met on various occasions in private. A brief, unhelpful, interim report was issued in 1970.[61] No further action has been taken.

As was made clear during the debates, the problem is not one of statehood in the strict sense: it is not doubted that small territories may be fully States in the sense of international law.[62] The question is rather a political and constitutional one. Of course it might be said that small States were not 'able ... to carry out' the obligations of the Charter, but since United Nations membership is commonly regarded as an important form of international certification, that aspect of Article 4 has tended to be disregarded in practice.[63] At present the Maldives is the smallest member in terms of area (298 square kilometres) and Grenada by population (96,000). Proposals for change included a United States' proposal for a form of associate membership (which would involve amendment of the Charter),[64] and a British proposal that small States should undertake, on admission, not to exercise voting rights or to be available for election to other United Nations organs, in return for a nominal budgetary assessment.[65]

It is evident that the pressure for change has come from a few States only, that response has been luke-warm, and that the prospects for formal change are not great. In any event it might have been thought that the United Nations, having swallowed the camel of a majority membership of small States, should not balk at the gnat of a relatively few very small States.[66] It is of

[59] *SCOR* 1505th mtg., 27 Aug. 1969; 1506th mtg., 29 Aug. 1969, 6.

[60] *UNMC* Vol. 6 No. 9, 33–4.

[61] S/9836, 15 Jun 1970.

[62] *Supra*, p. 36; Secretary-General's Introduction to the Annual Report, 1966–7: *GAOR* 22nd. Sess., Suppl. 1A, 20–1.

[63] It was on this ground that Liechtenstein was refused League membership: Gunter (1974), 68 *AJ* 496–501; Kohn (1967), 61 *AJ* 547–57; Raton, *Liechtenstein, History and Institutions of the Principality* (1970), 58–66. An enquiry by the Vatican in 1944 was rebuffed on similar grounds: *infra*, p. 156. Fawcett states that 'by a sensible convention, Liechtenstein, Monaco, San Marino and Andorra are not regarded as potential U.N. members': in O'Brien, ed., *New Nations*, 315n. See also Hambro's Foreword to Goodrich, Hambro and Simons, *Charter of the United Nations* (3rd edn., 1969), vi.

[64] S/9836, Annex I.

[65] Ibid., Annex II.

[66] Cf. Mendelson (1972), 21 *ICLQ* 609–30, 621–3, 630.

interest that Western Samoa, having previously rejected membership, changed its mind in 1976 and was admitted without dissent.[67]

[67] For Western Samoa's previous attitude see Davidson, *Samoa mo Samoa* (1967), 425. On 'Micro-States' in general see also Unitar, *Status and Problems of Very Small States and Territories* (1969); Blair, *The Ministate Dilemma* (rev. edn., 1968); Fisher (1968), 62 *PAS* 164–70; de Smith, in Fawcett and Higgins, eds., *International Organization. Law in Movement* (1974), 64–78; Plischke, *Microstates in World Affairs* (1977). Cf. UN *Jur. Ybk.* 1975, 153.

5. The Criteria for Statehood applied: Some Special Cases

5.1 GENERAL CONSIDERATIONS

THE CRITERIA for statehood, examined in Chapters 2 and 3, are clearly flexible enough to allow a variety of entities with differing circumstances to be classified as States. It cannot be assumed that all territorial entities will necessarily have the same rights and obligations, or the same particular status; nor that, because an entity has special or unusual characteristics, it does not qualify as a State under those criteria. The recurring problem of 'special cases' in this area thus involves a relation between two fundamental principles: the principle that the status of an entity is to be determined, not by reference to any general concept, but from the specific circumstances and constituent instruments;[1] and the principle that statehood is a general legal status with a certain, sometimes fairly nominal, regime of rules. It follows that, in analysing the problems which arise here, general descriptions—such as 'internationalized territory', 'protectorate', or 'fief'—are unhelpful. 'Special cases' must have *some* legal status, even if, for whatever reason, they do not qualify as States. They clearly are not *terrae nullius*, and there is no reason of principle or practice why they should not be subject to relevant international legal rules.[2] Moreover many of these entities do in

---

[1] *International Status of South West Africa* I.C.J. Rep. 1950 p. 128, 150 *per* Judge McNair; *Tunis and Morocco Nationality Decrees*, Ser. B No. 4 (1920), 27.

[2] The Valleys of Andorra are a paradigm example both of the irrelevance of general descriptions ('fief') and of the difficulty of classification of *sui generis* entities. Andorra is still, as the Court of Appeal of Montpellier stated, 'a *"co-seigneurie"* or vestige of feudal institutions which is under the joint protection of the President of the French Republic, as successor to the rights of the [French] Counts of Foix, and the Spanish Bishop of Urgel:' *Re Boedecker & Ronski* (1962) 44 ILR 176, 178; although the term 'protection' is not strictly accurate: the co-princes are joint sovereigns over the territory. I have discussed the status of Andorra elsewhere: see (1977) 55 *RDISDP* 259–73. The conclusion there reached is that, although proximate to statehood, Andorra is probably not independent of France, at least in its international relations, in view of the uncertainty and ambiguity of the relation between Andorra and the French co-prince. On Andorra see further Bélinguier, *La Condition juridique des vallées d'Andorre* (1970); Rousseau, in *Symbolae Verzijl* (1958), 337–46; *Les Problèmes actuels des vallées d'Andorre* (1970), and Kiss, 2 *Pratique français* 469–79.

fact play, or have in the past played, a significant part in international relations.

There are, or have been, a very large number of such 'anomalous' or special cases:[3] it is impossible, and unnecessary, to deal with them all here. However, some raise particular problems of difficulty and importance for the general law of international status; others have intrinsic historical and political importance and warrant some examination. Moreover the question of the relation between special legal status and statehood requires consideration. Three such entities are examined here in detail: Taiwan; the Vatican City (together with the Holy See); and the Free City of Danzig (with which is compared Cyprus). References will be made to other special cases where appropriate.

5.2 ENTITIES UNRECOGNIZED AS SEPARATE STATES: TAIWAN (FORMOSA)

The relation between recognition and statehood has been seen to be close but not inseparable: entities which conform to the requirements for statehood are States, independently of recognition, although recognition may be, especially in borderline cases, strong evidence of conformity with those requirements.[4] This view of the relationship is confronted with its most pertinent test in the case of Taiwan, which, although it would appear to comply in all respects with the criteria for statehood based on effectiveness, is universally agreed not to be a State, and is recognized by no one as such.

(1) *Historical background*

Taiwan (Formosa) became part of the Chinese Empire in 1683, and remained so, despite internal vicissitudes, until the Treaty of Shimonoseki of 1895, by Article 2(b) and (c) of which Formosa and the Pescadores were ceded to Japan.[5] The islands remained Japanese until 1945. In the Cairo Declaration of 1 December 1943 the Allies declared their 'purpose . . . that all the territories Japan has stolen from the Chinese, such as Manchuria,

---

[3] See further Verzijl, *International Law* II, *passim*; Ydit, *Internationalized Territories* (1961).
[4] *Supra*, p. 23.
[5] 87 *BFSP* 799.

Formosa and the Pescadores, shall be restored to the Republic of China'.[6] Paragraph (8) of the Potsdam Proclamation of 26 July 1945 affirmed that 'The terms of the Cairo Declaration shall be carried out and Japanese sovereignty shall be limited to the islands of Honshu, Hokkaido, Kyushu, Shikuku, and such minor islands as we determine.'[7] In the Instrument of Surrender of 2 September 1945, Japan undertook to carry out the provisions of the Potsdam Proclamation.[8] The Japanese forces in Taiwan thereafter surrendered to the Commander-in-Chief of the Republic of China.[9]

Civil war within China between the Government of the Republic, and the proclaimed People's Republic under Mao Tse Tung had been continuing since 1928. On 8 December 1949 the Republic of China's forces retreated to Taiwan, establishing there the provisional capital of that government. With certain exceptions other States remained neutral during the war:[10] it is clear that the People's Republic, on its establishment on the mainland, was a genuine revolutionary government, not a 'puppet' of any other State.

On 25 June 1950 the Korean War broke out: official Chinese participation is that war dated from November 1950. As an immediate result of the hostilities, President Truman ordered the Seventh Fleet to patrol the Taiwan Straits and to prevent attacks by either government on the other.[11] This unilateral action appears to have constituted an intervention in the still continuing, though consolidated, civil war between the two Chinese governments,[12] although its justification appears to have been not 'collective self-defence' of Taiwan but individual action in a case of threats to the international peace and 'security of the Pacific area'.[13] Meanwhile negotiations for a final Peace treaty with Japan were proceeding.[14] The Peace Treaty was in fact signed on 8 July 1951 by forty-eight Allied Powers (excluding

[6] (1944) 38 *AJ Supp.* 8.
[7] 13 *DSB* 137.
[8] Whiteman, 3 *Digest* 486–7.
[9] Ibid. 487–8.
[10] But cf. G.A. Res. 505 (VI), 1 Feb. 1952 (25–9:24).
[11] 23 *DSB* 5.
[12] Cf. 225 *UNTS* 57, 64; Hoyt (1961), 55 *AJ* 45–76, esp. 58–71.
[13] In 1953 the order was amended to allow Nationalist attacks on the mainland: 28 *DSB* 209.
[14] See Whiteman, 3 *Digest* 477–625.

the U.S.S.R. and China), and Japan.[15] By Article 2(b) of the Treaty Japan renounced 'all right, title and claim to Formosa and the Pescadores'; in whose favour was not stated. Mr. Dulles said at the time that 'the differences of opinion are such that [the disposal of Formosa] could not be definitively dealt with by a Japanese peace treaty to which the Allied powers, as a whole, are parties. Therefore the treaty merely takes Japan formally out of the Formosa picture, leaving the position otherwise unchanged.'[16]

Japan, in a separate peace treaty with the Republic of China, 'recognized' its renunciation of title to Formosa without further specification.[17] The treaty was stated to apply to 'all the territories under the control of the Government of the Republic of China'.[18] A Joint Declaration of 1956 between Japan and the U.S.S.R. ended the formal state of war between them, without referring to the problems of territorial disposition.[19] In 1954 a Mutual Defence Treaty was signed between the United States and the Republic of China, providing for collective self-defence of the Pacific territories of the two parties; the territory of the Republic was defined to mean Formosa and the Pescadores, with provision for extension to other territories by agreement.[20]

The question of Taiwan has been since 1949 bound up with two other issues: that of the recognition of the opposing governments, and that of the representation of China in the United Nations. A major reason for this entanglement of issues has been the continued insistence by both parties on the unity of all China including Taiwan, the only difference between them being over the government entitled to govern, and thus to represent, that China.[21] By 1976 the People's Republic had been recognized by a considerable majority of States: the Republic of China continued however to be recognized by some, including the United States.[22] On 25 October 1971 the People's Republic was seated in the General Assembly and the Republic of China

[15] 136 *UNTS* 45.
[16] 25 *DSB* 461–3; Whiteman, 3 *Digest* 538.
[17] (1952) 138 *UNTS* 38, Art. 2.
[18] Ibid. 52.
[19] 263 *UNTS* 99.
[20] 161 *BFSP* 598, Art. VI.
[21] For the various views see Jain (1963), 57 *AJ* 25–45.
[22] No State has ever had formal diplomatic relations with, or recognized, the two governments at the same time. Cf. (1975) 79 *RGDIP* 174–5, 791.

expelled.[23] On the other hand, although it is increasingly isolated from diplomatic intercourse, Taiwan continues to maintain strong informal and trade relations with many other States, and, in general, the *status quo* has remained unchanged.

(2) *The present legal status of Taiwan*

Debate on the legal status of Taiwan, which has been extensive,[24] has concentrated on the issue of the acquisition of territory by China. Little attention has been paid to the question why, even if Taiwan became Chinese territory in 1952 or at some other time, it is not now a State. The refusal of the governments involved to contemplate a 'two China' position has no doubt contributed to this neglect: however, it has not been shown in what way that refusal prevents or impairs the legal status which Taiwan would, presumably, otherwise have. Moreover, if a State has in fact come into existence on Taiwan then questions of the previous disposition of the territory become irrelevant. But since it may be argued that the Republic of China's right to administer Taiwan is as delegate rather than as sovereign, the issue of territorial status must first be dealt with.

Assuming for the time being that Taiwan is not a separate State, three views are possible.[25] It is arguable that Taiwan was returned to China by 1949, as a result of the cancellation by the Republic of China in 1941 of the Treaty of Shimonoseki, or, more plausibly, as a result of the transfer of administrative authority by Japan to the Republic of China pursuant to the Cairo and Potsdam Declarations. This is the view taken by both Chinese governments:[26] moreover, before the Korean War, the

[23] G.A. Res. 2758 (XXVI) (76–35:17). A U.S. draft resolution provided for dual representation of China. Ambassador Bush, in proposing the item, stated that . . . 'the U.N. should take cognizance of the existence of both the People's Republic of China and the Republic of China . . . [It] should not be required to take a position on the respective conflicting claims . . . pending a peaceful reconciliation of the matter as called for by the Charter' (A/8442: 10 *ILM* 1100). The draft resolution was not put to the vote. See also 11 *ILM* 561–73; 1972 UN *Jur. Ybk.* 154–6, para. 8.

[24] See especially Hungdah Chiu, ed., *China and the Question of Taiwan* (1973); O'Connell (1956), 50 *AJ* 405–16; Chen and Lasswell, *Formosa, China and the United Nations* (1967); Chen and Reisman (1972), 81 *Yale LJ* 599–671; Morello, *The International Legal Status of Formosa* (1966); Bueler, *U.S. China Policy and the Problem of Taiwan* (1971); Weng, in Leng and Chiu, eds., *Law in Chinese Foreign Policy* (1972), 123–77.

[25] Cf. O'Connell (1956), 50 *AJ* 405, 406; Weng, op. cit. 126–35 (who enumerates six positions and rejects all of them).

[26] For details see Jain (1963), 57 *AJ* 25, 33–8. This view is supported by Phillips (1957), 10 *Western Pol. Q.* 276–89; Hungdah Chiu, op. cit. 171.

United States also seems to have committed itself to this alternative.[27] On this view, all that remained to be done by the Japanese Peace Treaty was the confirmation of Japan's relinquishment of sovereignty in 1945.

However, it is submitted that Taiwan remained formally Japanese territory until the Peace Treaty. The arguments against the other view are elaborated elsewhere;[28] and it is not necessary to regard the Cairo and Potsdam Declarations as merely a 'statement of intent' in order to disagree with it.[29] The presumption in favour of the established rule that cession of territory at the end of a war must await the peace treaty is a strong one, and it is quite consistent that the terms of the treaty have been in part pre-arranged in binding form between the belligerents. In other words, the peace treaty could have ceded Formosa to no other than 'the government of China': the problem was that, in 1951, there was no agreement between the signatories as to which government that was. Until 1952 then, the position of the Republic of China in Taiwan was that of belligerent occupant and, after 1949, government-in-exile of China.

The second and the third alternatives referred to are in agreement on this point, but differ as to the effect of the Peace Treaty itself. The second view is that the Peace Treaty, by which Japan merely relinquished its title and claims, left the position otherwise unchanged, and thus left sovereignty over Taiwan undetermined. This view was, until recently, consistently espoused by both British and United States governments. It was put in the following way, for example, by Sir Anthony Eden in a written answer in 1955:

[The Cairo] Declaration was a statement of intention that Formosa should be retroceded to China after the war. This retrocession has, in fact, never taken place, because of the difficulties arising from the existence of two entities claiming to represent China, and the differences amongst the Powers as to the status of these entities. The Potsdam

---

[27] On Jan. 1950 President Truman stated that 'the United States and the other Allied Powers have accepted the exercise of Chinese authority over the Island', and Secretary of State Acheson stated that 'when Formosa was made a province of China nobody raised any lawyer's doubts about that' (Chiu, op. cit. 221–2). The State Department subsequently affirmed this position in replies to the Senate: ibid., 223–4. But cf. *USFR* 1949/IX, 271.

[28] Jain (1963), 57 *AJ* 25, 32–8; Kirkham (1968), 6 *Can. YIL* 144–63.

[29] Cf. Eden's statement, cited below; and *H.C. Deb.* Vol. 595 col. 1140, 19 Nov. 1958.

Declaration ... laid down as one of the conditions for the Japanese Peace that the terms of the Cairo Declaration should be carried out. In September 1945, the administration of Formosa was taken over from the Japanese by Chinese forces at the direction of the Supreme Commander of the Allied Powers; but this was not a cession, nor did it in itself involve any change of sovereignty. The arrangements made with Chiang-Kai-Shek put him there on a basis of military occupation pending further arrangements, and did not of themselves constitute the territory Chinese.

Under the Peace Treaty of April, 1952, Japan formally renounced all right, title and claim to Formosa and the Pescadores; but again this did not operate as a transfer to Chinese sovereignty, whether to the People's Republic of China or to the Chinese Nationalist authorities. Formosa and the Pescadores are therefore, in the view of Her Majesty's Government, territory the *de jure* sovereignty over which is uncertain or undetermined.[30]

The third view is that Japanese relinquishment in 1952 had the legal effect of transferring sovereignty with respect to Taiwan and the Pescadores to the government occupying the territory, that is, the Republic of China; although quite how this transfer came about is a matter of some obscurity. It cannot be argued, for example, that the Japanese relinquishment left Taiwan *terra nullius*,[31] since after 1952 as before the island continued to be controlled by an effective, organized government. It is arguable that Japanese relinquishment, which took place against a background of a commitment to return Taiwan to 'China', and the continued occupation of Taiwan by a recognized government of 'China', operated to revest sovereignty in China *qua* State (without specifically determining the government entitled to exercise that sovereignty).[32] As a mode of transfer of territory this would undoubtedly be unique; but on the other hand, it seems unlikely that Taiwan in 1952 became in effect a condominium of the forty-eight signatories to the Japanese Peace

[30] *H.C. Deb.* Vol. 536 col. 159 (w.a.), 4 Feb. 1955. See also ibid., cols. 158–64, 26 Jan. 1955; *H.L. Deb.* Vol. 212 col. 497–8, 13 Nov. 1958; ibid., Vol. 213 col. 216, 11 Dec. 1958; ibid., Vol. 278 col. 897, 5 Dec. 1966; *H.C. Deb.* Vol. 738 cols. 185–6 (w.a.), 19 Dec. 1966; Brownlie, *Principles,* 112–13. For the American position see e.g. Dulles (1954), 31 *DSB* 896: 'technical sovereignty over Formosa and the Pescadores has never been settled ... [T]he future title is not determined by the Japanese peace treaty, nor is it determined by the peace treaty which was concluded between the Republic of China and Japan ...'
[31] O'Connell (1956), 50 *AJ* 405, 414; (1952), 29 *BY* 423–35, 427. For the concept of *terra nullius* see *infra*, pp. 179–81.
[32] Harvey (1959), 30 *World Aff. Q.* 134–53, 144.

Treaty, in particular where such a *condominium* or joint power of disposition was unexpressed and substantially unclaimed by the parties. Nor did the treaty leave the status of Taiwan to be determined, for example, by the four Principal Powers: in the absence of specific enumeration or definition of such special dispositive authority, none can be presumed.[33]

However this may be, it seems clear that the *present* status of Taiwan (assuming again that it is not a separate State) is that it is Chinese territory, rather than territory subject to a *condominium*, or territory the title to which is undetermined. The major powers have now more or less unequivocally recognized the status of Taiwan as Chinese territory. For example a Joint Communiqué issued by the United States and the People's Republic in 1972 stated:

The China side reaffirmed its position ... the Government of the People's Republic of China is the sole legal government of China; Taiwan is a province of China which has long been returned to the motherland; the liberation of Taiwan is China's internal affair ... The United States acknowledges that all Chinese on either side of the Taiwan Strait maintain there is but one China and that Taiwan is a part of China. The United States Government *does not challenge that position*. It reaffirms its interest in a peaceful settlement of the Taiwan question by the Chinese themselves ...[34]

The British position, despite protestations, also changed markedly in 1972: in announcing the exchange of ambassadors with the People's Republic the Foreign Secretary stated the position as follows: 'the Government of the United Kingdom acknowledge the position of the Chinese Government that Taiwan is a province of the People's Republic of China ... We think that the Taiwan question is China's internal affair to be settled by the Chinese people themselves ...'[35] It follows that, even if, before

---

[33] To the same effect Kirkham (1968), 6 *Can. YIL* 144, 150; Chiu, op. cit. 130–2; Bueler (1971), 27 *The World Today*, 256–66, 263. The contrary view is argued by Wright (1955), 49 *AJ* 318–38; Chen & Reisman (1972), 81 *Yale LJ* 599, 654; Chen and Lasswell, op. cit. 77. Cf. Morello, op. cit., who argues that the Republic of China has obtained title to Formosa by prescription. The problem with this argument is that the Republic's title, in view of its claim to be 'the Government of China', is not adverse to the People's Republic.

[34] 11 *ILM* 445 (emphasis added).

[35] *H.C. Deb.* Vol. 833 cols. 31–8, 32, 13 Mar. 1972. Chen & Reisman, op. cit. 619n. state that the British statement marks a reversal of the earlier British position.

1971, the Powers retained dispositive authority with respect to Taiwan, their express recognition of the proposition that Taiwan remains part of China, together with the failure of any State to maintain diplomatic relations with both governments, must be taken as an acquiescence in the continued Chinese claim that the territory is part of metropolitan China, and thus, in effect, a relinquishment of any such dispositive authority. On either view, Taiwan is, if not a separate State, part of the unitary State of China. The question remains whether Taiwan, which has for more than twenty-five years been a distinct and *de facto* independent territorial unit, constitutes a separate State in international law. In other words, what is the status of territory occupied by a government-in-exile claiming to do so as the government of an existing State? There are three difficulties with the view that, as a long established effective entity, Taiwan must be regarded as a State.[36]

First, if the Nationalists had by 1952 lost all claim to being the government of China, then effective cession to them of Taiwan would seem to have been a violation of the agreed terms of the peace, as well as intervention in the civil war in China. As has been suggested, the Peace Treaty did not render Taiwan capable of appropriation, even notionally, by just any State or government—the validity of continued Nationalist occupation hinged on the Nationalist claim to be the 'government of China'. Secondly, if, as is suggested above, Taiwan became in 1952 a part of China, then, presumably, continued American patrolling of the Straits of Taiwan would have constituted illegal intervention in the civil war, and an attempt to disrupt the territorial integrity of China.[37] This might very well have

---

[36] A view adopted by Caty, *Statut Juridique des Etats Divisés* (1969), 23–30; Kirkham (1968), 6 *Can. YIL* 144–63; Wright (1955), 49 *AJ* 318–27.

[37] It is clear that the change in the U.S. position in 1950 was designed to give legal support to the unilateral U.S. action in 'neutralizing' the Taiwan Straits: see Harvey, op. cit. 137–8; Philips, op. cit. 279–80. This point was frankly conceded by Dulles in a conversation with Ambassador Koo on 20 Oct. 1950: 'If the United States already regarded Taiwan as purely Chinese territory, not only must the question of the representation of the Chinese government be solved immediately [*sed quaere*] but the United States would lose her grounds for despatching the Seventh Fleet to protect Taiwan . . .' (Chiu, op. cit. 237). The legality of the intervention was also based on precisely this ground by a Department of State legal adviser: Maurer (1958), 39 *DSB* 1005–11.

brought into play the rule that an entity is not a State if created through a violation of the rules relating to the use of force.[38]

However, this difficult problem—as in the Manchurian crisis but for different reasons—did not really arise. For the third difficulty with the view that Taiwan is not a separate State has been in practice determinative. The point is that there is even now universal agreement, not just of other States but of the chief parties concerned, that Formosa is not a State but is instead part of a larger China. The Republic of China on Taiwan, as well as the People's Republic in Peking, insist that there is only one Chinese State; and that view has been acquiesced in, or even explicitly recognized, by, it seems, all other international actors. As O'Connell pointed out in 1956, 'a government is only recognized for what it claims to be'.[39] Statehood is a claim of right,[40] and in the absence of any claim to secession the status of Taiwan can only be that of a part of the State of China under separate administration.

(3)   *Conclusions*

The conclusion must be that Taiwan is not a State, because it does not claim to be, and is not recognized as such: its status is that of a consolidated local *de facto* government in a civil war situation. The Republic of China may even be precluded, by its actions since 1949, from attempting to assert separate sovereignty over the island, although the finally effective secession of part of a State may never be excluded in practice. But this is not to say that Formosa has no status whatever in international law.[41] It is a party to various conventions binding its own territory.[42] Courts faced with specific issues concerning its status may treat it on a *de facto* basis as a 'well defined geographical, social, and political entity (with) . . . a Government which has undisputed control of the island'.[43] Conflicts between its limited status in international law and the policies of particular statutes or contracts may be reconciled or avoided, especially in a municipal forum, by

[38] *Supra*, pp. 106–8.
[39] (1956) 50 *AJ* 405, 415. The contrary proposition is not of course true: a government may be recognized for *less* than it claims.
[40] Cf. *supra*, p. 119.
[41] It has no U.N. status: Stavropoulos (1973), 7 *Int. L.* 70–7, 71.
[42] *Supra*, p. 145.
[43] *A.G.* v. *Sheng* (1960) 31 ILR 349.

interpretation.[44] Internationally the Government of Formosa is a well established *de facto* government, capable of committing the State to at least certain classes of transaction. It has also been argued that the principle of self-determination applies, so that Taiwan may not be transferred to the control of the People's Republic without the consent of the people.[45] In any case, attempts to solve the problem of Taiwan otherwise than by peaceful means must now constitute a situation 'likely to endanger the maintenance of international peace and security' under Article 33 of the Charter: this view is held, as we have seen, by both the British and United States governments. To this extent, while there is no strict 'juridical boundary' between the parties, there does appear to be a frontier for the purposes of the use of force.

5.3   ENTITIES RECOGNIZED AS STATES 'FOR SPECIAL REASONS': THE VATICAN CITY AND THE HOLY SEE

The legal status of the Vatican City and the Holy See have been the subject of much controversy.[46] Since the fourth century the Papacy has played a significant part in international relations. The temporal power of the Papacy however dates from the ninth century, when the Papal States were created by Pepin-le-Bref and his son Charlemagne.[47] The territorial extent of the Papal States varied, but, with brief revolutionary interruptions from 1793 to 1801 and 1809 to 1814,[48] they

---

[44] Thus for the purposes of a charterparty, Formosa, though unrecognized in any capacity by the U.K., was a 'government': *Luigi Monta of Genoa* v. *Ceckofracht Ltd.* [1956] 2 All E.R. 769.

[45] Chen and Lasswell, *Formosa, China and the United Nations* (1967), *passim*; Chen and Reisman (1972), 81 *Yale LJ* 599, 655–669; Wright (1955), 49 *AJ* 318, 333–5; and Bueler (1971), 27 *The World Today* 256, 263–4, also support the self-determination argument, which has however received little support in State practice.

[46] The best treatment is that of Kunz (1952), 46 *AJ* 308–14. See also Sereni, *The Italian Conception of International Law* (1943), 188, 231–2, 292–4; Oppenheim I, 250–5; Rousseau *DIP* II, 353–77, and works cited *infra*.

[47] For the early history of the Papacy in international law see Pallieri & Vismara, *Acta Pontifica Juris Gentium usque ad Annum MCCIV* (1946); Verzijl, *International Law* II, 308–38.

[48] The Papal Dominions were returned to the Holy See by the Final Act of the Conference of Vienna, Art. 103: (1815) 64 *CTS* 453, to which the Pope was not a signatory.

continued as the territorial base for the central government of the Catholic Church.

Until 1870, therefore, the Roman States under Papal government constituted one of the ordinary independent States of Europe in a still disunited Italy. In 1870, as the final step in the *risorgimento*, Italian troops occupied and, after plebiscite, annexed the territories.[49] The Italian Law of Guarantees of 1871 extended personal inviolability to the Pope and established the freedom of the Apostolic Palaces,[50] but the Papal States from their annexation ceased to exist as a State.[51] It was accordingly stated by various writers[52] that the Holy See had no international status after 1870. A settlement of the Roman Question was at length achieved in 1929, by the Lateran Treaty, in which Italy recognized both 'the sovereignty of the Holy See in the field of international relations as an attribute that pertains to the very nature of the Holy See, in conformity with its traditions and with the demands of its mission in the world',[53] and 'the State of the Vatican City under the sovereignty of the Supreme Pontiff.'[54] The purpose of the Lateran Treaty was summarized in the Preamble: 'And whereas it is a duty, for the purpose of assuring the absolute and visible independence of the Holy See, to guarantee to it an indisputable sovereignty in the international domain, it has been recognized as necessary to constitute, under special conditions, the Vatican City and to recognize the full ownership, and the exclusive and absolute dominion and sovereign jurisdiction of the Holy See over the same . . .' The status of the Vatican City is still regulated by the Lateran Treaty

[49] 62 *BFSP* 352 ff. for documentation. The annexation was a violation of a Franco-Italian Treaty of 1864: 55 *BFSP* 461.

[50] 65 *BFSP* 638.

[51] *Thome Guadalupe* v. *Assoc. Italiana di S. Cecilia* (1937) 8 AD No. 48; cf. *Re Esposito* (1899) 2 *Rdi* 551, cited Ireland (1933), 27 *AJ* 271–89, 283–4. *Contra* Cumbo (1948), 2 *ILQ* 603–20.

[52] e.g., Hall, *International Law* (7th edn., 1917), 308, 334n. Oppenheim (1st edn., 1905) I, 252 described the Holy See as 'not an international person' but as possessing 'a quasi international position'. This position was understandable, given Oppenheim's view that the only true legal persons were States (*supra*, p. 14 n. 47).

[53] 130 *BFSP* 791, Art. 2.

[54] Art. 26: cf. Art. 3, which recognized 'full possession and exclusive and absolute power and sovereign jurisdiction of the Holy See over the Vatican, as at present constituted . . .' The right of active and passive legation was confirmed: Arts. 12, 19. In addition certain Church properties outside the Vatican were privileged (Art. 15): they remained however 'Italian territory': *Padri Benedetti* v. *Nunzi* (1957) 24 ILR 214; *Trenta* v. *Ragonesi* (1938) 8 AD No. 93; 9 AD No. 173; *In re Moriggi* (1939) 9 AD No. 172.

and the associated constituent documents.[55] Three issues arise from this set of facts: the status of the Vatican City, the status of the Holy See, and the relation between them.

(1) *The international status of the Vatican City*

The State of the City of the Vatican, as constituted in 1929, is the smallest area in the world which claims to be a State. Its population, which is official and non-permanent,[56] is nominally 1,000. Italy carries out a number of governmental functions in respect of the Vatican City: Italian police patrol the Piazza S. Pietro;[57] the Italian railway, water, and sanitation systems support the enclave which is also dependent upon Italy for freedom of transit and communications. Moreover, unlike other States the Vatican City exists not to support its inhabitants but to provide a base for the central administration of a non-State entity, the Catholic Church. For these reasons, some writers have denied that the Vatican City constitutes in any way a State.[58]

It cannot be denied that the position of the Vatican City is peculiar and that the criteria for statehood in its case are only marginally—if at all—complied with. However peculiarity is not itself grounds for denying statehood, especially when other factors point directly to the opposite conclusion. And, as we have seen, recognition by other States is of considerable importance especially in marginal or borderline cases. The chief peculiarity of the international status of the Vatican City is not size or population—or lack of them—but the unique and complex relation between the City itself and its government, the Holy See. That relation is discussed later in this section. The international status of the Holy See itself contributed to the acknowledgment of the statehood of the Vatican, once Italy had ceded the territory and recognized the Vatican City.[59]

[55] Peaslee, *Constitutions of Nations* (3rd edn., 1969) III, 1184–1230.

[56] See the Law respecting Citizenship and Residence in the Vatican City of 7 June 1929: 130 *BFSP* 1018. Male children who reach the age of 25 normally lose Vatican nationality automatically: female children lose the nationality on marriage. Cessation of residence, or of official employment, in the Vatican City also determines nationality.

[57] Lateran Treaty, Art. 3: cf. also Arts. 6, 7.

[58] Rousseau (1930), 37 *RGDIP* 145–53, and *DIP* II, 375–7; Siotto-Pintor (1932), 41 *HR* 247–361, 319–32; Mendelson (1972), 21 *ICLQ* 609–30, 611–12.

[59] Fitzmaurice described the Vatican, for the purposes of the Draft I.L.C. Convention on the Law of Treaties, as an 'entit(y) recognized as being (a) State( ) on special grounds': *ILC Ybk.* 1956/II, 107, 118.

Moreover, it is not clear what legal consequence is sought to be drawn from the denial of the statehood of the Vatican City. Its functions certainly are special to itself, but it is believed that, for the purposes of international law it is capable of being termed a State. Its sovereign immunity is determined by the Italian courts in the same way as for other States.[60] It has exclusive legislative authority, and civil and criminal jurisdiction within its territory.[61] Italy agreed in 1929 not to intervene in the 'exclusive jurisdiction' of the State of the Vatican.[62] The Holy See has jurisdiction 'in conformity with the provisions of international law' over all persons with a 'fixed residence within the State of the Vatican'.[63] As government of the Vatican City, the Holy See is clearly independent: indeed it provides an unusual example of a small entity which is more independent in political than in the functional fields. It is a party to numerous treaties, multilateral and bilateral.[64] Under article 24 of the Lateran Treaty:

With regard to the sovereignty pertaining to it in the field of international relations, the Holy See declares that it wishes to remain and will remain extraneous to all temporal disputes between nations, and to international congresses convoked for the settlement of such disputes, unless the contending parties make a joint appeal to its mission of peace; nevertheless, it reserves the right in every case to exercise its moral and spiritual power. In consequence of this declaration, the State of the Vatican will always and in every case be considered neutral and inviolable territory.

The neutrality of the Vatican was recognized by all the belligerents in World War II.[65] The Vatican City is a member

---

[60] Hence medical contracts, having 'a technical and non-political character' are not immune, being acts *jure gestionis: Baronci* v. *Ospedale del Bambino Gesu* (1957) 24 ILR 215; cf. the immunity of the Sovereign Order of Malta in respect of the same class of matters: *Scarfò* v. *Sovereign Order of Malta* (1957) 24 ILR 1. It appears that the immunity of the Holy See was regarded as submerged by that of the Vatican City: *sed quaere.*

[61] *In re Dalla Torre* (1936) 8 ILR 250 (libel). The Piazza S. Pietro remains part of the Vatican, despite Italian police power there under the Treaty: *Levantesi* v. *Governor of Rome* (1940) 10 AD No. 25.

[62] Lateran Treaty, Art. 4.

[63] Ibid., Art. 9.

[64] *Infra*, p. 153.

[65] On 10 July 1943 President Roosevelt assured Pope Pius XII that 'the neutral status of Vatican City as well as of the Papal domains throughout Italy will be respected' throughout the Italian operations: *USFR* 1943/II, 926-7. The Acting-Secretary of State, on 2 Mar. 1944, stated that 'Germans, Japanese and other enemy diplomatic missions

of the Universal Postal Union[66] and the International Telecommunications Union.[67] It is not however a member of any political international organization. In 1944 tentative enquiries were made by the Holy See as to membership in the United Nations. Secretary of State Hull replied that

it would seem undesirable that the question of membership of the Vatican State be raised now. As a diminutive state the Vatican would not be capable of fulfilling all the responsibilities of membership in an organization whose primary purpose is the maintenance of international peace and security. In a number of cases diminutive states were refused admission to the League on this ground. Membership in the organization would not seem to be consonant with the provisions of Article 24 of the Lateran Treaty, particularly as regards spiritual status and participation in possible use of armed force. Non-membership would not preclude participation of the Vatican State in social and humanitarian activities of the organization nor impair its traditional role in promotion of peace by its usual influence.[68]

From this, fairly considerable, body of practice it would appear that the Vatican City is a State in international law, despite its size and special circumstances. However, before any definite conclusion can be reached, some reference to the international status of the Holy See is necessary.

(2) *The international status of the Holy See*[69]

The Holy See is the central administrative organ of the Catholic Church: it consists of the Pope, the College of Cardinals, and the central departments which govern the Church. It is a non-territorial body with a long history in international affairs. Before 1870 that involvement was associated with the govern-

accredited to Holy See should be given the option of entering Vatican City upon the arrival of Allied troops in the Italian Capital': ibid., 1944/IV, 1315. The British view was that no such option should be given since, technically, Axis diplomats would lose their immunity if apprehended outside the limits of Vatican City: loc. cit. See also Wright (1944), 38 *AJ* 452–7.

[66] 186 *UNTS* 356; 639 *UNTS* 368 ('sovereign country').

[67] 193 *UNTS* 189 ('country' listed in Annex 1 ('Etat de la Cité du Vatican' is so listed); otherwise 'sovereign country': Art. 1 (2)).

[68] *USFR* 1944/I, 960–3, 962. He added that 'protection of the integrity of the Vatican as an independent State would not be increased by membership'. No formal membership application has ever been made. In 1964 the Holy See acquired observer status at the U.N.: see Lucien-Brun, [1974] *AFDI* 536–42.

[69] See also de la Brière (1937), 20 *RDI* 29–48; Le Fur, *Le Saint-Siège et le droit des gens* (1930).

ment of the Papal States, so that no problem of the separate legal status of the Holy See arose in practice. However it seems clear that the Holy See did have a separate international status before 1870.[70] After the annexation of the Papal States in 1870, other States continued to accredit envoys to, and to receive Legates from, the Holy See,[71] and the Pope continued to make concordats with foreign States.[72] Though some writers denied that the Holy See had any international standing at all after 1870,[73] the true position is that it retained after the annexation of the Papal States what it had always had, a degree of international personality, measured by the extent of its existing legal rights and duties, together with its capacity to conclude treaties and to receive and accredit envoys. Writers have differed as to whether this personality was particular[74] or general.[75] It does not appear that the status of the Holy See, as distinct from the Papal States under its government, was, or was intended to be, nullified by the events of 1870.[76] Certainly the Holy See then ceased to be the government of a State, but its international position had been, at least in part, independent of its territorial competence; as Palmerston pointed out, the territorial competence was justified by the international position of the Pope as head of the Catholic Church.[77]

(3) *The relation between the Holy See and the State of the City of the Vatican*

Since 1929 the State of the City of the Vatican, and its government the Holy See, have achieved general recognition.[78]

---

[70] Kunz (1952), 46 *AJ* 307, 309–11; Sereni, op. cit. 188; Ehler (1961), 104 *HR* 1–68, 8.

[71] Graham, *The Rise of the Double Diplomatic Corps in Rome* (1952); Eustache (1972), *Grotius SP* 90–161, and *La Prassi Italiana di Diritto Internazionale (1861–1887)*, 303–34, 420–421.

[72] Cf. *Concordat (Germany) Case* (1957) 24 ILR 592; Wagnon, *Concordats et Droit International* (1933); de la Brière (1936), 63 *HR* 371–468; Ehler (1961), 104 *HR* 1–68.

[73] *Supra*, p. 153, n. 52.

[74] Brownlie, *Principles*, 68.

[75] Kunz (1952), 46 *AJ* 308, 310.

[76] Cf. *Ponce v. Roman Catholic Apostolic Church* 210 U.S. 296, 318 (1907) *per* Fuller C.J.

[77] Cited in Smith, *GB & LN* I, 220–1; cf. O'Connell, *International Law* I, 86.

[78] In 1973, 88 States maintained diplomatic relations with the Holy See. The U.S.S.R. has always refused to recognize the legal status of either the Holy See or the Vatican State, but its practice has not always been consistent with this profession: cf. Okeke, *Controversial Subjects of Contemporary International Law* (1974), 70–2.

The relation between them is however a matter of some uncertainty. There are three possibilities: that the only international legal person is the Vatican City;[79] that the only legal person is the Holy See which, as part of its activities, controls a certain territory and population;[80] or that there are two distinct legal persons, the Vatican and the Holy See.[81] In view of the entirely nominal character of the statehood of the Vatican, the second alternative has considerable attraction: however, the third hypothesis—that is, of dual personality—has been more generally accepted in the literature[82] and in practice.[83] For example, both the Vatican City and the Holy See are parties to a number of multilateral treaties. The Vatican City is a party to the Universal Postal Union and the International Telecommunications Union.[84] The Holy See is listed as a member of the International Atomic Energy Agency,[85] and is nominated as a contributor to the work of the functional agencies of the United Nations.[86] It would be helpful, and indeed significant, if accessions to multilateral treaties by the Vatican City had been restricted to cases where the primary application of the treaty was to the territory of the Vatican itself, whilst accession by the Holy See had taken place in cases of humanitarian treaties or treaties which were relevant to the more general religious or cultural purposes of the Holy See. To some extent (for example, with the functional international organizations) this may perhaps be the case: however practice with respect to multilateral treaties generally has been inconsistent. Thus the 'Vatican City' signed the International Wheat Agreement of 1956[87] and the Conven-

---

[79] Higgins (1929), 10 *BY* 214–17; *semble*, Oppenheim (8th edn.) I, 254–5.

[80] Siotto-Pintor (1932), 41 *HR* 247, 331–2; Mendelson (1972), 21 *ICLQ* 609, 611–12; Verhoeven, *Reconnaissance*, 170–6.

[81] Kunz, op. cit.; Sereni, op. cit. 231 & n; Ehler, op. cit. 9; Anzilotti (1929), 9 *Rdi* 165–176; Pallieri (1930), 53 *Riv. Int. di Scienze Sociali* 195–221.

[82] See also the works cited in Oppenheim (8th edn.) I, 254n. 2; Okeke, op. cit. 65–78.

[83] Cf. Art. III (1), Spanish Concordat (1953): 160 *BFSP* 698.

[84] *Supra*, p. 156 n. 66. But cf. the discrepancy between 186 *UNTS* 656 (where the Vatican City is listed as having ratified the 1952 Brussels Postal Convention) and 639 *UNTS* 368 (where the Holy See is listed as having ratified the 1964 Vienna Postal Convention.)

[85] But in 293 *UNTS* 359, the Statute of the IAEA is stated to have been ratified by the Vatican City: cf. 471 *UNTS* 334.

[86] Cf. G.A. Res. 3654 (XXV), 4 Dec. 1970.

[87] 270 *UNTS* 104 (ratified 9 July 1956); also 604 *UNTS* 378.

tion on the Recovery Abroad of Maintenance,[88] but the 'Holy See' signed the 1958 Convention on the Recognition and Enforcement of Foreign Arbitral Awards,[89] and the 1965 Convention on Transit Trade of Land-Locked States.[90] On the other hand, the Holy See has ratified the two Vienna Conventions on Diplomatic and Consular Relations,[91] the conventions on the laws of war,[92] and various conventions relating to cultural property and copyright.[93] Equally, some bilateral treaties are concluded with the Holy See, [94] others with the Vatican State.[95]

On the basis that there exist two legal persons—the Holy See and the State of the City of the Vatican—a further question arises as to the exact legal relation between them. This has variously been described as a real union,[96] or a form of vassalage.[97] The purposes of classification in this context must however be borne in mind. On the whole, terms such as 'vassal' or 'real' or 'personal union', while they may accurately describe a particular state of affairs and thus aid comprehension of it, do not carry with them general or distinctive legal characteristics.[98] To some extent the desire to particularize or categorize the relationship between the two entities reduces itself to a semantic dispute. In any case the analogy with a real union does not seem particularly useful;[99] that of vassal State, though better, is probably also inappropriate.[100] The position would appear to be

---

[88] 268 *UNTS* 32, 84 (unratified).

[89] 330 *UNTS* 38 (unratified).

[90] 597 *UNTS* 42 (unratified).

[91] 500 *UNTS* 204; 596 *UNTS* 261.

[92] 75 *UNTS* 287 (ratified 21 Feb. 1951).

[93] 216 *UNTS* 132; 260 *UNTS* 219; 287 *UNTS* 351.

[94] Apart from the Concordats see e.g. 260 *UNTS* 319. The Holy See also ratified the Convention and Protocol relating to the Status of Refugees (1951, 1967): 189 *UNTS* 137; 606 *UNTS* 268. The 1951 Convention was ratified with the reservation that 'the application of the Convention must be compatible in practice with the special nature of the Vatican City State and without prejudice to the norms governing access to and sojourn therein. . .'

[95] See the list in Okeke, op. cit. 74–6.

[96] Sereni, op. cit. 293; Ehler, op. cit. 10–11.

[97] Kunz (1952), 46 *AJ* 308, 313; Cumbo (1948), 2 *ILQ* 603, 613–14.

[98] *Infra*, pp. 186, 288.

[99] A real union is normally understood as a union of governments of two distinct territorial entities. This does not adequately describe the relation between the Vatican and the Holy See: cf. Ehler, op. cit. 10–11.

[100] States are usually subject to their government: the requirement of independence relates to the governments of *other* States.

that the relation is one of State and government, but with the peculiarity that the government in question, the Holy See, has an additional non-territorial status, which is in practice more significant than its status *qua* government of the City of the Vatican. A fairly exact parallel would exist if the United Nations were granted sovereignty over some small territory which was then recognized as a State. In such a case the status of the United Nations *qua* government of the territory concerned would not derogate from its general legal status *qua* international organization. *Mutatis mutandis* the same has been true of the Holy See after 1929.[101]

5.4 'INTERNATIONALIZED TERRITORIES': THE FREE CITY OF DANZIG

(1) *The Concept of 'internationalized territories'*

A persistent form of organization of territories disputed between States on strategic or ethnic or other grounds has been the establishment of autonomous entities under a form of international protection, supervision or guarantee. Such entities have been referred to generically as 'internationalized territories'.[102] But there appears to be no legal—as distinct from political—concept of 'internationalized territory': in fact the cases discussed vary considerably in nature and extent. For example, some territories, such as the Memel Territory (1924– 39)[103] or the Saar Territory (1920–35, 1945–57)[104] were

---

[101] Cf. the (probably particular) legal personality of the Sovereign Order of St. John of Malta: Breycha-Vauthier and Potulicki (1954), 48 *AJ* 554–63; Farran (1954), 3 *ICLQ* 217–34; Brownlie, *Principles*, 88; Verhoeven, *Reconnaissance*, 176–82; *Nanni* v. *Pace & Sovereign Order of Malta* (1935) 8 A.D. No. 2; *Répertoire suisse* I, 498–9.

[102] Ydit, *Internationalized Territories* (1961); Marazzi, *I Territori Internazionalizzati* (1959).

[103] See Convention & Statute of the Memel Territory (1924), 29 *LNTS* 87, 95. Art. 2 of the Convention accorded the Territory 'under the sovereignty of Lithuania, ... legislative, judicial, administrative and financial autonomy within the limits prescribed by the Statute . . .' See *Interpretation of the Statute of the Memel Territory (Merits)* Ser. A/B No. 49 (1932), 33–4, and cf. Minority Opinion, 56–7; Ydit, *Internationalized Territories*, 48–50; Kalijarvi (1936), 30 *AJ* 204–14.

[104] There were indeed two different 'Saar Territories'. The first Saar Territory was ceded to France for fifteen years (1920–35) by Arts. 45–50 of the Treaty of Versailles, as compensation for war damage. Germany renounced 'the government of the territory' (Art. 49) but remained residual sovereign. The territory itself was regarded, by German Courts at least, as still part of the Reich: *Saar Territory (Trade Marks) Case* 7 AD No. 24 (1934). Convictions in the Territory were convictions 'in Germany' for the purpose of a

established as autonomous areas within States, but with a form of international protection. Other 'international' territories, such as the International City of Tangier,[105] or the International Settlement of Shanghai (1845–1955),[106] were rather an extension and institutionalization of the system of capitulations than a protectorate or other distinct entity.

More significant for our purposes are those entities established on territory not part of another State and given substantial powers of internal self-government. For example, the Free City of Cracow was established by Article 6 of the Final Declaration of the Congress of Vienna as 'in perpetuity a free, independent City, strictly neutral, under the protection of Russia, Austria and Prussia'.[107] Perpetuity in this case lasted until 1846, when the territory was, by agreement between the protecting Powers (but without the consent of the organs of the Free City), annexed by Austria.[108] Ydit considers that it was 'never a viable State entity' in view of the threats to its independence from the protecting States on the one hand and Poland on the other.[109]

Another failed 'Free City' in modern times was the Free City of Trieste, which was to be constituted as an autonomous entity under Article 21 of the Italian Peace Treaty of 1947, with its 'integrity and independence' to be guaranteed by the Security Council.[110] Under its Permanent Statute a Governor, national of

law concerning recidivism: *Status of the Saar Territory Case* (1930) 5 AD No. 18. Inhabitants of the territory under Art. 296 of the Treaty of Versailles retained German nationality: *Muller* v. *Roeckling Bros.* (1923) 3 *Rep. MAT* 883. See also the Protocol between the German Government and the Saar Basin Territory (1921) 5 *LNTS* 208 Art. II. The Saar Territory was returned to Germany in 1935 after a plebiscite: see Ydit, *Internationalized Territories*, 44–5; Temperley, op. cit. II, 176–84; Bisschop, *The Saar Controversy* (1924); Rousseau, *DIP* II, 414–18. However it was, after a fashion, reconstituted and given *de facto* autonomy in part of the French zone of occupation in 1945. See *Rendition of Suspected Criminal (Saar Territory) Case* (1955) 22 ILR 512; *Statute of Saar Territory Case*, ibid. 630; Whiteman, 3 *Digest* 392–425; Freymond, *The Saar Conflict 1945–1955* (1960); Rousseau, *DIP* II, 418–23. The Territory was reincorporated into the German Federal Republic from 1 Jan. 1957. See French-G.F.R. Agreement of 27 Oct. 1956, 162 *BFSP* 957.

[105] For details see Ydit, *Internationalized Territories*, 154–84; Stuart, *The International City of Tangier* (2nd edn., 1955); Gutteridge (1957), 33 *BY* 296–302; Delore (1941), 35 *AJ* 140–5; del Castillo (1951), 20 *RIFDG* 18–25, 165–80; Rousseau, *DIP* II, 430–40.

[106] Ydit, *Internationalized Territories*, 127–53.

[107] (1815) 2 *BFSP* 12. See also Additional Treaty relative to Cracow, ibid. 74; and Constitution, ibid. 80.

[108] 35 *BFSP* 1088.

[109] *Internationalized Territories*, 95–108, 107; cf. Verzijl, *International Law* II, 502–3. For the short-lived Free City of Fiume see ibid. 503–4; Ydit, op. cit. 51–9; 120 *BFSP* 685.

[110] 49 *UNTS* 3, 137–9.

neither Yugoslavia nor Italy, was to be appointed by the Security Council, and to administer the territory in conjunction with a local executive and legislature, but with considerable personal authority: the Governor was to be subject only to the direction of the Security Council.[111] The Territory was to have its own foreign affairs powers: it was not subject to the veto of any one State. But, as the London Agreement of 1954 states, 'it . . . proved impossible to put into effect the provisions of the Italian Peace Treaty relating to the Free Territory . . .'[112] The particular difficulty was the appointment of a Director—but this was symptomatic of wider, irreconcilable, differences of interest between the parties.[113] Accordingly, after seven uncontemplated years of Allied (United Kingdom–United States) Military Government in Zone 'A' of the proposed Territory, and of Yugoslavian administration of Zone 'B', the parties principally concerned agreed that Zone 'A', with minor rectifications and including the port itself, should be reoccupied by Italy, and that Zone 'B' should continue to be administered by Yugoslavia.[114] Despite the abandonment of the Trieste proposal, the Italian Council of State held in 1961 that Italy had not regained sovereignty over Zone 'A':

If . . . the object of the Memorandum had been to renew the full, normal and final exercise of sovereignty by Italy over Zone A and in consequence to recognize that Yugoslavia had an absolute right of sovereignty over Zone B, then the Memorandum would have purported to modify the terms of the Treaty of Peace. But the Memorandum was not an instrument which could technically achieve such an object for the reason, if for no other, that the other signatories of the Treaty of Peace did not participate in the Memorandum . . . Though politically and in fact the Memorandum created a new state of affairs, in law it was based on Annex VII of the treaty, which gives the Allied military commands the right to administer their respective Zones . . .[115]

---

[111] Ibid., Annex VI, 186–97.

[112] 235 *UNTS* 99, Art. 1 (Italy, U.S.A., U.K., Yugoslavia).

[113] Ydit, *Internationalized Territories*, 231–72.

[114] Trieste was to remain a Free Port (Art. 5). Minority guarantees were provided (Annex II): Schwelb (1955), 49 *AJ* 240–8.

[115] *Società Teatro Puccini* v. *Commissioner-General of the Government for the Territory of Trieste* 40 ILR 43, 47–8. Courts in the Territory have continued to be 'Italian' by the same process of redelegation: *C.E.A.T.* v. *Società Hungaria* (1951) 18 ILR 81; *Soc. Immobiliare Roma-Trieste* v. *Stabilimento Tipografico Triestino e Soc. Editrice del 'Piccolo'* (1952) 19 ILR 145.

But this anomalous situation did not appear to have any significant international legal effects.[116] Politically it cannot be said that these experiments in internationalization have been very successful.[117] However, the classification of such territories as States, either generally or for specific purposes, remains a matter of some interest. A significant example of an internationalized territory was the Free City of Danzig, a brief account of which follows.

(2) *The legal status of the Free City of Danzig*[118]

The Free City of Danzig (like the Memel Territory in respect of Lithuania) was established in 1919 to ensure Poland's access to the sea, while safeguarding the interests of the inhabitants. On the other hand, unlike the Memel Territory, Danzig was not ceded to the State in whose interests it was created, but put under a special regime. By Article 100 of the Treaty of Versailles, Germany renounced its rights over the territory delineated there in favour of the Principal Allied and Associated Powers, who in turn undertook 'to establish the town of Danzig, together with the rest of the territory . . . as a Free City. It will be placed under the protection of the League of Nations.'[119] The Constitution of the Free City, drawn up by its representatives in agreement with a High Commissioner appointed by the League, was also placed under League guarantee.[120] Differences as to the Treaty provisions were to be decided, in the first instance, by the High Commissioner, but ultimately by the League. By Article 104 the

---

[116] See further Whiteman, 3 *Digest* 68–109; Udina, *Scritti sulla Questione di Trieste* (1969); Gervais (1947), 51 *RGDIP* 134–54; Conforti (1955), 38 *Rdi* 568–83. On 1 Oct. 1975, Italy and Yugoslavia announced their agreement to a 'final settlement' of the Trieste situation, accepting as permanent (with minor amendments) the 1954 interim settlement: *Keesing's* 1975, 27428A; (1976) 80 *RGDIP* 949–51. The Treaty of Osimo (in force 3 April 1977) is apparently regarded as superseding the London Agreement of 1954, on what basis is not clear. See further Udina (1977), 60 *Rdi* 405–41.

[117] This is the theme of Ydit, *Internationalized Territories, passim.*

[118] Ydit, *Internationalized Territories*, 50–1, 185–230; Brownlie, *Principles*, 63–4; Verzijl, *International Law* II, 500–2, 510–45; Hostie, *Questions de Principe relatives au statut international de Dantzig* (1934); Lewis (1924), 5 *BY* 89–102; Morrow (1937), 18 *BY* 114–26; Mason, *The Danzig Dilemma* (1946); Levesque, *La Situation internationale de Dantzig* (1924); Makowski (1923), 30 *RGDIP* 169–222; Redslob, *Le Statut international de Dantzig* (1926); Piccioni (1921), 28 *RGDIP* 84–106; Rousseau, *DIP* II, 423–30; and see the interesting analysis by Skubiszewski, 'Gdansk and the Dissolution of the Free City' in *Menzel Festschrift* (1975), 470–85.

[119] 112 *BFSP* 64–7, Art. 102.

[120] Ibid., Art. 103.

Powers undertook to negotiate a treaty between Poland and Danzig providing *inter alia* for Poland to undertake Danzig's foreign relations: this was done by the Treaty of Paris of 9 November 1920,[121] which, despite its enforced character, was 'an international agreement governed by international law' between Poland and Danzig.[122]

Two issues have arisen about this rather complex set of relations: whether Danzig was a 'State', and whether the relationship between Danzig and the League, or Danzig and Poland, constituted a protectorate. However, while there are various legal consequences attaching to statehood, the same cannot be said of 'protectorate'. The legal significance of the relationship between Poland and Danzig does not depend upon whether we term it a 'protectorate'. In fact, although Poland had important rights in respect of Danzig territory, the local administration did not cease to be independent in respect of all other matters. Moreover, while Poland had charge of Danzig's foreign relations, this was, as the Permanent Court held, a combination of an agency arrangement with a right of veto:

. . . the rights of Poland as regards the foreign relations of the Free City are not absolute. The Polish Government is not entitled to impose a policy on the Free City nor to take any step in connection with the foreign relations of the Free City against its will. On the other hand, the Free City cannot call upon Poland to take any step in connection with the foreign relations of the Free City which are opposed to her own policy . . .[123]

In view of Article 102 of the Treaty of Versailles, there might be more basis for terming the Danzig–League of Nations relation a protectorate, but once again no legal consequences ensue from such determination. As the Court held:

the League of Nations, as guarantor of the Constitution of the Free City [had] the right . . . as well as the duty, to intervene in the event of an erroneous application by Danzig of its constitution . . .[124]

Thus:

though the interpretation of the Danzig Constitution (was) primarily

[121] 6 *LNTS* 190.
[122] *Jurisdiction of the Courts of Danzig*, Ser. B No. 15 (1928), 17.
[123] *Free City of Danzig and the I.L.O.*, Ser. B No. 18 (1930), 13.
[124] *Treatment of Polish Nationals in the Danzig Territory*, Ser. A/B No. 44 (1932), 21.

an internal question of the Free City, it may involve the guarantee of the League of Nations, as interpreted by the Council and by the Court.[125]

On the other hand, although this has been denied by most commentators,[126] it seems clear that the Free City was a State in the sense in which that term has been defined.[127] Danzig had its own nationality.[128] It was bound by, and had the benefit of, 'the ordinary rules governing relations between States . . . With regard to Poland, the Danzig Constitution, despite its peculiarities, (was) . . . the Constitution of a foreign State'.[129] In contentious proceedings before the Court it was entitled to appoint a judge *ad hoc* under Article 71(2) of the Rules of Court, which refers to 'an existing dispute between two or more States or Members of the League of Nations',[130] Complaints by Poland with regard to breaches by Danzig of its Constitution were matters of Danzig's 'domestic jurisdiction': the status of Danzig was not such as to eliminate 'the ordinary legal distinction between matters of a domestic and of an international character'.[131] Danzig was eligible for membership of international organizations such as the League, subject to the Polish right of veto. The obligations of membership would, of course, be 'international obligations for the Free City' and not for Poland.[132] Significantly, the *Lotus* presumption applied in Danzig's favour, in cases of doubt: 'The port of Danzig is not Polish territory and therefore the rights claimed by Poland would be exercised in derogation of the rights of the Free City. Such rights must

---

[125] *Consistency of Certain Danzig Legislative Decrees with the Constitution of the Free City*, Ser. A/B No. 65 (1935), 13: but cf. Judge Anzilotti (diss.), 24.

[126] Morrow (1937), 18 *BY* 114, 126; Ydit, *Internationalized Territories*, 224; Lewis (1924), 5 *BY* 89, 100 ('*sui generis*'); Marek, *Identity and Continuity*, 168n.; Skubiszewski, op. cit. 471–4.

[127] Hostie, *Questions de principe relatives au statut international de Danzig* (1934); de Weck, *La Condition juridique du Conseil du Port et des Voies d'Eau de Dantzig* (1933), 74.

[128] Treaty of Versailles, Art. 105.

[129] *Treatment of Polish Nationals in Danzig*, Ser. A/B No. 44 (1932), 23–4.

[130] *Polish War Vessels in the Port of Danzig*, Ser. A/B No. 43 (1931), 7.

[131] *Treatment of Polish Nationals in Danzig*, Ser. A/B No. 44 (1932), 23–4.

[132] *The Free City of Danzig and the International Labour Organization*, Ser. B. No. 18 (1930), 15; *per* Judge Anzilotti, sep. op., 22. That Danzig, despite its political association with Poland, was not assimilated to Polish territory appears from the provisions of the U.K.–Poland Agreement and Secret Protocol of 25 Aug. 1939, providing *inter alia* that an attack on Danzig was an action threatening 'directly or indirectly the independence of Poland': Agreement, Art. 2(1), Protocol Art. 2: Cmd. 6616.

therefore be established on a clear basis.'[133] And this *jurisprudence constante* in favour of the statehood, for purposes of international law, of the Free City is supported by municipal decisions in a variety of jurisdictions.[134]

Danzig suffered the same fate as Poland, being invaded by Germany on 1 September 1939. The City was annexed; but was committed to Polish administration in 1945 'pending the final determination of Poland's western frontier'.[135] The Polish Supreme Court has since referred to Danzig as 'united with the rest of the territory of the Polish State on a basis of complete equality',[136] but the British view, at least in 1945, was that Danzig would not come under Polish sovereignty until a final settlement.[137]

(3) *Recent trends in internationalization: Cyprus*

It is clear then that internationalized territories such as Danzig may qualify as States under international law. However, they are undoubtedly artificial creations in every sense, and the political failures of internationalization since 1945, for example in the cases of Trieste and Jerusalem,[138] have led to different devices being adopted to achieve substantially the same political ends. A good example of this trend is the case of Cyprus, which, rather than being established under a particular regime, was granted independence subject to significant constitutional and treaty limitations. Despite appearances, Cyprus and Danzig have much in common, both politically and so far as their juridical status is concerned.

[133] *Polish War Vessels in the Port of Danzig*, Ser. A/B No. 43 (1931), 18. In *Polish Postal Service in Danzig*, Ser. B. No. 11 (1925), 39–40, the *Lotus* presumption was not applied in Danzig's favour because the relevant provisions as interpreted were clear.

[134] *The Blonde* [1921] P. 155, 163–4 *per* Duke P.; [1922] 1 A.C. 313, 338–9 (P.C.); *Danzig Pension Case* (1929) 5 AD No. 41; *In re M. (Danzig Conviction Case)* (1933) 7 AD No. 23; *U.S. ex rel. Zeller* v. *Watkins* 167 F.2d. 279 (1948); *In re Nix* (1951) 18 ILR 260; cf. *In re Kruger* (1951) ibid. 258.

[135] Protocol of the Proceedings of the Berlin Conference, 2 Aug. 1945: 145 *BFSP* 852, 866 (VIII B, 'Western Frontier of Poland').

[136] *L. & J.J.* v. *Polish State Rys.* (1948) 22 ILR 77. Skubiszewski argues convincingly for Polish title over Gdansk by consolidation: op. cit. 480–5.

[137] *H.C. Deb.* Vol. 414 pp. 292–3, 10 Oct. 1945 (Bevin); cf. ibid. Vol. 415 cols. 406–7, 31 Oct. 1945. Polish sovereignty over Gdansk was apparently acknowledged by Britain and the United States in 1976, when they agreed to return to Poland gold previously the property of the Free City: see (1977) 81 *RGDIP* 575.

[138] *Infra*, p. 333.

The Republic of Cyprus became independent on 16 August 1960, at which time its population was divided into tightly organized and mutually antagonistic ethnic groups (80 per cent Greek, and 20 per cent Turkish). Independence was preceded by drawn-out negotiations between the Governments of Greece and Turkey, resulting in a basic agreement[139] which was then approved with certain amendments by the British Government, and accepted by representatives of the Greek and Turkish communities on Cyprus.[140] The Constitution thus framed was formally brought into effect by a United Kingdom Order-in-Council under authority conferred by a United Kingdom statute.[141] Britain retained two 'sovereign base areas' and certain other military rights.[142]

The 1960 Constitution itself has 199 articles, forty-eight of which are expressed to be unalterable.[143] By Article 181 (itself unalterable), the Treaties of Alliance[144] and Guarantee[145] are given constitutional force. As a result Cyprus is bound, apparently in perpetuity, to accept tripartite military forces on its territory.[146] The purpose of the force is stated to be 'to resist any attack or aggression, direct or indirect . . . against the independence or the territorial integrity of the Republic of Cyprus'.[147] Considered in isolation the Treaty of Alliance appears unexceptional, but some of the provisions of the Treaty of Guarantee cast doubt on its legality. By Article IV of the latter Treaty, in the event of breach by Cyprus of certain undertakings, and in default of common action by the three guarantor powers, each of them 'reserves the right to take action with the sole aim of reestablishing the state of affairs created by the present Treaty.' And Cyprus undertakes to 'ensure' respect for its

[139] Basic Structure of the Republic of Cyprus, London, 19 Feb. 1959: 164 *BFSP* 219.

[140] Emilianides, *Mélanges Séfériades* (1961) II, 629–39; Xydis, *Cyprus, Reluctant Republic* (1973).

[141] S.I. 1960 No. 1363, under the Cyprus Act, 1960. Cf. 25 ILR 27.

[142] 164 *BFSP* 219; Cyprus Act, s. 2; Treaty of Guarantee, ibid. 388, Art. 3; Higgins, *Development*, 33–4; *Mizrihi* v. *Republic of Cyprus* (1963) 41 ILR 25.

[143] Art. 182 (1), Annex III; *Cmd.* 1093 (1960), 91–172. Although the present status of the Constitution is uncertain, it still serves to illustrate the limitations on Cypriot independence which are very likely to continue, under whatever forms. See further Polyviou, *Cyprus in search of a Constitution* (Nicosia, 1976).

[144] 164 *BFSP* 557.

[145] Ibid. 388.

[146] Treaty of Alliance, Art. III.

[147] Ibid., Art. II.

Constitution, to maintain its independence and security, and to prohibit 'any activity likely to promote, directly or indirectly, either union with any other State or partition of the Island.'[148] Interpreted liberally, the Treaty of Guarantee would appear to allow unilateral military intervention by each of the Powers in a wide variety of circumstances, and to demolish the domestic jurisdiction of Cyprus in the most important areas. Not surprisingly, the Government of Cyprus subsequently argued that Article IV was null and void as in breach of the Charter.[149] Alternatively, it might well have argued that the exercise of any right of military intervention ensured by the Treaty became illegal on Cyprus's admission to the United Nations. Presumably though, Article IV, which in terms 'reserves' the right to take unspecified action, must be interpreted by reference to the Charter, so as not to include any right of intervention except where consistent, in particular, with Articles 2(4) and 51. But Turkey has claimed the right to intervene in Cyprus with armed force under certain circumstances, and has done so on a number of occasions.

As a result of civil disturbances between the two Cypriot communities, a United Kingdom Truce Force, with the consent of the Cyprus Government, was formed in an attempt to restore order: the British view was that this Force was not operating under Article IV of the Treaty of Guarantee, but only by consent of the territorial sovereign.[150] The Truce Force was, on 27 March 1963, replaced by the United Nations Force in Cyprus (UNFICYP), the activities of which are continuing.[151]

Cyprus was admitted by unanimous vote to the United Nations on 24 August 1960: no question of its independent statehood has been raised by other States or in international organizations.[152] As has been seen, its theoretical international independence is rather greater than it is in practice or according to its constitution.

---

[148] Treaty of Guarantee, Art. I.

[149] *SCOR* 1098th mtg., 27 Feb. 1964, 15–31; *BPIL* 1964/I, 3–11, 8–9. For contrary British argument see ibid., 11–12. Cf. Shwelb (1967), 61 *AJ* 952–3.

[150] *SCOR* 1098th mtg., 27 Feb. 1964, 13; *BPIL* 1964/I, 7–8. Cf. *Nissan* v. *A.G.* [1970] A.C. 179, 206 *per* Lord Reid; 215, *per* Lord Morris; 223, *per* Lord Pearce; 237, *per* Lord Pearson; cf. 230, *per* Lord Wilberforce.

[151] See Bowett, *United Nations Forces* (1964), 552–60; Seyersted, *United Nations Forces in the Law of Peace and War* (1966), 79–85, 427–47.

[152] But cf. Higgins, *Development*, 33–4 (Cyprus 'very close to the borderline of lack of true independence').

The case of Cyprus illustrates the predominantly formal character of the criterion of independence, and the way in which statehood may coincide with substantial lack of actual independence. Given the intractable nature of the Cyprus situation, it is doubtful that any more formal arrangement for international control would have been more successful. But it could equally be said that the various limitations on Cypriot sovereignty in effect introduce internationalization by the back door.[153]

[153] Cf. however Rousseau, *DIP* II, 447–8. See further Lavroff (1961), 65 *RGDIP* 527–45; E. Lauterpacht (1960), 9 *ICLQ* 253–6; Dendas, in *Schätzel Festschrift* (1960), 71–103; Tsoutsos, *Politique et droit dans les relations internationales* (1967), 89–141; and Ehrlich, *Cyprus, 1958–1967* (1974). For materials on the 1974 crisis see 13 *ILM* 1254 and cf. *supra* p. 118, n. 157.

PART II: THE CREATION OF STATES IN INTERNATIONAL LAW

> [T]he proposition that the origination of a State is always and necessarily an historical fact happening beyond the realm of international law is an unfounded doctrinal *a priori*, contradicted by the facts of international law itself. (Verzijl, *International Law* II, 62–4, 63.)

ALTHOUGH international law does not, in general, 'create' States,[1] it does contain rules providing workable criteria for statehood, as we have seen: moreover, by determining in at least some cases the rights and duties of the participants during the process by which a State is formed, it also, *pro tanto*, regulates that process.[2]

In this section are examined the various contexts in which, and methods by which, new States are created. These include: the original creation of States on unoccupied territory; the creation and status of dependent States and other entities; grants by or forcible seizure of independence from a previous sovereign; the consolidation of autonomous or separate parts of 'divided States', and the various forms of amalgamation or merger into 'unions of States' with distinct legal personality. It must be emphasized that these distinctions between the various 'modes' of creation of new States, like the distinctions between the various 'modes' of acquisition of territory, do not provide a rigid, overriding formula. They are rather a convenient categorization of the various distinct ways in which, historically, new States have been created; and they thus provide a basis for discussion of particular problems, and for application of the basic, overriding, criteria discussed in Part I.

[1] Erich (1926), 13 *HR* 427–507, 442; Arangio-Ruiz, 7–8.
[2] Cf. Marek, *Identity and Continuity*, 1–2; Kelsen (1929), 4 *RDI* 613–41.

6. Original Acquisition and Problems of Statehood

6.1 GENERAL CONSIDERATIONS

THE QUESTION of the legal status of native tribes and other polities outside the ambit of the European political system was long one of the great issues of international law. Victoria's *De Indis*,[1] for example, written to vindicate the private and public rights of the Central American Indians, is only the best known work of an extensive literature concerned with the problem.[2] The point of the debate was twofold: to examine the moral propriety of European actions, and to determine the legal effect of the various transactions of the explorers and colonizers. Given the relatively non-peremptory nature of international law at the time, the former was probably the more important: nevertheless State practice, with at least some consistency, did attach significance to the legal incidents of the acquisition of territory from, and the government of, native tribes and other entities in the Americas, Africa, and Asia. That it still may do so is evident from the Advisory Opinion of the International Court in the *Western Sahara Case*.[3] At least a summary statement of the position is in order here.

In its essentials, the problem concerned acquisition of territory and its effects. Central to the traditional law was the notion of territory unoccupied and unacquired—*terra nullius*. Such territory could be acquired merely by occupation sufficiently effective.[4]

---

[1] *De Indis et de Jure Belli Relectiones* (1532, publ. posth., 1557).

[2] Lindley, 10–23 and works there cited. See also Alexandrowicz (1968–9), 43 *BY* 205–208; (1963) 39 *BY* 441–8; (1959) 35 *BY* 162–82.

[3] I.C.J. Rep. 1975, p. 12.

[4] It has been argued that, at least prior to 1800, discovery alone, or discovery accompanied by symbolic acts, was sufficient to establish title to *terra nullius*: Keller, Lissitzyn, and Mann, *Creation of Rights of Sovereignty through Symbolic Acts 1400–1800* (1938); Simsarian (1938), 53 *Pol. Sc. Q.* 111–28. The better view is that neither was sufficient to create a valid title, although they might establish a right in the State concerned to perfect its title by effective occupation: cf. Judge Huber, *Island of Palmas Case* (1928), 2 *RIAA* 829, 845–6; Jennings, *Acquisition of Territory*, 4, 29. In the various African arbitrations, discovery, while no doubt relevant, was never treated as decisive: see e.g. the *Island of*

On the other hand, where territory was already occupied or acquired, cession, conquest (and possibly prescription) were the appropriate modes.[5] But the category *terra nullius* was not self-defining, nor did practice bear out the positivist assumption that territory was either unoccupied or part of an existing State. *Terra nullius* was a residual category; and it is necessary to determine in what cases, before European colonization, territory was regarded as occupied whether by native States or other entities with a degree of political organization. A second, in practice more controversial, issue was the legal effect of acquisition of territory on the status of its inhabitants: did they possess any continuing international legal rights under the treaties, whether of cession or protection, and if so, how were these to be exercised? In this area clarity of analysis is particularly difficult to attain; the notions of absolute State sovereignty and of international law as the law of the Concert of Nations which gained currency in the nineteenth century, together with the fact that that law allowed in any case very extensive freedom of action to its subjects, both tend to confuse and blur the issues. Appeal to particular conventional rights was misleading (and was sometimes intended to be) when general international law provided adequate, though unpalatable, grounds for action. For modern commentators this complexity is increased in that the intertemporal law requires assessment in the light of the law in force at the relevant time, so that concepts foreign to modern international law may still produce important effects under that law.[6] But a distinction may be made between the actual legal effects of transactions which took place at a certain period, and the juristic theories then accepted as explaining the transactions. The intertemporal law certainly does not require the continued

---

Bulamu Arbitration (1870): Hertslet, *Map of Africa by Treaty* (3rd edn., 1909) III, 988; *Delogoa Bay Arbitration* (1875), ibid. 996. To the same effect *Johnson and Graham's Lessee* v. *McIntosh* (1823) 5 L.ed. 681, 692–3 *per* Marshall C.J.; Lindley, 26.

[5] Similarly, the common law distinguished between conquered or ceded and settled territory. In the former case, existing laws and customs applied until changed; in the latter, the common law was, so far as applicable, received *ab initio*. See *Anon* (1722) 2 P. Wms. 75, 24 E.R. 646; *Blankard* v. *Galdy* (1692) 4 Mod. 222, 87 E.R. 359; *Bl. Comm.* I, 108–9. But *Calvin's Case* (1608) 7 Co. Rep. Ia, 77 E.R. 377, 398, which is sometimes cited in this context, only established a distinction between conquest of a Christian Kingdom and conquest of an infidel kingdom: cf. also Littleton's note, 1 Salk. 49, 91 E.R. 46.

[6] Cf. *Right of Passage Case* I.C.J. Rep. 1960 p. 6, 37; *Island of Palmas Case* (1928) 2 *RIAA* 829, 845.

acceptance of the latter, except to the extent that they were embodied in the transactions themselves. Nor does it require exclusive concentration on the older law. At the least, continued effective exercise is necessary for the retention of rights which by modern standards were wrongfully acquired:[7] such rights may therefore be more readily lost. Moreover in certain cases new peremptory norms of general international law, or new conventional or customary rules, may require some degree of restitution of defeated rights or interests.[8]

More fundamentally, three reservations may be made concerning the law as propounded by late nineteenth-century writers.[9] In the first place, that view of the law was itself 'new', for the older writers were considerably more willing to accord legal personality to native tribes both before and after European penetration of their territories.[10] Moreover, it was a view of the law which, though dominant, was not unchallenged at the time, and was far from unchallengeable.[11] In the second place, State practice, though it sometimes relied on the positivist view, was by no means unambiguously in its favour. The common law's continuing insistence on even colonial protectorates as extraterritorial to the dominions of the Crown was an example of the influence of older doctrine and practice.[12] Thirdly, the positivist practice was, so far as legal basis existed for it, to a great degree conventional. By insisting on its version of paramountcy of the Crown over the Indian Native States, Great Britain enforced agreement where none was necessary; and the legal foundation of paramountcy was that very enforced consent. These points, so far as they relate to dependent statehood, will be discussed further in the next Chapter.

Finally brief mention will be made here of those rather rare cases where new States (as distinct from colonies or dependent entities) have been created on unoccupied or abandoned territory.

---

[7] Judge Huber, *Island of Palmas Case*, op. cit.

[8] For *jus cogens* see *supra*, p. 81. See also *infra*, Chs. 13, 14.

[9] e.g. Westlake, *Collected Papers* (ed. Oppenheim, 1911), 139–57; Lorimer, *Institutes of the Law of Nations* (1883) I, 101.

[10] Lindley, 17–20; *infra*, p. 176.

[11] Cf. O'Connell (1960), 54 *PAS* 77–84, 81.

[12] *Infra*, p. 201. Baty, (1921–2) 2 *BY* 109–21, 109 stated that 'the conception of a Protectorate has vitally altered its character within our own memory'.

6.2 INTERNATIONAL STATUS OF NATIVE COMMUNITIES

(1) *Statehood of native communities*

It appears that at least some communities were generally regarded not only as legal occupants of their territory but as fully sovereign States in international law.[13] Although some writers required a certain degree of civilization as a prerequisite for statehood,[14] it had long been established that the only necessary pre-condition was a degree of governmental authority sufficient for the general maintenance of order,[15] and subsequent practice was not sufficiently consistent or coherent to change that position. Although in many cases an extensive system of capitulations and concessions was established,[16] Asian States such as (for example) China, the Ottoman Empire,[17] Afghanistan, Japan, Korea, Thailand (Siam),[18] and the Maratha Empire in India[19] were early recognized as sovereign States subject to international law. This did not of course mean that identical rules were applied to such States as were by European States *inter se*, but that is to be explained not by any distinction between 'civilized' and 'barbarous' States but because many of those rules were what would now be called regional customs rather than general international law.[20]

Nor were African communities necessarily disqualified from statehood. The independence of the Kingdom of Swaziland, for example, was explicitly recognized by Great Britain and the

[13] See the excellent discussion in Lindley, 10–47; and Alexandrowicz, *An Introduction to the History of the Law of Nations in the East Indies* (1967). See also Sinha, *New Nations and the Law of Nations* (1967), 12–27; Syatauw, *Some Newly Established Asian States and the Development of International Law* (1961), 48–52; Sastri (1953), 2 *Indian YBIA* 133–52.

[14] In particular Westlake, in *Collected Papers*, 139–57, 145, who required a 'native government capable of controlling white men or under which white civilization can exist'.

[15] *Supra*, p. 73 and authorities there cited.

[16] Especially in the earlier, mercantile, period these were not always unequal: Alexandrowicz, op. cit., Ch. 6, and *The European-African Confrontation. A Study in Treaty Making* (1973), 20–8, 83–91.

[17] *Supra*, p. 13.

[18] *Temple Case* I.C.J. Rep. 1962 p. 6.

[19] *Right of Passage Case* I.C.J. Rep. 1960 p. 6, 38.

[20] McNair, *International Law Opinions* I, 65; cf. Judge Spender diss., *Temple Case* I.C.J. Rep. 1962, p. 6, 128; *Right of Passage Case* I.C.J. Rep. 1960, p. 6, 37, 91–2.

South African Republic in 1881 and 1884.[21] Morocco,[22] Algeria,[23] and Tunisia were regarded, it seems, as independent States in the relatively short period between their devolution from the Ottoman Empire and the institution of protectorates by France and Spain.[24] In the Pacific, Hawaii, Tonga,[25] and, probably, Samoa[26] were so recognized. In general, foreign States looked for communities with 'indisputable pretensions to independence',[27] wherever situated and governed under whatever forms: between such communities, with the reservations already made, the general rules of international law were applied.

(2) *Legal personality of native communities not regarded as States*

A further question was whether communities organized on territory, but not possessing a sufficiently coherent and organized government to be termed States, were nevertheless in law occupants of their territory, so that it might only be acquired by cession or conquest, and not by occupation. Classic international

---

[21] Pretoria Convention (1881), 72 *BFSP* 900, Art. 24; London Convention (1884) 75 *BFSP* 5, Art. 12. A further convention of 1890 provided for the regulation of Swazi affairs 'with the consent of the Swazi Government': 82 *BFSP* 1062, Art. 1. Cf. also *Sobhuza II* v. *Miller* [1926] A.C. 518, 522. Zanzibar was another example: see the *Island of Lamu Arbitration* (1889) Hertslet, op. cit. III, 891, 898; ibid. I, 300–30. For Abyssinia, ibid. II, 421–63.

[22] In the *Western Sahara Case*, the International Court described Morocco in 1884 as 'a State of a special character', due to its decentralized structure: I.C.J. Rep. 1975 p. 12, 44–5.

[23] Bedjaoui, *Law and the Algerian Revolution* (1961), 17–22.

[24] Also Mössner, *Grotius SP 1972*, 197–221, 205, 209, 217. There were 367 treaties, declarations and agreements (not all public in character) between the Barbary Powers and European States: ibid. 212–13. See also Alexandrowicz, *The European-African Confrontation*, 18–28; de Montmorency (1918), 4 *Grotius ST* 87–94; *The Madonna del Burso* 4 C.Rob. 169, 165 E.R. 574 (1802) *per* Sir Wm. Scott: *The Magellan Pirates* 1 Sp.Ecc.&Ad. 81, 164 E.R. 47, 48; Bynkershoek, *Quaestionum Juris Publici Libri Duo* (1737) I, §§ 122–30. Gentili, cited by Bynkershoek as a proponent of the contrary view, seems to have regarded the Barbary pirates as distinct from the King of Barbary: *Hispanicae Advocationis Libri Duo* (1661) I, xv, §§ 67–8.

[25] See the Treaties of Friendship with France (65 *BFSP* 373), Germany (67 *BFSP* 167) and Great Britain (70 *BFSP* 9).

[26] See Moore, 1 *Digest* 27; but cf. McNair, op. cit. 66 (Samoa not 'a foreign State' for the purposes of the Naturalization Act, 1870, s. 6). See also the cases cited *supra*, p. 73; and Johnston, *Sovereignty and Protection* (1973), Ch. 4.

[27] Stamford Raffles to Lord Minto, 10 June 1811 (Malay States), cited in Harlow & Madden, eds., *British Colonial Documents 1774–1834*, 65. The orthodox test of independence was also applied, for example, by the King of Italy to the legal status of tribes in the area controlled by the Barotse Kingdom: (1905) Hertslet, op. cit. III, 1074. Cf. also *Foster* v. *Globe Venture Syndicate Ltd.* [1900] 1 Ch. 811, Farwell J. (status of tribes of Suss (Morocco)).

law had allowed, in Victoria's words, that 'the aborigines undoubtedly had true dominion in both public and private matters, and . . . neither their princes nor private persons could be despoiled of their property on the ground of their not being true owners'.[28] On the other hand, in a development parallel to those mentioned already, writers in the later nineteenth century inclined to the view that only 'sovereignty' was sufficient to preclude occupation, and that, to quote Westlake again 'an uncivilized tribe [could] grant by treaty such rights as it understands and exercises, but nothing more.'[29] At the Berlin Conference of 1885, this conflict of opinion was quite explicit. A Declaration relating to conditions for effective occupation of African territory[30] provided merely for public notification of any annexation or protectorate, together with an obligation to assure a sufficient authority in the territory to protect acquired rights and freedom of trade.[31] Taken by themselves these conditions were unobjectionable, but the omission of further conditions was significant. The United States delegate observed that

Modern international law follows closely a line which leads to the recognition of the right of native tribes to dispose freely of themselves and of their hereditary territory. In conformity with this principle my government would gladly adhere to a more extended rule, to be based on a principle which should aim at the voluntary consent of the natives whose country is taken possession of, in all cases where they had not provoked the aggression . . . [The Declaration] only points out the

---

[28] *De Indis*, I, prop. 24, § 334 (1532).

[29] Westlake, op. cit. 151. To the same effect Judge Huber in the *Island of Palmas Case*, (1928) 2 *RIAA* 829, 858: contracts with . . . '*native princes* or *chiefs* of *peoples* not recognized as members of the community of nations . . . are not, in the international law sense, treaties or conventions capable of creating rights and obligations such as may, in international law, arise out of treaties . . .' As it stands, this is tautologous; nor does it exclude the possibility that in at least some cases such agreements could have direct legal effects. It should also be noted that the native tribes in question were apparently at a very low level of organization: even then, their grants were capable of having 'indirect legal effects' (ibid.). The Cayuga Indians of North America were also stated not to be a 'legal unit of international law': *Cayuga Indians Claim* (1936) 6 *RIAA* 173, 176: their treaty of cession of lands was treated as a contract (186–7). Keller, Lissitzyn, and Mann, op. cit. 9, treat 'the acts of natives' quite generally 'merely as facts that showed the actual situation as to possession', or as 'akin to symbolic acts of possession' (140). Cf. also Fawcett, *British Commonwealth*, 113, 127n.

[30] 76 *BFSP* 4, 19.

[31] Arts. 34, 35.

minimum of the conditions which must necessarily be fulfilled ... [I]t is reserved for the respective signatory powers to determine all the other conditions from the point of view of right as well as fact which must be fulfilled before an occupation can be recognized as valid.[32]

Both Lugard[33] and Alexandrowicz[34] argue that this view was tacitly accepted at the Conference, though, in view of the reaction of some of the participants,[35] this may be doubted. Equally, when the *Institut de Droit International* examined the question of acquisition of territory at Lausanne in 1888, it endorsed substantially the same rules as established by the Berlin Conference;[36] but failed to accept the proposal ... 'That occupation by a civilized State of territory in Africa not occupied by any other civilized State ought to have as its basis arrangements with the chiefs of the aboriginal tribes.'[37]

But it is one thing to deny an entity statehood on grounds such as lack of independence or coherent organization,[38] and another to determine that the territory on which the entity is established is *terra nullius*. Different criteria were rightly applied to determine the two distinct statuses, which were not exhaustive. Thus land was *terra nullius* only if it was, in Blackstone's words, 'desart and uncultivated' or 'uninhabited'.[39] Thus the proposals not accepted in the 1880s do now represent, and it is submitted always have represented, general international law. Lindley, after a lengthy examination of the point, concluded that: 'in order that an area shall not be *territorium nullius* it would appear ... to be necessary and sufficient that it be inhabited by a political society, that is, by a considerable number of persons who are permanently united

---

[32] C.4361, 209; cited Westlake, op. cit. 140.

[33] *The Dual mandate in British Tropical Africa*, 11.

[34] *The European-African Confrontation*, 47.

[35] Cf. the German reply: Westlake, op. cit. 141 ('delicate questions, upon which the conference hesitated to express an opinion').

[36] Wehberg, ed., *Institut de Droit international, table général des resolutions 1875–1956* (1957), 68–9, Art. 1.

[37] 10 *Annuaire* 181–2. On the other hand, a resolution that 'aboriginal tribes and the territory inhabited by them are outside "the community of the law of nations"' was also defeated: loc. cit.

[38] Cf. the status of the 'Mauritanian entity' in the late nineteenth century: *Western Sahara Case* I.C.J. Rep. 1975 p. 12, 57, 63–4.

[39] *Bl. Comm.* I, 108. Keller, Lissitzyn, and Mann state that 'the presence of a savage population, of aborigines, or of nomadic tribes engaged in hunting and fishing' is consistent with territory being *terra nullius*, but give a more extensive interpretation to that formula than practice warrants: op. cit. 4.

by habitual obedience to a certain and common superior, or whose conduct in regard to their mutual relations habitually conforms to recognized standards.'[40] Put negatively, this involves the proposition that only 'an unsettled horde of wandering savages not yet formed into civil society,'[41] or, more neutrally, only nomadic tribesmen lacking all regular political organization, could be regarded as not legal occupants of their territory. In the light of modern anthropological knowledge it can be seen that unoccupied territories as so defined were few indeed: only Australia[42] and the South Island of New Zealand[43] were treated as falling within that category, apart from scattered islands or totally uninhabited tracts. Certainly, almost the whole of Africa was treated as occupied territory, and the method of acquisition was overwhelmingly that of cession or, in some cases, conquest.[44] Nor were the treaties so obtained always illusory or a mere sham.[45]

[40] Lindley, 22–3. Cf. Allott, in Widstrand, ed., *African Boundary Problems* (1969), 15; O'Connell, op. cit. 80–1.

[41] Wheaton, *Elements* Pt. I, Ch. 2, § 17; Moore, 1 *Digest* 15.

[42] *Cooper* v. *Stuart* (1889) 14 A.C. 286, 291 *per* Lord Watson, cited Lindley, 40–1; Evatt, *Grotius SP 1968*, 16–45, 18–19. See also *White* v. *McLean* (1890) 24 S.A.L.R. 97, 100 *per* Boucaut J.; *Coe* v *Commonwealth* (1978) 18 A.L.R. 592, 596 *per* Mason J.

[43] Lindley, 41–2. Evatt states that the position on South Island was 'uncertain as between occupation and cession': ibid. 38 *et seq.*, 43. But in a Colonial Office opinion of 1839 Sir James Stephen took the view, quite firmly, that the Maoris had sovereignty at least over North Island; this was the basis for the Treaty of Waitangi of 6 February 1840: 89 *CTS* 873, and see 38 *Parl. Papers* (1840) 238; 51 *Law Officers Opinions* 4–7, and *Hoani Te Heuheu Tukino* v. *Aotea District Maori Land Board* [1941] A.C. 308. Stephen's opinion concentrated on details of British recognition (legislative and executive) of 'New Zealand' as a 'Substantive and independent State'. See also: *Correspondence relative to New Zealand*, 1840 No. 38, 68–9. Pennington authoritatively stated British policy in an earlier letter to Stephen of 22 June 1839 (ibid., No. 11, 33–4): 'any assumption of authority beyond that attaching to a British Consulate, should be strictly contingent upon the indispensable preliminary of the territorial cession having been obtained by amicable negotiation with, and free concurrence of, the native chiefs.' However, after 1840 New Zealand was treated as a settled colony in that English law applied: *WiParata* v. *Bishop of Wellington* (1877) 3 N.Z. Jr. (N.S.) 72, 77–8; *Milirrpum* v. *Nabalco Pty. Ltd.* (1971) 17 F.L.R. 141, 235 *per* Blackburn J. Keller, Lissitzyn and Mann, op. cit. 11 take the view that North America was *terra nullius* and so open to occupation, but that view is contradicted by the jurisprudence of the Supreme Court, as well as by the fact that in an overwhelming number of cases cession by treaty was the mode actually adopted: O'Connell (1960), 54 *PAS* 77, 80–1.

[44] e.g. Southern Rhodesia; Samkange, *Origins of Rhodesia* (1968); *In re Southern Rhodesia* [1919] A.C. 211. But for the infrequency of cases of occupation in Africa see Alexandrowicz, *The European-African Confrontation*, 12–13.

[45] Allott, op. cit. 14, and for examples see Lugard (1893), 1 *Geographical Journal* 53–5; Brunschwig (1965), 5 *Cahiers d'études africaines* 5–56, 11.

This restrictive view of the concept of *terra nullius* has been affirmed by the International Court in the *Western Sahara Case*. After succintly defining the concept,[46] the Court continued:

Whatever differences of opinion there may have been among jurists, the State practice of the relevant period indicates that territories inhabited by tribes or peoples having a social and political organization were not regarded as *terrae nullius*. It shows that in the case of such territories the acquisition of sovereignty was not generally considered as effected unilaterally through 'occupation' of *terra nullius* by original title but through agreements concluded with local rulers. On occasion, it is true, the word 'occupation' was used in a non-technical sense denoting simply acquisition of sovereignty; but that did not signify that the acquisition of sovereignty through such agreements with authorities of the country was regarded as an 'occupation' of a *'terra nullius'* in the proper sense of these terms. On the contrary, such agreements with local rulers, whether or not considered as an actual 'cession' of the territory, were regarded as derivative roots of title, and not original titles obtained by occupation of *terrae nullius*.[47]

This formulation was approved, or a substantially similar test was adopted, by Judges Gros,[48] Dillard,[49] Ammoun,[50] de Castro,[51] and Judge *ad hoc* Boni.[52] Applying this test, the Court held, unanimously, that the presence of nomadic tribes with a degree of political and social organization precluded the territory from being regarded as *terra nullius*.[53] The *Western Sahara Case* thus provides a decisive refutation of the criterion of 'civilization' as a test for *terra nullius*.

---

[46] I.C.J. Rep. 1975 p. 12, 39: 'a determination that Western Sahara was a *"terra nullius"* at that time of colonization by Spain would be possible only if it were established that at that time the territory belonged to no-one in the sense that it was then open to acquisition through the legal process of "occupation".'

[47] Loc cit.

[48] Ibid. 75: 'the independent tribes travelling over the territory, or stopping in certain places, exercised a *de facto* authority which was sufficiently recognized for there to have been no *terra nullius*.'

[49] Ibid. 124: 'independent tribes with a degree of political and social organization'. The conclusion of treaties of protection was also regarded as relevant: 'you do not *protect* a *terra nullius*.'

[50] Ibid. 85–7.

[51] Ibid. 171.

[52] Ibid. 173.

[53] I.C.J. Rep. 1975 p. 12, 34–40; criticized by Levy (1976), 2 *Brooklyn JIL* 289–307, 295–7. Cf. the reservations of Judges Gros (74–5) and Dillard (123–4) as to the relevance and propriety of determining the *terra nullius* point.

6.3   ACQUISITION OF TERRITORY
FROM NATIVE COMMUNITIES

(1) *Status of native treaties of cession*

It follows from what has been said that a necessary condition for valid acquisition of nearly all inhabited territory was the consent of the native chiefs or peoples involved. To this extent native treaties had legal significance. What other significance they had depended on the status of the local signatories at the time of signature. If the native community was a State, or possessed a degree of legal status, then the treaty was either generally or *pro tanto* of an international kind.[54] However, that did not mean that the community remained a State—or retained its lesser international status—subsequent to the treaty. Before cession or protectorate, the status and interpretation of the treaty depended on the status of the community: subsequently, the status of the community depended to a large extent on the treaty and, in some cases, on subsequent practice or usage. Even where the treaty purported to guarantee benefits to the community or its members in perpetuity, cessions of territory tended in practice to be regarded as absolute. Although the classic writers had agreed that such conditional treaties of cession (which were in practice very common) were binding according to their terms,[55] the difficulty was that the ceding party became, upon the execution of the treaty, a municipal unit within a larger State; in Chief Justice Marshall's words, a 'domestic dependent nation'.[56] The binding nature of such stipulations might have been assured by a rule that they constituted essential conditions of transfer, and thus bound the territory rather like a servitude, or that they constituted an equitable duty in the nature of an estoppel in favour of the previous occupants.[57] That line of argument was not however pursued.

---

[54] Cf. *Right of Passage Case* I.C.J. Rep. 1960 p. 6, 91–2 *per* Judge Moreno Quintana.

[55] Vattel, *Droit des gens* I, Ch. XVI, § 193; Wolff, *Jus Gentium*, Ch. I, § 83; although the latter allowed the possibility of prescription in favour of the new sovereign (§ 84).

[56] *Worcester* v. *State of Georgia* 8 L.ed. 483 (1832). See Snow, *The Problem of Aborigines in the Law and Practice of Nations* (1919), 125 ff.; Green, *Canada's Indians: Federal Policy, International & Constitutional Law* (1969), 8–15.

[57] Patterson A-J., *R.* v. *Syliboy* [1929] 1 D.L.R. 307, 314; cited by Green, op. cit. 13–14.

(2) *Legal effects of native treaties*

If the direct effects of such treaties were of little importance, there remained the possibility of indirect effects.[58] Certainly *vis-à-vis* third States, such treaties were prime evidence of title to territory,[59] being both necessary and, subject to the Berlin Act,[60] sufficient for territorial sovereignty. Beyond that, however, their effects were limited, unless the native community retained international status by means of a protectorate agreement. This was because a variety of rules—non-justiciability,[61] the Act of State doctrine,[62] or the non-self-executing nature of treaties in common law courts[63]—prevented municipal courts from attributing legal consequences to or otherwise enforcing nominally international agreements. And this was so even where the 'treaty' concerned was concluded subsequent to the original cession, when the native community had lost any international status.[64] The only possibility, a largely fortuitous one, was recovery in an international forum under the ordinary rules of international responsibility.[65] So in general it remains true that the legal protection of native communities was afforded not by the original

---

[58] Cf. Judge Huber, *supra*, p. 178, n. 29.

[59] See e.g. 76 *BFSP* 755 ff. (German Cameroons), where the British Government recognized as valid a title by cession obtained, as against itself, under false pretences: cited Lindley, 34–5.

[60] *Supra*, pp. 178–9. In the *Clipperton Island Arbitration* (1932) 26 *AJ* 390, the arbitrator declined to apply the Berlin Act to territory outside Africa as against a non-signatory (Mexico).

[61] *U.S.* v *Kagama* 118 U.S. 228, 234 (1886); *Lone Wolf* v. *Hitchcock* 187 U.S. 553, 564–6 (1903); cited by Green (1975), 4 *Anglo-Am. LR* 137–62, 142.

[62] *Ex-Rajah of Coorg* v. *East India Co.* (1860) 24 Beav. 300.

[63] *Hoani Te Heuheu Tukino* v. *Aotea District Maori Land Board* [1941] A.C. 308. See now the Treaty of Waitangi Act, 1975 (N.Z.), confirming and adopting measures of implementation of 'the principles of the Treaty . . .'

[64] Cf. *Ol Le Ngojo* v. *A.G.* (1913) 5 *Kenya LR* 70. *Quaere* as to the proper law of the agreement (ibid. 91–2). Green suggests that such agreements are governed by the 'general principles of law' applied by the arbitrator in the *Abu Dhabi* case: 18 ILR 144 (1951): see *Canada's Indians: Federal Policy, International and Constitutional Law* (1969), 10–11. In *Warman* v. *Francis* (1958) 20 D.L.R. (2d) 627, 631, such treaties were described as 'in the nature of a special agreement based on goodwill and expediency made by the Crown with a body of inhabitants'.

[65] e.g., *Cayuga Indians Claim* (1926) 6 *RIAA* 173, where Great Britain was awarded $10,000 on behalf of part of the tribe pursuant to the Treaty of Ghent, 1814: 63 *CTS* 421. The Indian treaty (with the State of New York in 1789) was held merely to create municipal rights.

instruments,[66] but by municipal law,[67] and, where applicable, international protection of minorities and colonial territories.[68]

(3) *Grants of territory to private persons*

One of the legal consequences of the political organization of native tribes was their capacity to grant land to private persons for their use and occupation.[69] When the territory was ceded to or otherwise acquired by another State, the principle of acquired rights required due respect for those interests: the cases clearly demonstrate the capacity either of chiefs themselves[70] or of the tribe acting by its customary procedures to create proprietary interests requiring such respect. But restrictions upon that power included a strict application of the *nemo dat* rule,[71] and scrutiny of the transactions to ensure that they were freely and properly made for adequate consideration.[72]

6.4   ORIGINAL OCCUPATION OF TERRITORY BY A NEW STATE

The two processes of occupation of unacquired territory and the creation of new States do not normally coincide, for the sufficient reason that the effective and exclusive governmental control of territory necessary for its acquisition is rarely

---

[66] A further difficulty was that of demonstrating identity of personality between the original parties and the claimants: e.g. *In re Southern Rhodesia* [1919] A.C. 211, 231–4; *Milirrpum* v. *Nabalco Pty. Ltd.* (1971) 17 F.L.R. 141, 183–98 (Blackburn J., Northern Territory S. Ct.).

[67] For U.S. and Canadian authority see also Cohen (1947–8), 32 *Minn. LR* 28–59; Symposium (1974), 68 *PAS* 265–300; Galey (1975), 8 *Human Rights J.* 21–39; Wilkinson and Volkman (1975), 63 *Calif. LR* 601–61; Green (1975), 13 *Osgoode Hall LJ* 233–49; Levy (1975), 63 *Calif. LR* 848–85; Washburn (1976), 40 *Law. Cont. P.* 12–24. See also *Tee-Hit-Ton Indians* v. *U.S.* 348 U.S. 272 (1955); *Calder* v. *A.G. of British Columbia* (1973) 34 D.L.R. (3d) 145; *Administration of Papua and New Guinea* v. *Guba & Doriga* [1973] P.N.G.L.R. 603; *Milirrpum* v. *Nabalco Pty. Ltd.* (1971) 17 F.L.R. 141.

[68] See e.g. I.L.O. Convention No. 107, 'Protection and Integration of Indigenous and other Semi-Tribal Populations in independent Countries' (1957) 328 *UNTS* 247, Art. 11; Bennett (1972–3), 46 *BY* 382–92.

[69] Cf. the opinion of Pratt and Yorke (1720); Chalmers, *Opinions of English Lawyers* (1814) I, 195.

[70] *Fijian Land Claims (Burt Claim)* (1923) Nielsen 588, 596–7; and cf. *In re Southern Rhodesia* [1919] A.C. 211, 235–6.

[71] *Webster Claim* (1925) Neilsen 540, 543.

[72] See Lindley, 316–21, 316. For land grants subsequent to the acquisition of the territory see e.g. *Johnson & Graham's Lessee* v. *McIntosh* 5 L.ed. 681 (1823).

sustainable by any collection of individuals lacking a previous political organization. Colonization, direct or indirect, has been much the more usual method of acquisition and settlement. However, in a very few cases new States have been established on territory previously not part of any State, or on territory abandoned or ceded by its previous occupants.[73] These cases, which are now of historic interest only, included Liberia,[74] the Boer Republic,[75] and the Free State of the Congo.[76] The creation of Israel was also, in certain respects, similar to an original creation on abandoned territory.[77]

[73] Verzijl, *International Law* II, 64–5; Lindley, 89–90, citing Vattel, *Le Droit des Gens* I, § 206; Verhoeven, *Reconnaissance*, 12.

[74] Lindley, 111–12; Alexandrowicz, *The European-African Confrontation*, 44–5; Hertslet III, 1130–40.

[75] Hertslet I, 222–49.

[76] Nys, *The Independent State of the Congo in International Law* (n.d.), 20–1; Reeves (1909), 3 *AJ* 99–118; Hertslet II, 541–604.

[77] *Infra*, p. 247. For another attempt see Horn (1973), 12 *Col. JTL* 520–56.

7. The Creation and Status of Dependent States and other Dependent Entities

7.1 GENERAL PRINCIPLES

A PERENNIAL problem in the law and practice of territorial status has been the various types of dependent entities. Many of these did not qualify as independent States but they appeared to enjoy legal personality distinct from any other State. The existence of such 'dependent States' seemed to nineteenth-century writers strange and anachronistic. Oppenheim referred to their existence as an 'anomaly', and still does.[1] They were a legal puzzle, but useful in providing a contrast with 'real' or 'full-sovereign' States.[2] With the more liberal view of international personality taken in modern practice, the notion of a 'half-sovereign' or 'dependent State' is unnecessary.[3] However, there still exist protectorates and other territorial entities subject to divided competence; and problems of dependent status continue to arise.

The variety of dependent status in practice has been considerable: almost every permutation of rights and powers can be instanced from virtual plenary independence to practical absorption in another State. As a result, terminology in this field tends to be confused—perhaps inevitably so, since, even if an appropriate term is chosen to describe the relation at its inception, changes in the relation may render that term confusing and inappropriate. It is therefore a cardinal principle that the legal incidents of a given relation are to be determined not by any inference from the label attached to it ('protectorate', 'suzerain', 'vassal', etc.) but from an examination of the constituent documents and the circumstances of the case. This principle was affirmed by the Permanent Court in *Nationality Decrees in Tunis and Morocco*:

---

[1] *International Law* (1st edn.), 101; cf. (8th edn.), 119, omitting part only of the passage; and cf. the authorities cited in Kamanda, 36–9; Rousseau, *DIP* II, 290–300.

[2] Cf. Judge Anzilotti, *Austro-German Customs Union Case*, (1931) Ser. A/B No. 41, 57; for the Austrian argument, Ser. C. No. 53, 89–90.

[3] *Supra*, p. 70; *infra*, p. 421.

The extent of the powers of a protecting State in the territory of a protected State depends, first, upon the Treaties between the protecting State and the protected State establishing the Protectorate, and, secondly, upon the conditions under which the Protectorate has been recognized by third Powers as against whom there is an intention to rely on the provisions of these Treaties. *In spite of common features possessed by Protectorates under international law*, they have individual legal characteristics resulting from the special conditions under which they were created, and the stage of their development.[4]

In this Chapter we shall concentrate on the various forms of protectorate, both because this was and remains the most common 'category' of dependent entity, and because it best illustrates the general problems of analysis and classification. Some further 'categories' are briefly noted in a concluding section.

7.2   PROTECTORATES AND PROTECTED STATES

The protectorate arrangement involves a consensual transaction—most usually a treaty[5]—between two or more subjects of international law, whereby the dependent entity surrenders to the protecting State or States at the least the conduct of its foreign relations, and in other cases responsibility for such relations together with various rights of internal intervention, without being annexed by or formally incorporated into the territory of the latter.[6] Protection of one State by another is one of the oldest features of international relations. Grotius regarded an 'unequal alliance', with one State having rights of 'protection, defence and patronage' over another, as quite consistent with the sovereignty of the latter: a view which was shared by virtually all the classic writers on international law.[7] In the nineteenth

---

[4] Ser. B No. 4 (1923), 27. The words italicized in the authoritative French text of the judgment read: 'Malgré les traits communs qui présentent *les protectorats de droit international* . . .' This makes the point much more clearly: indeed, the word 'under' in the English text is almost certainly a mistranslation.

[5] For a protectorate by unilateral declaration cf. Egypt after 1914: 109 *BFSP* 436; Verzijl, *International Law* II, 427–34.

[6] Cf. Jenkyns's definition, approved in *Sobhuza II* v. *Miller* [1926] A.C. 518, 523. And see Verhoeven, *Reconnaissance*, 230–55.

[7] *De Jure Belli ac Pacis* I, Ch. 3, §§ 21–3; Vattel, *Le Droit des gens* I, §§ 5–8, 192; Wolff, *Jus Gentium* (1764 ed.), ch. 1, §§ 80–1. Pufendorf is less categorical: *De Jure Naturae et Gentium* VIII, ch. 9, § 906.

century, however, such flexible interpretation came to be regarded as archaic. According to Baty, 'the old conception of a really independent, but protected, State had disappeared' by 1815.[8] Instead a variety of political forms was developed, which sought to derive the greatest advantage for European States in terms of accessibility of markets or bases, and non-availability of territory to competitors, with the least disadvantages in terms of actual administrative responsibility. To these political forms the term 'protectorate' was usually applied, despite their diversity and the essential freedom of action of the protecting as against the protected entity. The result was doctrinal confusion. If we are to discuss under the same heading such diverse phenomena as the ancient protected States in Europe, and the disguised colonies in Africa, some initial distinctions are required.[9] Judge Huber, in the *Island of Palmas Case*, distinguished between international and colonial protectorates, reserving to the former the title of a 'true protectorate'.[10] Much the same distinction has been made, in British constitutional practice, between 'protectorates' (that is, of colonial type) and protected States under the British Nationality Act, 1948.[11] But it will be seen that international protectorates fall again into two categories: those entities which, despite protection, themselves qualify as States under the criteria already discussed; and those which, while not so qualifying, still enjoy some separate legal personality, including legal rights *vis-à-vis* the protecting State. For the sake of convenience, the former class will be referred to as *protected States*, the latter as *international protectorates*.

(1) *Protected States*

We have seen that the legal independence of a State is consistent with a considerable degree of actual dependence. The priority of formal over actual independence[12] in assessing

---

[8] (1921–2) 2 *BY* 109, 116, In fact, the change occurred later in the century, in the period 1870–95. For a full account see Johnston, *Sovereignty and Protection: A Study of British Jurisdictional Imperialism in the Late Nineteenth Century* (1973).

[9] Kamanda, 143–5 also distinguishes three types; but only after excluding *a priori* both European (23) and colonial (25) protectorates. As we shall see, it is impossible to be so categorical in fact.

[10] (1928) 2 *RIAA* 829, 858.

[11] Parry, *Nationality and Citizenship Laws of the Commonwealth and Ireland* (1957), 356–63.

[12] *Supra*, p. 69.

whether an entity is a State means that quite extensive delegation of competences by treaty can coexist with statehood. Treaty provisions do not, in general, derogate from formal independence;[13] the question is then how extensive the loss of actual independence must be, under protectorate arrangements, before the local entity can no longer be regarded as a State. As a general rule it may be said that the exercise of delegated powers pursuant to protectorate arrangements is not inconsistent with statehood if the derogations from independence are based on local consent, do not involve extensive powers of internal control, and do not leave the local entity without some degree of influence over the exercise of its foreign affairs. For example, metropolitan authority to conclude treaties for the protected entity and to implement them in the latter's territory is inevitably inconsistent with local statehood: since modern international relations may involve practically every aspect of governmental powers within a State, control of this sort implies a discretion to intervene internally over the whole range of governmental powers. But this is an unusually clear case: it may be helpful to consider various examples of delegation of responsibility, as it were on a continuum from virtually complete independence to loss of actual independence such that statehood is in question.

The clearest case is that where the only obligation is to attend to the advice of the 'protecting' Government (so long as there is no obligation to accept that advice).[14] Under its Treaty of Friendship of 8 August 1949, Bhutan agreed to be 'guided by the advice of the Government of India in regard to its external relations': in return, India undertook 'to exercise no interference in the internal administration of Bhutan'.[15] Bhutan's external relations remain its own; and it clearly satisfies the basic criterion of independence.[16] Equally clear is the case of San Marino,

---

[13] *Supra*, p. 53.

[14] Cf. Kelantan, *supra*, p. 61; Brunei, *infra*, p. 197.

[15] 157 *BFSP* 214; Art. 2; Whiteman, 1 *Digest* 451; Kamanda, 140–3. For the U.K.-Bhutan Treaty of 29 Nov. 1865, providing for 'perpetual friendship', with disputes between Bhutan and other States made subject to British arbitration, see Aitchison (4th edn., 1909) II, 285–308, 303. The Treaty appears to be still in force: HMSO, *Index of British Treaties, 1101–1958* II, 297.

[16] An *a fortiori* case was Nepal. Although it was at least politically dependent upon the British East India Co. in the nineteenth century, its dependence was of a relatively nominal character. British recognition was accorded in 1923: 119 *BFSP* 448. However

which has undertaken not to accept the protection of any other power than Italy.[17]

The next step, as it were, and perhaps the central case of protected statehood, is the conduct by the protecting State of the foreign affairs of the protected State as agent, pursuant to agreement. For example, under the arrangement whereby Liechtenstein has delegated to Switzerland the conduct of its foreign affairs: 'Diplomatic steps of the Principality in its relations with other States are carried out by Switzerland only from case to case and inasmuch as they are the subject of a special instruction of the Government of the Principality.'[18] There can be no doubt that such an arrangement is entirely consistent with local independence.[19] This is equally so where the conduct of foreign affairs by the protecting State is accompanied by a right

because of its isolation and non-involvement in international relations it remained largely unrecognized: see the U.S. recognition of 5 Mar. 1947, referring to 'the independence which [Nepal] has long enjoyed': Whiteman, 2 *Digest* 206–8. See also the Indian-Nepalese Treaty of 31 July 1950: 94 *UNTS* 3. On Nepal see further Verhoeven, *Reconnaissance*, 9–11; Verzijl, *International Law* II, 356–7; Whiteman, 1 *Digest* 453.

[17] Treaty of Friendship and *'Bon Voisinage'*, 1939: 143 *BFSP* 537, Art. 1; revising an earlier Treaty of 1897; 90 *BFSP* 960, Art. 46. San Marino is a member of various international organizations, though W.H.O. membership was refused, largely on financial grounds: Higgins, *Development*, 47. It is a party to the Statute of the International Court (*supra*, p. 139, n. 53). It carries on its own international relations. Art. 1 of the 1939 Treaty probably does not constitute San Marino a protectorate at all: in any case the treaty is subject to denunciation at six months' notice (Art. 58. For San Marino's position in the E.E.C., see *infra*, p. 193, n. 40). Sereni describes San Marino as under Italian 'protection' but not as a protectorate: *The Italian Conception of International Law* (1943), 290–1. Cf. *USFR* 1944/IV, 290: '. . . Since the Republic of San Marino has been generally recognized by this Government as an independent State (see extradition treaty between U.N. and San Marino proclaimed 12 June 1908) the Department knows no reason why we should not entertain representations directly from the accredited representative of the Republic.'

[18] Note of 18 June 1973: *SCOR* 29th yr., Sp. Supp. No. 2, 120. For the Exchange of Notes of 21/24 Oct. 1919 see 127 *BFSP* 844; cf. 23 *NRG(3d.)* 543. Liechtenstein is linked to Switzerland by postal (2 *LNTS* 306) and customs unions (21 *LNTS* 232). It is a party to the Statute of the International Court: G.A. Res. 363 (IV), 1 Dec. 1949 (40–2:2). See also Raton, *Liechtenstein. History and Institutions of the Principality* (2nd rev. edn., 1970); Kohn (1967), 61 *AJ* 547–57; *Répertoire suisse* I, 305–12; *Nottebohm Case (Second Phase)* I.C.J. Rep. 1955, p. 4, 20. On representation generally see Sereni (1948), 73 *HR* 69–166. For U.N. depositary practice cf. 1975 UN *Jur. Ybk.* 196–9.

[19] Western Samoa is another case: Unitar Study No. 3, *Status and Problems of Very Small States and Territories* (1969), 115–16; Davidson, *Samoa mo Samoa: the emergence of the independent state of Western Samoa* (1967). For the N.Z.–Western Samoan Treaty of Friendship of 1 Aug. 1962, see [1962] *NZTS* No. 5. For the Exchange of Letters concerning Diplomatic Representation etc. see [1963] *NZTS No. 11*. For U.N. Membership, *supra*, p. 141, n. 67.

to advise on other matters, or by other non-essential competences. Tonga before 1970 is an example. By a Treaty of Amity of 18 May 1900, the King agreed to have 'no relations of any sort with foreign Powers concerning the alienation of any land or any part of his sovereignty, or any demands for monetary compensation',[20] an agreement apparently restricting part only of the King's foreign affairs power. By Article II Great Britain undertook to protect Tonga, and was accorded access to the island 'for this, or for similar purposes'. A British Agent was given consular jurisdiction in certain criminal and civil cases involving non-natives.[21] The Agent was not to interfere in internal affairs unless the interests of British subjects or foreigners was concerned, although he might tender advice at the request of the King and his Government.[22]

Finally, in a number of cases a protectorate has been regarded as a State despite the existence of an agency arrangement for the conduct of foreign affairs, combined with a right to veto. This was so, as we have seen, with Danzig.[23] However, such situations are close to the borderline of lack of independence: it would seem necessary to establish some degree of effective exercise of local authority despite the veto. The former British protected States in the Arabian Gulf are a case in point:[24] Bahrain may be taken as an example. By Agreement of 22 December 1881,[25] the Chief of Bahrain undertook 'to abstain from entering into negotiations or making treaties of any sort with any State or Government other than the British without the consent of the said British Government, and to refuse permission to any other Government than the British to establish diplomatic or consular agencies or

---

[20] 107 *BFSP* 521, Art. 1.

[21] Arts. IV, V. The jurisdiction was replaced by a further Agreement of 7 Nov. 1928: 128 *BFSP* 272.

[22] Art. III. Cf. Kamanda, 68–73; Whiteman, 1 *Digest* 450–1. For Tonga's position before the ILC, see *ILC Ybk.* 1974/II (1), 25, 27–8; ibid., 1972/II, 4–10.

[23] *Supra*, p. 163.

[24] *Sc.* Kuwait, Bahrain, Qatar and the Trucial States of Oman (now the United Arab Emirates). For Muscat and Oman see *infra*, p. 209. See in general Husain Al-Baharna, *The Legal Status of the Arabian Gulf States* (1968).

[25] Aitchison (1933), XI, 237. On Bahrain generally see Al-Baharna, 31–5; Whiteman, 1 *Digest* 440–2; Kamanda, 76–8; E. Lauterpacht (1958), 7 *ICLQ* 541–52. Adamiyat, *Bahrain Islands. A Legal and Diplomatic Study of the British-Iranian Controversy* (1955), and (more dispassionately) Tadjbakhche, *La Question des Îles Bahrein* (1960) argue for the imprescriptibility of Iranian rights over Bahrain. Cf. *supra*, p. 38.

coaling depots in (his) territory, unless with the consent of the British Government.'[26]

By a further Exclusive Agreement of 13 March 1892, the Sheikh undertook not to enter into any agreement or correspondence with any Power other than the British Government; not to consent, without British consent, to the residence in Bahrain of the agent of any other Government, and not to alienate in any way any part of his territory except to the British Government. Subsequent agreements also provided for prior consultation or approval of the grant of concessions for sponge- or pearl-fishing, or oil exploration.[27] Similar agreements were made with Kuwait in 1899,[28] Qatar in 1916,[29] and the Trucial States in 1892.[30]

The position of the States under these agreements has been a matter of some controversy. Although the British Government has repeatedly qualified them as 'independent States under the protection of Her Majesty's Government',[31] commentators have tended to deny their independence,[32] and even that they had any measure of separate personality at all.[33] In view of British disclaimers of any authority in or responsibility for the 'internal affairs of the British protected States in the Persian Gulf',[34] this latter view certainly underestimates the degree of separate personality of the Gulf States.[35] Whether they retained a sufficient degree of independence under these arrangements to be regarded as protected States as here defined, on the other hand, is uncertain.[36]

[26] The Agreement preserved local competence with respect to correspondence with neighbouring States on business of minor importance.

[27] Lauterpacht (1958), 7 *ICLQ* 110, 112.

[28] 166 *BFSP* 111; Whiteman, 1 *Digest* 442–6; Kamanda, 74–6; Al-Baharna, 40–6.

[29] Whiteman, 1 *Digest* 447; Aitchison (1933) XI, 258; Al-Baharna, 36–9.

[30] Aitchison (1909) XII, 165–86; Whiteman, 1 *Digest* 447; Kamanda, 81–3; Al-Baharna, 25–30.

[31] e.g. *H.C. Deb.* Vol. 445 cols. 1681–2, 17 Dec. 1947 (Bahrain).

[32] Al-Baharna regards the Gulf States (Oman excepted) as having some international status but as not independent States: ibid. 79–80. But they did have, he argues, 'independent governments': ibid. 139; cf. 91.

[33] Kamanda, 85–8, 158 (based on the erroneous assumption that the Colonial Laws Validity Act, 1865 and the Foreign Jurisdiction Acts authorize plenary intervention in the affairs of the Gulf States: cf. McNair, *Law Officers Opinions* I, 42, 44; [1965] *BPIL* 108 (Tonga)); Pillai and Kumar (1962), 11 *ICLQ* 108–30, 125.

[34] *H.C. Deb.* Vol. 711, w.a. col. 108, 3 May 1965; Al-Baharna, 30; [1965] *BPIL* 2; 278 *UNTS* 266.

[35] Cf. Verhoeven, *Reconnaissance*, 14–15.

[36] The 1899 Treaty with Kuwait was terminated in 1961 (166 *BFSP* 112; *infra*, p. 205); those of 1880 and 1892 with Bahrain were terminated by an unpublished Treaty of

The equivocal nature of local independence in these types of case, and the need to resort to ancillary criteria such as recognition, is well illustrated by the Principality of Monaco, which is recognized as an independent State in special treaty relations with France.[37] It is a member of a number of international organizations, and party to a substantial number of treaties, bilateral and multilateral.[38] It conducts its own foreign relations, subject to prior understanding with the French Government under Article 2 of the 1918 Treaty: as a result Oppenheim does not classify it as a 'protectorate' in the strict sense.[39] Nevertheless (and this is true also of San Marino) its inclusion in the customs area of the European Economic Community appears to result from Article 227(4) of the Rome Treaty, although France is not strictly speaking 'responsible' for its 'external relations'.[40] On the other hand it may be doubted whether Monaco is genuinely independent so as to qualify for statehood. The powers reserved to France under the various treaties are extensive: Monaco has undertaken 'to exercise its rights of sovereignty entirely in accord with the political, military, naval, and economic interests of France',[41] and not to alienate its territory except to France.[42] The succession to the Crown 'may only be transmitted to a person possessing French or Monegasque nationality, and agreeable to the French Government',[43] and in default of succession 'the territory of Monaco shall form, under the protectorate of France, an autonomous State called the State of Monaco'.[44] The French

---

Friendship on 15 Aug. 1971 (*Keesing's* 1971, 248434); and that of 1916 with Qatar was similarly terminated on 1 Sept. 1971 (*loc. cit.*). After lengthy negotiations, the Trucial States federated in 1971 to form the United Arab Emirates: see the Agreement of 27 Feb. 1968: Al-Baharna, 328–31. Their Exclusive Agreements were terminated as from 2 Dec. 1971. All four States are now United Nations members.

[37] Under Agreements of 1865 (55 *BFSP* 407), 1918 (111 *BFSP* 727) and 1963 (in Gallois, *Le Régime International de la Principauté de Monaco* (1964), 243–8). See also Kiss, *Pratique française* II, 462–9; Rousseau, *DIP* II, 332–9.

[38] See Gallois, op. cit. 260–8; Rollet, *Liste des Engagements Bilatéraux et Multilatéraux . . . Souscrits par la France* (1973), 158–61.

[39] Oppenheim (8th edn., 1955) I, 193n.

[40] Art. 227(4): 'The provisions of this Treaty shall apply to the European territories for whose external relations a Member State is responsible.' See Reg. 1496/68: *J.O. des Comm. Eur.* 1968 No. L.238/I, Art. 2.

[41] 1918 Treaty, Art. 1.

[42] Ibid., Art. 3.   [43] Ibid., Art. 2.

[44] Ibid., Art. 3: this provision O'Connell terms 'a contingent reversion of sovereignty': *International Law* I, 290.

Government may introduce armed forces into Monaco either by request or 'in an emergency, after notification . . . for upholding the security of the two countries',[45] a provision reminiscent of the retained powers of the United Kingdom over the Caribbean Associated States.[46] The two States are united by an extensive customs union: as a result transfer of gold from Monaco to a foreign State was held by the *Cour de Cassation* to constitute an export 'from French territory'. [47] The inclusion of Monaco in the category of protected States is probably a result not of any indisputable qualifications for statehood but of its widespread recognition and acceptance as a State.

To summarize, it can be seen that a necessary prerequisite for independence under a regime of protection in the retention of substantial authority in internal affairs (including implementation of international obligations); some degree of understanding with regard to and influence over the exercise of foreign affairs powers; and that metropolitan competences be expressly based on delegation by treaty or other instrument. Where these elements are not present, then in the absence of general recognition (as with Monaco), the entity in question is not to be regarded as a protected State as here defined, though it may possess some lesser degree of personality.

(2) *International protectorates*

International protectorates are those territories the governments of which, having agreed to protection, retain a separate international status but lack in some respect the qualifications for statehood as defined. This is a residual category, and the status of particular international protectorates can vary widely.

Perhaps the most controversial case is that of Morocco, which although generally recognized as a State was subjected to a fairly elaborate system of capitulations and spheres of influence. The General Act of the International Conference at Algeciras relating to the affairs of Morocco provided for extensive reforms 'basées sur le triple principe de souveraineté et de l'indépendance de Sa

---

[45] 1918 Treaty, Art. 4.

[46] *Infra*, pp. 374–5.

[47] *Ditzler, Reith & Buess* v. *Customs Administration* (1940) 11 AD No. 21. Cf. *Bayetto* v. *Administration d'Enregistrement* (1946) 13 ILR 22 (Monaco, by virtue of its relationship with France, a belligerent and not a neutral in World War II: its nationals not therefore subject to sequestration of property). To the same effect cf. *infra*, p. 208.

Majesté le Sultan, de l'integrité de Ses Etats et de la liberté économique sans aucune inégalité.'[48] In 1912 the Treaty of Fez brought the major part of Morocco under French protectorate.[49] A much smaller coastal area was recognized as within the Spanish sphere of influence, and subsequently reduced to a Spanish protectorate.[50] Under the Treaty of Fez, French rights in Morocco included the right to station military forces in the territory at discretion to maintain order and the security of commercial transactions (Article II); the right to require necessary legislative reforms to be carried out by the Sultan, and the right to appoint a French Resident to be in charge of all matters concerning foreigners in Morocco, as well as to be 'le seul intermédiaire du Sultan auprès des représentants étrangers et dans les rapports que ces représentants entretiennent avec le Gouvernement marocain.'[51] Decrees of the Sultan required prior French consent (Article VI), as also did the grant by him of concessions or the making of public or private loans (Article VIII). By 1925 the French Zone had been brought under practically direct French control, only the judicial system remaining formally distinct.[52] At first sight it would appear then that Morocco had by no means sufficient independence under these arrangements to be regarded as an independent State.[53] Even if, which is not clear, Morocco retained its formal independence, it would seem to have been under the substantial control of another State. However in the *Case concerning United States Nationals in Morocco* the International Court held that Morocco retained substantial international personality.

It is not disputed by the French Government that Morocco, even under the Protectorate, has retained its personality as a State in international law. The rights of France in Morocco are defined by the Protectorate Treaty of 1912 . . . Under this Treaty, Morocco remained a sovereign State, but it made an arrangement of a contractual character whereby France undertook to exercise certain sovereign powers in the name and on behalf of Morocco, and, in principle, all the international relations of Morocco . . .[54]

[48] 99 *BFSP* 141. Cf. also the Madrid Convention of 1880: 71 *BFSP* 639, 814.
[49] 106 *BFSP* 1023; Kamanda, 99–102.
[50] 106 *BFSP* 1025.
[51] Art. V.
[52] Kamanda, 105–6.
[53] Ibid., 108.
[54] I.C.J. Rep. 1952, p. 176, 185, 188.

The passage is well known, but rather difficult to interpret. It is, for the reasons already stated, difficult to regard Morocco after 1912 as a Protected State,[55] although the passage does confirm at least the possibility of protected statehood in the sense in which that term is used here. On the other hand, the widespread prior recognition of the Sultan, the complexity and internationalized nature of the arrangements in Morocco,[56] and the insistence by France (and by French courts)[57] on the continued statehood of Morocco perhaps militated in favour of its notional independence. In particular, recognition may, as we have seen, in some circumstances compensate for any lack of positive qualifications for statehood. But the recognition of Moroccan independence at Algeciras in 1906 antedated the Treaty of Fez, with which it can only be regarded as inconsistent.

In the alternative, it might be argued that, while Morocco was a 'State' in international law, it was not a 'sovereign' or 'independent' State.[58] Certainly the term 'State' has no fixed and inevitable meaning, and it is sometimes used to refer to territorial entities with a degree of international personality, but without independence. But the use of the term in two such different and distinct senses can only lead to confusion. The term 'State' may mean 'territorial legal person' in particular contexts, but as a general rule it appears to be reserved for independent States as distinct from other legal persons, territorial or not.[59] Moreover the International Court in the passage cited does appear to have been using the term in the latter more general sense. It is difficult otherwise to interpret the phrases 'remained a sovereign State' and 'an arrangement of a contractual nature'.

The position appears to be that where independent States become subject to protectorates which substantially restrict that independence, they are nevertheless, by a sort of convention, regarded as States for at least some purposes. For example, they

[55] Cf. Verzijl, *International Law* II, 451.

[56] Judge van Eysinga, diss., *Phosphates in Morocco*, Ser. A/B No. 74 (1938), 32.

[57] See e.g. *Govt. of Morocco* v. *Laurens* (1930) 5 AD No. 75; *Ménier* v. *P.L.M. Ry. Co.* (1938) 11 AD No. 25; *Re Hamou* (1955) 22 ILR 60.

[58] Kamanda, 187; Fitzmaurice (1953), 30 *BY* 1–70, 2, proposing 'that not all States are fully independent sovereign States; and that statehood in the international sense may be possessed by not fully sovereign entities—that, in fact, statehood is an attribute of any territorial entity which enjoys some real degree of sovereignty (*sic*) in the *international* field' (his itals).

[59] See also *supra*, pp. 31–5.

continue the personality of the State before protectorate so that its treaties remain in force.[60] Their international relations, the exercise of which is normally vested in the protecting State, remain formally distinct.[61] Their rulers are normally accorded sovereign immunity, at least in the protecting State's courts.[62] They retain their own nationality, for municipal purposes at least, if not internationally.[63] Their relations with the protecting State are 'contractual' in nature, and continue to be governed by international law.[64] Their status is terminated in substantially the same way as that adopted for Protected States.[65] And this is, upon reflection, a natural process. The protectorate relation is not in general aimed at annexation but at secure separate government. Moreover, an entity may well begin as a Protected State but gradually lose substantial independence: Zanzibar is one example.[66] Where the rights of other States are not infringed, as the rules referred to seek to ensure, and given local consent or acquiescence, there is normally no point in further particularization of status, which, moreover, local pride aims at retaining. The conclusion is then that international protectorates form a separate class of territorial entities, with a certain distinct legal personality, and, subject to the terms of the protectorate instruments, assimilated for many purposes to Protected States.

As well as Tunisia and Morocco,[67] almost all the protectorates in Asia, the Middle East, and North Africa fell into this category. For example, Brunei is the only remaining British international protectorate. The case is an instructive one, in that the Sultanate was originally a Protected State under its Protectorate Agreement of 17 September 1888.[68] That agreement provided that 'The State of Brunei shall continue to be governed and administered by the said Sultan . . . and his successors as an independent State, under the protection of Great Britain; but such protection shall confer no right on Her Majesty's Government to interfere with the internal administration of that State further than is herein

---

[60] *Infra*, p. 203. [61] *Infra*, p. 202. [62] *Infra*, p. 208.
[63] *Infra*, p. 208. [64] *Infra*, p. 203. [65] *Infra*, p. 205.
[66] Cf. Kamanda, 56–65.

[67] Kamanda, 99–113; Whiteman, 2 *Digest* 204–6, 229–30; Verzijl, *International Law* II, 443–52. The Moroccan protectorates were terminated by joint Declarations in 1956: 162 *BFSP* 958 (France); ibid. 1017 (Spain); and for Tunisia, by Protocol of 20 Mar. 1956; ibid. 963.

[68] Westlake, *International Law* Pt. I, 124.

provided.'[69] Succession disputes and interstate disagreements were subject to British arbitration under Articles II and III respectively: Brunei agreed to abide by and carry into effect such decisions. Brunei's foreign relations were to be 'conducted by Her Majesty's Government';[70] and cessions of territory by Brunei required British consent.[71] Britain was granted consular jurisdiction over British subjects.[72] The decisive change from Protected State to international protectorate as here defined came in 1906, when the Sultan agreed to the appointment of a British resident, whose 'advice must be taken and acted upon on all questions in Brunei, other than those affecting the Mohammedan religion, in order that a similar system may be established to that existing in other Malay States now under British protection.'[73] Thereafter, although formally a Protected State, Brunei lacked actual independence and must be considered an international protectorate.[74] Other examples were Sikkim,[75] Zanzibar,[76] the French protectorates in Indochina,[77] and (probably) the Maldive Islands.[78]

(3) *Colonial protectorates*

Judge Huber in the *Island of Palmas Case* described African (colonial) protectorates as merely 'a form of internal administra-

---

[69] 79 *BFSP* 240, Art. I.

[70] Art. III.   [71] Art. VI.   [72] Art. VII.

[73] Supplementary Agreement, 2 Jan. 1906: 25 *Hertslet C.T.* 32, Art. 1. Cf. the Agreement of 29 Sept. 1959, in substantially the same terms: 164 *BFSP* 38.

[74] Lindley, 193–4; Kamanda, 91–4 (on the Malay States in general). For an interesting analysis of the extension of European protection over the Malay States see Rubin, *Piracy, Paramountcy and Protectorates* (1974). In 1971 a new agreement was signed by the United Kingdom and the Sultan of Brunei: under it Brunei has full internal self-government, but the United Kingdom retains responsibility for external affairs (with only a limited form of joint consultation). See *Keesing's* 1971, 25036A; cf. S.I. 1974 No. 1895. Although the United Kingdom has argued that Brunei is a sovereign State and not, accordingly, a Chapter XI territory, this view has been rejected by the General Assembly: e.g. G.A. Res. 32/27, 28 Nov. 1977 (127–0: 14, U.K.n.p.).

[75] Whiteman, 1 *Digest* 451–2; Kamanda, 139–40, 143; Aitchison (4th edn., 1909) II, 309–44. On 26 Apr. 1975 Sikkim was in effect incorporated into India: see Agreement of 8 May 1973; (1973) 13 *Indian JIL* 620; (1975) 79 *RGDIP* 536–8. Fischer, [1974] *AFDI* 201–14 regards the situation as coming within Chapter XI of the Charter. For background to the troubled relations between India and Sikkim see Rao, *India and Sikkim 1814–1970* (1972).

[76] Kamanda, 56–65; *Jani v. Jani* (1952) 18 ILR 54.

[77] Kamanda, 113–28.

[78] Ibid., 73–4; 164 *BFSP* 390.

tion of a colonial territory on the basis of autonomy for the natives'.[79] This possibility is confirmed by s. 1 of the Foreign Jurisdiction Act, 1890 (U.K.), which provides that the Crown may enjoy 'within a foreign country' jurisdiction as ample 'as if Her Majesty had acquired that jurisdiction by the cession or conquest of territory'. The Act clearly contemplates plenary jurisdiction over a 'foreign country' without that country technically becoming part of the dominions:[80] this conflict of characterization between municipal and international law in relation to colonial protectorates lies at the heart of the problem. According to Alexandrowicz,

> The transformation of the classic protectorate into the colonial protectorate was in its essence not a legal but a political development ... It was the arrangement adopted behind the scenes of the Berlin Conference by which the signatory powers gave each other *carte blanche* to absorb protected States, which led to a deformation of the Protectorate as such. It has been emphasised that such an arrangement could not affect the validity of the treaties of protection with Rulers, for *pacta tertiis nec nocent nec prosunt*. The colonial protectorate is the outcome of a para-legal metamorphosis and has no place in international law as a juridically justifiable institution. It was at most a political expedient.[81]

Justifiable or not, it is clear that, *qua* protectorate, the colonial protectorate was not a separate juridical institution at all: the whole point of identifying it as colonial was that the extent of governmental authority with respect to the territory was plenary. It may also be that the territory concerned became, in international law, part of the metropolitan State's territory, not upon the conclusion of the treaty but by subsequent 'grant, usage, sufferance or other ... means'. But it is clear that the transition could occur, so that an entity with some of the distinguishing marks of a protectorate would be classified as, internationally, part of another State. As we have seen, it is a basic principle that the status of any dependent entity is to be determined by examination of its actual position, and not by inference from its title.[82] The absence of formal annexation was not a barrier to

[79] (1928) 2 *RIAA* 329, 358.

[80] Cf. Report of the Resumed Nigeria Constitutional Conference, 1958, Cmnd. 569, Annex II, 42; Al Baharna, 89–90; Fawcett, *British Commonwealth*, 119.

[81] *The European-African Confrontation*, 69–81, 80–1; cf. his (1968) 123 *HR* 117–214, 189–205.

[82] *Supra*, p. 186.

characterization of territory as part of a particular State, where the authority exercised was in fact plenary. The only qualifications to be made is that the metropolitan State, if it insisted on the separateness of the protectorate, might create unilateral legal obligations with respect to the protectorate. But, in view of the slight protection accorded to native treaties by international law at the time, even this is doubtful.

Colonial protectorates were, with two exceptions,[83] restricted to Africa, and may well have been a direct consequence of the General Act of the Berlin Conference, which assimilated colonies and protectorates, requiring for both effective occupation and notification to other powers.[84] Even though many protectorate agreements over what came to be regarded as colonial protectorates are treaties in international form made with recognized African States (for example, Swaziland),[85] or tribes with a certain legal status (for example Somaliland),[86] the continuous accretion of powers by usage and acquiescence to the protecting State was—by virtue of the Berlin Act procedure— opposable to the parties to that Act and in practice a matter at the protecting State's discretion. As a result, the protecting State had international full powers: it was competent, for example, to cede protected territory without consent and in breach of the protectorate agreements.[87] But that is not to say that international

[83] Aden Protectorate and the British Solomon Islands. For the former, see Kamanda, 88–91; Robbins (1939), 33 *AJ* 700–15. But even there the British view was that the protection agreements were 'of a kind recognized in international law, which imposed both legal and moral obligations on the signatories': [1963] *BPIL* 148; see also [1964] *BPIL* 12–20; [1966] *BPIL* 6–7, 50–2; [1967] *BPIL* 18–20. The protectorates became independent in conjunction with Aden Colony on 30 Nov. 1967 as the People's Republic of South Yemen. For the latter, 78 *BFSP* 691; 21 *Hertslet C.T.* 1178.

[84] *Supra*, pp. 178–9; Johnston, *Sovereignty and Protection* (1973), 167–225.

[85] 86 *BFSP* 61.

[86] 76 *BFSP* 101; 77 *BFSP* 1263.

[87] A point directly raised by the Ethiopia–Somalia boundary dispute. By an agreement of 1897 Britain ceded to Ethiopia certain traditional grazing lands of the Somali herdsmen under British protection: 89 *BFSP* 31, despite absence of local acquiescence or consent. The areas were returned to Ethiopia by a further Agreement of 1954: *UKTS* No. 1 (1955). In the House of Commons the validity of the 1897 Treaty was challenged: the Minister of State replied 'that the 1897 Treaty is an international instrument, whereas the other Agreements were not'. *H.C. Deb.* Vol. 537 cols. 1676–88, 1686 (25 Feb. 1955). See also ibid., Vol. 562 w.a. col. 149 (19 Dec. 1955); Latham Brown (1956), 5 *ICLQ* 245–64; Kamanda, 65–8, 205–14; Lindley, 183–4; Lewis (1967), 66 *African Aff.* 104–22; Hamilton, 'Ethiopia's Frontiers: The Boundary Agreements and their Demarcation, 1896–1956' (Oxford, MS., D.Phil. 1974), 55–167.

law was completely irrelevant to the relationship. As has been said it is at least arguable that the continued affirmation of the terms of protection agreements constituted an estoppel binding the metropolitan State to those terms. This would explain the otherwise insoluble conflict between the British view that the protectorate agreements were 'binding and valid',[88] and the view that, as against third States, such agreements were, or had become, a basis for plenary title to the territory in question. The location of status, *vis-à-vis* contract, in a colonial protectorate was thus reversed.[89]

(4) *Legal effects of protectorates*

Some of the legal effects of protectorate arrangements will be briefly reviewed.

(*i*) *Relations inter se of protected and protecting State*

It is sometimes suggested that the relations *inter se* of protecting and protected State are necessarily domestic or municipal.

In his report of the *Spanish Zone of Morocco Claims* Judge Huber stated that: 'Les rapports entre le protecteur et le protégé sont donc à envisager comme une affaire intérieure entre ces deux Puissances; vis-à-vis de l'étranger, les responsabilités du protecteur et du protégé, *tout en étant juridiquement distinctes*, se fondent en une seule, à la charge de la Puissance protectrice.'[90] But this was in the context of international responsibility for an international protectorate, where it appears that claims for redress against the protectorate are to be addressed to the Protecting Power. For those purposes, the relations between the two entities are irrelevant, for the liability for international torts is not to be reduced as against third States and without their consent merely by reason of the existence of a protectorate.[91] Judge Huber's remarks are not to be taken as a general assertion of the internal

---

[88] *H.C. Deb.* Vol. 537 col. 1683 (Somaliland); *supra*, p. 200, n. 83.

[89] For the problems of characterization of colonial protectorates in British courts, see Polack (1963) 26 *MLR* 139–55; Kato, [1969] *Public Law* 219–35; *Ex parte Mwenya* [1960] 1 Q.B. 241, 297 ff. *per* Lord Evershed M.R., discussed by Fawcett, *British Commonwealth*, 130–4. But cf. *Ex parte Thakrar* [1974] 1 Q.B. 684, 702 *per* Lord Denning M.R., discussed (1974–5) 47 *BY* 353–4. For an interesting account of the effect of the British cases on administration of the East African protectorates see Morris, in Morris and Read, *Indirect Rule and the Search for Justice* (Oxford, 1972), 41–70.

[90] (1928) 2 *RIAA* 615, 648 (emphasis added).

[91] Loc. cit.

municipal nature of such *inter se* relations. That argument has in fact been maintained, most notably by Fitzmaurice in a commentary on the *United States Nationals in Morocco* case:

Since France under the Treaty [of Fez] had the conduct of Morocco's international relations, her own relations with Morocco could hardly be of that character, nor Morocco's with her, or France would have been in the position of, in effect, carrying on relations with herself—or with Morocco through herself. Franco-Moroccan relations must therefore lie on the internal, not the international, plane.

[A]lthough France (or any other Protecting State in a similar position) is 'bound' by the instrument establishing the Protectorate, a dispute about its interpretation or application could not be an *international* dispute.[92]

But if the relation is 'inherently non-international' then presumably it is municipal, and presumably also liable to be changed by municipal legislation without the consent of the protected entity. Thus, unless the relation is binding under international law, it is not legally binding at all, a view inconsistent both with international practice and the judgment of the International Court in the *United States Nationals in Morocco Case* itself. If the relation was 'inherently non-international', the plea of domestic jurisdiction would be in principle an absolute bar to international discussion of protectorate problems—which is not so.[93] In one class of cases only is the protectorate relation 'inherently non-international': that is, the class of colonial protectorates, which are treated as equivalent to annexed territories. In all other cases the relation is in principle governed by international law.[94]

This issue arose in the *Rann of Kutch Arbitration* which concerned the relations between Sind, which in 1843 became part of British India, and the vassal State of Kutch. Although it was agreed that international law applied to the relations of the two entities before 1843,[95] Pakistan argued that it ceased to apply thereafter.[96] This argument was at least impliedly rejected in the Opinion of the Chairman, Lagergren (with whom Judge Entezam con-

[92] (1953) 30 *BY* 2–6, 4–5 (emphasis his); cf. *supra*, pp. 194–6.
[93] *Nationality Decrees in Tunis and Morocco*, Ser. B No. 4 (1923).
[94] Kamanda, 29; but cf. 126. Fawcett, *British Commonwealth*, 138–40 takes a middle view.
[95] (1968) 7 *ILM* 633, 657.
[96] Ibid. 657–60.

curred): he regarded the 'Rao of Kutch and the British Government in Sind', before 1947, as 'contending sovereigns' for the purpose of claims to an exercise of jurisdiction over the disputed territory.[97] The decision was therefore reached by applying international law to the evidence of official acts and claims before 1947, and not on the basis of any *uti possidetis* rule, as applied to purely *constitutional* boundaries. Judge Bebler, who dissented as to part of the boundary, was more emphatic: 'the relations between the British and Kutch were those of suzerain and vassal as defined in specific clauses in treaties; these clauses replaced certain rules governing the intercourse of nations under International Law; rules of International Law not replaced by such clauses remained valid and equally binding on both partners.'[98]

(ii) Protectorates and State succession

Problems of State continuity or State succession with respect to protectorates involve at least two distinct issues: the continuity of pre-protectorate treaties upon the commencement of a protectorate, and the position of the fully-independent State upon the termination of the protectorate.

The situation with respect to pre-protectorate treaties is the more straightforward: practice supports, with some consistency,[99] the view that treaties binding a State before its protection continue to bind it after the conclusion of a protectorate agreement and until annexation. Formally, of course, this is a case of continuity, not succession. The rule was affirmed by the International Court in the *United States Nationals in Morocco Case*,[100] and by the Rapporteur on State Succession with respect to Treaties (Waldock), who proposed as a special rule that 'Unless terminated or suspended in conformity with its own provisions or with the general rules of international law: (a) A treaty to which a State was a party prior to its becoming a pro-

---

[97] Ibid. 675.

[98] Ibid. 696; cf. 699.

[99] O'Connell, *State Succession* II, 31–2, 48–9 (Madagascar); 45 (Zanzibar); 46–8 (Tunisia); 49–50 (Korea); 50–3 (Morocco); Kamanda, 214–18; Lindley, 308–12; I.L.A., *The Effect of Independence upon Treaties*, Ch. 16; Pereira, *La Succession d'états en matière de traité* (1969), 83.

[100] I.C.J. Rep. 1952, p. 179, 188. See also *Spanish Zone of Morocco*, Claim 51 (1925) 2 *RIAA* 722, 725.

tected State continues in force with respect to that State . . .'[101]
This draft article was deleted from the 1972 Draft Articles,[102]
although there was little dissent from the proposition that pre-
protection treaties remained in force so long as the protected
entity retained its international status.[103]

More difficult is the problem of the continuity of, or successsion
to, treaties with respect to 'new States' formed by the termination
of a protectorate. The Rapporteur's commentary on this point
reflects with some accuracy the conflicting considerations:

Logically, it may be urged, the same reasoning should be applied to
treaties concluded with reference to a protected territory *during the
period of protection*. In other words, if a treaty had been concluded by the
protecting Power *on behalf of* or *in the name of* the protected State, the
treaty should be considered as a treaty of the protected State itself and
be binding upon it after independence. But if a treaty had been
concluded by the protecting Power simply in its own name, and merely
"extended" to the protected State, the question of succession should be
governed by the same rules as in the case of a treaty "extended" to a
colonial territory.[104]

Despite this logical consideration, it was thought that the
application of many treaties to protected States or territories was
only formally the result of representation or agency, and was—
with the possible exception of 'non-colonial' protectorates such
as those in Europe[105]—politically indistinguishable from the
application of treaties to colonies generally. As a result the
Rapporteur proposed that treaties to which a protected State
became a party 'in its own name and by its own will' should
continue in force, whereas those applied by the metropolitan
State should be subject to the normal rules of succession.[106] Again

---

[101] *ILC Ybk.* 1972/II, 3.

[102] *ILC Ybk.* 1972/I, 133 ff.

[103] Although some members supported the inclusion of Art. 18 in the Draft, a majority
took the view that the Convention was only 'intended to deal with future cases of
succession, which would not include many cases of protectorates.' There was no explicit
disagreement with the substance of the draft article, although M. Bedjaoui thought that,
in practice, the situation did not arise since prior treaties 'had ceased to be applied during
the period of the protectorates': ibid. 137.

[104] Ibid. 1972/II, 5. Cf. Zemanek (1965), 116 *HR* 181–300, 196–202.

[105] *ILC Ybk.* 1972/I, 139 (Ushakov).

[106] *ILC Ybk.* 1972/II, 3. For the earlier practice, see O'Connell, *State Succession* II, 141–
150.

the substance of this proposal received considerable support,[107] but a clear majority favoured its exclusion from the Draft Articles, either because of the difficulties of application,[108] inconsistency with recent practice,[109] the primacy of the principle of self-determination under the Charter,[110] or the practical irrelevance of the problem for the future.[111] It was also pointed out that in particular situations the theory of representation and agency could provide a satisfactory degree of continuity.[112]

Colonial protectorates, on the other hand, are treated as colonies for the purposes of State succession.[113]

(iii) Termination of protected status[114]

The way in which dependent status is normally terminated illustrates the status itself. Protected States usually achieve complete independence quite simply, either by a gradual process of transfer of power, the reverse of that by which the protecting State originally established its jurisdiction, or by treaties between protecting and protected States resulting in full and immediate independence. The case of Kuwait is instructive.[115] The protectorate treaty of 1899 and subsequent instruments[116] were, it seems, superseded over a period of time. For example, Kuwait was admitted to UNESCO on 18 November 1960, after the United Kingdom Government in a letter to the Director-General had affirmed that Kuwait was 'responsible for the conduct of her international relations'.[117] An Exchange of Notes between Kuwait and the United Kingdom of 1961 provided:

---

[107] *ILC Ybk.* 1972/I, 134 (Tammes), 135 (Câmara), 136 (Quentin-Baxter), 139 (Bilge), 141 (Ago): cf. 138 (Tsuruoka). In his summary, the Rapporteur reaffirmed that Draft Article 18(2) 'reflected the relevant State practice': ibid. 148.

[108] Ibid. 137 (Bedjaoui), 146 (Reuter), 147 (Kearney).

[109] Ibid. 138 (Bedjaoui), 139 (Ushakov).

[110] Ibid. 135 (Reuter), 135–6 (Alcívar), 145–6 (Tabibi).

[111] Ibid. 134 (El-Erian), 137–8 (Bedjaoui), 140 (Ustor, Singh).

[112] Ibid. 135 (Reuter); but cf. 138 (Bedjaoui).

[113] Ibid., 1972/II, 4. Thus the Swaziland Order in Council (*S.R.&O.* 1903, No. 531), consequent upon the annexation of the South African Republic, recited that 'all the rights and powers of the late . . . Republic with respect to Swaziland have, by virtue of the conquest and annexation of the said . . . Republic passed to His Majesty . . .'

[114] See also Kamanda, 295–304.

[115] *Supra*, p. 192.

[116] 166 *BFSP* 111; Al Baharna, 322–4.

[117] Al Baharna, 114.

1. The Agreement of the 23rd of January, 1899, shall be terminated as being inconsistent with the sovereignty and independence of Kuwait.

2. The relations between the two countries shall continue to be governed by a spirit of close friendship . . .[118]

As one would expect from the terminology of the Notes, both Governments took the view that 'it was not the Exchange of Notes on 19th June which conferred independence on Kuwait. Kuwait was already independent and had been for some time . . .'[119] This view has been disputed both by commentators[120] and by the Soviet Union in the Security Council proceedings concerning Kuwait's United Nations admission.[121] But if jurisdiction can be acquired in a State by 'grant, usage (or) sufferance' there seems to be no reason why such jurisdiction may not be relinquished in the same way. The problem is one of evidence, not of principle.

International protectorates—including entities with very much less international status than that enjoyed by Kuwait after 1899—are also as a rule granted independence by a process of consent. The Indian Native States are discussed elsewhere.[122]

The constitution of the Malaysian Federation raised similar issues and was dealt with in the same way. In 1963 Brunei declined to join the Federation, after failure to agree *inter alia* over oil revenues.[123] The British Government, whilst advising accession, regarded Brunei's constitution as an internal matter for the Sultan: no power existed to compel federation.[124] Brunei thus remains a separate 'State under British protection'.[125]

On the other hand, termination of colonial protectorates follows a course much more like the cession of or granting of independence to colonies in the strict sense. Such consensual

---

[118] 166 *BFSP* 112.

[119] *H.C. Deb.* Vol. 645 col. 952 (31 July 1961). Cf. Whiteman, 2 *Digest* 182–4; Pearcy (1961), 45 *DSB* 604, 606.

[120] Pillai & Kumar (1962), 11 *ICLQ* 108–30; O'Brien and Goebel, 'U.S. Recognition Policy', 165–7.

[121] *Supra*, p. 135.

[122] *Infra*, p. 210. The British Government did not regard the statutory termination of suzerainty over the Indian states as unilateral, because of the assent to that Act prior to its passage; *H.C. Deb.* Vol. 454 cols. 1719–40, 30 July 1948.

[123] *Keesing's* 1963, 19716.

[124] *H.C. Deb.* Vol. 669 cols. 31–6, 10 Dec. 1962; ibid., Vol. 680 cols. 1034–5, 9 July 1963.

[125] Ibid., Vol. 756 w.a. col. 29, 11 Dec. 1967. Cf. supra, p. 198 n. 74.

elements in the grant of independence as do exist can best be explained on grounds of self-determination. For example, certain islands administered as part of the South Arabian Federation were, at the inhabitants' request, ceded to Oman rather than made part of the new People's Republic of South Yemen in November 1967.[126] But no option of separate independence was offered, and Britain remained the only State competent to cede the protected territory. Colonial protectorates are, then, in the same position as colonies with regard to the grant of independence.[127]

(iv) Other legal effects

A summary review of other legal effects of protectorates supports the distinctions drawn here between the various categories of protectorate. Thus protectorate arrangements which preserve the status of the protected entity are arrangements 'of a contractual nature', and so non-opposable to third States:[128] colonial protectorates, on the other hand, whether or not as a result of the Berlin Act, came to be regarded as territorial arrangements opposable as against third States upon effective occupation and notification.[129] Territory of protected States or international protectorates may not be ceded without the consent

---

[126] [1967] *BPIL* 18–20; cf. [1964] *BPIL* 12–20; [1966] *BPIL* 6–7, 50 2.

[127] Swaziland again provides an interesting example. Independence was granted in two stages: in 1967 the Swaziland Constitution Order (S.I. 1967 No. 241) vested general authority in the King of Swaziland and local legislative and executive bodies, although the British High Commissioner retained substantial powers. Swaziland was reclassified as a protected State in British constitutional law under the new constitution. But that constitution was revoked and a new one established for the 'sovereign independent Kingdom' of Swaziland by the Swaziland Independence Order, 1968 (S.I. 1968 No. 1377 & Schedule), pursuant to the Swaziland Independence Act, 1968. That the position of the local authorities before independence was derivative is confirmed by the unilateral form by which independence was granted. See further Poulose, *Succession in International Law. A Study of India, Pakistan, Ceylon and Burma* (1974), 31–53.

[128] *Nationality Decrees in Tunis in Morocco*, Ser. B No. 4 (1923), 27; McNair, *Law Officers Opinions* I, 41–6. U.S. rights in Morocco were retained over a lengthy period, notwithstanding the French Protectorate: *U.S. Nationals in Morocco* I.C.J. Rep. 1952, p. 176.

[129] McNair gives two examples of the change in view: a Colonial Office Memorandum of 1891, based on the Berlin Act (op. cit. 46–52); and a Report by Reid and Lockwood of 1895 concluding 'that the existence of a protectorate in an uncivilized country imports the right to assume whatever jurisdiction over all persons may be needed for its effectual exercise' (ibid. 54–5).

or authorization of the protected entity:[130] this is not true of colonial protectorates.[131] Where a protectorate has separate personality, international obligations may be attributed to it separately;[132] although the protecting State, if responsible for the conduct of the protected entity's foreign relations, may be liable as guarantor for international wrongs attributable to the latter.[133] In practice, international claims are often brought against the protecting State alone.[134] International protectorates are not necessarily bound by treaties[135] or declarations of belligerency[136] by the protecting State, although in both cases the matter is largely one of interpretation and intent. In determining the neutrality or otherwise of the European protected States in World War II, the Department of State applied the criterion of enemy use or occupation: Andorra, Liechtenstein, and San Marino were all regarded as neutral.[137] Monaco, on the other hand, had been 'considered enemy occupied territory since November 1942'.[138] Citizens of international protectorates had a status intermediate between nationals and aliens of the protecting State, and were referred to as *protégés, ressortissants,* or protected persons.[139] Protected States, of course, retained their own nationality.[140] And, finally, sovereign immunity was uniformly accorded the heads of Protected States and international protectorates,[141] but not the chiefs of colonial protectorates.[142]

---

[130] Jenner, FO 83/2286, 29 June 1833 (Ionian Islands); McNair, op. cit. 39.

[131] For the Ethiopia-Somalia dispute, *supra*, p. 200, n. 87.

[132] *Phosphates in Morocco*, Ser. A/B No. 74 (1938), 25–7 ('international obligations of Morocco and France').

[133] *Spanish Zone of Morocco Claims* (1925) 2 *RIAA* 615, 648–9 ('une espèce de garantie'); O'Connell, *State Succession* II, 43.

[134] *Phosphates in Morocco*, Ser. A/B No. 74, 32–3 *per* Judge van Eysinga (diss.).

[135] Al Baharna, 84–114; Kamanda, 200–5.

[136] *The Ionian Ships* (1855) 2 Sp. Ecc. & Ad. 212; 164 E.R. 394, Smith, *GB & LN* I, 67–76; *Kantrantios* v. *Bulgaria* (1926) 3 AD No. 27 (Samos); Kamanda, 225–45.

[137] *USFR* 1944/IV, 294.

[138] Ibid. 293–4.

[139] Kamanda, 246–58; Al Baharna, 122–8; Jones (1945), 22 *BY* 122–9; *National Bank of Egypt* v. *Austria-Hungary Bank* (1924) 3 *Rep. MAT* 236, 238; *Re Ho* (1975) 5 A.I.,R. 304.

[140] e.g. Liechtenstein: *supra*, p. 190, n. 18.

[141] e.g. *Sultan of Johore* v. *Abukukar* [1952] A.C. 318; *Government of Morocco* v. *Laurens* (1930) 5 AD No. 75; *supra*, pp. 61–2. See also Al Baharna, 145–51; Kamanda, 222–5.

[142] *Chief Tschekedi Khama* v. *Ratshosa* [1931] A.C. 784 (Bechuanaland).

7.3　OTHER CASES

(1) *Special treaty relations*

In British practice the term 'special treaty relations' is often used to describe Protected States with full powers of self-government and only peripheral legal links with the protecting State. Bahrain was referred to in 1947 as an 'Independent State under the protection of Her Majesty's Government and in special Treaty relations with them'.[143]

The term is thus synonymous with legal independence, and implies links of alliance and guarantee based on consent. As a term of art it is however more than usually inexact. The Sultanate of Muscat and Oman, for example, was not described as in 'special treaty relations' with Great Britain, but rather as a 'sovereign and independent State'.[144] One would have thought that the relation between the two States, which involved international guarantees of Muscat's independence,[145] an undertaking of non-alienation without British consent,[146] certain rights of extra-territorial jurisdiction,[147] and an arrangement for the conduct of (though not responsibility for) Muscat's foreign relations,[148] were sufficiently close to be termed 'special'. There could however be no doubt about Muscat's legal independence.[149]

(2) *Vassal States and suzerainty*

The term 'vassal' and 'suzerain' derive from feudal law, and their translation into the field of international relations is a ready source of confusion.[150] The term 'vassal' refers sometimes to an entity subject to suzerainty, and sometimes to States gradually breaking away from an Empire, that is to say, devolving States. This latter problem is discussed in the next Chapter.

---

[143] *H.C. Deb.* Vol. 445 col. 1681 (17 Dec. 1947).

[144] *GAOR* A/C 109/SR 409, 8 (26 Apr. 1966).

[145] Franco-British Declaration (1862): *Aitchison* XI, 226.

[146] 100 *BFSP* 591; renewed periodically and terminated in 1958: 163 *BFSP* 490.

[147] *UKTS* No. 44 (1951). See also Kamanda, 78–81; Whiteman, 1 *Digest* 447–50; Al Baharna, 47–54.

[148] *H.C. Deb.* Vol. 574 cols. 870–2 (29 July 1957).

[149] Al Baharna, 47; *Muscat Dhows Case* (P.C.A., 1905) Scott I, 95; to which Muscat was not however a party; queried by E. Lauterpacht (1958), 7 *ICLQ* 99–109, 109n.54.

[150] On the nineteenth century origins of the term in international relations, see Kelke (1896), 12 *LQR* 215–27.

Suzerainty may be defined as a relation between a dominant and a dependent State the incidents of which are in part defined by treaty or agreement, and in part by a *lex specialis* peculiar to that relation or that class of relations. It differs from protectorate only in that certain of its incidents are more likely to be undefined, or to involve general claims of supremacy. Although suzerainty is practically obsolete, one important example —the Indian Native States until 1947—deserves some mention.[151]

Although the British Government regarded the Native States as extraterritorial and accorded their rulers sovereign immunity and the general right to internal self-government, they claimed various rights, including 'the conduct of international relations, the exercise of jurisdiction over Europeans and Americans, interference to settle disputes as to succession to the State, the suppression of gross misrule in the State, and the regulation of armaments and the strength of Military Forces.'[152] Arrangements with the Indian States was substantially similar although the tendency in British practice to regard 'paramountcy' as some specific legal condition irrespective of local consent should not be allowed to obscure the fact that their status depended on the specific agreements, documents and consents in each case.[153] Equally the British claim that 'the principles of international law have no bearing upon the relations between the Government of India ... and the native States under the suzerainty of Her Majesty. The paramount supremacy of the former presupposes and implies the subordination of the latter,'[154] seemed to be founded on the erroneous view that international law only governed the relations of independent and equal States.[155] The Native States were not independent, and their status was not that of Protected States as here defined. But neither were they equivalent to colonial protectorates. The incidents of their status are very similar to those attaching to international pro-

[151] See Sen, *The Indian States* (1930); Lee Warner, *The Native States of India* (1910); Somervell (1930), 11 *BY* 55–62; Fawcett, *British Commonwealth*, 126–9; Poulose, *Succession in International Law. A Study of India, Pakistan, Ceylon and Burma* (1974), 31–53.

[152] *Maharaja of Tripura* v. *Province of Assam* (1948) 22 ILR 64.

[153] Maine, in Ilbert, *The Government of India* (3rd ed., 1915), Ch. V; cited Lindley, 196.

[154] Off. Gaz. of India, 21 Aug. 1891, cited Fawcett, *British Commonwealth*, 126; Indian Statutory Commission Report, 1928–9, Cmd. 3302, §§ 18, 57. This view owed much to Lee Warner, op. cit. 28 ff., and Westlake. For criticism see Sen, *The Indian States, passim.*

[155] *Rann of Kutch Award, supra*, p. 202; Alexandrowicz, *Introduction to the History of the Law of Nations in the East Indies* (1967), 20–3.

tectorates.[156] By 1947 the Crown had evidently changed its mind, because its position then was quite inconsistent with the view that the States were merely municipal units of the Empire. Despite 'paramountcy', the Indian States were regarded as free to accede to India or Pakistan or neither: no constitutional authority was thought to exist to force such accession, although the British Government advised in favour of that course.[157] The Indian Independence Act 1947, s. 7 merely provided for the 'lapse' of suzerainty over the Indian States, so that it was arguable that those States which had not acceded were rendered fully independent.

The most important such case was that of Hyderabad, which had been in the 'most independent' class of native States prior to 1947. Its full independence was however shortlived: Hyderabad was blockaded and then invaded and annexed by India in September 1948. The Security Council, while hostilities were in progress, accepted the Nizam's complaint of aggression as an agenda item and admitted his representative to its deliberations, apparently under Article 35(2).[158] It was unable, by virtue of Hyderabad's surrender, to decide on any specific action.[159]

(3) *Autonomy and residual sovereignty*

Autonomous areas are regions of a State, usually possessing some ethnic or cultural distinctiveness, which have been granted separate powers of internal administration, to whatever degree, without being detached from the State of which they are part. For such status to be of present interest, it must be in some way internationally binding upon the central authorities.[160] Given such guarantees, the local entity may have a certain status, although since that does not normally involve any foreign relations capacity, it is necessarily limited. Until a very advanced stage is reached in the progress towards self-government, such

---

[156] Cf. Kamanda, 203–4.

[157] *H.C. Deb.* Vol. 439 cols. 2451–2 (10 July 1947); ibid., Vol. 452 cols. 1360–2 (23 June 1948).

[158] *SCOR* 3rd yr. Suppl., Sept. 1948, 5 (S/986); Higgins, *Development*, 51–2; Eagleton (1950), 44 *AJ* 277–302; *contra* Das (1949), 43 *AJ* 57–72.

[159] *SCOR* 3rd. yr. No. 109, 357th mtg., 16 Sept. 1948: Eagleton, op. cit. 277–81, 294–299. See also *USFR* 1948/V, 360–1, 373, 411, 417. On the Kashmir dispute see Gupta, *Jammu and Kashmir* (1968).

[160] Cf. the Memel Territory, *supra*, p. 160.

areas are not States. A good example of the problem of 'autonomous areas' is provided by Tibet.[161] Tibet had been said to be under the 'suzerainty' of China since the eighteenth century, but the incidents of the relation had remained obscure. By 1910 the weakness of central government in China made Tibetan independence at least arguable.[162] In a treaty of 1904 with Great Britain, Tibet undertook not to dispose of territory, not to pledge its revenue, not to grant concessions to, or admit representatives of, any 'foreign Power' without British consent.[163] That Treaty was confirmed by a Convention of 1906 between Great Britain and China, the terms of which suggest that the phrase 'foreign Power' in the earlier treaty was not intended to exclude China.[164] This is confirmed by the Russo-British Treaty of 1907 by which the parties, 'reconnaissant les droits suzerains de la Chine sur le Thibet', agreed to respect the territorial integrity of Tibet, not to interfere in its internal affairs, and not to negotiate with Tibet except through the Chinese Government as intermediary.[165] Thus the Agreement of 1908 amending Trade Regulations in Tibet between Great Britain, China, and Tibet, was concluded with the 'representative' of the 'High Authorities of Tibet' acting 'under the directions of the Chinese plenipotentiary'.[166] In 1910, therefore, Tibet possessed a considerable degree of *de facto* independence, conditioned by Chinese power with respect to Tibetan foreign affairs, and by the claims of China, in fact unexercised, to some greater degree of control. In 1911 the Manchu dynasty collapsed: with it, it has been argued, collapsed also the claims of China over Tibet, since these were based on a personal allegiance under feudal law.[167] That this might have happened can perhaps be conceded: on the other hand, neither China nor Great Britain thought that this was, at

---

[161] See Lamb, *The McMahon Line. A Study in the Relations between India, China and Tibet, 1904 to 1914* (1966); Rubin (1968), *China Q.* No. 35, 110–54; International Commission of Jurists, *The Question of Tibet and the Rule of Law* (1959); Alexandrowicz (1954), 48 *AJ* 265–74. Cf. the strikingly similar problem of Outer Mongolia prior to 1945: *supra*, p. 68, n. 192.

[162] Alexandrowicz (1954), 48 *AJ* 265, 275; International Commission of Jurists, op. cit. 85.

[163] Ibid. 78–91; 98 *BFSP* 148, Art. 9.

[164] 99 *BFSP* 171, Art. III.

[165] 100 *BFSP* 555; but cf. International Commission of Jurists, op. cit. 81–2.

[166] 101 *BFSP* 170. Only Great Britain and China were to ratify the Agreement.

[167] Alexandrowicz (1954) 48 *AJ* 265, 270.

any rate automatically, so. The crucial document of the period was the Simla Convention of 1914, intended to be signed by China, Tibet, and Great Britain, but because of disagreement over boundaries signed by the latter two only. The Simla Convention was thus not binding upon China, but it would seem to constitute good evidence of what the parties thought Tibet's status was at the time—or, perhaps, what they hoped Tibet could successfully claim. Article 2 stated: 'The Governments of Great Britain and China recognizing that Tibet is under the suzerainty of China, and recognizing also the autonomy of Outer Tibet, engage to respect the territorial integrity of the country, and to abstain from interference in the administration of Outer Tibet ...'[168] It would seem to follow then, despite the various possibilities,[169] that Tibet was not in 1914 regarded as independent, but that at least part of the country possessed substantial autonomy. This has always been the British view,[170] and it was also, apparently the Chinese view in 1951.[171] It may still be that Chinese actions in Tibet after 1951 have been illegal on other grounds.[172]

In cases of 'autonomous regions', such as Tibet or Oman,[173] normal classifications of 'sovereignty' and statehood are only applicable with difficulty, and the facts are often obscure and controversial. The case of Tibet, in particular, highlights the rather arbitrary way in which, for their own purposes, the 'Powers' decided upon a particular course of action, and thus, in effect, determined the status of a people. But from the point of view of a study of statehood, the problems of classification are

[168] International Commission of Jurists, op. cit. 85–7, 124–7.

[169] On the disputed declaration of independence of 1912 see Rubin (1965), 59 *AJ* 586–590; and (1966) 60 *AJ* 812–14; McCabe, ibid. 369–71. The matter is also of importance in relation to the India-China boundary: see Rubin (1960), 9 *ICLQ* 96–125; Sharma (1965), 59 *AJ* 16–47. See also International Commission of Jurists, *Tibet and the Chinese People's Republic* (1960), 139–66.

[170] 151 *BFSP* 89.

[171] China-Tibet Agreement on Administration of Tibet, 1951: 158 *BFSP* 731. Cf. however the Sino-Indian Agreement of 29 April 1954 concerning Indian Trade and Intercourse with the 'Tibet Region of China': Lamb, op. cit. II, 638–41. The 1954 Agreement appears to assume either termination or cancellation of British treaties relating to Tibet: *loc. cit.*

[172] Cf. G.A. Res 1353 (XIV), 21 Oct. 1959 (45–9:26); 1723 (XVI), 20 Dec. 1961 (56–11:29); 2079 (XX), 18 Dec. 1965 (43–26:22); Higgins, *Development*, 123–5, 222.

[173] As to which see Al Baharna, 239–49; Kelly, *Chatham House Memoranda* 1959 (13); (1961) 19 *ICLQ* 552; SCOR 783rd mtg., 20 Aug. 1957.

mitigated by the fact that neither suzerainty nor sovereignty necessarily exclude international obligations or international inquiry with respect to autonomous regions. The effect is rather, as pointed out already, to alter the burden of proof.

(4) *Spheres of influence*

Spheres of influence were agreements by two or more States delimiting the areas of territory, in particular in Africa, within which each party would be permitted by the other party or parties to operate. Their force was strictly contractual;[174] and they gave no legal rights over the territory itself as against its occupants. They are accordingly outside the scope of this study.[175]

---

[174] Cf. 88 *BFSP* 1287, cited Lindley, 212–13. To the same effect, *Western Sahara Opinion* I.C.J. Rep. 1975 p. 12, 56.

[175] See generally McNair, *Law Officers Opinions* I, 55–8; Lindley, 207–36; Rutherford (1926), 20 *AJ* 300–25.

8. Devolution

8.1 INTRODUCTORY

THE TWO most important methods by which new States are formed are the grant of independence by the previous sovereign, and the forcible seizure of independence by the territory in question.[1] These will be referred to as devolution and secession respectively. The crucial distinguishing feature is the presence or absence of metropolitan[2] consent, although in some circumstances this distinction is formal and may even be arbitrary.[3] Thus the relevance of metropolitan consent varies in different situations, especially when the principle of self-determination is at issue. The contrast between Biafra and Guinea-Bissau[4] demonstrates this difference, but equally it demonstrates the importance attached in State practice to metropolitan consent to the formation of a new State on part of its territory.

Grants of independence can take different forms: in particular it is useful to distinguish between immediately effective grants of independence, and gradual devolution or accretion of power in a local unit, such that the latter eventually is classified as a separate State. Immediate, or relatively immediate, grant of independence is by far the most common modern method of transfer of governmental authority. The exercise of, and limits upon, this power are considered in the next section. The process of gradual devolution of power was adopted in the case of the British Dominions before 1945, and there have been other instances. Though now less common than the relatively immediate formal transfer of power, gradual devolution thus has considerable historical importance: it is considered in the following sections of this Chapter.

---

[1] International Law Association, *The Effect of Independence on Treaties* (1965), 1; O'Connell, *State Succession* II, 88, 101 ('revolutionary' and 'evolutionary secession').

[2] The term 'metropolitan' refers here to the State on whose territory the new State is to be created (and to the government of that State): cf. *infra*, p. 359.

[3] Brownlie (1961), 8 *Rev. of Cont. L.* 19–40, 26–7.

[4] *Supra*, p. 102; *infra*, Chapter 9.

8.2   EXPLICIT GRANTS OF INDEPENDENCE

Like the competence to cede territory, the competence to transfer governmental power to a new State on part of the metropolitan territory is an attribute of State sovereignty.[5] There is however this difference, that in the latter case a new legal person is created, and the legal position of third States is *pro tanto* affected. The power is thus an important one, but it would seem that there are relatively few legal limitations to its exercise. That this is so is no doubt due to the absence of any political desire, and, perhaps, any need, to regulate the number of new States.

A variety of means has been used to transfer competence to the local entities: municipal legislation,[6] the termination of treaties of protection,[7] the conclusion of an agreement in the nature of a treaty between the former sovereign and the new State,[8] or a combination of some of these methods. That the constitution of a State results from, and is contained in, municipal legislation of another State might be thought a derogation from the independence of the former. In Kelsen's words, for a new State, 'ce qui importe, c'est que ces normes aient pour principe de validité une Constitution créé indépendamment des constitutions des autres États';[9] and it is sometimes argued that this cannot be so when the constitution is a municipal law of another State. This issue arose in an interesting way in *Buck* v. *Attorney General*,[10] when a number of former citizens of the colony of Sierra Leone sought a declaration in a British court that the Sierra Leone (Constitution) Order in Council, 1961 was *ultra vires* the British Settlements Act 1887 and void. The Court of Appeal denied that it had jurisdiction to determine the matter, for several reasons: that the independence of Sierra Leone was achieved not by the Order in Council but by the Sierra Leone Independence Act, 1961; and that in any event a British court could not 'make a declaration

---

[5] Pufendorf, *De Jure Naturae et Gentium Libri Octo* VII, Ch. 3, § 690; *supra*.

[6] Cf. Roberts-Wray, in Anderson, ed., *Changing Law in Developing Countries* (1963), 43–62; *Liyanage* v. *R.* [1967] 1 A.C. 259, 286.

[7] *Supra*, p. 205.

[8] e.g., Articles of Agreement for a Treaty between Great Britain and Ireland, 6 Dec. 1921, 26 *LNTS* 10.

[9] (1929) 4 *RDI* 613–41, 616; cf. *supra*, pp. 74–6; Fawcett, *British Commonwealth*, 94–106.

[10] [1965] Ch. 745.

impugning the validity of the constitution of a foreign or independent State, at any rate where that is the object of the action. This may be put as a matter of international comity, or upon the ground of effectiveness.'[11] But two more fundamental reasons could have been given, one of which the Court assumed, the other of which was, in at least one of the judgments, more explicit.

In the first place it is necessary to distinguish between the validity of the grant of independence to a State, and the validity of its constitution. In international law only the former is necessary, since a State may be created without a formal constitution, or may change its independence-constitution by municipally illegal means without any discontinuity of international personality.[12] The invalidity of the Sierra Leone Constitution in British law would have left unaffected the independence of Sierra Leone. The validity of its constitution, in accordance with the law of Sierra Leone, would still have been a matter for the courts of Sierra Leone to decide.

A second closely related point was made by Diplock L.J.

> As soon as Sierra Leone became independent, the Order in Council ceased to have any effect as an Order in Council, that is, as an exercise of the sovereign power of the United Kingdom Government . . . Whatever effect it then had was as part of the law of a foreign sovereign State, into the validity of which this court has no jurisdiction to enquire. Whether it was valid during the *punctum temporis* during which it was in force before Sierra Leone became independent is a subject-matter in which the parties have no interest. No legal rights or liabilities can depend upon it . . .[13]

The assumption by a new State of a constitution established by a law of the previous sovereign is thus a matter both formally and substantially distinct from the validity of that law under the municipal law of the previous sovereign. The achievement of State independence by grant thus complies with Kelsen's requirement, because the *'principe de validité'* of the new

---

[11] Ibid. 768 *per* Harman L.J. Leave to appeal was refused: [1965] 1 W.L.R. 860.

[12] *Infra*, p. 405.

[13] Ibid. 771–2; cf. *per* Russell L.J., 773. Compare *Sabally and N° Jie* v. *Attorney-General* [1965] 1 Q.B. 273, where the Court enquired into the constitutional validity of prerogative acts with respect to a self-governing, but not then independent, territory (Gambia).

constitution is not its legality under the law of the grantor, but the fact of its assumption as the constitution of the State.[14]

The consent of the former sovereign is none the less, as has been stated, an important element in the statehood of the newly emergent entity. In a study of United States recognition policies with respect to sixty new States, O'Brien and Goebel note that forty-five States were accorded 'instantaneous' or even 'antici-patory' recognition.[15] Such recognition would have been quite improper, absent the consent or acquiescence of the previous sovereign.[16] Although it has been said that the mere declaration by the metropolitan State that independence has been granted is not of itself sufficient,[17] modern practice demonstrates with some consistency the proposition that, *prima facie* a new State granted full formal independence by the former sovereign has the international right to govern its territory as a State.[18] Certain exceptions to this principle do however exist, and these must now be considered.

(1) *Purported but illusory grants of independence*

Where a State purports to grant independence to a particular territory, but in fact retains substantial authority over the territory, then, clearly, the grant is ineffective, although questions of responsibility may arise.[19]

(2) *Partial or incomplete grants of independence*

The problem of partial grants of independence is more difficult. There is of course no general prohibition against a State granting a certain degree of autonomy, or certain rights to act in the international sphere without granting plenary competence.

[14] Cf. De Smith, *The New Commonwealth and its Constitutions* (1964), 6–7.

[15] O'Brien and Goebel, 'U.S. Recognition Policy', 207 ff., esp. 212. In only two cases (India and Burma) was recognition anticipatory of independence by more than a few days. Of the thirteen cases of delayed recognition, three (Senegal, Guinea and probably Morocco) were political and two, Nepal and Yemen, were probably the result of the isolation of the entities in question. In the other eight cases subsisting disputes, or doubts about independence, were regarded as justifying the withholding of recognition. Cf. also Myers (1961), 55 *AJ* 701–20, 703; Verzijl, *International Law* II, 66–89; Verhoeven, *Reconnaissance*, 12–19.

[16] *Infra*, p. 257.

[17] Hone, *Report of International Law Conference, 1960*, 14–16, cited O'Brien and Goebel, 'U.S. Recognition Policy', 308n.

[18] *Supra*, p. 44.

[19] Cf. Syria and Lebanon after 1943: *supra*, pp. 66–8.

The status of an entity granted partial competence is sometimes uncertain: the situation approximates to that of gradual accretion of power, discussed later. Although the view has been taken that 'international law [makes] it impossible to create an "international person", responsible only for certain specific fields of external affairs of any one territory'[20] it is by no means clear that this is so. On the other hand, where a State has undertaken to grant full independence or self-determination to a particular territory, a partial grant will not absolve it from, and may be a breach of, that obligation.

(3) *Grants in violation of self-determination*

We have discussed already the problem of purported secessions in breach of self-determination, and in particular the case of Rhodesia.[21] The problem of grants of power in violation of self-determination also requires discussion. In practice, two different situations have arisen. A metropolitan State may seek to avoid the obligation of self-determination by granting independence to a quite unrepresentative fraction of the people of a territory. Alternatively, an attempt may be made to divide a particular territory so as to avoid an obligation to grant independence to the territory as a whole.

(i) *Grants to unrepresentative governments within self-determination units*

Where an obligation exists to grant self-determination to a particular territory, it is quite clearly possible for an administering authority in effect to circumvent its obligation by granting independence to an entrenched and unrepresentative minority. On the other hand, self-determination does not necessarily involve the establishment of a democracy based on the principle of 'one vote, one value', and the administering authority has a measure of discretion in determining the persons in the territory to whom the grant of authority will be made. Thus where the traditional authorities within the territory retain the support of the people, the United Nations has approved transfers of power to those authorities (for example in Swaziland, the United Arab Emirates, and Malaysia). It has also approved constitutional

---

[20] Report of the Singapore Constitutional Conference, Cmnd. 147 (1957), cited O'Connell, *International Law* (1st edn.) I, 310n.

[21] *Supra*, pp. 103–6.

arrangements which gave a certain preferential position to an indigenous ethnic group (for example in Fiji).[22]

But it remains true that the transfer of authority must be to a government which possesses the support of, and thus can fairly be said to be representative of, the people. The most important recent instance has been Rhodesia. Both the General Assembly and the Security Council have repeatedly 'Request[ed] the United Kingdom Government not to transfer under any circumstances to its colony of Southern Rhodesia, as at present governed, any of the powers or attributes of sovereignty, but to promote the country's attainment of independence by a democratic system of government in accordance with the aspirations of the majority of the population.'[23]

On the view taken by the United Nations,[24] the United Kingdom retains authority over Southern Rhodesia, and thus has the competence to transfer power to the territory. However the exercise of that competence is now restricted, not only by the principle of self-determination but also by explicit United Nations resolutions to which the United Kingdom has assented.[25]

(ii) *Grants disruptive of the 'territorial integrity' of a self-determination unit*

United Nations' practice in self-determination matters reveals two distinct, and to some extent conflicting, rules: the rule that 'all peoples have right to self-determination',[26] and the rule that 'Any attempt aimed at the partial or total disruption of the national unity and the territorial integrity of a country is incompatible with the purposes and principles of the Charter of the United Nations.'[27] This latter rule was restated in the Declaration on Principles of International Law of 24 October 1970 . . .

Nothing in the foregoing paragraphs shall be construed as authorizing or encouraging any action which would dismember or impair, totally

---

[22] Cf. Rigo Sureda, *The Evolution of the Right of Self-Determination* (1973), 182–3.

[23] e.g., S.C. Res. 202 (1965), 6 May 1965 (7–0:4), para. 5.

[24] *Supra*, pp. 103–6.

[25] See also G.A. Res. 2023 (XX) (90–11:4), para. 4 (Aden). The Assembly has also condemned in general terms the imposition of 'non-representative regimes and arbitrary constitutions': e.g. Res. 2878 (XXVI), 20 Dec. 1971 (96–5:18), para. 6.

[26] G.A. Res 1514 (XV), para. 2.

[27] Ibid., para. 6.

or in part, the territorial integrity or political unity of sovereign and independent States conducting themselves in compliance with the principle of equal rights and self-determination of peoples as described above and thus possessed of a government representing the whole people belonging to the territory without distinction as to race, creed or colour.

Every State shall refrain from any action aimed at the partial or total disruption of the national unity or territorial integrity of any other State or country . . .[28]

The principle of self-determination is, as we have seen, a principle of positive international law.[29] The status of the 'territorial integrity' rule, so far as it relates to self-determination units which are not States, is less certain. It is, at least, an established part of United Nations practice, and it may well be regarded as a presumption as to the operation of self-determination in particular cases. Certainly, the division of a self-determination unit into fragments for the purpose of avoiding the principle of self-determination is illegal: for example, the division of South-West Africa into 'Bantustans' or native homelands has been universally condemned.[30] For present purposes, the consequences of the 'territorial integrity' rule in practice may be summarized as follows.

(1) In principle, self-determination units must be granted self-determination as a whole. Only if the continued unity of the territory is clearly contrary to the wishes of the people or to international peace and security will schemes for partition meet with approval of United Nations organs.[31]

(2) As has been stated, attempts to disrupt the territorial integrity of a self-determination unit so as to evade the principle of self-determination are illegal. This principle would appear not to apply to established metropolitan States, assuming always

[28] G.A. Res. 2625 (XXV), 24 Oct. 1970 (adopted without vote).

[29] *Supra*, pp. 85–102.

[30] See e.g. S.C. Resns. 323 (1972), para. 2 (13–0:1); 366 (1974), para. 5(6) (15–0:0); Dugard, *The South West Africa/Namibia Dispute* (1973), 236–8, 431–5; D'Amato (1966), 4 *JMAS* 177–92; Umozurike, *Self-Determination in International Law* (1972), 133–7. Cf. also *Namibia Opinion* I.C.J. Rep. 1971 p. 6, 57.

[31] Partition was approved in the cases of Ruanda and Burundi, Palestine, and the British Cameroons. For West Irian see *infra*, p. 382. See also Rigo Sureda, op. cit. 143–51; Chapter 14 *infra*.

that the dismemberment is a free act of the government of the State and not the result of external illegal force.[32]

(3) A further aspect of practice under the rubric of 'territorial integrity' has been the disapproval of alienations of territory of self-determination units without local consent. For example, Assembly Resolution 2066 (XX) of 16 December 1965 'Invite[d] the administering Power to take no action which would dismember the Territory of Mauritius and violate its territorial integrity . . .'[33] Practice has not, however, been particularly consistent.[34]

(4) The problem of 'colonial enclaves' is sometimes treated as an aspect of the self-determination rule.[35] It is however better regarded as an exception to the rule, and in this discussion of limitations on the competence to grant independence must be dealt with separately.

(4) *Grants of independence in furtherance of illegal policies: the Transkei?*

The question of the limits, if any, on the power of a State to grant independence to a portion of its territory—which power has hitherto been regarded as more-or-less unfettered—was raised squarely by the purported grant of independence by South Africa to the Transkei, on 26 October 1976.

(i) *Origins of the Transkei: The Bantustan policy*

The policy of 'separate development' of racial groups within South Africa is long-established: its ultimate extension was the dismemberment of areas of the Republic by the creation of self-governing 'bantustans' which would then be granted independence. Such a process, it was thought, would justify the denationalization of these South Africans who historically belonged or were thought to belong to the ethnic group for which the bantustan was formed.[36] The Transkei, for example,

---

[32] *Supra*, pp. 106–18. For Transkei, and the Bantustans within South Africa see *infra*, pp. 222–7.

[33] Para. 4 (89–0:18).

[34] See further *infra*, p. 382.

[35] e.g. Rigo Sureda, op. cit. 218–19.

[36] For background to the bantustan policy see Barber, *South Africa's Foreign Policy 1945–70* (1973), 231–42; 'Report of the Special Committee on the Policies of *Apartheid* of the Government of the Republic of South Africa', *GAOR* 18th Sess., A/5497 (1963), 52–4; Hill, *Bantustans: the Fragmentation of South Africa* (1964). For discussion in the context of the

was accorded 'self-government' in 1963.[37] The South African Status of the Transkei Act, 1976[38] purported to grant independence to the Transkei: section 1 provides as follows:

(1) The territory known as the Transkei and consisting of the districts mentioned in Schedule A, is hereby declared to be a sovereign and independent state and shall cease to be part of the Republic of South Africa.

(2) The Republic of South Africa shall cease to exercise any authority over the said territory.

The Act contains rather unusual provisions purporting to determine the citizenship of the Transkei,[39] and including in that 'grant' broad categories of former South African citizens with little or no effective link with the Transkei.[40] Quite apart from the doubtful legality of this form of mass deprivation of nationality, these provisions of the Act demonstrate with some clarity the racially discriminatory nature of the bantustan policy, which is aimed at preserving the bulk of South Africa for its minority white population.[41] The South African Act also provides a procedure for resolution of disputes over the citizenship provisions.[42]

'independence' of the bantustans see R. F. & H. J. Taubenfeld, *Race, Peace, Law, and Southern Africa* (N.Y., 1968), 156–8. Harding, *Unabhängigkeit der Transkei* (Hamburg, 1976).

[37] Transkei Constitution Act No. 48 of 1963; see Kahn (1963) 80 *SALJ* 473–82; Richings (1976), 93 *SALJ* 119–126; Booysen & ors. (1976), 2 *S.Af. YBIL* 1–35.

[38] 15 *ILM* 1175; and see *Keesing's* 1976, 28061–3.

[39] Act, s. 6(1), Schedule B.

[40] Schedule B, paras. (f) and (g) purport to revoke the South African citizenship of, and to confer Transkeian citizenship on, anyone who 'speaks a language used by the Xhosa or Sotho speaking section of the population of the Transkei . . .' or who 'is related to any member of the population contemplated in paragraph (f) or has identified himself with any part of such population or is culturally or otherwise associated with any member or part of such population'.

[41] The Constitution of the Republic of Transkei (15 *ILM* 1136), Ch. 7, does not apparently confer automatic local nationality on all the persons referred to in Schedule B of the South African Act. S. 58(2) provides that 'Any person, who has been found in the manner to be prescribed by or under an Act of Parliament, to be predominantly Xhosa-speaking or Sotho-speaking and to be a member of, or descended from, or ethnically, culturally or otherwise associated with, any tribe resident in a district of Transkei *shall be registered as and become* a citizen of Transkei.' This is ambiguous, but is apparently regarded as providing an option to register. Those not exercising the option, apparently, become stateless. See Dean (1978), 11 *CILSA* 57–67; cf. Oliver (1976), 2 *S.Af.YBIL* 143–154.

[42] S. 6(2). Ss. 4, 5 provide in apparently peremptory form for devolution and continuation in force of various treaties and agreements with South Africa or other States.

The South African Act, and the local Republic of Transkei Constitution Act, appear, with one qualification, to vest full formal independence in the local authorities in the Transkei. That qualification relates to the citizenship provisions of the South African Act: it is a derogation from formal independence for another State to control the grant of nationality of a putative State. However, as a matter of local (Transkeian) law it is uncertain whether the South African Act has this effect: the Transkeian Legislative Assembly has plenary authority,[43] the validity of its legislation cannot be impugned in any court,[44] and the Constitution itself may be freely amended in the ordinary manner and form.[45] Whatever the correct interpretation of section 58 (2) of the Constitution, therefore, the local authorities seem to retain eventual control over who will be regarded as Transkeian nationals under Transkeian law.

The General Assembly has consistently condemned the bantustan policy and asserted that no independent bantustan would be recognized as a State. Thus Resolution 2775E (XXVI) of 29 November 1971, condemned 'the establishment by the Government of South Africa of Bantu homelands (Bantustans) and the forcible removal of the African people of South Africa and Namibia to those areas as a violation of their inalienable rights, contrary to the principle of self-determination and prejudicial to the territorial integrity of the countries and the unity of their peoples.'[46] Resolution 3411D (XXX) of 28 November 1975 reaffirmed this position and '[Call[ed] upon all Governments and organizations not to deal with any institutions or authorities of the bantustans or to accord any form of recognition to them.'[47] On 27 October 1976 the Assembly again condemned the Bantustan policy and rejected the 'independence' of the Transkei as 'invalid'.[48] Meanwhile the Organization of African Unity in July 1976 had invited 'all States ... not to accord recognition to any Bantustan, in particular, the Transkei

[43] Constitution, s. 21.
[44] Ibid., s. 21(4).
[45] Ibid., s. 75.
[46] Para. 1 (105–2:2). See also G.A. Resns. 2923E (XXVII), 15 Nov. 1972, para. 2 (100–4:21); 3151G (XXVIII), 14 Dec. 1973, para. 14(88–7:2); 3324E (XXIX), 16 Dec. 1974, para. 10 (95–13:14).
[47] G.A. Res. 3411D(XXX) (99–0:8).
[48] G.A. Res. 31/6A (134–0: 1 (U.S.)). To the same effect G.A. Res. 32/105N (140–0:0).

whose so-called independence is scheduled for the 26 October 1976.'[49] In fact no third State has, at this writing, recognized the Transkei.[50]

(ii) *The status of the Transkei*

The status of the Transkei as an entity granted formal independence by the previous sovereign and claiming to be a State is thus squarely raised. The various resolutions and statements referred to, although unanimous in effect, are somewhat diffuse in their justification of the non-recognition of the Transkei—assuming, as seems clear, that such non-recognition goes to the status, or lack of it, of the entity in question. For example, Resolution 2775E (XXVI) refers to the principle of self-determination and to 'the territorial integrity of the countries and the unity of their peoples'. But self-determination, as we have seen,[51] has only a limited application to independent metropolitan States: the incidents of the principle in such cases are negative—the duty of non-intervention—and hardly peremptory. Nor does practice demonstrate any general requirement that the government of a metropolitan State be representative of its people (although it is of course for almost all purposes *the* representative of that people), or that it should act with respect to its population in accordance with the principle of self-determination.[52] The principle of 'territorial integrity' does not provide a permanent guarantee of present territorial divisions, nor does it preclude the granting of independence to portion of the metropolitan territory, even where such a grant is contrary to the wishes of the majority of the people of the metropolitan State.[53]

The second justification for non-recognition generally given is that the Transkei lacks independence in view of its economic and political reliance on South Africa: thus the Organization of African Unity resolution referred to its 'fraudulent pseudo-independence'.[54] Where the creation of an entity is attended by

[49] Res. 493 (XXVII); 15 *ILM* 1221.

[50] See e.g. *Australian Foreign Affairs Review* Nov. 1976, 591–5; *U.S. Digest* 1976, 20–1; (1977) 33 *Annuaire Suisse* 166–7; Fischer, [1976] *AFDI* 63–76).

[51] *Supra*, p. 101.

[52] *Supra*, p. 36.

[53] Cf. the Irish Free State: *infra*, p. 238.

[54] O.A.U. Res. 493 (XXVII), para. 4.

serious illegalities, as seems to be the case here, it may be that the presumption in favour of the independence of entities granted full formal independence by the metropolitan State is displaced.[55] None the less, in cases of devolution the criterion of independence is predominantly formal, and there have been other cases of small States very substantially dependent on a former metropolis or third State.[56] It seems doubtful whether the difference in degree of actual dependence is very much greater in the present case.

But on balance it may be concluded that, as an entity the creation of which was attended by serious illegalities, which is not supported (as were the Congo,[57] Lesotho and so on) by the principle of self-determination, and which remains substantially dependent on South Africa for its subsistence, Transkei would seem not to be independent for the purpose of statehood in international law. However, in view of the relatively formal nature of the criterion of independence in these types of case, this judgement remains somewhat precarious, and it certainly could not justify the *permanent* and unequivocal non-recognition which the resolutions cited appear to contemplate.

The third possible justification for non-recognition is that the Transkei, as an entity created directly pursuant to a fundamentally illegal policy of *apartheid*, is for that reason, and irrespective of its degree of formal or actual independence, not a State. As we have seen, some such rule as this seems justifiable with respect to self-determination,[58] and the illegal use of force.[59] The relevance of the concept of *jus cogens* in this context has also been referred to.[60] *Apartheid* as such, a particular institution adopted in one country, is probably not illegal as a matter of customary international law;[61] but it provides a clear case of a policy

[55] Cf. *supra*, p. 44.

[56] The Transkei is 43,798 sq. km. (16,675 sq m.) in area. It imports about 90 per cent of its food supplies; and is heavily reliant on remittances from workers in the Republic of South Africa for its national income. But it has a sea-coast, and unlike some of the Bantustans has a relatively coherent territory.

[57] *Supra*, p. 46.

[58] *Supra*, p. 106.

[59] *Supra*, p. 118.

[60] *Supra*, p. 84.

[61] For the International Convention on the Suppression and Punishment of the Crime of *Apartheid*, annexed to G.A. Res. 3068 (XXVIII), 30 Nov. 1973 (91–4:26), see 13 *ILM* 50. The Convention came into force on 18 July 1976: 15 *ILM* 983. It makes no express reference to the bantustans: but cf. Art. 2(c).

predicated on a fundamental denial of equality on the grounds of race or ethnic origin.[62] There is considerable support for the principle of racial equality and non-discrimination as a principle of general international law and even of *jus cogens*.[63] It is clear (and apparent from Schedule B of the South African Act itself) that the creation of the Transkei was an integral part of a policy which violates this fundamental principle.[64] It may therefore be that a third fundamental criterion of legality regulating the creation of States has been added to the two discussed earlier in this study; although in view of the rather generalized formulations of the non-recognition policy so far, and of the availability of another ground of non-acceptance of the Transkei as a State, this conclusion is necessarily tentative.[65]

(5) *Colonial enclaves and other rights of pre-emption*

Where a State undertakes by treaty or otherwise not to dispose of territory except in a certain way, that undertaking may well limit its competence to grant independence to portion of its territory. Perhaps the most common instance is the so-called right of pre-emption.[66]

A further limitation on the right to grant independence in practice has been the problem of colonial enclaves—of which, again, Gibraltar provides perhaps the best remaining example. The view taken by a majority of the General Assembly has been that colonial enclaves constitute in effect an exception to the self-determination rule, and that the only option is for the administering authority to transfer the enclave to the enclaving State. The wishes of the population of the enclave are not

[62] The important International Convention on the Elimination of all Forms of Racial Discrimination, 1966 (660 *UNTS* 195) expressly and particularly prohibits 'racial segregation and *apartheid*' (Art. 3). As at 31.12.76 there were ninety-two parties to the Convention.

[63] See esp. Judge Tanaka, diss., *South West Africa Cases (Second Phase)* I.C.J. Rep. 1966 pp. 6, 284–316; Brownlie, *Principles*, 578–80 and works there cited. And cf. *supra*, p. 81.

[64] That racial equality and non-discrimination is observed *within* the Transkei is of course not to the point: the illegality relates to the non-observance of the principle within South Africa as a whole, and to the very act of creation of the Transkei which was an aspect of that non-observance.

[65] See also the thorough discussion by Norman (1977), 12 *New England LR* 585–646; Witkin (1977), 18 *Harvard ILJ* 464–7, 605–27; Roth (1976), 9 *NYUJILP* 205–35; (1977) 81 *RGDIP* 582–5. A further 'independent' homeland, Bophuthatswana, was created on 6 Dec. 1977.

[66] e.g. Art. X of the Treaty of Utrecht, 1713:28 *CTS* 325 (Gibraltar); *infra*, p. 381.

regarded as relevant. This practice, and its legal status, will be discussed elsewhere.[67]

(6) *Derogations from grants of independence*

Where a metropolitan State grants independence to a particular territory, it would seem to be necessary that it should grant the attributes necessary for the exercise of that independence. For example, it is established that State property in a territory passes without compensation to the government of an independent State established in the territory.[68] One would have thought then that the former sovereign would not be justified in removing a substantial proportion of the State property in the territory prior to independence, since that would be to derogate from the grant itself. Although there have been instances of this sort of depredation, it has been relatively infrequent, and practice is accordingly undeveloped.

8.3 RELINQUISHMENT OF SOVEREIGNTY WITHOUT GRANT

If States are, in principle, free to relinquish sovereignty over territory in favour of another State, existing or to be created, they are also free to relinquish sovereignty without making any positive disposition of the territory in question. Whether that territory immediately becomes part of another State by 'instantaneous occupation',[69] or becomes *terra derelicta* and so susceptible of appropriation by another State, or becomes subject to a power of disposition (not necessarily equivalent to territorial sovereignty in the normal sense of that term) in a group of major Powers,[70] or possibly the United Nations,[71] then falls to be determined. These problems are discussed as they arise elsewhere in this study.

---

[67] *Infra*, p. 377.
[68] ILC Draft Articles on Succession of States in respect of Matters Other than Treaties, Arts. 5–8, A/9010/Rev. 1, 43–7; Arts. 9, 11, 12–15: *ILC Ybk* 1975/I, 73 ff.
[69] Cf. Taiwan, *supra*, p. 150.
[70] *Infra*, p. 313.
[71] *Infra*, p. 325.

8.4 THE GRADUAL DEVOLUTION OF GOVERNMENTAL POWER: GENERAL PRINCIPLES

(1) *Preliminary considerations*

Where a grant of independence occurs *uno ictu*, as we have seen, relatively few legal problems arise. This is not so in the case of the gradual transfer to or accretion of powers in a local unit over a period of time, where problems of characterization can be particularly acute.[72] To some extent these problems are similar to those, discussed in the last chapter, that occur with dependent entities such as protectorates and vassal States; indeed, the terms 'vassal' and 'suzerain' are sometimes used to describe relationships of devolution. However in the case of dependent entities, there are usually legal instruments in treaty form regulating the relation, and the difficulty is commonly that of reconciling assertions of continued legal personality with loss of actual independence. In the case of devolving entities, on the other hand, the relation tends to be poorly defined, or defined only in non-international instruments or understandings, such as municipal legislation or (in the case of the British Empire) constitutional conventions. Here the difficulty is that of reconciling formal dependence with substantial practical autonomy or independence. Before independence, the essence of the problem is that of divided responsibility; for from the time the local unit is accorded significant powers of self-government, the international responsibility of the metropolitan unit is attenuated in fact, with the consequent destruction, for many practical purposes, of the single 'international unit'. After independence, which may not be any clearly defined point in time, the problem is rather how to reconcile the fact of independence with the history of dependence, aspects of which may well survive. No doubt in principle this is only another application of the basic criteria for statehood: none the less, the application of these criteria to an ill-defined and flexible process of transfer of power presents particular problems in practice, which warrant separate consideration.

---

[72] Cf. Fitzmaurice's reference to the situation where the 'conclusion of a treaty may be part of a process (or even constitute the act) whereby the State not fully *sui juris* is becoming so, and is throwing off the status of dependency': *ILC Ybk.* 1958/II, 33.

The devolution of the States of the British Empire has received the most attention from writers, and will be taken as an example here, but other cases have occurred; in particular the States arising out of the disintegration of the French[73] and Ottoman Empires.[74]

(2) *The 'unitary State' theory*

According to one influential view of the devolutionary process, there are no such difficulties of application: until all substantial legal links between the local and metropolitan territories are severed, the former remains subordinated for all international purposes to the latter.[75] No matter how extensive the devolution of administration or governmental functions, the local unit remains subordinate and without status in international law until either devolution is complete or the entity is formally recognized as independent. This view of Imperial sovereignty continued to be asserted by Great Britain, with at least a degree of acquiescence on the part of the Dominions, until well after the 1926 Imperial Conference. It had, on the international plane, the corollary that Great Britain, Ireland, and the Dominions and Colonies, constituted together a single unitary State in international law, under the sovereignty of an indivisible Crown; the relation between the various territorial units being governed by municipal and not international law.[76] But what happened in practice was by no means so simple. Responsible government was introduced in Canada in 1848, and in South Africa and the Australian States shortly after. This involved a substantial degree of local, in particular fiscal, autonomy.[77] By 1900 the degree of autonomy included the negotiation of, or optional accession to, commercial

---

[73] On the French Union see Kiss, *Pratique Française* II, 524–67; Whiteman, 1 *Digest* 544–82; Gonidec, [1960] *Public Law* 177–89; O'Connell, *International Law I*, 356–9. On the Netherlands Union, see ibid. 359–61; Van Panhuys (1958), 5 *NILR* 1–31.

[74] See Altug, *Turkey and Some Problems of International Law* (1958), 108–36; Al Baharna, 232–7. For Crete and Samos, see *infra*, pp. 233–7; for the Barbary States, *supra*, p. 177. The Philippines in the period 1934–46 was also in this category: O'Brien & Goebel, 'U.S. Recognition Policy', 176–7; Fischer, *Un Cas de décolonization. Les États-Unis et les Philippines* (1960).

[75] Cf. Harding, 5 May 1860, on Canada: Smith, *GB & LN* I, 48–50, 49.

[76] Keith, *Imperial Unity and the Dominions* (1916), *passim*; Oppenheim (8th edn.), 208.

[77] Porritt, *The Fiscal and Diplomatic Freedom of the British Oversea Dominions* (1922) (dealing with the period 1778–1837 only); Keith, *Selected Speeches and Documents on British Colonial Policy 1763–1917* (1918) II, 51–142. Cf. Ewart (1913), 7 *AJ* 268–84.

treaties and agreements.[78] The Dominions became members of the League of Nations, and several of them were mandatories under the League. They were accorded by Great Britain the right to separate diplomatic representation from 1920; and the legislative supremacy of the Westminster Parliament was conventionally restricted by 1926, and restricted in British law by 1931. In 1926 the Imperial Conference cited as established the principle of 'the equality of status existing among the Members of the British Commonwealth',[79] but at no stage were the Dominions formally and explicitly recognized as independent States.

There arises then, as Fawcett says, 'an antinomy between the dependent status of the overseas territories and their capacity for self-government',[80] or, more exactly, their actual and substantial self-government. But this is to assume the continuance of dependent status despite a substantial degree of autonomy. We may term this view the 'unitary State theory'; it holds that no middle position is possible between the continued sovereignty of the metropolitan State, and the plenary sovereignty of the local unit; local autonomy falling short of complete independence is a matter of exclusively domestic concern; local powers even in the international sphere exist merely by delegation from the sovereignty of the metropolitan State, and are therefore (in international law)[81] freely revocable.

But another view seems tenable. In a situation of substantial local autonomy, the exercise by the local unit of international competence could be regarded not as a mere delegation or agency from the metropolitan State, but as the exercise of separate and independent powers, though limited to whatever degree by the position of the metropolitan State. On this view, the relations between the local unit and the metropolitan State would be international in the same way as relations between a

[78] For details see O'Connell, in *International Law in Australia* (1965), 1–33, 2–16; International Law Association, *Effects of Independence on Treaties* (1965), 22–8; Jacomy-Millette, *Treaty Law in Canada* (1975), 5–13. But cf. Dicey, *Introduction to the Study of the Law of the Constitution* (7th edn., 1908), 119–20; and his Introduction to the 8th edn., 1915, xxix–xxxii.

[79] Cmd. 2768, 7: *infra*, p. 241.

[80] Fawcett (1949), 26 *BY* 86–107, 93.

[81] Not necessarily in municipal law: cf. *Campbell* v. *Hall* (1774) 1 Cowp. 204 *per* Lord Mansfield C.J.; *Ndlwana* v. *Hofmeyr* [1934] AD 229, 237 ('Freedom once conferred cannot be revoked').

suzerain and vassal State. The precise legal status of the devolving unit would of course remain to be determined, and might well pass through two stages of development. In the first stage, it would as a result of its actual exercise of certain limited competences in the international sphere be regarded as possessing a distinct, though limited, legal personality. In the second stage, its autonomy would be such that it qualified as a State under the criteria discussed above, in which case continuing legal relations with the metropolitan State would be reinterpreted, in international law, as a type of consensual link, or agency. In the first stage, the competence might well be revocable, at least as a matter of international law. In the second stage, on the other hand, the competences of the devolved unit would have become irrevocable, by virtue of the fact that the devolving unit qualified as a State. The history of Dominion status is of interest in demonstrating that devolving entities can achieve statehood as it were along the way, before the full transfer of responsibility for all purposes from the metropolitan State. The application of these general principles to devolving units may now be considered in rather more detail.

(3) *General principles of the status of devolving entities*

It is clear, in the first place, that whether a particular territorial unit has separate international standing, or is merely a subordinate constitutional unit of a metropolitan State, is not a matter of domestic jurisdiction of that State, nor is it determined conclusively by the municipal law of the State concerned. The fact that until the Statute of Westminster (1931), Canada was still, in British law, a 'colony'[82] was not decisive as to its international status. The extent of a particular State is clearly not just a matter of assertion, legislative or otherwise.

The question then is whether international law requires complete separation from the metropolitan State, or whether some lesser degree of political separation will suffice, before the local unit may be adjudged sufficiently independent to qualify as a State. The matter was considered by the Permanent Court of International Justice in *Lighthouses in Crete and Samos*.[83] The

---

[82] Interpretation Act, 1889 (U.K.), s. 18(2).

[83] Ser. A/B No. 71 (1937); considered briefly by Fawcett, *British Commonwealth*, 90–1; Brownlie, *Principles*, 115.

question there was whether the Ottoman Empire, which had originally included the islands of Crete and Samos as part of its territory, retained power in 1913 to make a concession agreement in favour of a French company, involving *inter alia* lighthouses on the two autonomous islands. Since Ottoman rights over the islands were transferred to Greece by Article 12 of the Treaty of Lausanne,[84] Greece would ordinarily have been bound to respect prior rights legally acquired. However Greece contended that the Empire's power to make such contracts so as to bind the islands had ceased by 1913, by virtue of the autonomy and the internationalized status of the two islands. The Court held, by eleven votes to three (Judges Hurst, Hudson, and Judge *ad hoc* Séfériades dissenting) that Greece was bound by the concession over the lighthouse on Crete, and by thirteen to one (Judge *ad hoc* Séfériades dissenting) that Greece was also bound with respect to the lighthouse on Samos. The matter was complicated by the form of the question before the Court, which accepted as *res judicata* a previous decision holding that the concession contract was valid (that is, by Ottoman law).[85] The question ostensibly before the Court then was the date at which Crete and Samos were 'detached' from the Empire.[86] But this was not the fundamental issue, as Judge Hurst pointed out:

If it is to be assumed as a consequence of the finding by the Court in its judgement of 1934 that the said contract was duly entered into because it was duly entered into according to the Ottoman law in force at the time, it must be shown that the Ottoman law in question was also in force in Crete and in Samos at that time. This is a question entirely independent of the date of the detachment of Crete and Samos from the Ottoman Empire.[87]

[84] 117 *BFSP* 543; *infra*, p. 306.

[85] Ser. A/B No. 62 (1934).

[86] According to the terms of Art. 9 of Protocol XII of the Treaty of Lausanne, 1923.

[87] Ser. A/B No. 71, 109. That the form of the question was a mere confusion is clear. *Nemo dat quod non habet*: a State can no more grant a concession treaty where it has no jurisdiction in respect of the matter subject to the concession than it can cede territory not under its sovereignty or disposition: cf. *Island of Palmas Case* (1928) 2 *RIAA* 829, 842. The real point at issue was in fact expressly reserved by the Court in the previous case: Ser. A/B No. 62, 28. In any event, even if the majority view of the international law position was right, it might still be the case that the concession was by Ottoman law invalid, since because different legal systems operated in the different territories, more remained to be done by the Ottoman authorities before the concession became binding. It is to this possibility, as much as to the first, that Judge Hurst's comment is directed—but the point was in fact assumed in France's favour by all the judges (Judge Hurst included). Cf. *Dupire* v. *Dame Dupire-Constantinoff* (1937) 8 A.D. No. 26 (Bulgaria).

Despite this confusion, the matter was in substance dealt with by all the judges, according to whether or not they accepted the implied view of the law in the question as argued by the parties. Thus the majority judgment is an endorsement of the 'unitary State' theory as defined above:

The issue, reduced to its essence, may be stated as follows: had every political link between the Ottoman Empire and the islands of Crete and Samos disappeared at the time of the conclusion of the contract in dispute . . . The Court finds that this has not been shown by the Greek Government. Notwithstanding its autonomy, Crete had not ceased to be a part of the Ottoman Empire. Even though the Sultan had been obliged to accept important restrictions on the exercise of his rights of sovereignty in Crete, that sovereignty had not ceased to belong to him, *however it might be qualified from a juridical point of view.* That situation persisted until the time when Crete was separated from the Ottoman Empire by treaties, which were treaties of cession . . . These treaties are subsequent to the conclusion of the contract in dispute.[88]

Judge Hurst dissented as to the validity of the concession with respect to Crete, because 'at the date of the contract of 1913 Crete enjoyed a full measure of autonomy'.[89] Judge Hudson was even more explicit:

It is unnecessary to attempt to place the Crete of this period in a precise legal category. Nor is it necessary . . . to set forth the complete extent of the Cretan autonomy. It will suffice to say that after 1899 the Ottoman Government exercised no governmental powers in Crete, and that although the Sultan's flag was ceremoniously flown in Crete until February 1913, the government of this island was entirely in the hands of the High Commissioner and the Cretans themselves, subject in certain respects to the approval of the four European States. In its external relations, the Cretan Government acted independently of the Ottoman Government also, and it concluded or acceded to various international conventions . . . If it can be said that a theoretical sovereignty remained in the Sultan after 1899, it was a sovereignty shorn of the last vestige of power. He could neither terminate nor modify the autonomy with which Crete had been endowed against his will and with the sanction of the four European States. A juristic conception must not be stretched to the breaking-point, and a ghost of a hollow sovereignty cannot be permitted to obscure the realities of this situation.[90]

---

[88] Ser. A/B No. 71, 103 (emphasis added).
[89] Ibid. 109.   [90] Ibid. 127.

Judge van Eysinga's separate Opinion goes on the ground that, although in other areas Crete was autonomous and the Empire accordingly without power to make valid concessions, lighthouses were a matter of 'Imperial interest' and accordingly reserved to the metropolitan power.[91]

The majority judgment would seem to be decisive in favour of the unitary State theory. But it seems to ignore both the internationalized nature of Cretan autonomy (binding on the Porte), and the compelling force of the *nemo dat* principle in this context. If Crete enjoyed a 'full measure of autonomy' under international guarantee, and that autonomy included the matter of lighthouses, it is difficult to avoid the conclusion that the Ottoman concession was an intervention in Cretan affairs. Judge van Eysinga, whose judgment is not open to this criticism, made the same point:

The administration of lighthouses is a service which in most States belongs to their domestic jurisdiction. But there are cases in which, on the one hand, lighthouses are imperatively demanded in the interest of international navigation, while, on the other hand, the State in whose territory the lighthouse would have to be operated, is not in a position to provide for its administration and maintenance . . . The lighthouse service covers the whole of the Ottoman Empire except in so far as certain parts of that Empire are excepted from it. Here we have a case of 'Imperial interest' which was primarily a matter of concern to international shipping . . . The international interest thus continuously manifested tended to preserve the character as 'Imperial interest' of all these services for which the Sublime Porte itself had to support the responsibility.[92]

It may be objected that this begs the question, which is whether Crete was a 'State' so as to have its internal affairs interfered with. But Judge van Eysinga certainly treats it as a State for all but Imperial purposes.[93]

Moreover, the reasons given by the majority to support their view that the Empire was still competent with regard to Cretan affairs are, with respect, unconvincing. The basic test is formulated as follows:

---

[91] Ibid. 114–15, citing a British reservation relating to lighthouses in the Irish State Treaty, 26 *LNTS* 9, Art. VII & Annex.

[92] Ser. A/B No. 71, 113–14.

[93] Cf. Ydit, *Internationalized Territories*, 109–26.

The wide forms of autonomy conferred on the territories in question could only be taken into consideration for the solution of the present dispute, if they justified the conclusion that the autonomous territories were already, at the date of the contract, detached from the Ottoman Empire to the extent that every political link between them and the Sublime Porte had been severed, so that the Sultan had lost all power to make contracts in regard to them.[94]

This is, however, ambiguous. It could mean that autonomy is only relevant if its result is to deprive the Sultan of the power to grant concessions within that area of competence; this is Judge van Eysinga's view. But it could also mean that, until 'every political link' (whatever) had been severed, the Sultan continued to have that power; and the subsequent formulation (*'no* link subsisted on that date') shows that this is so.[95] But this cannot be correct. The fact that 'political links' continue to exist between Canada and Great Britain (e.g. the North Atlantic Treaty Organization) is no ground for allowing to Great Britain sovereign power with respect to Canadian affairs.[96] The Court's reliance on the Treaty of London (regarded as 'decisive') seems on the contrary equally misplaced; as Judge Hudson pointed out, the provisions of the Treaty are quite 'equivocal'.[97] The terms of Article 4 of the Treaty are quite consistent with its being merely an abandonment of any claim to territory (including residual jurisdictional competences) rather than a cession of territory which the Empire did not then, in any real sense, possess. In any event, if Crete was in fact independent, the Treaty of London would have been *res inter alios acta*. No other evidence was adduced as to Crete's dependence on the Empire. As to Samos, on the other hand, the Court was in substantial agreement.[98]

[94] Ser. A/B No. 71, 103.

[95] Loc. cit. It is perhaps unfortunate that the arguments of the parties concentrated on the question when Crete and Samos were 'detached' from the Empire: cf. Ser. C No. 82, 77–8, 143–4, 146–50, 174–5, 219.

[96] If the term 'political' is given a narrower meaning—i.e. relating to a single community—still the majority opinion gives no indication of which links are to be 'political' in this narrower sense—which is of course the crucial issue.

[97] Cf. Ser. A/B No. 71, 103, and Judge Hudson, 127. By Art. 4, the Sultan ceded to the Allied Sovereigns 'all rights of sovereignty and all other rights which he possessed over that island': 107 *BFSP* 656, 893.

[98] Samos, though internally autonomous, paid an annual tribute to the Sultan, and had considerably less external independence than Crete. But the factor regarded as most significant was Samian acquiescence in previous concessions granted to the French

It follows that the only basis on which the case can be upheld is that lighthouses constituted an Imperial interest, and a residual competence of the Empire, recognized by the protecting powers. A degree of confirmation of this conclusion is provided by *Claim No. 11* in the subsequent *Lighthouses Arbitration*, where the Permanent Court of Arbitration, refusing to hold the matter *res judicata* by the 1937 decision, held Crete jointly liable for actions before 1913 which caused damage to the claimant French company.[99] It is clear therefore that Crete was an 'international person' capable of being held internationally responsible for its acts, before 1913, and that the majority judgment in the earlier *Lighthouses* case is not authority for the contrary proposition.

We may conclude then that when the stage is reached at which the local unit is substantially independent of the metropolitan State, not only internally but over a range of international matters, infringement by the metropolitan State of the local State's autonomy constitutes intervention. Since it is clear that international law does not require complete independence before denominating governmental units as 'States', we may take this point as the critical date of 'independence', for the purposes of the application of rules of international law which have as their object independent States. When this point is reached is a matter of judgement. One might formulate the test as follows: a devolving unit is to be considered independent when it possesses virtually complete internal autonomy and some substantial competences in international relations, which the metropolitan State is bound by law, convention or treaty to respect,[100] and when the remaining restrictions on its freedom of action *vis-à-vis* the metropolitan State, in both internal and

company, and in the maintenance by it of the lighthouse fees, until 1915 and later: Ser. A/B No. 71, 111 (Judge Hurst). As to Samos, then, it may be said that the dissentients in substance concurred in Judge van Eysinga's 'Imperial interest' view. But cf. *Katrantsios* v. *Bulgaria* (1926) 3 AD No. 27 (Samian neutrality in Balkan war).

[99] (1956) 23 ILR 81, 83 ff.

[100] It is sometimes argued that the local autonomy must be established by law, and that a conventional autonomy is insufficient. For example in *Madzimabamuto* v. *Lardner-Burke* [1969] 1 A.C. 645, 723 the majority of the Privy Council, after referring to the convention of non-interference in the external affairs of Southern Rhodesia, stated that this . . . 'was a very important convention but it had no legal effect in limiting the legal power of Parliament'. Lord Pearce, dissenting, agreed on this point: ibid. 732–3. On that view only a Statute, or instrument having statutory force, could effectively grant independence to a British territory. As a matter of British municipal law this may be so; but as a matter of international law it is more doubtful. Cf. *infra*, p. 242.

external affairs, are not such that, if they were consented to by an existing State, the obligations or fetters so created would be inconsistent with the legal independence of that State. After the critical date, remaining fetters on local autonomy are to be explained on grounds of agency or representation. After this point, remaining fetters are subject to political negotiation and the normal rules of acquiescence and consent.

8.5   THE PRINCIPLES APPLIED: THE DEVOLUTION OF STATES WITHIN THE BRITISH COMMONWEALTH[101]

It is generally accepted that the Dominions (Canada, Australia, South Africa, New Zealand, and Newfoundland) had not attained before 1914 any substantial international status, though they were internally autonomous and exercised certain international competences.[102]

It was the events of 1914–18, and in particular the issues of Imperial defence and finance, which brought about effective Dominion independence.[103] Imperial federation, mooted on various occasions, proved completely unacceptable on these grounds.[104] Rejection of the only alternative made rapid Dominion independence virtually certain. The question is at what point international practice accepted the implications of these events.

It is, at any rate, quite clear that the Dominions (apart from

[101] In addition to works already cited, see Keith, *The Sovereignty of the British Dominions* (1929); *The Constitutional Law of the British Dominions* (1933); Noel-Baker, *The Present Juridical Status of the British Dominions in International Law* (1929); Fawcett, *The British Commonwealth in International Law* (1965); Dawson, *The Development of Dominion Status 1900–1936* (1937); Jacomy-Millette, *Treaty Law in Canada* (1975), 5–41; and Kidwai (1976), 9 *UQLJ* 76–117.

[102] *Supra*, p. 230. Newfoundland, though a Dominion, cannot be placed in the same category as the other four Dominions. It was not a League Member. Its constitution was suspended in 1933, and in 1940, after a plebiscite, it became a province of Canada: see Whiteman, 1 *Digest* 533–4. The Irish Free State was established by the 1921 State Treaty and associated legislation: its chequered relations within the Commonwealth are described elsewhere: Dawson, op. cit. 230–3, 437–52; Hancock, op. cit., Chs. 3, 6; Whiteman, *Digest* 510–13. In 1948 it became the Republic of Eire, and seceded from the Commonwealth, although retaining special relations with the U.K. under the Ireland Act, 1949. See also *State* v. *Hynes* (1961) 100 I.L.T. 145. British India had a special status in the period 1919–47: see *infra*, p. 406.

[103] Cf. *South West Africa Cases (Merits)* I.C.J. Rep. 1966 p. 6, 397–9 *per* Judge Jessup diss.

[104] See Cheng, *Schemes for the Federation of the British Empire* (1931); Kendle, *The Round Table Movement and Imperial Union* (1975).

Newfoundland) had achieved independence within the British Empire, or the Commonwealth, as it was coming to be called, by 1939. Both Canada and South Africa declared war upon Germany independently of Great Britain:[105] Eire remained neutral.[106] But these manifestations of independence were only the exercise of competences established long before.[107]

The consequences of Dominion independence were various, and have been amply discussed elsewhere. The Dominions achieved plenary treaty-making power,[108] and the right of legation.[109] The Crown became in practice divisible with respect to each independent Dominion—a development only reluctantly accepted by Empire theorists.[110] The *inter se* doctrine (that is, the doctrine that inter-imperial relations were governed by a form

[105] Joseph, *Nationality and Diplomatic Protection. The Commonwealth of Nations* (1969), 42–3; Fawcett, *British Commonwealth*, 78; Mansergh, *Documents and Speeches on British Commonwealth Affairs 1931-1952* (1953) I, 461–572. It had previously been thought impossible that the Dominions could declare war separately of the United Kingdom: see e.g. Noel-Baker, 229–30, 330–42; Oppenheim (8th edn.) I, 206n.; Dawson, 63–4 (distinguishing 'active' from 'passive' belligerency).

[106] Mansergh, op. cit. I, 512–13.

[107] *A.G. for Canada* v. *A.G. for Ontario* [1937] A.C. 326, 349 *per* Lord Atkin; cf. *Jolley* v. *Mainka* (1933) 49 C.L.R. 242, 283–4 *per* Evatt J.; *Theodore* v. *Duncan* [1919] A.C. 696, 706. But see Judge Anzilotti, sep. op., *Danzig and I.L.O.*, Ser. B No. 18 (1930), 21–2.

[108] Apart from the Treaty of Versailles (*infra*, p. 243) the Dominions were of course parties to the various multilateral treaties concluded under the auspices of the League. The first bilateral treaty entered into by a Dominion on its own separate authority seems to have been the Canadian–United States Halibut Fisheries Treaty of 2 March 1923: 117 BFSP 382; Lewis (1923–4), 4 *BY* 168–9; (1925) 6 *BY* 31–43; Mackenzie, ibid. 191–2. A Senate reservation seeking to apply the treaty to the Empire as a whole was abandoned upon Canadian insistence: see Dawson, 254–8. For the dispute over the Treaty of Lausanne see *infra*, pp. 244–5. For Dominion treaty making generally see International Law Association, *The Effects of Independence on Treaties* (1965), Ch. 3; Stewart, *Treaty Relations of the British Commonwealth of Nations* (1939); McNair, *The Law of Treaties* (1938), 67–76 and *The Law of Treaties* (1961), 111–17; Noel-Baker, 164–203; Fawcett, *British Commonwealth*, 209–10; Jacomy-Millette, op. cit. 13–22. The incidents of the treaty-making power *vis-à-vis* other Dominions and the United Kingdom itself were regulated by the Imperial Conferences of 1923 and 1926: Dawson, 272 ff., 337–51. As a result Mackenzie King argued in 1924 that treaties, even if in heads-of-State form, which were negotiated by a particular government should bind only that government: ibid. 285–6.

[109] Noel-Baker, 147–56; Harvey, *Consultation and Co-operation in the Commonwealth* (1952), 173–204; Fawcett, *British Commonwealth*, 197–201. It was announced in 1920 that Canada would appoint a Minister to the United States: Dawson, 202; but no appointment was in fact made until 1926. By then, the Irish Free State had already appointed a Minister to the United States: ibid. 314–15. Within the Commonwealth, diplomatic representatives were, and are, entitled 'High Commissioners', although their status, functions, and, since 1948, their immunities, are essentially the same as those of foreign ambassadors: Jennings (1953), 30 *BY* 320–51, 321–4.

[110] O'Connell (1957), 6 *ICLQ* 103–25; Fawcett, *British Commonwealth*, 79–83.

of municipal law rather than by international law) lost whatever independent validity it may have had.[111] The British Empire was in effect dissolved—or, perhaps more precisely, it continued its legal personality in the form of the United Kingdom and dependencies, while the Commonwealth of Nations, a kind of residual international organization, replaced it so far as relations between the United Kingdom and the various Dominions were concerned.[112] Where the British Government continued to perform acts on behalf of the Dominions, these were based upon relations of agency or representation.[113] The Dominions acquired their own citizenship, though Dominion citizens retained British nationality as well.[114] Problems of State succession were in general treated on the basis of a considerable political continuity—although in some cases there was no succession at all but rather the continuation of treaties made by the Dominions prior to independence.[115] Certain other residual links remained.[116]

For present purposes, the interesting problem is that of determining the 'critical date' of Dominion independence, although in an evolution as gradual and ill-defined as that of the Dominions in the period 1919–39 the search is rather for a *scintilla iuris* than for any single definable moment in time having

[111] Jennings (1953), 30 *BY* 320–51; Wilson (1957), 51 *AJ* 611–17; Noel-Baker, 289–305. Fawcett, *British Commonwealth*, 144–94 concludes that the doctrine was never recognized either as a rule of customary international law or as part of the general law of the Commonwealth, but derived its validity from express stipulations (194); *contra* Keith, *The Constitutional Law of the British Empire* (1933), 78–85. In *In re Labrador Boundary* 43 T.L.R. 289 (1927) the Privy Council determined a boundary dispute between Canada and Newfoundland by the application *inter alia* of the watershed rule, which was regarded as 'consistent with the doctrine of international law' (294).

[112] For legal problems of the Commonwealth see Fawcett, *British Commonwealth*, 76–87; Noel-Baker, 359–72; Latham, in Hancock, *Survey of British Commonwealth Affairs*, Vol. I *Problems of Nationality 1918–1936* (1937), 510–630; Harvey, op. cit.

[113] A degree of representation continued, for example, with respect to naval matters: Dawson, 359–62.

[114] The 1929 Report of the Conference on the Operation of Dominion Legislation, para. 74, stated that the 'status of the Dominions in international relations . . . not merely involve[s] the recognition of these communities as distinct juristic entities, but also compel[s] recognition of a particular status of membership of those communities for legal and political purposes' (cited Dawson, 387–8). The Report was approved by the 1930 Imperial Conference: ibid. 399. For Commonwealth nationality, see Joseph, op. cit.; Fawcett, *British Commonwealth*, 182–6; Jones, *British Nationality Law* (rev. edn., 1956); Parry, *Nationality and Citizenship Laws of the Commonwealth* (2 vols., 1957, 1960).

[115] See generally O'Connell, *State Succession* I, 36–57; and in O'Brien, *New Nations*, 7–41 for the general argument relating to 'localized' treaties.

[116] Jennings (1953), 30 *BY* 330–51.

significant legal effects. The continuity of political development minimized the legal changes, or extended them over a longer time. But the changes did occur—moreover, it is only after the status of the various entities has been determined that precise analysis of the particular transactions becomes possible. The former, at least, may be attempted here. Three different dates have been suggested as critical. Earliest is the separate signature of the Dominions to the Treaty of Versailles, and their separate membership of the League (1918–19).[117] Alternatively it is suggested that the political formulations, and the recognition of equality between Great Britain and the Dominions in the period 1923–6 constitute a sort of 'recognition' by the former.[118] Thirdly, it might be said that the Statute of Westminster, 1931, marking the renunciation by Great Britain of ultimate legislative authority over the Dominions is the conclusive date.[119] It is convenient to treat these suggestions in reverse order.

It is submitted that the Statute of Westminster, despite its considerable municipal importance, neither established nor recognized Dominion independence in the international sense, for the following reasons. First, it was expressly founded on the previous agreements of the 1926 and 1930 Imperial Conferences,

[117] Fawcett, *British Commonwealth*, 88–106. For details see Dawson, 178–201.

[118] In particular, the so-called Balfour Declaration concerning the 'Status of Great Britain and the Dominions': Cmd. 2758 (1926); Dawson, 331–2; which read, in part, as follows: 'one most important element . . ., from a strictly constitutional point of view, has now, as regards all vital matters, reached its full development—we refer to the group of self-governing communities composed of Great Britain and the Dominions. Their position and mutual relation may be readily defined. *They are autonomous Communities within the British Empire, equal in status, in no way subordinate one to another in any aspect of their domestic or external affairs, though united by a common allegiance to the Crown, and freely associated as members of the British Commonwealth of Nations* . . . Equality of status, so far as Britain and the Dominions are concerned, is thus the root principle governing our Inter-Imperial Relations. But the principles of equality and similarity, appropiate to *status*, do not universally extend to function. Here we require something more than immutable dogmas. For example, to deal with questions of diplomacy and questions of defence, we require also flexible machinery—machinery which can, from time to time, be adapted to the changing circumstances of the world.'

[119] The Statute, entitled 'An Act to give effect to certain resolutions passed by Imperial Conferences held in the years 1926 and 1930', referred to the 'established constitutional position' of non-interference, and provided *inter alia* that . . . 'No Act of Parliament of the United Kingdom passed after the commencement of this Act shall extend, or be deemed to extend, to a Dominion as part of the law of that Dominion, unless it is expressly declared in that Act that that Dominion was requested, and consented to, the enactment thereof' (s. 4).

and on the admitted equality of the Dominions.[120] Second, it was
a measure of British municipal law, which applied immediately
to Canada, South Africa and the Irish Free State, but which,
under section 10, did not in substance apply as part of the law to
Australia or New Zealand until adopted by the Parliaments of
those Dominions.[121] Australia did not adopt it until 1942
(retrospectively to 1939);[122] but it seems unnecessary to treat
Australia in 1936 as 'dependent' while Canada was at the same
time 'independent'. That the Statute constituted a relinquishment
of legislative authority is admittedly of some force; but is not, it
is submitted, conclusive. A State cannot by its municipal
measures define the scope of its international authority.[123]
Equally one cannot merely from the relinquishment of an
authority or power infer that the relinquishing State in fact had
the right to exercise that authority or power.[124] And, crucially,
it is accepted that the Statute of Westminster is repealable at will
by the Westminster Parliament.[125] That it will not do so without
Dominion consent is a matter of convention, and not of law.
There is accordingly no ground for preferring the legal
formulation of the rule by Great Britain to its conventional
formulation by the parties concerned in 1926.

[120] But cf. *Madzimabamuto* v. *Lardner-Burke* [1969] 1 A.C. 645, 722: 'It was necessary to
pass the Statute of Westminster, 1931, in order to confer independence and sovereignty
on the six Dominions therein mentioned . . .' To the same effect, *semble*, Keith: cf. his
Dominion Autonomy in Practice (rev. edn., 1929), 65–6: 'not ordinary States of international
law'; with *The Constitutional Law of the British Dominions* (1933), 56–7: 'no adequate ground
for denying international personality a State character'. But in a note on the Statute
((1932), 13 *BY* 115–16) H.A.S. stated that 'its chief importance is constitutional rather
than international'. Cf. *GB&LN* I, 47–67 which still appears to adhere to the indivisibility
of the Empire. The Statute of Westminster was also held to have no effect on pre-existing
extradition treaties: *Ex parte O'Dell and Griffen* [1953] 3 D.L.R. 207. In *Moore* v. *A.G.*
[1935] A.C. 484 (P.C.), the Irish Free State was held legally competent to abrogate the
Irish Free State (Agreement) Act, 1922 (U.K.) as a result of the Statute of Westminster,
and notwithstanding that to do so was a breach of the 'contractual' obligations of the
1921 Treaty. Wheare, *The Statute of Westminster and Dominion Status* (5th edn., 1954), does
not discuss the international status of the Dominions (ibid. 94), but rather the effects of
the Statute on the constitutional law of the Dominions and the Commonwealth.

[121] Cf. the South African Status of the Union Act, 1934: Dawson, 422.

[122] Statute of Westminster Adoption Act, 1942 (Aust.); cf. Statute of Westminster
Adoption Act, 1947 (N.Z.).

[123] *Supra*, p. 232.

[124] Cf. *supra*, pp. 235–6.

[125] That is, it is repealable at will as a matter of British law: *British Coal Corporation* v.
The King [1935] A.C. 500, 520 *per* Viscount Sankey L.C. For the contrary argument,
Cowen (1952), 15 *MLR* 282–96; (1953), 16 *MLR* 273–48; Fawcett, *British Commonwealth*,
98–9.

But to determine which of the other two possible dates—1919 and 1923–6—involved the emergence of the Dominions as independent States is more difficult. In 1919 the Dominions each signed, and the Dominion Parliaments separately approved ratification of, the Treaty of Versailles; and four Dominions became separate members of the League. They thus acquired a distinct legal personality, for all purposes of the League.[126] Mandates, for example, were entrusted directly to the various Dominions,[127] and not (with one exception)[128] to the Empire as a whole. Under Article 1 of the Covenant, a member was required to give 'effective guarantees of *its* sincere intention to observe *its* international obligations'. It is accordingly very difficult to argue that the Covenant did not apply to the relations of the Dominions *inter se*,[129] although in a celebrated controversy in 1924 the contrary was indeed argued by the British Government.[130]

The international status acquired by the Dominions in 1919 was considerable. However, neither separate Dominion signature of the Treaty of Versailles nor separate membership of the League of Nations was in itself quite unequivocal. The League Covenant allowed the admission to membership of any 'fully self-governing State, Dominion, or Colony' (Art. 1), with the inference that Dominion status was something between that of 'Colony' and 'State'.[131]

Moreover, the signatures to the Treaty were also equivocal, in that the separate Dominion signatures followed not in

---

[126] Keith, *Dominion Home Rule in Practice* (1921), 37; *The Constitutional Law of the British Dominions* (1933), 47; Noel-Baker, Ch. IV; Fawcett, *British Commonwealth*, 76–9. Smuts's view was that the Dominions were 'signatories as component independent States of the British Empire': Dawson, 219. On the other hand Salmond thought that the Treaty merely gave them 'a voice in the management of the international relations of the British Empire as a single, undivided unity': ibid. 226.

[127] Whiteman, 1 *Digest* 707–8; *In re Tamasese* [1929] NZLR 209; *Jolley* v. *Mainka* (1933) 49 C.L.R. 342, 281–4; Oppenheim (8th edn.) I, 199 n.4.

[128] Charteris (1923–4), 4 *BY* 137–52, 146–7 (Nauru). The Mandate authority was delegated to Australia.

[129] Fawcett, *British Commonwealth*, 76–7; Keith, *The War Governments of the British Dominions* (1921), 157.

[130] For the exchange of views over Irish registration with the League of the State Treaty, see 27 *LNTS* 449–50; Dawson, 315–16.

[131] Cf. *supra*, pp. 131–2. In the Rules of the Paris Conference, the British Empire was treated as one of five 'Powers with general interests'; the Dominions and India as among the twenty-three 'belligerent Powers with special interests': Dawson, 181.

alphabetical order, but under the heading 'British Empire' and after those of the British delegation.[132] This may be regarded as a typographical incident rather than an acknowledgment of Dominion subordination, though the Canadian Prime Minister thought it conferred upon the Dominions 'the doubtful advantage of a double signature'.[133]

On the other hand, the Balfour Declaration itself was, so far as the independence of the Dominions is concerned, also equivocal. It referred to the equal status of the Dominions as already established in practice;[134] and it was regarded by some commentators, at least,[135] as not having made a substantial difference to the existing position.[136] In view of its terms, however,[137] it is difficult to accept that, after 1926, the Dominions remained merely dependent entities. The importance of the events of 1923–6, and in particular the Balfour Declaration, was its affirmation of an equality of status which had, in the period 1920–3 been under a certain persistent, if not overt, attack.[138] Thus the Chanak Incident,[139] the controversy over the Treaties of Lausanne[140] and Locarno[141] and the recognition of the Soviet Union[142] were all examples of what may be regarded as a Foreign Office campaign to assert the 'diplomatic unity of the Empire'. Typical of the uncertainties of this period was the controversy over the negotiation and signature by Britain of the Treaty of Lausanne.[143] The Canadian Prime Minister, Mackenzie King, appeared at first to have taken the view that,

[132] Ibid. 178–99; Fawcett, *British Commonwealth*, 146–51.

[133] Ibid. 148.

[134] *Supra*, p. 241. Cf. Resolution IX of the Imperial War Conference, 1917: Dawson, 175–6.

[135] Keith, *The Sovereignty of the British Dominions* (1939), 20–2; Smith (1926–7), 12 *Cornell LR* 1–12; Corbett & Smith, *Canada and World Politics* (1926), 161; Hurst, in *Great Britain and the Dominions* (1928), 3–104.

[136] But the South African Prime Minister Hertzog stated, after the 1926 Conference, that 'As a result of the work of the Imperial Conference the old Empire no longer exists . . . All that remained was a free alliance of England and the six Dominions . . .': Dawson, 112. Contrast his view before the Conference: ibid. 104.

[137] *Sc.* 'autonomous Communities . . . equal in status, in no way subordinate one to another in any aspect of their domestic or external affairs'.

[138] Dawson, 36–54.

[139] Ibid. 234–51.

[140] Ibid. 258–72.

[141] Ibid. 316–24.

[142] Ibid. 295–6.

[143] 117 *BFSP* 543.

although Canada would, by ratification of the Treaty, cease to be at war with Turkey, no other specific legal consequences would ensue.[144] This position could be explained on grounds of representation: since, in 1914, Britain's declaration of war automatically involved Canadian belligerency, a British conclusion of peace would automatically terminate that belligerency. But, since no further Canadian authorization existed with respect to the terms of the peace, no further Canadian obligations were involved by its conclusion. However, the view taken by Mackenzie King remained unclear, since he subsequently distinguished between 'the purely legal and technical position in which this Dominion may be placed and the moral obligations which arise under treaties depending upon . . . the representative capacities' of the negotiating parties.[145] This latter view, as Keith pointed out,[146] was quite consistent with the continued unity of the Empire.

In the period 1919–25, therefore, the situation remained uncertain. For some purposes, at least, the Dominions were, or were treated as, States:[147] for others, they seemed to remain portions of an ostensibly undivided Empire.[148] The importance of the Imperial Conferences of 1923 and 1926, then, was the reaffirmation by the various governments of the principle of Dominion equality, in the form of a binding convention. To be sure, formal independence was still lacking, and steps were taken, pursuant to the 1926 Declaration, to remove the various derogations from formal independence.[149] But, after 1926 it became possible, as it had not been before, to express inter-Dominion relations, with certainty and clarity, on the basis of agency and representation. For these reasons, the Balfour Declaration can properly be taken as the critical date of the independence of the Dominions,[150] although of course, in view

---

[144] Dawson, 260–1.

[145] Ibid. 268–9, cf. 265. But in 1927, it was stated flatly that 'Canada has not ratified the pact of Locarno and is not a party to it.': ibid. 319.

[146] *The Sovereignty of the British Dominions* (1929), 390–6.

[147] Cf. the Paris Convention for the Regulation of Aerial Navigation, 1919: 112 *BFSP* 931, Art. 40 (signed in the same way as the Treaty of Versailles, and separately ratified).

[148] Cf. the excellent analysis by Schwarzenberger, *International Law* I, 90–1. To the same effect Harvey, *Consultation and Cooperation in the Commonwealth* (1952), 279–80.

[149] Dawson, 354–421 for details.

[150] In addition to Noel-Baker, the following writers take this view, though with some hesitancy in many cases: Dunn (1926–7), 13 *Virginia LR* 354–79, 365–6, 373; Scott

of their pre-existing legal personality for League and other purposes, this difference was in practice only one of degree.[151]

(1927), 21 *AJ* 95–101, 99; Verzijl *International Law* II, 208–10, 220; O'Connell, in *International Law in Australia*, 18; Brownlie (1961), *Rev. of Cont. L.* 19–40, 34. Cf. Johnston (1927), 21 *AJ* 481–9. Latham, after citing Hertzog's view of the Balfour Report (*supra*, p. 244, n. 136) describes the view as 'legitimate and, in the event, correct': op. cit. 530. The Balfour Declaration was followed by a wider acceptance of the distinct general legal personality of the Dominions. They were, for example, separately invited to become original parties to the Pact of Paris, 1928: Dawson, 357–9. For the official British view see *H.C. Deb.* Vol. 208 cols. 535–8, 29 June 1927. Cf. the more reserved account of Rousseau *DIP* II, 214–64.

¹⁵¹ The status of Southern Rhodesia before 1965 deserves brief mention here. By 1964, Southern Rhodesia had achieved virtually complete internal autonomy, and Britain had expressly accepted a convention of non-interference in internal affairs: see De Smith, *The New Commonwealth and its Constitutions* (1964), 38–43; Palley, *The Constitutional History and Law of Southern Rhodesia 1888–1965* (1966); Devine, [1973] *Acta Juridica* 1, 40–62. Beadle C.J. in *Madzimabamuto* v. *Lardner-Burke* (1968) 39 ILR 61, 198–9, 209, 238, argued that Rhodesia in 1964 had an irrevocable partial international personality on which a declaration of independence could be based. The Privy Council, at the other extreme, denied it any status at all: *supra*, p. 237, n. 100. The British Government's view was that UDI was a violation of the conditions upon which autonomy and non-interference were granted; and that Southern Rhodesia thereupon reverted to dependent status: Rigo Sureda, *The Evolution of the Right to Self-Determination* (1973), 88–9; Fawcett (1965–6), 41 *BY* 103–121, 113; Devine, op. cit. 45–6. Cf. also Lewis J. in *Madzimabamuto* v. *Lardner-Burke* (1966) 39 ILR 61, 93. This view is certainly more consistent with the argument in the text as to devolutionary status: on the other hand, Rhodesia in 1964 was comparable to the Dominions in 1914 rather than 1918 or 1926, in view of the former's lack of substantial external affairs capacity in practice (cf. Palley, op. cit. 726), and, *semble*, of the fact that in Rhodesia's case fundamental constitutional legislation was outside the ambit of the convention: Fawcett, op. cit. 104–5. In contrast, the Dominions' conventional autonomy in 1920 was unconditional: cf. Dawson, 124–5, 423–31.

9. Secession

9.1 SECESSION AS A METHOD OF THE CREATION OF STATES

UNTIL THIS century, secession[1] was certainly the most conspicuous, as well as probably the most usual, method of the creation of new States. The period 1776–1900 saw, amongst other cases, the American War of Independence, the revolution of the former Spanish colonies of South and Central America, the secession of Greece from the Ottoman Empire and of Belgium from the Netherlands. In this century, new States have been more often created with the consent of the former sovereign, especially of course in the colonial situation. However, attempts at secession, which may be defined as the creation of a State by the use or threat of force and without the consent of the former sovereign, have been frequent. For example, there have been successful secessionary creations in the cases of Indonesia, North Korea, North Vietnam, Bangladesh, and Guinea-Bissau. In addition, there is the rather exceptional case of Israel, which was created by force without the consent of the previous administration, and on territory vacated by it.[2] Many more attempts at secession have failed—for example, those in Katanga and Biafra.

It may be said once again that the distinction between devolution and secession may be in some cases a rather arbitrary one.[3] Elements of forcible seizure and free grant of independence may be combined, and other elements—a process in the nature

---

[1] We are not here concerned with revolutionary changes of government within the same State: it is established that such changes do not in general affect the continuity of the State: *infra*, p. 405. For this reason the term 'secession', which is restricted in its meaning to revolutionary creations of new States, is preferred. Cf. Marek, *Identity and Continuity*, 62.

[2] On Israel see Moore, ed., *The Arab-Israeli Conflict* (1974) esp. Vol. I; Martin, *Le Conflict israelo-arabe* (1973); Cattan, *Palestine and International Law* (1973); Feinberg, *On an Arab Jurist's Approach to Zionism and the State of Israel* (1971); Alexander (1951), 4 *ILQ* 423–30, and the essays in (1968) 33 *Law & Contemporary Problems* 1–182. The creation of Israel from the Mandated territory of Palestine, with its mixture of elements of secession, occupation and international dispositive authority, was undoubtedly *sui generis*: cf. Rosenne (1950), 77 *JDI* 1141–73, 1141. It is not dealt with in this study.

[3] *Supra*, p. 215.

of consolidation (as in Vietnam and Korea)[4] or the intervention of a group of Great Powers (as in Greece and Belgium)[5]—may also be present. None the less certain questions arise specifically in relation to the secessionary situation. In particular, the application of the criteria for statehood to situations where statehood is disputed by the previous sovereign, and may thus be acutely controversial; the relation between third State recognition and status; the legality of secession in modern international law, and the legal incidents of the process by which a seceding unit attains international status—these questions require consideration here.[6] In the first place the application of the criteria for statehood— and in particular the criterion of independence—to cases of secession must be dealt with.

9.2   THE CRITERIA FOR STATEHOOD IN SECESSIONARY SITUATIONS

(1)   *The relevance of recognition*

Politically, and to a significant extent also legally, recognition of secessionist regimes has always been regarded as important. Its precise legal effects however require examination. In this context three types of recognition—recognition of statehood on the part of the previous sovereign (here termed 'metropolitan recognition'), recognition of statehood on the part of third States, and belligerent recognition—must be distinguished.

(i)   *Metropolitan recognition*
It is clear that, if the former sovereign recognizes as a State a

---

[4] *Infra*, p. 281.

[5] *Infra*, p. 320.

[6] There is a considerable body of literature on general problems such as civil war, neutrality, intervention, and so on, which include secessionary situations together with other, distinct, problems. For example on civil war see Rosenau, ed., *International Aspects of Civil Strife* (1964); Pinto (1965), 114 *HR* 451–558; Oglesby, *Internal War and the Search for Normative Order* (1971); Dhokalia (1971), 11 *Indian JIL* 219–50; Falk, ed., *The International Law of Civil War* (1971); Luard, ed., *The International Regulation of Civil Wars* (1972); Khairallah, *Insurrection under International Law* (1973); Zorgbibe, *La guerre civile* (1975); Bennouna, *Le Consentement à l'ingérence militaire dans les conflits internes* (1974). On intervention see Stanger, ed., *Essays on Intervention* (1964); Jaquet, *Intervention in International Politics* (1971); de Lima, *Intervention in International Law* (1971). There is a considerable amount of material on particular secessionist conflicts (as to which see *infra*) but virtually nothing on secession in general: cf. Mayer (1968), 3 *Manitoba L J* 61–74; Yakemtchouk, *L'Afrique en droit international* (1971), 40–50; Verhoeven, *Reconnaissance*, 19–21, 29–32.

local unit exercising *de facto* control over certain territory, then that entity is, at least *prima facie*, a State.[7] The problem is rather the status of a *de facto* entity effectively controlling certain territory, in the absence of metropolitan recognition. As we have seen,[8] there was a conflict in the early doctrine on this point. Pufendorf, arguing from the notion of allegiance to the former sovereign, regarded metropolitan recognition as necessary to statehood: Vattel, on the other hand, took the view that, at least in some situations, metropolitan recognition was unnecessary.[9] The question was not entirely settled by the American War of Independence, since, on any view, French recognition of the United States of North America was premature;[10] and since British recognition, in 1783,[11] was itself not long delayed. Any doubts that might have remained were settled by the controversy over the independence of the former Spanish colonies in South America. The colonies declared their independence at various times after 1809, and, despite fluctuating fortunes, maintained that independence against Spain for a considerable time without being accorded any formal recognition.[12] By 1822 several of the secessionist regimes were subsisting without any effective Spanish opposition and with relative stability: none the less Spain refused to countenance recognition.[13] The question of third State recognition was thus squarely raised. In June 1822 President Monroe extended United States recognition of Colombia.[14] British recognition of Buenos Ayres followed on 2 February 1825; that of Colombia on 18 April 1825, and that of Mexico on 28 December 1826.[15] In response to Spanish protests, Canning distinguished three 'descriptions of Recognition':

---

[7] *Supra*, pp. 42–4, 216–18

[8] *Supra*, p. 9.

[9] Frowein (1971), 65 *AJ* 568–71 and works there cited.

[10] Treaty of Amity and Commerce of 6 Feb. 1778: 46 *CTS* 477, and Separate and Secret Act of the same date: ibid. 457.

[11] Preliminary Articles of Peace, Paris, 30 Nov. 1782: 48 *CTS* 225; Definitive Peace Treaty, 3 Sept. 1783: ibid. 489, pursuant to 22 Geo. III c. 46. The Netherlands extended recognition in a Treaty of Amity and Commerce of 4 Oct. 1782: ibid. 135.

[12] See Smith, *GB & LN* I, 115–20; McNair, *Law Officers Opinions* II, 327–37; Moore, 1 *Digest* 74–84; Paxson, *The Independence of the South American Republics* (1903); and esp. Webster, *Britain and the Independence of Latin America 1812–1830* (2 vols., 1938).

[13] Smith, *GB & LN* I, 142 ff.

[14] Moore, 1 *Digest* 85–96.

[15] Smith, *GB & LN* I, 151–2.

1st. The Recognition *de facto* which now substantially subsists.
2nd. The more formal Recognition of Diplomatic Agents.
3rd. The Recognition *de Jure*, which professes to decide upon the Title, and thereby to create a Certain Impediment to the Rights of the former Occupant.[16]

As to the third of these, in his view it was:

for the two Contending Parties themselves to settle the Question of Title,—not for third Parties to interfere ... The practical question, then, is,—How long should the *de facto* System of Recognition be maintained, to the Exclusion of the Diplomatic, and when should the latter be adopted?[17]

To which, in a later dispatch, the answer was given that:

To continue to call that a possession of Spain, in which all Spanish occupation and power had been actually extinguished and effaced, could render no practical service to the Mother Country;—but it would have risked the peace of the World. For all political communities are responsible to other political communities for their conduct:—that is, they are bound to perform the ordinary international duties, and to afford redress for any violation of the rights of others by their citizens or subjects.

Now, either the Mother Country must have continued responsible for acts over which it could no longer exercise the shadow of a controul; or the Inhabitants of those countries, whose independent political existence was, in fact, established, but to whom the acknowledgment of that independence was denied, must have been placed in a situation in which they were either wholly irresponsible for their actions, or were to be visited for such of those actions as might furnish ground of complaint to other Nations, with the punishment due to Pirates and Outlaws ...

[N]o other choice remained for Gt. Britain, or for any other Country having intercourse with the Spanish American Provinces but to recognize, in due time, their political existence as States, and thus to bring them within the pale of those rights and duties, which civilized Nations are bound mutually to respect, and are entitled reciprocally to claim from each other.[18]

---

[16] F.O. 139/49, 8 Aug. 1822 (ibid. 124–6); repeated *inter alia* Canning to Ward, F.O. 50/9, 9 Sept. 1825 (ibid. 126).
[17] Loc. cit.
[18] Ibid. 162, 166–7 (25 Mar. 1825). Cf. (to the same effect) Adams, 6 Apr. 1822: Moore, 1 *Digest* 87–8.

Canning's distinction between *de jure* and diplomatic recognition and his application of it to the Spanish-American colonies are of great importance. It is commonly assumed that the third 'description' of recognition—that relating to the 'question of right' between the belligerents—is equivalent to modern *de jure* recognition.[19] It is however clear that this was, and is, not so: rather this recognition 'of right' was a reflection of the then influential principle of legitimacy,[20] which was, in a sense, the successor to Pufendorf's principle of allegiance.[21] No international legal consequences—at least so far as third States were concerned—were to be deduced from the failure of metropolitan recognition, provided that the local entity was effectively independent, and the military opposition of the metropolitan State had, to all intents and purposes, ceased. The point was made with even greater clarity by Dr. Lushington in 1820:

His own opinion on the subject was, that when colonies had once acquired independence for themselves, it was at the option of other governments either to acknowledge their independence or not, according to the views of policy which they might entertain. It was indeed a matter of pure necessity to make such an acknowledgment on account of the great inconvenience and injustice that would otherwise attend the existence of an unsettled and unrecognized State ... [N]either the law of nations, nor any peculiar relations between England and Spain, withheld us from recognizing the independence of South America ...[22]

Canning's second description of recognition, then, was the equivalent of modern *de jure* recognition, and it followed from the South American precedents that metropolitan recognition was not a precondition for statehood, if effective independence had been achieved. And that, as we shall see, is in principle the modern rule.[23]

---

[19] Smith, *GB & LN* I, 126–7.

[20] Before the Congress at Aix-la-Chapelle in 1818, there was a distinct possibility of European intervention to secure Spanish sovereignty in South America. By the combined efforts of the U.S. and Great Britain this was averted: however, fear of such intervention was the major factor behind the Monroe Doctrine of 1822. See generally Webster, op. cit. I, 14–15; Oppenheim (8th edn.) I, 313–19; Moore, 6 *Digest* 373–9, 401–4.

[21] Smith, *GB & LN* I, 168–9; Kane, *Civil Strife in Latin America: A Legal History of U.S. Involvement* (1972), 21; and cf. Webster, op. cit. I, 26–34.

[22] *Parl. Deb. N.S.* Vol. II, pp. 378–80, 11 July 1820; cited Paxson, op. cit. 196–8.

[23] *Infra*, p. 266.

(ii) Recognition by third States

Although it was thus established that absence of metropolitan recognition did not preclude statehood, diplomatic recognition by third States was treated as important and, indeed, was commonly regarded as constitutive. Canning's memorandum of 25 March 1825, already cited,[24] had a distinctly constitutive aspect, as did his famous boast that he had 'called the New World into existence to redress the balance of the Old'.[25] The memorandum of 1825 had seemed to infer that the existence of a separate 'political community' was insufficient, and that recognition was required before such a Community was brought within the 'pale of those rights and duties' involved in international law. However, in practice the South American States had been regarded as legally responsible for their acts before recognition: indeed all political contacts short of formal recognition were regarded as legitimate and desirable.[26] Whatever formal view of recognition may have been entertained,[27] in practice recognition was—in the South American situation—substantially declaratory of existing rights and duties.[28]

(iii) Recognition of belligerency

A third form of recognition in situations of insurgency or secession was recognition of belligerency. Where a secessionary

[24] *Supra*, p. 250.
[25] *Parl. Deb. N.S.* Vol. 16 col. 397, 12 Dec. 1826; Temperley, *The Foreign Policy of Canning 1822–1827* (1925), 154.
[26] Christopher Robinson reported on 6 Feb. 1817 (Smith, *GB & LN* I, 268–70) that it was 'allowable for any Nation . . . to maintain public relations with Countries in the situation of the Insurgent Provinces, after a certain Time. But it will be a Question of general expediency, when and under what, Modifications, that right should be asserted'. The flags of the various seceding States were also recognized for commercial purposes, and vessels flying those flags were not treated as piratical (cf. Monroe, 19 Jan. 1816: 3 *BFSP* 119; Smith, *GB & LN* I, 271–5). Consuls were appointed; and, of course, revolted territory was not treated as *terra nullius*: Moore 1 *Digest* 43–5. Lushington (*supra*, p. 251) accurately stated that, 'mercantile concerns were conducted as if we had recognized the independence of South America'.
[27] It is probable that the point did not—at least explicitly— occur to contemporary statesmen: cf. Canning to Stuart, 1 Dec. 1825: 'I . . . continue to think this mode of Recognition better calculated for the advantage and dignity of the State to be recognized than any form of words distinctly expressing Recognition . . . because the assumed Independence is therein admitted, not created . . .' (Webster, op. cit. I, 292).
[28] Cf. Harcourt's distinction between recognition and intervention: *Letters by Historicus on some Questions of International Law* (1863), 6; cf. ibid. 4 where the status of revolted subjects is said to be 'a question of mixed law and fact'.

movement had achieved a certain degree of governmental and military organization, problems of responsibility, the desire to remain neutral in the conflict, and also to maintain commercial relations, impelled a certain *de facto* recognition of the situation even while the conflict was continuing. This informal *de facto* recognition gradually emerged as a distinct formal status: by virtue of recognition of belligerency third States were entitled to maintain a strict neutrality between the parties to the conflict, and the insurgents achieved a separate, though temporary, legal status. The institution of recognition of belligerency was established only towards the end of the South American conflict—and, then in a situation where plenary recognition would probably have been justified.[29] It found its most significant application in the American Civil War.[30] The position was authoritatively formulated by Wheaton:

Until the revolution is consummated, whilst the civil war involving a contest for the government continues, other States may remain indifferent spectators of the controversy, still continuing to treat the ancient government as sovereign, and the government *de facto* as a society entitled to the rights of war against its enemy; or may espouse the cause of the party which they believe to have justice on its side. In the first case, the foreign State fulfils all its obligations under the law of nations; and neither party has any right to complain, provided it maintains an impartial neutrality. In the latter, it becomes, of course, the enemy of the party against whom it declares itself, and the ally of the other; and as the positive law of nations makes no distinction, in this respect, between a just and an unjust war, the intervening State becomes entitled to all the rights of war against the opposite party.

If the foreign State professes neutrality, it is bound to allow impartially to both belligerent parties the free exercise of those rights which war gives to public enemies against each other; such as the right of blockade, and of capturing contraband enemy's property.

But the exercise of those rights, on the part of the revolting colony or province against the metropolitan country, may be modified by the obligation of treaties previously existing between that country and foreign States.[31]

[29] For the development of the notion of belligerent rights see Smith, *GB & LN* I, 265–281. U.S. recognition of belligerency was effected by a neutrality proclamation of 1 Sept. 1815: Moore, 1 *Digest* 171–2. British recognition was effected by an Order-in-Council of 12 July 1819: Smith, *GB & LN* I, 276.

[30] Ibid. 302–12, 322–5; McNair, op. cit. II, 358–65; Moore, 1 *Digest* 184–93.

[31] Wheaton's *Elements* (8th edn., 1866 (ed. Dana)) Pt. I, § 23.

Recognition of belligerency became permissible in two situations: where the metropolitan government itself unequivocally treated the insurgents as an organized belligerent force, in particular by exercise of belligerent rights on the high seas;[32] or where, in the judgment of other States, the insurgent force had achieved the character of an organized government, capable of carrying on hostilities in accordance with the laws of war, and of accepting responsibility for its actions.[33] Recognition of belligerency was however improper unless the third State's interests were materially affected: it tended in practice to be restricted to civil wars fought at least in part on the high seas, since the main legal incident of belligerency was the right of both parties to search neutral ships for contraband on the high seas.

For present purposes, the institution of belligerent recognition is only of peripheral importance: nevertheless, certain points may be made. In the first place, in secessionary situations belligerent recognition was sometimes used as a substitute for, rather than an intermediate step towards, recognition of the entity in question as a State. This was certainly so with the South American territories, and to some extent it was so with Greece.[34]

Secondly, even in the absence of formal recognition of belligerency it is likely that the insurgents—so long as they maintained a certain degree of territorial and administrative effectiveness—had certain legal rights. Their ships were not to be treated as pirates, nor were they, so far as third States were concerned, merely in the position of traitors.[35] On the other hand, third States were not entitled to assist or foment the rebellion—or rather, since war was, in the nineteenth century, legally permissible, they had the option of non-intervention or the commission of an act of war against the metropolitan State.

[32] The U.S. proclamation of a blockade of the Confederate States was regarded by Britain as justifying recognition of belligerency: this view was upheld, by implication, in the *Alabama Arbitration*: Moore, 1 *IA* 653. See also Oglesby, *Internal War and the Search for Normative Order* (1971), vi–vii; *Smith* v. *Stewart* (1869) 2 *Am. I.L.C.* 66, 68.

[33] Report of Karslake, Selwyn and Phillimore of 14 Aug. 1867 (Crete): McNair, op. cit. I, 143.

[34] Dana in a note to § 23 of Wheaton's 8th edn. gave as the first of the tests of belligerency: 'the existence of a *de facto* political organization of the insurgents, sufficient in character, population and resources, to constitute it, if left to itself, a State among the nations, reasonably capable of discharging the duties of a State . . .' It was thus, in his view, 'a *quasi* political recognition' (loc. cit.). For Greece see *infra*, pp. 319–20.

[35] Cf. Lauterpacht, *Recognition*, Ch. 18.

The effect of recognition of belligerency was thus threefold: it formalized the legal status of the insurgents; it gave rise to a duty of non-intervention with respect to both parties, and it entailed the acceptance of the exercise of belligerent rights by both parties.

The point that, at least in traditional international law, non-intervention was an option rather than a duty is of considerable importance. It followed that recognition of belligerency was, in a fundamental sense, voluntary, and the obligation of neutrality with respect to both parties which was entailed in recognition of belligerency was self-imposed. Since third States retained the right to make war, neutrality in civil as well as international conflicts remained discretionary. Recognition of belligerency was thus not a peremptory institution but a permissible expression of a certain legal relation—neutrality. Only where the metropolitan Government itself unequivocally recognized local belligerency was recognition by third States in any way enjoined. For this reason, neutrality between belligerents could be set aside if there existed, for example, a treaty of alliance or other commitment with the metropolitan State.[36] Again, since the legal incidents of recognition of belligerency—and in particular the duty of neutrality *vis-à-vis* the metropolitan government—were self-imposed, recognition of belligerency could properly, and exceptionally, be said to be constitutive.[37] The status of recognition of belligerency in civil war situations was thus, even in nineteenth-century practice, somewhat precarious.[38]

(2) *The traditional test of independence in a secessionary situation*

It remains to determine just when third State recognition became permissible, or, in other words, when the seceding entity qualified as a State. Nineteenth-century practice—apart from cases of intervention to secure independence, such as Belgium, and, to some extent, Greece[39]—established that a seceding territory could properly be recognized as a State if it governed

---

[36] Cf. Wheaton, cited *supra*, p. 253. The Portuguese alliance was one of the reasons for the British treatment of Brazil, which differed from that accorded the Spanish American States: cf. Smith, *GB & LN* I, 180–97.

[37] Charpentier, *Reconnaissance*, 95–109; *contra* Chen, *Recognition*, 333–51. Cf. *ILC Ybk.* 1975/I, 45 (Reuter), 49 (Ushakov).

[38] See further, *infra*, p. 268.

[39] *Infra*, p. 319.

its territory effectively and with sufficient stability, such that there was no real likelihood of the previous sovereign (whether because of the latter's virtual relinquishment of the struggle or its defeat in the field) reasserting its position. For example, in a letter to Lieven concerning the prospective Austrian recognition of Greece, Canning formulated the test as follows.

It is to be presumed that when the Austrian Plenipotentiaries speak of the acknowledgement of the Morea and the islands as an independent State, they intend that acknowledgement to be subject to the qualification that such State shall have shown itself substantially capable of maintaining an independent existence, of carrying on a Government of its own, of controlling its own military and naval forces, and of being responsible to other nations for the observance of international laws and the discharge of international duties.

These are questions of fact. By acknowledgement we can only acknowledge what is. We have never recognized in Spanish America any State in whose territory the dominion of the mother-country has not been practically extinguished, and which has not established some form of government with which we could treat.[40]

The position was summarized by Harcourt . . .

When a sovereign State, from exhaustion or any other cause, has virtually and substantially abandoned the struggle for supremacy it has no right to complain if a foreign State treat the independence of its former subjects as *de facto* established; nor can it prolong its sovereignty by a mere paper assertion of right. When on the other hand, the contest

---

[40] 40 *BFSP* 1216, 4 Sept. 1826; reaffirmed ibid., 1222. Cf. the Marquis of Landsdown, *Parl. Deb. N.S.* Vol. X, col. 974, 15 Mar. 1824, cited Paxson, op. cit. 224. The Earl of Liverpool, agreed that 'there could be no right [to recognize] while the contest was actually going on . . . so long as the struggle in arms continued undecided' (col. 999). But the timing of the actual decision, he asserted, was peculiarly a matter for the executive.

In August 1823 the U.S. had also declined to recognize or aid the Greeks, pleading the constitutional incapacity of the President to declare war on Turkey, and the fact that Greek independence was not yet 'undisputed, or disputed without any rational prospect of success': 11 *BFSP* 300 (Adams).

In an opinion of 6 June 1844, Dodson advised that 'in December 1830 . . . the course of events had shown that the separation between Belgium and Holland consequent on the Revolution in the former country would be final . . .' However, the 'independent political existence of Belgium had not . . . at that time assumed any definite shape'. It was, in his view, impossible to determine whether Britain had recognized Belgium as at 6 Aug. 1831: Smith, *GB & LN* I, 245–7. The same strict test was applied by the British government to the Confederacy: e.g. Russell to Mason, 2 Aug. 1862: 55 *BFSP* 733, cited Lauterpacht, *Recognition*, 17. See also Wright, in Falk, ed., *The International Law of Civil War*, 30–109.

is not absolutely or permanently decided, a recognition of the inchoate independence of the insurgents by a foreign State is a hostile act towards the sovereign State . . .[41]

The strictness of this position is in marked contrast to the position in the case of States granted independence by the previous sovereign, where a minimal degree of *de facto* control may suffice.[42] This strict view—which was normally applied to particular cases in a cautious and highly conservative manner— represented the position at the beginning of this century: it was reaffirmed by the Commission of Jurists in the *Aaland Islands Case*.[43] Its status in modern international law is discussed in the following section.

(3) *Independence and secession in modern international law*

Modern methods of warfare and communications, and the strong pressures favouring intervention on behalf of one or other of the belligerents in a civil war, make it much less likely that established secessionary entities, in the absence of special circumstances, could survive sixteen or so years (as did Venezuela, for example) before attracting third party recognition. The extremely cautious application of the criteria for independence, which a feature of nineteenth-century practice, is thus by no means so marked in modern practice. Indeed the question is whether the criteria themselves are the same. It will be argued that there is now established an important distinction between secession within a metropolitan State and the secession of a self-determination unit and, in particular, of a non-self-governing territory. The secession of a self-determination unit, where self-determination is forcibly prevented by the metropolitan State, will in general be reinforced by the principle of self-determination, so that the degree of effectiveness required as a precondition to recognition will be less extensive than in the case of secession within a metropolitan State.[44] It follows that there is no longer one comprehensive test for secessionary independence. The various possibilities will be discussed in turn.

---

[41] Op. cit. 9. Cf. Moore, 1 *Digest* 78 (Adams, 1818).
[42] *Supra*, p. 218.
[43] *Supra*, p. 45.
[44] *Supra*, p. 46.

(i) The secession of a self-determination unit

It is necessary to distinguish between secession in pursuance of, and in violation of, self-determination. Where the territory in question is a self-determination unit it may be presumed that any secessionary government possesses the general support of the people: secession in such a case, where self-determination is forcibly denied, will be presumed to be in furtherance of, or at least not inconsistent with, the application of self-determination to the territory in question.[45] On the other hand, it is possible for a seceding government manifestly to lack general support.

(a) *Secession in furtherance of self-determination*   State practice since 1945 in relation to secessions of this type has not been entirely consistent: this is attributable at least in part to the fact that self-determination as a positive legal principle has itself undergone a considerable evolution since 1945. However in three of the earlier cases of seceding territories, at least some degree of international recognition was extended at a relatively early stage.

The Indonesian situation was the first of these. Indonesian nationalist leaders declared the Republic of Indonesia independent on 17 August 1945: there followed a protracted conflict, both military and diplomatic, with the Netherlands before sovereignty was formally transferred on 27 December 1949.[46] The events of this period have been described elsewhere:[47] what is of interest here is that, although Indonesia was probably not a fully independent State before December 1949, it was accorded in various ways a certain—even considerable—legal status during the conflict. It was recognized as a *de facto* government by the Netherlands itself,[48] and by a number of other States: in addition several States accorded *de jure* recognition. The Security Council consistently assumed jurisdiction with respect to the dispute,

---

[45] Cf. Judge Ammoun, sep. op., *Western Sahara Case* I.C.J.Rep. 1975 p. 12, 99–100.

[46] Round Table Conference Agreement, 2 Nov. 1949: 69 *UNTS* 200. The agreement refers to the 'Government of the Republic of Indonesia' (cf. Art. 1). For the Linggadjati Agreement of 25 March 1947, see Taylor, *Indonesian Independence and the United Nations* (1960), Appendix 3. For the Renville Agreement of 17 Jan. 1948 see ibid., Appendix 4.

[47] Taylor, op. cit.; Rajan, *The United Nations and Domestic Jurisdiction* (1961), 139–51; Hyde (1949), 49 *Col. LR* 955–66; Sastroamidjojo & Delson, ibid. 344–61; Verzijl, *International Law* II, 82–5; Jessup, *Birth of Nations*, 43–92.

[48] Linggadjati Agreement, Art. 1, 17.

basing this, in part at least, on the status of the Republic.[49] It was allowed to participate in those proceedings as a 'State' under Article 32 of the Charter.[50]

The status of the Democratic Republic of Vietnam after the declaration of independence in 1945 was complicated by the conflicting grants of authority by France to various local governments, and by the claims of both governments to represent Vietnam as a whole. As in the Indonesian case, various States recognized the Democratic Republic: France also extended a somewhat equivocal *de facto* recognition.[51] The Democratic Republic was a participant at the Geneva Conference of 1954 which temporarily partitioned the country. This 'divided State' situation and the right to reintegration provided for in the 1954 Agreements, further complicated the situation: nevertheless, in the events which occurred, the Democratic Republic became a separate State in the territory north of the line of partition: its separate statehood must probably be dated from 1956.[52]

These complicating features were not present in the case of Algeria. The Algerian Republic was proclaimed on 19 September 1958 and after protracted hostilities was granted formal independence by France on 3 July 1962.[53] After some hesitation,[54] the General Assembly took the matter up in 1960 and 1961, calling upon the parties to negotiate 'with a view to implementing the right of the Algerian people to self-determination and independence respecting the unity and territorial integrity of

---

[49] Rajan, op. cit. 139–51.

[50] *Supra*, p. 137.

[51] 149 *BFSP* 657.

[52] *Infra*, p. 285.

[53] Whiteman, 2 *Digest* 133–4, pursuant to the Evian Agreements of 13 Mar. 1962 (1962), 66 *RGDIP* 686–92. Pt. III of the Agreements would appear itself to have recognized Algerian statehood ('A défaut d'accord sur ces procédures, chacun des deux États pourra saisir directement la Cour international de justice'). See generally Bedjaoui, *Law and the Algerian Revolution* (1961); O'Ballance, *The Algerian Insurrection 1954–1962* (1967); Gordon, *The Passing of French Algeria* (1966); Fraleigh, in Falk, ed., *The International Law of Civil War* (1971), 179–243; Yakemtchouk, op. cit. 36–40; and esp. Belkherroubi, *La Naissance et la reconnaissance de la République Algérienne* (1972); and the notes by Charpentier, Flory, and Touscoz in *AFDI* 1954–63.

[54] The question of Algeria was deleted from the agenda in 1955: G.A. Res. 909 (X), 25 Nov. 1955 (adopted without vote). In 1957 two innocuous and uncontroversial resolutions were accepted: G.A. Resns. 1012 (XI), 1184 (XII). In 1958 a considerably stronger draft resolution failed to be adopted (35-18:28): *UN Ybk.* 1958, 79–82.

Algeria.'[55] Algeria had also been recognized, before 3 July 1962, by a certain number of States.[56]

Two more recent successful secessions may be compared with these earlier cases. The Bangladesh situation has been discussed already.[57] Despite the presence of Indian troops on its territory, its doubtful stability, the refusal of Pakistani recognition until 1974, and the probable illegality of Indian intervention, Bangladesh was rapidly and virtually universally recognized as a State. Perhaps even more in point, for present purposes, is the case of Guinea-Bissau. The African Independence Party of Guinea and the Cape Verde Islands was formed in September 1956 by Amilcar Cabral; it tood up overt armed resistance in 1963, and by 1970 claimed to have liberated a large part of the country.[58] Security Council Resolution 322 (1972) recognized the PAIGC as 'legitimate representative()' of Guinea-Bissau.[59] On 26 September 1973 the PAIGC formally proclaimed the independence of Guinea-Bissau. By the end of 1973, it had been recognized by forty States including the Soviet Union, the People's Republic of China, and India.[60] General Assembly Resolution 3061 (XXVIII) welcomed 'the recent accession to independence of the people of Guinea-Bissau, thereby creating the sovereign State of the Republic of Guinea-Bissau.'[61] General Assembly Resolution 3181 (XXVIII) approved 'the credentials of the representatives of Portugal, on the clear understanding that they represent Portugal as it exists within its frontiers in Europe and that they do not represent the Portuguese-dominated Territories of Angola and Mozambique nor could they represent Guinea-Bissau, which is an independent State.'[62] By 31 May

---

[55] G.A. Res. 1724 (XVI), 20 Dec. 1961 (62-0:38, France n.p.); cf. G.A. Res. 1573 (XX), 19 Dec. 1960 (63-8:27, France n.p.).

[56] Twenty-nine States recognized Algeria by April 1961: Bedjaoui, op. cit. 112-38. Belkherroubi argues that the creation of Algeria was a case of secession rather than devolution, and that the Evian Accords were an international agreement between France and the G.P.R.A., a belligerent government with a degree of international personality: op. cit. 85-98 *et seq.* Cf. Zorgbibe, *La guerre civile*, 136-40, who is critical.

[57] *Supra*, pp. 115-17.

[58] Davidson, *The Liberation of Guiné* (1969).

[59] *SCOR* 1677th mtg., 22 Nov. 1972 (15-0:0).

[60] See the valuable note by Rousseau (1974), 78 *RGDIP* 1166-71; and Zorgbibe, *La guerre civile*, 140-1.

[61] G.A. Res. 3061 (XXVIII), 2 Nov. 1973, para. 1 (93-7:30). See further *supra*, p. 136.

[62] G.A. Res. 3181 (XXVIII), 17 Dec. 1973 (amendment referring to Guinea-Bissau adopted 93-14:21; resolution as a whole adopted 108-0:9).

1974 (five weeks after the overthrow of the former Portuguese government) Guinea-Bissau had been recognized by eighty-four States. Its admission to the United Nations was recommended unanimously by the Security Council on 12 August 1974.[63] But an Agreement Granting Independence between Portugal and Guinea-Bissau was not concluded until 26 August 1974:[64] pursuant to paragraph (1) of that agreement, Portugal extended *de jure* recognition on 10 September 1974.[65] It is quite clear, and is implicit in the Agreement of 26 August 1974, that Guinea-Bissau was very widely recognized as a State before—even well before—its recognition by Portugal. This would not have been so had the traditional criterion for secessionary independence, discussed above, been applied.[66]

The following conclusions would seem to be possible.

(1) In principle, self-determination is predicated on a free and effective choice by the people of the territory concerned:[67] where such a choice is available, no particular problem arises with respect to secession.

(2) Where, however, the metropolitan State forcibly denies self-determination to the territory in question, this primary option is not available. In such cases the principle of self-determination operates in favour of the statehood of the seceding territory, provided that the seceding government can properly be regarded as representative of the people of the territory.

(3) Recognition will thus, it seems, be proper even though the independence of the territory is not 'disputed without rational hope of success'.[68]

(4) However, the practice in the cases reviewed has not been either unequivocal or entirely consistent:[69] it is thus difficult to

[63] S.C. Res. 356 (1974).

[64] 18 *ILM* 1244. The Agreement is phrased in terms of recognition rather than grant of independence; it refers, e.g., to 'the territory of the Republic of Guinea-Bissau' (para. (3)).

[65] For the status of the Cape Verde Islands see *infra* p. 435, n. 10.

[66] Cf. Rousseau, op. cit. 1168–9. But see the rather equivocal statements about recognition in *U.S. Digest* 1973, 17; ibid., 1974, 8–9, 14; (1976) 12 *Rev. belge* 334–6; [1975] *Italian YIL* 299–300.

[67] *Western Sahara Case* I.C.J. Rep. 1975 p. 12; *infra* Chapter 14.

[68] Adams, cited *supra*, p. 256, n. 40.

[69] For example in the Vietnamese situation, both for ideological reasons and because of the factors enumerated above. Another possible situation to which the traditional criteria were applied was that of Tibet in 1951, although it may be doubted whether Tibet was a self-determination unit, or whether an indigenous government ever exercised

agree that the normal requirement of effective government has been entirely displaced. Rather, the criterion in this type of case would appear to be one of qualified effectiveness: the metropolitan government cannot rely on the advantages of incumbency against a liberation movement which is supported by the population and controls substantial territory. At least if the Guinea-Bissau precedent is regarded as determinative, the situation would appear to be that the principle of self-determination operates as it were to transfer legal sovereignty to the self-determination unit, legitimizing recognition of it by other States.

(5) It cannot be said that the situation is clear or particularly satisfactory. It is not clear at what stage during a liberation conflict recognition becomes permissible, nor is it easy to formulate any satisfactory test for determining the statehood of the seceding entity before its complete success. This situation is exacerbated by the decline of neutrality in situations of established civil war:[70] in both Vietnam and Guinea-Bissau there was a considerable degree of intervention in favour of both parties to the conflict. Recognition of statehood in such cases seems to have replaced recognition of belligerency, and the notion of reciprocal intervention has proved persuasive.[71] It may be that the effect of self-determination on the criteria for secessionary independence is twofold: in situations such as Guinea-Bissau or Algeria, where the insurgents control substantial areas of the territory and where their legitimacy or representativeness is acknowledged, self-determination will operate to legitimize recognition that would otherwise be premature. In any event, where a self-determination unit achieves actual independence, recognition may be immediate: the requirements of stability and permanence emphasized in nineteenth-century practice do not seem to apply. Bangladesh, the stability and permanence of which must have remained in question, was rapidly recognized by almost all States.[72]

(6) These considerations only apply in the case of secessionary

---

more control or authority than that traditionally recognized as pertaining to Tibet as an autonomous area: cf. *supra*, pp. 212–14.

[70] Cf. the works cited *supra*, p. 248, n. 6.

[71] Falk, *Legal Order in a Violent World* (1968), 124–5; and cf. Kaplan, in Rosenau, ed., *International Aspects of Civil Strife* (1964), 92–121.

[72] *Supra*, pp. 115–17. For the civil war in the Yemen see Boals, in Falk, ed., *The International Law of Civil War*, 303–47.

movements by an entire (or virtually entire) self-determination unit. Different considerations apply to secessions of parts of self-determination units.[73]

(b) *Secession in violation of self-determination*   The situation is quite otherwise where the secession occurs in derogation of the principle of self-determination as applied to the territory as a whole. The Rhodesian situation, which is the most significant example of this, has been discussed already.[74] The principle of self-determination does not here qualify the operation of the principle of effectiveness but operates as a distinct and overriding criterion, suspending statehood until the constitutional and governmental structure is consistent with the principle of self-determination.

(c) *The relevance of the illegal use of force*   This situation has been discussed in Chapter 3. It is argued that the use of force in furtherance of self-determination, though it may be illegal *vis-à-vis* the metropolitan State, will not impede recognition of the independence of the local unit.[75]

(ii) *Secession within a metropolitan State*

Where part of a metropolitan State attempts to secede, different considerations apply. Numerous instances of secession could be given, but it is sufficient to describe the two most significant modern cases—Katanga and Biafra.

The situation in the former Belgian Congo at independence in 1960 has been described already.[76] A secessionist regime in the province of Katanga, under the leadership of Moise Tshombe and with a considerable degree of external support, declared its independence eleven days after the Congo itself became independent. The secession was not ended until 21 January 1963: during that time the Katangan government was considerably more stable than the central government of the Congo,

[73] This was the case with North Korea and East Germany, although in both cases the 'divided State' situation was a complicating factor: see *infra*, Chapter 10. For the attempted secession of Anguilla see *infra*, p. 374.

[74] *Supra*, pp. 103–6.

[75] *Supra*, p. 118.

[76] *Supra*, pp. 42–4.

though that stability was somewhat factitious, given substantial external involvement, and the revenues of the *Union Minière*.[77]

It is quite clear that Katanga was not a State, nor did it, at any time between 1960 and 1963, remotely approach general acceptance as such. Despite its claim to self-determination, it was recognized by no State.[78] Although the United Nations Force in the Congo was formally impartial as to the outcome of internal conflicts, its mandate included the promotion of the territorial integrity of the entire Congo,[79] and in fact it was instrumental in ending the secession.[80]

The status of the Katangan regime was also, indirectly, an issue in the *Expenses Opinion*. The International Court was asked to determine whether the costs of ONUC were 'expenses of the Organization' under Article 17(2) of the Charter. The Court stated that, in order to answer the request, it was not necessary to determine the validity of the specific resolutions authorizing the Congo (or Middle East) operations. However, the Majority Opinion went on to hold the operations *intra vires* on the ground that, not constituting 'enforcement measures' under Chapter VII, their direction was not within the exclusive preserve of the Security Council under the Charter, nor did they require a finding under Article 39 of a threat to or breach of the peace or act of aggression. The Court stated:

It is not necessary for the Court to express an opinion as to which article or articles of the Charter were the basis for the resolutions of the Security Council, but it can be said that the operations of ONUC did not include a use of armed force against a State which the Security Council, under Article 39, determined to have committed an act of aggression or to have breached the peace. The armed forces which were utilized in the Congo were not authorized to take military action against any State. The operation did not involve "preventive or

[77] For details see McNemar, in Falk, *The International Law of Civil War*, 244–302; Leclercq, *L'ONU et l'affaire du Congo* (1964); Hoskyns, *The Congo since Independence* (1965).

[78] Cf. Lemarchand (1962), 56 *Am. Pol. Sc. R.* 404–14. S.C. Res. 169, 24 Nov. 1961 (9-0:2), *inter alia*, deplored 'all armed action in opposition to the authority of the Government of the Republic of the Congo, specifically secessionist activities and armed action now being carried on by the Provincial Administration of Katanga with the aid of external resources and foreign mercenaries, and *completely reject[ed]* the claim that Katanga is a "sovereign independent nation".'

[79] Cf. Simmonds, *Legal Problems arising from the United Nations Military Operations in the Congo* (1968), 289–92; Bowett, *United Nations Forces* (1964), 153–254.

[80] O'Brien, *To Katanga and Back: A UN Case History* (1962), 261–7.

enforcement measures" against any State under Chapter VII and therefore did not constitute "action" as that term is used in Article 11.[81] It follows more or less explicitly from this that Katanga was at no time a 'State' for the purposes of the Charter.[82] In the Biafran situation the same conclusion must be reached. The secession of Biafra was declared on 30 May 1967[83] and terminated on 12 January 1970.[84] Biafra received less substantial external support than Katanga: it was an indigenous secession with some claims to self-determination in the political sense.[85] Again unlike the Katangan case there was no substantial United Nations involvement, although the O.A.U. was a strong supporter of the central government.[86] Five States recognized Biafra unconditionally, although none of these established diplomatic relations with it.[87] The vast majority of States adjudged that Biafra did not qualify for recognition as a State: indeed, there was no case even of belligerent recognition in the civil war.[88] Once again it must be the case that Biafra was not a State.[89]

[81] I.C.J. Rep. 1962 p. 151, 177. Judges Spiropoulos (180), Spender (182), and Morelli (224–5) expressed no opinion. Judge Koretsky, diss. (267–72), was more equivocal. Only Judge Moreno Quintana expressly disagreed: he regarded the Katangan regime, apparently, as 'a belligerent community recognized under international law as possessing a legal personality' (246). Judge Bustamante, diss. (297 ff.) thought that, although 'the new tutelary functions of the United Nations in respect of new States' might well be *intra vires*, they were not contemplated by the Charter as expenses.

[82] In the pleadings in the *Expenses Case*, only a few governments even indirectly adverted to the problem. Upper Volta was critical of what it regarded as a denial of self-determination (*Pleadings*, 123). South Africa regarded ONUC as an intervention in the domestic jurisdiction of the Congo, and an uncontemplated maintenance of the artificial unity of a State (265–6; cf. Evensen's reply, 358). Denmark referred to 'the local regime in Katanga' as 'revolting provincial authorities' (160).   [83] 6 *ILM* 665–80.

[84] See Cronje, *The World and Nigeria. The Diplomatic History of the Biafran War 1967–1970* (1972); Nwankwo and Ifejika, *The Making of a Nation: Biafra* (1964); Kirk-Greene, *Crisis and Conflict in Nigeria. A Documentary Sourcebook 1966–1969* (2 vols., 1971).

[85] e.g., Statement of French Council of Ministers, 31 July 1968: Kirk-Greene, op. cit. II, 245–6, 329–31; Cronje, op. cit. 194–6. Also *infra*, p. 269; Post (1968), 44 *Int. Aff.* 26–39; Nayar (1975), 10 *Texas ILJ* 321–45; Calogeropoulos-Stratis, *Le Droit des peuples à disposer d'eux-mêmes* (1973), 342–8.

[86] Kirk-Greene, op. cit. II, 172–3, 244–5, 328; Tiewul (1975), 16 *Harvard ILJ* 259–302.

[87] The most significant of these recognitions (Tanzania) was extended for moral and humanitarian reasons, rather than in the conviction that Biafra was a State: Kirk-Greene, op. cit. II, 202–11, and Nyerere's remarkable 'Memorandum on Biafra's Case', 4 Sept. 1969: ibid. 429–39.

[88] Criticized by Higgins, in Luard, ed., *The International Regulation of Civil Wars* (1972), 169–86, 175.

[89] Loc. cit.; also Ijalaye (1971), 65 *AJ* 551–9; Elias (1971), 5 *Nigerian LJ* 1–18;

The conclusion seems then to be that, in cases where the principle of self-determination does not operate, the criterion for statehood of seceding territories remains in substance that established in the nineteenth century: that is, the maintenance of a stable and effective government over a reasonably well defined territory, to the exclusion of the metropolitan State, in such circumstances that independence is either in fact undisputed, or manifestly indisputable.[90]

(iii) Secession fomented by external illegal force

This situation is examined in Chapter 3.[91]

9.3   CERTAIN INCIDENTS OF SECESSION IN MODERN INTERNATIONAL LAW

Certain incidents of secession in modern international law also require at least brief consideration.

(1) The legality of secession in modern international law[92]

The Charter of the United Nations, which is in this matter expressive of general international law, forbids the use of force (except in self-defence) 'in . . . international relations' or 'against the territorial integrity and political independence of any State'. Civil conflicts, whether aimed at changes of government or at secession would appear not to involve a use of force in international relations, and thus to be exempt from this prohibition. On the other hand, neither does international law provide for any 'right to secession or rebellion'. In principle, as

---

Adaramola (1970), 4 *Nigerian LJ* 76–84; Panter-Brick (1968), 44 *Int. Aff.* 254–66; *contra* Nwogugu (1974), 14 *Indian JIL* 13–53; Okeke, *Controversial subjects of contemporary international law* (1974), 165.

[90] *Supra*, p. 256.

[91] *Supra*, p. 106.

[92] Various unsuccessful attempts have been made, inspired by notions of monarchical or democratic legitimacy, to outlaw revolutions aimed at changes of government within a State: for details see Marek, *Identity and Continuity*, 51–5. These have taken the form of refusal of political recognition rather than denial of the effectiveness of the new government, and it remains true that, in the matter of governments, international law looks to '*de facto* sovereignty and complete governmental control', rather than to 'illegitimacy or irregularity of origin': *Tinoco Arbitration* (Taft C.J.) (1923) 1 *RIAA* 369, 381.

Lauterpacht pointed out 'International law does not condemn rebellion or secession aiming at the acquisition of independence.'[93] This position was affirmed by the International Law Commission in its discussion of the principle of non-recognition of territorial acquisition by illegal force. Article 11 of the Draft Declaration on Rights and Duties of States,[94] which embodied that principle, was amended by limiting it to acquisition 'by another State' to eliminate the case of secession.[95]

However, in various resolutions relating to both the Katangan and the Rhodesian secessions, the Security Council has characterized a secession as illegal. For example, Resolution 169 (1961) on the Congo *inter alia* '*Strongly deprecate[d]* the secessionist activities illegally carried out by the provincial administration of Katanga, with the aid of external resources and manned by foreign mercenaries ...' and '*Declare[d]* that all secessionist activities against the Republic of the Congo are contrary to the *Loi fondamentale* and Security Council decisions and specifically *demand[ed]* that such activities ... cease forthwith.'[96]

In the case of Southern Rhodesia, from the very first United Nations resolutions have referred to the Smith government as an 'illegal racist minority regime'.[97]

The question is whether this language indicates the existence of legal rules prohibiting secession.[98] It is not thought that this is so, for the following reasons. First, if the seceding entity is acting illegally under international law, it follows that the entity is a subject of international law, although the main object of the resolutions cited was to deny to the entities in question any international status. Secondly, in the debates on the resolutions there is little or no reliance on legal rules prohibiting secession:[99] rather, reference is made to the municipal illegality of the acts in

---

[93] *Recognition*, 8; and (1928) 22 *AJ* 105–30, 128.

[94] Cf. *supra*, p. 107.

[95] *ILC Ybk.* 1949, 112–13 (9–1).

[96] S.C. Res. 169 (1961) (9–0:2), paras. 1, 8.

[97] *Supra*, p. 103.

[98] Equally, resolutions proclaiming the 'legitimacy' of particular 'wars of national liberation' raise the question of a legal right to rebellion: cf. *supra*, p. 110; *infra*, p. 270; and Ginsburg, in Baade, ed., *The Soviet Impact on International Law* (1965), 66–98.

[99] e.g., the only reference to the issue in the debates on S.C. Res. 169 (1961) referred the illegality to the municipal law of the Congo: *SCOR* 974th mtg., 15 Nov. 1961, 9 (Loutfi, UAR).

question.[100] Any international illegality associated with secession movements, before their consolidation as States, relates to the existence of foreign intervention (as in Katanga) or the existence of a threat to international peace and security (as in Rhodesia). The position is therefore that secession is neither legal nor illegal in international law, but a legally neutral act the consequences of which are, or may be, regulated internationally. The various legal regulations will now be briefly referred to.

(2) *Belligerency and insurgency in modern civil war*

The role of the institution of belligerent recognition in nineteenth-century civil wars has been briefly discussed earlier in this chapter.[101] It was an intermediate legal status, involving some legal capacity, but not equivalent to statehood. Other legal incidents of civil wars—the laws of war, intervention and the like—were at least notionally attached to recognition of belligerency, which was thus in theory a relatively monolithic and identifiable form of regulation. Unfortunately, this can no longer be said to be true, if it ever was. Recognition of belligerency assumed the existence of relatively stable territorial units contesting the war in accordance with the rules and customs of international conflict. Modern civil war tends to be less centralized, less territorial, guerilla war.[102] Even when civil war has been conducted from a more or less coherent territorial base, the unwillingness of metropolitan or central governments to accord insurgents any form of status, and the political delicacy of third State recognition of belligerency, have operated to internalize even prolonged civil wars.[103] There is no clear twentieth-century case of recognition of belligerency: and the failure to recognize the parties to the continuing civil war in Spain as belligerents, it has been persuasively argued, has resulted in the desuetude of the doctrine of recognition of belligerency.[104] Other candidates, such as 'recognition of

---

[100] Elias, in Ch. 6 ('The legality of illegal regimes in Africa') of his *Africa and the Development of International Law* (1972) discusses only the legal position of revolutionary governments, and makes no reference to secession. Cf. Bennouna, op. cit. 60–3.

[101] *Supra*, pp. 252–5.

[102] Cf. Higgins, in Luard, ed., op. cit. 172.

[103] Falk, *Legal Order in a Violent World* (1968), 121n.

[104] Oglesby, *Internal War and the Search for Normative Order* (1971); Falk, op. cit. 124–5; Higgins, op. cit. 171.

insurgency', have failed to establish themselves in doctrine or practice.[105] Instead, recognition of insurgents as the government (as in Spain) or as a new State (as in Biafra) has effectively replaced belligerent recognition—despite the prematurity of the former, in most cases.[106] And intervention on behalf of both parties—whether or not under the cover of recognition—has become virtually a universal phenomenon in civil wars of all types.[107]

If international law is effectively to regulate civil conflict, it must do so by regulating specific problems rather than through the medium of some more general legal status such as belligerency. Fortunately, these problems are to a large extent outside the scope of this study, but some brief reference to the more important issues follows.

(3) *The application of the laws of war to civil conflicts*

Under the *ancien régime* of rules relating to belligerent status, the laws of war applied to civil conflict when belligerency was recognized. Before that point, the treatment of rebel forces in accordance with those rules, if it occurred, was merely a concession of the central government. With the decline of belligerency the problem of the application of general standards of conduct of war to civil wars has proved troublesome, and has attracted a voluminous literature. Common Article 3 of the 1949 Geneva Conventions of the Laws of War provides for the application of certain minimum standards 'in the case of armed conflict not of an international character'.[108] Since secessionist regimes are *ex hypothesi* not signatories to the convention, the

---

[105] Cf. however Castrén (1965), 5 *Indian JIL* 443–54; Lauterpacht, *Recognition*, 270–8; Chen, *Recognition*, 398–407. See further Verhoeven, *Reconnaissance*, 100–140.

[106] Recognition of insurgents as a government of a new State occurred for example in the Algerian, Indonesian, and Guinea-Bissau conflicts: *supra*, p. 258.

Other forms of recognition of groups (National Liberation Movements and the like) attempting to seize control of particular territory have evolved in practice. The status accorded such entities by third-State recognition is probably non-opposable; recognition would appear to be constitutive of such consequences, if any, as the recognizing State wishes to attach to it.

On 'National Liberation Movements' see Klein (1976), 36 *ZfV* 618–53; Verhoeven *Reconnaissance*, 140–67, Ronzitti, *Le guerre di liberazione nazionale e il diritto internazionale* (1974); Bennouna, op. cit. 159–70; Fisher (1975), 3 *Syracuse JILC* 221–54. Cf. Lazarus, [1974] *AFDI* 173–200, who is critical. See also 1975 UN *Jur. Ybk.* 176.

[107] Kaplan, in Rosenau, ed., *International Aspects of Civil Strife* (1964), 92–121.

[108] 75 *UNTS* 32.

application of Article 3 has met with difficulties in practice:[109] moreover its operation is limited to persons taking no active part in the hostilities. The status of combatants in a civil war is thus left to the limited mercy of the customary law and the discretion of the central or metropolitan government.[110] However, recent attempts have been made to extend the international laws of war (as distinct from the minimum protection of common Article 3) to certain types of civil conflict. Article I (4) of Protocol I additional to the Geneva Conventions, relating to the Protection of Victims of International Armed Conflicts (1977) extends the notion of international armed conflict to include. . .

'armed conflicts in which peoples are fighting against colonial domination and alien occupation and against racist régimes in the exercise of their right of self-determination. . .'[111]

(4) *The problem of intervention: aid to seceding regimes*

Again, the question of legality of intervention in aid or opposition to a revolutionary or secessionary force is highly controversial. There is little agreement on a satisfactory and comprehensive regulation of intervention, but once again the matter is largely outside the scope of this study. The argument that, exceptionally, aid or intervention is permissible to liberation movements in self-determination territories has been referred to already.[112]

(5) *Problems of continuity and commencement*

One of the peculiarities of secession is that an effective territorial entity can subsist for a period of time without any, or with only a provisional, legal status. If the entity subsequently establishes itself as a State, problems of commencement, continuity, and responsibility arise. The legal position here is clearer: it is discussed in a later chapter.[113]

---

[109] Greenspan, *The Modern Law of Land Warfare* (1959), 619–27; Rubin (1972), 21 *ICLQ* 472–96; Umozurike (1971), 11 *Indian JIL* 205–18; Zorgbibe, *La guerre civile*, 178–201.

[110] See also Baxter (1951), 28 *BY* 323–45, 333–8; Bierzanek, in *Mélanges Andrassy* (1968), 54–77; Abi-Saab (1972), 3 *Annales d'Études Internationales* 93–117; Taulbee (1972), 12 *Indian JIL* 185–99; Meyrowitz, [1971] *Rev. Belge* 56–72; Veuthey, ibid. 505–39; Nurick and Barrett (1946), 40 *AJ* 563–83.

[111] (1978) 72 *AJ* 457. In addition to the works cited already see Graham (1975), 32 *Washington & Lee LR* 25–63; Bond, ibid. 65–78; Forsythe (1975), 69 *AJ* 77–91.

[112] *Supra*, pp. 113–14.

[113] *Infra*, pp. 392–6.

10. The Divided States

10.1 GENERAL PRINCIPLES: THE CATEGORY 'DIVIDED STATES'

IN THE decade after the Second World War, certain territorial entities which had previously been either States (Germany, China) or colonial possessions (Vietnam, Korea) found themselves divided into two or more separate units of administration.[1] It has been argued that this phenomenon of the 'divided State' is a special juridical category of State, requiring separate treatment.[2] Caty, for example, argues that: 'il y a État divisé lorsque la ligne partegeant l'État ne peut être considerée comme une frontière au sens juridique du terme.'[3] But the question whether a particular administrative line can be considered a frontier 'au sens juridique du terme' assumes a specific, unique sense of the term 'frontier', whereas a demarcation line within a State may be a frontier for certain juridical purposes, but not others. For example the General Assembly's Declaration elaborating Charter Principles of 1970 states in part:

Every State . . . has the duty to refrain from the threat or use of force to violate international lines of demarcation, such as armistice lines, established by or pursuant to an international agreement to which it is a party or which it is otherwise bound to respect. Nothing in the foregoing shall be construed as prejudicing the positions of the parties concerned with regard to the status and effects of such lines under their special regimes or as affecting their temporary character.[4]

---

[1] Cf. also the division of Austria after 1945 (*infra*, p. 310), and the Anglo-Egyptian Sudan 1899–1956: Whiteman, 1 *Digest* 280–1, 2 *Digest* 217–18, 14 *Digest* 487–90; Baddour, *Sudanese-Egyptian Relations* (1960); Coret, *Le Condominium* (1960), 165–76. More recently, ethnic or other conflicts within States have tended to cause territorial polarization not unlike the 'divided State' situations discussed in this Chapter: e.g. Cyprus (*supra*, p. 169).

[2] Caty, *Le Statut juridique des états divisés* (1969); Martinez-Agullo (1964), 91 *JDI* 265–284; Whiteman, 1 *Digest* 320–38; but cf. the more summary treatment by Verzijl, *International Law* II, 307. See also Mendelson, 171–203; Verhoeven, *Reconnaissance*, 36–52.

[3] Caty, 15.

[4] G.A. Res. 2625 (XXV), Annex. For the travaux préparatoires see e.g. A/7326 (1968), 28–30; A/7619 (1969), 27–8, 38; A/8018 (1970), 33, 65, 90, 120.

There are then two distinct questions; the juridical status of a particular frontier for a given purpose, and the question whether a particular frontier is the frontier between two States. The latter carries certain implications for the former: thus an interstate frontier is, with hardly any exceptions, a frontier for the purposes of the use of force, but, as Resolution 2625 (XXV) recognizes, the contrary is not necessarily the case. These two questions are relevant to the various divided States, but they are equally relevant elsewhere. As we have seen, territorial entities can vary substantially in status, and the juridical status of frontiers can similarly vary. Treating divided States as a juridical category blurs the similarity of issues between the different types of case. In Caty's study, at least, there is a further disadvantage, in that the prototype 'divided State' is taken to be Germany—in part because of its intrinsic interest, but in part perhaps because of the extensive practical and theoretical analysis to which the German question has been subjected.[5] For example, in Caty's view 'Dans les deux cas du Vietnam et de la Corée, seul un traité de paix peut écarter l'hypothèse d'un Etat global. Il en est de même en Allemagne.'[6] But the cases are quite different. If 'Germany' continues to exist, it must be because there are subsisting legal reasons for its existence. The same could not be said of 'Vietnam' before 1975 or of 'Korea' now. Indeed, it is doubtful if it ever was true of 'Vietnam'. An intention for eventual unification, and the reaffirmation that ceasefire lines are 'temporary' are not necessarily such subsisting legal reasons, since either may be as consistent with two States as with one.[7] Again, the point is not whether two entities are bound, on whatever terms, to the reunification of the nation and their reabsorption into a single State; but whether they do in truth constitute parts of a single State.

This is not to say that the various cases of divided States which occurred shortly after the Second World War did not have important political similarities. They marked, as it were, the front line of the 'Cold War'. They were created, on the whole, at the same time and for much the same reasons. With the partial exception of China, relatively permanent settlements have been

[5] Cf. Caty, 17, 74.
[6] Ibid. 57.
[7] See also ibid. 52, 56; but cf. 80.

achieved, also at the same time (sc.1970–3) and for much the same reasons. That China, despite resolution of the question of United Nations representation, is an exception to this generalization is probably due to the fact that the China problem, in the general view, is incapable of a compromise settlement.[8] The divided States are none the less worth consideration: separately, because of their considerable interest and importance; together as demonstrating the marked tendency towards consolidation of status of existing political and administrative entities, despite political, and to some extent legal, impediments tending to prevent such consolidation. What is erroneous is to treat the 'divided States' as a special juridical category, the subject of legal rules different in kind from those applying to States in general.[9]

In this Chapter Germany will be discussed in some detail, both because of its continuing importance and as an instance of the particularity of the 'divided State' situation. In view of recent events, the other cases are given more summary treatment.

10.2 THE 'TWO GERMANIES'[10]

On 18 September 1973 the Federal Republic of Germany and the German Democratic Republic were admitted, without opposition, to the United Nations.[11] Both are now widely recognized,[12] and the once controversial issue of their separate statehood is now moot. But the transactions affecting Germany since 1945 still deserve analysis: there remain Great Power competences relating to 'Germany as a whole', the 'international enclave' of Berlin, and claims to continuity of or identity with pre-1945 Germany.

---

[8] *Supra*, pp. 143–52; *infra*, p. 286.

[9] See further *infra*, p. 286. Waldock stated that the 'circumstances of each of these so-called divided States are . . . altogether too special for them to provide guidance in regard to questions of succession': *ILC Ybk.* 1972/II, 43.

[10] The literature is voluminous. See Caty, 31–41, 47–51, 57–73; Bathurst and Simpson, *Germany and the North Atlantic Community* (1956); Bishop (1955), 49 *AJ* 125–47; van Laun (1951), 45 *AJ* 267–85; Münch (1962), 89 *JDI* 5–51; Wright (1952), 46 *AJ* 299–308; Mann, *Studies in International Law* (1973), 634–59, 660–706; Pinto (1959), 86 *JDI* 313–425; Tsoutsos, *Politique et Droit dans les Relations Internationales* (1967), 19–85; and the works cited *infra*.

[11] S.C. Res. 355 (1973), 22 June 1973; G.A. Res. 3050 (XXVIII), 18 Sept. 1973; cf. 12 *ILM* 217; Battati, [1973] *AFDI* 211–31.

[12] (1975) 79 *RGDIP* 156–7; 13 *ILM* 500.

(1) *Quadripartite control and its effects on Germany*

With the collapse of German resistance, there was by 5 June 1945 no longer an effective or recognized government of Germany.[13] The Allied Powers assumed 'supreme authority with respect to Germany',[14] which, in accordance with previous arrangements, was divided into four Zones of Occupation, with a 'special Berlin area' under quadripartite control.[15] In the absence of a reformed German government, this would normally have led to the extinction of Germany by *debellatio*, as Kelsen pointed out:[16] however, the Berlin Declaration was stated not to effect the annexation of Germany,[17] and the Allied Control Council subsequently achieved a degree of recognition as 'the Government of Germany'.[18] Thus, it was said, 'Germany continued to exist as a State, and German nationality as a nationality'.[19] This remarkable arrangement—'government in commission', as it has been called[20]—was taken both in practice and in the predominant doctrine[21] to involve the legal continuity of pre-1945 Germany; although it is difficult to see how this would have been so, absent the Allied Control Council's claim to act as its government, or general recognition of the non-extinction of Germany.

In practice the government of Germany was entrusted to the respective Commanders-in-Chief of the Four Powers, jointly with respect to Germany as a whole, and each separately in his own Zone of Occupation, acting officially as the agent of the Powers, though instructed by his own government.[22] On this

---

[13] Berlin Declaration, 145 *BFSP* 796.

[14] Loc. cit.

[15] Protocol on Zones of Occupation in Germany, 12 Sept. 1944: 227 *UNTS* 279, as amended: ibid. 298; Statement on Control Machinery in Germany, 5 June 1945: 145 *BFSP* 803; affirmed at Potsdam, ibid. 852. For details see Sharp, *The Wartime Alliance and the Zonal Division of Germany* (1975).

[16] (1945) 39 *AJ* 518–26, 519.

[17] 145 *BFSP* 796.

[18] e.g., Exchange of Notes with Spain concerning German Enemy Assets (1949): 147 *BFSP* 1058. This probably involved the termination of the war as a matter of international law: Bathurst and Simpson, op. cit. 45–6. For termination in municipal law see Ottensooser (1952), 29 *BY* 435–42; Kunz (1952), 46 *AJ* 114–19.

[19] *R.* v. *Bottrill ex parte Kuechenmeister* [1947] 1 K.B. 41 (F.O. certificate).

[20] Jennings (1946), 23 *BY* 112–41.

[21] Ibid. 139–40; Bathurst and Simpson, op. cit. 33–41; Mann, op. cit. 652–8; *Re Lachinger* (1954), 21 ILR 43.

[22] Bathurst and Simpson, op. cit. 41–5.

view, Germany was not a condominium of the Powers,[23] but the government of Germany was carried on by them, according to the instruments establishing the occupation regime. But those instruments remained largely executory, and separate governmental entities evolved in the Soviet and Western Zones of Germany.

(2) *The creation of the Federal Republic of Germany*

Shortly after the breakdown of the Allied Control Council, the three Western Allies established a subordinate government in their zones—the Federal Republic of Germany. At this period, unilateral creation of such subordinate entities was probably not illegal: each occupying Power was '*de jure* entitled to exercise governing authority in respect of [its] zone of occupation in Germany and might therefore establish subordinate organizations to act on its behalf.'[24] Nevertheless, the Western Allies were already taking the view that the Federal Republic was entitled to some special status: a Declaration of 19 December 1950, for example, stated that 'The Three Governments consider that the Government of the Federal Republic is the only German Government freely and legitimately constituted and therefore entitled to speak for the German people in international affairs.'[25] The authority of the Federal Republic was further extended by a Tripartite Convention on Relations of 26 May 1952, as amended.[26] Under that Convention the 'Occupation regime' in the Federal Republic was purportedly terminated, and it was stated that 'The Federal Republic shall have accordingly the full authority of a sovereign State over its internal and external affairs.'[27] However, that authority was not unlimited: 'In view of the international situation, which has so far prevented the unification of Germany and the conclusion of a peace settlement the Three Powers retain the rights and responsibilities, heretofore exercised or held by them, relating to Berlin and to Germany as

---

[23] Cf. Coret, *Le Condominium* (1961), 215–27.

[24] *H.C. Deb.* Vol. 735 w.a. col. 204, 7 Nov. 1966.

[25] [1964] *BPIL*276. Cf. the Declaration of 3 Oct. 1954, cited by Baade, in Stanger, ed., *West Berlin: The Legal Contest* (1966), 53–160, 67. The 1949 Protocol relating to the incorporation of Germany into the European Community of Nations treats the Federal Republic as equivalent to 'Germany': 185 *UNTS* 308.

[26] 331 *UNTS* 327.

[27] Ibid., Art. 1(2).

a whole, including the reunification of Germany and a peace settlement . . .'[28] It is clear that the three Allies had no competence to relinquish quadripartite authority without Soviet consent; but that consent was granted by Soviet recognition on 13 September 1955, retrospective to 1949.[29] This, as Mann pointed out, involved the 'ratification and validation of the action taken in 1949 in creating the Federal Republic'.[30] The Federal Republic thereafter achieved general recognition as a State.

(3) *The creation of the German Democratic Republic*

In much the same way the Soviet Union on 7 October 1949 created a local government—the German Democratic Republic. A treaty of 20 September 1955 accorded it general freedom of action with respect to its 'domestic and foreign policy', but express reservation was made, in the preamble, of the 'obligations of the Soviet Union and of the German Democratic Republic under existing international agreements relating to Germany as a whole'.[31] But Western recognition of this purported transfer of power was withheld: that the German Democratic Republic was a separate State was consistently denied by the various Western governments.[32] Four different arguments were proposed in the period 1955–70. General non-recognition[33] is not of course supportable on a ground for denying statehood; though it might be regarded as a summary of other, more particular contentions. Nor could it be argued that the quadripartite agreements made independence legally impossible:[34] secession from international

---

[28] Ibid., Art. 2.

[29] Mann, *Studies in International Law* (1973), 671.

[30] Loc. cit.

[31] 226 *UNTS* 201. Cf. the treaty of 1964 in which the G.D.R. and the U.S.S.R. affirmed 'the existence of two sovereign German States', stated that unification could be achieved only by agreement between them, but reserved 'the rights or obligations of the Parties under bilateral or other international agreements at present in force, including the Potsdam Agreement': 553 *UNTS* 249, Arts. 7, 9.

[32] In a 1968 debate on Rhodesia, a telegram from the G.D.R. was circulated not under Rule 6 but unofficially. Answering a Soviet complaint, the U.K. stated that the telegram was 'not a communication from a State': *SCOR* 1445th mtg., 24 Aug. 1968, 3. The U.S. (loc. cit.) and Canada (ibid. 7) agreed. A proposal to invite the G.D.R. to participate was rejected: ibid. 17 (2–9:4). Cf. [1966] *BPIL* 160.

[33] e.g. *Internaional Registration of Trade Mark (Germany) Case* (1959) 28 ILR 82.

[34] Cf. the certificate in *Carl Zeiss Stiftung* v. *Rayner & Keeler* [1967] A.C. 853, criticized by Mann, op. cit. 674–9. The House of Lords was compelled by the certificate to take the view it did: either the G.D.R. was a subordinate government or it was nothing.

authority is presumably possible in the same way as secession from national authority. A third persistent argument alleged lack of effective independence from the Soviet Union:[35] continuance of the German Democratic Republic over a considerable period of time, and the fairly nominal criteria for effectiveness where no military opposition to secession continued, made this objection difficult to sustain.[36] Finally, it seems to have been argued that the creation of the German Democratic Republic was a violation of the principle of self determination as applied to 'Germany as a whole' by the Potsdam Agreement.[37] But self-determination, in the Potsdam Agreement, was heavily qualified by reliance on strategic considerations, and coexisted with extensive quadripartite powers, extending to the contemplated dismemberment of Germany.[38] In the context the objection could hardly be regarded as convincing.

(4) *Residual quadripartite competences over 'Germany as a whole'*

It follows that both the Federal Republic and the Democratic Republic must be taken to have established themselves, by processes analogous to devolution and secession respectively, before the agreements of 1970–3.[39] It followed that the term 'Germany' in legal documents might well be construed to bear a non-technical, or even a non-specific, meaning.[40] Relations between the two German States might also possess certain special characteristics, a phenomenon discussed elsewhere.[41]

[35] e.g. [1963] *BPIL* 71–2.

[36] Cf. *supra*, p. 266; Wright (1961), 55 *AJ* 959–65. Mann in 1967 referred to the G.D.R. as an 'insurgent regime': op. cit. 693–4. *Contra* Grewe (1962), 56 *AJ* 510–13.

[37] Baade, op. cit. 69.

[38] Cf. the terms of the Berlin Declaration: 'The Governments ... will hereafter determine the status of Germany or of any area at present being part of German territory': 145 *BFSP* 796. For earlier plans for dismembering Germany see Wheeler-Bennett and Nicholls, *The Semblance of Peace*, 131–3, 172.

[39] To the same effect e.g. Wright, op. cit.; Pinto (1959), 86 *JDI* 312–425; Baade, op. cit.; *contra* Caty, 31–9, 52–64. The transactions of 1970–3 are as follows: U.S.S.R.–F.R.G. Non-Aggression Treaty, 12 Aug. 1970: 9 *ILM* 1026; Quadripartite Agreement on Berlin, 3 Sept. 1971: 10 *ILM* 895; F.R.G.–G.D.R., Treaty on the Basis of Intra-German Relations, 21 Dec. 1972: 12 *ILM* 16. See also 13 *ILM* 878. Cf. Rohn (1969), 16 *Rev. of Cont. L.* 7–16.

[40] e.g. *Re Delacher* (1962) 40 ILR 5; *Austrian Citizens (Entitlement to Compensation) Case* (1960) 32 ILR 153.

[41] *German Inter-Zonal Trade Case* (1965) 45 ILR 37; and cf. the decision of 31 July 1973 on the constitutionality of the Treaty of Relations, noted (1976) 70 *AJ* 147–54. Cf. *supra*, p. 240.

The establishment of the two German States must also have limited or extinguished the competences of the Four Powers with respect to their affairs, at least to the extent that these competences were not reserved in the various instruments. Such reservations have usually been made in rather general terms;[42] they apparently involve the reunification of Germany and the conclusion of a formal peace treaty. It is not necessary to examine their precise extent here, but it is doubtful whether they are particularly peremptory. Their relevance to the issues of identity and continuity is referred to later.[43]

(5) *The status of Berlin*[44]

As we have seen, a 'special Berlin area' under an inter-Allied Governing Authority was established in 1945.[45] Its collective operation ceased by 1948,[46] but Greater Berlin has always been regarded as extra-territorial to the Federal Republic.[47] Both the Soviet Union and the Democratic Republic claim that, while West Berlin is extra-territorial to the Federal Republic, East Berlin is an integral part of the Democratic Republic and thus, presumably, exempt from quadripartite control.[48] In view of the insistence by the other three powers on the continuing quadripartite authority over the whole of Berlin,[49] it is not clear by what method the Democratic Republic has acquired

[42] e.g. 1952 Tripartite Convention, Art. 2: 331 *UNTS* 327; 1955 Convention (U.S.S.R.–G.D.R.), *supra*, p. 276, n. 31; 1972 Treaty, Art. 9 ('bilateral and multilateral international treaties and agreements relating to them').

[43] *Infra*, pp. 280–1.

[44] In addition to the works cited already, see Lush (1965), 14 *ICLQ* 742–87; Doeker, Melsheimer and Schröder (1973), 67 *AJ* 44–62; Simpson (1957), 6 *ICLQ* 83–102; Caty, 64–73; Zorgbibe, *La Question de Berlin* (1970); Stanger, *West Berlin: the Legal Context* (1966); Green (1963), 10 *NILR* 113–38; Bathurst (1962), 38 *BY* 255–306; Feller (1977), 51 *ALJ* 272–6.

[45] 227 *UNTS* 279, Art. 1.

[46] Cf. 138 *UNTS* 123.

[47] e.g., Bathurst, op. cit.; Jessup (1949), 43 *AJ* 92–5; cf. *Hartje* v. *Yugoslav Military Mission* (1954) 21 *ILR* 116. See also Schiedermair, [1973] *AFDI* 171–87.

[48] In a note of 19 June 1974 (A/9648), the U.S.S.R. stated that there was no basis for 'asserting that the status of Berlin, the capital of the Sovereign State of the German Democratic Republic, and that of West Berlin, which was under the occupation of the three Powers, were identical'.

[49] In reply to the Soviet note, the three Western Powers reaffirmed their view that 'any change in the status of greater Berlin would require the agreement of all four Powers which continued to exercise their quadripartite rights in all four sectors of the city': A/10087 (1975), reaffirming A/9855 (1974) and cf. the Soviet reply, A/10084 (1975); and (1976) 80 *RGDIP* 214–15, 884–5. See further (1977) 81 *RGDIP* 494, 613–14, 772–4.

sovereignty over East Berlin. Certainly it could do so by prescription over a period of time, but the factors tending to acquisition of territory by prescription are less cogent in this situation than those tending to acquisition of statehood by the Democratic Republic by the process of secession. In particular there is no exact analogy in the law relating to acquisition of territory to the secessionary creation of the new State. In the latter case, the factors compelling recognition— the need to treat with the *de facto* government, the need to recognize an effective nationality, and so on—are more pressing: where the case involves merely acquisition of territory by an existing State such factors, though still relevant, may be effectively dealt with through recognition of *de facto* control.[50]

The separate status of Berlin—within whatever limits—was the subject of and was in general confirmed by a Quadripartite Agreement and Associated Arrangements of 3 September 1971.[51] The Four Powers 'acting on the basis of their quadripartite rights and responsibilities, and of the corresponding wartime and postwar agreements and decisions of the Four Powers, which are not affected'[52] agreed that there would be no use or threat of force 'in the area'[53] and that the *de facto* situation would not be changed unilaterally.[54] West Berlin was declared 'not to be a constituent part of the Federal Republic of Germany and not to be governed by it';[55] but the arrangement whereby the normal diplomatic representation of West Berlin was entrusted to the Federal Republic was reaffirmed.[56] The effect of the Agreement was summarized in a Note to the Chancellor of the Federal Republic: 'Our Governments will continue, as heretofore, to exercise supreme authority in the Western Sectors of Berlin, within the framework of the Four Power responsibility which we share for Berlin as a whole.'[57]

[50] Cf. *infra*, pp. 396–9.
[51] 10 *ILM* 895; see Doeker & ors. (1973), 67 *AJ* 44–62.
[52] 10 *ILM* 895, Preamble, para. 2.
[53] Ibid., Pt. I(2). [54] Ibid., Pt. I(4).
[55] Ibid., Pt. II(B), Annex II(1).
[56] Ibid., Pt. II(D), Annex IV.
[57] 10 *ILM* 901. See also the Final Quadripartite Protocol of 3 June 1972: 11 *ILM* 734, affirming that the agreements do 'not affect quadripartite agreements or decisions previously concluded or reached', and approving the various ancillary agreements; all of which came into force and remain in force together (Arts. 1, 3). See further Catudal (1976), 25 *ICLQ* 766–800.

(6) *Issues of identity and continuity*

The German Democratic Republic has never claimed identity with pre-1945 Germany: on the other hand the Federal Republic has often been regarded as wholly[58] or partly[59] identical with pre-1945 Germany. Although such claims can of course become binding *inter partes* by consent, acquiescence or estoppel,[60] there is little to support the claim to any general continuity of the two entities—at least, so far as it is a legal claim.[61] On the hypothesis of the extinction of Germany in 1945, the creation of a new State under a different constitutional regime on part only of its territory could hardly establish a relation of continuity opposable to third States.[62] On the more generally accepted hypothesis of the continuity of pre-1945 Germany under the auspices of the four Powers, then the creation of the Federal Republic occurred by devolution on part only of the territory of pre-1945 Germany, which again provides tenuous support for any general claim to continuity. This is particularly so in that the quadripartite government of Germany retained functional and territorial competences with respect to Germany as a whole and Berlin. It is to these powers, which may be traced directly to the assumption of supreme authority over Germany in 1945, that one must look to find a body of legal relations formally continuous with pre-1945 Germany. But, if 'Berlin' remains, in a sense, formally the territory of pre-1945 Germany, it seems most unlikely, in view of its links with the two Germanies and the absence of effective quadripartite control, that it can still be regarded as a State identical with that older Germany. The competences have, on this view, become so residual that they have ceased to be 'sovereignty' in any meaningful sense.[63]

[58] e.g. *Simon* v. *Taylor* [1975] 2 Ll. Rep. 38; Mann, op. cit. 680 ff. (and works there cited), 704; *Concordat (Germany) Case* (1957) 24 ILR 592.

[59] e.g. Decision of the Federal Constitutional court of 31 July 1973: (1976) 70 *AJ* 147–154, 150 (referring to its earlier jurisprudence); cf. Koenig, [1973] *AFDI* 147–70; *In re Dirks' Patent* (1957), 30 ILR 54. But cf. Treaty on the Basis of Inter-German Relations, 1972: 12 *ILM* 16, Art. 4.

[60] *Infra*, Chapter 16.

[61] The often cited declaration that the Federal Republic was alone 'entitled to speak for Germany as the representative of the German people' (*supra*, p. 275; Mann, op. cit. 683) is not necessarily such a claim—or not, at any event, a claim to the legal identity of the Federal Republic with pre-1945 Germany. Cf. Kunz (1955), 49 *AJ* 68–76, 74–5.

[62] For claims to reversion see *infra*, p. 414.

[63] Tomuschat, in Bathurst *et al.*, *Legal Problems of an Enlarged European Community* (1972), 154–61, 160; but cf. Brownlie, *Principles*, 83.

Subsequent action by the Federal Republic with respect to pre-1945 German treaties[64] and other legal relations[65] would seem then to be based either on a special regime of succession or on novation.

10.3 OTHER CASES OF 'DIVIDED STATES'

(1) *Korea after 1947*[66]

In 1945 the Japanese colony of Korea was occupied by Soviet and United States military administrations to the north and south, respectively, of the 38th parallel.[67] Unlike Germany, where quadripartite action was based on an assumption of supreme governmental authority, the status of the United States and the Soviet Union in Korea was that of belligerent occupants. In 1947, after the failure of a tripartite Agreement aimed at the unification of Korea,[68] the United States referred the problem of Korea to the General Assembly. Elections under United Nations surveillance followed: these were restricted to the south. As a result, the Assembly declared 'that there has been established a lawful government (the government of the Republic of Korea) having effective control and jurisdiction over that part of Korea where the Temporary Commission was able to observe . . .'[69] Such action went well beyond that permitted to a belligerent occupant, and amounted in effect to a secession under international auspices from Japan. In 1949 the Assembly stated that 'the Republic of Korea is a peace-loving State within the meaning of Article 4 of the Charter, is able and willing to carry out the obligations of the Charter, and should therefore be admitted to

[64] e.g. British-German Extradition Treaty of 1872, 62*BFSP* 5; 'reapplied' to British-West German relations by a treaty of 23 Feb. 1960, 358 *UNTS* 39. Cf. O'Connell, *State Succession* II, 81–7.

[65] e.g. *UKTS* No. 42 (1964); [1964] *BPIL* 120 (acceptance of liability for damage done to U.K. nationals by Germany pre-1945); Israel–F.R.G. Reparations Agreement, 1952: 162 *UNTS* 206, 272.

[66] See Caty, 44–6, 52–7; Whiteman, 1 *Digest* 320–5, 2 *Digest* 172–82, 3 *Digest* 477–559; Gordenker, *The United Nations and the Peaceful Unification of Korea* (1959); Potter (1950), 44 *AJ* 709–13; Goodrich, *Korea. A Study of United States Policy in the United Nations* (1956); Green (1951), 4 *ILQ* 462–8; Jessup, *Birth of Nations*, 19–42.

[67] Whiteman, 3 *Digest* 486–9.

[68] 20 *UNTS* 259; Whiteman, 3 *Digest* 506–7.

[69] G.A. Res. 195 (III), 12 Dec. 1948 (46–6:1).

the United Nations.[70] There were several differences at this time between the Republic of Korea, and the Democratic People's Republic of Korea. The former had been established under international supervision in circumstances which lent support to its government's representative character; and it had been widely recognized. It would seem to have qualified as a State before 1951, having established, in accordance with the principles discussed in the preceding Chapter, effective independence after secession.[71] The status of the Democratic People's Republic was less clear. In the first place, its effective independence was in doubt, since it had been established by nomination of a single belligerent occupant without any form of international supervision. It had been recognized by very few States. It was probably, in 1950, only a *de facto* regime in the process of seceding from the territorial sovereign, but which had not at that stage established its effective independence. This situation did not alter during the Korean War, since that conflict related at least in part to the very existence of a divided Korea, or its unification under one or other of the claimant governments.[72] But in 1951 Japan, 'recognizing the independence of Korea, renounce[d] all right, title and claim to Korea, including the islands of Quelpart, Port Hamilton and Dagelet.'[73] Article 2(a) is open to various interpretations. It could be that, as with Formosa,[74] Japan merely renounced its sovereignty over the territory in question, leaving at large the status of the various entities in the territory. On that view, presumably, the Democratic People's Republic of Korea would have become a State in 1951, assuming that it had, by that date, established its separate independence from the former belligerent occupant.[75] Alternatively, it could be that, in

[70] G.A. Res. 296 (IV), 22 Nov. 1949 (50–6:3). The RoK's application for membership had been vetoed by the U.S.S.R.: *SCOR* 423rd mtg., 8 Apr. 1949 (9–2:0). A DPRK application was not considered: ibid., 410th mtg., 16 Feb. 1949 (2–8:1).

[71] But cf. *Kanda v. State of Japan* (1961) 32 ILR 170.

[72] On the Korean War see Hoyt (1961), 55 *AJ* 45–76; Higgins, *United Nations Peacekeeping 1946–1967* II, 153–214.

[73] Japanese Peace Treaty, 136 *UNTS* 45, Art. 2(a). Neither Korean government was a party to the Treaty. Cf. O'Connell (1952), 29 *BY* 423–35, 427–8.

[74] *Supra*, p. 146.

[75] In the period 1950–3, the Security Council consistently refused hearings to the DPRK under Art. 32, although the RoK was invited to attend under its equivalent, Art. 39 of the Provisional Rules: *SCOR* 473rd mtg., 25 June 1950, 4, 15; ibid., 474th mtg., 27 June 1950, 7. In the alternative it was argued that action concerning a 'breach of the peace' did not relate to a dispute, and Art. 32 was inapplicable: e.g. ibid., 494th mtg., 1

recognizing the independence of 'Korea' (which was taken to mean the Republic of Korea)[76] and in simultaneously renouncing its claims to the whole of Korea, Japan transferred territorial sovereignty over the whole of the Korean peninsula to the Republic of Korea, so that after 1951 the Democratic People's Republic of Korea continued its secession against a new territorial sovereign, the Republic of Korea. In view of the formal acceptance by all parties of the principle of the unity of Korea in 1951, and the general recognition of the Republic of Korea as entitled to represent internationally the whole of Korea, the latter view is perhaps the better one; on the other hand the Republic of Korea has never exercised effective jurisdiction over the whole of Korea,[77] and Article 2(a) of the Japanese Peace Treaty does not very readily lend itself to interpretation in terms of transfer, rather than renunciation, of sovereignty.

The United Nations has since 1953 frequently reaffirmed 'that the objectives of the United Nations remain the achievement by peaceful means of a unified, independent and democratic Korea under a representative form of government, and the full restoration of international peace and security in the area.'[78] However, it is clear that there now exist two Korean States, though both profess the aim of eventual unity.[79] The boundary between them has been consolidated into a full-scale juridical boundary for the purpose amongst other things, of the use of force. An Agreement on Basic Principles of National Unity of 4 July 1972 laid down *inter alia* that unification was to be effected by peaceful means and not the use of force:[80] this constitutes express recognition by the parties of the situation created in 1953.[81] At what point the Democratic Republic became a

Sept. 1950, 5–6, 20, 21, 22. See also ibid., 409th mtg., 15 Feb. 1949, 12, 18; 585th mtg., 1 July 1952, 6, 10.

[76] Cf. (1975) 79 *RGDIP* 468–9.

[77] Art. 10 of the Military Armistice Agreement of 27 July 1953 (1953 *U.N. Ybk.* 136) accepted the 'civil and relief jurisdiction' of each side with respect to its territory. The RoK was not, but the DPRK was, a signatory.

[78] G.A. Res. 811 (IX), 11 Dec. 1954 (50–5:4), para. 2; see also Res. 2668 (XXV), 7 Dec. 1970 (67–28:22).

[79] Cf. *In re Al-Fin Corporation's Patent* [1970] Ch. 160, overruling *Re Harshaw Chemical Co.'s Patent* (1964) 41 ILR 15. See further [1970] R.P.C. 70.

[80] *Keesing's* 1972, 25488A.

[81] Cf. (1975) 79 *RGDIP* 468–9. For U.N. Membership see *supra*, p. 136.

separate State is however less clear. It was accepted at the time of the *Pueblo* incident that the Democratic Republic's twelve-mile territorial sea was opposable to the United States.[82] The date of the Korean ceasefire (July 1953) may perhaps be taken as the date of the secession of the Democratic Republic from the Republic of Korea. That date has the twin merit of being the point at which the boundary between the two entities became firmly established, and of marking the last substantial attempt at a settlement of the Korean problem by unilateral military force.

(2) *Vietnam after 1945*[83]

The legal status of Vietnam, which had been the subject of much bitter controversy, is no longer so, since the Paris Agreement of 1973, the victory of the Provisional Revolutionary Government, and the formal reunification of the two Vietnamese States in July 1976.[84] Like Korea, and unlike Germany, Vietnam had never been a unified, independent State before the *de facto* partition effected by the Geneva Agreements of 1954.[85] There had of course been a substantial secession movement—the Democratic Republic of Vietnam[86]—and conflicting or equivocal acts of recognition[87] or 'grants of independence' by France to various authorities.[88] No French-established Vietnamese government could claim even formal authority over Vietnam as a whole before 1954.[89] The failure to hold elections to reunite the

---

[82] The Republic of Korea claimed only three miles: the U.S. argument thus accepted the Democratic Republic's capacity to extend its maritime frontier. The Ethiopian representative suggested that an invitation to North Korea to attend as a party to the dispute would be in order: *SCOR* 1389th mtg., 27 Jan. 1968, 2. The meeting adjourned without reaching any decision.

[83] See Cameron, *Vietnam Crisis. A Documentary History* (2 vols., 1972); Caty, 42–4, 52–6; Blanchet, *La Naissance de l'État associé du Vietnam* (1954); Partan (1966), 46 *Boston ULR* 281–316; Thierry, [1955] *AFDI* 168–74; Moore, *Law and the Indochina War* (1972); Falk, ed., *The Vietnam War and International Law* (4 vols., 1968–76); Murti (1967), 7 *Indian JIL* 369–96; Schick (1968), 17 *ICLQ* 953–95.

[84] *Keesing's* 1976, 27917A.

[85] Cameron, op. cit. I, 286–318.

[86] *Supra*, p. 259.

[87] e.g. Cameron, op. cit. I, 77–8 (1946); ibid. 414 (1948).

[88] Ibid. 80–2; cf. 161 *BFSP* 649 (unsigned).

[89] For the rather equivocal U.S. and U.K. recognition of the RVN in 1950, see Cameron, op. cit. 145–7; O'Brien and Goebel, 'U.S. Recognition Policy', 147–51. But G.A. Res. 620 (VII), 21 Dec. 1952 (40–5:12) affirmed the statehood of [the republic of] Vietnam: its application for U.N. membership was thrice vetoed by the U.S.S.R.: e.g. *SCOR* 603rd mtg., 19 Sept. 1952, 11.

country under the Geneva Agreements[90] meant the continuance of *de facto* separate entities in north and south: these came generally to be accepted as States. This situation was at least tacitly accepted by the 1973 Paris Peace Agreements.[91]

The Vietnamese situation before 1975 bore a certain resemblance to that in Korea. In both cases there existed for a time rival *de facto* governments: in both cases there was eventually established a ceasefire line binding both parties, after open conflict between them. The lines so established subsequently became, by a process of recognition, acquiescence and consolidation, effectively the boundaries between two States. Nevertheless the Vietnamese situation has certain peculiarities. In particular, the early and effective establishment of the Democratic Republic in 1945, and the subsequent, albeit partial, recognition of that government by the previous sovereign, were without parallel in the case of Korea. In the latter case the creation of a regime in the North was clearly a violation of the relevant agreements, so that the judgment that the government of the Republic of Korea, established under United Nations auspices and recognized as such by the previous territorial sovereign, was *de jure* the government of the whole State of Korea was a possible one, at least until 1953. With Vietnam, the Democratic Republic preceded its rival; its creation was not, internationally, illegal; and it achieved a measure of recognition. The permanent establishment of separate zones in Vietnam in 1956 must probably be taken to mark the establishment of two separate States,[92] neither of which, in

---

[90] Final Declaration, Art. 7: Cameron, op. cit. I, 373.

[91] (1973) 22 *ICLQ* 379–82, esp. Arts. 1, 2, 4, 9, 15. The 1973 Agreement was not internally consistent: it attributed territory to the Democratic Republic, a right of self-determination and a domestic jurisdiction to the Republic of Vietnam, and a right of veto over unification to both parties, but maintained that the boundary between them was not only 'provisional' (which is consistent with separate statehood), but was not all a 'political or territorial boundary'. But it is difficult to see what consequences were intended to flow from that denial, apart from a reaffirmation of the political goal of unification of Vietnam. Cf. H. A. Kissinger's analysis of the Agreement: *U.S. Digest*, 1973, 6–8.

[92] Cf. Johnson, in Falk, ed., *The Vietnam War and International Law* I, 211–13; Brownlie, *Legal Aspects of the Armed Conflict in Vietnam* (1969); Oppenheim (8th edn.) I, 173–4, 258; Hull and Novgorod, *Law and Vietnam* (1968), 53; *contra* Thierry, [1955] *AFDI* 168–78; Wright (1966), 60 *AJ* 750, 756–9, 187–95. Cf. the rather equivocal U.S. view: (1966) 60 *AJ* 565, 570, 584. The Democratic Republic of Vietnam claimed a territorial sea of 12 miles: the Republic of Vietnam claimed only three miles: U.S. Dept.

law or in fact, ever extended over the whole territory of 'Vietnam'.[93]

(3) *China after 1948*

The legal status of Taiwan, and its relation to China, have been discussed already.[94] Although Caty excludes the Chinese situation from the rubric 'divided State', on the ground that Formosa is a separate State,[95] the contrary would appear to be the case: indeed, of the four situations discussed by him, only China now constitutes, according to his definition, a 'divided State'. But, for the reasons that have been given, neither that category nor any general conception of divided statehood is of value in analysing the precise legal status of Taiwan.

10.4   CONCLUSIONS

Examination of these few cases demonstrates fairly clearly the unhelpful character of the rubric 'divided State'. The better view is that until 1951 Formosa remained Japanese; the Republic of China was in effect a government-in-exile occupying the islands with the consent of the Allies.[96] That Formosa became part of China in 1951 resulted as much from the continuing claims of the Republic of China as from the Japanese Peace Treaty itself. So China only became a 'divided State' in 1951, and then not unequivocally.

If Korea was ever a divided State, it can only have been for the relatively brief period between the Japanese Peace Treaty

of State, *Geographic Bulletin* No. 3, Oct. 1969. It is not altogether clear that the Gulf of Tonkin incident occurred outside the 12-mile limit: in any case the U.S. stated it had no objection to the DRVN authorities being invited to appear before the Security Council (under what provision was not stated): *SCOR* 1140th mtg., 5 Aug. 1964, 15. Two statements of the DRVN were subsequently circulated as 'official documents of the Security Council'. The Council made no determination as to the merits of the dispute: ibid., 1141 mtg., 7 Aug. 1964.

[93] For problems of State succession prior to unification see Nguyen-Huu-Tru, *Quelques problèmes de succession d'États concernant le Vietnam* (1970); O'Connell, *State Succession* II, 144–148. The State succession situation since 1975 is unclear; but the Socialist Republic of Vietnam was accepted, on 15 Sept. 1976, as successor to the Republic of Vietnam as Member of UNESCO (with one dissentient); *Keesing's* 1976, 28004B. Cf. (1977) 8 *NYIL* 157. For U.N. Membership, see *supra*, p. 136 n. 38.

[94] *Supra*, p. 143.

[95] Caty, 23–30.

[96] *Supra*, p. 147.

and the termination of the Korean War. Thereafter the Democratic People's Republic consolidated its position north of the ceasefire line. Vietnam was probably never a unified independent State: if it possessed any formal unity that was in the period 1954–6, as a result of the Geneva Agreements and the absence of any claim to separate statehood on the part of the Democratic Republic of Vietnam. Despite its equivocations the Paris Peace Agreement of 1973 recognized the effective separation of Vietnam into two States—though, to be sure, that separation proved to be temporary.

In the case of Germany the position of the occupying Powers, and the subordination of the local authorities to them, may have supported for a time the claim to a 'global State'. But after 1954, with the independence or putative independence of these local authorities, the central 'state' authority came to appear less substantial: apart from the special status of Berlin, such competences as remain appear to be of a rather nominal kind.

Although, then, these cases present more differences than similarities, it may be admitted that an entity divided *de facto* into separate parts can continue to be regarded as a single State, whether because of the claims to and third State recognition of that unity, or because of overriding principles of legality in such cases. China is an example: but so too is Cyprus since 1975. But such cases are to be referred to the general criteria of statehood, not to any special category of the 'divided State'.

11. Unions and Federations of States

11.1 THE CLASSIFICATION OF POLITICAL UNIONS

PERMANENT links between States can of course take a multitude of forms, and they are of little interest in an examination of territorial status unless they involve either the creation of a relation of dependency between one State and another, or the partial or total merger of the States concerned in a new political entity; or else, what may amount to the same thing, the creation of joint and autonomous institutions for the conduct of some or all of the affairs of the States concerned.[1] These latter types of union have traditionally been accorded separate treatment in textbook discussions of statehood and legal personality;[2] and it is indeed the case that certain typical forms of union (such as federations) raise interesting problems of personality and responsibility.[3]

However, the fundamental principle in the context of political union, no less than in the context of dependent status,[4] is that the incidents of a particular arrangement are to be determined only by an examination of *that* arrangement, and not by deductions from some *a priori* category or construction. The only overriding principles—apart of course from the general principles of consent and the like—are those relating to the attribution of legal personality, especially the general criteria for statehood. The point was made succinctly by Kunz: 'Les conceptions des

---

[1] One of the issues in the *Western Sahara Case* was the status of the so-called 'Mauritanian entity' at the time of the colonization of the Spanish Sahara (*c.* 1884). The Court held that 'despite some form of common activity . . . the absence . . . of any common institutions or organs, even of a quite minimal character' among the tribes and emirates in question precluded them from constituting 'a personality or corporate entity distinct from the several emirates and tribes which composed it'. The entity was accordingly incapable of enjoying any 'form of sovereignty in Western Sahara': I.C.J. Rep. 1975 p. 12, 63.

[2] Oppenheim (8th edn.) I, 169-8; Verzijl, *International Law* II, Ch. 4; O'Connell, *International Law* I, 293-7; Whiteman, 1 *Digest* 373-429; Rousseau, *DIP* II, 96-213.

[3] See also Kunz, *Staatenverbindungen* (1929); Pilotti (1928), 24 *HR* 441-546; Kaufman (1924), 3 *HR* 177-290; Rapisardi-Mirabelli (1925), 7 *HR* 345-93; Conforti (1964), 18 *Dir. Int.* 324.

[4] *Supra*, p. 182.

différents liaisons d'Etates ne sont pas conceptions normatives, ne sont pas des conceptions du droit, mais des conceptions de classification fournies par la doctrine.'[5] International lawyers commonly distinguished four typical kinds of political union: real and personal unions, federations, and confederations.[6] These were not mutually exclusive or exhaustive categories, but were rather discrete pairs of frequently occurring contrasting institutions. Of the four 'classical' types, only federation has continued to be a durable form of political organization—and then only through increasing *de facto* political centralization. However, with the virtual completion of the process of decolonization, the recurrence of various forms of voluntary political union other than federation is likely, and some brief discussion of the problems of characterization is worth while. It is however also likely—and the limited post-1945 experience confirms this—that future political unions will be *sui generis* entities in transition towards more stable forms of organization. A related trend is that towards functional unification through regional organizations—although the European Communities, which represent the best example of this type, may well be an exceptional case.[7]

Apart from the problem of characterization which will be adverted to in a little more detail in the following sections, the main legal problems of voluntary union have been those of succession to domestic and international obligations. In most cases the political union of two or more States coexists with substantial political and administrative continuity within the entities concerned, and a much more extensive degree of 'succession' to legal relations—extending even to membership in international organizations[8]—has accordingly been the practice.[9] It is however unnecessary to go into these questions in any detail here.[10]

---

[5] Kunz (1930), 11 *RDILC* 835–77, 849.

[6] Pufendorf, *De jure Naturae et Gentium* VII, ch. 5; Vattel, *Le droit des gens* I, Ch. 1 §§ 8–11; Wheaton, *Elements* Pt. I, Ch. 2, §§ 40–59.

[7] *Infra*, p. 295.

[8] O'Connell, *State Succession* II, 190–200.

[9] Ibid. 54–87; and (1963) 39 *BY* 54–132.

[10] The I.L.C. Draft Articles on State Succession with respect to Treaties (1972) distinguish 'union of States' from 'newly independent States' and provide for a much more extensive degree of continuity in the former case: Arts. 26, 27. See also *ILC Ybk.* 1972/II, 18–44; 1972/I, 158–81, 271–3.

11.2   FEDERATION, CONFEDERATION, AND OTHER FORMS OF POLITICAL UNION

There follows a brief account of the more common forms of political union.

(1)   *Real and personal unions*[11]

The classical treatises made a distinction between 'personal' and 'real' unions of States. Broadly, a personal union was said to exist 'where States, which are wholly separate and distinct, have the same ruling prince.'[12] Great Britain and Hanover from 1714 to 1837, and the independent Commonwealth monarchies at the present time, may be regarded as examples of personal unions.[13] The relation between States in personal union varies considerably: however, they are clearly separate international entities—a result achieved, in the context of the Commonwealth, by the 'divisibility of the Crown'.[14] With the decline in monarchical institutions, personal unions are likely to be increasingly rare.

On the other hand 'Where States are not only ruled by the same prince, but are also united for international purposes by an express agreement, there is said to exist a real union.'[15] The phrase 'united for international purposes' is however somewhat of an equivocation. Rather than a general description of 'unitary' States formed by treaty, the term 'real union' has in practice been restricted to those cases where two international units share joint institutions for example for the purposes of foreign affairs, defence, or finance. The union of Austria–Hungary from 1867 to 1918 was regarded as a 'real union'.

Nevertheless labels are no substitute for analysis, and in particular the term 'real union' seems to lack precise legal meaning. It is significant that the Permanent Court saw no need to adopt the terminology in its discussion of the relation betweeen Austria and Hungary. The court held that: 'the frontier between Hungary and Galicia was in August 1914 an international

[11] Verzijl, *International Law* II, 133–59.

[12] Rivier, *Principes du droit des gens* (1896) I, 77; Moore, 1 *Digest* 21.

[13] The union of Denmark and Iceland (1918–44) is also classified as a personal union, although Denmark was also responsible for Iceland's international relations until 1940; Whiteman, 1 *Digest* 366–8; 2 *Digest* 156–61. The U.S. recognized Iceland's independence on 1 July 1941, but the Act of Union was not abrogated until 17 June 1944.

[14] *Supra*, pp. 239–41.

[15] Rivier, op. cit. 97–9; Moore, 1 *Digest* 22.

frontier, Galicia then being part of the Austrian Monarchy ...
Although Austria and Hungary had common institutions based
on analogous laws passed by their legislatures, they were none
the less distinct international units.'[16]

(2) *Federations and confederations*

Of greater present-day significance is the distinction between
federation and confederation, which can be described as a
distinction of principle based on a difference in the degree of
decentralization of the latter as compared with the former. A
federation, it has been said, exists 'when the following features
may be found in a political entity': '(1) a division of powers
between a central and regional government; (2) a certain degree
of independence between central and regional governments; (3)
direct action on the people by the central and regional
governments; and (4) some means of preserving the constitutional
division of powers ...'[17] As such federation represents a major
form of State organization.[18] Internationally it is usual for the
central government to have full authority over foreign affairs,
although the local States may retain minor competences. As a
result it is said that: 'The federal state ... constitute(s) a sole
person in the eyes of international Law.'[19] But the difficulty with
such statements of the law is that they either assume a constant
entity—the 'federation'—with constant legal incidents, or they
are circular. Thus Fitzmaurice stated that: 'a constituent State of
a Federation can never be a State *internationally* or, as such, party
to a treaty—for the treaty will bind the Federation, and will
bind the constituent State not as such, but only as an
(internationally) indistinguishable part of the Federation.'[20] But
this is either far too categorical, or it assumes the only federation
properly so-called to be that State 'the local units of which are
indistinguishably part' of the larger unit.[21] The question is—of

---

[16] *Advisory opinion regarding the delimitation of the Polish-Czechoslovakian Frontier (Question of Jaworzina)*, Ser. B. No. 8 (1923), 42–3 (interpretation of the term 'international frontier'). On the status of Austria–Hungary before and after 1918 see *infra*, p. 404, n. 20.

[17] Bernier, *International Legal Aspects of Federalism* (1973), 5.

[18] See also Kunz, op. cit., and (1931) 12 *RDILC* (3d) 130–44, 280–302; Okeke, *Controversial Subjects of contemporary international law* (1974), 35–62; Halajzuk (1931), 12 *OZfOR*.

[19] Montevideo Convention, 1933, Art. 2: 165 *LNTS* 19.

[20] *ILC Ybk.* 1956/II, 118 & n.

[21] Loc. cit. (referring to Switzerland).

which entities is this true?[22] In reality there are entities which, though they may be termed federations, are indistinguishable from unitary States:[23] there are those which, though federations in the sense defined, are for all or most international purposes the same as unitary States:[24] there are federations which are called 'confederations' but which are closer to the former type:[25] there are entities, the local units of which are regarded as sovereign and the central government as their agent;[26] and there are entities which, though claiming to be unitary States, operate very much like loose unions of separate States.[27] It would appear to be necessary to add to Bernier's four, purely formal, criteria of federations a fifth, substantive, one: the central government's powers must include substantially the whole foreign affairs power, together with autonomous authority extending to aspects of the internal affairs of the local States. Given all five criteria it remains true that 'the practically complete supersession of the international personality of the Member States must, as a matter of positive law, be regarded as still constituting one of the . . .

[22] Cf. Bernier, op. cit. 34–5. It is noteworthy that Kunz, in order to formulate a coherent (unitary) theory of federal States, finds it necessary to distinguish between real and '*soi-disant*' federal States—a distinction which predetermines the conclusion reached as to the particular categories.

[23] e.g. India and Brazil.

[24] e.g. Australia, the United States, and Canada.

[25] Switzerland: Huber (1909), 3 *AJ* 62–98; Wildhaber (1974), 12 *Can. YIL* 211–21. On the cantons see further *Répertoire suisse* I, 531–66.

[26] Such entities will often be termed 'confederations', but terminology is not consistent. The Federation of Mali was probably such a case: Cohen (1960), 36 *BY* 375–84. It used to be thought, following U.S. doctrine, that the distinction between federation and confederation was a rigid one: the central organs of a federal State could act with direct effect on subjects in the constituent 'States,' whereas the central organs of a confederation were restricted to acting through or upon the local States themselves. But the better view is that, in a confederation, the local units remain States in the general sense, having merely delegated certain competences to the central organs, whereas in a federation there is only one State in that sense, even if the local units retain some degree of international competence. The distinction is thus, in practice, one of degree only (although there may be a presumption in favour of local or central authority as a result of the apparent choice of structure). Cf. Oppenheim (8th edn.) I, 182 with the original statement at 173. Certain acts of the European Communities, it will be noted, may have direct legal effect in the Member States, although the Communities at present constitute a decentralized union more in the nature of a confederation than a federation. Historically confederations have tended to be transitional organizations of unifying States: e.g. the Confederation of North American States (1778–87), the German Confederation (1815–66); but cf. the Swiss Confederation (1291–1798, 1815–48).

[27] The United Arab Republic (1958–61): *infra*, pp. 294–5.

main distinguishing features of the federal system.'[28] Nevertheless the following points may be noted.

(i) To the extent that the constitution does not abrogate the international law rights of the local units these may be treated as continuing.[29]

(ii) International law may, in the absence of any overriding provision in the law of the union, govern the relations *inter se* of federal States.[30] Various reasons for this have been given: either international law is regarded as imported into the constitutional law of the union,[31] or the local units are regarded as, to the extent of their autonomy, independent States and so bound by international law,[32] or the basic rationale of international law rules is regarded as no less applicable to federations than to relations between independent States.[33]

(iii) In certain federal States, the treaty executing power may not be granted to the full extent to the central unit;[34] or reasons of prudence or expedience may prevent central assumption, by way of treaty, of extensive State-reserved powers.[35] This can militate in practice against the full exercise by federal States of treaty-making powers, or it may allow the local units to commit the responsibility of the central government by refusal to implement treaties.

(iv) In some federal States the local units may retain a certain treaty-making competence, either with the consent of the central government (as in the United States), or without it (as in the Soviet Union). The presumption in such cases is in favour of the treaty binding the State as a whole rather than the local unit; but this is only a presumption.[36]

[28] Lauterpacht, *International Law and Human Rights* (1950), 458. To the same effect Bernier, op. cit. 146; Kunz, op. cit. 867.

[29] *Principality of Monaco v. Mississippi* 78 L.ed. 1282 (1934); cf. Bernier, op. cit. 121–46.

[30] *Island of Palmas Case* (1928) 2 *RIAA* 828, 840; Cowles (1949), 74 HR 657–756.

[31] *Bremen (Hansa City of) v. Prussia* (1925) 3 AD No. 266.

[32] *Wurttemberg & Prussia v. Baden* (1927) 4 AD No. 86; cf. *Mellenger v. New Brunswick Development Corporation* [1971] 1 W.L.R. 604, 608 (Lord Denning M.R.), 611 (Salmon L.J.). *Sed quaere.*

[33] *New Jersey v. Delaware* 291 U.S. 361, 380 (1934), *per* Cardozo J.

[34] This is the case in Canada: *A.G. for Canada v. A.G. for Ontario* [1937] A.C. 326; but not in Australia: *R. v. Burgess ex parte Henry* (1936) 55 C.L.R. 608; or the U.S.: *State of Missouri v. Holland* 252 U.S. 416 (1920).

[35] e.g. Australia and India: Bernier, op. cit. 169–71.

[36] Brownlie, *Principles*, 79. The final Draft Articles on the Law of Treaties included an Article (5(2)) to the effect that 'States members of the federal union may possess the

(v) It is probably the case that the central government is internationally responsible for any act of a local unit which results in a default or violation of international obligations of the State.[37] The governing principle here appears to be that the central government may not plead its constitutional law to avoid its international obligations,[38] although the matter is not entirely free from doubt.[39]

(vi) Finally, local States may, in accordance with the federal constitution, be recognized as possessing some, or even substantial, international personality: the best-known, but probably anomalous, cases are those of the Ukraine and Byelorussia, constituent Republics of the Soviet Union.[40]

(3)   *Unusual formations*

States may form such political associations as they wish, and some of the unions or associations in fact created have proved extraordinarily difficult to characterize.[41] The best modern example is the United Arab Republic (1958–61), formed ostensibly as a unitary State by the union of Egypt and Syria and dissolved three years later by the secession of the latter.[42] By acquiescence and agreement, all international obligations of both States continued to bind the Republic with respect to the territory of the relevant subdivision. After 1961 these obligations continued in force, and by a special arrangement the separate United Nations memberships of Syria and Egypt (which retained the title of United Arab Republic) were revived without formal readmission. In retrospect, therefore, despite the claims to, and

capacity to conclude treaties if such capacity is admitted by the federal constitution and within the limits there laid down.' After vigorous debate this was eventually excluded from the Vienna Convention: see Bernier, op. cit. 14–17; Steinberger (1967), 27 *ZfV* 411–28. Cf. Vienna Convention, Art. 3.

For the treaty-making competence of the Canadian provinces, see Jacomy-Millette, *Treaty Law in Canada* (1975), 69–105. For a very full account of the treaty-making power in federations see Wildhaber, *Treaty-Making Power and Constitution* (Basel, 1971), 254–342.

[37] Bernier, op. cit. 83–120; cf. Pres. Verzijl, *Hycinth Pellat Case* (French-Mexican M.A.T., 1929) 5 AD No. 90.

[38] McNair, *International Law Opinions* I, 36–7, citing a note of Fox to Webster, 12 Mar. 1841.

[39] Cf. *Cayuga Indians Claim* (1910) 6 *RIAA* 173, 186–8.

[40] *Supra*, p. 132.

[41] Cf. Verzijl, *International Law* II, 199–206.

[42] Cotran (1959), 8 *ICLQ* 346–90; Young (1962), 56 *AJ* 482–8; Rousseau (1962), 66 *RGDIP* 413–17; O'Connell, *State Succession* II, 71–4, 169–70.

recognition of, the Republic as a unitary State,[43] it appears in reality to have been a loose association the existence of which was not inconsistent with the continuing and substantial international personality of its component parts.

(4) *Associated States*

Certain 'associated States' constitute fully independent States which have delegated foreign affairs, defence or other powers to another State: Western Samoa is the best example. Others, it is thought, are not States but have separate international status by virtue of the relevant association agreements. These include Puerto Rico, the Cook Islands, and Niue. Associated status is dealt with further elsewhere.[44]

11.3 UNIONS OF STATES IN INTERNATIONAL ORGANIZATIONS

As we have seen, international organizations may have particular or general international personality if this is the intention of the States parties, express or implied, and (where general international personality is claimed) also 'indispensable' to the performance of the intended functions.[45] The formation of an organization or league, performing international acts on behalf of member States, is clearly a step in the direction of some sort of confederal State, at least where important or 'sovereign' rights are abandoned to the organization in question.

But the question whether any particular organization approaches statehood in any respect can only be determined on the facts of the particular case.

In this context the European Communities, the most extensive attempt at regional integration, deserve brief mention.[46] The European Communities can be said to fall between international organizations merely co-ordinating areas of State policy, and a confederation or league in part directing them. As the German Federal Constitutional Court has stated, 'Community law is

---

[43] Whiteman, 2 *Digest* 230–3.

[44] *Infra*, p. 370.

[45] *Supra*, pp. 25–6.

[46] For an account of the structure and workings of the Communities see Robertson, *European Communities* (3rd edn., 1973), Ch. 6; Lasok and Bridge, *An Introduction to the Law and Institutions of the European Communities* (1973).

neither a component part of the national legal system nor international law, but forms an independent system of law flowing from an autonomous legal source, for the Community is not a State, especially not a federal State, but a *sui generis* community in the process of progressive integration, an "inter-State institution" within the meaning of Article 24(1) German Constitution.'[47] There is much scope for development within the Treaties, and an assessment of the international status of the Communities must depend not just on the Treaties themselves but on the extent to which their machinery has been used to create binding common policies pre-empting individual State action. It is clear so far that the activities of the various community organs can be explained on the basis of an extensive delegation of power from Member States, which remain sovereign, though with the exercise of their powers considerably limited.[48] The Court of Justice of the European Communities has tended to give an expansive interpretation to the powers of Community organs: thus the monopolies jurisdiction of the European Economic Community was held to cover, by way of their local subsidiaries acting as agents, the activities of companies in Switzerland and the United Kingdom (at that time a non-member).[49] In argument the Advocate-General said of the European Commission '. . . it has not all the powers of a State, but all the attributed powers necessary for the execution of its tasks. In the field of its competence—and that covers the field of cartels—the Community has quite as much power as a State, provided that it is a question of cartels affecting competition in the Common Market.'[50]

In an earlier decision, *Re the European Road Transport Agreement*, the Court gave an extensive interpretation to the exclusive treaty-making power of the Community within its fields of

---

[47] *Internationale Handelsgesellschaft mbH* v. *Einfuhr-und Vorratsstelle für Getreide und Futtermittel* [1974] 2 CMLR 540. Thus the European Court has no jurisdiction under Art. 177 of the E.E.C. Treaty to rule on matters of international law which bind member States outside the framework of Community law: *Wandeweghe* v. *B.C.I.* [1973] E.C.J. Rep. 1329. See also Schermers (1975), 12 *CMLR* 77–90. On the other hand, the Court has jurisdiction to determine the validity of *Community* acts under general international law: *International Fruit Co. NV* v. *Produktschap voor Groeten en Fruit (No. 3)* [1975] 2 CMLR 1.

[48] Cf. *Administration des Douanes* v. *Société Cafés Jacques Value* [1975] 2 CMLR 336 (Cour de Cassation, France).

[49] *I.C.I. Ltd.* v. *Commission of the European Communities* 21 CMLR 557 (1972).

[50] Ibid. 602; and see Mann (1973), 22 *ICLQ* 35–50.

interest under Article 228 of the Rome Treaty, despite the argument that such competence was not explicitly granted and could not be presumed.[51] Thus the internal regulation by the Community of common policy can preclude member States individually from acting whether internally or internationally in respect of that field: understandably the Council of Ministers has shown some reluctance to allow the full implications of the terms of the Treaty as so interpreted.[52] Nevertheless machinery for an unprecedented degree of functional unification exists under the Treaties: to what extent it will be developed in practice remains to be seen.

[51] 20 CMLR 335 (1971). Art. 228 provides for negotiation by the Commission of all agreements contemplated by the Treaty. The Court held that the phrase 'any other appropriate provisions' in Art. 75(1)(c) of Title IV ('Transport') included the conclusion of international agreements. Cf. also its important pronouncement in *N.V. Algemeine transport- en Expeditie Ondernenning Van Gend en Loos* v. *Nederlandse Tariefcommissie* [1963] CMLR 105, 129: 'the Community constitutes a new legal order in international law, for whose benefit the States have limited their sovereign rights, albeit within limited fields, and the subjects of which comprise not only the member-States, but also their nationals.'

[52] Norton (1973), 7 *Int. L.* 589–611. Cf. *Re the OECD Understanding on a Local Cost Standard* [1976] 1 CMLR 85; *Officier van Justitie* v. *Kramer & ors.* [1976] 2 CMLR 440.

PART III: THE CREATION OF STATES IN INTERNATIONAL ORGANIZATIONS

IN THE types of case discussed in Part II we have been concerned with what may be called 'local', usually discretionary, creations of new States. But in many cases—and this is as true of the nineteenth century as of the twentieth[1]—international action has been determinative: international organizations or groups of States—especially the so-called 'Great Powers'—have exercised a collective authority to supervise, regulate, and condition such new creations. In some cases the action takes the form of the direct establishment of the new State: a constitution is provided, the State territory is delimited, a Head of State is nominated.[2] In others it is rather a form of collective international recognition— although the distinction is not a rigid one. Alternatively, various international regimes have been established for particular territories or groups of territories, with eventual independence in view—in particular, the Mandate and Trusteeship systems, and the procedures established under Chapter XI of the Charter. In the next Chapter, the general issues of international disposition relating to the creation of States will be discussed, and in the two following Chapters, the three territorial regimes aimed at independence or self-government.

[1] But cf. Briggs (1950), 44 *PAS* 169–80, 170.
[2] For example Albania (1913–23), Korea (1948), Libya (1952), Austria (1955).

12. International Dispositive Powers

> Prince Bismark observes that the question is whether or not the powers are agreed to recognize the independence of Roumania ... Europe alone has the power to sanction independence. She has then to ask herself under what conditions she will adopt that important decision. (*Protocols of the Berlin Conference* (1878) 69 *BFSP* 982; cited Munro, *The Berlin Congress* (1918), 33.)
>
> From time to time it happens that a group of great Powers, or a large number of States both great and small, assume a power to create by a multilateral treaty some new international regime or status, which soon acquires a degree of acceptance and durability extending beyond the limits of the actual contracting parties, and giving it an objective existence. This power is used when some public interest is involved, and its exercise often occurs in the course of the peace settlement at the end of a great war. (Judge McNair, sep. op., *South West Africa (Status) Case* I.C.J. Rep. 1950, p. 128, 153.)

12.1 INTRODUCTORY

As THESE remarks suggest, a quantity of political practice attests the existence of certain international powers or capacities to bring about territorial change, and to create new States or entities approximating to States, with effects extending beyond the immediate contracting parties.

The relation between the legal principles of equality and consent and this area of international practice is unclear; and the problem has been neglected to a degree.[1] Three general areas may be distinguished; the exercise of powers of disposition by means of multilateral treaty or declaration; their exercise on a

---

[1] See however Verzijl, *International Law* II, 97–104; Brownlie, *Principles*, 138–9, 175–82; Langer, *Seizure of Territory*, 6–16; Dickinson, *Equality of States*, 124–31, 138–45, 292–310; Lande (1967), 62 *Pol. Sc. Q.* 259–86, 398–417.

more or less organized basis of collective recognition, and their exercise by permanent international organizations.

12.2   TERRITORIAL DISPOSITIONS BY MULTILATERAL TREATY

(1)   *Dispositions in treaties of peace*

(i)   *The nineteenth-century practice*

The difficulty with assessing nineteenth-century practice in the matter of powers of disposition concerning the creation of new States hinges on the claim of the Great Powers to some sort of primacy with respect to the territorial *status quo* in Europe, the Near East, and later, Africa; a claim that major political changes, for their validity, required 'the assent of Europe'.[2] But the dispositive acts that here concern us took the form of a series of multilateral arrangements the validity of which must first be referred to the consent or acceptance of States (or other entities) concerned. Only if we find that these international acts are squarely based upon a claim of right deriving from Great Power hegemony does the question whether the European system constituted some special form of international organization or para-statal entity arise.

A survey of territorial dispositions by multilateral treaty during the nineteenth century reveals a fairly consistent practice of Great Power agreement on the action to be taken, either at the request or with the subsequent consent of the States affected, and a general refusal to allow such changes to be brought about unilaterally. For example, the Congress of Vienna, *inter alia*, confirmed the third partition of Poland of 1795,[3] created the Free City of Cracow,[4] and the German Confederation,[5] enlarged and neutralized the Swiss Confederation,[6] and united Belgium with the Kingdom of the Netherlands.[7]

---

[2] Cf. Bismark, cited *supra*, p. 301.

[3] Act of the Congress of Vienna, 9 June 1815: 2 *BFSP* 7, Arts. 1–5, Annexes I, II.

[4] Ibid., Arts. VI–X, Annex III. Cracow's separate existence continued until 1846 when it was annexed by Austria: Treaty of Vienna, 6 Nov. 1846; 35 *BFSP* 1088. Cf. *supra*, p. 161.

[5] Act of the Congress of Vienna, Arts. 53–64, Annex IX.

[6] Ibid., Arts. 34, 74–80, Annex XI A. For Swiss accession see Annex XI B.

[7] Ibid., Arts. 65–6, 73, Annex X.

To these dispositions the States present at the Congress, and the Princes and Free Cities involved, were invited to accede,[8] although the term 'invitation' was not intended to imply any degree of free choice in the smaller States or principalities. As Peterson points out: 'The lesser or "small" Powers were denied equality of representation; they had no voice in the decisions except as they were required to ratify what the Great Powers had done; and they had no choice but to accept a settlement which the concert had agreed upon and which it stood ready to enforce.'[9]

Much the same was true of the interventions to secure the independence of Greece (1827) and Belgium (1831), which are dealt with elsewhere under the rubric of collective recognition.[10]

By the Treaty of Paris, 1856, the Principalities of Moldavia and Wallachia were accorded substantial independence under the suzerainty of the Porte and the collective guarantee of the Powers.[11] The two principalities united in 1859 as Roumania,[12] Serbia too was guaranteed an autonomous administration under Turkish suzerainty.[13] Serbia's independence was recognized by the Treaty of Berlin, subject to certain conditions.[14]

But the most controversial issue at the Congress of Berlin was the question of Roumania, the independence of which was only recognized on condition of the retrocession to Russia of part of Bessarabia.[15] Of this in particular it could be said that 'The Congress of Berlin offers one of the most exteme cases of the concerted action of the Great powers, taking and carrying out decisions affecting smaller nations without their consent ...'[16]

---

[8] Ibid., Art. 119.

[9] Peterson (1945), 60 *Pol. Sc. Q.* 522–54, 552. See generally, Albrecht-Carrié, *The Concert of Europe* (1968), 23–5; Seaman, *From Vienna to Versailles* (1955), 1–15; Nicholson, *The Congress of Vienna* (1946).

[10] *Infra*, p. 319.

[11] 46 *BFSP* 8, Arts. 22–5; also 48 *BFSP* 81 ff., 49 *BFSP* 454 ff.

[12] Marriott, *The Eastern Question* (4th edn., 1940), 285–308; Verzijl, *International Law* II, 372–8.

[13] 46 *BFSP* 8.

[14] 69 *BFSP* 749, 13 July 1878, Arts. 34–42. The conditions were accepted by Serbian Proclamation of 10 Aug. 1878: 69 *BFSP* 1109. Bulgaria also became an autonomous tributary Principality: 69 *BFSP* 749, Arts. 1–5. Montenegro's ancient independence was recognized (Art. 31); and Boznia-Herzegovina given over to the administration of Austria-Hungary (Art. 25).

[15] Ibid., Arts. 43–5.

[16] Lande (1967), 62 *Pol. Sc. Q.* 259, 265.

Other relatively peremptory acts of Great Power 'mediation' in this period included the imposition of an 'international government' on Crete (1897–1913),[17] and the intervention of Albania in 1913. The latter case is of particular interest. As a result of British mediation after the first Balkan War (1912–13), the problem of Albania was referred to the six Powers by Article III of the Treaty of London.[18] By a subsequent Organic Statute, Albania was constituted an autonomous principality under the guarantee of the six Powers;[19] its boundaries were delimited,[20] and its civil and fiscal administration placed under an international commission for ten years.[21] However these provisions remained executory and Albania was occupied by various belligerents during the Great War.[22] Various alternative dispositions for Albania were proposed—including partition[23] and an 'A' mandate[24]—but President Wilson's insistence on the 'territorial integrity' of Albania prompted a reversal of the British and French positions.[25] Albania was admitted to the League in 1920, against the recommendation of the Fifth Committee,[26] but its frontiers remained uncertain until the Conference of Ambassadors issued a Declaration regarding the integrity of the Frontiers of Albania on 9 November 1921.[27]

[17] See the Collective Notes of 2 March 1897: 91 *BFSP* 175; Albrecht-Carrié, 291–2; Verzijl, *International Law* II, 387–9; Ydit, *Internationalized Territories*, 109–26; Dutkowski, *L'Occupation de la Crète 1897–1909* (1952). For the Provisional Statute of 1897 and subsequent Constitutions of 1899 and 1907, see Ser. C. No. 82, 92–131. On the status of Crete in this period, cf. *supra*, pp. 223–7. The *de facto* union of Crete with Greece dated from 1909, and the technical surrender of Turkish sovereignty—to the Powers, not to Greece—was effected by the Treaty of London, 1913, Art. 4: 107 *BFSP* 656.

[18] Loc. cit., referring 'le soin de régler la délimitation des frontières de l'Albanie et toutes autres questions concernant l'Albanie.'

[19] 9 *NRG* (3d) 650, Art. 1.

[20] Protocol of Florence, 17 Dec. 1913; in Ser. C. No. 5 (II), 266. See also *Monastery of Saint-Naoum (Albanian Frontier)*, Ser. B No. 9 (1924), 9–10.

[21] Organic Statute, Arts. 4–5.

[22] Marriott, op. cit. 471–2; Ydit, *Internationalized Territories*, 29–33.

[23] Secret Treaty of London, 1915, Art. III: 112 *BFSP* 973.

[24] 113 *BFSP* 810, 816, 831. Italy eventually renounced the possibility of an Albanian mandate: *H.C. Deb.* Vol. 131 col. 1625, 8 July 1920.

[25] Cf. his note of 10 Feb. 1920, and the British and French Reply of 14 Feb.: 113 *BFSP* 842, 846.

[26] The Fifth Committee had doubted whether the '*de jure* recognition by the Powers in 1914 could be considered as effective': *LNOR Ctee. mtgs.* 1st Ass., II, 191. But Albania was admitted by 35–0:7. See *LNOJ* Sp. Supp. No. 5, 28; Walters, *A History of the League of Nations* (1952) I, 123; Ser. C No. 5 (II), 156–8; Graham, *The League of Nations and the Recognition of States*, 25–6, 65–6; Briggs, *Law of Nations*, 108–13.

[27] 117 *BFSP* 452.

In general, the dispositions referred to above, though concluded under the aegis of the 'Concert of Europe', were consented to by parties affected: the actual exercise of authority by the powers—with certain exceptions—did not in fact extend beyond negotiation, conciliation and the exercise of political influence between disputants. The relevant dispositions of the Treaty of Paris were assented to by Turkey and Russia, and, to the extent that they altered the position of Turkish provinces in Europe, did so to their manifest advantage.[28] The Berlin Conference of 1885 and the Algeciras Conference of 1906 raised no difficulties. The exceptions referred to all relate not to Europe as a whole but to the affairs of the Ottoman Empire—so much so that Holland described the action of the Great Powers there as 'a sort of *corpus iuris publici orientalis*'.[29] The three most important cases for our purposes were the Bessarabian controversy at the Congress of Berlin in 1878; the imposition of an International Government on Crete in 1897, and the action taken with respect to Albania in the period 1913–22. But it is clear that no general rule can be established from these cases. The compulsory retrocession of Bessarabia was admittedly an extreme example. Roumania's claims were, however, as the British Secretary of State pointed out: 'not wholly free from question, first, because they' (sc. Roumania and Serbia) 'are not as yet independent Governments, and, secondly, because by allying themselves to Russia they placed their rights in the hands of that Power, which did not think them entitled to be made parties to the Treaty of San Stefano . . .'[30] Moreover, the Roumanian Declaration of Independence of 3 June 1877 referred expressly to their desire—and even the need—for confirmation of that independence by international agreement.[31] On the other hand, Roumania was before 1878 substantially independent, and little compensation was offered it for the loss of Bessarabia.[32] The better view would appear to be that the retrocession was substantially illegal, and brought about only by Russian threats of force and her superior strategic position. The British Plenipotentiary was thus instructed

[28] *Supra*, p. 303.
[29] Holland, *The European Concert in the Eastern Question* (1885), 2; cf. Lande, op. cit. 282; Langer, *Seizure of Territory*, 9–11.
[30] 69 *BFSP* 832.
[31] 68 *BFSP* 871.
[32] Cf. Protocols of the Conference (Nos. 9–10): 69 *BFSP* 972, 978.

to protest 'against a violation of international law, for which there seems to be little excuse, and which cannot be justified by reference to the purpose of which the war was undertaken.'[33] The question of Crete in 1897 saw the collective military intervention of the Powers in a vain attempt to prevent war between Greece and Turkey.[34] Subsequent action there must be regarded in part as a consequence of Greek consent following her defeat in the Thirty Days War, and in part as an expression of that local hegemony of the Powers over the Ottoman Empire, already referred to.

The problem of Albania in 1913 is of rather less difficulty, in that intervention there was a direct result of Article 3 of the Treaty of London, delegating to the Powers the settlement of the Albanian question.[35] However, the dispositions of 1913–14 were not effectively executed; and the Allies appear to have taken the view that further disposition of Albanian territory remained in their hands. It may be doubted whether their freedom of action was complete: President Wilson's view was that the agreements of 1913 had established a State territory for Albania which the Allies were not subsequently at liberty to dismember. The question arose in a modified form in the *Affair of the Monastery of Saint Naoum (Albanian Frontier)*.[36] In that case, although the Court unanimously accepted that the Conference of Ambassadors, by its decisions of 9 November 1921, had effectively delimited Albanian territory,[37] it is significant that this power was referred to the consent and acquiescence of the parties given in 1921,[38] rather than at any earlier date. Moreover the power was, it was held, not unlimited: although 'the Conference, whose mission it was to "settle the frontiers of Albania" had, in the fulfilment of its task, a certain amount of latitude'[39] they had no power to alter any decision once made, or even to rectify it on grounds of

---

[33] Salisbury to Russell, 8 June 1878: ibid. 834.

[34] *Supra*, p. 304.

[35] *Supra*, p. 304.

[36] Ser. B No. 9 (1924).

[37] 'The character of the decision of November 9th 1921 has been discussed before the Court. Its legal foundation is to be found in the fact that the Principal Powers, acting through the Conference of Ambassadors, had the power to render a decision.' Ser. B. No. 9, 14. Cf. Lauterpacht, *Recognition*, 68n.

[38] Ser. B No. 9, 13.

[39] Ibid. 16.

error.[40] Their decision was, it was held,[41] in the nature of 'arbitration'. There was thus no question of any supranational authority of the Powers—authority which presumably would have included power to change a decision for sufficient reason— either with respect to Albania in particular or Europe generally.

The question of the validity of Great Power action taken without the consent of 'minor' Powers arose directly in the case concerning the *Jurisdiction of the European Commission of the Danube between Galatz and Braila*.[42] The European Commission of the Danube had been established by the Treaty of Paris in 1856, and its jurisdiction extended to Galatz, in Roumania, by Article 53 of the Treaty of Berlin, 1878 which also, as we have seen, recognized Roumania as independent of the Ottoman Empire.[43] The Commission's jurisdiction was further extended, to Braila, by the Treaty of London of 10 March 1883.[44] 'Roumania did not sign this Treaty, or take part in the Conference by which it was drawn up, the Conference having refused to admit her delegates except in a consultative capacity.'[45] Article 346 of the Treaty of Versailles[46] reaffirmed the *de facto* position existing before the war, and this was incorporated in the Definitive Statute of the Danube of 23 July 1921, to which Romania was also a party.[47] The Court held, by nine votes to one, that the jurisdiction of the Commission did extend as far as Braila, by interpretation of the treaties of 1919 and 1921; but it was not suggested that the Treaty of London of 1883 had had that effect. The fact, that, since 1883 'the European Commission had exercised some powers on the sector from Galatz to Braila, no matter what the legal ground and nature may have been'[48] was a reason for construing the post-war treaties as referring to the previous *de facto* situation:

[40] The court found that the 1913 Protocols had left the St. Naoum frontier undermined: ibid. 16 ff. It expressly did not decide whether, if the frontier had been fixed, it could have been validly altered in 1921: ibid. 21–2. Presumably that would have required an analysis of the terms by which the Parties had in 1921 accepted the competence of the Conference of Ambassadors.

[41] Ibid. 15, approving the *Jaworzina Frontier Opinion*, Ser. B No. 8 (1923), 29.

[42] Ser. B No. 14 (1927).

[43] *Supra* p. 303. Turkey was, but Roumania was not, a party to the Treaty.

[44] 74 *BFSP* 1231.

[45] Ser. B No. 14 (1927), 11.

[46] 112 *BFSP* 1.

[47] 114 *BFSP* 535, Arts. V, VI.

[48] Ser. B No. 14, 27.

but it was not relied upon to prove Romanian acquiescence in the Treaty of London, much less 'any supra-national' competence of the Powers to bind Romania without its consent.[49]

The conclusion must be, then, that nineteenth-century precedents do not support the claim of the Great Powers to any legal hegemony in the territorial affairs of Europe.[50] The competence, referred to already,[51] to create 'objective' settlements derives not from the position of the Powers *per se*, but from the importance of the common interests involved, and the express, tacit or implied acceptance of the States concerned.

(*ii*)   *The First World War settlements*[52]

Apart from a relatively few immediate dispositions,[53] by far the greater proportion of dispositive clauses in the peace treaties of 1919–23 either recognized pre-existing States, or delegated authority to the Powers or the League to decide on the future regime of territories concerned.[54] In this respect these treaties differ from those of the nineteenth century: the continuing and explicit authority of the Allied Powers, and in particular of the Principal Allied and Associated Powers (Great Britain, the United States, France, Italy and, for certain purposes, Japan) after 1918 was very extensive. Nevertheless, the principle of consent was, with one exception, maintained: no general

---

[49] Ibid. 75 *per* Judge Nyholm. Cf. Judge Negulesco, diss., 89–91, 95.

[50] Academic authority has been very thoroughly canvassed by Dickinson, *Equality of States*, 126–31 (writers affirming equality), 131–45 (writers doubting or denying equality): his conclusion (145) is equivocal; see also 173–5, 292–311. The conclusion in the text is also supported by Lande, op. cit. 282–6; Albrecht-Carrié, 22, 59; Dupuis, *Le Principe d'équilibre et le concert européen* (1909), 496; Nys (1899), 1 *RDILC* (2d) 271–313, 279; Langer, *Seizure of Territory*, 10–11; and cf. Westlake, in *Collected Papers* (1914), 92–101. But in his *International Law* (2nd edn., 1910) I, 321–5, Westlake cites Salisbury's reference to the 'federated action of Europe'. Lawrence, in *Essays on Some Disputed Questions in Modern International Law* (1884) 191–213, 209 refers to 'what can hardly be distinguished from a legal right to settle disputed questions . . .'

[51] *Supra*, p. 301; and cf. *infra*, pp. 315–19.

[52] The main Treaties concluded were as follows: Versailles, 1919 (112 *BFSP* 1); St. Germain-en-Laye, 1919 (ibid. 317); Neuilly, 1919 (ibid. 781); Trianon, 1920 (113 *BFSP* 186); and Lausanne, 1923 (117 *BFSP* 543), replacing the unratified Treaty of Sèvres, 1920 (113 *BFSP* 652).

[53] Belgium was restored to independence: Versailles, Arts. 31–9; Saint-Germain, Art. 83; Trianon, Art. 67. The British protectorate over Egypt, and the French protectorates over Monaco and Morocco were recognized: see e.g. Versailles, Arts. 147–54, 436, 144–146 respectively.

[54] See also *infra*, pp. 313–15, 325.

authority was claimed to impose particular duties on third parties.[55] The exception, again, was Bessarabia, claimed by Romania, but which was not in the gift of the Allies.[56] None the less, the British government recognized 'the reunion of Bessarabia and Romania',[57] which was confirmed by a treaty of 1920, to which Russia was not a party.[58] Both the United States[59] and the Soviets[60] protested. Once again it seems that a transaction resulting in the transfer of Bessarabia was substantially illegal.[61]

(iii) *The Second World War settlements*[62]

The Second World War settlements, in their dispositive elements, were less complex and far-reaching than those of 1919–23. Internationalization was not regarded as the panacea for all intractable conflicts of nationality: where the earlier settlements saw the creation of Danzig, Fiume, the Memel and Saar Territories, and the formation of a large number of Mandated Territories, the later ones saw only the unsuccessful Trieste experiment, [63] the unilateral establishment by France of a new Saar Territory,[64] and the, rather reluctant, transfer, with one addition, of still existing Mandates to an analogous Trusteeship system.[65] In the former case a large number of new States had come into existence: in the latter, the emphasis was on the re-establishment of States which had 'disappeared' during the hostilities. Disputes arose, not about whether these States should

---

[55] Judges Altamira and Hurst, diss., *Free Zones Case*, Ser. A/B No. 46 (1932), 89 (no disagreement with the majority on this point). But cf. the cases of conditional recognition of new States: *infra*, pp. 322–3.

[56] Bessarabia was not among the extensive territories detached from Russia by the Treaty of Brest-Litovsk, 1918: 123 *BFSP* 740.

[57] *USFR* 1920/III, 431.

[58] 113 *BSFP* 647, Arts 1–3.

[59] *USFR* 1920/III, 433.

[60] Ibid. 434.

[61] Spector, *Rumania at the Paris Peace Conference* (1962), 101–2, 222–5; Langer, *Seizure of Territory*, 29–31; Temperley, op. cit. IV, 213–36. But a Romanian-German Mixed Arbitral Tribunal in *Wildermann* v. *Stinnes* held that Bessarabia had ceased to be Russian territory in 1917 by a process of secession and union with Romania, a process recognized by the Allies: (1925) 4 *Rep. MAT* 842, 847. But cf. 42 *UNTS* 3, Art. 1; Whiteman, 3 *Digest* 131–8.

[62] See generally Whiteman, 3 *Digest* 1–623; Wheeler-Bennett and Nichols, *The Semblance of Peace. The Political Settlement after the Second World War* (1972).

[63] *Supra*, pp. 161–3.

[64] *Supra*, p. 160.

[65] *Infra*, p. 341.

be re-established, but over their territory and form of government. Most importantly, in the former case peace treaties had been concluded with virtually all the belligerents: in the latter, the most important enemy power had never beeen in a position to sign a formal peace treaty. The replacement of the German government by a Quadripartite Allied government, and the subsequent division of the Reich into two German States, necessitated a prolonged, piecemeal, method of settlement, a 'functional peace treaty'. In fact, the entire post-war settlement was to some extent functional, in this sense: decisions were taken at a series of inter-Allied Conferences which were regarded as binding and which were in fact final. By assuming complete control over the government of Germany and Austria, the Allied Powers acquired virtually complete dispositive control over them; and in other respects their combined authority, together with the presence of their armies in 'liberated' Europe, meant that the smaller Allied Powers had little choice but to acquiesce in their decisions. Of this Poland, an Allied not an enemy State, provided much the best example. For present purposes, two problems may be referred to.

(a) *The re-establishment of annexed or conquered States* Perhaps the most interesting such case was that of Austria. The annexation of Austria by Germany in 1938 was a clear violation of Article 80 of the Treaty of Versailles;[66] nonetheless, at least *de facto* recognition of the Anschluss was quite general.[67] This general recognition notwithstanding, the Moscow Declaration of 1 December 1943 affirmed that the *Anschluss* was 'null and void', and declared a joint 'desire to see re-established a free and independent Austria'.[68] Austria in the period 1938–45 thus appears to have been regarded as in the same legal position as Ethiopia and Albania; its 'sovereignty . . . not . . . destroyed but only suspended'.[69] In the absence of any claimant Austrian government or government-in-exile, the collapse of the German government in June 1945 necessitated the assumption by the

---

[66] Whiteman, 3 *Digest* 425–77; Clute, *The International Legal Status of Austria 1938–1955* (1962), 1–22; Lemkin, *Axis Rule in Occupied Europe* (1944), 108–16; Langer, *Seizure of Territory*, 155–206; Marek, *Identity and Continuity*, 338–68; H. Wright (1944), 38 *AJ* 621–637.

[67] Marek, *Identity and Continuity*, 343–6; Clute, op. cit. 8–12.

[68] (1944) 38 *AJ Supp.* 7.

[69] Lemkin, op. cit. 115. See further *infra*, Ch. 17.

Allies of governmental authority in Austria,[70] leading eventually to the Austrian State Treaty of 1955, terminating control machinery in Austria, and recognizing 'that Austria is re-established as a sovereign, peaceful, independent and democratic State'.[71] Austria was not regarded as a World War II belligerent,[72] and Article 21 provided that reparations would 'not be exacted from Austria arising out of the existence of a state of war after 1st September 1939'.[73]

On the view taken by the Allies after 1943, it seems then that Austria was a State throughout.[74] On that view, governmental authority with respect to Austria was divided between the Austrian Government and the Allied Commission for Austria. It was not that, after 1945, Austria *qua* State was 'limited in her capacity for action under international law';[75] rather that the government of Austria was shared between different instrumentalities.

Ethiopia, also, had been invaded and annexed in violation of the Covenant, and the Kellogg-Briand Pact.[76] The annexation had received some degree of recognition, but its nullity was in effect affirmed by the Peace Treaty with Italy.[77] Albania, where a puppet government had been established in union with Italy,[78] was also restored to independence, acts of the puppet government between 1939 and 1943 being recognized as null and void.[79]

(b) *Poland 1939–1946* Preservation of the legal existence of Poland, after its partition between the U.S.S.R. and Germany in 1939,[80] was an *a fortiori* case, since the invasion of Poland was

[70] 145 *BFSP* 846, 850; 146 *BFSP* 504; Mair, in *RIAA, Four Power Control in Germany and Austria* (1956), Pt. II; Wheeler-Bennett and Nichols, op cit. 465–86.
[71] 217 *UNTS* 223, Art. 1. For the negotiations see Whiteman, 3 *Digest* 437–68.
[72] Lemkin, op. cit. 116n.36.
[73] Potsdam Proclamation, Pt. VII; 145 *BFSP* 852; Feis, *Between War and Peace. The Potsdam Conference* (1960), 65–9, 274–9.
[74] Cf. 1946 Agreement, Art. 3; Clute, op. cit. 130–8; *infra*, pp. 418–19.
[75] Brandweiner, in Lipsky ed., *Law and Politics in the World Community* (1953), 221–42, 225, describing Austria as a 'Protected State'.
[76] Marek, *Identity and Continuity*, 263–82; Langer, *Seizure of Territory*, 132–54.
[77] 49 *UNTS* 747, Arts. 33–8, 74; Bentwich (1945), 22 *BY* 275–8.
[78] *Supra*, p. 65; Langer, *Seizure of Territory*, 245–53; Marek, *Identity and Continuity*, 331–337; Lemkin, op. cit. 99–107; *Case of Gold Looted by Germany from Rome in 1943* (1953) 20 ILR 441, 450–1; cf. *Monetary Gold Removed from Rome* I.C.J. Rep. 1954 p. 19.
[79] 49 *UNTS* 747, Arts. 27, 31, 74. For Korea and Formosa after 1945, see *supra*, pp. 281, 286.
[80] Secret Protocol to the Non-Aggression Pact of 23 August 1939: 143 *BFSP* 503; Grenville, 200.

the *casus belli,* and even the older doctrine preserved the legal existence of the State *pendente bello.*[81] The disagreement between the Allies over Poland in the period 1944–1946 related rather to the composition of the Polish Government, and the boundaries of Poland, and is thus of marginal relevance for present purposes.[82] But, whatever the legalities of the Allied action,[83] there can be no doubt as to their extensive *de facto* dispositive control.

(2) *Dispositions anticipatory of peace treaties*

The phenomenon of dispositions anticipatory of peace treaties has been little remarked.[84] There is however nothing special about a formal peace treaty as distinct from *ad hoc* settlement of specific issues on a basis of consent. The question is not what type of treaty is necessary, but what are the rights and duties of States concerned, and which issues remain open for disposition. The problem here is a slightly different one: that is, the legal basis of dispositions made by certain States—usually the Great Powers—before formal peace treaties, but affecting the rights of defeated or other States. Various examples might be given,[85] but the case of Poland in 1919 is illustrative.

The creation of a Polish State was one of the Fourteen Points,[86] and a cardinal war aim of the Entente Powers.[87] Even before the withdrawal from Polish areas of German troops, the Polish National Committee in London had been accorded a certain status by recognition as a co-belligerent and the government of a future State of Poland.[88] After the armistice and the withdrawal of German troops, the Polish National Committee became the basis for a generally effective government in Poland; one which may be considered to have been recognized by the admission of

[81] *Infra,* p. 407.

[82] See this writer, 'The Polish Question at Yalta and Potsdam' (1977), *Studies for a New Central Europe* Ser. 4 Nos. 1–2, 89–100. See also Whiteman, 3 *Digest* 177–392; Wheeler-Bennett and Nicholls, op. cit., index ref. 'Poland'; Feis, op. cit. 31–8, 203–34; Clemens, *Yalta* (1970), 8–28, 173–215; Woolsey (1944), 38 *AJ* 441–8; (1945) 39 *AJ* 295–300; H. Wright, ibid. 300–8; Marek, *Identity and Continuity,* 417–526.

[83] Cf. Lauterpacht, *Recognition,* 353n.1.

[84] But cf. Brownlie, *Principles,* 138–9, 175.

[85] For the institution of the Mandate system in 1919, see *infra,* p. 314, for the Pacific Islands Trust Territory in 1947, see *infra,* p. 347.

[86] Temperley, op. cit. I, 192–5.

[87] Cf. Temperley, op. cit. I, 181, 183, 191, 199, 335–8; ibid. IV, 238.

[88] Smith, *GB & LN* I, 234–5 (15 Oct. 1917).

Polish plenipotentiaries at the Paris Peace Conference on 18 January 1919.[89] Thus, although Poland was formally recognized by Articles 87–93 of the Treaty of Versailles (to which it was a signatory), there can be no doubt that the Polish State had been effectively reconstituted well before signature of the Treaty.[90]

The same is true, in varying degrees, of the other States created in the period 1918–20: that is, Czechoslovakia,[91] the Serb-Croat-Slovene State (Yugoslavia),[92] Armenia,[93] and the Hedjaz.[94] A general provision covered 'States now existing or coming into existence in future in the whole or part of the former Empire of Russia',[95] and may be taken to have included Latvia, Lithuania and Estonia,[96] Finland,[97] and the more transient political formations elsewhere on the fringe of the Russian Empire (Azerbaijan, the Ukraine, etc.). Of course, since the criteria for statehood take priority over other forms of territorial transfer,[98] it may be that these 'anticipatory dispositions' were of a rather special kind.

(3) *Dispositions delegated to groups of States*

As we have seen, the territorial sovereign can, in general, dispose of its territory at discretion: there is nothing contrary to principle therefore in delegation by the territorial sovereign to a group of States of authority to decide on the future status of a particular

[89] Temperley, op. cit. V, 158; *contra* Chen, *Recognition*, 201.

[90] *Deutsche Continental Gas Gesellschaft* v. *Polish State* (1929) 5 AD No. 5; Herz (1936), 17 *RDILC* 564; Blociszewski (1921), 28 *RGDIP* 5–83; (1924), 31 *RGDIP* 89–144; *infra*, p. 390.

[91] Versailles, Arts. 81–6; Saint-Germain, Arts. 53–8; Trianon, Arts. 48–52; Temperley, op. cit. IV, 237–77; V, 159–60; Perman, *The Shaping of the Czechoslovak State* (1962); Hobza (1922), 29 *RGDIP* 385–409.

[92] Saint-Germain, Arts. 46–52; Neuilly, Arts. 36–41; Trianon, Arts. 41–4; Temperley, op. cit. IV, 170–217; V, 158–9.

[93] Sèvres, Arts. 88–93; omitted from Treaty of Lausanne, after Armenia's reincorporation into Russia.

[94] Sèvres, Arts 98–110; Lausanne, Art. 16 (general terms only). The Hedjaz was listed as an original Member of the League by the Treaty of Versailles, Annex to Part I; but did not ratify the Treaty. After a two year war the Hedjaz was united with the Nejd under King Ibn Sa'ud as the Kingdom of Hedjaz, Nejd and Dependencies: 130 *BFSP* 789; after 1932 called Saudi Arabia. For British recognition (1927), 134 *BFSP* 273; for Turkish recognition (1929), 131 *BFSP* 491.

[95] Versailles, Arts. 116–17; Saint-Germain, Art. 87; Neuilly, Art. 58; Trianon, Art. 72; Sèvres, Art. 135.

[96] Laserson (1943), 37 *AJ* 233–47; Graham, *The Diplomatic Recognition of the Border States* (1935); Hackworth, 1 *Digest* 201.

[97] *Supra*, p. 44.

[98] *Infra*, p. 396.

territory. The reference may take various forms: the overt cession of sovereignty to designated States, with the further disposal of the territory left at their discretion, is the most obvious, but is only one possibility. Subject to any relevant rule of law, the question is one of intent. But, at least where a particular purpose is stated or implied, it is unlikely that renunciation in favour of a group of States can be interpreted as involving 'even a momentary or technical lodgement of sovereignty'.[99]

In the *Jaworzina Case* the Permanent Court was concerned with the authority of the Principal Allied and Associated Powers under the post-World War I treaties to delimit the Polish-Czechoslovak frontier. Their decision on the question, the Court held,

> was taken in accordance with a common desire on the part of all concerned to arrive at a final settlement of the dispute between Poland and Czechoslovakia. In this respect it has much in common with arbitration . . . Only by a settlement emanating from a duly authorised body could the whole dispute be disposed of without leaving any important point for subsequent decision, and the task with which the Conference of Ambassadors was entrusted be fulfilled.[100]

As a result, the Council of Ambassadors having completed their task, no further power remained to alter or vary the boundary in the absence of fresh consent of the parties concerned.[101] Much the same limitation appears to have applied to the five-Power authority over Albania in 1919.[102] Perhaps the best example of dispositive authority delegated to groups of States was that of the Principal Allied and Associated Powers with respect to the establishment of the Mandate System under Article 22 of the League Covenant.[103] It is interesting to note that the Mandates over former Turkish territories were allocated by the Supreme Council in April/May 1920,[104] although the territories had not

---

[99] Judge Jessup, diss., *South West Africa Case (Second Phase)* I.C.J. Rep. 1966 p. 6, 422; *infra*, p. 345. Cf. also 18 *BFSP* 780 (Belgium).

[100] Ser. B No. 8 (1923), 29; *supra*, p. 307.

[101] Ibid. 37–8.

[102] *Supra*, p. 306.

[103] 112 *BFSP* 1, Art. 119; Temperley, op. cit. VI, 503–4.

[104] Ibid. 134–69, 505.

then been relinquished by Turkey.[105] The view appears to have been taken (and it found some support in the terms of Article 22)[106] that the 'A' Mandates had come into force irrespective of formal Turkish consent.[107] The Treaty of Lausanne provided for renunciation by Turkey of all territories outside its new boundaries, 'le sort de ces territoires . . . étant reglé ou à regler par les intéressés'.[108] Any formal illegality in this proceeding can thus be seen to have been cured by subsequent ratification.[109]

By contrast, the authority of the Principal Allied Powers after 1945 was not, with one exception, perpetuated by express delegation in the various peace treaties. The exception was the future disposition of the Italian colonies;[110] and even then, the Allies were unable to agree, and the substance of the matter was referred, under Annex XI of the Treaty, to the United Nations.[111]

(4) *International status of dispositions pursuant to multilateral treaties*

The dispositions discussed above were in general either carried out pursuant to the consent of affected parties, or, as in the case of Bessarabia in 1878, were probably illegal. There is however at least some authority for the proposition that international settlements, regimes, or institutions, once established, may acquire, as it is said, 'objective' or 'dispositive' effect, and thus become valid and binding *erga omnes*.[112] Given the modern rule that consent to a settlement may not be coerced by illegal force,[113] this area of law may well be important in validating at least those parts of peace settlements which are consistent with the general interest. In a series of cases, international tribunals have accorded to territorial regimes, when elements of public

---

[105] The 'A' Mandates came into force on 29 Sept. 1923. Turkey ratified the treaty of Lausanne on 31 Mar. 1924: 117 *BFSP* 543.

[106] *Sc.* 'colonies and territories which, as a consequence of the late war, *have ceased to be under the sovereignty* of the States which formerly governed them' (my itals.). Cf. the Harbord Report on Armenia, 16 Oct. 1919: 'The Covenant . . . (appears) to recognize in advance the dismemberment to some degree of the Ottoman Empire'; cited Temperley, op. cit. IV, 55.

[107] Cf. Temperley, op. cit. VI, 37; Brownlie, *Principles*, 138.

[108] 117 *BFSP* 543, Art. 16.

[109] Other cases of delegation to the Principal Allied and Associated Powers included Danzig (*supra*, p. 163), Memel (*supra*, p. 160) and Fiume (*supra*, p. 161).

[110] Italian Peace Treaty, 49 *UNTS* 747, Art. 23.

[111] *Infra*, p. 331. For Formosa, see *supra*, pp. 144-9.

[112] Cf. Judge McNair, *supra*, p. 301; Wright (1917), 11 *AJ* 566-79, 573.

[113] *Supra*, p. 106.

interest are involved, characteristics of permanence, opposability, and to a degree, unalterability, not possessed by ordinary conventional transactions.[114] In the *Aaland Islands Case*, the question arose whether the provisions of the Peace of Paris, 1856,[115] demilitarizing the islands, had survived the war, and bound the new State of Finland. The Commission of Jurists reported that the demilitarization of the islands, though not a servitude, was a matter of 'general European interest'.[116]

This 'true objective law', it was held, had three results. The demilitarized status of the islands survived even a general European war; it could be relied upon by, and was opposable to, third parties such as Sweden or Finland; and it could not, as 'a settlement regulating European interests . . .', 'be abolished or modified either by the acts of one particular Power or by convention between some few of the Powers which signed the provisions of 1856'.[117] A further illustration is the Opinion of the International Court in the *South West Africa (Status) Case*. There the Court unanimously held that the Mandate for South West Africa had continued to exist after the demise of the League of Nations in 1946, because of the general public interest involved. The Mandate had, in Judge McNair's words, 'a special legal status, designed to last until modified in the manner indicated by Article 22 . . .'[118]

These cases illustrate the elements of permanence and opposability of dispositive settlements. Their unalterability is perhaps more contentious. In the *Aaland Island Case*, as has been seen, the Commission denied the possibility of modification *inter se* by some of the States parties. In two cases before the Permanent Court the same problem arose, though in neither was discussion of it particularly satisfactory.

In the *Austro-German Customs Union Case*,[119] the Majority

[114] Cf. *Reparations Case* I.C.J. Rep. 1949 p. 174, 179; *supra*, p. 25; *Namibia Opinion* I.C.J. Rep. 1971 p. 6, 56; *supra*, p. 125.

[115] 46 *BFSP* 23.

[116] *LNOJ* Sp. Supp. No. 3 (1920), 17; cited with approval by Judge McNair, *Status Opinion* I.C.J. Rep. 1950 p. 128, 153–4.

[117] *Report*, 18. The demilitarized status of the Islands was reaffirmed by a Convention of October 1921 (10 States): 9 *LNTS* 212, designed 'to supplement, without prejudice thereto, the obligations assumed by Russia in the Convention of March, 30, 1856'.

[118] I.C.J. Rep. 1950 p. 128, 155. Even more strikingly, the Court held by 12 votes to 2 that supervision of the Mandate was to be carried out by the General Assembly. See further *infra*, p. 341.

[119] Ser. A/B No. 41 (1931); *supra*, p. 50.

Judgment apparently took the view that the Geneva Protocol of 1922 had extended Austrian and German obligations with respect to Austrian independence, beyond the provisions of Article 88 of the Treaty of Versailles. The Protocol (to which seven States, not including Germany, were parties by signature or accession) was, it was held, 'a special and distinct instrument open to the accession of all Powers, whether signatory to the Peace Treaty or not . . . [and having its] own value and on that account a binding force capable in itself of independent application'.[120] The Majority Judgment is on this point in the nature of a separate opinion, since six of the seven judges held the proposed customs union a violation of both Article 88 and the 1922 Protocol.[121] Only Judge de Bustamante held the customs union incompatible with the Protocol but not Article 88. What is of interest is that Judge Anzilotti found it

an arguable question whether the States who in 1922 signed the Geneva Protocol were in a position to modify *inter se* the provisions of Article 88, which provisions . . . form an essential part of the peace settlement and were adopted not in the interests of any given State, but in the higher interest of the European political system and with a view to the maintenance of peace. However that may be as regards the obligations devolving upon Austria the Protocol is covered by the provisions of Article 88.[122]

Bearing in mind the strong joint dissenting opinion, the actual decision thus seems to rest on a point unargued in the Court's Opinion and in part at least conceded in the crucial Separate Opinion, for the view that the proposed union violated Article 88 is difficult to support.[123] But it was arguable that the 1922 Protocol did not derogate from Article 88 but constituted merely an extension or reinterpretation of that Article, which was contrary neither to its terms nor to the general European interest involved. The view that the Protocol was binding on its signatories would then seem to be supportable.

In the *Oscar Chinn Case*[124] the majority held that the provisions of the Berlin Act of 1884–5 regarding freedom of commerce in

120 Ibid. 48–9.
121 Ibid. 53.
122 Ibid. 64.
123 *Supra*, p. 49.
124 Ser. A/B No. 63 (1934).

the Congo Basin[125] had been materially amended, by some of the parties to that Act, by the Convention of Saint Germain of 1919.[126] Judge van Eysinga, dissenting, held that, since the General Act created 'a highly internationalized regime . . . recognized, as henceforward a part of public international law . . . a regime, a statute, a constitution . . .'[127] it could not be modified *inter se* by only some of the Signatories. Judge Schücking agreed,[128] and Judge Hurst left the point open.[129] However it was again arguable that the post-war settlement was of such a nature that multilateral adjustment of the 1885 Act was permissible between consenting parties.[130]

The converse proposition is less debatable: if some of the parties to a multilateral dispositive settlement can vary its provisions *inter se*, such variations cannot effect non-consenting States.[131]

The conclusion then is that, apart from any asserted primacy or hegemony of groups of States either generally or with respect to a particular region, multilateral territorial settlements may well possess certain special features as a matter of general international law.[132] They are relatively impervious to termination by operation of law, for example by way of the *rebus sic stantibus* doctrine, the effects of war, or even the disappearance of some of the original parties. Although they may probably—at least in the absence of any stipulation to the contrary—be amended by agreement between some of the Parties *inter se*, such amendments are not to affect the rights of the other signatories and will, in general, be restrictively interpreted.[133] Moreover, where the settlement relates to some general international interest in respect of territory or political status, it may be held

[125] 76 *BFSP* 4.
[126] 112 *BFSP* 901; Ser. A/B No. 63 (1934), 84.
[127] Ibid. 132, 134.
[128] Ibid. 148.
[129] Ibid. 122-3.
[130] Cf. however General Act, art. 36, cited Judge van Eysinga, ibid. 133.
[131] *United States Nationals in Morocco* I.C.J. Rep. 1952 p. 176, 199 (Majority opinion), 217 (Joint diss. op.).
[132] There is a useful discussion in McNair, *Law of Treaties* (1961), 255-71, esp. 268-9, citing some of the above material, and also Judge Huber, diss., *The Free City of Danzig and the I.L.O.*, Ser. B No. 18 (1930), 29. To the contrary, Schwarzenberger, *International Law* II, 735-736; Erle-Richards, 'Introduction' to Oakes and Mowat, ed., *The Great European Treaties of the Nineteenth Century*, v-xi.
[133] Cf. *Oscar Chinn Case*, Ser. A/B No. 63 (1934), 84.

to be dispositive in character, so as to bind third parties, whether by virtue of the rules of State succession,[134] or otherwise.

12.3 PROBLEMS OF COLLECTIVE RECOGNITION

(1) *The concept of 'collective recognition'*[135]

As we have seen, recognition in modern practice is the formal acknowledgement by existing States of the normal political consequences flowing from the status of the entity to be recognized. As such, it may be either an individual or a collective act. But for those adopting a constitutive view of recognition, individual recognition presents serious difficulties: and consequently both Lauterpacht and Jessup have argued for 'the establishment of a standard [collective] procedure for the recognition of new States'.[136]

In practice, however, certification of status is achieved in a variety of ways—as is appropriate to a system in which such certification is in principle of evidential importance. Thus in some situations collective acknowledgment of status is of substantial probative value:[137] in others, its effect is to consolidate or legitimize a *de facto* situation (for example, Goa), or, conversely, to underwrite a particular status so as to prevent the operation of the principle of acquisitive prescription (as with Namibia or Rhodesia). In more normal situations, the collective acknowledgment of status that might have been effected by a system of organized collective recognition is achieved by admission to the United Nations. It cannot be expected, then, that collective recognition will ever play a major role in matters of territorial status: on the other hand in a number of cases it has been of considerable importance. Three examples may be cited.

In the case of Greece (1822–30),[138] the Powers intervened to

---

[134] On the classical distinction between 'dispositive' and 'personal' treaties in the law of State succession see O'Connell, in O'Brien, ed., *New Nations*, 7–41; and further, in Bos, ed., *The Present State of International Law and other Essays* (1973), 331–8. See also Waldock's Commentary on Draft Articles 22 and 22 (*bis*) on State Succession with Respect to Treaties: *ILC Ybk.* 1972/II, 44–59, and works there cited; and for discussion, ibid., 1972/I, 247–54, 258–66, 275–6.

[135] Lauterpacht, *Recognition*, 67–9, 165–74, 253–5; Chen, *Recognition*, 221–3; Verhoeven, *Reconnaissance*, 521–33; Hackworth, 1 *Digest* 173–4.

[136] Jessup, *A Modern Law of Nations* (1946), 43–67, 45; cf. Chen, *Recognition*, 221.

[137] e.g. Albania: *infra*, pp. 321–2.

[138] Marriott, op. cit. 193–224; Anderson, *The Eastern Question*, 53–77; Albrecht-Carrié, 99–128; Crawley, *The Question of Greek Independence* (1930).

propose a settlement[139] only when the Greek insurrection appeared in danger of defeat. With the rejection of the Treaty of London by the Porte, the Conference of Ambassadors agreed on a joint military expedition to expel the forces of Mehemet Ali,[140] and on the placing of the mainland under provisional guarantee.[141] When Turkey accepted the mediation offered in the Treaty of London,[142] the Powers had acquired, in effect, full dispositive authority over Greece. This was exercised in 1830 and thereafter, when Greece was established as an independent State,[143] its Monarch nominated, and various supplementary matters regulated.[144] Mediation and 'collective recognition' had turned into a much more general dispositive authority.

The same is true of Belgium, which in 1830 declared its independence from the Netherlands.[145] In contrast with the Greek case, Great Power intervention was almost immediate. The first of a long series of Protocols between the Ministers of the five Great Powers in London called in strong terms for an armistice;[146] then, after its acceptance by the Belgian Provisional Government and the Government of the Netherlands[147] a further Protocol recited that 'the very object of the union of Belgium with Holland is destroyed', and began to concert 'such new arrangements, as may be most proper for combining the future independence of Belgium with the stipulations of Treaties, with the interests and security of other Powers, and with the preservation of the balance of Europe'.[148]

On 14 October 1831 the Ambassadors announced their

[139] St. Petersburg Protocol, 1826: 14 *BFSP* 629; Treaty for the Pacification of Greece, London, 6 July 1827: ibid. 632.

[140] 16 *BFSP* 1084.

[141] Ibid. 1094.

[142] Treaty of Adrianople, Art. 10: ibid. 647; and further Declaration, 17 *BFSP* 195.

[143] Protocol of 3 Feb. 1830, Art. 1: 17 *BFSP* 192.

[144] 18 *BFSP* 597–637; 19 *BFSP* 2–54. A further Treaty of 20 November 1852 (Great Britain, Bavaria, Russia, France, Greece) relative to the Succession to the Crown of Greece amended the rules relating to the succession: 41 *BFSP* 36. The King of Greece was invited to attend 'comme directement intéressé à prendre part à une transaction destinée à assurer le repos à venir de la Grèce'.

[145] See Oakes and Mowat, *The Great European Treaties of the Nineteenth Century*, 126–57; Albrecht-Carrié, op. cit. 60–98; Fleury de Lannoy, *Histoire diplomatique de l'indépendence belge* (1930).

[146] 18 *BFSP* 728.

[147] Ibid. 731, 734.

[148] Ibid. 749.

'definitive agreement' on twenty four articles . . . 'comme devant servir à la séparation de la Belgique d'avec la Hollande et régler toutes les questions auxquelles ont donné lieu cette séparation, ainsi que l'indépendance et la neutralité de la Belgique.'[149] Article VII of the Twenty Four Articles provided that Belgium would become an independent and permanently neutral State. No alteration of this proposed settlement was envisaged; and, on the Netherlands rejecting it,[150] the Five Powers forthwith signed a treaty 'relative to the separation of Belgium from Holland' with Belgium alone, reciting the Twenty Four Articles, and formally guaranteeing their execution.[151] Dutch protests continued until 1839, when all parties concluded practically identical treaties embodying the Twenty Four Articles. The Netherlands recognized the separation of Belgium as effective (though from what date was not stated); the Treaty of 15 November 1831 was declared to be no longer binding, and the re-enacted Articles were again 'placés sous la garantie de Leurs dites Majestés'.[152] Lauterpacht has sought to justify the Belgian case on grounds of 'collective intervention';[153] but the parties themselves seemed to have acted as much upon the assumption of a continuing right to enforce and regulate the terms of the Congress of Vienna.[154] On that view the present relevance of the Belgian precedent is limited.[155]

Finally, some mention should be made of Albania.[156] Whatever its exact status in 1921, the effect of the decision of the Council of Ambassadors in certifying its statehood was considerable. The United States had refused recognition before 1921 on the grounds of lack of governmental stability: however the Department of State on 9 May 1922, while reaffirming doubts about the stability of the government, stated that 'The international status of Albania has . . . been so affected by the decisions regarding that

---

[149] Ibid. 893.
[150] Ibid. 906.
[151] London, 15 Nov. 1831 : ibid. 645.
[152] 27 *BFSP* 990, 1000.
[153] *Recognition*, 10n.; but cf. 62n.
[154] For the Dutch protest and the Allied reply, see 19 *BFSP* 57, 73.
[155] See also Smith, *GB & LN* I, 245–7; Moore, 1 *Digest* 110; Harcourt, *Letters by Historicus* (1863), 5–6. In the *Case concerning Sovereignty over certain Frontier Land* I.C.J. Rep. 1959 p. 209, 213, the International Court stated that the 'separation of Belgium from the Netherlands was sanctioned by the Treaty of London of 19 April 1839 . . .'
[156] *Supra*, pp. 304, 306–7.

country which were taken by the Conference of Ambassadors on November 9, 1921, that the Department is no longer disinclined, in principle, to recognize that country . . .'[157] Recognition followed on 28 July 1922.

(2) *Collective recognition in international organizations*

Membership of universal political organizations is commonly restricted either to 'States' (as with the United Nations) or to entities which, whatever their formal status, possess substantial independence (as with the League). Admission to the former type, in particular, is thus strong evidence of the necessary status. However it is clear that such admission does not constitute recognition by the other members as a whole, or, it seems, even by those voting in favour of admission.[158] The admissions practice of the two organizations has been examined in Chapter 4.

(3) *Collective conditional recognition*

Conditional recognition has been defined as 'recognition the grant or continuance of which is made dependent upon the fulfilment of stipulations other than the normal requirements of statehood . . .'[159] It was, though not general practice, an accepted mode of recognition in the last century.[160] The new States which emerged after the First World War were required, as a condition of their recognition and, in some cases, of the transfer of disputed territory to them, to accept and sign treaties protecting minority rights in their territories. In forwarding the text of a revised Minorities Treaty to be signed by Poland under Article 93 of the Treaty of Versailles, Clemenceau stated:

It has for long been the established procedure of the public law of Europe that when a State is created . . . the joint and formal recognition by the great Powers should be accompanied by the requirement that such State should, in the form of a binding international convention, undertake to comply with certain principles of government. This principle, for which there are numerous other precedents, received the most explicit sanction when, at the last great assembly of European

---

[157] *USFR* 1922/I, 598; Hackworth, 1 *Digest* 196-8.
[158] Aufricht (1949), 43 *AJ* 679-704; Chen, *Recognition*, 215-16.
[159] Lauterpacht, *Recognition*, 358. See generally Moore, 1 *Digest* 73-4; Hackworth, 1 *Digest* 192-5; Whiteman, 1 *Digest* 119-33; Chen, *Recognition*, 265-9; Lauterpacht, *Recognition*, 357-64 and (1945) 22 *BY* 185-90; Verhoeven, *Reconnaissance*, 648-56.
[160] Cf. Hall, *International Law* (8th edn., 1924), 113-14.

Powers—the Congress of Berlin—the sovereignty and independence of Serbia, Montenegro and Roumania were recognized . . .[161]

These cases, relating to the treatment by the new States of minorities included in their territory by peace settlements, would seem to be unobjectionable. However, the institution of conditional recognition has been criticized,[162] and would seem only to be justified in cases where some substantial *quid pro quo* is offered in return for the undertaking. States are not entitled to refuse to treat unrecognized States as such except upon compliance with legally irrelevant conditions: what are bargained, in cases of conditional recognition, are the political favours that may accompany friendly relations between States.[163] In any case, breach of a condition attached to a grant of recognition (that is, where the breach does not relate to the continuance of the entity concerned as a State) does not avoid the recognition, but is to be treated as 'the violation of an international obligation'.[164] Collective conditional recognition is thus of some, but not substantial, value in imposing obligations on new States.

12.4 TERRITORIAL DISPOSITIONS BY INTERNATIONAL ORGANIZATIONS

(1) *General principles*

Just as States may delegate to groups of States authority to dispose of their territory, so they may delegate such authority to international organizations. The main legal difficulty is whether the constitution of the organization allows its members to exercise the delegated authority by means of its procedures and with the use of its facilities. That problem only arises when the constitution permits decisions by majority vote. In the League of Nations period it did not therefore arise, but it has done so on various occasions under the Charter. As will be seen, United Nations practice supports the conclusion that at least certain delegated

---

[161] 112 *BFSP* 225. For the Treaty of 28 June 1919, see ibid. 232. Cf. Temperley, op. cit. V, 112–49, 143; *Acquisition of Polish Nationality*, Ser. B No. 7 (1923), 15–16.

[162] Chen, *Recognition*, Jessup, op. cit. 48; Lauterpacht (1945), 22 *BY*, 185, 190. Cf. Lauterpacht, *Recognition*, 361–2 (Finland).

[163] An analogy is U.N. membership—to which, it has been held, irrelevant conditions may not be attached: *Admissions Case* I.C.J. Rep. 1948 p. 65.

[164] Resolutions of the *Institut de Droit International* 1936, Art. 6; Whiteman, 2 *Digest* 119. For collective non-recognition, see *supra*, pp. 120–8.

functions may properly be exercised by United Nations organs without the consent of all Member States.[165] It may also be that particular international organizations possess, pursuant to their constitutions, certain powers of disposition. In either case the question depends on the particular issues and the terms of the particular treaty. Some relevant cases will be discussed here.

(2) *The Concert of Europe*

The status of the Concert of Europe in nineteenth-century international relations has been discussed already,[166] and the conclusion reached that the precedents do not support the claim of the major Powers to any legal hegemony in the territorial affairs of Europe. At the Conference of Aix-la-Chapelle in 1818, a British memorandum recorded the view that, although the settlement of 1815 constituted a 'Great Charter, by which the territorial system of Europe has been restored to order', yet that settlement could 'hardly be stated to give any special or superior security to the parts of the European system thus regulated, as compared with those parts which were not affected by the negotiations ... and which rest for their title upon anterior treaties or public acts of equal and recognized authority.' Rather, in the British view, the true function of the Powers in Europe was

without ... transgressing any of the principles of the law of nations or failing in the delicacy which they owe to the rights of other States ... to interpose their good offices for the settlement of differences subsisting between other States, to take the initiative in watching over the peace of Europe, and finally in securing the execution of its treaties in the mode most consonant to the convenience of all the parties.[167]

The Vienna settlement and the Holy Alliance were not, on this view, a system of collective guarantee of the territorial and political *status quo*, or an arrangement for the government of Europe by the major powers, but a form of mediation backed by political primacy, a semi-organized system of good offices combined with powerful political interests.[168]

[165] *Infra*, pp. 325-8.   [166] *Supra*, pp. 305-8.

[167] British Memorandum, October 1818: Albrecht-Carrié, op. cit. 36.

[168] Cf. Protocol of the Conference at Aix-la-Chapelle, para. 4:6 *BFSP* 18; and the Duke of Argyll, cited Satow, *International Congresses* (1920), 1-2. Cf. also Castlereagh's memorandum of 19 June 1821: 8 *BFSP* 1160. The conflict of opinion between Britain, Austria and Prussia is the theme of Holbraad, *The Concert of Europe* (1970); see also Nichols, *The European Pentarchy and the Congress of Vienna, 1822* (1971); Bourquin (1953), 83 *HR* 381-459.

(3) *The League of Nations*

With certain exceptions, the League of Nations did not possess dispositive powers with respect to States or other territorial entities. There was, it is true, a certain political continuity between the Council of Ambassadors of the Powers and the Council of the League.[169] Nevertheless the voting procedure in the Council under Articles 4 and 5 of the Covenant was such that, in general, decisions contrary to the interests of Member States could not be taken without their consent.[170] Protective or dispositive powers were in fact delegated to the League or assumed under the Covenant with respect to the independence of Austria and Hungary,[171] the protection of the Free City of Danzig,[172] the government of the Saar Basin,[173] and the supervision of the Mandate system.[174]

(4) *The United Nations and territorial dispositions*

(i) *General principles : delegated and inherent authority*

The question, adverted to already, whether an international organization can undertake functions not authorized by its constitution but by some extraneous treaty has arisen in relatively acute form in United Nations practice. We must first distinguish three categories of 'United Nations acts': that is, acts pursuant to the Charter; acts not illegal under the Charter, the authority to perform which derives from extrinsic delegation; and acts not authorized by the Charter, but which States members may perform individually or collectively and have chosen to perform in the course of proceedings of the United Nations. For example, the admission of Libya in 1955 was an act pursuant to the Charter; the establishment of Libya by the General Assembly under Article 23 and Annex XI of the Italian Peace Treaty was

---

[169] Albania had argued before the Assembly that the League was successor to the European concert of nations, and thus had power to delimit Albanian frontiers, a contention rejected unanimously on 2 October 1921. See *Monastery of St. Naoum Case*, Ser. B No. 9 (1924), 10.

[170] For voting procedure in the exercise of dispositive functions see *Interpretation of the Treaty of Lausanne*, Ser. B No. 12 (1925) discussed *infra*, p. 346 in its application to the Mandate system.

[171] Versailles, Art. 80; Saint-Germain, Art. 88 (Austria); Trianon, Art. 73 (Hungary).

[172] Versailles, Arts. 102–3; *supra*, pp. 163–5.

[173] Versailles, Arts. 49; *supra*, p. 160.

[174] *Infra*, Chapter 13.

(subject to what will be said below)[175] an act performed under delegated authority; whilst the recognition of the new State, even if it had been performed by unanimous resolution under United Nations auspices, would have been an act in the third category, an act of individual members, not an act of the organization itself at all. Acts in the first category will always be acts of the Organization, and expenses incurred in doing them will be 'expenses of the Organization' under Article 17. Acts in the third category, whatever their legal effect, will never be acts of the Organization, nor will expenses incurred by 'expenses of the Organization'. But it appears to be the case that acts in category 2 ('delegated' or 'extramural' functions) may sometimes be 'acts' (and thus involve 'expenses') of the Organization, depending on the relation they bear to the purposes of the United Nations.[176]

These questions of acceptance by the United Nations of delegated dispositive authority were discussed, albeit obliquely, by Judge Lauterpacht in his separate opinion in the *Voting Procedure Case*.[177] There the question was the voting procedure to be adopted by the General Assembly in carrying out the supervision of the South West Africa Mandate, authority to do which had been accepted by the Court in the *Status of South West Africa Case*.[178] The Majority Opinion chose merely to interpret the phrase 'degree of supervision' in the *Status Case*[179] as extending to substance only and not procedure, on the ground, *inter alia*, that the General Assembly was bound to adopt the voting procedure provided for it under the Charter.[180] They did not however go on to argue the crucial point whether, on this assumption, the Court in 1950 had been correct in allowing the Assembly to exercise Mandate functions, a point which could not be answered merely by interpretation of that decision. Moreover, if the General Assembly could not have altered its voting procedure in order to carry out delegated functions, it might have seemed equally arguable that it could not carry out

---

[175] *Infra*, p. 331.
[176] This formulation follows from the *Expenses Opinion* I.C.J. Rep. 1962 p. 151, 167–178; cf. the subtly different view of Judge Fitzmaurice, sep. op., 205, 214n., 215.
[177] I.C.J. Rep. 1955 p. 67.
[178] I.C.J. Rep. 1950 p. 128.
[179] Ibid. 138.
[180] I.C.J. Rep. 1955 p. 67, 74–5; Judge Basdevant, 82.

delegated functions (that is, functions unauthorized by the Charter) at all.[181]

Judge Lauterpacht, on the other hand, was more careful:

it cannot be said, by way of an absolute rule, that in no circumstances may the General Assembly act by a system of voting other than that laid down by the Charter . . . On the other hand . . . it does not seem to me permissible . . . to hold that a modification of the system of voting is permitted every time when the Organization acts under a treaty other than its own constitutional Charter. The correct rule seems to lie half-way between these two solutions. the available practice and considerations of utility point to the justification of a rule which recognizes in this matter a measure of elasticity not inconsistent with the fundamental structure of the Organization. Within these limits, it is in my view a sound legal proposition that such modification is permissible under the terms of a general treaty, in the general international interest, and in relation to institutions and arrangements partaking of an international status—in particular, in cases in which the General Assembly acts in substitution for a body which has hitherto fulfilled the functions in question.[182]

It seems permissible to extrapolate from this passage a similar principle relating to delegated functions in general: that is, that the United Nations may undertake such functions provided that they come within the general purposes of the Organization and that their exercise is not 'inconsistent with the fundamental structure of the Organization'. Such functions, if we accept the Majority's reasoning in the *Expenses Case*,[183] will be not only 'acts' but will result, where appropriate, in 'expenses' of the Organization.

The argument may be summarized as follows: where an organ of the United Nations performs an act pursuant to and *intra vires* the Charter, that act is an act of the United Nations for all purposes. Where an act is not illegal (that is, not forbidden by the Charter, or in Judge Lauterpacht's terms not 'contrary to the fundamental structure of the United Nations') and is authorized by the appropriate organ by its normal voting procedure, that

---

[181] The Majority Opinion in the *Voting Procedure Case* relies essentially on the proposition that the Assembly possessed Mandate functions pursuant to the Charter, rather than by delegation: *infra*, p. 351.

[182] I.C.J. Rep. 1955 p. 67, 111–12. But cf. Judge Fitzmaurice (diss.), *Namibia Case* I.C.J. Rep. 1971 p. 6, 285–9, where the effect of Judge Lauterpacht's Opinion is misstated.

[183] But cf. Brownlie, *Principles*, 680–2; Gross (1963), 17 *Int. Org.* 1–35.

act will be an act of the Organization, provided that it comes within the purposes of the United Nations under Articles 1 and 2.[184] As will be seen, United Nations practice in the area of delegated functions supports these propositions.[185]

The next question, in the context of dispositions by United Nations organs, must be the extent of dispositive authority possessed by those organs under the Charter. This is important both in itself and in relation to the problem of delegated power: for if the exercise of dispositive authority by United Nations organs is not merely not authorized but by some implication prohibited under the Charter, then equally exercise of dispositive power by delegation must be regarded as prohibited. The two relevant organs, of course, are the General Assembly and the Security Council.

(a) *General Assembly*

It is, first of all, clear that the Assembly has no general powers of decision making: with certain exceptions its powers are recommendatory and advisory only. However, there are exceptions to this, and in our context powers of admission to membership (which bind non-consenting members to a code of conduct *vis-à-vis* the newly admitted entity), and in particular termination of Trusteeship status,[186] demonstrate that, although the Assembly possesses no general dispositive powers under the Charter, it is not necessarily contrary to its 'constitutional structure', in certain circumstances, for such powers to be conferred upon it.[187]

(b) *The Security Council*

The powers of the Security Council in relation to international peace and security are much more extensive. Its powers under Chapter VII would seem to be limited only by the discretion, and the voting procedure, of the Security Council in applying them. However Judge Fitzmaurice was again prepared to imply a limitation concerning 'territorial rights'. In his view:

Even when acting under Chapter VII of the Charter itself, the Security

---

[184] But cf. Judge Fitzmaurice's stricter view, *Namibia Opinion* I.C.J. Rep. 1971 p. 6, 284–290.

[185] *Infra*, pp. 329–33.

[186] *Infra*, pp. 341–4.

[187] But cf. Judge Fitzmaurice's conclusion: I.C.J. Rep. 1971 p. 6, 283: 'The Assembly has no power to terminate any kind of administration over any kind of territory.'

Council has no power to abrogate or alter territorial rights, whether of sovereignty or administration. Even a wartime occupation of a country or territory cannot operate to do that. It must await the peace settlement. This is a principle of international law that is as well established as any there can be,—and the Security Council is as much subject to it (for the United Nations is itself a subject of international law) as any of its individual member States are. The Security Council might, after making the necessary determinations under Article 39 ... order the occupation of a country or piece of territory *in order to restore peace and security*, but it could not thereby, or as part of that operation, abrogate or alter territorial rights;—and the right to administer a mandatory territory is a territorial right without which the territory could not be governed or the mandate be operated. It was to keep the peace, not to change the world order, that the Security Council was set up.[188]

It can be admitted that annexations of territory may not be effected during hostilities, but transfers of territory may take place either by consent of parties affected before a formal peace settlement (and the Security Council would be competent, if such transfer was regarded as necessary to 'maintain or restore international peace and security', to require and enforce it), or by the creation in compliance with the principle of self-determination of a new State in the territory affected. The point is that such action would seem to be fully authorized by the terms of Chapter VII;[189] and that the exercise of dispositive authority by the Council cannot therefore be said to be contrary to the 'structure' of the Charter. Whether it would be contrary to the 'purposes and principles of the United Nations' would of course depend on the specific case. Certain instances of territorial disposition by United Nations organs will now be discussed.

(ii) Functions pursuant to the peace treaties

By contrast with the extensive delegations to the League, only a few powers were delegated to the United Nations pursuant to the Second World War settlements. For our purposes two cases are relevant.

(a) Trieste

As has been seen, the Free City of Trieste, created under

---

[188] *Namibia Opinion* I.C.J. Rep. 1971 p. 6, 294.

[189] The International Court has consistently favoured a liberal interpretation of U.N. powers: Lauterpacht, *Development*, 274–7.

Article 21 of the Italian Peace Treaty, was to have its 'integrity and independence ... assured by the Security Council ...'[190] The Australian representative argued that the Charter did not authorize the Council:

> to give any general guarantee of integrity and independence to a particular territory ... Before the Council may act, there must be a dispute or a situation which might lead to international friction or give rise to a dispute or a threat to the peace, or a breach of the peace. These powers operate independently of any peace treaties drawn up by the Council of Foreign Ministers, and they operate in respect of all territories, including Trieste.
>
> The proposals now before the Security Council, however, are to the effect that the Council should accept various new responsibilities and, in particular, the responsibility of assuring the integrity and independence of the Free Territory. The acceptance of such responsibility is clearly not authorized by the Charter.[191]

This view was not accepted by a majority of the Council: various Members emphasized the connection between the Trieste problem and international peace and security,[192] and the practical necessity for the Council to co-operate in reaching a solution to the Trieste problem.[193] The Secretary-General went further, and argued for a general competence in the Council to perform acts not coming under specific Articles of the Charter, but incidental to the responsibility for international peace and security—always of course 'subject to the purposes and principles of the United Nations'.[194] Jurisdiction was thus accepted:[195] however the Security Council was unable to agree on the choice of a Governor[196] and the Trieste problem was at length settled by bilateral negotiations without Council participation.[197]

(b) *Disposition of Italian Colonies in Africa*[198]

As we have seen, the Italian colonies in Africa had been placed

---

[190] 49 *UNTS* 3, Annex VII; *supra*, p. 161.

[191] *SCOR* 89th mtg., 7 Jan. 1947, 5–7; cited Kahng, *Law, Politics and the Security Council* (1964), 75–7.

[192] France, U.S.S.R.: ibid. 15–6, 9.

[193] U.S.A.: ibid. 11.

[194] *SCOR* 91st mtg., 10 Jan. 1947, 44–5; Kahng, op. cit. 77.

[195] Ibid. 60 (10:1 (Aust.)).

[196] *S.C. Rep. 1946–51*, 314; *S.C. Rep. 1952–5*, 110, 134–5.

[197] *Supra*, p. 162.

[198] Whiteman, 3 *Digest* 4–32; Ydit, *Internationalized Territories*, 68–71; Jessup, *Birth of Nations* (1974), 211–54.

at the disposal of the four Allied Powers by Article 23 of the Italian Peace Treaty: such disposal was to be determined within a year of the Treaty coming into force. The four Powers failed to agree on the disposition of the territories,[199] and in accordance with Annex XI paragraph (3) of the Treaty the matter was 'referred to the General Assembly of the United Nations for a recommendation, and the Four Powers agree[d] to accept the recommendation and to take appropriate measures for giving effect to it.'[200]

The Assembly recommended that Libya should be constituted 'an independent and sovereign State ... not later than 1 January 1952';[201] that Italian Somaliland 'shall be an independent sovereign State ... at the end of ten years from the date of the approval of a Trusteeship Agreement by the General Assembly', and that, in the meantime, the territory 'be placed under the International Trusteeship System with Italy as the Administering Authority';[202] and that Eritrea's disposition should await a report of a Commission, appointed to consider, *inter alia*, the wishes of its inhabitants, and Ethiopian interests (especially its 'legitimate need for adequate access to the sea'.)[203] Although there was considerable debate over the disposition of particular territories, it was not contended that the exercise by the Assembly of the power of effective decision was in any way improper or *ultra vires*. Expenses incurred in carrying out the recommendations were treated as expenses of the Organization charged on the general fund.[204] On the other hand, both the terms of Annex XI and the subsequent documentation make it clear that the technical power of disposition remained with the four 'Administering Powers': the United Nations recommendation only bound them by virtue of their prior agreement.[205] In fact Resolution 289A (IV) was duly executed according to its terms,

---

[199] Whiteman, 3 *Digest* 6–14.

[200] 49 *UNTS* 214.

[201] G.A. Res. 289A (IV), Pt. A (49–0:9).

[202] Ibid., Pt. B (48–7:3).

[203] Ibid., Pt. C (47–5:6). Res. 289A (IV), 21 Nov. 1947, was passed as a whole by 48–1 (Ethiopia):9.

[204] Ibid., Pt. D, para. 2.

[205] Cf. the case of Palestine in 1947, when the administering Power's reference of the matter to the Assembly was certainly sufficient to validate Res. 181 (II) *qua* recommendation; although the lack of further agreement probably prevented it from having, in the circumstances, more than recommendatory force.

by the Administering Powers and the United Nations working in concert.[206]

(iii) *Functions pursuant to the Mandate and Trusteeship Systems*

The functions assumed by United Nations organs with respect to the dispositive aspects of the Mandate and Trusteeship systems are discussed in the following chapter.

(iv) *Other cases*

(a) *West Irian*

Although Indonesia had been granted independence by the Netherlands in 1949,[207] the latter took the view that West New Guinea (West Irian) had not been included in the grant, and its status and disposition thus became the subject of a lengthy dispute between the two States. In 1962 it was agreed that, subject to the consent of the General Assembly, 'the Netherlands (would) transfer administration of the territory to a United Nations Temporary Executive Authority established by and under the jurisdiction of the Secretary-General' which would in turn 'transfer the administration to Indonesia in accordance with Article XII.'[208] The United Nations Administrator was to have full authority 'to administer the territory for the period of the U.N.T.E.A. administration in accordance with the terms of the present agreement'.[209] All the costs of the administration were to be met by Indonesia and the Netherlands jointly:[210] the two governments were also to furnish consular protection for inhabitants of the territory.[211] General Assembly approval of the

[206] A U.N. Commissioner for Libya was appointed; a constitution drawn up; boundaries delimited; and economic and financial arrangements made. Libya became independent on 24 Dec. 1951: G.A. Res. 515 (VI), 1 Feb. 1952 (53–9:0). See Pelt, *Libyan Independence and the United Nations* (1970). Italian Somaliland was placed under a ten-year trusteeship, approved on 2 Dec. 1950: G.A. Res. 442 (V) (44–6:0). Ethiopia argued that the agreement was improperly concluded in that, as a 'State directly concerned' under Art. 79, Ethiopia had not been consulted: A/C.4/L. 102, rejected 34–6:7: *GAOR* 5th sess., 4th Ctee., 176th mtg. Eritrea was eventually (on 11 Dec. 1952) federated as an 'autonomous unit . . . under the sovereignty of the Ethiopian Crown': G.A. Res. 390 (V), 2 Dec. 1950 (45–5:6); G.A. Res. 617 (VII), 17 Dec. 1952 (51–0:5).

[207] *Supra*, p. 258.

[208] 437 *UNTS* 273, Art. II. See Czerapowicz, *International Territorial Authority: Leticia and West New Guinea* (1975); Bowett, *United Nations Forces*, 255–61.

[209] Art. V. Cf. *Aide-Mémoire* concerning the Modalities of the Transfer of Authority over West New Guinea: 537 *UNTS* 310.

[210] Agreement, Annex III.

[211] Ibid., Art. XXIV, Annex II.

delegation of authority to the Secretary General was duly given,[212] and the Temporary Executive Authority took over responsibility for the territory on 1 October 1962. Authority was eventually and without disturbances handed over to Indonesia after 1 May 1963. Although other aspects of the West Irian controversy raise serious questions of legality and propriety,[213] it was not contended, nor in view of the peace-keeping nature of the United Nations' role was it arguable, that participation in the transfer of authority was *ultra vires*.

(b) *Jerusalem*

Under Part III of the General Assembly's partition resolution for Palestine, the City of Jerusalem was to be established 'as a *corpus separatum* under a special international regime ... administered by the United Nations ...'[214] Detailed administration was to be delegated to the Trusteeship Council, which was to draw up a Statute for the City. The 'special international regime' never came into effect, for reasons described elsewhere.[215]

(v) *Conclusion*

No other significant powers of territorial administration or disposition have been delegated to United Nations organs since 1945. The record, such as it is, demonstrates that the difficulties with such delegations derive not from any assumed incompetence of the United Nations to exercise dispositive powers, but from the political feasibility of the particular situation.

12.5   THE NOTION OF 'INTERNATIONAL DISPOSITIVE POWERS'

Although this review of the practice since 1815 has demonstrated the diversity and importance of the various issues grouped here under the rubric of international dispositive powers, it may be conceded that there are no very specific primary rules or competences in this area, apart from general principles of consent

[212] G.A. Res. 1752 (XVII), 21 Sept. 1962 (88–1 (Senegal):14).
[213] *Infra*, p. 382, n. 132.
[214] G.A. Res. 181 (II), 29 Nov. 1947.
[215] See Bovis, *The Jerusalem Question 1917–1968* (1971); E. Lauterpacht, *Jerusalem and the Holy Places* (1968); Blum, *The Juridical Status of Jerusalem* (1974); Jones (1968), 33 *Law & Cont. Problems* 169–82.

and the like. Indeed, the principle of consent, as it applies to States as the primary international actors, virtually ensures that this is so. But in a fundamentally decentralized society, the exercise of competences of this sort is distinctive, and they may well continue to play an important role in international relations. This has certainly been the case with the specific regimes considered in the following two Chapters.

13. Mandates and Trust Territories

13.1 GENERAL

IN THE previous Chapter brief reference was made to the Mandate system, established by the Principal Allied and Associated Powers in conjunction with the League of Nations, under Article 22 of the Covenant.[1] The Mandate system was replaced after World War II by the International Trusteeship System under Chapters XII and XIII of the Charter. The two systems had the same general aims: in particular the encouragement of the 'well-being and development' of the peoples of the various territories, and of their 'progressive development towards self-government or independence',[2] although this second aim was only implicit in the Covenant. Both accepted the principle of the international responsibility of the administering State for carrying out these aims, 'securities for performance' being provided in the Covenant and the Charter, and in the various individual agreements. The systems thus constituted a rejection of annexation of former German, Turkish, and Italian colonies, and the assertion of international interest at a much earlier stage in the process towards independence than the international law of the time otherwise allowed.[3] In particular, the principle of self-determination, as the International Court has twice explicitly affirmed, was made applicable to Mandates and Trust territories, which therefore constitute, as it were, the primary type of self-determination territory.[4] With the termination of the Australian Trusteeship for New Guinea,[5] the ordinary trusteeship system is, for practical purposes, at an end.[6] There remain however two

---

[1] *Supra*, p. 314.
[2] Charter, Art. 76b.
[3] *Status of South West Africa Case* I.C.J. Rep. 1950, p. 128, 131.
[4] *Namibia Opinion; Western Sahara Opinion, supra*, p. 96.
[5] For details see (1975) 49 *ALJ* 695–6; (1975) 79 *RGDIP* 1184–7.
[6] Although from time to time various proposals have been made for trusteeships under Charter Art. 77(1)(c) ('territories voluntarily placed under the system by States responsible for their administration'), no such new trusteeships have been created. For details of Mandated and Trust Territories 1919–77, see Appendix 2.

territories: South-West Africa (Namibia), the Mandate for which was revoked by General Assembly Resolution 2145 (XXI) in 1966, but which is still the subject of contention between the United Nations and South Africa;[7] and the strategic Trusteeship of the Pacific Islands, negotiations for the termination of which are continuing.[8]

The Namibia controversy apart, the details of the two systems are now of relatively minor importance.[9] However, some discussion of the contentious issues of disposition, revocation, and termination is called for, both by the continuing disputes or potential disputes over the two remaining territories, and because of the light this may throw on more general issues of international territorial disposition.[10]

[7] See Whiteman, 1 *Digest* 706–31, 13 *Digest* 756–8; Dugard, *The South West Africa/Namibia Dispute* (1973), and works cited *infra*.

[8] Negotiations for the future status of the territory as a whole have not resulted in agreement: see Green (1974), 9 *Texas ILJ* 175–204; Metalski (1974), 5 *Cal. Western ILJ* 162–83; Heine, *Micronesia at the Crossroads* (1974). As a result, the U.S. has proposed a Commonwealth of the Northern Mariana Islands in Political Union with the U.S.: see 14 *ILM* 344; (1975) 79 *RGDIP* 1128–32; (1976) 70 *AJ* 557–8. The population of the Northern Marianas approved the Covenant by plebiscite on 17 June 1975; and the Covenant was approved by Act of Congress of 24 Mar. 1976: 15 *ILM* 651. But the U.S. proposes not to bring the Covenant into full force until the termination of the Trusteeship Agreement for the Trust Territory as a whole, in the 1980–1. See *U.S. Digest* 1973, 59–62; ibid. 1974, 54–63; ibid. 1975, 97–104; ibid. 1976, 56–61. Cf. also Bergsman (1976) 6 *Cal. Western ILJ* 382–411; McHenry, *Micronesia: Trust Betrayed* (1975); Lucchini, [1975] *AFDI* 155–74; Erstad (1976), 50 *Temple L.Q.* 58–92; Dempsey (1976), 9 *NYUJILP* 277–302; and see further Whiteman, 1 *Digest* 769–839; de Smith, *Micro-States and Micronesia* (1970), 119, 188.

[9] The literature on Mandates and Trust Territories is voluminous. See especially Wright, *Mandates under the League of Nations* (1930); Toussaint, *The Trusteeship System of the United Nations* (1956); Thullen, *Problems of the Trusteeship System* (1964); Duncan Hall, *Mandates, Dependences and Trusteeship* (1948); Véicopoulos, *Traité des territoires dépendants* (1960, 1971, 2 vols.); Chowdhuri, *International Mandates and Trusteeship Systems; A Comparative Study* (1955), and works cited *infra*. And cf. Verhoeven, *Reconnaissance*, 21–9.

[10] There was an extensive debate over the location of 'sovereignty' in Mandates and Trust Territories: see Oppenheim (8th edn.) I, 213–15, 235–9; Brownlie, *Principles*, 181–182; Wright, *Mandates under the League*, 90–2; Toussaint, *The Trusteeship System of the United Nations* (1956), 319–39; Leeper (1951), 49 *Michigan LR* 1199—210; Roche (1954), 58 *RGDIP* 399–437; Whiteman, 1 *Digest* 635–50. The better view is that the concept was inapplicable to international regimes of divided competences such as the Mandate and Trusteeship systems: see esp. Judge McNair, sep. op., *Status Opinion* I.C.J. Rep. 1950, p. 128, 150. Thus the grant of a Mandate was not a cession of territory to the administering power: ibid. 132 (Majority Opinion). The Trusteeship Agreement for Somaliland expressly vested 'sovereignty' in the people of the territory: 118 *UNTS* 225, Art. 24. This probably expressed in strong terms the proposition that the inhabitants were entitled to self-determination in respect of the territory.

13.2   TERMINATION OF MANDATES AND TRUSTEESHIPS

(1) *Termination of Mandates*

(*i*) *During the period of the League*

Neither the Mandate Agreements nor Article 22 of the Covenant contained express provision for the termination of Mandates, though Article 22 did state that 'the degree of authority, control, or administration to be exercised by the Mandatory shall, if not previously agreed upon by Members of the League, be explicitly defined in each case by the Council.' In fact only four Mandates—the 'A' Mandates for Iraq, Syria, the Lebanon, and Transjordan—were terminated by independence before the dissolution of the League in 1946, and of these only the Mandate for Iraq was actually terminated by agreement between the new State, the Mandatory and the Council.[11] The history of the termination of the other three Mandates is of considerable interest, both in itself and as illustrating the nature of the Mandate regime.

On 28 September 1941 General Catroux proclaimed the independence of Syria and Lebanon;[12] and governmental authority was gradually transferred to local governments over a period of some years.[13] These declarations notwithstanding, the French government, on the whole, took the view that the Mandates remained formally in existence until terminated by the League Council, and that the continued existence of the Mandates justified continued French rights with respect to Syria and Lebanon,[14] including the right to impose a treaty of future relations. The United States withheld recognition of independence until September 1944, but at no stage regarded the non-termination of the Mandate as a relevant consideration. Rather, the view was consistently taken that the independence of the two States, provided it was sufficiently effective, could be recognized as consistent with the object and purpose of the Mandate, notwithstanding the absence of formal termination by the

---

[11] *LNOJ* (1932), 1212, 1347; Bentwich (1930), 11 *BY* 193–5; Wright (1931), 25 *AJ* 436–46. See also, *supra*, p. 57, n. 132.

[12] *USFR* 1941/III, 786.

[13] *Supra*, pp. 66–8.

[14] *USFR* 1941/III, 790–1, 809; ibid., 1942/IV, 616; ibid., 1943/IV, 956 ('non-recognition by most foreign States justified in itself a continuing exercise of the mandatory power'); ibid., 1944/V, 785, 811.

League.[15] The same view was expressed, in strong terms, by Syria.[16] The British government attempted to mediate between the United States and France, and in the process took a somewhat equivocal view on the matter of termination:[17] however British action, and in particular the ultimatum of May 1945,[18] was quite inconsistent with the retention by France of substantial authority over Syria or Lebanon.

In the event, no formal League action was taken to terminate the Mandate, which disappeared 'with graceless reluctance'.[19] No treaty with France formally terminating the French administration was concluded, and the League Assembly at its final session merely welcomed 'the termination of the mandated status of Syria, the Lebanon, and Transjordan, which have, since the last Session of the Assembly [i.e. in 1939], become independent members of the world community'.[20] Syria and Lebanon both became original members of the United Nations.

The same position was taken by both the United States and the United Kingdom when the independence of Transjordan was recognized by the conclusion of a treaty of alliance on 22 March 1946.[21] In an *Aide-Mémoire* the British Embassy stated that objections to the form by which Transjordan acceded to independence were

answered by the fact that (a) their intention to grant independence to Transjordan was announced at an early session of the United Nations Assembly in London, where it was not challenged by any delegate, and (b) that the final assembly of the League of Nations passed a resolution approving and welcoming this action . . . In the light of the above and of the welcome given by the United Nations Assembly in January to the announcement of His Majesty's Government's intention to recognise

---

[15] Ibid., 1942/IV, 647–8, 665; ibid., 1943/IV, 966, 987, 1007 ('no useful purpose would be served by an academic debate on the juridical technicalities of this complex situation. The validity of the French thesis is dubious, at best, and for practical purpose the League mandate must be regarded as being in suspense'); ibid., 1944/V, 774, 782, 785, 795–7; ibid., 1945/VIII, 1197.

[16] Ibid., 1944/V, 786.

[17] Cf. ibid. 1941/III, 802, with ibid. 1942/IV, 646. See also 1943/IV, 900; 1945/VIII, 1041; *H.C. Deb.* Vol. 393 col. 157, 27 Oct. 1943.

[18] *USFR* 1945/VIII, 1124.

[19] Longrigg, *Syria and Lebanon under French Mandate* (1958), 317.

[20] *LNOJ* 21st Ass. (1946) Sp. Supp. No. 194, 58. Cf. the Franco–Lebanese Agreement of 24 Jan. 1948; 173 *UNTS* 101, and the Franco–Syrian Financial Agreement of 7 Feb. 1949; Rollet, 199.

[21] 146 *BFSP* 461. There is no reference in the treaty to termination of the Mandate.

Transjordan as an independent State . . . His Majesty's Government feel that, in so far as general international approval is required for setting up Transjordan as an independent State, such approval has in fact been manifestly given.[22]

The legality of this process was subsequently also challenged by Poland in the Security Council when Transjordan's application for United Nations membership was under discussion,[23] although the Polish representative did not appear to contend that Transjordan's independence was a legal impossibility without the consent of the League Council or conversion to trusteeship. Rather he doubted whether Transjordan had in fact attained independence, and claimed that the consent of the General Assembly was a condition precedent to any such independence. Great Britain contended that such consent had in fact been given.[24] In any case Jordan was eventually admitted to membership in 1955.

It is clear, then, that the three Mandates were effectively and validly terminated without the consent of the appropriate organ of the League. Several explanations for this are possible.

It may be that 'A' Mandates, having already 'provisional independence', were subject to different procedures regarding termination, though it is difficult to accept that this could be so, in view of the fact that Article 22 of the Covenant applied equally to all classes of Mandate.[25] The better view would appear to be that approval by the Council was not a condition precedent to valid termination of a Mandate where such approval, for whatever reason, could not be obtained. Termination of a Mandate involved compliance with the basic purpose of the Mandate,[26] and a determination of political fact—that effective

---

[22] *USFR* 1946/VII, 799–800. The U.S. view was that 'formal termination of the mandate . . . would be generally recognized upon the admission of [Trans-Jordan] into the United Nations as a fully independent country': ibid. 798.

[23] *SCOR* 1st yr., 2nd sess. Suppl. No. 4, 70–1 (S/133); Higgins, *Development*, 30–1.

[24] In particular by G.A. Res. 11(I), 9 Feb. 1946, clause 3 (adopted unanimously) noting with approval the Mandatory's intention to grant independence to Transjordan.

[25] This was the U.S. view in 1946: *USFR* 1946/VII, 797. But the principle of self-determination, though more immediately relevant to the 'A' Mandates, was not confined to them.

[26] Throughout the Syria–Lebanon conflict the U.S. emphasized that the independence of the two States was a right recognized and guaranteed by the Mandate: cf. ibid., 1943/IV, 1008.

self-government existed.[27] In default of Council approval, recognition by individual States and appropriate action by the General Assembly was regarded as sufficient validly to terminate the Mandate. The propriety to this view would seem to be incontrovertible; otherwise the dissolution of the League would have deprived the mandated people of the self-government of independence which it was a purpose of the Mandate system to guarantee.[28]

In one other case—viz. the loss by Japan of its right to administer the Pacific Islands Mandate—dispositive elements of a Mandate were altered. What was terminated there was not the Mandate but the authority of the Mandatory: the matter is closer to revocation than to termination, and is dealt with below.[29] Once again no League approval for the change was forthcoming: the matter was left for the United Nations to solve.

(ii)   After the dissolution of the League

Only two Mandates survived the dissolution of the League without being transferred to the Trusteeship system—Palestine and South-West Africa. With regard to both, the General Assembly unequivocally asserted its authority, the Mandatories having each made requests about the future disposition of their respective territories. Assembly action with respect to Palestine has been referred to already:[30] it is clear that, at the least, Resolution 181 (II) was effective to terminate the Mandate for Palestine, although its relevance for the future disposition of the territory was disputed.

The General Assembly also refused a South African request for permission to annex South-West Africa,[31] and instead, when it became clear that the territory would not be brought under trusteeship, asserted authority to carry out the supervisory functions of the Mandate. In this it was upheld by the International Court in the *Status Opinion*. The Court held unanimously that the Mandate had survived the dissolution of

---

[27] Cf. Report of P.M.C., June 1931 (Iraq): Briggs, *Law of Nations*, 74–5; discussed by Hales (1937), 23 *Grotius ST* 85, 117.

[28] To the same effect, Duncan Hall, op. cit. 265–6; Longrigg, op. cit. 362. See further, *infra*, p. 350 ff.

[29] *Infra*, p. 347.

[30] *Supra*, p. 331.

[31] G.A. Res. 65(I), 14 Dec. 1946 (37–0:9).

the League and by 12 votes to 2 (Judges McNair and Read dissenting) that the supervisory functions were to be exercised by the Assembly.[32] The case was not directly concerned with termination, as distinct from supervision, functions, but in the light of United Nations practice, the rationale behind the Opinion, and the South African request for permission to annex, there can be little doubt that the Assembly had the authority to terminate the Mandate. The extent of this authority will be discussed further in the context of revocation.[33]

(iii) By transfer to Trusteeship

All the 'B' Mandates, and all but one of the 'C' Mandates, were in fact terminated by transfer to the Trusteeship system. Yet again no League Council approval for this disposition was forthcoming, though the League Assembly did 'take note' of the new system.[34] Approval of the new arrangements was a matter, in practice, of the General Assembly acting with the Mandatory.[35] The validity in principle of this transfer from Mandate to Trusteeship system was never challenged.[36] The matter is now of little interest, except that it emphasizes again the role of the Charter and the General Assembly in the winding-up of the old system, and in the maintenance in various ways of the principles embodied in both old and new.

(2) Termination of Trusteeships

Each Trusteeship was terminated by agreement between the Assembly and the Administering Authority, and in most cases after plebiscites under United Nations' authority had been conducted. The matter has been discussed elsewhere.[37]

---

[32] I.C.J. Rep. 1950, p. 128, 136–7; 155–62 (Judge McNair); 169 (Judge Read).

[33] *Infra*, pp. 350–5.

[34] Assembly Resolution of 17 Apr. 1946: *LNOJ* Sp. Supp. No. 194, 254. For the arguments from rejection of the 'Chinese' draft resolution purporting to transfer supervisory functions to the U.N. see Judge Jessup, diss., *South-West Africa Cases (Second Phase)* I.C.J. Rep. 1966, p. 6, 347–8; *contra* Judge Fitzmaurice, diss., *Namibia Opinion* I.C.J. Rep. 1971, p. 6, 247–9.

[35] Cf. Charter, Arts. 79, 85 (1).

[36] The term 'States directly concerned' in Art. 79 did however lead to controversy: Parry (1950), 27 *BY* 164–85.

[37] Whiteman, 1 *Digest* 897–911, 13 *Digest* 679–90; Toussaint, op. cit. 125–42; Marston (1969), 18 *ICLQ* 1–40.

(3) *Legal effects of termination*

One issue in the *Northern Cameroons Case*[38] was the legal effect of termination of trusteeship under Chapter XII. In its application under Article 19, the jurisdictional clause of the Trusteeship Agreement, the Republic of Cameroon (formerly the French Trust Territory of the Cameroons) alleged that the United Kingdom had failed to lead the peoples of Northern Cameroons (who had voted in a plebiscite for union with Nigeria rather than Cameroon) to self-government according to Article 76(b) of the Charter; and in particular that the administrative union of the Northern Cameroons with Nigeria before independence was in breach of the Trusteeship Agreement.[39] The Court held that the action was inadmissible irrespective of jurisdiction: 'the proper limits of its judicial function do not permit it to entertain the claims submitted to it, with a view to a decision having the authority of *res judicata* between the Republic of Cameroon and the United Kingdom. Any judgment which the Court might pronounce would be without object.'[40] The reason why the Court could not pronounce a judgment 'capable of effective application' was that the General Assembly in approving Resolution 1608(XV) had disposed of all the legal issues—at least, those relating to the basic trusteeship obligations as distinct from individual rights of United Nations members, such as for example to equality of treatment. The effect was that 'no question of actual legal rights [was] involved'.[41]

It was to the General Assembly of the United Nations that the Republic of Cameroon directed the argument and the plea for a declaration that the plebiscite was null and void. In paragraphs numbered 2 and 3 of resolution 1608(XV) the General Assembly rejected the Cameroon plea. Whatever the motivation of the General Assembly in reaching the conclusions contained in those paragraphs, whether or not it was acting wholly on the political plane and without the Court finding it necessary to consider here whether or not the General Assembly based

---

[38] I.C.J. Rep. 1963, p. 15.

[39] A similar argument had been rejected by the General Assembly: *GAOR* 15th Sess., Supp. No. 16A; Doc. A/PV. 994, 77 (64–23:10).

[40] I.C.J. Rep. 1963, p. 15, 38.

[41] Ibid. 37.

its decision on a correct interpretation of the Trusteeship Agreement, there is no doubt . . . that the resolution had definitive legal effect . . .[42]

Three basic issues were involved at this stage of the case: whether the Republic of Cameroons had any legal rights in the due administration of the British Cameroons under the Trusteeship; whether such rights (if they existed) survived the termination of the Trusteeship; and, thirdly, whether, even if such rights existed and survived, the Court ought in the circumstances to adjudicate upon them. Although the *dispositif* of the Majority Judgment appears to be phrased in terms of the third alternative, it is quite clear that the decision is based on the second. The Court held that, even if legal rights in the general administration of the Trusteeship existed prior to April 1961, termination of the Trusteeship 'had definitive legal effect' as regards any such rights. As to the first point, the majority expressed no clear opinion.[43] As to the third point, it is again unclear what the majority would have done if it had held that the Cameroon had subsisting legal rights in the Trusteeship Agreement. The difficulty was that any judgment potentially affected a State not a party to the proceedings before the Court, so that presumably the Court must have asked that third State (Nigeria) whether it wished to intervene, and if not, dismissed the case for lack of jurisdiction. But in fact the case was dismissed on grounds of inadmissibility.[44]

It follows that in determining a Trusteeship Agreement the General Assembly Resolution has a more than recommendatory effect, and belongs to that category of matters over which the Assembly possesses actual 'executive' authority. It may be asked how this is so, given the incapacity of the Assembly in most areas to create legal obligations for States. The answer would seem to be that the Assembly's function here is a determinative one—

---

[42] Ibid. 32; Judge Wellington Koo, 57. Judge Fitzmaurice's opinion is on different grounds: if individual States had rights in the system, no General Assembly resolution could determine them (120). But they have no such rights (108 ff.)

[43] Cf. *infra*, p. 366, n. 47.

[44] That G.A. Res. 1608 (XV) had definitive legal effect is not to deny that the Court was seised of a legal issue—*viz.* the propriety of the administrative union of the Northern Cameroons province with Nigeria. But that legal issue was 'remote from reality' and could have, at the time of judgment, no legal consequences. Hence the inadmissibility. For the interesting municipal analogy to the *Northern Cameroons Case*, see *Buck* v. *A.G.* [1965] Ch. 745 (C.A.) discussed *supra*, pp. 216–8.

that it is designated by the Charter to decide particular matters of political fact, applying principles of self-determination implicit in the Trusteeship instruments.[45] It is obviously necessary, as Judge Wellington Koo pointed out, that in these matters there be some *finis litium*. The General Assembly, exercising these functions, puts an effective end to the Trusteeship. The territory is then incorporated in or associated with another State ('self-government') or becomes itself independent—in either case a new situation has arisen, the legality of which cannot be open to question.

13.3   REVOCATION OF MANDATES AND TRUSTEESHIPS

(1) *Revocation of Mandates during the period of the League*

It is natural that the question of revocation was not much discussed at the time of the creation of the Mandates system.[46] It cannot however be assumed that because the matter was not dealt with, revocation is legally impossible.[47] On the contrary, considering the notions of 'mandate' and 'trust' it seems more likely that revocation was implicit in the whole system: otherwise a Mandatory guilty of flagrant violation of the whole purpose of the Mandate would go unchecked. In the words of the Privy Council in a somewhat different context, 'certain legal incidents attach *de jure* to the relationship which is constituted by the grant of authority on the one hand . . . and the exercise of that authority by the recipient of it on the other according to his mandate. It is not that this arises out of some unexpressed stipulation: it is annexed to the relationship.'[48] On this view then, in the absence of express or clearly implied exclusion of it, revocation was 'annexed to the relationship' and a legal possibility under the

---

[45] Cf. Brownlie, *Principles*, 176.

[46] But cf. Smuts's original proposal, *The League of Nations—A Practical Suggestion* (1919), reprinted in Hunter Miller, *The Drafting of the Covenant* II, 32: 'in case of any flagrant and prolonged abuse of this trust the population concerned should be able to appeal for redress to the League, who should in a proper case assert its authority to the full, even to the extent of removing the mandate, and entrusting it to some other state, if necessary.'

[47] The arguments against revocability of Mandates are nowhere better put than in Judge Fitzmaurice's dissenting opinion in the *Namibia Case*, I.C.J Rep. 197 p. 6, 264–79. See also Slonim, *South West Africa and the U.N.: an International Mandate in Dispute* (1973).

[48] *In re Southern Rhodesia* [1919] A.C. 211, 214: the quotation in the text is preceded by the passage: 'in the present case . . . their Lordships do not propose to deal with the question referred to them under any terms of art peculiar to municipal law. They desire to take a broader view . . .'

Mandate system. And there was in fact respectable authority during the League period in favour of the existence of a power of revocation for fundamental breach, exercisable by the League Council, although the power was never in fact exercised.[49] The International Court in the *Namibia Case* had little difficulty in assenting to the existence of such a power.[50]

Several problems remain however. There is first of all authority for the view that any power of revocation might inhere in the Principal Allied and Associated Powers in whose favour Germany and Turkey renounced title over their colonial possessions.[51] The arguments against this view are nowhere better expressed than in Judge Jessup's important dissenting judgment in the *South West Africa Cases (Second Phase)*:

the argument that the Principal Allied and Associated Powers had any such residual or reversionary rights is devoid of merit . . . It needs no elaborate demonstration to show that Article 119 of the Treaty of Versailles did not involve a cession of territory to the Allies; the idea of a cession which would have meant even a momentary or technical lodgement of sovereignty over the former German colonies was wholly at variance with the agreed settlement of this colonial problem . . . The Allies acquired the right to allot the mandates and thereafter became *functi officio*. The mandatories were mandatories on behalf of the League and not of the Powers . . .[52]

Given, then, that it was for the Council rather than the five Powers to exercise the power of revocation a problem of voting procedure arises. Since the normal voting procedure in the Council was unanimity, and since non-Council members, parties to disputes before the Council, were entitled to attend, it is arguable that the Council could never have revoked a Mandate without the consent of the Mandatory.

[49] Lauterpacht, *Private Law Sources and Analogies of International Law* (1927), 200–1; Hales, op. cit. 120–2; Wright, *Mandates under the League*, 520–2; Dugard (1968), 62 *AJ* 78–97, and authorities there cited. Cf. also Lauterpacht, 3 *Collected Papers* 29–84, 70–76 (1972).

[50] *Namibia Opinion* I.C.J. Rep. 1971, p. 16, 48–9 (Majority Opinion); 131 (Judge Petrèn), 146 (Judge Onyeama), 210–16 (Judge de Castro). Cf. Judge Fitzmaurice, diss., 275–8.

[51] Judges Spender and Fitzmaurice, joint diss. op., *South-West Africa Cases (First Phase)* I.C.J. Rep. 1962 p. 319, 482 and n.3; cf. Written Statement of the U.S.A., *Pleadings, Status Opinion*, 137–9.

[52] I.C.J. Rep. 1966 p. 6, 421–2: cf. *R.* v. *Christian* [1924] S.Af.L.R. 101, 106 *per* Ross-Innes C.J.

To this, two answers may be given. The Mandatory could have been first expelled from the League under Article 16, paragraph 4, by vote of the Council less the State concerned, upon which the Mandatory's title to vote disappeared. Violation of Article 22 would have been grounds for expulsion.[53] Alternatively it was argued by Judge Lauterpacht in the *Voting Procedure Case* that a 'constitutional convention' had grown up during the existence of the League so that 'the opposing vote of the mandatory State could not in all circumstances adversely affect the required unanimity of the Council . . .'[54] Support for this view was found in *Interpretation of the Treaty of Lausanne*, where the Court applied the *nemo judex* principle to hold parties to a dispute unable to exercise their veto in the Council.[55] Significantly, that too was a case in which the Council was designated to exercise a 'referred' function affecting dispositively the rights of States. Whichever position is taken, it follows that unilateral revocation of a Mandate by the League Council was a legal possibility.

Thirdly, there is the question whether independent judicial determination of the fundamental breach of the Mandate was a condition precedent to revocation by the political organ.[56] In the normal case such a determination would have been desirable in the interests of fairness: there are, however, several considerations which suggest that it was not imperatively required. In the first place, the material breach might be so flagrant that judicial determination was superfluous: moreover immediate international action might have been necessary to avoid damage to the interests the Mandate was designated to protect—for example, in a case of genocide of the people of a Mandated territory. Perhaps more fundamentally however, we need to consider exactly what happens when a Mandate is revoked. It has already been suggested that in exercising its 'executive' or 'dispositive' functions the Council and the General Assembly are both rather in the position of referees than holders of 'residual sovereignty'.

[53] Oppenheim (8th edn.) I, 383n.2.

[54] I.C.J. Rep. 1955 p. 67, 98–106, esp. 105–6.

[55] Ser. B No. 12 (1925), 32. The Treaty of Lausanne, Art. 3 (2) provided for the Council to determine a boundary in dispute between Turkey and Iraq: but cf. Judge Klaestad, I.C.J. Rep. 1955 p. 67, 85 ff. See also Lauterpacht, *Development*, 161.

[56] Dugard (1968), 62 *AJ* 78, 79–81 for a review of authority. See also Judge Dillard, I.C.J. Rep. 1971 p. 12, 167–8; *contra* Judge Fitzmaurice, ibid. 299–301.

In revoking a Mandate (or Trusteeship) the political organ is declaring that, as a result of acts contrary to its fundamental obligations, the Mandatory is no longer entitled to exercise its administrative function. Just as the Mandate is an international status impressed on territory, so the administrative authority of the Mandatory is a limited political status which can be avoided by acts fundamentally contrary to the purposes for which the status exists. While the Mandatory complies with its obligations, the Mandate is of course irrevocable, but it is difficult to allow that, following its material breach, a Mandatory would remain entitled to retain its position: the League Council's function would have been not precisely to deprive the Mandatory of its status, but to declare the legal results of the Mandatory's own act.[57] When the General Assembly revoked the Mandate for South-West Africa, the resolution declared that South African violation of the Mandate amounted to a disavowal of the Mandate, and decided that the Mandate 'is therefore terminated, and that henceforth South-West Africa comes under the direct responsibility of the United Nations'.[58] And there was precedent for adopting a declaratory rather than executory form of words. The Japanese Mandate for the Pacific Islands was, according to some views, revoked by virtue of Japanese violation of the demilitarized status of the Mandate, and this despite any authoritative League finding on the matter. The matter was argued before the Security Council by the U.S. Representative Austin in the following terms:

The United States Government does not consider that there is any obstacle to the placing of these islands under trusteeship in accordance with the Charter as soon as the Security Council approves the draft agreement.

As a result of the war, Japan has ceased to exercise, or to be entitled to exercise, any authority in these islands . . . In utter disregard of the mandate, Japan, contrary to the law of nations, used the territories for aggressive warfare against the U.S. and other Members of the United Nations. Japan, by her criminal acts of aggression, forfeited the right and capacity to be the mandatory Power over these islands. The termination of Japan's status as the Mandatory power over the islands

---

[57] There is a certain analogy in the procedure for termination of an ordinary treaty on the grounds of material breach by one party: Art. 60 of the Vienna Convention on the Law of Treaties, but cf. Judge Fitzmaurice, *Namibia Opinion* I.C.J. Rep. 1971 p. 16, 266n.

[58] G.A. Res. 2145 (XXI), 27 Oct. 1966 (114–2:3).

has been frequently reaffirmed: in the Cairo Declaration of 1943, subsequently reaffirmed in the Potsdam Declaration and in the instrument of surrender accepted by the powers responsible for Japan's defeat . . . In the above circumstances, it is the view of my Government that the conclusion of a trusteeship agreement pursuant to the Charter, for the former Japanese mandated islands clearly can take effect at this time, and does not depend upon, and need not await, the general peace settlement with Japan.[59]

Although some other delegations expressed their reservations about this argument,[60] the Security Council did proceed to approve the Trusteeship Agreement. The islands were arguably in the unusual position of being in each of the three categories of territory to which the Trusteeship System applied: apart from Article 77 (1)(c), the extensive wording of which may have been intended to deal with this question,[61] it is arguable that the dispositive authority involved in the new appointment was that of the Security Council as a whole, pursuant to the fundamental breach by Japan.[62]

(2) *Revocation of Trusteeships*

Revocation has fortunately never been an issue in relation to any of the ordinary Trusteeships, all of which have been terminated in the normal way by agreement between the General Assembly and the Administering Authority.[63] There

[59] *SCOR* 133rd mtg., 26 Feb. 1947, 413: Whiteman, 1 *Digest* 772.

[60] *SCOR* 2nd Yr., 116th mtg., 7 Mar. 1947, 464 (U.K.). The U.S. view is challenged by Toussaint, op. cit. 87–92, and Marston (1969), 18 *ICLQ* 1, 29 ff., both on the assumption that the traditional rules of disposition of State territory apply to the Trusteeship institution. Interestingly, the islands under Japanese sovereignty occupied by the U.S. were treated in a different way. The Trusteeship Agreement over the Islands merely stated 'Whereas Japan, as a result of the Second World War, has ceased to exercise any authority in these islands . . .': 8 *UNTS* 189, 190. In the Peace Treaty of 1951, Japan accepted 'the action of the U.N. Security Council extending the trusteeship system to the Pacific Islands formerly under mandate to Japan': 136 *UNTS* 48, Art. 2(b).

[61] Art. 77(1)(c) refers to 'administration': it is at least arguable that this was intended to override the principle *nemo dat quod non habet:* Parry, op. cit. 166–7; cf. Toussaint, op. cit. 87–92.

[62] On the Pacific Islands Mandate 1944–7, see Russell, *History of the Charter,* 573–89; Gilchrist (1944), 22 *For Aff.* 635–43; James, Emerson *et al., American Pacific Dependencies* (1949), Ch. 8.

[63] Charter, Art. 85. Cf. Opinion of Legal Counsel concerning the termination of the Trusteeship Agreement for the Territory of New Guinea, T/11757, 18 Oct. 1974, paras. 1–2.

can be however little doubt that revocation was a legal possibility: the argument about revocation of Mandates apply with at least equal force to Trusteeships.[64]

Once again however the Strategic Trusteeship of the Pacific Islands administered by the United States is a special case. Arguably, since the Charter explicitly gives to the permanent members of the Council a veto over all but procedural matters, the *nemo judex* principle invoked by the Permanent Court in *Interpretation of the Treaty of Lausanne* was overridden, thus effectively excluding revocation. Nevertheless, the United States in negotiating the terms of the Trusteeship Agreement renounced the use of the veto, and adopted the equally effective method of refusing to accept the Trusteeship on any other than the terms proposed by it.[65] Article 15 of the Trusteeship Agreement reads: 'The terms of the present agreement shall not be altered amended or terminated without the consent of the administering authority.'[66] The debate on Article 15 suffered from a confusion between the terms of the agreement and its term of validity, two quite different things. The article as it stands is unclear, and one is required to assume that if the 'terms' of an agreement were terminated, the 'term' of the Trusteeship itself would also be brought to an end. As there may well be a distinction between trusteeship status and the agreement regulating that status, this is not perhaps an inevitable assumption, though undoubtedly the intended one. In proposing and insisting on Article 15, the United States delegate offered an interpretation of Chapter XII

[64] No proposals were made to the San Francisco Conference with respect to termination or revocation of trusteeships, although both Ecuador and Venezuela proposed at the Conference that the Assembly might declare independence under specified conditions: 10 *UNCIO* 655. Egypt subsequently proposed the inclusion of specific termination and revocation provisions in the Charter: after considerable debate this proposal was dropped: ibid. 547–8. Instead, the delegates of the U.K. and the U.S. in a Joint Statement (Annex C to the Report of the Rapporteur of Committee II/4, 20 June 1945), stated in part that if a State was expelled or withdrew from the U.N., 'and did not voluntarily consent to the transfer of the Trust to another authority, the resulting situation could only be judged by the General Assembly and the Security Council on its merits in the light of all the circumstances prevailing at the time. It is impossible to make provision in advance for such a situation.' (Ibid. 620–1). This statement was not adopted as an expression of the views of the Committee, but it was approved by France and Egypt: ibid. 601–2.

[65] The debate is in Whiteman, 1 *Digest* 834–8.

[66] 8 *UNTS* 198. A U.S.S.R. amendment to read: 'The terms of the present agreement may be altered or amended, and the term of its validity discontinued by the decision of the Security Council' was defeated (8–1:2): *SCOR* 124th mtg., 2 Apr. 1947, 679.

inconsistent both with the reasoning above and with subsequent United States argument in the *Namibia Opinion*:

. . . the whole theory of the Trusteeship System is based on the fact that there must be, in any case, at least two parties to any trusteeship agreement. It would be an astonishing interpretation of the Charter to assume that the function of determining the terms of the agreement should be given exclusively to that party which, under the Charter, has only the function of approval. An amendment leaving the terms of an agreement and the power of termination to the Security Council alone is a violation of the spirit of the Charter and of the theory of agreement . . .[67]

This argument assumes that the Charter intended Trusteeships to be permanent and irrevocable, no matter how violative of the terms and purposes of the agreement the behaviour of the administering power. If this were so then there would appear to be no distinction between the position of administering power and the position of a territorial sovereign, since it would then be a characteristic of the former, as of the latter, that violation of agreements with respect to the territory did not impair in any way the continued rights of the State concerned over the territory.[68] However in the context of strategic trusteeship, the argument was perhaps more acceptable, resulting merely in the replacement of one veto by another. No other Trusteeship Agreement contains a termination provision. It is submitted that the validity of the United States argument is restricted to the special circumstances of strategic trusteeship.

(3) *Revocation of Mandates by United Nations organs*

Reference has been made already to Resolution 2145(XXI), by which the General Assembly declared the Mandate for South West Africa revoked. After the failure of negotiations between the United Nations and South Africa, the Security Council referred the matter to the Court. The Court held by thirteen votes to two (Judges Fitzmaurice and Gros dissenting) that the Mandate had been validly revoked.[69] This may be regarded as

---

[67] Ibid. 670.

[68] It is not accidental that at a crucial stage of this argument against revocability, Judge Fitzmaurice is driven to rely on the *Lotus* presumption, which is, we have seen, a characteristic of sovereignty with respect to territory: *infra*, pp. 354–5.

[69] I.C.J. Rep. 1971 p. 16. For non-recognition see *supra*, pp. 124–8.

a continuation of the quite extensive history of United Nations involvement in Mandates and their termination. Charter authority to wind up the system, whether by transfer to Trusteeship or otherwise, was consistently asserted, as we have seen.

In supporting the legality of revocation, the Majority Opinion relied strongly on the treaty character of the Mandates institution:

In examining this action of the General Assembly it is appropriate to have regard to the general principles of international law regulating termination of a treaty relationship on account of breach. For even if the mandate is viewed as having the character of an institution ... it depends on those international agreements which created the system and regulated its application ... By stressing that South Africa 'has, in fact, disavowed the Mandate', the General Assembly declared in fact that it had repudiated it. The resolution in question is therefore to be viewed as the exercise of the right to terminate a relationship in case of a deliberate and persistent violation of obligations which destroys the very object and purpose of that relationship ...[70]

Whatever its validity might have been during the existence of the League, the difficulty with this argument is that the United Nations is not the contractual successor of the League in respect of Mandates *qua* treaties. It was on the ground of status, as distinct from contract, that the Court in 1950 held the General Assembly entitled to exercise supervisory powers[71], although subsequent cases, notably the Majority Opinion in the *Hearing of Petitioners Case*,[72] tended to treat the Assembly as if it were a universal successor. This point was forcibly made by Judge Fitzmaurice:

There is no doubt a genuine difficulty here, inasmuch as a regime like that of the mandates system seems to have a foot both in the institutional and the contractual field. But it is necessary to adhere to at least a minimum of consistency. If, on the basis of contractual principles, fundamental breaches justify unilateral revocation, then equally it is

[70] I.C.J. Rep. 1971 p. 16, 46–7. For criticism see also Schwarzenberger, *International Law* (1976) III, 168 ff.; cf. 176–7.

[71] I.C.J. Rep. 1950 p. 128, 141–2 (Majority Opinion); 153–5 (Judge McNair).

[72] I.C.J. Rep. 1956, p. 23. The point is not clear: in any case, assuming that the Majority Opinion (apart from Judge Winiarski) did adopt the wider view, there was still a majority of 7–6 in favour of the 'status' view. See especially the Judge Lauterpacht, 36 ff.

the case that contractual principles require that a new party to a contract cannot be imposed on an existing one without the latter's consent (novation). Since in the present case one of the alleged fundamental breaches is precisely the evident non-acceptance of this new party, and of any duty of accountability to it (such acceptance being, *ex hypothesi*, on contractual principles, *not* obligatory), a total inconsistency is revealed as lying at the root of the whole Opinion of the Court in one of its most essential aspects.[73]

The question then is on what grounds the exercise by the General Assembly of supervision and revocation functions can be justified. The Majority Opinion in 1950 based its holding on the essential nature of supervision in the Mandates system, and on the inseverability of the Mandatory's legal position from the existence and exercise of these powers of supervision: 'To retain the rights derived from the Mandate and to deny the obligations thereunder could not be justified.'[74] This suggests that the exercise of mandate functions by the United Nations finds its legal basis in a form of estoppel. South Africa had applied to the United Nations for permission to annex the Mandate, as we have seen.[75] This, and its continued possession of South-West Africa (as well as certain admissions by it of its position in doing so)[76] constituted an affirmation of the entire Mandate; that is, a form of estoppel, so that the absence of actual consent by South Africa to the continuance of the Mandate and its supervision could not be denied.[77] Clearly again, if supervision was to be carried out, it had to be by the United Nations: 'It cannot be admitted that the obligation to submit to supervision has disappeared merely because the supervisory organ has ceased to exist, when the United Nations has another international organ performing similar, though not identical, supervisory functions. These general considerations are confirmed by Art. 80 paragraph 1 of

---

[73] I.C.J Rep. 1971 p. 12, 267. Against the 'automatic succession' view see also Bowett, *International Institutions* (3rd edn., 1976), 337–8; Chiu (1965), 14 *ICLQ* 83–120, 103–6; Brownlie, *Principles*, 653–4; cf. *Barcelona Traction (Preliminary Objections)* I.C.J. Rep. 1964 p. 6, 38–9.

[74] I.C.J. Rep. 1950 p. 128, 133. This assumes that South Africa had no other legal title to administer the territory: it is clear that this is so. See e.g. Judge Jessup diss., *South West Africa Cases (Second Phase)* I.C.J. Rep. 1966 p. 6, 418.

[75] *Supra*, p. 340.

[76] Dugard, 99–100, 102–3, 115: cf. Slonim (1975), 69 *AJ* 640.

[77] I.C.J. Rep. 1950 p. 128, 135–7.

the Charter ...'[78] There was unquestionably a 'legislative' element in the Court's 1950 ruling as to supervision: it is not therefore unsound. This operation is, as Judge Lauterpacht has pointed out, one akin to the *cy-près* doctrine in the English law of trusts: 'in order to render effective a general charitable intention in face of the impossibility of applying it according to the literal language of its author'.[79] The legitimacy of this view is supported by the following considerations.

First, a trustee is essentially a person with limited title, one who is estopped from denying the rights of his beneficiary. The application of the 'equitable' principles (to use the terminology of English law) of estoppel and trust against a Mandatory and in favour of the beneficiary is entirely consistent with the nature of the Mandate institution.[80]

Second, it has been argued above that the Mandate is a territorial institution terminable only by consent while it is being executed according to its terms, but avoided for fundamental breach on the Mandatory's part. Revocation is thus essentially declaratory, though like other forms of termination, it may have 'definitive legal effect'. There is nothing historically or constitutionally inappropriate in the General Assembly's exercising such a role, since, as has been seen, dispositive rights in this area have consistently been claimed and exercised.

Third, it is submitted that the restriction, expressed in the 1950 Opinion and subsequently reaffirmed, that the General Assembly may not exceed the 'degree of supervision' of Mandates exercised by the Council is not relevant here, though clearly correct in the context of normal supervision. There is a distinction to be made between supervision and termination functions. Supervision functions are powers related to the continuing exercise of the Mandate: they are expressed in the Mandate agreement and defined and limited by its terms. Termination functions, on the other hand, are left to be inferred from the structure of the Mandate system and general principles of law.

---

[78] Ibid. 136.

[79] *Hearing of Petitioners Opinion*, I.C.J. Rep. 1956 p. 23, 48; Lauterpacht, *Development*, 279; Judge de Castro, sep. op., *Namibia Opinion*, I.C.J. Rep. 1971 p. 16, 198–9.

[80] Cf. however the differing expressions of opinion by the Majority and Judge McNair as to the relevance of municipal law analogies in the interpretation of the mandates system: *Status Opinion* I.C.J. Rep. 1950 p. 128, 132; 147–8.

If the Mandate survived, so must the various modes of termination. That the *Status Opinion* reservation as to 'degree of supervision' required adjustment in cases where the Mandatory was in breach of its obligations is evident from the *Voting Procedure Opinion*.[81] *A fortiori* where the Mandatory has repudiated, or otherwise fundamentally breached the Mandate itself,[82] and where what is at issue is not supervision but termination.

It remains to consider the argument against revocation by the Assembly. Judge Fitzmaurice, after establishing that General Assembly power could not properly be based on treaty succession, continues:

> If, in order to escape this dilemma ... a shift is made into the international institutional field, what is at once apparent is that the entities involved are not private persons or corporate entities but sovereign States. Where a sovereign State is concerned, and where also it is not merely a question of pronouncing on the legal position, but of ousting the State from an administrative role which it is physically in the exercise of, it is not possible to rely on any theory of implied or inherent powers. It would be necessary that these should have been given concrete expression in whatever are the governing instruments. If it is really desired or intended, in the case of a sovereign State accepting a mission in the nature of a mandate, to make the assignment revocable upon the unilateral pronouncement of another entity, irrespective of the will of the State concerned, it would be essential to make express provision for the exercise of such a power.[83]

There are two elements to this argument. First, it is said that revocability must be expressed in the instruments, and cannot be implied from the Mandate institution. The arguments against this view have been discussed already:[84] in particular, it seems incongruous to insist that the power of revocation be expressed in the constituent documents when, with only one exception, those documents make no mention whatsoever of powers of termination. If termination powers are to be implied, why not

[81] I.C.J. Rep. 1956 p. 23, 31–2 (Majority Opinion): see also Judge Winiarski, 33; Judge Lauterpacht, 36 ff.

[82] The Assembly treated both South Africa's rejection of the Mandate, and its application of the doctrine of *apartheid* to the territory, as fundamental breaches of the Mandate. That the former is so is clear: for argument as to the latter, see Judges Tanaka and Jessup, *South West Africa Cases (Second Phase)* I.C.J. Rep. 1966 p. 6, 290 ff., 426 ff.; *contra*, Judge *ad hoc* Van Wyk, 139–215. And cf. [1967] *BPIL* 18.

[83] I.C.J. Rep. 1971 p. 12, 267–8.

[84] *Supra*, pp. 344–5.

powers of revocation? More subtly, however, Judge Fitzmaurice's argument is a variant of the *Lotus* presumption; that is, the presumption against limitations upon State sovereignty.[85] But to rely upon that presumption here is to beg the question.

The presumption clearly does not apply to acts performed on the territory of other States, and its application by the Permanent Court to acts on the high seas was acutely controversial. The whole point, which Judge Fitzmaurice appears only to assume, is whether a Mandated territory is to be treated as if it were the territory of the Mandatory, or of the local population under tutelage, for the purposes of revocation for fundamental breach. It is ironic that the main argument against revocation should be a deduction from that sovereignty which the Mandate system was designed to replace.[86]

---

[85] *Supra*, p. 33.

[86] The United Nations now regards itself as the *de jure* government of Namibia, pending a proper act of self-determination: it has formed a Council for Namibia to exercise that authority. See its Decree No. 1 on Natural Resources of Namibia (1974), and *U.S. Digest* 1975, 85–90; (1976) 9 *CILSA* 277–81; (1977) 8 *NYIL* 166–8; Herman (1975), 13 *Can. YIL* 306–322. For recent developments see S.C. Res. 385 (1976), 20 Aug. 1976.

14. Non-Self-Governing Territories: the Law and Practice of Decolonization

> It is for the people to determine the destiny of the territory and not the territory the destiny of the people. (Judge Dillard, sep. op., *Western Sahara Case* I.C.J. Rep. 1975 p. 12, 122.)

14.1 INTRODUCTORY

BEFORE 1945 there was very little general international concern with colonial problems, and still less with the advancement of colonial peoples to self-government. The Mandate and Trusteeship systems of course contained machinery for progressive development towards independence or self-government of certain colonial territories, but their ambit was restricted, and has remained so.

However, at the San Francisco Conference more extensive provision for colonial territories was made—in the form of Chapter XI of the Charter, entitled 'Declaration Regarding Non-Self-Governing Territories'.[1] The Chapter, which contains only Articles 73 and 74, is an attempt to apply somewhat similar ideas to those embodied in Article 22 of the Covenant to a far broader category of territory. Our concern here is only with the dispositive aspects of Chapter XI, and of the extensive practice pursuant to Chapter XI. The status of that practice has historically been a matter of acute controversy, but a large majority of States has on the whole taken an extensive view of Chapter XI. By Article 73,

Members of the United Nations which have or assume responsibilities for the administration of territories whose peoples have not yet attained a full measure of self-government recognize the principle that the interests of the inhabitants of these territories are paramount, and accept as a sacred trust the obligation to promote to the utmost, within

---

[1] See G.A. Res. 9 (I), 9 Feb. 1946; and for the *travaux préparatoires*, Russell and Muther, *A History of the United Nations Charter* (1954), 813–24.

the system of international peace and security established by the present Charter, the well-being of the inhabitants of these territories . . .

and there follow five specific undertakings relating to the development of the peoples concerned, progress towards self-government, the furtherance of international peace and security, economic development, and the regular transmission of certain information to the Secretary-General.[2] An important development in the practice pursuant to Article 73 was the Declaration on the Granting of Independence to Colonial Countries and Peoples,[3] which, like certain other Assembly Declarations, has achieved in practice a quasi-constitutional status.[4] Clause 7 of the Declaration places it on a par with the Universal Declaration of Human Rights and the Charter itself. Article 5 requires that: 'immediate steps shall be taken, in Trust and Non-Self-Governing Territories . . . to transfer all powers to the peoples of those territories, without any conditions or reservations, in accordance with their freely expressed will and desire, without any distinction as to race, creed or colour, in order to enable them to enjoy complete independence or freedom'. United Nations practice under Chapter XI, and the Colonial Declaration as an integral part of that practice, have been explicitly approved by the International Court. In the *Namibia Case* the Court stated that:

the concepts embodied in Article 22 of the Covenant were not static but were by definition evolutionary, as also therefore was the concept of the sacred trust . . .
The parties to the Covenant must consequently be deemed to have accepted them as such. That is why, viewing the institutions of 1919, the Court must take into consideration the changes which have occurred in the supervening half century, and its interpretation cannot

---

[2] The best study, of an extensive literature, is Rigo Sureda, *The Evolution of the Right of Self-Determination* (1973). See also Sud, *The United Nations and Non-Self-Governing Territories* (1965); Ahmad, *The United Nations and the Colonies* (1974); El-Ayouty, *The United Nations and Decolonization. The Role of Afra-Asia* (1971); Rajan, *The United Nations and Domestic Jurisdiction* (2nd edn., 1961), 133–222; Barbier, *Le Comité de décolonization des Nations-Unies* (1974); Nawaz (1962), 11 *Indian YIA* 3–47; van Asbeck (1947), 71 *HR* 345–472, and the works cited *infra*.

[3] Often referred to as the Colonial Declaration: G.A. Res. 1514 (XV), 14 Dec. 1960 (89–0:9).

[4] Cf. Asamoah, *The Legal Significance of the Declarations of the General Assembly of the United Nations* (1966), 163–85.

remain unfettered by the subsequent development of law, through the Charter of the United Nations and by way of customary law . . .[5]

This may be regarded as equally true of Article 73 of the Charter, based as it is on Article 22 of the Covenant; and indeed the Court explicitly affirmed the applicability of self-determination to non-self-governing territories under the Charter.[6] In the *Western Sahara Case*, after referring to this passage, the Majority Opinion reaffirmed 'the validity of the principle of self-determination':[7] in its view, Spain, as an administering power, 'has not objected, and could not validly object, to the General Assembly's exercise of its powers to deal with the decolonization of a non-self-governing territory . . .'[8] Thus the 'right of [the Spanish Sahara] population to self-determination' was 'a basic assumption of the questions put to the Court'.[9] The Court's reply to those questions, equally, was based upon 'existing rules of international law'.[10] On the other hand, the Court stated, 'the right of self-determination leaves the General Assembly a measure of discretion with respect to the forms and procedures by which that right is to be realized.[11] In view of the fact that a considerable majority of non-self-governing territories have achieved self-government in some form or other, the exercise of this 'procedural discretion' by the General Assembly in respect to the remaining territories (most of them small and relatively non-viable) has assumed great practical importance—it was indeed the issue before the Court in the *Western Sahara Case*. Before considering these specific problems of application, some brief account of the development of Chapter XI in practice since 1945 is in order.

14.2   THE DEVELOPMENT IN PRACTICE OF CHAPTER XI
OF THE CHARTER

(1)   *The definition of 'non-self-governing territories'*

Article 73, like Article 22, is imprecisely worded. It refers to

[5] I.C.J. Rep. 1971 p. 16, 31.

[6] *Supra*, p. 96.

[7] I.C.J. Rep. 1975 p. 12, 33. The Court referred to Res. 1514 (XV) as providing 'the basis for the process of decolonization which has resulted since 1960 in the creation of many States which are today Members of the United Nations': ibid. 32.

[8] Ibid. 24.   [9] Ibid. 36.

[10] Ibid. 30, 37.   [11] Ibid. 36.

'territories whose peoples have not yet attained a full measure of self-government', and binds 'Members of the United Nations which have or assume responsibilities for the administration of such territories to the obligations set out. The meaning of these terms is not self-evident, and has not been entirely settled by subsequent practice. The matter is a little advanced by the distinction established in Article 74 between 'the territories to which this Chapter applies' and 'their [sc. Member States'] metropolitan areas'. One can at least infer that Chapter XI applies only to defined 'territories' whose 'peoples' as a whole are not 'fully self-governing'. This would exclude from Chapter XI the problem of minorities not inhabiting a clearly defined territory but scattered throughout a State. Member States are bound in their behaviour towards minorities not by Chapter XI by the more general human rights provisions of Chapter IX, and in particular by Articles 55 and 56.[12]

The basic difficulty remains: how is one to distinguish between 'territories' which are, and those which are not, part of the metropolitan State, although both may be equally 'non-self-governing' in fact? The question itself assumes that a territory falls outside the ambit of Chapter XI if it is 'metropolitan', no matter what the conditions in, or actual status of, the territory in fact. But the term 'metropolitan' is no clearer than 'non-self-governing', and it is not clear that the two are mutually exclusive. Article 74 contrasts two kinds of territories defined in rather different ways: 'metropolitan' is presumably a reference to the history of the area concerned as part of a State (and perhaps to its geographical contiguity with the rest of the State). 'Non-self-governing' appears to refer not to history or geography, but to the present political situation. It would seem to be quite possible that 'metropolitan areas' should be at the same time 'non-self-governing' ones. Or alternatively, if the antithesis established in Article 74 is a true one, a territory might cease to be 'metropolitan' when it becomes 'non-self governing', whatever its history.[13]

The usual, and more restrictive view, is that Chapter XI was intended to apply only to 'territories, known as colonies at the

---

[12] This interpretation is confirmed by the *travaux préparatoires*: cf. 6 *UNCIO* 296; 10 *UNCIO* 495-8.
[13] This was the contention of Belgium in 1952 (the so-called 'Belgian Thesis'): see Whiteman, 13 *Digest* 697-8. See also *infra*, p. 362.

time of the passing of the Chapter'.[14] In particular, according to Principle IV of Resolution 1541 (XV), '*Prima facie* there is an obligation to transmit information in respect of a territory which is geographically separate and is distinct ethnically and/or culturally from the country administering it.' Thereafter, according to Principle V,

Once it has been established that such a *prima facie* case of geographical and ethnical or cultural distinctness of a territory exists, other elements may then be *inter alia*, of an administrative, political, juridical, economic or historical nature. If they affect the relationship between the metropolitan State and the territory concerned in a manner which arbitrarily places the latter in a position or status of subordination, they support the presumption that there is an obligation to transmit information under Article 73e of the Chapter.

Given these, relatively restrictive, criteria, the next problem has been to determine which territories are within the ambit of Chapter XI.

(2) *The ambit of Chapter XI in practice*

In the first instance, the extent of Chapter XI was determined by the replies of States to a letter from the Secretary-General requesting information about non-self-governing territories.[15] As a result, 74 territories under eight different administering States were enumerated in Resolution 66 (I)[16] as territories with regard to which information under Article 73e had been or was intended to be submitted. This method was not well calculated to produce a comprehensive application of Chapter XI to non-self-governing territories: nevertheless, the only objections to the enumeration of territories in Resolution 66 (I) were made by States with claims to sovereignty over certain of those territories (Guatemala over British Honduras; Panama over the Panama Canal Zone; and Argentina over the Falkland Islands).

After the admission in 1955 of Spain and Portugal to United Nations membership, the issue of their various territories was raised. Spain eventually agreed to comply with Assembly

---

[14] G.A. Res. 1541 (XV), Annex, Principle I; Nawaz (1962), 11 *Indian YIA* 3, 13. But Art. 73 expressly refers to after-acquired territories: it would be strange if the characteristics of colonies in 1945 only were to be relevant in such cases.

[15] A/74, 29 June 1946; authorized by G.A. Res. 9 (I).

[16] 13 Dec. 1946 (27–7:13).

recommendations, and after considerable debate nine Portuguese territories were also designated as non-self-governing.[17]

In 1962, with the impending secession of Southern Rhodesia, the Assembly also, by Resolution 1747 (XVI), declared it to be a non-self-governing territory.[18] The British contention was that, since Southern Rhodesia was a 'self-governing colony' in British constitutional law, it did not have the status of a 'Non-Self-Governing Territory' under the Charter, and that any United Nations declaration to the contrary was therefore *ultra vires*.[19] This view was rejected by the Fourth Committee and by the Assembly itself. In any event, as we have seen, in 1965 the British Government itself, by the Southern Rhodesia Act, claimed 'responsibilities for the administration' of Southern Rhodesia, so that the territory would seem to have reverted to non-self-governing status then.[20]

In addition, certain territories which are no longer reported on by Administering States continue to be considered by the Committee of Twenty-Four: these included (until recently) the Comoro Archipelago,[21] and the French Territory of the Afars and Isaas (formerly French Somaliland),[22] and still include the West Indies Associated States,[23] and Puerto Rico.[24]

[17] G.A. Res. 1542 (XV), 15 Dec. 1960 (68–6:17). See *UN Repertory*, Supp. III, Vol. 3, Art. 73, paras. 105–29; Wohlgemuth, 'The Portuguese Territories and the U.N.' *Int. Conc.* No. 545 (Nov. 1963). The Portuguese arguments were set out in Nogueira, *The U.N. and Portugal: A Study of Anticolonialism* (1963).

[18] G.A. Res. 1747 (XVI), 28 June 1962 (73–1:27, Portugal and U.K. n.p.).

[19] *GAOR* 17th sess., 4th Ctee., 1360th mtg., A/C.4/SR.1360, 11 ff.

[20] *Supra*, p. 246.

[21] In a referendum held on 22 December 1974, the inhabitants of the four islands voted overwhelmingly (94 per cent) for independence. On one island (Mayotte) there was however a majority in favour of continued association with France. In negotiations for independence, attempts were made to secure separate self-determination, or at least substantial constitutional guarantees, for the inhabitants of Mayotte. The then local government rejected these attempts and on 6 July 1975 unilaterally declared their independence. This was accepted (with respect to the three main islands) by France on 9 July, and the Comoro Islands were recognized thereafter by a number of other States, and admitted to the U.N. on 12 Nov. 1975. The situation on Mayotte remains unresolved. See (1975) 80 *RGDIP* 793–7; Ostheimer, *The Politics of the Western Indian Ocean Islands* (1975), 73–101; and on the decision of the French Constitutional Court, Ruzié (1976), 103 *JDI* 392–405; Favoreu, [1976] *Rev. de Droit Public* 557–581. The General Assembly has rejected the continued French occupation of Mayotte as a violation of the 'national unity of the Comorian State . . .': G.A. Res. 31/4 (XXXI), 21 Oct. 1976 (102–1:28). See also G.A. Res. 32/7, 1 Nov. 1977 (121–0:17, France n.p.).

[22] *Infra*, p. 377.   [23] *Infra*, p. 374.

[24] *Infra*, p. 372. For a list of Chapter XI territories and their eventual political statuses see Appendix 3.

3. *Application of Chapter XI to non-colonial territories*

We have already discussed whether Chapter XI was intended to apply only to territories of the colonial type, or, to put it another way, to what extent the term 'Non-Self-Governing' should be read in any of the wider senses of which it would seem to be capable. United Nations practice, with one possible exception, has so far at least followed the former view. But its action over Rhodesia may lead us to inquire into the possibilities of such a wider application. As we have seen, the Assembly was not prepared to accept that the degree of internal autonomy possessed by Southern Rhodesia in British constitutional law before 1965, or thereafter in fact, prevented it from being non-self-governing. Substantially, the reason was that the Smith regime's effective control in Rhodesia was, in Fawcett's words: 'based upon a systematic denial in its territory of certain civil and political rights, including in particular the right of every citizen to participate in the government of his country, directly or through representatives elected by regular, equal and secret suffrage.'[25] There are two possible interpretations of the Assembly action in this case, assuming that it was indeed *intra vires*. It may be that, irrespective of the racial composition or democratic nature of the local government, Rhodesia always had been 'non-self-governing', and that Britain's failure to report on it under Article 73e was either a breach of that Article, acquiesced in by the Assembly, or else a tacit assertion tacitly accepted that 'constitutional considerations' prevented the transmission of information, under the proviso to Article 73e. However, it may be that Southern Rhodesia would not have been considered 'non-self-governing' but for the element of denial of human rights: in other words, as a territory it was self-governing, but its people as a whole were not. Comparison with the various Resolutions establishing criteria for self-governing fortify this latter conclusion and it may also be politically the more accurate.[26]

If the latter view is correct, some interesting possibilities arise. For example, the people of South Africa are not 'self-governing' in the sense stipulated. The Government of South Africa has 'responsibilities for the administration of territory' (viz. South

---

[25] (1965–6) 41 *BY* 103–21, 112.
[26] Cf. also the case of Bangladesh: *supra*, pp. 115–17.

Africa itself) 'whose peoples have not yet attained a full measure of self-government'. The reason why South Africa may not be treated as 'Non-Self-Governing' perhaps is not so much the dichotomy in Article 74 between metropolitan and non-self-governing territories as the implied distinction in Article 73 between 'Members of the United Nations' and non-self-governing territories. It would follow that Rhodesia might, even if its statehood were conceded, be treated by the United Nations as 'non-self-governing' until either it fulfils the conditions laid down in Resolution 742 (VIII) or as admitted to United Nations membership. The situation could also arise in which a United Nations member did have 'responsibilities' (for example, at the invitation of a puppet government) for the administration of the territory of a recognized State. Such situations may well be, in practice, equivalent to those of colonial type, and it is thought that (at least where the 'subject' State is not a United Nations member) the argument that Article 73 applies only to colonies and not to States need not prevail. The situation might also arise in the case of a protectorate or 'special treaty arrangement' between two States, especially where the arrangement served the purpose of widespread denial of human rights in the subject State. Such cases have not generally been treated as within the ambit of Chapter XI.[27]

14.3   THE INTERNATIONAL STATUS OF NON-SELF-
GOVERNING TERRITORIES

(1) *'Sovereignty' and Non-Self-Governing Territories*

Article 73 applies to United Nations members 'which have or assume *responsibilities for the administration of* territories' which are non-self-governing. Clearly, the phrase 'responsibilities for the administration of' includes, but is not limited to, colonies under the sovereignty of an administering Power. Protectorates and other forms of administration[28] are also included. It would appear therefore that Chapter XI is not directly concerned with problems of sovereignty: none the less, it is sometimes asserted

---

[27] Cf. Fischer, [1974] *AFDI* 201–14 (Sikkim); and *supra* p. 198 n. 74 (Brunei).
[28] e.g. Kowloon: *infra*, p. 380. The Panama Canal Zone is not reported on: see *infra*, p. 434, n. 6.

that administering States are *ipso facto* not sovereign with respect to their Chapter XI territories.[29] It is not clear either that Chapter XI purports to deprive administering States of sovereignty over colonial territories, or that subsequent practice could have that effect.[30] On the other hand, to the extent that 'sovereignty' implies the unfettered right to control, or to dispose of, the territory in question, the obligations in Article 73b, and the associated principle of self-determination, substantially limit the sovereignty of an Administering State.[31] In the *Right of Passage Case*, a majority of the Court accepted that Portugal retained sovereignty over its enclaves in India.[32] This view was denied only by three judges; and by one of these (Judge Badawi) only on an interpretation of the original grant.[33] Judge Kojevnikov thought that 'Portugal did not possess, and does not possess, any sovereign rights over Dadra and Nagar-Aveli', but gave no reasons for his finding.[34] Judge Moreno Quintana, in a rather obscure paragraph,[35] denied the existence of a right of passage: a claim implying 'survival of the colonial system, without categorical and conclusive proof' in his view flew 'in the face of the . . . Charter'.[36] This appears to be less a denial of title than a use of self-determination to shift the burden of proof of rights normally appurtenant to title.

The view that Chapter XI does not affect territorial title was also affirmed in the *Western Sahara Case*: the court held that the request, relating to the future status of a non-self-governing territory, did not relate to 'existing territorial rights or sovereignty over territory'.[37]

(2) *The use of force and non-self-governing territories*

The relation between the principle of self-determination and

---

[29] Bedjaoui, *ILC Ybk.* 1975/I, 49; Calogeropoulos-Stratis, *Le Droit des peuples à disposer d'eux-mêmes* (1973), 113; Rigo Sureda, op. cit. 353; cf. his more cautious formulation at 223.

[30] Cf. Jennings, *Acquisition of Territory*, 78–87.

[31] Cf. *Western Sahara Case* I.C.J. Rep. 1975 p. 12, 145 (Judge de Castro).

[32] I.C.J. Rep. 1960 p. 6, 39. See also ibid. 48–9 (Judge Basdevant); 65–6 (Wellington Koo); 99 (Spender); 123–4 (Judge *ad hoc* Fernandes).

[33] Ibid. 51.

[34] Ibid. 52.

[35] Cf. *infra*, p. 414.

[36] I.C.J. Rep. 1960 p. 6, 191–6.

[37] I.C.J. Rep. 1975 p. 12, 28.

the rules relating to the illegal use of force has been discussed already:[38] modern practice establishes a distinct connection between the two, such that, even where a particular use of force is illegal, its effects may be treated as valid provided that they are consistent with the principle of self-determination in its application to the territory in question.

A somewhat related issue arose in the *Right of Passage Case.* There the question of the status of the enclaves after the insurrection was in issue, for if Portugal had remained sovereign—as it would appear to have done according to ordinary rules of acquisition of territory—then its right of access to the enclaves would surely also have remained. The majority judgment side-stepped the issue completely by considering the problem of sovereignty and the right of passage only as at December 1954, before the insurrection. India was held not culpable, because its refusal of access was an exercise of the power to regulate transit.[39] The Majority Opinion thus failed, as President Klaestad pointed out, to consider fully the merits of the case.[40] Only two majority judges did consider the point, apart from the two dissentients.[41] Judge Spiropoulos, for example, stated:

It is a fact that after the departure of the Portuguese authorities, the population of the enclaves set up a new autonomous authority based upon the will of the population. Since the right of passage assumes the continuance of the administration of the enclaves by the Portuguese, the establishment of a new power in the enclaves must be regarded as having *ipso facto* put an end to the right of passage.[42]

Apart from the more direct effects on statehood discussed in Chapter 3, the principle of self-determination may thus entail that the sovereignty of an administering State in a Chapter XI territory is more readily displaced, even in the case of annexation by the use of force, provided of course that the principle of self-determination is not itself violated.[43] However, as the International Court emphasized in the *Western Sahara Case,* 'the

---

[38] *Supra*, pp. 106–18.
[39] I.C.J. Rep. 1960 p. 6, 44–5.
[40] Ibid. 47.
[41] Ibid. 115 (Judge Spender); 125 (Judge *ad hoc* Fernandes).
[42] Ibid. 53. Cf. Judge Armand-Ugon: ibid. 87.
[43] Cf. Brownlie, *Principles*, 577–80; Jennings, *Acquisition of Territory*, 85–6.

application of the right of self-determination requires a free and genuine expression of the will of the peoples concerned . . .'[44] and any use of force to alter the status of such a territory—except possibly where self-determination is forcibly denied by the administering Power—is in principle illegal under the Charter.

(3)   *The legal personality of dependent peoples*

The Declaration elaborating Charter principles annexed to Resolution 2625(XXV) states, *inter alia:* 'The territory of a colony or other self-governing territory has, under the Charter, a status separate and distinct from the territory of the State administering it; and such separate and distinct status under the Charter shall exist until the people of the colony or non-self-governing territory have exercised their right of self-determination in accordance with the Charter.'[45] It seems clear from this and other formulations[46] of the principle of self-determination, that where the principle applies, it does so as a right of the people concerned, rather than as a form of *jus quaesitum tertio.* Of course, another State may well be interested in the result of an act of self-determination, in that it may stand to gain, or regain, territory: but to treat self-determination as a right of that State would be to deny the reality of the alternative options open to the self-determining unit.[47]

However, in certain cases this clear distinction between the right of a dependent people to choose its own political future, and the contingent interest of a neighbouring State in the results

---

[44] I.C.J. Rep. 1975 p. 12, 32; ibid. 121–2 (Judge Dillard).

[45] Cf. *supra*, pp. 91–5.

[46] Colonial Declaration, para. 2: 'all peoples have the right to self-determination'.

[47] See also Brownlie, *Principles*, 66. In the *Northern Cameroons Case* I.C.J. Rep. 1963, p. 15, the question of the legal interest of the Republic of Cameroon in the results of an exercise of self-determination by the Northern Cameroons province was in issue, although the majority side-stepped the point by holding that the matter had been already settled by the Assembly. Nevertheless the Court referred to 'the indisputable fact that if the result of the plebiscite in the Northern Cameroons had not favoured joining the Republic of Nigeria, it would have favoured joining the Republic of Cameroon' (28). It is unclear whether this meant that the Republic of Cameroon had a legal interest in the matter, or was intended merely as a demonstration of the reason for the *actio popularis* (as the majority considered it) in the jurisdiction clause (Art. 19) of the Trusteeship Agreement. Judges Spender (95–6), Fitzmaurice (109–11), Morelli (137–8) held that the Cameroons had no personal legal interest: as did Judge Wellington Koo (46). Judges Badawi and Bustamante, and Judge *ad hoc* Beb a Don dissenting thought that the Republic of Cameroons did have a special interest: (152, 163, 193 resp.).

of the exercise of that right, has been confused. In particular, the General Assembly has treated certain territories, not as self-determination units but as enclaves of a claimant State, with the result that, in the latter case, the only acceptable future status has been the surrender of the territory to the claimant. This practice is examined later.[48]

14.4 TERMINATION OF NON-SELF-GOVERNING STATUS: THE FORMS OF SELF-GOVERNMENT

(1) *Termination of non-self-governing status*

(i) Criteria for self-government

A territory ceases to be 'non-self-governing' when it has achieved self-government, or rather, in the terms of Article 73, 'full' self-government. The question is which political statuses will be regarded as satisfying this requirement. In view of the omission of the term 'independence' from Article 73,[49] it is clear that other possibilities were contemplated, and despite the emphasis in the Colonial Declaration on 'independence', the Assembly has fairly consistently allowed three alternatives:

A Non-Self-Governing Territory can be said to have reached a full measure of self-government by:
(a) Emergence as a sovereign independent State;
(b) Free association with an independent State; or
(c) Integration with an independent State.[50]

In general terms therefore, there can be no doubt about what is meant by 'full-self-government'. However it has sometimes been argued that the attainment of a certain standard of material, political, social, and educational progress in a given territory is legally a prerequisite to 'self-government' in terms of Article 73. The obligations of the Administering State to 'promote the well being of the inhabitants' and the specific obligations in Article 73a and 73c, are certainly capable of this interpretation:

---

[48] *Infra*, p. 377.

[49] On the controversy at San Francisco about inclusion of 'independence' in Ch. XI, see Russell and Muther, *A History of the U.N. Charter*, 815; 10 *UNCIO*, 677–8.

[50] G.A. Res. 1541 (XV), Annex, Principle VI; cited in the *Western Sahara Case* I.C.J. Rep. 1975 p. 12, 32.

nevertheless a majority of the General Assembly has generally taken the view that, while material and political progress is a correlative of political independence, the former is not a precondition of the latter; that the two should be promoted together, and that ultimately political self-determination is the basis of the enjoyment of other rights.

(ii) *Determination of cessation of non-self-governing status*

Although it has sometimes been suggested that United Nations authorization is necessary before the reporting obligation concerning a former non-self-governing territory ceases,[51] this would appear not to be the case. The matter is not one within domestic jurisdiction of Administering States, on the other hand, since it relates to fulfilment of their legal obligations under Chapter XI. The position was stated by the General Assembly to be as follows: 'Chapter XI of the Charter embodies the concept of Non-Self-Governing Territories in a dynamic state of evolution and progress towards a "full measure of self-government". As soon as the territory and its peoples attain a full measure of self-government, the obligation ceases. Until this comes about, the obligation to transmit information under Article 73e continues.'[52]

This is the natural interpretation of Chapter XI itself, which provides for no termination functions to be exercised by United Nations organs. This is not to say that the United Nations has no competence whatsoever with respect to termination of non-self-governing status. United Nations supervision or surveillance of any act of self-determination is clearly desirable to ensure the freedom of choice so made, and has been common under Chapter XI.[53] Where the relevant mode of self-determination is independence, admission to the United Nations constitutes probably unchallengeable evidence that a territory has ceased to be non-self-governing. More specific powers with respect to decolonization have also, on occasion, been delegated to United Nations organs.[54]

[51] Cf. Higgins, *Development*, 111.

[52] Res. 1541 (XV), Annex, Principle II. Cf. the terms of the 1970 Declaration of Principles: 'such separate and distinct status under the Charter shall exist until the people of the colony or self-governing territory have exercised their right of self-determination in accordance with the Charter ...' (Res. 2625 (XXV), Annex).

[53] *UN Repertory*, Supp. III, vol. 3, 92–9; Johnson, *Self-Determination within the Community of Nations* (1967).

[54] Cf. West Irian: *supra*, pp. 332–3; Dallier (1973), 27 *RJPIC* 41–60.

A distinct problem which has arisen under Chapter XI is that of territories claimed by Administering States to be 'self-governing' or 'independent' while still being treated as non-self-governing by the General Assembly. This has occurred both where the new status was claimed to be independence,[55] and where the new status was claimed to be free association.[56] The case of the French Territory of Afars and Isaas was somewhat similar, but France did not submit information after 1947.[57]

It seems then that non-self-governing status ceases automatically upon the achievement of full self-government: whether full self-government has in fact been achieved is to be decided by the Administering State and the General Assembly together, either specifically or by some such unequivocal act as admission to United Nations membership. In the absence of agreement, the situation becomes one for political negotiation.

(2) The forms of self-government

The three methods of self-government referred to in principle VI of G. A. Resolution 1541 (XV)[58] will be referred to in turn.

(i) Independence

No specific problems arise in the case of Territories choosing independence, unless the Territory concerned is small.[59] In the terms of the Colonial Declaration and in practice, independence has been the central and most usual form of self-government.[60]

(ii) Incorporation in another State

Principle VIII of the Annex to Resolution 1541 (XV) provides

---

[55] e.g. Oman: *UN Repertory* Supp. III, No. 3, 56–9; Higgins, *Development*, 18n.; *supra*, p. 213. Cf. Brunei, *supra*, p. 198 n. 74.

[56] e.g. the West Indies Associated States; *infra*, p. 374.

[57] *UN Repertory* Supp. III, No. 3, 33–4, 56; Unitar Study, *Small States and Territories* (1971), 103–4; Rigo Sureda, op. cit. 64–7, 71–2, 203–12; Umozurike, op. cit. 226–35; Rabier and Angrand (1975), 49 *RJPIC* 473–85. See further *infra* p. 377 n. 110.

[58] *Supra*, p. 367.

[59] *Supra*, p. 139.

[60] Of approximately 100 Chapter XI territories in the period 1945–78, 59 achieved joint or separate independence (this includes Grenada, Surinam, and Singapore, which had a previous status of self-government). Seven territories were integrated with the metropolitan State; 6 with other States. Seven are now Associated States. About 17 are still dependent territories, whether or not reported on; the status of a further three (Brunei, East Timor, Western Sahara) is controversial or uncertain. See further Appendix 3.

for integration 'on the basis of complete equality' with an independent State as a method of self-government. Principle IX requires the integrating territory to have attained 'an advanced stage of self-government with free political institutions'.

Incorporation with the metropolitan State has occurred in a number of cases, either with[61] or without[62] express United Nations approval. Singapore, Sabah, and Sarawak were incorporated in the Federation of Malaysia, with United Nations approval. Such incorporation, as a result of an act of self-determination, remains a practical option of self-government, although claims to incorporation in the metropolitan State tend to be regarded by the General Assembly with some suspicion.

An alternative avenue for integration is that of claims by third States to the territories in question. So far, four territories have been integrated with other States on grounds of national unity rather than self-determination (viz. Goa and dependencies, and French Establishments in India, both assimilated into Indian territory; Ifni (Morocco), and São João Batista de Ajudá (Dahomey)).[63] These claims raise special problems and are dealt with separately.[64]

(iii) Association

The requirements for association as a form of self-government are formulated as follows by Resolution 1541 (XV):

PRINCIPLE VII
(a) Free association should be the result of a free and voluntary choice by the peoples of the territory concerned expressed through informed and democratic processes. It should be one which respects the individuality and the cultural characteristics of the territory and its peoples, and retains for the peoples of the territory which is associated with an independent State the freedom to modify the status of that territory through the expression of their will by democratic means and through constitutional processes.

---

[61] Greenland (1953), Surinam (1954; independent 1975), Netherlands Antilles (1954), Alaska and Hawaii (1959).

[62] French Polynesia, French Caledonia, French Guiana, and Reunion (1947).

[63] West Irian and the Western Sahara are further possible examples: *infra*, p. 382, n. 132, 384

[64] *Infra*, pp. 377–84.

(*b*) The associated territory should have the right to determine the internal constitution without outside interference, in accordance with due constitutional processes and the freely expressed wishes of the people. This does not preclude consultations as appropriate or necessary under the terms of the free association agreed upon.[65]

Association represents one of the more significant possibilities of self-government for the future, especially in the case of islands and archipelagos too small to be economically and politically stable States. Nevertheless its status as a coequal form of self-government for Chapter XI territories has not gone unchallenged, and recent controversies relating to Puerto Rico and to the West Indies Associated States demonstrate the need for a more detailed analysis of the concept of association than is provided by Principle VII of Resolution 1541.

(*a*) *Association arrangements in practice since 1952* The first formal instance of 'free association' was the case of Puerto Rico[66] in 1952. In that case the arrangement was the product of a compromise between a desire for local self-government and perceived economic exigencies.[67] 'Commonwealth status' as it was termed,[68] was granted in 1952 pursuant to Act of Congress[69] and was approved by referendum. The arrangement is stated to be 'in the nature of a compact': it is contained in large part in the Puerto Rican Federal Relations Act, 1950 as amended.[70] Puerto Rican citizens have automatic United States citizenship, and enjoy some, though not all, of the protections afforded by the United States Constitution.[71] Acts of Congress apply to Puerto Rico unless they are for some reason locally inapplicable.[72] The local government has considerable, though by no means complete, internal autonomy, but only vestigial international competence. This arrangement was approved by the United

---

[65] Cf. the development of the concept of association in G.A. Resns. 567 (VI), 648 (VII), and 742 (VIII).

[66] Reisman, *Puerto Rico and the International Process, New Roles in Association* (1975); Cabranez (1967), 16 *ICLQ* 531–9; Hector (1973), 6 *NYUJIL* 115–37; and articles by Cabranez, Benitez, and Martinez in (1973), 67 *PAS* 1–27.

[67] Cf. Rousseau (1974), 78 *RGDIP* 1182–7.

[68] Ibid. 1185.

[69] Text in Reisman, op. cit. 124.

[70] Ibid. 126.

[71] Ibid. 35–9.

[72] *U.S.* v. *Vargas* 370 F. Supp. 908 (1974); *Caribtan Corp.* v. *O.S.H.R.C.* 493 F. 2d. 1064 (1974); *Hodgson* v. *U.E.S.P.* 371 F. Supp. 56 (1974).

Nations in 1953,[73] whereupon the United States ceased transmitting information under Article 73e.

In some respects, the Puerto Rican association arrangements provide an unsatisfactory model. There is little or no participation in international affairs, and relatively little countervailing participation in metropolitan affairs.[74] Internal autonomy is restricted, especially in legislative and judicial matters. As a result, the Committee of Twenty Four moved in 1972 to reinstate Puerto Rico on the list of territories subject to its consideration, and on 30 August 1973 proclaimed 'the inalienable right of the Puerto Rican people to self-determination'.[75] Partly in response to these criticisms there has been some progress towards a renegotiation of the arrangement.[76]

Despite these problems, it may be pointed out that Puerto Rico has been regarded by the United States Government since 1952 as entitled to opt for a different status—either complete independence[77] or integration with the United States. This was reaffirmed by a United States–Puerto Rican Commission on the Status of Puerto Rico, which reported in August 1966.[78] In 1967 the present arrangement was reaffirmed in a further referendum. Substantive defects in the terms of association have thus, it seems, been ratified by the people of Puerto Rico.[79]

Perhaps a more satisfactory precedent for future association relationships is that of the Cook Islands. In this case, association was chosen by means of an election under United Nations surveillance;[80] the arrangement came into effect on 4 August 1965. The terms of association are contained in the Cook Islands Constitution Act 1964 as amended.[81] The Islands have full internal self-government;[82] although the Head of State of the Cook Islands is the Queen in right of New Zealand,[83] and

[73] G.A. Res. 748 (VIII), 27 Nov. 1953 (26–16:18).
[74] Puerto Rico elects one non-voting Commissioner to Congress. It does not participate in Presidential elections. But cf. *U.S.* v. *Valentine* 288 F. Supp. 957 (1968).
[75] Reisman, op. cit. 184–6.
[76] Ibid. xii, 113–23. See further *U.S. Digest* 1974, 51–2; ibid. 1975, 90–2.
[77] Cf. President Eisenhower, (1953) 29 *DSB* 841; Whiteman, 1 *Digest* 400; discussed by Reisman, op. cit. 43–5.
[78] Cabranez (1967), 16 *ICLQ* 531, 536–9.
[79] Cf. Reisman, op. cit. 44–50.
[80] G.A. Res. 2005 (XIX), 18 Feb. 1965; A/5962, 20 Aug. 1965.
[81] Act No. 69 of 1964; as amended by Act No. 2 of 1965.
[82] Act No. 69 of 1964, s. 3.
[83] Constitution, s. 2.

executive power is accordingly vested in her,[84] that power is exercised on the advice of a local Executive Council.[85] New Zealand retains responsibilities for the external affairs and defence of the Cook Islands, those responsibilities to be discharged after consultation by the Prime Minister of New Zealand with the Premier of the Cook Islands.[86] Legislation of the New Zealand Parliament does not extend to the Islands as part of its law unless requested and consented to by the Government of the Islands.[87] The Legislative Assembly has the power to amend the Constitution upon compliance with certain special manner and form provisions.[88] Such amendment procedures could be used to declare the Islands fully independent.

In 1965 the General Assembly, with some hesitation, approved this arrangement as giving the people of the Islands 'control of their internal affairs and of their future', resolved that 'since the Cook Islands have attained full internal self-government, the transmission of information in respect of the Cook Islands under Article 73e of the Charter of the United Nations is no longer necessary'; but at the same time reaffirmed 'the responsibility of the United Nations, under General Assembly resolution 1514 (XV), to assist the people of the Cook Islands in the eventual achievement of full independence, if they so wish, at a future date.'[89] These two operative paragraphs of Resolution 2064 (XX) were the product of a compromise between members who considered that the association arrangement was itself a definitive act of self-determination and others who regarded it as merely an interim—and not very satisfactory—accommodation.[90] The arrangement has however proved durable and acceptable to the Islanders; in any event the apparent distinction relied on in the 1965 debates is not an exact one, since New Zealand itself has explicitly accepted the right of the Cook Islands to choose independence.[91]

The value of the Cook Islands case as a precedent is

---

[84] Ibid., s. 12.
[85] Ibid., ss. 4, 7.
[86] Act, s. 5.
[87] Constitution, s. 46.
[88] Ibid., s. 41.
[89] G.A. Res. 2064 (XX), 16 Dec. 1965 (78–0:29), paras. 5, 6.
[90] There is an account of the debates in Allen, *Int. Conc.* No. 560 (Nov. 1966), 40–9.
[91] See also Kilbride (1965), 1 *NZULR* 571–6; Stone (1966), 1 *J. Pac. H.* 168–77.

considerable: a similar arrangement was approved for Niue in 1974,[92] and other instances of association have been proposed.[93]

The cause of associated statehood has, however, suffered somewhat of a reverse with the refusal of the United Nations to approve arrangements made between the United Kingdom and certain Caribbean islands under the West Indies Act 1967. These arrangements were merely noted in Resolution 2257 (XXII):[94] subsequently the United Kingdom ceased reporting. Resolution 2422 (XXIII), paragraph 3

> Strongly regrett[ed] the . . . decision of that [*sc.* the U.K.] Government to cease transmitting information on Antigua, Dominica, Grenada, St. Kitts-Nevis-Anguilla and St. Lucia . . .[95]

By Resolution 2701 (XXV) the Assembly

> Consider[ed] that, in the absence of a decision by the General Assembly itself that the Territories of Antigua, Dominica, Grenada, St. Kitts-Nevis-Anguilla, St. Lucia and St. Vincent have attained a full measure of self-government in terms of Chapter XI of the Charter, the Government of the United Kingdom . . . should continue to transmit information under Article 73e of the Charter with respect to those territories . . .[96]

The situation remains unresolved.[97] The problem in this case, apart from the general failure of consultation and communication, is that the West Indies Act 1967 leaves with the United Kingdom a substantial degree of power to intervene in local affairs, so that the division of authority between defence and

[92] See the Niue Constitution Act, 1974. G.A. Res. 3155 (XXVIII), 14 Dec. 1973 (128–0:0) approved a proposed 'act of self-determination' and appointed a special mission to observe it: G.A. Res. 3285 (XXIX), 13 Dec. 1974 (adopted without vote) recognized that Niue had achieved self-government in free association with New Zealand and approved cessation of transmission of information under Art. 73e.

[93] e.g., for the Northern Marianas: 14 *ILM* 344, and for the Cocos (Keeling) Islands: see Australian Senate, Standing Committee on Foreign Affairs and Defence, *United Nations Involvement with Australia's Territories* (1975), 99–104.

[94] G.A. Res. 2357 (XXII), 19 Dec. 1967 (86–0: 27).

[95] G.A. Res. 2422 (XXIII), 18 Dec. 1968 (87–4; 16).

[96] G.A. Res. 2701 (XXV), 14 Dec. 1970 (86–2: 18).

[97] Cf. Broderick (1968), 17 *ICLQ* 368–403; Fawcett, [1967] *ASCL* 709–11; Spackman, *Constitutional Development in the West Indies 1922–1968* (1975), 375–413, 533–41; Phillips, *Freedom in the Caribbean. A Study in Constitutional Change* (1977), 78–93. On the Anguillan secession see Fawcett, [1968] *ASCL* 785–8; Cmnd. 4510 (1970); Anguilla Act, 1971 (U.K.); Brisk, *The Dilemma of a Ministate: Anguilla* (1969); Simmonds, in *Mélanges W. J. Ganshof van der Meersch* (1972), 435–47, and in (1972) 21 *ICLQ* 151–7.

foreign affairs on the one hand, and internal matters on the other is not adhered to.[98]

Failure on both sides to reach an accommodation over the British Associated States must be regretted, because association would appear to be a satisfactory solution to the problem of small islands and territories, which have otherwise to choose from the options of unwelcome federation, unacceptable dependency, or perhaps impracticable statehood.[99]

(b) *The international legal status of Associated States* It is sometimes asserted that Associated States lack international status in view of metropolitan responsibilities for foreign affairs and defence which have been a feature of each of the arrangements concluded so far.[100] It is of course not possible to establish *a priori* rules: like international protectorates, to which they bear a certain resemblance, the status of particular Associated States depends primarily on the specific instruments.[101] None the less, association is a distinct status developed in United Nations practice. It seems necessary first to generalize as to the terms upon which association is likely to be acceptable as a form for self-government in accordance with that practice, and especially with Resolution 1541 (XV).[102] The terms upon which United Nations approval of association is likely to be given are as follows:

---

[98] The Act provides that the U.K. Government's responsibilities are to include matters of nationality and citizenship (s. 2(1)(b)), and succession to the throne (s. 2(1)(c)), but most importantly 'any matter which *in the opinion of H.M.'s Government* in the U.K. is a matter relating to defence (whether of an associated state *or of the U.K. or of any other territory* for whose government H.M.'s Government in the U.K. are wholly or partly responsible) or to external affairs' (s. 2 (1)(a), my italics. See also ss. 3(2); 7(2).) Broderick's comment is that 'it is difficult to see . . . how the U.K. Government could relax its legislative authority further and still be in a position to control the discharge of its international responsibilities': op. cit. 371–2. This may however beg the question just what are the international responsibilities of the U.K. The view that the Associated States are 'not yet entities in international law' (402), if it is indeed correct, is a corollary of the U.K.'s reluctance to commit itself to an arrangement based on consent rather than dependence, not a reason for it. New Zealand's relations with both the Cook Islands and Niue preclude this form of unilateral intervention, despite the former's responsibility for foreign affairs and defence.

[99] Cf. Unitar Study, op. cit. 181–8; De Smith, in Fawcett and Higgins, eds., *International Organisation: Law in Movement* (1974), 64–78.

[100] Cf. Broderick (1968), 17 *ICLQ* 368, 402.

[101] *Supra*, p. 186.

[102] *Supra*, p. 370; and cf. Reisman, op. cit. 78–50.

(1) The association must be freely chosen by the inhabitants of the territory.
(2) The terms of association must be clearly and fully set down, in a form binding on the parties.
(3) The associated territory must have substantial powers of internal self-government.
(4) The reserved powers of the State accepting the regime of association (which will usually be those of foreign affairs and defence) should not involve substantial discretions to intervene in the internal affairs of the Associated State.[103]
(5) There must be a procedure for termination of the association which should be:
  (a) at least as easily available to the Associated State as to the government of the metropolitan State;
  (b) capable of being regarded as a continued expression of the right to self-determination of the people of the Associated State.

On this basis, it cannot simply be asserted that Associated States lack all international status. They are clearly not separate independent States, but equally they are not for international purposes merely part of the metropolitan State. Relations between the metropolitan State and its associate are not a matter within the domestic jurisdiction of the former.[104] The relation is binding under the municipal law of both parties.[105] Further, given that association arrangements are accepted in practice as satisfying the principle of self-determination, and are accepted on the basis of undertakings and arrangements to which the metropolitan State is committed, it cannot be argued that association relations are, as a matter of international law, revocable at the will of the metropolitan State.[106] And, finally, it is clear that those territories which have so far achieved associated status have remained self-determination units, able both in international and municipal law to choose other more permanent forms of self-government. For all these reasons it may

---

[103] This is not of course to preclude further arrangements between the Associated State and the metropolitan State for other forms of representation or assistance, so long as these comply with the basic principles summarized here.

[104] Cf. Fawcett, [1968] *ASCL* 786–7.

[105] *U.S.* v. *Valentine* 288 F. Supp. 957, 981 (1968) (Puerto Rico).

[106] Cf. Reisman, op. cit. 44–5.

be concluded that, under association arrangements accepted by the United Nations as fulfilling the requirements of self-government under Chapter XI, the Associated State will acquire substantial international personality. More specific problems—such as membership in international organizations—can only be worked out in particular cases.[107]

(iv) Colonial enclaves and rights of revindication

A persistent and troublesome aspect of United Nations practice in the context of Chapter XI is the problem of the so-called 'colonial enclave':[108] the small territory claimed by a neighbouring State, for whatever reason, without regard to the principle of self-determination. Various territories have, in decolonization practice so far, been disposed of as colonial enclaves rather than as self-determination units:[109] moreover, of the remaining sixteen or so non-self-governing territories no less than eight might be said to fall into this category.[110] The conflict in United Nations practice which is thus apparent has its roots in the Colonial Declaration itself. Article 2 provides that 'All peoples have the right to self-determination; by virtue of that right they freely determine their political status and freely pursue their economic, social and cultural development . . .' Article 6 of the Declaration on the other hand states that 'Any attempt aimed at the partial or total disruption of the national unity and the territorial integrity of a country is incompatible

[107] Cf. Reisman's rather optimistic analysis: ibid. 51–104. And see Leibowitz, *Colonial Emancipation in the Pacific and the Caribbean. A Legal and Political Analysis* (1976), for a general account.

[108] Cf. Rigo Sureda, op. cit. 214–19; Franck and Hoffman (1976), 8 *NYUJILP* 331–386.

[109] In particular, Ifni, São João Batista di Ajudá and the French and Portuguese enclaves in India. West Irian is a further possible example. For Western Sahara see *infra*, p. 379; for East Timor see *infra*, p. 384.

[110] Sc. Belize (British Honduras), Falkland Islands (Malvinas), Gibraltar, Hong Kong, Macao, the British Indian Ocean Territory, Mayotte and the Panama Canal Zone. This is not to say that all of these are regarded by the General Assembly as colonial enclaves, still less that all of them are properly defined as such. Somalia's claim to French Somaliland, for example, was rather a claim for independence for the territory concerned, upon which, it was hoped, it would choose union with Somalia: Rigo Sureda, op. cit. 71–72. The territory in fact became independent as Djibouti in June 1977 and was admitted to the UN without opposition: GA Res. 32/1, 20 Sept. 1977; (1978) 82 *RGDIP* 254–5. For a survey of some of the claims see Mathy (1974), 10 *Rev. belge* 167–205; (1975) 11 *Rev. belge* 129–60; Barbier, op. cit. 564–87. For the British Indian Ocean Territory see *infra*, p. 435, n. 9.

with the purposes and principles of the Charter . . .' It has been argued that, in the case of small non-viable territories claimed by a contiguous State, Article 6 takes priority over Article 2, so that the only option for decolonization of the territory is its transfer to the claimant State.[111] This problem was in issue in the *Western Sahara Case*. The Spanish Sahara has been claimed by Morocco and Mauritania:[112] the General Assembly[113] asked the Court *inter alia* to determine what were the legal ties, if any, between the territory and Morocco, on one hand, and the Mauritanian entity, on the other hand, at the time of Spanish colonization (1884). Before the Court, Algeria, Morocco and Mauritania each adopted distinct positions on the relation between Articles 2 and 6 of the Colonial Declaration

Morocco has expressed the view that the General Assembly has not finally settled the principles and techniques to be followed, being free to choose from a wide range of solutions in the light of two basic principles: that of self-determination indicated in paragraph 2 of resolution 1514 (XV), and the principles of the national unity and territorial integrity of countries, enunciated in paragraph 6 of the same resolution . . .

Mauritania maintains that the principle of self-determination cannot be dissociated from that of respect for national unity and territorial integrity; that the General Assembly examines each question in the context of the situations to be regulated; in several instances, it has been induced to give priority to territorial integrity, particularly in situations where the territory has been created by a colonizing Power to the detriment of a State or country to which the territory belonged . . .

Algeria states that the self-determination of peoples is the fundamental principle governing decolonization, enshrined in Articles 1 and 55 of the Charter and in General Assembly resolution 1514 (XV); that, through successive resolutions which recommend that the population should be consulted as to its own future, the General Assembly has recognized the right of the people of Western Sahara to exercise free and genuine self-determination; and that the application of self-determination in the framework of such consultation has been accepted

---

[111] Cf. also the territorial claims with respect to Mauritania and Bahrain, discussed *supra*, p. 38. Cf. Rigo Sureda, op. cit. 176–7.

[112] See Rigo Sureda, op. cit. 72–4, 212–15; Jacquier (1974), 78 *RGDIP* 683–728; Rezette, *The Western Sahara and the Frontiers of Morocco* (1975); Barbier (1976), 30 *RJPIC* 67–103; Levy (1976), 2 *Brooklyn JIL* 268–307; Frank and Hoffman, op. cit.; Trout, *Morocco's Saharan Frontiers* (1969).

[113] G.A. Res. 3292 (XXIX), 13 Dec. 1974 (87–0:43).

by the administering Power and supported by regional institutions and international conferences, as well as endorsed by the countries of the area.[114]

The Majority Opinion, after examining the historical material, concluded that, although 'legal ties' did exist between the Western Sahara and the two claimant entities before colonization, these were not of such a character as to affect the exercise by the Western Sahara of its right to self-determination,[115] which required 'a free and genuine expression of the will of the peoples concerned'.[116] The 'colonial enclave' problem did not therefore need to be dealt with in the Majority Opinion, although certain inferences can be drawn from passages of the Opinion. Three judges in their separate opinions were however more explicit. Judge Dillard expressed the firm view that self-determination remains in all cases the 'cardinal principle', which cannot be overridden by territorial claims of third States.[117] Judge Singh appeared to take the view that only dismemberment of a pre-colonial State by the colonizer would justify reintegration rather than self-determination.[118] Judge Petrèn, on the other hand, thought that the principle of 'territorial integrity' was, in United Nations practice, co-ordinate to self-determination, and that the precise legal relation between them remained undeveloped: the position was thus, in his view, *de lege ferenda*.[119] The difficulties with this view, are considerable: since the question is a definitional one which bears on the relation between an asserted general principle of law (self-determination) and a possible

---

[114] I.C.J. Rep. 1975 p. 12, 29–30.

[115] On the issue of the 'legal ties' the Majority (14–2, Judges Ruda and de Castro dissenting in the case of Morocco; 15–1, Judge de Castro dissenting in the case of Mauritania) was itself divided. Judges Ammoun and Forster regarded the ties as particularly substantial, amounting in effect almost to territorial sovereignty: cf. Judge Ammoun, ibid., *passim*; Judge Forster, ibid. 103. On the other hand, Judges Gros, Ignacio-Pinto, Dillard and Petrèn regarded any ties that existed as insubstantial; indeed in Judge Gros's view they were not legal at all but sociological: ibid. 75 and cf. the capital analysis of Judge Dillard, ibid. 119, 125–6. On this point these judges agreed with Judges de Castro and Ruda in dissent. The Majority Opinion—to the effect that legal ties of personal allegiance existed but that these, not being equivalent to sovereignty, could not affect the application of the principle of self-determination to the territory—was a distinct and rather awkward compromise between mutually inconsistent positions.

[116] Ibid. 21 (Majority Opinion); cf. 36.

[117] Ibid. 120 n. 1.

[118] Ibid. 75: cf. 76.

[119] Ibid. 79–80, cf. 112.

exception to it (the territorial integrity rule), it is necessary to the existence of the former that the latter be capable of enunciation at least in reasonably precise terms—otherwise the exception would destroy the rule. Morocco's assertion that in decolonization questions the Assembly has the option of choosing either 'self-determination' or 'territorial integrity' reduces both to procedural policies or processes.[120] It is significant that the Majority Opinion expressly avoided this position: in its view, self-determination is the fundamental principle, and the existence of claims such as those of Morocco or Mauritania was relevant only in that it might influence the Assembly in the exercise of its 'discretion with respect to the *form* and *procedure* by which that right [sc. self-determination] is to be realized.'[121]

To a considerable extent the problem of so-called colonial enclaves is outside the scope of this study. There follows however a brief, and necessarily tentative, summary of the legal position.

1. As we have seen already, Chapter XI does not displace the sovereignty of an administering authority with respect to colonial territory.[122] By parity of reasoning, one would expect that, where the territorial sovereign is not the administering authority, its sovereignty would also not be displaced by Chapter XI. This conclusion is perhaps not quite inevitable, since Chapter XI might have been intended to override third party sovereignty in the interests of the inhabitants of the territory concerned.[123] However, it is not clear by what authority the original Members of the United Nations could achieve such a displacement, and even more pertinently, it is not clear that they intended to do so. It follows that third States sovereign with respect to Chapter XI territories retain that sovereignty, and with it, presumptively, the right to retrocession of the territory under whatever treaty or arrangement is relevant. This is the case with Kowloon,[124] and

---

[120] Cf. Umozurike, op. cit. 86–7, 183.

[121] I.C.J Rep. 1975 p. 12, 36.

[122] *Supra*, p. 363.

[123] Cf. Charter Art. 103, which refers however only to 'obligations under any . . . international agreement'.

[124] Kowloon was leased to Britain for 99 years by a Convention of 9 June 1898: 90 *BFSP* 17; cf. *In re Wong Hon* [1959] *H.K.L.R.* 601. In 1972 the Committee of Twenty Four recommended that Hong Kong and Macau and their dependencies (including Kowloon) be excluded from the list of Territories to which the Colonial Declaration is applicable:

the Panama Canal Zone,[125] both 'leased' territories. *Mutatis mutandis*, it is also arguably the case with Gibraltar—at least on the assumption that the latter is not a true colonial enclave.[126]

2. Where there is a territorial dispute with respect to a non-self-governing territory, the same principle will apply if the disputing State is in law a dispossessed sovereign. In practice, however, such a situation is most unlikely, in view of the likelihood of extinction of pre-colonial claims by lapse of time, consent or prescription.[127]

3. As a matter of general principle, one would expect that Chapter XI refers to existing territories within their established boundaries.[128] Use of the 'territorial integrity' rule to revert to some earlier territorial formation would thus appear to be prohibited—with the possible exception of 'colonial enclaves'.[129]

4. However, administering States would appear not to be at liberty to divide up or dismember self-determination territories in violation of self-determination. Territories formed by such

(1972) 9 *UNMC* No. 7, 36. No formal action has been taken, but the Committee no longer considers information on these two territories. The People's Republic of China has rejected offers of retrocession of both territories; cf. (1976) 80 *RGDIP* 235–7.

[125] *Infra*, p. 434, n. 6.

[126] By Article X of the Treaty of Utrecht, 13 July 1713: 28 *CTS* 325, Spain ceded to Great Britain 'the full and entire propriety of the town and castle of Gibraltar'. Although this has been interpreted to involve a cession of sovereignty, it is not clear from Article X that this was so. The 'propriety' was yielded 'without any territorial jurisdiction', and in the case of any grant, sale, or alienation by Great Britain of Gibraltar, Spain was entitled to first preference. The General Assembly has called upon Great Britain to negotiate a transfer of Gibraltar to Spain: see e.g. Res. 2429 (XXIII), 18 Dec. 1968 (67–18:34): and cf. Res. 3286 (XXIX), 18 Dec. 1974 (adopted without vote); despite the expressed wishes of the Gibraltarians in favour of the *status quo*. The British position is that Gibraltar is a self-determination territory, which, so long as the inhabitants desire it, may properly remain under British administration. Britain does however concede that a grant of plenary independence to Gibraltar would violate Art. 10 of the Treaty of Utrecht: A/AC.109/P.V. 543, cited Rigo Sureda, op. cit. 283. Rigo Sureda contests this: a grant of independence does not, in his view, constitute a violation of a pre-emption clause (ibid. 285–8, and cf. 193–8), and, in any event, Article 73 of the Charter prevails over the Treaty of Utrecht in case of conflict. Thus, in Rigo Sureda's view, only the 'colonial enclave' rule justifies the Assembly's position on Gibraltar. See also Fawcett (1967), 43 *Int. Aff.* 236–51; Carrington, *Chatham House memoranda*, 1958 (1); [1966] *BPIL* 84–99.

[127] On the Belize (British Honduras) dispute, which is the other substantial dispute of this type, see Bloomfield, *The British Honduras–Guatemala Dispute* (1973); Humphreys, *The Diplomatic History of British Honduras 1638–1907* (1961); Wadell (1951), 55 *AJ* 459–69. G.A. Res. 3432 (XXX), 8 Dec. 1975 (110–9:16) unequivocally asserted Belize's right to self determination: see [1976] *Public Law* 205–9.

[128] Higgins, *Development*, 104; Rigo Sureda, op. cit. 216–17.

[129] *Infra*, p. 384.

dismemberment are not self-determination units, but are subject to the 'territorial integrity' rule.[130] Examples might be the British Indian Ocean Territory,[131] and (possibly) Mayotte. It is submitted that this is the only satisfactory explanation of the West Irian case.[132]

5. Apart from these specific and rather exceptional cases, the problem arises where a political claim (whether or not disguised by legal argumentation) is made to a specific territory on ethnic or strategic grounds, or on the basis of pre-colonial rights, real or imagined.

6. It is clear that these political considerations will not affect the application of self-determination to a Chapter XI territory, where the claimant State was not sovereign with respect to the territory prior to colonization. Other forms of legal connections, such as personal allegiance, will not suffice. The point was made quite explicitly by the International Court in the *Western Sahara Case*:

... the Court's conclusion is that the materials and information presented to it do not establish any tie of territorial sovereignty between the territory of Western Sahara and the Kingdom of Morocco or the Mauritanian entity. *Thus* the Court has not found legal ties of such a nature as might affect the application of resolution 1514 (XV) in the decolonization of Western Sahara and, in particular, of the principle of self-determination through the free and genuine expression of the will of the peoples of the territory.[133]

7. Where the claimant State was sovereign with respect to the territory in question before colonization, the problem is more difficult. The statement cited above might suggest, *a contrario*, that pre-colonial sovereignty *would* affect the operation of self-

---

[130] Cf. *supra*, pp. 220–2.

[131] Rigo Sureda, op. cit. 199–202; Allen, *Int. Conc.* No. 560 (1966); *infra*, p. 435 n. 9.

[132] When Indonesia achieved independence in 1950, West New Guinea, which had been for administrative purposes part of Netherlands New Guinea, remained under Dutch control. In 1962 the territory was transferred to Indonesia (*supra*, p. 332). G.A. Res. 1752 (XVII), 21 Sept. 1962 (88–1 (Senegal): 14) approved the arrangement for the transfer. In 1969 an 'act of free choice' was held, pursuant to Res. 1752: the decision in favour of continued Indonesian sovereignty was noted by G.A. Res. 2504 (XXIV), 19 Nov. 1969 (84–0:30). See generally Rigo Sureda, op. cit. 70–1, 77–8, 143–51, 228–33; Taylor, *Indonesian Independence and the U.N.* (1960), 235–9, 440–6; van der Kroef (1963), 7 *Orbit* 120–49; Bone, *The Dynamics of the Western New Guinea (Irian Barat) Problem* (1958, 1962); Henderson, *West New Guinea. The Dispute and its Settlement* (1973). Cf. the pertinent criticism by Pomerance (1974), 12 *Can. YIL* 38–66.

[133] I.C.J. Rep. 1975 p. 12, 68 (emphasis added).

determination, and this was also, as we have seen, the view of Judges Singh and Petrèn.[134] Even if this is so, three conditions would need to exist.

(a) The 'legal tie' would have to have been one of State sovereignty. A relationship with a non-State entity would not suffice.[135]

(b) The claimant State would have to be the 'same' State as the pre-colonial sovereign. Such identity exists in the case of Spain with respect to Gibraltar, and Morocco with respect to the Spanish Sahara; but the Court explicitly denied any legal identity or reversion of Mauritania.[136] Equally, it is difficult to agree with the suggestion that post-1957 India was legally the same State as the Maratha sovereign of the Portuguese enclaves.[137]

(c) Thirdly, it is reasonably clear that pre-colonial sovereignty *per se* could not give rise to a right of reversion, since such sovereignty might have been peacefully and voluntarily surrendered.

8. More fundamentally, however, this exercise of 'relating back' colonial territories in order to allow for pre-colonial claims would appear to be a violation of the principle of the inter-temporal law not justified by anything in Chapter XI or any other principles of international law. The better view would appear to be Judge Dillard's: given the impossibility of redrawing colonial boundaries or of picking and choosing among Chapter XI territories in order to apply mutually inconsistent rules, it must be the case that self-determination is the cardinal principle, which applies generally—subject to what has been said above— to all Chapter XI territories.[138]

---

[134] *Supra*, p. 379.

[135] Thus the relation between the 'Mauritanian entity', which the Court held not to be a State (ibid. 57–8), and the Spanish Sahara could not, for that reason alone, affect the application of self-determination to the territory in question.

[136] Loc. cit.

[137] *Infra*, p. 415.

[138] However the Majority Opinion in the *Western Sahara Case* by inference at least approved the Assembly's treatment of Ifni as a colonial enclave: I.C.J. Rep. 1975 p. 12, 34–5. Cf. also their reference, in this context, to cases where the 'General Assembly has dispensed with the requirement of consulting the inhabitants of a given territory. Those instances were based either on the consideration that a certain population did not constitute a "people" entitled to self-determination, or on the conviction that a consultation was totally unnecessary, in view of special circumstances': ibid. 33.

9. However, if there exists a further exception to the fundamental principle of self-determination, in the shape of 'colonial enclaves', international practice supports its application only in the most limited circumstances: that is, to minute territories which approximate, in the geographical sense,[139] to 'enclaves' of the claimant State, which are ethnically and economically parasitic upon or derivative of that State, and which cannot be said in any legitimate sense to constitute separate territorial units. Such a category would include Gibraltar, the French and Portuguese settlement in India, and apparently, Ifni. It would not include island territories—which are by definition not enclaves: the General Assembly has given only lukewarm support to Argentina's claim to the Falkland Islands.[140] Equally, it would not include larger, relatively more viable territories such as the Western Sahara[141] or Portuguese Timor.[142] To such territories, as the International Court affirmed, the principle of self-determination applies as of right.[143]

[139] Robinson (1959), 49 *Annals of the Association of American Geographers* 283–95.

[140] Cf. G.A. Res. 3160 (XXVIII), 14 Dec. 1973 (116–0:14) which restated the view that 'the way to put an end to this colonial situation is the peaceful solution of the conflict of sovereignty between the Governments of Argentina and the United Kingdom with regard to the aforementioned islands . . .' On the Falklands see Rigo Sureda, op. cit. 80–82; Cohen, [1972] *AFDI* 235–62; Metford (1968), 44 *Int. Aff.* 463–81; Goebel, *The Struggle for the Falkland Islands* (1927); Waldock (1948), 25 *BY* 311–53; and (1975) 80 *RGDIP* 773–4.

[141] For further material on the Western Sahara dispute see 14 *ILM* 1503–15. A 'Declaration of Principles' of 14 Nov. 1975 between Spain, Morocco and Mauritania proposed a joint administration of the two latter States, pending an expression of 'views of the Sahara population': ibid. 1512–13. The General Assembly, by Res. 3458 (XXX), Part A (88–0:41), reaffirmed the 'right of the people of the Spanish Sahara to self-determination'; but by Res. 3458 (XXX), Part B (56–42:34) 'took note' of the tripartite agreement and requested the interim administration to ensure that the population was able to exercise its right of self-determination 'through free consultations'. A form of consultation was carried out; and Morocco and Mauritania, by agreement of 14 April 1976, partitioned the territory, despite armed resistance by a portion of the population, with Algerian assistance. Cf. (1977) 81 *RGDIP* 306–7.

[142] In Dec. 1975, Indonesia invaded Portuguese Timor, which it purported to annex on 17 July 1976: (1976) 80 *RGDIP* 958–9. The invasion was condemned *inter alia* by G.A. Res. 3485 (XXX), 12 Dec. 1975 (72–10:43). Cf. G.A. Res. 32/34, 28 Nov. 1977 (67–26:47).

[143] But cf. the comments of Moynihan (1976), 17 *Harvard ILJ* 465–502, 468–9; and the analysis in Franck and Hoffman (1976), 8 *NYUJILP* 331–86, 384–6. Also Franck (1976), 70 *AJ* 694–721.

PART IV: PROBLEMS OF COMMENCE,
CONTINUITY, AND
TERMINATION

15. The Commencement of States

DETERMINING THE date of the commencement of a new State may be particularly difficult: none the less it is, for certain purposes at least, sometimes necessary both in international and municipal fora.[1] The problem has two aspects: the precise application of the criteria of statehood to particular factual situations at the relevant period; and the application of various rules or presumptions which may attribute personality, at least in certain respects, to entities in the process of becoming States. These latter rules qualify the general principle that the attributes of statehood await the definitive constitution of the State; in practice, especially in secessionary situations, considerations of continuity and effectiveness may well render the qualifications— at least retrospectively—more important than the general principle.[2]

(1) *Problems of commencement in municipal courts*

Where municipal courts apply international law directly in order to determine matters of territorial or governmental status, no special problem arises. Where, however, the courts defer to executive recognition policies in such matters (as in the common law countries), effective *de facto* entities may be denied municipal status for lengthy periods of time.[3] As a result, it is established in Anglo-American jurisprudence that, as a general rule, '. . . when a government which originates in revolution or revolt is recognized by the political department as the *de jure* government of the country in which it is established, such recognition is retrospective in effect and validates all the actions and conduct of the government so recognized from the commencement of its

---

[1] Cf. Kelsen (1929), 4 *RDI* 613–41, 616.
[2] *Infra*, p. 392.
[3] *Supra*, pp. 15–16.

existence'.⁴ This, although something of a hallowed formula, is thoroughly misleading. In the first place, it is a rule of municipal law only, devised in order to mitigate the problems caused by judicial deference to executive recognition policy.⁵ It is not, as the Supreme Court implied in *Oetjen* v. *Central Leather Co.*, a result of the application of 'principles of international law'—at least in any other than the most indirect sense.⁶ Nor does recognition 'validate' governmental or State acts, in the sense of curing any illegalities involved: it is a rule of attribution rather than of validation.⁷ The phrase 'commencement of its existence' is also obscure.⁸ In the absence of executive pronouncement, the Courts have tended to relate 'commencement' back to the earliest date at which the entity in question was formed as a recognizable political entity, even though it may not then have been definitively established.⁹ As will be seen, this is perfectly proper, but it is not the same thing as relating commencement of a State or government only to the time of its establishment as such.

Finally, the 'retroactivity' rule itself is only a presumption: it will not apply where the executive act of recognition is intended to have only prospective effect;¹⁰ nor will it apply to invalidate transactions entered into by the previously recognized State or government with third parties,¹¹ or, generally, to bring within the competence of the newly recognized entity acts or events which were outside its effective control when they occurred.¹²

---

⁴ *Oetjen* v. *Central Leather Co.* 246 U.S. 297 (1918), citing *dicta* in *Williams* v. *Bruffy* 96 U.S. 176 (1877) and *Underhill* v. *Hernandez* 168 U.S. 250 (1897). The leading British authority is *Luther* v. *Sagor* [1921] 3 K.B. 432; see also *Lazard Bros.* v. *Midland Bank Ltd.* [1933] A.C. 289, 297; *Bank of Ethiopia* v. *National Bank of England & Liguori* (1937) 53 T.L.R. 751. See also Whiteman, 2 *Digest* 728–45; Chen, *Recognition*, 172–86; Lauterpacht, *Recognition*, 59–60; Jones (1935), 16 *BY* 42–55; Nisot (1943), 21 *Can. BR* 627–43.

⁵ de Visscher, *Théories et réalités* (4th rev. edn., 1970), 262–3.

⁶ Oppenheim, (8th edn.) I, 150 ('a rule . . . of convenience rather than principle'); Brownlie, *Principles*, 97–8: *contra* Chen, *Recognition*, 177–9.

⁷ Jessup, *A Modern Law of Nations* (1948), 66–7.

⁸ *Princess Paley Olga* v. *Weisz* [1929] 1 K.B. 718, 729 *per* Sankey L.J.

⁹ Chen, *Recognition*, 179–82, Cf. the dispute between British and American courts as to the commencement of the North American Confederation: Weis, *Nationality & Statelessness in International Law* (1956), 151–2; Chen, *Recognition*, 172–3 and cases there cited. See also *infra*, p. 392   ¹⁰ *Boguslawski* v. *Gdynia-Ameryka Linie* [1953] A.C. 11.

¹¹ *Civil Air Transport Inc.* v. *Central Air Transport Corp.* [1953] A.C. 70 (P.C.). Cf. *Guaranty Trust Co. of N.Y.* v. *U.S.* 304 U.S. 126 (1938); *Lehigh Valley R.R Co.* v. *State of Russia* 21 F. 2d. 396 (1927).

¹² *The Jupiter* (No. 3) [1927] P. 122, 250; *Boguslawski* v. *Gdynia Ameryka Linie* [1953] A.C. 11, 28–9 *per* Lord Porter. Cf. however *U.S.* v. *Pink* 315 U.S. 203 (1942), criticized by Lauterpacht, *Recognition*, 60n.2

(2) *Problems of commencement in international fora*

In an international forum, where national recognition policies provide evidence of, but are not conclusive as to, the status of particular entities, problems of commencement require the application of the general criteria of statehood to particular factual situations.[13] Since these situations tend to be complex, such application can be acutely difficult: it is none the less, in principle, suitable for judicial determination by any body in possession of those facts.[14] It is thus said that 'on the international plane there is no rule of retroactivity'.[15] This is true if it means that in international law recognition is effective *pro tanto* only when accorded. It is equally true if it means that an entity which clearly does qualify as a State at a particular moment will not in some way retrospectively lose its competence through subsequent extinction, merger, or other change of status. On the other hand, an entity whose status is doubtful at a particular time may well, if it becomes definitively established or generally recognized as a State, be regarded as having been a State also at that earlier time: in such cases, subsequent events are capable of giving form to a state of affairs which would otherwise have been equivocal. There is thus, in international practice, at least an element of retroactivity, not in any recognition accorded to a new State, but in its legal status while it is in the process of establishing itself.[16] Of course, much will depend on the particular claim: a court might well treat a claim to change of nationality[17] more strictly than a claim of responsibility[18] or a claim to particular State property under the control of the entity in question.

[13] This is equally true in a municipal forum where for whatever reason there is no binding determination of the Executive on the point: cf. the detailed examination by Hill J. of whether Odessa was within the territorial sovereignty of the R.F.S.F.R. in the period preceding April 1919: *The Jupiter (No 3)* [1927] P. 122.

[14] Chen, *Recognition*, 41, 176–7. Cf. the discussion by Vallat, *ILC Ybk.* 1974/II(1), 29–30; Verhoeven, *Reconnaissance*, 683–5.

[15] Brownlie, *Principles*, 98.

[16] Cf. the decision of a U.S.–Venezuelan Arbitral Tribunal in the case of *Jacob Idler* v. *Venezuela*, Moore, *IA* IV, 3491, 3527–8, 3542–4.

[17] Cf. the dispute between the British and American Commissioners under the Jay Treaty in the case of *Andrew Allen* (1799); Moore, *Int. Adj. (N.S.)* III, 238–52.

[18] In the *Reparations Case* the request for an opinion referred to 'the responsible *de jure* or *de facto* government'; I.C.J. Rep. 1949 p. 180. This was in context of claims against Israel for acts committed by Jewish terrorists in September 1948, when Israel was still establishing itself as a State and before its admission to the U.N. The Court did not advert to the possibility that Israel was not therefore responsible. See also *infra*, p. 392.

The reason for this element of retroactivity is to be found in the relatively conservative operation of the rules relating to acquisition of statehood by secession: where an entity which has enjoyed effective control of territory for a period of time is acknowledged as a State, there would appear to be little point in denying the entity's own characterization of its acts since its *de facto* establishment, especially in view of the well established rule that a seceding State will be held internationally responsible for acts performed by it *pendente bello*.[19]

In the application of these general considerations, international tribunals have thus tended, in much the same way as municipal tribunals but for somewhat different reasons, to date the commencement of the State in question from the earliest date at which it could be said to have been effectively in control of its territory.[20] Exceptions have related on the whole not to the competence of the new State *vis-à-vis* that territory, but to matters such as the adhesion of minorities in geographically or historically separate territories,[21] or relations of belligerency *vis-à-vis* non-recognizing States.[22]

[19] Chen, *Recognition*, 179–81.

[20] Mixed arbitral tribunals consistently held that the various States formed after World War I had come into existence prior to the relevant peace treaties: see e.g. *Deutsche Continental Gas–Gesellschaft* v. *Polish State* (1920) 5 AD No. 5; *Germany* v. *Reparations Commission (13th Question)* 1 RIAA (1924) 524–5; *Poznanski* v. *Lentz & Hirschfield* (1925) 4 *Rep. MAT* 353, and the cases cited under 'Beginning of State Existence' in AD Vols. 1–6. According to the Rules of the Paris Peace Conference (Protocol I of the Preliminary Peace Conference, 18 January 1919, Annex II) 'States in process of formation' were accorded the same status as 'Neutral Powers', but less status than 'belligerent Powers with special interests', with respect to representation at the Conference. Poland and Czechoslovakia were however placed in the latter category. Cf. Hunter Miller, *My Diary of the Conference at Paris*, xx, 331–4; and *supra*, pp. 312–13. Compare the stricter rule adopted in the case of transfer of territory between existing States: *Ottoman Public Debt Arbitration* (1925) 1 *RIAA* 554–5. Cf. also Marek, *Identity and Continuity*, 203, 212–13.

[21] In the *Aaland Islands Case*, the International Commission of Jurists advised that, before May 1918, 'the conditions required for the formation of a Sovereign State did not exist', and that, at that time, the population of the islands preferred a different status. In their view 'The fact that Finland was eventually reconstituted as an independent State is not sufficient to efface the conditions which gave rise to the aspiration of the Aaland Islanders and to cause these conditions to be regarded as if they had never arisen ... ' Thus ' ... even with reference to a *de facto* situation, it should be possible to invoke, if not the actual principle of non-retrospective action ... at any rate the primary reason on which it rests, which is dictated by justice and equity'. *LNOJ* Sp. Supp. No. 3 (Oct. 1920), 6, 10, 12. The Commission of Rapporteurs relied on the separate legal identity of Finland before 1914 to refute this argument: cf. *supra*, pp. 44–5.

[22] In the *Polish Upper Silesia Case* the Permanent Court held that 'Poland, as it was becoming constituted in the Russian territories occupied by the Central Powers, was

(3) *'Illegal entities' and problems of commencement*

A distinct problem arises in the case of an internationally illegal administration of territory which continues in existence either pursuant to an international settlement or to general (prescriptive) recognition. In such cases, is the commencement of the resulting entity (whether a State or a territorial administration) to be regarded as retroactive to the date of its assuming *de facto* control? For example, if the Rhodesian question were to be settled by the continuation of the existing polity under a reformed administration, would the statehood of the resulting entity be regarded as in some way retroactive, for example, to 1965? There is little or no practice on this point,[23] and explicit provision would probably be made in the agreements embodying the settlement. A distinction might be drawn between continuance of an entity pursuant to a positive international settlement of the dispute, and the continuance of an entity or administration originally illegal, but the illegality of which was cured by prescription or general recognition. In the former case, there would be no retroactivity unless specifically provided for: in the latter case, it may be that retroactivity would be presumed.[24] In any event, the acts of the illegal administration would presumably retain whatever limited validity they had before the settlement or recognition.

15.2 STATES *IN STATU NASCENDI*

The difficulties of exact application of the general criteria of statehood to the commencement of States are, in practice, mitigated by a number of rules attributing legal competence to entities in the process of formation, so as to enable them to bind the State once definitively formed, in accordance with the maxim

undoubtedly not at war with Germany', and, not being recognized as a belligerent by Germany, was not therefore a party at the armistice: Ser. A No. 7 (1926), 27–9.

[23] Manchukuo and the puppet States in Europe (*supra*, pp. 62–5) were regarded as mere agents of the belligerent occupants. The expelled sovereigns were given an extensive discretion to regulate the consequences of the acts of those administrations upon re-occupation. Cf. Art. 31 of the Italian Peace Treaty, 1947 (Albania): *supra*, p. 65.

[24] Recognition by the U.K. and the U.S. of the 'puppet' Lublin government of Poland, pursuant to the Yalta Agreement, was expressly prospective in effect: this was so because the Polish Provisional Government was intended to be a 'new' government. Cf. Yalta Declaration (1945), 12 *DSB* 215; *Gdynia Ameryka Linie* v. *Boguslawski* [1953] A.C. 11.

nasciturus pro jam nato habetur.[25] The more important of these rules
are as follows:

(1) In some situations a new State may be said to be the
continuation of an entity which possessed international personality before independence. International protectorates such as
Morocco and Tunisia provide a clear example.[26] Equally, the
British Dominions after 1926, and (on the view generally
accepted) India after 1947, were continuations of pre-independence legal persons.[27] Legal rights and obligations of those entities
(e.g. separate membership of international organizations) continued: these were cases of continuity, not succession. Whether
such a relation can be established between an entity possessing
no international but only internal constitutional status is more
doubtful.[28] Equally controversial was the claim made by the
Israel courts in the *Eichmann Case* that there was a sufficient
degree of continuity between the Palestine Mandate (or the
Jewish nation under the mandate) and Israel to justify the
exercise of jurisdiction by the latter over anti-Jewish crimes
committed during World War II.[29]

(2) It is well established that legal rights and liabilities of
successful insurgent governments continue to bind the State so
formed.[30] This is perhaps an incident of the continuity of legal
personality of the belligerent and the new State.[31] Recognition
of the belligerency of the claimant appears however to be
regarded as irrelevant.

(3) More difficult is the problem of pre-independence treaties

---

[25] Brownlie, *Principles*, 82.

[26] *Supra*, p. 195.

[27] *Infra*, p. 406, n. 35.

[28] Cf. the dispute over Finland in the *Aaland Islands Case*: *supra*, pp. 44–5.

[29] 36 ILR 52–3; on appeal, ibid. 304.

[30] Silvanie, *Responsibility of States for Acts of Unsuccessful Insurgent Governments* (1939), 1; de Beus, *The Jurisprudence of the General Claims Commission* ... (1938), 108–9; Ralston, *International Arbitral Law and Procedure* (1910), 232–3; Chen, *Recognition*, 326–7; and see *Bolivar Ry. Co. Claim* (1903) 9 *RIAA* 445; *Dix Claim*, ibid. 119. The rule was applied to seceding governments in a series of cases under the U.S.–Mexico Arbitration Convention of 11 Apr. 1839: see Moore, *IA* IV, 3426–32; Silvanie (1939), 33 *AJ* 78–103, 89–90. However contracts made before the formation of a provisional government and not subsequently ratified by it were held not binding: *Zander Claim*, Moore, *IA* IV, 3432–3. See also *Fogarty* v. *O'Donague* [1926] I.R. 531; and cf. *Irish Free State* v. *Guaranty Safe Deposit Co.* 215 N.Y. Supp. 255 (1927).

[31] For Draft Art. 13 of the ILC's Draft Articles on State Responsibility, which asserts this principle, see *ILC Ybk.* 1975/1, 62–71, 217–18. Cf. (1977) 16 *ILM* 1253.

or agreements, which are often made by the Government of a constitutional unit about to be granted independence by the metropolitan State. For example, the Government of the Congo concluded a Treaty of Friendship with Belgium on 29 June 1960, a day before independence.[32] The validity of these types of arrangement was a matter of some dispute in the International Law Commission: there the precise problem was the legal status of devolution agreements,[33] which, as the Special Rapporteur pointed out, were frequently concluded at the time of, or even just before, the grant of independence to a former colony.[34] The Draft Articles as agreed upon avoided the issue of the validity of such agreements, providing instead that their conclusion could not effect a novation of the predecessor State's obligations or rights.[35] During discussion of Draft Article 7, differing views were expressed as to the validity of agreements of this type. On the one hand Ago was inclined to the view that '... all agreements for the devolution of rights and obligations were international agreements, even though one of the parties might be an insurgent movement or an emergent State represented by a provisional government ... In his opinion, the international character of such an agreement would be unaffected even if the metropolitan power had described it as an instrument of internal public law.'[36] At the other extreme, Yasseen,[37] Bedjaoui,[38] and Ushakov[39] expressed strong doubts as to the validity of such agreements.

In the context of agreements made immediately before independence, a compromise between the two positions seems possible. The analogy of agreements concluded during minority might suggest a *locus poenitentiae* for the new State to disavow pre-independence agreements within a reasonable time after independence; in the absence of disavowal these agreements would be treated as affirmed. Suggestions along these lines were

---

[32] 164 *BFSP* 645. The U.S., by contrast, refused to conclude a similar treaty with the Philippines until the actual day of independence: see *USFR* 1946/VIII, 890–7, 937–9.

[33] Cf. *supra*, p. 229, n. 72.

[34] *ILC Ybk.* 1969/II, 54 ff.; ibid., 1972/I, 50, 56, 158.

[35] A/8710/Rev. 1., Art. 7.

[36] *ILC Ybk.* 1972/I, 55; cf. 52.

[37] Ibid. 53.

[38] Ibid. 53–4.

[39] Ibid. 51–2.

made by both Ustor[40] and Bartos.[41] This view would satisfy both the principle of continuity of treaty obligations, and the need to allow new States some opportunity to scrutinize agreements which may not have been freely entered into.[42]

(4) The capacity of entities *in statu nascendi* to acquire rights under other forms of international arrangement is also a matter of some difficulty. In the *Polish Upper Silesia Case* a majority of the Permanent Court held that Poland was not a party to, and could not rely upon, the Armistice Agreement with Germany or the Protocol of Spa. Poland *qua* State was not, in its view, a World War I belligerent; and the status of the Polish National Committee, recognized by the Allies but not by Germany, was insufficient to enable it to be regarded as a belligerent.[43] Lord Finlay dissented on this point: in his view . . .

It was common knowledge that if the Allies succeeded, the independence of Poland would be one of the terms of peace. All Parties to the Armistice must have contracted with this present to their minds, and it must have been intended that Poland, whose army had been fighting on the side of the Allies as an autonomous army, should be bound by the terms of the Armistice, and, when she came into existence as a recognized State, have the benefit of them. This would be a *jus quaesitum*, a right acquired for the new State as soon as it should come into existence . . . In my view the Allied States made the Armistice on behalf of Poland, which was about to become a State, as well as on their own behalf.[44]

This attractive argument was not adopted by the Court. However the law relating to treaties and third States is now better settled:[45] the question is one of intention, and there would appear to be no reason why contracting States should not confer rights upon an entity in the process of being, or yet to be, created; upon acceptance in writing, these rights or obligations would bind the new State. The difference between Lord Finlay and the majority

---

[40] Ibid. 52.

[41] *ILC Ybk.* 1963/II, 293, 297; cf. ibid., 1972/I, 52–3.

[42] Cf. the discussion of the issue in relation to State succession and matters other than treaties: *ILC Ybk.* 1968/II, 103 (Bedjaoui); ibid., 1973/I, 158 (Bedjaoui), 195 (Ushakov), 197 (Kearney).

[43] Ser. A No. 7 (1926), 27–8; *supra*, p. 390, n. 22. For the arguments, see Ser. C No. 11 126–30, 175–6.

[44] Ser. A No. 7, 84: cf. Schwarzenberger, *International Law* I, 132–4.

[45] Vienna Convention on the Law of Treaties, Arts. 34–7.

in the *Polish Upper Silesia Case* may well have been one of evidence rather than principle.[46]

If a *nasciturus* state can have rights conferred upon it by treaty, it is more doubtful whether such an entity could acquire rights by operation of law, for example through the law of State responsibility. In the *Northern Cameroons Case* it was argued *inter alia* that, since the relevant acts complained of by the Republic of Cameroon occurred before its independence or admission to the United Nations, these could not constitute international wrongs *vis-à-vis* the Republic. The majority judgment made no reference to the problem, since it dismissed the claim on other grounds. The point was, however, dealt with by several of the judges. Judge Bustamante (dissenting) argued that the Republic of Cameroons might . . .

demand the investigation of facts *prior* to its political emancipation, seeing that an undeniable link of dependence, a sort of successive solidarity, exists between the actual situation on the date of the Application and the events which previously played their part in bringing about that situation during the period of the trusteeship . . . A certain parallel may be found, in this connection, in the field of private law if one recalls the case of an infant who, on achieving full age, seeks to examine his guardian's acts of administration during his minority.[47]

On the other hand, Judge Fitzmaurice was firmly of the view that

since the Applicant State did not exist as such at the date of these acts or events, these could not have constituted, in relation to it, an international wrong, nor have caused it an international injury. An act which did not, in relation to the party complaining of it, constitute a wrong at the time it took place, obviously cannot *ex post facto* become one. Similarly, such acts or events could not in themselves have constituted, or retroactively have become, violations of the Trust *in relation to the Applicant State*, since the Trust confers rights only on Members of the United Nations, and the Applicant State was not then one, nor even, over most of the relevant period, in existence as a State and separate international *persona*.[48]

---

[46] Cf. Ser. A No. 7, 29: '*in case of doubt*, no rights can be deduced in favour of third States' (my italics).
[47] I.C.J. Rep. 1963 p.15, 169–70. Cf. 47 (Judge Wellington Koo).
[48] Ibid. 129.

The situation has been summarized as follows:

States not infrequently first appear as independent belligerent entities under a political authority which may be called and function effectively as a provisional government . . . Once statehood is firmly established, it is justifiable, both legally and practically, to assume the retroactive validation of the legal order during a period prior to general recognition . . . when some degree of effective government existed . . . [T]he principle of effectiveness dictates acceptance, for some legal purposes at least, of continuity before and after statehood is firmly established.[49]

This validation of acts of entities in the process of formation is based on, and limited by, the principle of effectiveness: transactions entered into by a provisional government bind the State, but transaction with individuals struggling to establish, but who have not yet established, a *de facto* regime require subsequent ratification. Where the *nasciturus* State possesses a distinct capacity, international rights and duties may be acquired: where it is still effectively submerged in another State, the mechanism of a *jus quaesitum tertio* is required.

15.3 NEW STATES AND THE ACQUISITION OF TERRITORIAL SOVEREIGNTY

The problem of the relation between acquisition of statehood and acquisition of territorial sovereignty has been discussed already.[50] The problem has two aspects: theoretical, in that it is necessary to reconcile the rules relating to acquisition of statehood (which necessarily[51] involves acquisition of some territory) with the traditional 'modes of acquisition of territory', which do not include the acquisition of territory by new States; and practical,

---

[49] Brownlie, *Principles*, 82.

[50] *Supra*, pp. 36–40.

[51] The proposition that statehood *necessarily* involves territorial sovereignty is generally accepted, and since there has in practice been no clear case where this was not so, the assumption has been accepted also for the purposes of this study. In theory, however, why should not an entity set up for a certain fixed period of time on territory granted for that purpose by another State, and which remained under the residual sovereignty of the grantor, be none the less, for the period of its separate existence, a State? This possibility is not really relevant for present purposes, since the cases under discussion involve conflicting or disputed claims to sovereignty over particular territory: in such a case, the position is, it is thought, that the conflict is to be settled, in the first instance, by the application of the criteria for statehood, and only secondarily by the rules relating to territorial disputes between States.

in that it is sometimes necessary to deal with claims to the whole territory of a new State, which claims must, if successful, result in the extinction of the State.

(1) *The acquisition of statehood as a 'mode of acquisition' of territory*

Traditional international law distinguished, not perhaps very helpfully, five modes of acquisition of territory, which were derived from the Roman law rules relating to transfer of land *inter vivos.*[52] It is clear that the acquisition of territory by a new State does not fit into this pattern: as Jennings points out,

'In transfers between existing States the law ... has been inspired chiefly by the seductive private law analogy of transfers of ownership in land. But where a new State arises the law has looked chiefly to the emergence of the new subject rather than the incidental transfer of territory; it has looked to the sovereign, rather than the territorial, element of territorial sovereignty.[53]

This problem—of 'placing' the acquisition of territorial sovereignty by a new State in the traditional scheme—has proved troublesome, especially to adherents of the declaratory theory of recognition.[54] It is, however, something of a false problem. International law provides that, where an entity qualifies as a State, certain rules *prima facie* enure to its benefit: it is entitled to the control and government of its territory (subject to boundary disputes and the like); it is entitled to protection against the use of force other than in self-defence by other States; and disputes or claims against it must be settled (apart from the mechanism of Chapter VII of the Charter) not only peacefully, but also with its consent.[55] There is thus a primary regime of rules for determining statehood, which rules, both logically and in practice, take priority over the rules relating to transfer of territory between existing States. If it is thought desirable to categorize acquisition of territory by new States as a distinct 'mode' of acquisition,[56]

---

[52] Cf. Oppenhiem (8th edn.) I, 545–6; Kelsen, *Principles* (1952), 207 ff.; Shoenborn (1929), 30 *HR* 85–187.

[53] Jennings, *Acquisition of Territory*, 8.

[54] Cf. Starke (1965–6), 41 *BY* 411–16, where it is suggested, as an explanation of recent practice at least, that such acquisition is a mode *sui generis* involving something like succession by dependent peoples as subjects of international law.

[55] *Supra*, pp. 32–4.

[56] Jennings, *Acquisition of Territory*, 11–12.

still the rules applicable are those relating to acquisition of statehood. This point was made with some clarity in a *consultation* of MM. Basdevant, Jèze, and Politis on the creation of Czechoslovakia:[57] the view that Czechoslovakia was created piecemeal by the 'cession' to it of particular parcels of territory in the post-war treaties in their view 'contredit le principe fondamental incontestable et incontesté selon lequel l'état existe dès que ses éléments constitutif sont réunis.'[58] This view proceeded, they stated,

de la prétention de traîter comme une cession territoriale la formation d'un État nouveau sur des térritoires que se sont détachés de trois États. Or, ce sont là deux situations nettement différentes, et les règles applicables à la première ne peuvent être transportées à la seconde . . . Il faut ici tenir compte de ce principe qu'un État existe dès que ses éléments constitutifs sont réunis et du fait que la Tchécoslovaquie a existé et agi comme un État dès le 28 octobre 1918. Les divers traités qui la visent constantent l'existence de l'État tchécoslovaque comme un fait déjà accompli.[59]

(2) *Claims to the entire territory of a new State*

This view of the primacy of the rules relating to the acquisition of statehood may be tested by examining situations where the entire territory of a new State has been claimed. The view has consistently been taken in such cases that the entity in question continued to exist as a State despite such claims.[60] Even assuming a valid territorial claim before the purported creation of the new State, the latter's claim to statehood is *ipso facto*, as it were, a secession from that territorial claim. In such a case, the continued existence of the new State as an effective territorial entity, and the protection afforded by Chapter VII of the Charter, combine to defeat the previous territorial claim. Jennings' conclusion is thus seemingly inevitable:

if the new State . . . is established with the disputed territory as its sole territory, and its Statehood is recognized, it would seem that another

---

[57] The *consultation* was one of three such opinions requested by the Czechoslovak government and annexed to the Request: Ser. C No. 68, 29 *et seq.* The case was not proceeded with.

[58] Ser. C No. 68, 58–9.

[59] Ibid. 51–3.

[60] *Supra*, p. 38.

claim to sovereignty over the territory *is* defeated. In short it is only where there is room for doubt or ambiguity in the definition of the new State's territory that a claim against the territory will survive. A sufficient number of recognitions of the new State clearly implying recognition of its title to the disputed territory would presumably destroy the claim.[61]

[61] *Acquisition of Territory*, 38 (his itals.). Note however the emphasis on recognition: cf. Jennings's quasi-constitutive position, *supra*, p. 17, n. 62.

16. Problems of Identity, Continuity, and Reversion

16.1 THE PROBLEM OF IDENTITY AND CONTINUITY: GENERAL CONSIDERATIONS

As we have seen, there is a fundamental distinction between State continuity and State succession: that is to say, between cases where the 'same' State can be said to continue to exist, despite changes of government, territory, or population, and cases where one State can be said to have replaced another with respect to certain territory.[1] *De lege lata* the whole of the law of State succession depends on this distinction, and it must therefore, presumably, be possible to distinguish cases of continuity from cases of succession. None the less in many situations in practice the distinction is arbitrary, and it may depend in particular cases not on the substance of a particular transaction but on the way in which that transaction was carried out.[2] The notion of 'continuity' has thus been criticized as misleading and over-general.[3]

Despite these criticisms, the concept is well established and, in default of abandonment of the State/government distinction, *a priori* necessary. Moreover, relations in other areas of international law are also subject to alteration at the will of the actors; nor can it be said that alternative notions of continuity are sufficiently well-defined to lead us to abandon the present position. Indeed the concept of continuity *prima facie* preserves legal relations despite changes in the subject of the relations: it is thus a desirable alternative to the present law of State succession, which, in most cases at least, is marked by a *prima facie* discontinuity of relations.

On the other hand, it must be admitted that, in many of the marginal cases, as well as in cases of States re-established after illegal occupation, notions of continuity contain a distinct element of legal fiction: in such instances, recognition, and the

---

[1] *Supra*, pp. 28–30, and authorities there cited.
[2] Cf. Sardinia—Italy: *infra*, p. 404, n. 17.
[3] Brownlie, *Principles*, 85–6.

claims to continuity made by the parties, may well be determinative. The point is that, in practice, claims to 'continuity' are made and recognized: there has been no general tendency to deal with the problems in a functional way, by reference to specific, more or less isolated, issues.

International lawyers have generally paid little more attention to these problems than to those of the definition and operation of the concept of statehood itself. Certainly, it is one thing to determine that entity A is a State at a particular time, and another to determine that entity A1, at some other time, is the 'same' State, for relevant purposes. However, allowing greater latitude to recognition and the views of the actors concerned, one would have thought that reasonable solutions to problems of identity could have been found by reference to the basic criteria of statehood as affecting the entities at the relevant times. A different approach has been adopted in Marek's leading study:[4] there, identity is defined by reference to the legal obligations of the State in question, rather than by application of the criteria for statehood. Thus Marek defines 'the identity of a State' as the identity of its international rights and obligations, before and after the event which called that identity in question, and solely on the basis of the customary norm 'pacta sunt servanda'.[5] Where a State is identical in the sense defined, it is by definition continuous as between the two occasions referred to. State continuity is merely 'the dynamic predicate of State identity'.[6] It is therefore impossible, in Marek's view, that a State should finally disappear, and then reappear as the 'same' State: the extinction of a State puts an end to any possible identity of continuity.[7]

To the view that State identity means identity of legal rights and obligations, several objections may be proposed. In the first place, the existence of a State might seem to be separate from the legal relations of that State, and certainly from its conventional legal relations. This is not to say that the State is some meta-legal 'thing': *qua* legal person it is, in a sense, merely the sum of its

---

[4] *The Identity and Continuity of States in Public International Law* (1954), 68–76.

[5] That is, excluding rights and obligations devolved by virtue of the rules of State succession; op. cit. 14.

[6] Ibid. 5–6.

[7] Ibid. 7–9; cf. the reference (581) to the impossibility of a 'miraculous resurrection' of a once-extinct State.

rights, duties, and notably, powers and immunities. But the assertion that the customary rights, etc. of entity A are the 'same' as those of entity A1, two weeks or two years later, may not be self-evident and is certainly not self-explanatory. Marek admits that, in a dynamic legal system, identity and continuity can only be relative;[8] and it seems just as meaningful to say that the customary rights etc. of the two entities are only the 'same' if the entities are, relatively, the 'same' as *vice versa*. For to say that a particular entity is the 'same' in this context (given that other entities may have equal rights) is merely to say that the relevant rights exist with respect to, or are attributed to, the same State— that is, the same, or substantially the same, territorial governmental entity. Particular rights, duties and powers, in terms of the creation of States, are not criteria for, but rather the consequences of statehood.[9] It therefore seems sensible to make continuity, identity, and extinction depend on variants of these basic criteria; that is, primarily, territory, population, and independent government, and, as subsidiary criteria (but criteria which may be particularly important in doubtful or marginal cases), permanence and recognition. Significantly, Marek is, in general, critical of recognition as a criterion of problems of identity.[10] However, the specific rules for continuity she proposes are at least as consistent with this view, which in addition avoids two problems raised by her analysis.

First, because in each case the same rights and obligations exist, is it impossible on Marek's view to distinguish cases of State continuity from cases of (postulated) universal succession, except by excluding *a priori* the category of succession.[11] But this is circular, because, as she rightly points out, the question of succession only arises after problems of continuity and extinction have been resolved: the two are mutually exclusive.[12] Secondly, it appears reasonable to postulate two types of State identity: the case of non-extinction despite change of circumstances, and the case of rebirth after temporary extinction. The second may, on one view at least, be said to have been the case with Syria after

---

[8] Op. cit. 4–5.
[9] *Supra*, pp. 32–5.
[10] *Identity and Continuity*, 129, 216.
[11] Ibid. 9–14.
[12] Cf. the discussion (*supra*, p. 280) relating to the 'identity' of the Federal Republic of Germany with pre-1945 Germany.

1961. The view proposed here allows for both alternatives: Marek's view *a priori* excludes the second.

It is argued then that the rules for determining identity and continuity are variants upon the basic criteria for statehood, with the addition of certain specific qualifying or particularizing rules. Thus, a State may be said to continue as such so long as the same governmental system continues to exist with respect to a significant part of a territory and population: its constitutional system need not be the same, as long as it is in fact independent as defined. In applying these criteria, which may often be equivocal, questions of recognition and acquiescence will be important;[13] and the view of the entity concerned, though not necessarily decisive, will be particularly relevant. A State may be said to be the 'same' State (with the consequence that the same legal rules, including conventional rules, *prima facie* continue to apply) where it is continuous in the sense defined; or where, after a temporary extinction, an entity with substantially the same constituent features is re-established.[14] In the latter case, because of the doubts inevitably raised by State extinction, recognition by other States will be of particular importance. These general principles will be, briefly, examined in the context of the specific accepted rules or presumptions concerning identity and continuity of States.

16.2 SOME APPLICATIONS OF THE CONCEPT OF CONTINUITY

Where a State retains substantially the same territory, and the same structure or system of government, over a period of time, there is quite clearly no change in personality. This 'central' case establishes that the problem of continuity, like that of statehood itself, cannot be settled by application of a constitutive theory of recognition:[15] in clear cases, at least, issues of identity and

---

[13] Where a situation is equivocal, continuity may well be non-opposable to non-recognizing States. In practice (e.g. in the Syrian case) no objections have been raised: the honorific aspects for the State in question are usually regarded as more important than any adverse legal consequences of continuity for other States.

[14] Marek rejects this view on the basis that 'territorial changes have no effect on the identity of States: it is not territory which determines that identity' (21). But this does not refute the proposition that extensive territorial change may be one of several criteria for continuity (cf. ibid. 23–4).

[15] Cf. however Marek, *Identity and Continuity*, 4.

continuity will be opposable *erga omnes*. The other view would involve the proposition that a State could evade treaty obligations by alleging on insubstantial grounds a change of personality.

Problems do however arise where the constitutive elements of statehood undergo substantial change. The following rules are established.

(1) *Territorial changes*

(i) *In General*

It is established that acquisition or loss of territory does not *per se* affect the continuity of the State.[16] This may be so even where the territory acquired or lost is substantially greater in area than the original or remaining State territory. The presumption of continuity is particularly strong where the constitutional system of the State prior to acquisition or loss continues in force.[17]

(ii) *'Imperial States'*

The presumption of continuity despite territorial change is somewhat dramatically illustrated by the case of 'imperial' States.[18] The United Kingdom remains the same State despite the loss since 1920 of a massive Empire: indeed its continuity has never been questioned. Turkey was also regarded as a continuation of the Ottoman Empire.[19] The cases of Austria and Hungary are more doubtful.[20]

[16] Ibid. 15–24. For I.L.C. *travaux* on what became Art. 10 of the Draft Articles on State Succession with respect to Treaties (the 'moving treaty frontiers' rule) cf. Waldock, *ILC Ybk.* 1969/II, 52–4; and the debates ibid. 1972/I, 43–50, 152–4, 156–8, 182, 276.

[17] This is probably the justification for the view that the Kingdom of Italy was created in the period 1848–70 by the enlargement of, and was thus identical with, Sardinia-Piedmont: Marek, op. cit. 191–8; Romano (1912), 6 *Rdi* 345; *Costa v. Military Service Commission of Genoa*, 9 A.D. No. 13 (1939); *Gastaldi v. Lepage Hemery* (1929) 5 A.D. No. 43. The Sardinian Constitution remained in force throughout the Risorgimento. *Contra*: Anzilotti (1912), 6 *Rdi.* Cf. also the Secretariat legal opinion on the continued U.N. membership of Malaya as Malaysia, stressing that the federation was achieved by the admission into Malaya of Singapore, Sabah, and Sarawak: *Jur. Ybk.* 1963, 161.

[18] Cf. Gentili's argument for the continuity of the Roman Empire: *On the Law of War* (1612) I, c. 23 esp. 192–3: 'an empire does not come to an end if it survives even in some tiny part . . . [A] slight degree of preservation keeps up preservation.'

[19] *Ottoman Debt Arbitration* (Arbitrator Borel, 1925) 3 AD No. 57; *Roselius & Co. v. Karsten & Turkish Republic* (1926) ibid., No. 26.

[20] The Treaties of Saint-Germain and Trianon assumed continuity of Austria and Hungary with the two kingdoms of the Dual Monarchy (as to which cf. *supra*, p. 291, n. 16). The problem depended in large part on the view taken of the status of the kingdoms before 1918. Marek, op. cit., 199–236 denies that either Austria or Hungary before 1918 possessed separate international status, and thus denies the possibility of

(2) *Changes in population*

Changes in population are of course concomitants of territorial changes (in the absence of a transfer of populations), and the same considerations apply.[21]

(3) *Changes in government*

It has long been established that, in the case of an 'internal revolution, merely altering the municipal constitution and form of government, the State remains the same; it neither loses any of its rights, nor is discharged from any of its obligations'.[22] Despite the question-begging nature of this and other formulations, the rule that revolution *prima facie* does not affect the continuity of the State in which it occurs has been consistently applied to the innumerable revolutions, *coups d'état* and the like in the nineteenth and twentieth centuries.[23] After some hesitation, it was for example established that the R.F.S.F.R. (later the Soviet Union) was a continuation of Imperial Russia.[24] *A fortiori*, continuity is not affected by alterations in a municipal constitution according to its own amendment provisions; or by a change in the name of the State;[25] or by non-recognition of the revolutionary government of a State.[26] Although it is sometimes

continuity. The same view was taken by Commissioner Parker, *Administrative Decision No. 1* (Tripartite Claims Commission, 1927) 6 RIAA 203, 209–10; and by the Austrian courts: see e.g. *Railway Pension (Austria) Case* (1923) 2 AD No. 34. See also Udina, *L'estinzione del Impero Austro-Ungarico nel diritto internazionale* (2nd edn., 1933), 15–37. The continuity thesis was upheld by Arbitrator Beichmann: *Reparations Commission* v. *German Government* (1924) 1 *RIAA* 440–1; and by courts in other States: e.g. *In re Ungarische Kriegsproduckten A.G.* (1920) 1 AD No. 45. See also *Répertoire suisse* III, 1291–2, 1337–52.

[21] Cf. the case of Poland, *infra*, pp. 409–12.

[22] Wheaton, *Elements* (8th ed., 1866) I, § 22, citing Grotius, *De Jure Belli ac Pacis* II, Ch. 9 § 8; Pufendorf, VIII, Ch. 12, §§ 1–3.

[23] Marek, op. cit., 24–73 and works there cited. Cf. also *State* v. *Dosso* (Pakistan S.C., 1958) 27 ILR 22 *per* Muhammad Munir C.J.

[24] Marek, op. cit., 34–8; Grzybowski, *Soviet Public International Law. Doctrines and Diplomatic Practice* (1970), 92–5. Cf. *Agency of Canadian Car and Foundry Co. Ltd.* v. *American Can Co.* (1918) 253 F. 152, affd. (1919) 258 F. 363; *Russian Government* v. *Lehigh Valley Railroad Co.* (1919) 293 F. 133, affd. (1927) 21 F.2d. 396. British courts assumed continuity without argument (3 AD 35) until *Lazard Bros.* v. *Midland Bank Ltd.* [1933] A.C. 289, 297, 307–8 *per* Lord Wright. See also *Russian Roubles (Attempted Counterfeiting) Case* (Japan S.C. 1919) 1 AD No. 15; *Golovitschiner* v. *Dori* (Cairo Civil Tr., 1923) 2 AD No. 24; *Lowinsky* v. *Receiver in Bankruptcy* (Amsterdam D.C., 1932) 6 AD No. 16; *Banque de L'Union Parisienne* v. *Jaudon* (Paris C.A., 1933) 7 AD No. 32; *Weber* v. *U.S.S.R.* (Amsterdam C.A., 1942) 11 AD No. 74. Cf. also *In re petition of S.* (Hague 1957) 24 ILR 52 & n.

[25] *The Sapphire* v. *Napoleon III* 78 U.S. 164 (1871).

[26] *Tinoco Arbitration* (1924) 18 *AJ* 147.

argued that 'socialist revolutions', which result in a changed class-structure of the State, bring about a fundamental discontinuity in relations,[27] it is not at all clear whether this claim is directed to the notion of legal continuity of the State, or is a claim to a more liberal regime of succession. Neither the Soviet Union[28] nor the People's Republic of China[29] have asserted such discontinuity; while problems of succession of governments in the two cases have tended to be worked out on an *ad hoc* basis.

(4) Changes in international status

The possibility of continuity of personality between entities with varying degrees of personality or capacity has been referred to already.[30] Although Marek denies this possibility on *a priori* grounds,[31] it is established in practice that, for example, international protectorates or protected States continue the legal personality of the pre-protectorate State.[32] The position of mandated and trust territories is more doubtful: it would seem that there is no continuity,[33] except, possibly, in the case of 'A' Mandates.[34] Where there are substantial changes in the entity concerned, continuity may depend upon recognition (as in the case of India after 1947).[35] The predominant view was that Austria and Hungary after 1918 continued the legal personality of the two States of the Dual Monarchy, although this has been denied.[36] Where the change in status is a result of external

[27] Taracouzio, *The Soviet Union and International Law* (1935), 21; O'Connell, *State Succession* I, 19–21.

[28] Grzybowski, op. cit., 94.

[29] Hsiung, in Cohen, *China's Practice of International Law* (Harvard, 1972), 14–56, 36.

[30] *Supra*, p. 392.

[31] *Identity and Continuity*, 187.

[32] *Supra*, pp. 203–4.

[33] This is to be inferred from the discussion of the *Northern Cameroons Case: supra,* pp. 395–6.

[34] *Shehadeh* v. *Commissioner of Prisons* (1947) 14 AD No. 16. Israel for most purposes denied continuity with Palestine: cf. however the *Eichmann Case; supra,* p. 392.

[35] Britain and, after some debate, the U.N., took the view that India was a continuation of British India, and so retained U.N. membership; whereas Pakistan was a new State which therefore had to be admitted under Art. 4. This equation of India with British India was however questionable. See O'Connell, *State Succession* II, 127–30, 184–7, 277–88; Poulose, *Succession in International Law. A Study of India, Ceylon, Pakistan and Burma* (1974), 11–30; Schachter (1948), 25 *BY* 91–132, 103–9; Aufricht (1962), 11 *ICLQ* 154–170, 155–6. On the status of India before 1947, see Poulose (1970), 44 *BY* 202–12; Sunderam (1931), 7 *Grot. ST* 35–54; Mahatra, *India and the Commonwealth 1885–1924* (1965); Verhoeven, *Reconnaissance,* 16–18.

[36] *Supra*, p. 404, n. 20, and works there cited.

imposition (in particular of a puppet entity), continuity is not to be presumed, since, in the absence of general recognition, such an entity lacks any international status other than as agent of the belligerent.[37]

(5) *Belligerent occupation*

It is well established that belligerent occupation does not affect the continuity of the State:[38] as a result, governments-in-exile have frequently been recognized as governments of an enemy-occupied State *pendente bello*.[39] In the absence, at least, of constitutional continuity of the government-in-exile with the pre-occupation government of the State,[40] such recognition would appear to be constitutive and non-opposable.[41] The continuity of a State under belligerent occupation remains until the peace settlement, or, probably, until extinction by *debellatio*.[42]

(6) *Continuity and illegal annexation*

State practice in the period since 1930 has established, not without some uncertainty, the proposition that annexation of the territory of a State as a result of the illegal use of force does not effect the extinction of the State. The practice is discussed in more detail in the next Chapter.

(7) *Identity without continuity*

The case of Syria, which has been referred to already, demonstrates the possibility that a State which has for a time been extinguished may be re-established on the same or substantially the same territory and be regarded as for relevant purposes the same entity as before extinction. Syria's United Nations membership apparently revived upon its secession from the United Arab Republic in 1961, without the need for

---

[37] *Supra*, p. 64. Cf. the case of Poland, *infra*, p. 409.

[38] Marek, *Identity and Continuity*, 73–125.

[39] Marek, op. cit., 86–101; Whiteman, 1 *Digest* 921–30; Flory, *Le Statut International des Gouvernements Réfugiés et le cas de la France Libre 1939–1945* (1952); Oppenheimer (1942), 36 *AJ* 568–75.

[40] This was the case with the Polish Government in exile after 1939. However, constitutional continuity did not avail against an effective government recognized by the Allies of Potsdam. Cf. Lauterpacht, *Recognition*, 353n.

[41] Cf. *Polish Upper Silesia Case*, *supra*, pp. 394–5.

[42] *Infra*, p. 419. For the case of Germany after 1945, cf. *supra*, p. 274.

readmission.[43] The South African Republic also seems to have been regarded as the same State before and after a period of extinction (1877–81).[44] However, where State existence is terminated either by consent of the entities concerned (as with the United Arab Republic) or validly in accordance with international law at the time (as with the South African Republic), any subsequent assertion of 'identity' takes on decidedly fictional overtones, and may very well be non-opposable. This is especially so where (as with Poland from 1795 to 1918)[45] the period of extinction lasts for more than a few years.

Identity is more tenable in the case of States illegally but effectively annexed: in such situations, the formal legal identity of the State may be preserved over a period of time by the relevant legal rules and any corresponding obligations of non-recognition. This was, it seems, the case with Ethiopia, Austria, and Czechoslovakia, even though the international community extended substantial *de facto* recognition of extinction.[46] In practice, this situation appears to be treated as one of continuity without extinction, but the other view would seem to be at least arguable;[47] as well as politically more realistic where the annexed State is not represented by any claimant government-in-exile or insurgent movement.[48]

(8) *Multiple changes and State continuity*

Each of the rules or presumptions referred to have related to changes in one or other of the constituent elements of statehood. Where a State undergoes multiple changes, the problem is more difficult, and the role of recognition still more important. Examples of asserted identity despite multiple changes of this

[43] Young (1962), 56 *AJ* 482–8.

[44] An entity called the South African Republic existed during the periods 1852–77 and 1881–1900. Art. X of the Pretoria Convention, 1881 (72 BFSP 900) and Arts. X, VIII of the London Convention, 1884 (75 BFSP 5) clearly treat it as the same State during both periods.

[45] Identity was claimed by Polish courts: *Republic* v. *Felsenstadt* (1922), 1 AD No. 16; *Republic* v. *Weisholc* (1919), ibid., No. 17; *Republic* v. *Pantol* (1922) ibid., No 18; but was not recognized by other States.

[46] *Infra*, Chapter 17.

[47] Cf. *Land Registry of Waldsassen* v. *Towns of Eger and Waldsassen* (Bavaria, S.C., 1965) 44 ILR 50, 57–8.

[48] Cf. also the problem of reversion: *infra*, pp. 412–16; and for the I.L.C.'s view, *infra*, p. 415, n. 83.

type include Serbia after 1918[49] and Germany after 1945.[50] Perhaps the best example, however, is the case of Poland after 1945.

Pursuant to the Yalta and Potsdam Agreements, Poland's territory and population were radically redistributed, and an entirely different political and constitutional system was imposed.[51] The new government of Poland was doubtfully, if at all, independent. None the less, Poland after 1945 was treated in practice as the same State as Poland before 1939, so that, although there was in 1945 a succession of governments, there was at no time a succession of States, or the creation of a new Polish State not identical with pre-1939 Poland. For example, treaties made by the Polish government before 1939 generally continued in force.[52] The post-1945 government appears to have regarded itself as still bound by agreements or obligations entered into before 1945 by the Polish government-in-exile.[53] An Agreement for the Settlement of Lend-Lease and Other Claims of 28 June 1956 between the United States and Poland referred to the 'London' government and the post-1945 government indistinguishably as 'the Government of Poland'.[54] And a decision of the Polish Supreme Court in 1963 referred to the Concordat with Poland of 10 February 1925 as continuing to regulate the activities of the Catholic church in Poland until unilaterally terminated by a resolution of the Polish Council of Ministers of 12 September 1945.[55]

Practice points unequivocally then to the conclusion that

---

[49] Although a number of treaties between Serbia and other States continued in force, apparently on the assumption of continuity (O'Connell, *State Succession* II, 378–9), the better view seems to be that Yugoslavia (the Serb-Croat-Slovene State) was not a continuation of pre-1914 Serbia: Marek, op. cit. 237–62; *Artukovic v. Boyle* (1952) 107 F. Supp. 11. But a German-Yugoslav M.A.T. held that Yugoslavia was not a 'new State' for the purposes of Art. 297(h) of the Treaty of Versailles: *Katz & Klump v. Yugoslavia* 5 Rep. MAT 963 (1925). Cf. also Hackworth, 5 *Digest* 374–5.

[50] *Supra*, pp. 280–1.

[51] *Supra*, pp. 311–12.

[52] Dabrowa (1968–9), 2 *Polish YBIL* 50–62. *U.S. Treaties in Force 1978* lists *inter alia* the 1927 Extradition Treaty with Poland (92 *LNTS* 101), and the 1922 Agreement relating to the Funding of Polish Indebtedness (58 *LNTS* 97). The U.S.A. emphasized, in its negotiations with the Polish Provisional Government, that the 1931 Treaty of Friendship (*USFR* 1931/II, 933) was still in force: *USFR* 1945/V, 362.

[53] The Lend Lease Agreement of 1942 (103 *UNTS* 267) is also listed in *U.S. Treaties in Force 1978*. Cf. Harriman, *USFR* 1945/I *The Potsdam Conference*, 730.

[54] 273 *UNTS* 79.

[55] *Metropolitan Chapter in Poznán v. State Treasury* (1963) 47 ILR 24.

Poland before 1939 and after 1945 was the same State for relevant purposes, despite substantial changes in territory, population, and government. However, Marek has argued that post-1945 Poland was, if a State at all, a new State not identical with the pre-1939 Polish State, which continued to exist in the government-in-exile in London.[56] This position is however difficult to accept. The view that the Government established at Lublin under Soviet occupation was the government of a puppet State[57] is surely erroneous. Accepting, for present purposes, its puppet character, it was rather the puppet government of a State not extinguished by *debellatio*. The 'Lublin government' claimed to be the government of Poland, the pre-existing State, and, after some reconstruction, was recognized as such at Yalta. The 'London government' did not regard the Provisional Government as government of any other State than Poland.[58] Marek's position appears to be that the only proper course in 1945 would have been the replacement in Poland of the Polish government-in-exile, but this was not even Mikolajczyk's view,[59] nor of course was it that of the Allies. The problem can be tested in another way. If the elections which were due under the Yalta and Potsdam Agreements in 1946 and which were actually held in January 1947 had produced a government which might fairly have been regarded as representative, the problem of identity could hardly have been raised. Free elections were not held, but this violation of the Yalta-Potsdam Agreements was not made the basis for withdrawal of recognition: *a fortiori* it could hardly have retroactively invalidated the continued existence of the Polish State as a legal entity. Moreover, if the post-1945 Government had—assuming again its puppet character in 1945—become in some way a genuinely independent government at a later date, it would surely not have been debarred from claiming continuity with the Polish State as it had existed since 1919. The assumption which is crucial to Marek's thesis is that

---

[56] *Identity and Continuity*, 507–8.

[57] Ibid. 486.

[58] Ibid. 496.

[59] Apart from the re-establishment of the government-in-exile, three other possibilities were envisaged, two of which were 'outside the scope of [*sc.* municipal] legal procedure': *USFR* 1945/V, 119. After Mikolajczyk resigned as Premier of the government-in-exile in November 1944, the latter's re-establishment in Poland was only a remote possibility: cf. Rozek, *Allied Wartime Diplomacy. A Pattern in Poland* (1958), 183 ff.

the lack of independence of the government of a recognized State brings about the extinction of the State as a legal entity; or, perhaps more properly, that where a government which is recognized as the government of an existing State is not truly independent, then it must be regarded merely as the government of a different, puppet, State. It is very doubtful whether either of these assumptions is tenable. The total lack of independence of a separate entity over a period of time can of course lead to the extinction of the State, yet such a result is neither inevitable nor automatic. A State can continue to exist for example even if its government is reduced to relative impotence or even if its territory is wholly occupied.[60]

If the position be taken that, although the lack of independence by itself was insufficient to disturb the continuity of the Polish State, yet along with the other substantial changes in territory, population, and government, the total change was such as to have this effect, it is still necessary to consider the terms by which recognition was given to the new government. Although recognition is not decisive in matters of territorial and governmental status, it can hardly be denied that it will constitute important evidence of that status, particularly in doubtful or marginal cases. Marek cites at least some evidence of State practice in support of her contention: however, much of it is of dubious value. For example, Soviet action *vis-à-vis* the Lublin Government, which action was on Marek's hypothesis unilateral and illegal, can scarcely be entitled to much weight.[61] Equally, deductions from British practice with respect to the Polish forces are not impressive as evidence of the non-identity of the Polish People's Republic with pre-1945 Poland. In fact, it seems reasonably clear that the British position accorded with its recognition of the Republic as a new government, not a new State. The position of the Polish army in exile after 1945 was admittedly anomalous: nevertheless, section 9(8) of the Polish Resettlement Act 1947,[62] which retrospectively validated

---

[60] See also, *infra*, p. 417; and cf. the case of Czechoslovakia (1968–   ), *supra*, p. 58.

[61] But cf. Marek, *Identity and Continuity*, 511 ff.

[62] 'As respects any period between the first day of January 1945 and the passing of this Act, the powers conferred by subsection (1) of section 1 of the Allied Forces Act, 1940, shall be deemed to have been exercisable in relation to the said forces by reference to the law of Poland in force on that day and as if the said forces had not ceased to be recognized by *the Government of Poland,* and any Order in Council made under or by virtue of that Act shall be deemed to have had effect accordingly.' (Italics added.)

military discipline over the Polish forces, was based on the tacit assumption that the action is validated was otherwise illegal at common law.[63] Non-identity of the 'two States' was not the explanation. The conclusion must be that the creation and recognition of the post-1945 Polish government did not affect the identity or continuity of the Polish State.[64] It must be said, however, that where the elements of discontinuity become as extensive as with Poland in 1945, continuity will depend to a great extent on processes of claim and recognition.

16.3 REVERSION TO SOVEREIGNTY

The term 'reversion' in international law has various meanings, four of which require to be distinguished here.

(1) *Rights of reversion by treaty*

The simplest meaning of the term is as a description of the right to sovereignty contingent upon some future event—such as, for example, a failure of heirs of the ruling line.[65] Such rights are now rare. Provided that the future contingency is sufficiently defined, and (possibly) that its occurrence is not within the control of the reversioner, the entity in question may be an independent State.

(2) *Reversion of territorial enclaves*

The claim of a right of reversion with respect to so-called 'colonial enclaves' has been discussed already.[66] If it is a valid legal claim, it applies only to a very restricted category of territories.

(3) *Postliminium*

The notion of *postliminium* was derived by the classical international lawyers from Roman law, where it had involved

---

[63] Cf. also s. 9(2) (reference to the military law 'in force . . . under the law of Poland' as at 1 Jan. 1945).

[64] In 1954, the Lebanon, Spain, the Vatican and Cuba still recognized the Government-in-exile as the Government of Poland. But even they did not, it seems, adhere to the 'two States' theory.

[65] Cf. Monaco: Verzijl, *International Law* II, 472–3; *supra*, pp. 193–4.

[66] *Supra*, pp. 377–84.

reversion of persons or property to their status or ownership before capture by an enemy or alien nation.[67] The classical writers, strongly influenced by the municipal content of the Roman concept, dealt for the most part with matters of status and private property.[68] Where, by analogy with the status of individuals, *postliminium* was considered with respect to groups of people or nations, the answer generally given was that such nations had such a right only when they continued to exist as such, and that the right ceased to be applicable on the extinction of the nation. The classical treatises thus assumed as the foundation of the rule the proposition that 'the acquisition of a conquered town is only consummated by the treaty of peace, or by the entire subjugation or destruction of the State to which it belongs.'[69] A converse assumption was that *postliminium* did not survive a peace treaty, or the extinction of the State by *debellatio*:[70] this is stated by Oppenheim as the modern rule.[71] However, Vattel, with characteristic ambivalence, did suggest that, in the case of complete subjugation of a Nation, *postliminium* might continue to apply so long as the subjugated people 'ha[d] not voluntarily submitted, and ha[d] merely ceased to resist from lack of power, if its conqueror ha[d] not put aside his sword in exchange for the sceptre of a just and peaceful ruler . . .'[72] This extension of the principle went further than the proposition that restoration by an ally *pendente bello* precluded *debellatio*,[73] and involved a real reversion to sovereignty after extinction. Such a reversion was possible however only in a situation of unwilling subjugation, and then, in all probability, only for a relatively brief period of time, since thereafter the Nation's consent to subjugation might be presumed. Precedent for this extension was found in the case of Portugal, which was regarded as reverting to sovereignty after its invasion and annexation by Philip II of Spain (1580–1640).[74]

---

[67] Oppenheim (7th edn., 1952) II, 616–17.

[68] Grotius, *De Jure Belli ac Pacis* III, Ch. IX; Gentili, *De Jure Belli Libri Tres* (1612) III, Ch. XVII; Bynkershoek, *Quaestionum Juris Publici Libri Duo* (1737) I, Ch. XVI; Vattel, *Le Droit de Gens* Ch. XIV.

[69] Vattel, op. cit., § 212.

[70] Cf. Gentili, op. cit., § 623.

[71] (7th edn.) II, § 284 ('No Postliminium after Interregnum').

[72] Op. cit., § 213.

[73] *Infra*, p. 407.

[74] Ibid. and cf. Bynkershoek, op. cit., § 121.

(4) Reversion to sovereignty

The case of Portugal was perhaps the first claim to reversion in the sense which presently concerns us; that is, as a claim of a State to revert to the sovereignty, and thus reassume the rights of, an assertedly identical State extinguished some time previously.[75] The *locus classicus*, such as it is, is a passage from the dissenting opinion of Judge Moreno Quintana in the *Right of Passage Case*:

We must not forget that India, as the territorial successor, was not acquiring the territory for the first time, but was recovering an independence lost long since. Its legal position at once reverted to what it had been more than a hundred years before, as though the British occupation had made no difference . . .

To support the Portuguese claim in this case, which implies survival of the colonial system, without categorical and conclusive proof is to fly in the face of the United Nations Charter.[76]

It is not at all clear what *legal* consequences Judge Moreno Quintana sought to derive from this reversion: Alexandrowicz suggests that the basic incident is procedural, and that, in the absence of compelling evidence, limitations on the plenary sovereignty of the reversioner as it existed before colonization cannot be presumed.[77] It is not at all clear that such a presumption is necessary: the matter would appear to be covered by established presumptions and rules (including the rules of State succession) relating to the sovereignty of new States.[78] Moreover on the evidentiary point Judge Moreno Quintana was a sole dissentient.

Even allowing that reversion might in certain circumstances be arguable, it is clearly necessary that the reverting entity be 'identical' with the pre-colonization State. It is very doubtful indeed whether the Maratha Empire was in any sense identical

---

[75] Reversion is defined by Alexandrowicz as follows: 'There is a legal presumption that a State which lost its sovereignty but reverted to it (before the dust of history had settled), recovers a full and unencumbered sovereignty. The interpretation of rights and obligations connected with such sovereignty would therefore be in favour of the reverting State': (1969) 45 *Int Aff.* 465–80, 474.

[76] I.C.J. Rep. 1960 p. 6, 95; cf. *supra*, pp. 364–5.

[77] *Supra*, n. 75; cf. (1968) 123 *HR* 117–214.

[78] No distinction between reverting and non-reverting States in respect of treaty succession has been made: e.g. Algeria (O'Connell, *State Succession* II, 113, 223). Cf., however, Brownlie, *Principles*, 87–8.

with India after 1947.[79] In the *Western Sahara Case* Mauritania 'expressly accepted that the "Mauritanian entity" did not then [*sc.* in 1884] constitute a State; and also that the present statehood of Mauritania is not retroactive'.[80] The Court concluded that no legal ties of sovereignty could have existed which could avail Mauritania in its claim to the Spanish Sahara. It is also of interest that Algeria, which is one of the few States which, employing the criterion of territorial identity, might fairly be regarded as having reverted to sovereignty, has not claimed such a reversion.[81]

It must be concluded that, whatever the validity or usefulness of reversion as a political claim, there is little authority, and even less utility, for its existence as a legal claim.[82] The International Law Commission after some debate deleted the notion of reversion from its Draft Article 7 ('Date of Transfer of public property') of its Draft Articles on State Succession in Respect of Matters other than Treaties.[83]

---

[79] Alexandrowicz (1968), 123 *HR* 117, 166–7.

[80] *Western Sahara Opinion* I.C.J. Rep. 1975 pp. 12, 57.

[81] *Supra*, pp. 259 60. Bedjaoui, *Law and the Algerian Revolution*, 18 ff. argues that Algeria's sovereignty was never validly extinguished, and so revived with the belligerency of the N.L.F. Belkherroubi, rightly, regards Algeria as a 'new State', without discussing the question of reversion: *La naissance et la reconnaissance de la République algérienne* (1972).

[82] Cf. *supra*, p. 408 for 'identity' after temporary extinction.

[83] Draft Article 7 had originally provided that public property was to be transferred on the date at which the change of property occurred, but excepted, *inter alia*, cases 'where sovereignty has been restored and is deemed to be retroactive to the date of its termination'. *ILC Ybk.* 1973/I, 137. In explanation, the Special Rapporteur (Bedjaoui) instanced the cases of Poland in 1918 and Ethiopia and Albania in 1947 (although in the latter two cases the better view is that sovereignty was never extinguished, so that the problem of reversion did not arise): ibid., 1228th mtg. para. 60. This confusion between continuity and reversion was evident also in the debate. Members were unanimous in agreeing that a State invaded and illegally annexed did not thereby become extinct, but such a hypothesis was already, as was pointed out, excluded from the scope of the Draft Articles: cf. Tammes, ibid., 1229th mtg., para. 3; Ago, ibid., paras. 19–20; nor was it a case of succession: Ushakov, ibid., para. 31. The notion of reversion as at least a principle of international morality was generally accepted, although it was, in Hambro's words, a principle of a 'special and extraordinary character': ibid., paras. 14–17; cf. Yasseen, ibid., para. 11; Camara, ibid., para. 9; Kearney, ibid., para. 4. Ramangasoavina's comment is both representative and instructive: he 'supported the principle that when sovereignty was restored the transfer of public property was retroactive; that principle certainly reflected an idea of justice. However, the period during which sovereignty disappeared might be very long . . . Furthermore, after a State had seized a territory by force, it might try to obliterate all trace of the former sovereignty by destroying its property . . . [For example] in 1895 . . . the Kingdom of Madagascar had fallen into the hands of the French. Previously, the Kingdom of Madagascar had concluded

(*continued overleaf*)

international treaties . . . and had maintained diplomatic missions abroad. After being a protectorate for a year, Madagascar had become a colonial territory. It was difficult to consider that when it had attained independence 65 years later its sovereignty had been restored. Even if the principle of restoration were accepted in such cases, it would obviously be very difficult to reconstitute the property which had existed at the time of the original sovereignty.'

Ibid., paras. 23–4, and cf. Bedjaoui's reply: paras. 37–41. Reference to retroactivity of restored sovereignty was deleted from Art. 7 in the Drafting Committee: ibid., 1239th mtg., para. 21.

17. The Extinction of States

17.1 GENERAL PRINCIPLES

PARALLEL TO the problem of identity and continuity, discussed in Chapter 16, is that of extinction: in what circumstances does a State become extinct, so that the various incidents of succession are brought into play?[1] The rules or presumptions discussed in Chapter 16 are of course equally relevant here: as we have seen, a State is not necessarily extinguished by substantial changes in territory, population, or government, or even, in some cases, by a combination of all three. Continuation of a State entity under a regime such as a protectorate, with some degree of international personality, may preserve the legal identity of the State over a period of time. Belligerent occupation, *per se*, does not extinguish the State. And, generally, the presumption—in practice a strong one—is in favour of the continuance, and against the extinction, of an established State.[2] Extinction is thus, within broad limits, not affected by more or less prolonged anarchy within the State,[3] nor, within equally broad limits, by loss of substantial independence, where the original organs of the State remain formally separate and retain at least some semblance of effective control.[4]

On the other hand, effective submersion or disappearance of separate State organs in those of another State, over any considerable period of time, will result in the extinction of the State, so long at least as no substantial international illegality is

---

[1] The literature on extinction is not extensive. Apart from Marek, *Identity and Continuity*, and Langer, *Seizure of Territory*, see Raestad (1939), 20 *RDILC* 441–9; Oppenheim (8th edn.) I, 155–6; Verzijl, *International Law* II, 122–31 and the works cited *infra*.

[2] Cf. Marek, *Identity and Continuity*, 548.

[3] *Supra*, p. 46. In the Manchurian Crisis, various delegates to the League raised, mostly in a tentative manner, the question whether China, then in a state of considerable governmental disarray, still qualified as a State for the purposes of the protection afforded by the Covenant. There was however little support for this view. Cf. *LNOJ* Sp. Supp. No. 111, Annex X (December 1932), 333; Thorne, *The Limits of Foreign Policy*, (1972), 150–151. But Baty, then Legal Adviser to the Japanese Government, took a different view: (1934) 28 *AJ* 444–55.

[4] *Supra*, pp. 69–71.

involved.[5] This is particularly so where the previous State organs voluntarily relinquished separate identity; for example in the case of the union of two States.[6] More difficult is the case of annexation of the entire territory of a State by external force— a situation which occurred with some frequency in the period 1935–40. This problem of extinction by illegal annexation deserves at least brief treatment; although a full study of the problem is impossible within the limits of this work.

17.2   EXTINCTION AND ILLEGAL ANNEXATION

As we have seen, the various States (Ethiopia,[7] Austria,[8] Czechoslovakia,[9] Poland,[10] and Albania[11]) effectively submerged by external illegal force in the period 1935–40 were reconstituted by the Allies during, or at the termination of, hostilities. Despite a considerable degree of at least *de facto*, and in some cases *de jure*, recognition of annexation, the view was on the whole taken that the legal existence of these States was preserved from extinction: the maxim *ex injuria jus non oritur* was regarded, at least retrospectively, as more cogent than the competitive maxim *ex factis jus oritur*; and this despite the inconsistency of non-recognition practice in this period.[12] Indeed, the illegality of the extinction seems to have been regarded as constituting grounds for withdrawal of recognition (as with Austria in 1943). It is necessary however to distinguish between the States effectively submerged prior to the outbreak of World War II (Ethiopia, Austria, Czechoslovakia, and Albania), and those occupied and

---

[5] Cf. *In re Savini* (1927) 4 AD No. 106 (Montenegro); *Achikian v. Bank of Athens* (Cairo, Mixed Tribunal, 1923) 2 AD No. 7 (Armenia); *Nankivel v. Omsk All Russian Government* (1932) 237 N.Y. 150; 142 N.E. 569. For problems of 'identity' after extinction see *supra*, pp. 407–8; and for the problem of 'reversion' see *supra*, pp. 412–16.

[6] Austria, however, was not regarded as extinguished by the Anschluss, despite the acquiescence of its population in union with Germany. Cf. Brandweiner, in Lipsky, ed., *Law and Politics in the World Community* (1953), 221–42; Clute, *The International Legal Status of Austria 1938–1955, passim*; Grayson, *Austria's International Position 1938–1953: The reestablishment of an Independent Austria* (Geneva, 1953).

[7] *Supra*, p. 311.

[8] *Supra*, pp. 310–11.

[9] Marek, op. cit. 283–330; Langer, op. cit. 207–44; *Valk v. Kokes* (1950) 17 ILR No. 114.

[10] *Supra*, pp. 311–12, 409–12.

[11] *Supra*, p. 311; and cf. Lemkin, op. cit. 99–107.

[12] Cf. Green, in Schwarzenberger, ed., *Law, Justice and Equity* (1967), 152–67, 153–8.

annexed during the war (in particular Poland).[13] In the latter case, even the traditional law, based as it was more or less exclusively on the notion of effectiveness,[14] allowed belligerency on behalf of a subjugated State by an ally to prevent the extinction of the former.[15] On the other hand, *debellatio*, on the traditional view, occurred when all effective organized resistance to the invader had ceased. State practice in the cases of Ethiopia, Austria, Czechoslovakia, and Albania was on the whole inconsistent with that view;[16] the legal personality of the State was subsequently regarded as having been preserved, so as to form the basis for the reconstruction of the State, which was not required to await a peace treaty with the defeated belligerent.

17.3   EXTINCTION AND PRESCRIPTION

The difficulty remains: how long could it be said that the legal identity of the State was preserved, despite its lack of effective control, in face of effective but illegal annexation? Post-1945 practice has been of little assistance in determining this issue, since illegal invasion of a State for the purpose of its annexation has not occurred with any frequency.[17] The most significant case, that of the Baltic States, sheds little light on the problem either.[18] On the whole, few States have so far recognized the annexation of the Baltic States; on the other hand, it is difficult to deny that their continued 'existence' is as much a matter of 'cold-war politics' as law.[19] Marek's conclusion would appear to be to similar effect: after referring to 'the survival of those States, whose physical suppression, although not assuming the orthodox form of belligerent occupation, proved equally temporary or

[13] *Quaere* as to the present legal status of the Free City of Danzig: *supra*, p. 166. Turack (1968–9), 43 *BY* 209–16, 212 states, without argument, that the 'City State still exists in law'.

[14] Cf. de Visscher, *Théories et réalités* (4th rev. edn.), 188–91. See for example the cases of effective extinction of Madagascar (*supra*, p. 415), the South African Republic (*supra*, p. 205) and the Papal States (*supra*, pp. 152–3).

[15] Cf. Vattel, op. cit., *supra*, p. 413.

[16] Cf. however Lauterpacht, *Recognition*, 356.

[17] Cf. Bot, *Non-Recognition and Treaty Relations*, 60–4. Hyderabad is probably the only, and that a controversial, instance: *supra*, p. 211. For East Timor see *supra*, p. 384.

[18] On the Baltic States see Marek, op. cit. 369–416; Langer, op. cit. 262–70, 284; (1970) 80 *RGDIP* 890–1.

[19] Cf. Jessup, *Transnational Law* (1956), 62; *In re De-Sautels* 307 N.E. 2d. 576 (1974); [1966] *BPIL 82*.

transient' she states that 'At the same time, the final loss of independence, either by way of a legal settlement or by way of a total obliteration of the entire international delimitation of a State, signified its extinction.'[20] If, on the other hand, it is concluded that continued recognition of Latvia, Lithuania, and Estonia signifies their continued existence as States,[21] then it may be that the rule protecting State personality against illegal annexation has achieved relatively peremptory, permanent, force: the character as *jus cogens* of the rules relating to the use of force is no doubt relevant here.[22] The absence of more recent and explicit State practice is hardly regrettable; but it would seem to preclude any more conclusive assessment of the effect of continued effective but illegal annexation upon statehood. It may be said that the uncertainty of this position is common to that of prescription in general international law.[23] Equally, in view of the uncertainty of the position, the recognition practice of other States—in the context of extinction as of identity and continuity—assumes considerable importance.

[20] *Identity and Continuity*, 589.

[21] Cf. Brownlie, *Principles*, 82–3: 'illegal occupation cannot of itself terminate statehood ... [W]hen elements of ... *jus cogens* are involved, it is less likely that recognition and acquiescence will offset the original illegality.'

[22] Cf. *supra*, pp. 79–84.

[23] Cf. Johnson (1950), 27 *BY* 332–54; Radojković, in *Mélanges Andrassy* (1968), 225–36.

Conclusion

THE CRITERIA for statehood, and modern practice in the field, have been examined at length in this study, and there would be no point in repeating the conclusions reached in earlier Chapters. Four specific problems however deserve brief mention.

In the first place, the concept of 'sovereignty' as a criterion for plenary competence has been rejected.[1] Although that view gained a certain degree of acceptance among nineteenth-century writers, and is still accepted in Soviet, and in some Western doctrine,[2] the notion of 'sovereignty' has been seen to be both unhelpful and misleading. It is unhelpful since both the legal and the effective capacities, rights, immunities and so on of States may vary widely, within the limits established by the criteria for separate independence. It is misleading since it implies a necessary and overriding omnipotence which States do not possess in law or in fact. Rejection of 'sovereignty' as a criterion involves rejection of the old notion of the 'semi-sovereign State'. Those dependent[3] or devolving[4] or *sui generis*[5] entities which qualify as States under the general criteria do so despite specific limitations as to capacity and the like: entities which do not so qualify are not States, although they may retain a more limited legal personality. The adoption of this terminology both avoids confusion and accords with most modern practice.

Secondly, although the criteria for statehood do provide a general, applicable standard, the application of that standard to particular situations where there are conflicting and controversial claims is often difficult: it is here in particular that recognition and, equally importantly, other State practice relating to or implying a judgment as to the status of the entity in question is of particular importance.[6] Apart from its evidential value such recognition may render particular situations opposable to

---

[1] *Supra*, p. 71.
[2] Cf. Fitzmaurice, cited *supra*, p. 196.
[3] Cf. *supra*, pp. 188–94.
[4] *Supra*, pp. 230–8.
[5] *Supra*, p. 142.
[6] Cf. *supra*, pp. 20–5.

recognizing States, at least in the absence of general issues of the legality of those situations; and it may also play an important role in consolidating the legal status of effective but illegal situations. This is, as we have seen, particularly the case with problems of identity and extinction, where the general criteria tend in practice to be unhelpful and equivocal.

Thirdly, although statehood is thus a legal concept with a determinate, though flexible, content, it is probably[7] the only such concept in the field of legal personality. Other general terms (protectorate, suzerain, confederation, internationalized territory, and so on) may be more or less convenient *classifications* of common forms of organization; but they are classifications without positive legal consequences beyond those arising from the specific agreements or instruments in question, and they are thus, in one sense, not *legal* concepts at all.[8] It follows that the description of any given entity as, say, a 'protectorate' or a 'vassal' has no direct bearing on that entity's general legal status (or lack of it) *qua* State under the criteria referred to.[9] The 'common features' of, say, protectorates may make it unlikely that any entity classified as a protectorate could be sufficiently independent to qualify as a State; but that result is reached by direct application of the relevant criteria, and not by deduction from any other classification.[10]

Finally, the application of this last principle to problems of the creation of States requires some comment as to the 'modes' of creation distinguished in Sections II and III of this study.[11] Like the various accepted classifications of non-State entities, these modes of the creation of States are distinguished in this study because of relevant 'common features'. It is for example useful to distinguish cases of grant of independence by a former sovereign from cases of forcible seizure, since in the former case the criteria for statehood are likely to be more readily fulfilled: equally, problems of consolidation of 'divided States' (or entities illegally

---

[7] *Pace* Seyersted (1964), 34 *Acta Scandinavica* 3–112.

[8] Cf. Kunz, cited *supra*, p. 289.

[9] Cf. Andorra: *supra*, p. 142.

[10] Thus, the statehood of Liechtenstein (*supra*, pp. 132, 190) does not depend upon whether we regard the arrangement for the conduct of Liechtenstein's foreign relations by Switzerland (essentially a strict agency relationship) as qualifying Liechtenstein for the description 'protectorate'. Cf. the cases of San Marino (p. 189) and Western Samoa (p. 190).

[11] Cf. pp. 171, 299.

created but which subsist effectively over a period of time) raise similar difficulties and warrant discussion under the one rubric.[12] It remains true, as has been pointed out, that these classifications are in principle classifications of convenience; and that a particular entity may achieve statehood by a combination of different 'modes', or by recognition. Discrimination between different States, for example, for State succession purposes, on the basis of the different 'modes' by which each has come into existence is thus probably erroneous, in the absence of very special factors such as continuity of personality with a pre-independence protectorate,[13] or the extension of competence of a devolving territory with separate legal personality,[14] or administrative and political continuity of an entity formerly the member of a federation or other political union.[15]

[12] *Supra*, Chapter 10.
[13] *Supra*, pp. 203–5.
[14] *Supra*, p. 240, n. 15.
[15] *Supra*, p. 289, nn. 8–10; cf. Brownlie, *Principles*, 650–1.

Appendix 1. List of States and Territorial Entities Proximate to States (as at 31.12.77)

A. *States* (155)
(* signifies not a U.N.Member)

Afghanistan
Albania
Algeria
Angola
Argentina
Australia
Austria
Bahamas
Bahrain
Bangladesh
Barbados
Belgium
Benin (Dahomey)
Bhutan
Bolivia
Botswana
Brazil
Bulgaria
Burma
Burundi
Cambodia (Khmer Rep.)
Cameroon
Canada
Cape Verde Islands
Central African Empire (formerly Central African Republic)
Chad
Chile
China
Colombia
Comoro Archipelago
Congo

Costa Rica
Cuba
Cyprus
Czechoslovakia
Denmark
Djibouti
Dominican Republic
Ecuador
Egypt
El Salvador
Equatorial Guinea
Ethiopia
Fiji
Finland
France
Gabon
Gambia
Germany, Democratic Republic
Germany, Federal Republic
Ghana
Greece
Grenada
Guatemala
Guinea
Guinea-Bissau
Guyana
Haiti
Honduras
Hungary
Iceland
India
Indonesia

Iran
Iraq
Ireland
Israel
Italy
Ivory Coast
Jamaica
Japan
Jordan
Kenya
*Korea, Democratic People's Republic
*Korea, Republic of
Kuwait
Laos
Lebanon
Lesotho
Liberia
Libya
*Liechtenstein
Luxembourg
Madagascar
Malawi
Malaysia
Maldives
Mali
Malta
Mauritania
Mauritius
Mexico
*Monaco
Mongolia
Morocco
Mozambique
*Nauru
Nepal

Netherlands	Senegal	Tunisia
New Zealand	Seychelles	Turkey
Nicaragua	Sierra Leone	Uganda
Niger	Singapore	United Arab
Nigeria	Somalia	Emirates
Norway	South Africa	United Kingdom of
Oman	Southern Yemen	Great Britain and
Pakistan	Soviet Union	Northern Ireland
Panama	Spain	United States of
Papua-New Guinea	Sri Lanka	America
Paraguay	Sudan	Upper Volta
Peru	Surinam	Uruguay
Philippines	Swaziland	*Vatican City
Poland	Sweden	Venezuela
Portugal	*Switzerland	Vietnam
Qatar	Syria	Western Samoa
Romania	Tanzania	Yemen
Rwanda	Thailand	Yugoslavia
*San Marino	Togo	Zaire
São Tomé and	Tonga	Zambia
Principe	Trinidad and	
Saudi Arabia	Tobago	

B. *Entities proximate to States* (3)

Andorra	Holy See	Taiwan

C. *'State'-entities the status of which is uncertain or disputed* (10)

Bophuthatswana	Germany	Rhodesia
Brunei	Latvia	Transkei
Byelorussia	Lithuania	Ukraine
Estonia		

Appendix 2. League Mandates and United Nations Trusteeships

'A' Mandates

All 'A' Mandates were territories detached from Turkey by Article 16 of the Treaty of Lausanne, 1923. The terms of the Mandates were approved by the League Council: for Syria, Lebanon, and Palestine (including Transjordan) on 24.7.1922; for Iraq on 16.9.1922. Armenia was also intended to be placed under mandate, but the U.S.A. refused the responsibility, as did the League itself. Part of Armenia was then reconquered by Turkey, and part organized as a soviet republic in the U.S.S.R.[1]

Dependent Territory & Administering State	Independence, Termination, etc.	Relevant Resolution
Iraq (Great Britain)	No special mandate agreement; Treaty of Alliance 10.10.1922 and Protocols. Further treaty of 30.6.1930 provided for renunciation of Mandate and admission to League—effective 4.10.1932	*LNOJ* (1932), 1212, 1347
Palestine (Great Britain)	In force 29.9.1923. Not transferred to Trusteeship. U.N. partition plan (Nov. 1947) failed. Instead Great Britain withdrew unilaterally, 14.5.1948: State of Israel declared, and after first Arab-Israel War admitted to U.N. 11.5.1949	G.A. Res. 181 (II)
Transjordan (Great Britain)	Part of Palestine Mandate administered separately. By agreement of 20.2.1928 Great Britain recognized *de facto* independent Government. Further Treaty of Alliance 22.3.1946 extended United Kingdom's *de jure* recognition as State of Jordan: admitted to U.N. 14.12.1955.	G.A. Res. 11 (I); cf. *LNOJ* 21st Ass. 1946 Sp. Supp. No. 194, 58.
Syria (France)	In force 29.9.1923. Treaty of Alliance 9.9.1936 suspended by War. After Vichy collapse proclamation of 27.9.1941 gave status of 'independent republic'. French withdrew 1.1.1944. Syria an original Member of U.N.	*LNOJ* 21st Ass. Sp. Supp. No. 194, 58.
Lebanon (France)	In force 29.9.1923. Treaty of Alliance 13.11.1936 suspended by war. Proclamation of 27.9.1941 gave status of 'independent republic'. French withdrawal 1.1.1944: original Member of U.N.	*LNOJ* 21st Ass. Sp. Supp. No. 194, 58.

[1] Mandelstam, *La Société des Nations et les puissances devant le problème arménien* (Paris, 1925).

'B' Mandates

All 'B' Mandates were African territories of Germany detached by Articles 118–19 of the Treaty of Versailles, 1919. The terms of the Mandates were approved by the League Council: for Togoland and the Cameroons on 18.7.1922; for Tanganyika and Ruanda-Urundi on 20.7.1922.

Dependent Territory & Administering State	Independence, Termination, etc.	Relevant Resolution
Tanganyika (Great Britain)	Former German East Africa: transferred to Trusteeship 13.12.1946. Independent 9.12.61	G.A. Res. 63 (I) G.A. Res. 1642 (XVI)
British Togoland (Great Britain)	Transferred to Trusteeship 13.12.1946. United after plebiscite with new independent Republic of Ghana (fomerly Gold Coast): 6.3.1957	G.A.Res. 63 (I) G.A.Res. 1044 (XI)
French Togoland (France)	Transferred to Trusteeship 13.12.1946. After plebiscite divided into 2 new independent Republics of Rwanda & Burundi, effective 1.6.1962	G.A.Res. 63 (I) G.A. Res. 1746 (XVI)
British Cameroons (Great Britain)	Administered in 2 provinces separately. Transferred to Trusteeship 13.12.1946. After plebiscites, S. Cameroons joined new Republic of Cameroon 30.9.1961, N. Cameroon joined Nigeria: 1.6.1961	G.A. Res. 63 (I) G.A. Res. 1608 (XV)
French Cameroons (France)	Transferred to Trusteeship 13.12.1946. Independent as Republic of Cameroon 1.1.1960	G.A. Res. 63 (I) G.A. Res. 1349 (XIII)

'C' Mandates

These were, in terms of Article 22, 'territories . . . which, owing to the sparseness of their population, or their small size, or their remoteness from the centres of civilization, or their geographical contiguity to the territory of the Mandatory, and other circumstances, can be best administered under the laws of the Mandatory as integral portions of its territory, subject to the safeguards above mentioned in the interests of the indigenous population.' All 'C' Mandates were territories of Germany detached by Articles 118–19 of the Treaty of Versailles. The terms of the 'C' Mandates were approved by the League Council on 17.12.1920.

Dependent Territory & Administering State	Independence, Termination, etc.	Relevant Resolution
New Guinea (Australia)	Transferred to Trusteeship 13.12.1946. Administered together with Australian Territory of Papua: independent as Papua New-Guinea 16.9.1975	G.A. Res. 63 (I) G.A. Res. 3284 (XXIX)

Dependent Territory & Administering State	Independence, Termination, etc.	Relevant Resolution
Nauru (British Empire: N.Z., U.K., Aust.)	Administration delegated to Australia. Transferred to Trusteeship, November 1947. Independent 31.12.1968	G.A. Res. 140 (II) G.A. Res. 2347 (XXII)
Western Samoa (New Zealand)	Transferred to Trusteeship 13.12.1946. Independent 1.1.1962: special treaty relations with New Zealand	G.A. Res. 63 (I) G.A. Res. 1626 (XVI)
Pacific Islands (Japan 1920–1944; U.S.A. 1947–)	Used by Japan as a military base: occupied by U.S. troops during War, and thereafter administered by U.S. Terms of Strategic Trusteeship approved by S.C. 2.4.1947.[1]	S.C. Res. 21
South West Africa (South Africa)	Not brought under Trusteeship. Permission to annex refused by G.A. Mandate declared revoked for fundamental breach 27.10.1966. Territory renamed Namibia. Remains under South African control *de facto*.[2]	G.A. Res. 2145 (XXI) approved by S.C. Res. 264, 269, 276

'*Territories detached . . . as a result of the Second World War*' (Charter Art. 77 (1) (b)).

Note: The Japanese Pacific Mandate was, it seems, detached from Japan 'as a result of the Second World War': see *supra*, pp. 347–8. By Article 2 (d) of the treaty of Peace of 8 Sept. 1951, Japan renounced its rights under the Mandates System and accepted the action of the Security Council in placing the Pacific Islands under Strategic Trusteeship.[3] In addition three territories were detached from Italy by Article 23 and Annex XI of the Treaty of Peace 1947.[4] Of these, Libya became independent on 24.12.1951, and Eritrea was put under a United Nations Commission and ultimately federated with Ethiopia: see General Assembly Resolution 284 (VI). Only one territory was placed under Trusteeship.

Dependent Territory & Administering State	Independence, Termination, etc.	Relevant Resolution
Somalia (Italian Somaliland) (Italy)	Placed under Trusteeship for a fixed period of 10 years. Trusteeship Agreement approved 1950. United after plebiscite with former British Protectorate of Somaliland to form Somali Republic, 1.7.1960	G.A. Res. 289 (IV) G.A. Res. 442 (V) G.A. Res. 1418 (XIV)

[1] For termination see *supra*, p. 336.
[2] See further *supra*, pp. 336, 350–5.
[3] 136 *UNTS* 45, 48–50.
[4] 49 *UNTS* 3, 139, 214.

Appendix 3. The United Nations and Non-Self-Governing Territories, 1946–1977[1]

THE FOLLOWING table sets out all the territories so far treated as 'Non-Self-Governing' for the purposes of Article 73, together with an indication of local, national, or international action affecting the status of the territory in question. For further information consult the index reference for each territory.

A. *Territories listed in G.A.Res. 66 (I)*

Administering Authority and N.S.G. Territory	Comments	G.A. Res.
Australia		
Papua	Independent 16.9.1975 in union with former Australian Trust Territory of New Guinea	3284 (XXIX)
Belgium		
Belgian Congo	Independent as Democratic Republic of Congo, 15.8.1960. Now Zaire	1480 (XV)
Denmark		
Greenland	Voted in 1952 for union with Denmark: effective 1953	849 (IX)
France		
French West Africa	Information ceased 1957. Part of French Community under 1958 Constitution. Following territories independent:	
	Dahomey, 1 August 1960	1481 (XV)
	Guinea, 28 September 1958	1325 (XIII)
	Ivory Coast, 7 August 1960	1484 (XV)
	Mali (formerly French Sudan), 20 June 1960	1491 (XV)
	Mauritania, 28 November 1960	1631 (XVI)
	Niger, 3 August 1960	1482 (XV)
	Senegal, independent as part of Mali Federation, 20 June 1960; withdrew, 20 August 1960	1490 (XV)
	Upper Volta, 5 August 1960	1483 (XV)

[1] All territories not independent or self-governing remain subject to Article 73e unless stated. Where territories have achieved self-government through independence, in most cases no formal U.N. decision as to cessation of information has been taken, although of course admission of the new State to the U.N. could be taken as confirmation of the appropriateness of cessation of information.

Administering Authority and N.S.G. Territory	*Comments*	*G.A. Res.*
French North Africa	Information submitted on French protectorates of Morocco and Tunisia, but not on Department of Algeria.	
	Independent as follows:	
	Morocco, 2 March 1956	1111 (XI)
	Tunisia, 20 March 1956	1112 (XI)
	Algeria, 3 July 1962	1754 (XVII)
French Equatorial Africa	Information ceased in 1957. Various territories Associated States in French Community under 1958 Constitution. Independent as follows:	
	Central African Republic (Ubangi Shari), 13 August 1960	1488 (XV)
	Chad, 11 August 1960	1485 (XV)
	Congo (Brazzaville), 15 August 1960	1486 (XV)
	Gabon, 17 August 1960	1487 (XV)
French Somaliland (Djibouti)	French overseas territory: information discontinued 1957. Renamed French Territory of Afars and Issas.	
	Referendum 1967 voted 58% in favour of French connection.	2288 (XXI)
	Rejected by U.N. Independent 26 June 1977. U.N. Member.	2356 (XXII) 32/1 (1977)
Madagascar & Dependencies	Overseas territory, elected in 1958 to be Member State of French Community. Information discontinued 1958. Independent as Malagasy Republic, 26 June 1960.	1478 (XV)
French Establishments in Oceana (*viz.* French Polynesia)	French overseas territory 1946: integral part of French Republic. Information ceased 1947	
French Indochina	Associated States in French Union under 1946 Constitution. Information ceased 1948. Independent as follows:	
	Laos, 19 July 1949	995 (X)
	Cambodia, 9 November 1953	995 (X)
	Vietnam, 1956 (?)[2]	620C (VII)
French Establishments in India (Chandernagore, Pondicherry, Karikal, Mahe, Yanam)	Transferred to India, 1950–4 as Union Territory. Ratified by treaty of 28 May 1956.[3] Information ceased 1956	—

[2] *Supra,* pp. 284–5.

[3] Treaty of Cession of the Territory of the Free Town of Chandernagore, Paris, 2 Feb. 1951: 203 *UNTS* 155; Treaty ceding French Establishments in india, New Delhi, 28 May 1956: 162 *BFSP* 848. Cf. 49 ILR 484.

Administering Authority and N.S.G. Territory	Comments	G.A. Res.
New Caledonia and Dependencies	French overseas territory 1946: integral part of French Republic. Information ceased 1947	—
French Guiana and Reunion	Overseas Department of France and integral part of French Republic 1946. Information ceased 1947	—
Netherlands		
Netherlands Indies	Indonesia independent after liberation fight 1950: West Irian (West New Guinea) ceded to Indonesia in 1962 subject to U.N. supervised referendum in 1969—in favour of continued association	448 (V) 491 (VI) 1752 (XVI)
Surinam	Autonomous and equal part of Netherlands since 1954. Independent 25 November 1975	945 (X) 3413 (XXX)
Curacao (and other islands—Netherlands Antilles)	Autonomous and equal part of Netherlands since 1954	945 (X)
New Zealand		
Cook Islands	Asssociated with N.Z. under Cook Islands Act 1964–5; approved by G.A. 1965, after elections under U.N. surveillance	2064 (XX)
Tokelau Islands	Still dependent	
Niue Islands	Associated with N.Z. under Niue Constitution Act 1974	3285 (XXIX)
United Kingdom		
Aden (Colony & Protectorate)	After period of conflict with U.N., a Special Mission sent to Territory; British military base disbanded. Independent 30.11.67 as Southern Yemen.	1949 (XVIII) 2023 (XX) 2310 (XXII)
Bahamas	Independent July 1973, after voting for independence rather than association	3051 (XXVIII)
Barbados	Independent 30.11.1966	2175 (XXI)
Basutoland	Enclave within S. Africa. Independent as Lesotho, 4.10.1966	2003 (XX) 2134 (XXI) 2136 (XXI)
Bechuanaland Protectorate	Enclave within S. Africa. Independent as Botswana, 30.9.1966	2063 (XX) 2134 (XXI) 2137 (XXI)
Bermuda	Still dependent territory	3289 (XXIX)
British Guiana	Independent as Guyana, 26.5.1966	2133 (XXI)
British Honduras (Belize)	Claimed by Guatemala. Still dependent. U.N. has affirmed right to self-determination	3432 (XXX)

Administering Authority and N.S.G. Territory	Comments	G.A. Res.
British Somaliland Protectorate	Independent, together with Italian Trusteeship of Somaliland, as Somalia, 1.7.1960	1479 (XV)
Brunei	Protected State. Declined in 1963 to join Federation of Malaysia. Disputed as Ch. XI territory.	3159C (XXVIII)
Cyprus	Independent 16.8.1960, despite majority desire for *enosis* (union with Greece)	1489 (XV)
Dominica	Associated State with U.K. under West Indies Act 1967: not fully independent. U.K. ceased transmission of information, but not approved by G.A.	2422C (XXIII) 2707 (XXV)
Falkland Islands (Malvinas)	Claimed by Argentina: negotiation invited by G.A. Still dependent	2065 (XX)
Fiji	Independent 10.10.1970	1951 (XVIII) 2068 (XX) 2622 (XXV)
Gambia	Independent 18.2.1965	2008 (XX)
Gibraltar	Claimed by Spain, with U.N. support. Referendum held 10.9.1967, voted overwhelmingly in favour of U.K. sovereignty. Repudiated by G.A.	2353 (XXII)
Gold Coast (Colony and Protectorate)	Independent as Republic of Ghana, 6 March 1957	1118 (XVI)
Grenada	Associated State with U.K. under West Indies Act. Independent 7 February 1974	3204 (XXIX)
Hong Kong	British colony on S.E. coast of China; also Kowloon, leased for term of 99 years expiring 1997. No G.A. action	
Jamaica	Independent, 6 August 1962	1750 (XV)
Kenya (Colony and Protectorate)	Independent, 12 December 1963	1976 (XVIII)
Leeward Islands (Antigua; St. Kitts; Nevis-Anguilla, Montserrat)	Associated States under West Indies Act 1967. Anguilla seceded 11.7.1967. See note for Dominica.	
Malayan Union	Independent as Malaya 31.8.1957; later Federation of Malaysia 16.9.1963	1134 (XI)
Malta	U.K. ceased transmission 1949: resumed after constitution revoked in 1959. Independent 21 September 1964	Consensus 1.12.64

Administering Authority and N.S.G. Territory	Comments	G.A. Res.
Mauritius	Independent 12 May 1968	2232 (XXI)
Nigeria	Independent 1 October 1960	1492 (XV)
North Borneo (Sabah)	State within Federation of Malaysia, 16 September 1963	No res. See *UN Ybk*, 1963, 41–4
Northern Rhodesia	Part of Federation of Rhodesia and Nyasaland (1954–63). Independent as Zambia, 24 October 1964	Consensus 1.12.64
Nyasaland	Part of Federation of Rhodesia and Nyasaland (1954–63). Independent as Malawi, 6 July 1964	Consensus 1.12.64
Oman. Previously Sultanate of Muscat and Oman in special treaty relations with U.K.	Independence disputed between U.K. and U.N. (1963–70); admitted to U.N. in 1971	2754 (XXVI)
St. Lucia	Associated State under West Indies Act. See note for Dominica	
St. Vincent	Associated State (1969) under West Indies Act. See note for Dominica	
Sarawak	Claimed by Philippines. Part of Federation of Malaysia, 16 September 1963	No res. See *UN Ybk*. 1963, 41–4.
Seychelles	Independent, 29 June 1976	3287 (XXIX)
Sierra Leone	Independent, 27 April 1961	1623 (XVI)
Singapore	Became part of Federation of Malaysia, 16 September 1963. Withdrew, 9 August 1965: independent State	2019 (XX)
Swaziland	Former High Commission Territory: independent 6.9.1968	2063 (XX) 2134 (XXI)
Trinidad and Tobago	Independent, 31.8.1962	1751 (XVII)
Uganda Protectorate	Independent, 9.10.1962	1758 (XVII)
Western Pacific High Commission Territories (*viz.* Gilbert & Ellice Islands Colony,[4] British Solomon Islands Protectorate,[5] Pitcairn Islands)		3288 (XXIX) 3290 (XXIX)
	Still dependent	
Zanzibar Protectorate	Independent 9.12.1963—on 26.4.1964 became part of United Republic of Tanzania (together with Tanganyika)	1975 (XVIII)

[4] Administratively separated, Jan. 1976: now Gilbert Islands and Tuvalu. See (1975) 80 *RGDIP* 1165–7; G.A. Consensus, 32/407, 28 Nov. 1977.

[5] Internally self-governing, 31 Dec. 1975, pursuant to an Agreement of 21 May 1975. Independence proposed in 12–18 months. See *Keesings* 1975, 27297A.

Administering Authority and N.S.G. Territory	Comments	G.A. Res.
United States		
Alaska	Incorporated as 50th State of U.S.A. 3.1.1959	1469 (XIV)
American Samoa	Unincorporated U.S. territory	2069 (XX)
Guam	Unincorporated U.S. territory	2069 (XX)
Hawaii	Incorporated as 51st State, 21.8.1959	1469 (XIV)
Panama Canal Zone	'Leased' to U.S. by Panama. After objection, U.S. ceased transmitting information. Still dependent.[6]	
Puerto Rico	In association with U.S. via 'Commonwealth status', with an assurance of full independence if desired. Effective 25.7.1952	748 (VIII)
Virgin Islands	Unincorporated U.S. territory	2069 (XX)

B. *Territories subsequently determined to be Non-Self-Governing*

(1) *Territories not listed in Res. 66 (I) but treated as Non-Self-Governing in practice*

Administering Authority and N.S.G. Territory	Comments	G.A. Res.
Australia		
Cocos (Keeling) Islands	Transferred from Straits Settlement in 1955; subsequently reported on separately[7]	Consensus, 13.12.1974
France		
Comoro Archipelago	Not listed in Res. 66 (I); reported on until 1957. Independent 1975. Mayotte remains under French administration	3385 (XXX)
United Kingdom and France		
New Hebrides	Condominium: not listed in Res. 66 (I) but information submitted. Still dependent territory[8]	3290 (XXIX)

[6] On negotiations over the Zone see 13 *ILM* 390; Simpson (1975), 5 *Georgia JICL* 195–215; (1978) 82 *RGDIP* 278–82. For the Panama Canal Treaties see (1977) 16 *ILM* 1021. The Treaty recognizes Panamanian sovereignty over the Zone (Arts. I (2), III (1), VII (1)), and provides for the termination of U.S. control over the canal in 1999 (Art. II).

[7] Cf. Australian Senate, Standing Committee on Foreign Affairs and Defence, *United Nations Involvement with Australia's Territories* (Canberra, 1975), 61–7. Christmas Island, which was transferred in a similar manner in 1957, has not been reported on: ibid., 108–111.

[8] On the New Hebrides see Benoist, *La Condominium des Nouvelles-Hébrides et la Société Mélanesienne* (Paris, 1972); O'Connell (1968–9), 43 *BY* 71–146; Chiroux (1976), 30 *RJPIC* 309–30; (1975) 80 *RGDIP* 845–6; *UKTS* No. 61 (1976).

Administering Authority and N.S.G. Territory	Comments	G.A. Res.
United Kingdom		
British Indian Ocean Territory	4 groups of islands (including Diego Garcia) detached from Mauritius and Seychelles in 1965: 3 groups of islands returned to Seychelles after independence[9]	Cf. 3430 (XXX)

(2) Territories subsequently determined to be Non-Self-Governing

Portugal (See G.A. Res. 1542 (XV), para. 1)		
Cape Verde Archipelago	Independent 5 July 1975[10]	3363 (XXX)
Portuguese Guinea (Guinea-Bissau)	Declared independence 26.9.1973: Recognized by Portugal 10.9.1974	3061 (XXVIII)
São Tomé, Príncipe and Dependencies	Independent 12 July 1975[11]	3364 (XXX)
São João Batista de Ajudá	United with Dahomey 1961	No express approval; but cf. *UN Ybk.* 1961, 420, & Res. 1699 (XVI)
Angola (including the enclave of Cabinda)	Independent 11 November 1975. Civil war with foreign intervention[12]	
Mozambique	Independent 25 June 1975 pursuant to Agreement of 7 September 1974 between FRELIMO and Portugal[13]	3365 (XXX)
Goa and Dependencies (called the State of India)	Annexed by India, 18.12.61. Union Territory	No U.N. action
Macau and Dependencies[14]		
Portuguese Timor	Invaded by Indonesia 7 December 1975. Assembly and Council resolutions have demanded self-determination and Indonesian withdrawal	e.g. 3485 (XXX)
Spain (see G.A. Res. 1542 (XV), para. 5)		
Equatorial Guinea (Fernando Póo, Rio Muni)	Elections in 1968 under U.N. supervision. Independent as Guinea 12.10.1968	2384 (XXIII)

[9] See *Keesing's* 1976, 27620A, 27852B, 27871A. Only the Chagos Archipelago now remains of the Territory: in view of Mauritius' apparent acceptance of the position, its status as a Chapter XI territory must be considered doubtful.

[10] See 13 *ILM* 1244.

[11] 14 *ILM* 39.

[12] (1975) 79 *RGDIP* 1098–101; (1976) 80 *RGDIP* 555–74; (1977) 81 *RGDIP* 240–7.

[13] Ibid. 1179–81; 13 ILM 1467.

[14] See note for Hong Kong.

Administering Authority and N.S.G. Territory	*Comments*	*G.A. Res.*
Ifni	Province of Spain claimed by Morocco. Agreement in principle 10.10.1967, on practical implementation of self-determination between Spain and Morocco, approved by G.A.	2354 (XXII)
Spanish Sahara	Spanish province claimed by Morocco and Mauritania; partition agreement noted	3458 (XXX) A/B
United Kingdom (see G.A. Res. 1747 (XVI))		
Southern Rhodesia	Declared a Chapter IX Territory in 1962. U.D.I. by minority government, 1965: rejected by U.N. Unrecognized	1755 (XVII), etc.

Bibliography

GENERAL WORKS

AKEHURST, M., *A Modern Introduction to International Law* (3rd edn., London, 1977).

AMERICAN LAW INSTITUTE, *Restatement, Second. Foreign Relations Law of the United States* (1965).

ANZILOTTI, D., *Corso di Diritto Internazionale* (3rd edn., 1929).

BLAUSTEIN, A. P., SIGLER, J., and BREEDE, B. R., *Independence Documents of the World* (N.Y., Oceana, 2 vols., 1977).

BOS, M., ed., *The Present State of International Law and other Essays* (Deventer, 1973).

BOWETT, D. W., *Self-Defence in International Law* (Manchester, 1958).

BRIERLY, J. L., *The Basis of Obligation in International Law and Other Papers* (Oxford, 1958).

—— *The Law of Nations: an Introduction to the International Law of Peace* (6th edn., ed. Waldock, Oxford, 1963).

BRIGGS, H. W., *The Law of Nations* (2nd edn., N.Y., 1952).

BROWNLIE, I., *International Law and the Use of Force by States* (Oxford, 1964).

—— *Principles of Public International Law* (2nd edn., Oxford, 1973).

BYNKERSHOEK, C., *Quaestionum Juris Publici Libri Duo* (1737) (Oxford, 1930; Classics of International Law Series).

CRAWFORD, J. R., 'The Criteria for Statehood in International Law' (1976–7) 48 *BY* 93–182.

DE VISSCHER, C., *Problèmes d'interprétation judiciaire en droit international public* (Paris, 1963).

—— *Théories et réalités en droit international public* (4th rev. edn., Paris, 1970).

DICKINSON, E., *The Equality of States in International Law* (Harvard, 1920).

DOWDALL, H. C., 'The Word "State"' (1923) 39 *LQR* 98–125.

FAWCETT, J. E. S., *The Law of Nations* (2nd edn., London, 1971).

FAWCETT, J. E. S. and HIGGINS, R., eds., *International Organization: Law in Movement* (Oxford, 1974).

GENTILI, A., *Hispanicae Advocationis Libri Duo* (1661) (N.H., 1921; Classics of International Law Series).

GREEN, N. A. M., *International Law, Law of Peace* (London, 1973).

GRENVILLE, J. A. S., *The Major International Treaties 1914–1973. A History and Guide with Texts* (London, 1974).

GROTIUS, H., *De Iure Belli ac Pacis Libri Tres* (1646) (trans. F. W. Kelsey, Oxford 1925, 2 vols.; Classics of International Law Series).

GUGGENHEIM, P., ed., *Répertoire suisse de droit international public. Documentation concernant la pratique de la Confédération en matière de droit international public 1914–1939* (vols. i–iv, Basle 1975).

HACKWORTH, G. H., *Digest of international law* (Washington, 8 vols., 1940–4).

HALL, W. G., *A Treatise on International Law* (Oxford, 2nd edn., 1884).

HART, H. L. A., *The Concept of Law* (Oxford, 1961).

HIGGINS, R., *The Development of International Law through the Political Organs of the United Nations* (London, 1963).

—— *United Nations Peacekeeping 1946–1967. Documents and Commentary* (2 vols., London, 1970).

HOBBES, J., *De Cive, or, The Citizen* (ed. S. P. Lamprecht, N.Y., 1949).

HUNTER MILLER, D., *The Drafting of the Covenant* (N.Y., 2 vols., 1928).

HYDE, C. C., *International Law Chiefly as Interpreted and Applied by the United States* (2nd edn., Boston, 3 vols., 1947).

JAFFÉ, L. L., *Judicial Aspects of Foreign Relations* (Harvard, 1933).

JELLINEK, G., *Allgemeine Staatslehre* (1st edn., 1900).

JENNINGS, R. Y., 'General Course' (1967) 121 *HR* 327–605.

JESSUP, P. C., *A Modern Law of Nations* (N.Y., 1952).

—— *The Birth of Nations* (Columbia, 1974).

KEITH, A. B., ed., *Basic Documents in International Affairs 1918–1937* (2 vols., Oxford, 1938).

KELSEN, H., *Legal Techniques in International Law: A Textual Critique of the League Covenant* (Geneva, 1939).

—— *The Law of the United Nations: a critical analysis of its fundamental problems* (London, 1951).

—— *Principles of International Law* (2nd rev., edn., ed. Tucker, N.Y., 1966).

—— *The Pure Theory of Law* (2nd edn., trans. Knight, Berkeley, 1967).

LAUTERPACHT, E., ed., *International Law. Being the Collected Papers of Hersch Lauterpacht* (Cambridge, vols. 1–3, 1970–77).

LAUTERPACHT, H., *Private Law Sources and Analogies of International Law* (London, 1927).

LORIMER, J., *Institutes of the Law of Nations* (Edinburgh, 1883, 2 vols.).

MCNAIR, A. D., *Law of Treaties: British practice and opinions* (Oxford, 1938).

—— *The Law of Treaties* (Oxford, 1961).

MAREK, K., *Identity and Continuity of States in Public International Law* (Geneva, 1955).

MARTENS, KARL VON, *Nouvelles Causes célébres du droit des gens* (Leipzig, 1843).

MENDELSON, M. H., 'Acquisition of Membership in Selected International Organizations' (Oxford, MS.D. Phil. d.5229, 1971).

MOORE, J. B., *A Digest of International Law* (Washington, 8 vols., 1906).

MORGENTHAU, H. J., *Politics among Nations* (5th edn., N.Y., 1973).

NUSSBAUM, A., *A Concise History of the Law of Nations* (rev. edn., N.Y., 1954).

OAKES, A. and MOWAT, R. B., eds., *The Great European Treaties of the Nineteenth Century* (Oxford, 1918).

O'BRIEN, W. V., ed., *The New Nations in International Law and Diplomacy* (N.Y., 1965).

O'CONNELL, D. P., *State Succession in Municipal Law and International Law* (Cambridge, 2 vols., 1967).

—— *International Law* (2nd edn., London, 1970, 2 vols.).

——, ed., *International Law in Australia* (Sydney, 1965).

OPPENHEIM, L. F. L., *International Law* (1st edn., 2 vols. 1905; 8th edn., Vol. I, London, 1955; 7th edn., Vol. II, 1953).

PARRY, C., *Nationality and Citizenship Laws of the Commonwealth and the Republic of Ireland* (London, 1957–60, 2 vols.).

PARRY, C., and HOPKINS, C., *Index of British Treaties 1101–1968* (London, 3 vols., 1970).

PEREIRA, A. G., *La Succession d'États en matière de traité* (Paris, 1969).

PHILLIMORE, R., *Commentaries upon International Law* (2nd edn., London, 1871–4, 4 vols.).

PUFENDORF, S. VON, *De Iure Naturae et Gentium Libri Octo* (1672) (trans. C. H. & W. A. Oldfather, Oxford, 1934; Classics of International Law Series).

RAY, J., *Commentaire du Pacte de la société des nations* (Paris, 1930).

RIVIER, A., *Principes du droit des gens* (Paris, 1896, 2 vols.).

ROUSSEAU, C., *Droit international public* (Paris, 1953; 3rd edn., 1965).

—— *Droit international public*, Tome II, *Les sujets de droit* (Paris, 1974).

RUSSELL, R. B., assisted by MUTHER, J. G., *A History of the United Nations Charter; the role of the United States 1940–1945* (Washington, 1958).

SCHERMERS, H. G., *International Institutional Law* (Leiden, 1972–4, 3 vols.).

SCHWARZENBERGER, G., *International Law* (3rd edn., London 1957–76, 3 vols.).

—— *A Manual of International Law* (6th edn., London, 1976).

SMITH, H. A., *Great Britain and the Law of Nations* (London, 1932, 2 vols.).

SØRENSEN, M. ed., *Manual of public international law* (London, 1968).

STARKE, J. G., *An Introduction to International Law* (London, 7th edn., 1972).

—— *Studies in International Law* (London, 1965).

SYMPOSIUM, 'Genèse et Declin de l'État' (1976), 21 *Archives de Philosophie du Droit* 1–182.

TEMPERLEY, H. W. V., *A History of the Peace Conference of Paris* (London, 6 vols., 1920–4).

TUNKIN, G. I., *Theory of International Law* (trans. Butler, Harvard, 1974).

440   Bibliography

VATTEL, E. DE. *Le Droit des gens* (1758) (trans. C. G. Fenwick, Washington, 1916; Classics of International Law Series).

VERZIJL, J. H. W., *International Law in Historical Perspective* (Leyden, 1968–76, vols. 1–8), esp. vol. II, *International persons*.

VICTORIA, F. DE, *De Indis et de Iure Belli Relectiones* (1696) (trans. E. Nys, Washington, 1917; Classics of International Law Series).

WALDOCK, C. H. M., 'General Course' (1962) 106 *HR* 5–250.

WALTERS, F. P., *A History of the League of Nations* (Oxford, 2 vols., 1952).

WAMPACH, G., *Le Luxembourg neutre, Étude d'histoire diplomatique et de droit international public* (Paris, 1900).

WEHBERG, H., ed., *Institut de droit international. Table général des résolutions 1873–1956* (Basle, 1957).

WESTLAKE, J., *International Law* (Cambridge, 2 vols., 1904–1907).

—— *Collected Papers on public international law* (ed. L. Oppenheim, Cambridge, 1914).

WHEATON, H., *Elements of International Law* (Philadelphia, 1st edn., 1836; 3rd edn., 1846; 4th edn., (ed. Dana) 1866; reprinted Oxford, 1936; Classics of International Law Series).

WHITEMAN, M., *Digest of International Law* (Washington, 15 vols., 1963–1973).

WOLFF, C. F. VON, *Jus Gentium methodo scientifica pertractatum* (1764) (2 vols., Oxford, 1934; Classics of International Law Series).

CHAPTER I. STATEHOOD, RECOGNITION, AND INTERNATIONAL LAW

ALEXANDER-ALEXANDROWICZ, C. H., 'Doctrinal Aspects of the Universality of the Law of Nations' (1961) 37 *BY* 506–15.

—— 'The Theory of Recognition *in Fieri*' (1958) 34 *BY* 176–98.

—— 'The Quasi-Judicial Function in Recognition of States and Governments' (1957) 46 *AJ* 631–40.

ARANGIO-RUIZ, G., *L'État dans le sens du droit des gens et la notion du droit international* (Bologna, 1975, and in (1975) 26 *OZfOR* 3–36, 265–406).

BINAVINCE, E. S., 'Canadian Practice in Matters of Recognition', in R. St. J. MacDonald & ors., eds., *Canadian Perspectives on International Law and Organization* (Toronto, 1974), 153–83.

BORCHARD, E. M., 'Recognition and Non-Recognition' (1942) 36 *AJ* 108–10.

BOT, B. R., *Non-Recognition and Treaty Relations* (Leyden, 1968).

BRIGGS, H. W., 'Community Interest in the Emergence of New States: the Problem of Recognition' (1950) 44 *PAS* 169–80.

—— 'Recognition of States: Some Reflections on Doctrine and Practice' (1949) 43 *AJ* 113–21.

BROWN, P. M., 'The Effects of Recognition' (1942) 36 *AJ* 106–8.

—— 'La reconnaissance des nouveaux États et des nouveaux gouvernements' [1934] *Annuaire* 302–57.

BROWNLIE, I., 'The Relations of Nationality in Public International Law' (1963) 39 *BY* 284–364.

BUSHE-FOXE, P. L., 'The Courts of Chancery and Recognition, 1804–1831' (1931) 12 *BY* 63–75.

—— 'Unrecognized States: Cases in the Admiralty and Common Law Courts' (1932) 13 *BY* 39–48.

CHARPENTIER, J., *La reconnaissance internationale et l'évolution du droit des gens* (Paris, 1956).

CHEN, T. C., *The International Law of Recognition: with special reference to practice in Great Britain and the United States* (ed., L. C. Green, London, 1951).

DEVINE, D. J., 'The Status of Rhodesia in International Law' [1973] *Acta Juridica* 1–173; [1974] *Acta Juridica* 109–246.

ERICH, R. W., 'La Naissance et la Reconnaissance des États' (1926) 13 *HR* 427–507.

FROWEIN, J. A., 'Transfer or Recognition of Sovereignty: Some Early Problems in Connection with Dependent Territories' (1971) 65 *AJ* 568–71.

GROSS, E. A., 'The Peace of Westphalia 1648–1948' (1948) 42 *AJ* 20–41.

GUGGENHEIM, P., 'The Modern Conception of the Sovereign State' (1971) 3 *U. Tol. LR* 203–13.

HOSSAIN, Kamal, 'State Sovereignty and the U.N. Charter' (Oxford, MS. D. Phil d.3227, 1964).

HSIUNG, J. C., 'China's Recognition Practice and International Law', in J. A. Cohen, *China's Practice of International Law: Some Case Studies* (Harvard, 1972), 14–56.

JENNINGS, R. Y., 'The Progress of International Law' (1958) 34 *BY* 334–55.

—— 'Recognition De Jure and De Facto' *Report of International Law Conference, London 1962* (1963), 21–31.

JONES, J. W., 'The "Pure" Theory of International Law' (1935) 16 *BY* 5–19.

KETTNER, J. H., 'Subjects or Citizens: A Note on British Views respecting the Legal Effects of American Independence' (1976) 22 *Virginia LR* 945–67.

KIDD, C. J. F., 'Statehood and Recognition' (1970) 33 *MLR* 99–102.

KELSEN, H., 'La Naissance de l'État et la formation de sa nationalité. Les principes; leur application à la Tcéchoslovaquie' (1929) 4 *RDI* 613–41.

KELSEN, H., 'Recognition in International Law: Theoretical Observations' (1941) 35 *AJ* 605–17.

—— 'The Draft Declaration of the Rights and Duties of States: Critical Remarks' (1950) 44 *AJ* 259–76.

KOROWICZ, M. S., *Organisations internationales et souveraineté des États membres* (Paris, 1961).

KUNZ, J. L., 'Critical Remarks on Lauterpacht's "Recognition in International Law"' (1950) 44 *AJ* 713–19.

LACHS, M., 'Recognition and Modern Forms of International Cooperation' (1959) 35 *BY* 252–9.

LA FOREST, G. V., 'Towards a Reformation of the Law of State Succession' (1966) 60 *PAS* 103–11.

LAUTERPACHT, H., *Recognition in International Law* (London, 1948).

—— 'The Subjects of the Law of Nations' (1947) 63 *LQR* 438–560; (1948) 64 *LQR* 97–119; in 2 *Collected Papers* 487–533.

LE NORMAND, R., *La Reconnaissance internationale et ses diverses applications* (Paris, 1899).

MCMAHON, J. L., *Recent Changes in the Recognition Policy of the United States* (Washington, 1933).

O'CONNELL, D. P., 'State Succession and the Theory of the State' *Grotius Soc. Papers 1972*, 23–75.

—— 'La Personnalité en Droit International' (1963) 67 *RGDIP* 3–43.

OPPENHEIMER, F. E., 'Governments and Authorities in Exile' (1942) 36 *AJ* 568–95.

PATEL, S. R., *Recognition in the Law of Nations* (Bombay, 1959).

RAPISARDI-MIRABELLI, A., 'Le Congrès de Westphalie entre les puissances de l'Europe' (1929) 8 *Bibl. Viss.* 5–102.

REDSLOB, R., 'La reconnaissance de l'état comme sujet de droit international' (1934) 13 *RDI* 429–83.

REISMAN, W. M., and SUZUKI, S., 'Recognition and Social Change in International Law. A Prologue for Decision-making', in W. M. Reisman and B. M. Weston, eds., *Toward World Order and Human Dignity. Essays in Honour of Myres S. McDougal* (N.Y., 1976), 403–470.

RUDDY, F. S., *International Law in the Enlightenment. The Background of Emmerich de Vattel's Le Droit des Gens* (N.Y., 1975).

SALCEDO, J. A. C., *Soberania del Estado y Derecho Internacional* (Madrid, 2nd edn., 1976).

SALMON, J. J. A., *La Reconnaissance d'état: quatre cas: Mandchou Kuo, Katanga, Biafra, Rhodésie du Sud* (Paris, 1971).

SCHACHTER, O., 'The Development of International Law through the Legal Opinions of the United Nations Secretariat' (1948) 25 *BY* 91–132.

VERHOEVEN, J., *La Reconnaissance internationale dans la pratique contemporaine: les relations publiques internationales* (Paris, 1975).

WOOD, H. M., 'The Treaty of Paris and Turkey's Status in International Law' (1943) 37 *AJ* 262–74.

WRIGHT, Q., 'Recognition and Self-Determination' (1954) 48 *PAS* 23–37.

—— 'The Status of Germany and the Peace Proclamation' (1952) 46 *AJ* 299–308.

CHAPTER 2. THE CRITERIA FOR STATEHOOD

ANTONOWICZ, L., 'Definition of State in International Law Doctrine' (1966–7) 1 Pol. *YIL* 195–207.

BATY, T., 'Can an Anarchy be a State?' (1934) 28 *AJ* 444–55.

BOURQUIN, M., *L'État souverain et l'organization internationale* (N.Y., 1959).

BROCKELBANK, W. J., 'The Vilna Dispute' (1926) 29 *AJ* 483–501.

CAVARÉ, L., 'La Reconnaissance de l'Etat et le Manchukuo' (1935) 42 *RGDIP* 5–99.

CRANE, R. T., *The State in Constitutional and International Law* (Baltimore, 1907).

DAS, T., 'The Status of Hyderabad during the after British Rule in India' (1949) 43 *AJ* 57–72.

DELUPIS, I., *International Law and the Independent State* (Epping, 1974).

D'ENTRÈVES, A. P., *The Notion of the State* (Oxford, 1967).

DEVINE, D. J., 'The Requirements of Statehood Re-examined' (1971) 34 *MLR* 410–17.

DUMBAULD, E., 'Independence under International Law' (1976) 70 *AJ* 425–31.

EAGLETON, C., 'The Case of Hyderabad before the Security Council' (1950) 44 *AJ* 277–302.

—— *International Government* (3rd edn., N.Y., 1957).

FITZGIBBON, R. H., *Cuba and the United States 1900–1935* (N.Y., 1935).

FLORY, M., *Le Statut international des gouvernements réfugiés et le cas de la France Libre 1939–1945* (Paris, 1952).

FOUER, P. S., *The Spanish-Cuban-American War and the Birth of American Imperialism 1895–1902* (2 vols., N.Y., 1972).

FRITERS, G. M., 'The Prelude to Outer Mongolian Independence' (1937) 10 *Pac. Aff.* 168–89.

—— 'The Development of Outer Mongolian Independence' (1937) 10 *Pac. Aff.* 315–36.

—— *Outer Mongolia and its International Position* (London, 1951).

GANSOF VAN DER MEERSCH, W. J., *Fin de la souveraineté belge au Congo. Documents et réflexions* (The Hague, 1963).

GRAUPNER, R., 'Nationality and State Succession' (1946) 32 *Grot. ST* 87–120.

HAMZAVI, A. H., *Persia and the Powers. An Account of Diplomatic Relations 1941–1946* (London, 1946).

444 *Bibliography*

HASSOUNA, H. A., *The League of Arab States and Regional Disputes* (N.Y., 1975).

JENNINGS, R. Y., *The Acquisition of Territory in international law* (Manchester, 1963).

KANZA, T., *Conflict in the Congo* (Penguin, 1972).

KAVASS, I. (with SPRUDZS, A.), eds., *Baltic States: A Study of their Origin and National Development: Their Seizure and Incorporation into the U.S.S.R.* (International Military Law and History, Reprint Series, Vol. IV, N.Y., 1972).

KHADDURI, M., 'The France-Lebanon Dispute and the Crisis of November 1943' (1944) 38 *AJ* 601–20.

LANGER, R., *Seizure of Territory: the Stimson doctrine and related practices in legal theory and diplomatic practice* (Princeton, 1947).

LAPRADELLE, A. DE (with L. LE FUR and A. N. MANDELSTAM), *The Vilna Question* (London, 1929).

LAUTERPACHT, H., 'Restrictive Interpretation and the Principle of Effectiveness of Treaties' (1949) 26 *BY* 48–85.

—— 'Resort to War and the Covenant during the Manchurian Dispute' (1934) 28 *AJ* 43–60.

LEMKIN, L. *Axis Rule in Occupied Europe* (Washington, 1944).

LONGRIGG, S. H., *Syria and Lebanon under French Mandate* (London, 1958).

MAIN, E., *Iraq from Mandate to Independence* (London, 1955).

NEMZER, L., 'The Status of Outer Mongolia in International Law' (1939) 33 *AJ* 452–64.

NINČIĆ, D., *The Problem of Sovereignty in the Charter and in the Practice of the U.N.* (The Hague, 1970).

RHODES JAMES, R., ed., *The Czechoslovak Crisis 1968* (London, 1969).

RIPHAGEN, W., 'Some Reflections on "Functional Sovereignty"' (1975) 6 *NYIL* 121–65.

ROUSSEAU, C., 'L'indépendance de l'État dans l'Ordre International' (1948) 73 *HR* 171–253.

RUDZINSKI, A. W., 'Admission of New Members. The United Nations and the League of Nations' *Int. Conc.* No. 480 (April, 1952), 141–96.

SCELLE, G., 'La situation juridique de Vilna et de son territoire' (1928) 35 *RGDIP* 730–80.

SERENI, A. P., 'The Status of Croatia under International Law' (1940) 35 *Am. Pol. Sc. R.* 1144–51.

SHAFIK-G. SAÏD, *De Léopoldville à Kinshasa. La situation économique et financière au Congo ex-Belge au jour de l'indépendance* (Neuchâtel, 1969).

SUKIENNICKI, W., *La Souveraineté des Etats en droit international moderne* (Paris, 1927).

TÉKÉNIDÈS, G., 'La nature juridique des gouvernements institués par l'occupant en Grèce suivant la jurisprudence hellénique' (1974) 51 *RGDIP* 113–33.

TOUSCOZ, J., *Le Principe d'effectivité dans l'ordre international* (Paris, 1964).
UNITAR, Series No. 3, *Status and Problems of Very Small States and Territories* (N.Y., 1969).
VARSANYI, V., 'The Independence of Nauru' (1968) 7 *Aust. Lawyer* 161–6.
WEIS, P., *Nationality and Statelessness in International Law* (London, 1956).
WEISSBERG, G., *The International Status of the United Nations* (N.Y., 1961).
WILLIAMS, E. T., 'The Relations between China, Russia and Mongolia' (1916) 10 *AJ* 798–808.
WOLF, BARON VON DER OSTEN-SACKEN, *The Legal Position of the Grand Duchy of Finland in the Russian Empire* (London, 1912).
WRIGHT, Q., 'Note on the Manchurian Crisis' (1932) 26 *AJ* 342–348.
——— *Legal Problems in the Far Eastern Conflict* (N.Y., 1941).

CHAPTER 3. THE CRITERIA FOR STATEHOOD:
CRITERIA SUGGESTED AS A RESULT OF MODERN
DEVELOPMENTS IN INTERNATIONAL LAW

ANDERSON, C. A., 'Portuguese Africa: a brief history of U.N. involvement' (1974) 4 *Denver JILP* 133–51.
ASAMOAH, O. Y., *The Legal Significance of the Declarations of the General Assembly of the United Nations* (The Hague, 1966).
BAER, G. W., *Test Case. Italy, Europe and the League of Nations* (Stanford, 1967).
BARBIER, M., 'Le problème rhodésien: données actuelles et perspectives de solution' (1977) 81 *RGDIP* 735–71.
BARROS, J., *The Aaland Islands Question* (Princeton, 1968).
BATY, T., 'The Relations of Invaders to Insurgents' (1926–7) 36 *Yale LJ* 966–84.
BISSCHOP, W. R., 'Sovereignty' (1921–2) 2 *BY* 122–32.
BLUM, Y. Z., 'Reflections on the Changing Concept of Self-Determination' (1975) 10 *Israel LR* 509–14.
BOKOR-SZEGÖ, H., *New States in International Law* (Budapest, 1970).
BOND, J. E., 'Amended Article 1 of Draft Protocol to the 1949 Geneva Conventions: the Coming of Age of the Guerilla' (1975) 32 *Washington & Lee LR* 65–78.
BOWETT, D. W., 'Self-determination and Political Rights in the Developing Countries' (1966) 60 *PAS* 129–35.
BROWNLIE. I., 'Essay in the History of the Principle of Self-Determination' *Grotius Society Papers 1968*, 90–9.
CALOGEROPOULOS-STRATIS, S., *Le droit des peuples à disposer d'eux-mêmes* (Brussels, 1973).
CARR, E. H., *The Bolshevik Revolution 1917–1923* (London, 1950).
CASTAÑEDA, J., *The Legal Effects of United Nations Resolutions* (N.Y., 1969).

CHEN, L-C., 'Self-Determination as a Human Right', in W. M. Reisman and B. H. Weston, eds., *Toward World Order and Human Dignity: Essays in Honour of Myres S. McDougal* (N.Y., 1976), 198–261.

CHOWDHURY, S. R., *The Genesis of Bangladesh* (N.Y., 1972).

COETZEE, J. A., *The Sovereignty of Rhodesia and the Law of Nations* (Pretoria, 1970).

DELAVOIX, R., *Essai Historique sur la séparation de la Finlande et de la Russie* (Paris, 1932).

DEVINE, D. J., 'Rhodesia and the U.N.: the Lawfulness of International Concern—A Qualification' (1969) 2 *CILSA* 454–66.

DE VISSCHER, C., 'Positivisme et Jus Cogens' (1971) 75 *RGDIP* 5–11.

DE VISSCHER, F., 'La Question des Îles d'Aland' (1921) 2 *RDILC* 35–56; 243–84.

DINSTEIN, Y., 'Collective Human Rights of Peoples and Minorities' (1976) 25 *ICLQ* 102–30.

DOXEY, M. P., *Economic Sanctions and International Enforcement* (Oxford, 1971).

DRAPER, G. I. A., *The Red Cross Conventions* (London, 1958).

DUGARD, C. J. R., 'The O.A.U. and Colonialism: An Inquiry into the Plea of Self-Defence as a Justification for the Use of Force in the Eradication of Colonialism' (1967) 16 *ICLQ* 157–90.

EAGLETON, C., 'Excesses of Self-determination' (1953) 31 *For. Aff.* 592–604.

EEKELAAR, J. M., 'Principles of Revolutionary Legality' in Simpson, A. W. B. ed., *Oxford Essays in Jurisprudence* (2nd ser., 1973), 22–43.

EISEMANN, P. M., *Les Sanctions contre la Rhodésie* (Paris, 1972).

EL-AYOUTY, Y., *The U.N. and Decolonization. The Role of Afro-Asia* (Leyden, 1971).

EMERSON, R., 'Self-determination' (1971) 65 *AJ* 459–75.

—— *Self-Determination Revisited in the Era of Decolonization* (Harvard, 1964).

EVRIVIADES, M. L., 'The Legal Dimensions of the Cyprus Conflict' (1975) 10 *Texas ILJ* 227–64.

FALK, R. A., 'On the Quasi-Legislative Competence of the General Assembly' (1966) 60 *AJ* 782–91.

FAWCETT, J. E. S., 'Security Council Resolutions on Rhodesia' (1965–1966) 41 *BY* 103–21.

—— 'General Course' (1971) 132 *HR* 365–558.

—— 'Note' (1971) 34 *MLR* 417.

FENWICK, C. G., *Foreign Policy and International Law* (N.Y., 1968).

FITZMAURICE, G. G., 'The Future of Public International Law', *Institut de Droit International. Évolution et perspectives du droit international* (Basel, 1973), 196–363.

FORSYTHE, D. P., 'The 1974 Diplomatic Conference on Humanitarian Law: Some Observations' (1975) 69 *AJ* 77–91.

FRANCK, T. M., and RODLEY, N. S., 'After Bangladesh: The Law of Humanitarian Intervention by Military Force' (1973) 67 *AJ* 275–305.

—— 'The Law, the United Nations and Bangla Desh' (1972) 2 *Is. Ybk. HR* 142–75.

FUJITA, H., 'La guerre de liberation nationale et le droit international humanitaire' (1975) 53 *RDISDP* 81–142.

GRAHAM, D. E., 'The 1974 Diplomatic Conference on the Law of War: A Victory for Political Causes and a Return to the "Just War" Concept of the Eleventh Century' (1975) 32 *Washington & Lee LR* 25–63.

GUILHAUDIS, J. F., *Le Droit des peuples a'disposer d'eux-mêmes* (Grenoble, 1976).

HAUSER, R. E., 'International Protection of Minorities and the Right of Self-determination' (1971) 1 *Is. Ybk. HR* 92–102.

HIGGINS, R., 'International Law, Rhodesia and the United Nations' (1967) 23 *The World Today* 94–116.

HILL, CHESNEY, 'Recent Policies of Non-Recognition' *Int. Conc.* No. 243 (October 1933), 355–477.

HUNNINGS, N. M., 'The Legal Validity of State Independence Forcibly Acquired' (1962–3) 32 *Ybk. AAA* 58–65.

INDIAN MINISTRY OF EXTERNAL AFFAIRS, *Bangladesh Documents* (2 vols., New Delhi, 1971–2).

INTERNATIONAL COMMISSION OF JURISTS, 'East Pakistan Staff Study' *I.C.J. Review* No. 8 (June 1972), 23–62.

INTERNATIONAL COMMITTEE OF THE RED CROSS, *Commentary on the Geneva Conventions of the Laws of War* (4 vols., Geneva, 1958, ed. White, Coursier *et al.*).

JENKS, C. W., *Law in the World Community* (London, 1967).

JENNINGS, W. I., *The Approach to Self-Government* (London, 1956).

JOHNSON, C. D., 'Towards Self-determination—A Re-appraisal as Reflected in the Declaration on Friendly Relations' (1973) 3 *Georgia JICL* 145–63.

JOHNSON, D. H. N., 'The Effect of Resolutions of the General Assembly of the United Nations' (1955–6) 32 *BY* 97–122.

JOHNSON, H. S., *Self-determination within the Community of Nations* (Leyden, 1967).

KAUR, S., 'Self-determination in international law' (1970) 10 *Indian JIL* 479–502.

KOPUNGA, L. T., *The United Nations and Economic Sanctions against Rhodesia* (Toronto, 1973).

LACHS, M., 'The Law in and of the United Nations. Some reflections on the principle of self-determination' (1960–1) 1 *Indian YIL* 429–42.

LAUTERPACHT, H., "The Covenant as the "Higher Law"' (1936) 17 *BY* 54–65.

LEVIN, D. B., 'The Principle of Self-Determination of Nations in International Law' [1962] *Soviet Yearbook* 45–8.

MCDOUGAL, M. S., and REISMAN, W. M., 'Rhodesia and the United Nations: the Lawfulness of International Concern' (1968) 62 *AJ* 1–19.

MCNAIR, A. D., 'The Stimson Doctrine of Non-Recognition' (1933) 14 *BY* 65–74.

MCWHINNEY, E., 'The "New" Countries and the "New" International Law: the U.N.'s Special Conference on Friendly Relations and Co-operation among States' (1966) 60 *AJ* 1–33.

—— 'Non-Intervention and Self-Determination', in I.L.A., *Report of 56th Conference, New Delhi 1974*, 296–301.

MANI, V. S., 'The 1971 War on the Indian Sub-continent and International Law' (1972) 12 *Indian JIL* 83–99.

MAREK, K., 'Contribution à l'étude du jus cogens en droit international', *Réceuil d'études en hommage à Paul Guggenheim* (1967), 526–49.

MARSHALL, H. H., 'The Legal Effects of U.D.I.' (1968) 17 *ICLQ* 1022–1034.

MENON, P. K., 'The Right to Self-Determination. A Historical Appraisal' (1975) 53 *RDISDP* 183–200, 272–82.

MIDDLEBUSH, F. A., 'Non-Recognition as a Sanction of International Law' (1933) 27 *PAS* 40–55.

MOORE, J. B., 'An Appeal to Reason' (1931) 11 *For. Aff.* 547–88.

MOUSKHÉLY, M., 'La Naissance des États en Droit International Public' (1966) 70 *RGDIP* 469–85.

MUSTAFA, Z., 'The Principle of Self-Determination in International Law' (1971) 5 *Int. L.* 479–87.

NANDA, V. P., 'Self-Determination in International Law—A Tragic Tale of Two Cities—Islamabad (West Pakistan) and Dacca (East Pakistan)' (1972) 66 *AJ* 321–36.

—— 'Critique of the U.N. Inaction in the Bangladesh Crisis' (1972) 49 *Denver ILJ* 53–67.

NAWAZ, M. K., 'The Meaning and Range of the Principle of Self-determination' [1965] *Duke LJ* 82–101.

—— 'Bangladesh and International Law' (1971) 11 *Indian JIL* 251–68.

NEDJATI, Z., and LEATHES, G., 'A Study of the Constitution of the Turkish Federated State of Cyprus' (1976) 5 *Anglo-Am. L.R.* 67–92.

OBOZUWA, A. U., 'Some Legal Aspects of the Rhodesian Situation' (1975) 5 *Nig. J. Cont. L.* 1–43

OKEKE, C. N., *Controversial Subjects of International Law* (Rotterdam, 1974).

ONUF, N. G., 'Professor Falk on the Quasi-Legislative Competence of the General Assembly' (1970) 64 *AJ* 349–55.

PADELFORD, N. J. (with ANDERSSON, K. G. A.), 'The Aaland Islands Dispute' (1939) 33 *AJ* 465–87.

POMERANCE, M., 'The United States and Self-Determination: Perspectives on the Wilsonian Conception' (1976) 70 *AJ* 1–27.

REDSLOB, R., *Le Principe des nationalités* (Paris, 1930).

RIGO SUREDA, A., *The Evolution of the Right of Self-determination* (Leiden, 1973).

ROSENNE, S., *Law of Treaties. A Guide to the Legislative History of the Vienna Convention* (The Hague, 1970).

RUDOLPH, H., 'Rhodesia: Does South Africa Recognize it as an Independent State?' (1977) 94 *S. Af. LJ* 127–32.

RUZIÉ, D., 'Les sanctions economiques contre la Rhodésie' (1970) 97 *JDI* 20–56.

SALMON, J. J. A., 'Naissance et Reconnaissance du Bangladesh', *Multitudo legum, ius unum. Mélanges en honneur de Wilhelm Wengler* (Berlin, 1973) I, 467–90.

SALZBERG, J., 'U.N. Prevention of Human Rights Violations: the Bangladesh Case' (1973) 27 *Int. Org.* 115–28.

SCELLE, G., 'Quelques réflexions sur le droit des peuples à disposer d'eux-mêmes', *Fundamental Problems of International Law (Spiropoulos festschrift)* (Bonn, 1957), 385–92.

SCHEUNER, U., 'Conflict of Treaty Provisions with a Peremptory Norm of General International Law and Its Consequences' (1967) 27 *ZfV* 520–32.

SCHWARZENBERGER, G., 'International Jus Cogens' (1965) 43 *Texas LR* 455–78.

SCHWELB, E., 'Some Aspects of International Jus Cogens as Formulated by the International Law Commission' (1967) 61 *AJ* 946–75.

SHARP, R. H., *Duties of Non-Recognition in Practice 1775–1934* (Geneva, 1934).

SINHA, S. P., 'Has Self-Determination become a Principle of International Law Today?' (1974) 14 *Indian JIL* 332–61.

—— 'Is Self-Determination Passé?' (1973) 12 *Col. JTL* 260–73.

SKUBISZEWSKI, K., 'A New Source of the Law of Nations: Resolutions of International Organizations', *Guggenheim Festschrift* (Geneva, 1968), 508–20.

SLOAN, F. B., 'The binding force of a "Recommendation" of the General Assembly of the United Nations' (1948) 25 *BY* 1–33.

STARUSHENKO, G. B., 'The Abolition of Colonialism and International

Law' in Tunkin, G. I., ed., *Contemporary International Law* (Moscow, 1969), 77–96.

STEPHEN, M., 'Natural Justice at the U.N.: the Rhodesia Case' (1973) 67 *AJ* 479–90.

ŠUKOVIĆ, O., 'Principle of Equal Rights and Self-Determination of Peoples', in M. Šahović, ed., *Principles of International Law Concerning Friendly Relations and Cooperation* (Belgrade, 1972), 323–74.

SZTUCKI, J., *Jus Cogens and the Vienna Convention on the Law of Treaties. A Critical Appraisal* (Vienna, 1974).

THOMAS, A. V. W., and A. J., 'The Cyprus Crisis 1974–75: Political-Juridical Aspects' (1975) 29 *Southwestern LJ* 513–46.

TOURET, D., 'Le principe de l'égalite des droits des peuples et de leur droit à disposer d'eux-mêmes' (1975) 53 *RDISDP* 241–71.

UMOZURIKE, U. O., *Self determination in International Law* (Hamden, Conn., 1972).

VALLAT, F. A., 'The Competence of the U.N. General Assembly' (1959) 97 *HR* 203–91.

VAN DYKE, V., *Human Rights, the United States and the World Community* (N.Y., 1970).

VERDROSS, A., 'Forbidden Treaties in International Law' (1937) 31 *AJ* 572–7.

—— '*Jus Dispositivum* and *Jus Cogens* in International Law' (1966) 60 *AJ* 55–63.

WAMBAUGH, S., *A Monograph on Plebiscites* (N.Y., 1920).

—— *Plebiscites since the World War* (2 vols., Washington, 1933).

WILLIAMS, J. F., 'The New Doctrine of Recognition' (1932) 18 *Grot. ST* 109–29.

WILSON, J. H., *The Labour Government 1964–1970* (London, 1971).

WRIGHT, Q., 'The Goa Incident' (1962) 56 *AJ* 617–21.

ŽOUREK, J., *L'Interdiction de l'emploi de la force en droit international* (Leyden, 1974).

CHAPTER 4. ISSUES OF STATEHOOD BEFORE UNITED
NATIONS ORGANS

AUFRICHT, H., 'Principles and Practices of Recognition by International Organizations' (1949) 43 *AJ* 679–704.

BAILEY, S. D., *The Procedure of the Security Council* (Oxford, 1975).

CIOBANU, D., 'Credentials of Delegations and Representation of Member States at the United Nations' (1976) 25 *ICLQ* 351–81.

CLAUDE, I., 'Collective Legitimation as a Political Function of the U.N.' (1966) 29 *Int. Org.* 567–79.

DAVIDSON, J. W., *Samoa mo Samoa: The emergence of the independent State of Western Samoa* (Melbourne, 1967).

DOLAN, E., 'The Member Republics of the U.S.S.R. as Subjects of the Law of Nations' (1955) 4 *ICLQ* 629–36.

FEINBERG, N., 'L'Admission de Nouveaux Membres à la S.d.N. et à l'O.N.U.' (1952) 80 *HR* 297–393.

GOLD, J., *Membership and Non-membership in the International Monetary Fund* (Washington, 1974).

GRAHAM, M. W., *The League of Nations and the Recognition of States*, (Berkeley, 1933).

GROSS, L., 'Election of States to U.N. Membership' (1954) 48 *PAS* 37–59.

GUNTER, M. M., 'Liechtenstein and the League of Nations. A Precedent for the United Nations' (1974) 68 *AJ* 496–501.

—— 'What happened to the United Nations Ministate Problem?' (1977) 71 *AJ* 110–24.

HUDSON, M. O., 'Membership in the League of Nations' (1924) 18 *AJ* 436–58.

JACOBS, S., and POIRIER, M., 'The Right to Veto United Nations Membership Applications: The United States Veto of the Vietnams' (1976) 17 *Harvard ILJ* 581–607.

KOHN, W. S. G., 'The Sovereignty of Liechtenstein' (1967) 61 *AJ* 547–557.

MENDELSON, M. H., 'Diminutive States in the United Nations' (1969) 21 *ICLQ* 609–30.

MOWER, A. G., 'Observer Countries: Quasi-Members of the U.N.' (1966) 20 *Int. Org.* 66–83.

PIIP, A., 'Estonia and the League of Nations' (1920) 6 *Grotius ST* 35–44.

PLISCHKE, E., *Microstates in World Affairs. Policy Problems and Options* (Washington, 1977).

RATON, P., *Liechtenstein, History and Institutions of the Principality* (2nd rev. edn., 1970).

REISMAN, W. M., *Puerto Rico and the International Process: New Roles in Association* (Washington, 1974).

SCELLE, G., 'L'Admission des Nouveaux Members de la S.d.N.' (1921) 28 *RGDIP* 122–38.

SCHWARZENBERGER, G., *The League of Nations and World Order. A Treatise on the Principle of Universality in the Theory and Practice of the League of Nations* (London, 1936).

STEIN, E., *Some Implications of Expanding U.N. Membership* (N.Y., Carnegie Endowment for International Peace, 1956).

TIMASHEFF, N. S., 'Legal Aspects of the Grant of Three Seats to Russia in the U.N. Charter' (1945) 14 *Fordham LR* 180–90.

UIBOPUU, M. J., 'International Legal Personality of Union Republics of the U.S.S.R.' (1975) 22 *ICLQ* 811–45.

452   *Bibliography*

WEHRER, A., 'Le Statut International de Luxembourg et la S.d.N.' (1924) 31 *RGDIP* 169–202.

WILDHABER, L., 'Switzerland, neutrality and the U.N.' (1970) 12 *Malaya LR* 140–59.

CHAPTER 5. THE CRITERIA FOR STATEHOOD APPLIED: SOME SPECIAL CASES

ANGELO, A. H., 'Andorra: Introduction to a Customary Legal System' (1970) 14 *Am. J. L. Hist.* 95–111.

ANZILOTTI, D., 'La Condizione giuridica internazionale della Sancta Sede in seguito agli accordi del Laterano' (1929) 9 *Rdi* 165–76.

BATTAGLINI, G., 'Amministrazione e sovranità nell'ex Territorio libero di Trieste . . .', *Studi in Onore di Manlio Udina* (Milan, 1975) I, 71–156.

BÉLINGUIER, B., *La Condition juridique des Vallées d'Andorre* (Paris, 1970).

BISSCHOP, W. R., *The Saar Controversy* (London, 1924).

BLOCISZEWSKI, J., 'L'Affaire de Memel. La Décision de la Conférence des Ambassadeurs du 16 février 1923' (1923) 30 *RGDIP* 143–62.

BOWETT, D. W., *United Nations Forces* (London, 1964).

BREYCHA-VAUTHIER, A. C., and POTULICKI, M., 'The Order of Saint John in International Law' (1954) 43 *BY* 554–63.

BUELER, W. M., 'Taiwan; a problem of international law or politics?' (1971) 27 *The World Today* 256–66.

—— *United States China Policy and the Problem of Taiwan* (Boulder, 1971).

BUCCI, P. V., *Chiesa e Stato, Church-State Relations in Italy within the Contemporary Constitutional Framework* (The Hague, 1969).

CARDINALE, H. E., *The Holy See and the International Order* (The Hague, 1976).

CHEN, L. C., with LASSWELL, H. D., *Formosa, China and the United Nations* (N.Y., 1967).

CHEN, L. C., with REISMAN, W. H., 'Who owns Taiwan: A Search for International Title' (1972) 81 *Yale LJ* 599–671.

CHIU, HUNGDAH, ed., *China and the Question of Taiwan. Documents and Analysis* (N.Y., 1973).

CONFORTI, B., 'L'attuale situazione giuridica del Territorio di Trieste' (1955) 38 *Rdi* 568–83.

CRAWFORD, J. R., 'The International Legal Status of the Valleys of Andorra' (1977) 55 *RDISDP* 259–73.

CUMBO, A. P., 'The Holy See and International Law' (1948) 2 *ILQ* 603–620.

DAI, P., 'Recognition of States and Governments under International Law' (1965) 3 *Can. YIL* 289–305.

DALLABOND, J., 'L'Operation des Nations Unies à Chypre' (1976) 80 *RGDIP* 130–62.

DAKUSA, S., *Le Régime d'autonomie du Territoire de Klaidpeda* (1936).

DE LA BRIÈRE, R., 'Le Droit Concordataire dans la Nouvelle Europe' (1936) 63 *HR* 371–468.
—— 'Le Souveraineté du Saint-Siège et le Droit des Gens' (1937) 20 *RDILC* (3d) 29–48.
DEL CASTILLO, D. C., 'L'expérience internationale de Tangier' (1951) 20 *RIFDG* 18–25, 165–80.
DELORE, G., 'The Violation by Spain of the Statute of Tangier and its Consequences as they affect the United States' (1941) 35 *AJ* 140–5.
DENDAS, M., 'L'arrangement des problèmes de Chypre' *Schätzel Festschrift* (1960), 71–104.
DE WECK, N., *La Condition juridique du Conseil du Port et des Voies d'Eau de Dantzig* (Paris, 1933).
EHLER, S. Z., 'The Recent Concordats' (1961) 104 *HR* 5–68.
EHRLICH, T., *Cyprus 1958–1967* (Oxford, 1974).
EMILIANIDES, A. C., 'The Zurich and London Agreements and the Cyprus Republic', *Mélanges Séfériades* (Athens, 1961) II, 629–39.
EUSTACHE, F., 'Le Statut des Envoyés Pontificaux en France au XIX Siècle' *Grotius S. P. 1972*, 90–161.
EVRIVIADES, H. L., 'Legal Dimensions of the Cyprus Conflict' (1975) 10 *Texas ILJ* 227–64.
FARRAN, C. D'O., 'The Sovereign Order of Malta in International Law' (1954) 3 *ICLQ* 217–34.
—— 'The position of diminutive States in international law' *Schätzel Festschrift* (1960), 132–47.
FREYMOND, J., *The Saar Conflict 1945–1955* (London, 1960).
GERVAIS, A., 'Le Statut du Territoire Libre de Trieste' (1947) 51 *RGDIP* 134–45.
GRAHAM, R. A., *The Rise of the Double Diplomatic Corps in Rome. A Study in International Practice (1870–1875)* (The Hague, 1952).
GUTTERIDGE, J. A. C., 'The Dissolution of the International Regime in Tangiers' (1957) 33 *BY* 296–302.
HARVEY, R., 'The United States and the Legal Status of Formosa' (1959) 30 *World Aff. Q.* 134–53.
HOSTIE, J., *Questions de principe relatives au statut international de Dantzig* (Brussels, 1934).
HOYT, A. J., 'The U.S. Reaction to the Korean Attack' (1961) 55 *AJ* 45–76.
JAIN, J. P., 'The Legal Status of Formosa' (1963) 57 *AJ* 16–57.
JARRIGE, R. *La Condition internationale du Saint-Siège avant et après les Accords du Latran* (*Thèse*, Paris, 1930).
JENKS, C. W., 'The Interpretation and Application of Municipal Law by the P.C.I.J.' (1938) 19 *BY* 67–103.
KALIJARVI, T. W. V., 'The Problem of Memel' (1936) 30 *AJ* 204–15.
—— *The Memel Statute* (London, 1937).

KIRKHAM, D. B., 'The International Legal Status of Formosa' (1968) 6 *Can. YIL* 144–63.

KUNZ, J. L., 'The Status of the Holy See in International Law' (1952) 46 *AJ* 308–14.

LAVROFF, D. G., 'Le Statut de Chypre' (1961) 65 *RGDIP* 527–45.

LE FUR, L., *Le Saint-Siège et le droit des gens* (Paris, 1930).

LEVESQUE, G., *La Situation internationale de Dantzig* (Paris, 1924).

LEWIS, M. M., 'The Free City of Danzig' (1924) 5 *BY* 89–102.

LUCIEN-BRUN, J., 'Le Saint-Siège et les Institutions Internationales' [1964] *AFDI* 536–42.

MAKOWSKI, J., 'La situation juridique de la Ville Libre à Dantzig' (1923) 30 *RGDIP* 169–222.

MARAZZI, A., *I Territori Internazionalizzati* (Turin, 1959).

MASON, J. B., 'The Status of the Free City of Danzig under International Law' (1933) 5 *Rocky Mntn. LR.*

—— *The Danzig Dilemma* (California, 1946).

MAURER, E., 'Legal problems regarding Formosa and the Offshore Islands' (1959) 38 *DSB* 1005–11.

MORELLO, F. P., *The International Legal Status of Formosa* (The Hague, 1966).

MORROW, I. F. D., *The Peace Settlement in the German-Polish Borderlands*, (London, 1936).

——'The International Status of the Free City of Danzig' (1937) 18 *BY* 114–26.

NYS, E., 'La Papauté et le droit international' (1905) 37 *RDILC* 105.

O'CONNELL, D. P., 'Legal Aspects of the Peace Treaty with Japan' (1953) 29 *BY* 423–35.

—— 'The Status of Formosa and the Chinese Recognition Problem' (1956) 50 *AJ* 405–16.

OURLIAC, P., 'Existe-t-il une nationalité andorrane?', *Mélanges Maury* (Paris, 1960) I, 403–15.

OURLIAC, P. and ors., *Les Problèmes Actuels des Vallées d'Andorre* (Publications de l'Institut d'Etudes Politiques de Toulouse, No. 5) (Paris, 1970).

PALLIERI, G. B., 'Il rapporto fra Chiesa Cattolica e Stato Vaticano Secondo il Diritto Ecclesiastico e il Diritto Internazionale' (1930) 53 *Riv. Int. di Scienze Sociali* 195–221.

PALLIERI, G. B., with VISMARA, G., *Acta Pontifica Juris Gentium usque ad Annum MCCIV* (Milan, 1946).

PHILLIPS, C. S., 'The International Legal Status of Formosa' (1957) 10 *Western Pol. Q.* 276–87.

PICCIONI, C., 'Le Statut International de Dantzig' (1921) 28 *RGDIP* 84–106.

POLYVIOU, P. G., *Cyprus in Search of a Constitution* (Nicosia, 1976).

REDSLOB, R., *Le Statut international de Dantzig* (Brussels, 1926).
RIÈRA, G., 'L'Andorre' (1968) 72 *RGDIP* 361–80.
ROUSSEAU, CH., 'Le "État" de la Cité du Vatican' (1930) 37 *RGDIP* 145–153.
—— 'Les Vallées d'Andorre: Une Survivance Féodale dans le Monde Contemporain' *Symbolae Verzijl* (The Hague, 1958), 337–46.
SCHWELB, E., 'The Trieste Settlement and Human Rights' (1956) 49 *AJ* 240–8.
SCOTT, I., *The Roman Question and the Powers 1848–1865* (The Hague, 1969).
SERENI, A. P., *The Italian Conception of International Law* (N.Y., 1943).
SEYERSTED, F., *United Nations Forces in the Law of Peace and War* (Leyden, 1966).
SIOTTO-PINTOR, M., 'Les Sujets du Droit International Autres que les États' (1932) 41 *HR* 251–360.
SKUBISZEWSKI, K., 'Gdansk and the Dissolution of the Free City', in *Menzel Festschrift* (1975), 469 85.
STAVROPOULOS, C., 'Current Legal Problems of the U.N.' (1973) 7 *Int. L.* 70–7.
STUART, G. H., *The International City of Tangier* (2nd rev. edn., Stanford, 1955).
TSOUTSOS, A., *Politique et droit dans les relations internationales* (Paris, 1967).
UDINA, M., *Scritti sulla Questione di Trieste, Sorta in Sequito al Secondo Conflitto Mondiale ed i principali atti internazionali ed interni ad essa relativi* (Milan, 1969).
—— 'Gli accordi italo-jugoslavi di Osimo del 10 novembre 1975' (1977) 60 *Rdi* 405–41.
VILLAS, P., 'Les États Exigus en Droit International Public' (1954) 58 *RGDIP* 559–81.
VUKAS, B., 'Solution Définitive de la "Question de Trieste" par la Conclusion des Accords entre l'Italie et la Yougoslavie à Osimo (Ancona), le 10 Novembre 1975' [1976] *AFDI* 77–95.
WAGNON, H., *Concordats et droit international: fondement, élaboration, valeur et cessation du droit concordataire* (Gembloux, 1935).
WENG, B. S., 'The Legal Status of Taiwan' in Leng, S. C., Chiu, H., eds., *Law in Chinese Foreign Policy: Communist China and Selected Problems of International Law* (N.Y., 1972), 123–77.
WRIGHT, H., 'The Status of the Vatican City' (1944) 38 *AJ* 452–7.
WRIGHT, Q., 'The Chinese Recognition Problem' (1955) 49 *AJ* 318–327.
YDIT, M., *Internationalized Territories from the 'Free City of Cracow' to the 'Free City of Berlin'* (Leyden, 1961).
ZYDIS, S. G., *Cyprus, Reluctant Republic* (Paris, 1973).

CHAPTER 6. ORIGINAL ACQUISITION AND PROBLEMS
OF STATEHOOD

ALEXANDROWICZ, C. H., 'Freitas *versus* Grotius' (1959) 35 *BY* 162–82.

—— 'Paulus Vladimiri and the Development of the Doctrine of Coexistence of Christian and Non-Christian Countries' (1963) 34 *BY* 441–8.

—— *An Introduction to the History of the Law of Nations in the East Indies (16th, 17th and 18th Centuries)* (Oxford, 1967).

—— 'Puffendorf-Crull and the Afro-Asian World' (1968–9) 43 *BY* 205–8.

—— *The European-African Confrontation. A Study in Treaty Making* (Leiden, 1973).

ALLOTT, A. N., 'Boundaries and the Law in Africa' in C. G. Widstrand, ed., *African Boundary Problems* (1969), 9–21.

BATY, T., 'Protectorates and Mandates' (1921–2) 2 *BY* 109–21.

BENNETT, G. I., 'The I.L.O. Convention on Indigenous and Tribal Populations—The Resolution of a Problem of *Vires*' (1972–3) 46 *BY* 382–92.

BLUM, Y., 'The Missing Reversioner: Reflections on the Status of Judea and Samaria' (1968) 3 *Is. LR* 279–330.

BRUNET, R., *L'Annexion du Congo à la Belgique et le droit international* (Paris, 1911).

BRUNSCHWIG, H., 'La négociation du traité Makoko' (1965) 5 *Cahiers d'Études Africaines* 5–56.

COHEN, F. S., 'Original Indian Title' (1947–8) 32 *Minnesota LR* 28–59.

DE MONTMORENCY, J. E. G., 'The Barbary States in the Law of Nations' (1918) 4 *Grotius ST* 87–94.

EVATT, E., 'The Acquisition of Territory in Australia and New Zealand' *Grotius S. P. 1968*, 16–45.

FINNIGAN, R. A., 'Indian Treaty Analysis and Off-Reservation Fishing Rights: A Case Study' (1975) 51 *Washington LR* 61–95.

GALEY, M. E., 'Indigenous Peoples . . . and the Development of International Law on Human Rights' (1975) 8 *Human Rights J.* 21–39.

GILL, E. A., 'An Analysis of the 1868 Oglala Sioux Treaty and the Wounded Knee Trial' (1975) 14 *Col. JTL* 119–46.

GREEN, L. C., *Canada's Indians: Federal Policy, International and Constitutional Law* (Alberta, 1969).

—— '"Civilized" Law and "Primitive" Peoples' (1975) 13 *Osgoode Hall LJ* 233–49.

—— 'North America's Indians and the Trusteeship Concept' (1975) 4 *Anglo-America LR* 137–62.

HERTSLET, L., *Map of Africa by Treaty* (3rd edn., London, 1909, 4 vols.)

HORN, L. A., 'The Republic of Minerva: Nation Founding by Individuals' (1973) 12 *Col. JTL* 520–56.

KELLER, A. S., LISSITZYN, O. J., and MANN. F. J., *Creation of Rights of Sovereignty through Symbolic Acts 1400–1800* (Columbia, 1938).

LEVY, G. J., 'Comment on the Western Sahara Opinion' (1976) 2 *Brooklyn JIL* 289–307.

LEVY, N. H., 'Native Hawaiian Land Rights' (1975) 63 *Calif. LR* 848–885.

LUGARD, F. J. D., 'Treaty Making in Africa' (1893) 1 *Geographical Journal* 53–5.

—— *The Dual Mandate in British Tropical Africa* (Edinburgh, 1922).

MENSAH-BROWN, A. K. ed., *African International Legal History* (Unitar, N.Y., 1975).

MÖSSNER, J. H., 'The Barbary Powers in International Law (Doctrinal and Practical Aspects)' *Grotius S. P. 1972*, 197–221.

NYS, E., *The Independent State of the Congo in International Law* (Brussels, n.d.).

O'CONNELL, D. P., 'International Law and Boundary Disputes' (1960) 54 *PAS* 77–84.

REEVES, J. S., 'The Origin of the Congo Free State Considered from the Standpoint of International Law' (1909) 3 *AJ* 99–118.

SAMKANGE, S., *Origins of Rhodesia* (Nairobi, 1968).

SASTRI, K. A. N., 'Inter-State Relations in Asia' (1953) 2 *Indian YBIA* 133–52.

SIMSAURIAN, J., 'The Acquisition of Legal Title to *Terra Nullius*' (1938) 53 *Pol. Sc. Q.* 111–28.

SINHA, S. P., *New Nations and the Law of Nations* (Leyden, 1967).

SNOW, E., *The Problem of Aborigines in the Law and Practice of Nations* (Washington, 1919).

SYATAUW, J. J. G., *Some Newly Established Asian States and the Development of International Law* (The Hague, 1961).

SYMPOSIUM, 'The Rights of Indigenous Peoples: A Comparative Analysis' (1974) 68 *PAS* 265–300.

TORRELLI, H., 'Les Indiens du Canada et le droit des traités dans la jurisprudence canadienne' [1974] *AFDI* 227–49.

WASHBURN, W. E., 'The Historical Context of American Indian Legal Problems' (1976) 40 *Law & Cont. P.* 12–24.

WILKINSON, C. F., and VOLKMAN, J. H. 'Judicial Review of Indian Treaty Abrogation' (1975) 63 *Calif. LR* 601–61.

CHAPTER 7. THE CREATION AND STATUS OF
DEPENDENT STATES AND OTHER DEPENDENT ENTITIES

ADAMIYAT, F., *Bahrein Islands. A Legal and Diplomatic Study of the British-Iranian Controversy* (N.Y., 1955).

AL BAHARNA, H., *The Legal Status of the Arabian Gulf States* (Manchester, 1968).
—— 'The Fact-Finding Mission of the U.N. Secretary General and the Settlement of the Bahrein-Iran Dispute, May 1970' (1973) 22 *ICLQ* 541–52.
ALCOCK, E. A., *The History of the South Tyrol Question* (London, 1970).
ALEXANDROWICZ, C. H., 'The Legal Position of Tibet' (1954) 48 *AJ* 265–74.
—— 'The Afro-Asian World and the Law of Nations (Historical Aspects)' (1968) 123 *HR* 121–213.
CASTAGNO, A. A., 'The Somalia-Kenyan Controversy' (1964) 2 *JMAS* 165–88.
FAWCETT, J. E. S., 'Treaty Relations of British Overseas Territories' (1949) 26 *BY* 86–107.
FISCHER, G., 'Le nouveau statut de Sikkim' [1974] *AFDI* 201–14.
FITZMAURICE, G. G., 'The Law and Procedure of the International Court of Justice' (1953) 30 *BY* 2–5.
FENET, A., *La Question du Tyrol du Sud, un problème de droit international* (Paris, 1968).
GALLOIS, J. P., *Le Régime international de la Principauté de Monaco* (Paris, 1964).
GUIHO, P., *La Nationalité marocaine* (Rabat, 1961).
GUPTA, J. B. D., *Jammu and Kashmir* (The Hague, 1968).
HAMILTON, D., 'Ethiopia's Frontiers: The Boundary Agreements and their Demarcation, 1896–1956' (Oxford, diss., 1974).
INTERNATIONAL COMMISSION OF JURISTS, *The Question of Tibet and the Rule of Law* (Geneva, 1959).
—— *Tibet and the Chinese People's Republic* (Geneva, 1960).
INTERNATIONAL LAW ASSOCIATION, *The Effects of Independence upon Treaties* (London, 1965).
JENKYNS, H., *British Rule and Jurisdiction beyond the Seas* (Oxford, 1902).
JOHNSTON, W. R., *Sovereignty and Protection. A Study of British Jurisdictional Imperialism in the late Nineteenth Century* (Durham, 1973).
JONES, J. M., 'Who are British Protected Persons?' (1945) 22 *BY* 122–9.
—— *British Nationality Law and Practice* (Oxford, 1947).
KAMANDA, A. M., 'A Study of the Legal Status of Protectorates in Public International Law' (Thesis, Geneva, 1961).
KATO, L. L., 'Act of State in a Protectorate—in Retrospect' [1969] *Public Law* 219–35.
KELLY, J. B., 'Sultanate and Imamate in Oman' *Chatham House Memoranda*, 1959 (13).
LAMB, A., *The McMahon Line. A Study in the Relations between India, China and Tibet, 1904–1914* (2 vols., London, 1966).

LATHAM BROWN, D. J., 'The Ethiopia-Somaliland Frontier Dispute' (1956) 5 *ICLQ* 245–64.

LEWIS, I. M., 'Developments in the Somali Dispute' (1967) 66 *African Aff.* 104–22.

LITTLE, T., *South Arabia, Arena of Conflict* (London, 1968).

McCABE, D. A., 'Tibet's Declaration of Independence' (1966) 60 *AJ* 369–71.

MIRIAM, M. W., 'The Background of the Ethiopian-Somalian Boundary Dispute' (1964) 2 *JMAS* 189–219.

MORRIS, H. F., 'Protection or Annexation? Some Constitutional Anomalies of Colonial Rule', in H. F. Morris and J. S. Read, *Indirect Rule and the Search for Justice* (Oxford, 1972), 41–70.

PEARCY, G. E., '40 Newly Independent States: Some Politico-Geographic Observations' (1964) 45 *DSB* 604–11.

PILLAI, R., and KUMAR, M., 'The Political and Legal Status of Kuwait' (1962) 11 *ICLQ* 108–30.

PINTER, F., 'Changes in the South Tyrol Issue' [1977] *YBWA* 64–74.

POLACK, K., 'The Defence of Act of State in Relation to Protectorates' (1963) 26 *MLR* 139–55.

POULOSE, T. T., *Succession in International Law. A Study of India, Pakistan, Ceylon and Burma* (New Delhi, 1974).

RAO, P. R., *India and Sikkim 1814–1970* (New Delhi, 1972).

ROBBINS, R. R., 'The Status of Aden Colony and Aden Protectorate' (1939) 33 *AJ* 700–15.

ROLLET, H., *Liste des engagements bilatéraux et multilatéraux au 30 juin 1972 ; accords et traités souscrits par la France* (Paris, 1973).

RUBIN, A. P., 'The Sino-Indian Border Dispute' (1960) 9 *ICLQ* 96–125.

—— 'A Matter of Fact' (1965) 59 *AJ* 586–90.

—— 'Tibet's Declaration of Independence?' (1966) 60 *AJ* 812–14.

—— 'The Position of Tibet in International Law' *China Q.* No. 35 (1968), 110–54.

—— *Piracy, Paramountcy and Protectorates* (Kuala Lumpur, 1974).

RUTHERFORD, G. W., 'Spheres of Influence: an Aspect of Semi-Suzerainty' (1926) 20 *AJ* 300–25.

SEN, S. D. K., *The Indian Native States* (London, 1930).

SERENI, A. P., 'La Représentation en Droit International' (1948) 73 *HR* 69–166.

SHARMA, S. P., 'The India-China Border Dispute: An Indian Perspective' (1965) 59 *AJ* 16–47.

SOMERVELL, D. B., 'The Indian States' (1930) 11 *BY* 55–62.

VAN PANHUYS, H. F., *The Role of Nationality in International Law* (Leyden, 1959).

VARADARJAN, M. K., *The Indian States and the Federation* (Oxford, 1934).

WARNER, W. L., *The Native States of India* (London, 1910).
ZEMANEK, K., 'State Succession after decolonization' (1965) 116 *HR* 187–300.

CHAPTER 8. DEVOLUTION

ALTUG, Y. M., *Turkey and Some Problems of International Law* (Istanbul, 1958).
BALL, H. H., *The 'Open' Commonwealth* (Durham, 1971).
BARBER, J., *South Africa's Foreign Policy 1945–70* (London, 1973).
BOOYSEN, H. *et al.*, 'Comments on the Independence and Constitution of Transkei' (1976) 2 *S. Af. YBIL* 1–35.
BROWNLIE, I., 'Transition to Independence: the Legal Aspects' (1961) 8 *Review of Contemporary Law* 19–40.
CARTY, T., 'A Place for Scotland in International Law?', in J. P. Grant, ed., *Independence and Devolution. The Legal Implications for Scotland* (Edinburgh, 1976), 100–23.
CHARTERIS, A. H., 'The Mandate over Nauri Island' (1923–4) 4 *BY* 137–52.
CHENG, S. C., *Schemes for the Federation of the British Empire* (Columbia, 1931).
CORBETT, R. E., and SMITH, H. A., *Canada and World Politics. A Study of the Constitutional and International Relations of the British Empire* (London, 1926).
COWEN, D. V., 'Legislature and Judiciary: Reflections on the Constitutional Issues in South Africa' (1952) 15 *MLR* 282–96; (1953) 16 *MLR* 273–98.
COWEN, Z., *The British Commonwealth of Nations in a Changing World: law, politics and prospects* (Evanston, 1965).
D'AMATO, A. A., 'The Bantustan Proposals for South-West Africa' (1966) 4 *JMAS* 177–92.
DAWSON, R. M., *The Development of Dominion Status 1900–1936* (London, 1937).
DEAN, W. M. B., 'A Citizen of Transkei' (1978) 11 *CILSA* 57–67.
DE SMITH, S. A., *The New Commonwealth and its Constitutions* (London, 1964).
DICEY, A. V., *Introduction to the Study of the Law of the Constitution* (London, 7th edn., 1908; 8th edn., 1915).
DUNN, F. S., 'The New International Status of the British Dominions' (1926–7) 13 *Virginia LR* 354–79.
EWART, J. S., 'Canada. Colony to Kingdom' (1913) 7 *AJ* 268–84.
FAWCETT, J. E. S., *The British Commonwealth in International Law* (London, 1963).
FISCHER, G., *Un Cas de Décolonization. Les Etats-Unis et les Philippines* (Paris, 1960).

Fischer, G., 'La non reconnaissance de Transkei' [1976] *AFDI* 63–76.

Gonidec, P. F., 'La Communauté' [1960] *Public Law* 177–89.

Hancock, W. K., *Survey of British Commonwealth Affairs* vol. I. *Problems of Nationality 1918–1936* (London, 1937).

Harding, L., *Unabhängigkeit der Transkei* (Institute of African Studies, No. 4, Hamburg, 1976).

Harvey, H. J., *Consultation and Co-operation in the Commonwealth* (London, 1952).

Heydt, D. A., 'Nonrecognition of the Independence of Transkei' (1978) 10 *Case W. Res. JIL* 167–96.

Hill, C. R., *Bantustans. The Fragmentation of South Africa* (London, 1964).

Hone, R., 'International Legal Problems of Emergent Territories' *Report of International Law Conference, 1960* (London, 1960).

Hurst, C. J. B., 'The British Empire as a Political Unit' in *Great Britain and the Dominions* (Chicago, 1928).

Jacomy-Millette, A., *Treaty Law in Canada* (Ottawa, 1975).

Jennings, R. Y., 'The Commonwealth and International Law' (1953) 30 *BY* 320–51.

Johnston, V. K., 'Dominion Status in International Law' (1927) 21 *AJ* 481–9.

Joseph, C., *Nationality and Diplomatic Protection. The Commonwealth of Nations* (Leyden, 1969).

Kahn, E., 'Some Thoughts on the competency of the Transkeian Legislative Assembly and the Sovereignty of the South African Parliament' (1963) 80 *SALJ* 473–82.

Keith, A. B., *Imperial Unity and the Dominions* (Oxford, 1916).

—— *Selected Speeches and Documents on British Colonial Policy 1763–1917* (London, 1918, 2 vols.).

—— *The War Governments of the British Dominions* (London, 1921).

—— *Dominion Home Rule in Practice* (Oxford, 1921).

—— *Dominion Autonomy in Practice* (rev. edn., London, 1929).

—— *The Sovereignty of the British Dominions* (London, 1929).

—— *The Constitutional Law of the British Dominions* (London, 1933).

Kendle, J. E., *The Round Table Movement and Imperial Union* (Toronto, 1975).

Kidwai, M. H. M., 'International Personality and the British Dominions: Evolution and Accomplishment' (1976) 9 *UQLJ* 76–117.

—— 'External Affairs Power and the Constitutions of the British Dominions', ibid. 167–87.

Lewis, M. M., 'The Canadian-American Halibut Fisheries Treaty' (1923–4) 4 *BY* 168–9.

—— 'The Treaty Making Power of the Dominions' (1925) 6 *BY* 31–43.

MacKenzie, N., 'Two Recent Canadian Treaties' (1925) 6 *BY* 191–2.

Mackintosh, J. P., 'The Problem of Devolution—the Scottish Case', in J. A. G. Griffith, ed., *From Policy to Administration. Essays in Honour of William A. Robson* (London, 1976), 99–114.

Mahatra, S. R., *India and the Commonwealth 1885–1924* (London, 1965).

Mansergh, N., ed., *Documents and Speeches on British Commonwealth Affairs 1931–1952* (2 vols., London, 1953).

Myers, D. P., 'Contemporary Practice of the U.S. relating to International Law' (1961) 55 *AJ* 703–20.

Noel-Baker, P. J., *The Present Juridical Status of the British Dominions in International Law* (London, 1929).

Norman, G. E., 'The Transkei: South Africa's Illegitimate Child', (1977) 12 *New England LR* 585–646.

O'Connell, D. P., 'The Crown in the British Commonwealth' (1957) 6 *ICLQ* 103–25.

Olivier, W. H., 'Statelessness and Transkeian Nationality' (1976) 2 *S. Af. YBIL* 143–54.

Palley, C., *The Constitutional History and Law of Southern Rhodesia 1888–1965 with Special Reference to Imperial Control* (Oxford, 1966).

Patenaude, L., *Le Labrador à l'heure de la contestation* (Montreal, 1972).

Porritt, E., *The Fiscal and Diplomatic Freedom of the British Overseas Dominions* (Oxford, 1922).

Poulose, T. T., 'India as an Anomalous International Person (1919–1947)' (1970) 44 *BY* 202–12.

Richings, F. G., 'The Applicability of South African Legislation in the Self-Governing Bantu Territories' (1976) 93 *SALJ* 119–26.

Roberts-Wray, K., 'The Legal Machinery for the Transition from Dependence to Independence', in J. N. D. Anderson, ed., *Changing Law in Developing Countries* (London, 1963), 43–62.

Roth, L., 'Transkei: A Tale of Two Citizenships' (1976) 9 *NYUJILP* 205–35.

Scott, J. B., 'The British Commonwealth of Nations' (1927) 21 *AJ* 95–101.

Smith, H. A., 'The British Dominions and Foreign Relations' (1926–7) 12 *Cornell LQ* 1–13.

Stewart, R. B., *Treaty Relations of the British Commonwealth of Nations* (London, 1939).

Sunderam, L., 'The International Status of India' (1931) 17 *Grotius ST* 35–54.

Taubenfeld, R. F., and H. J., *Race, Peace Law, and Southern Africa (Background Paper and Proceedings of the Tenth Hammarskjöld Forum)* (N.Y., 1968).

Van Panhuys, R., 'International Aspects of the Reconstruction of the Kingdom of the Netherlands in 1954' (1958) 5 *NILR* 1–31.

WHEARE, K. C., *The Statute of Westminster and Dominion Status* (5th edn., London, 1953).

WHITE, W. W., *The Status in International Law of the fragments of the Ottoman Empire* (Dissertation, Chicago, 1935).

WILSON, R. R., 'Some Questions of Legal Relations between Commonwealth Members' (1957) 51 *AJ* 611–17.

WITKIN, M. F., (Note on the Transkei Constitution Act of 1976) (1977) 18 *Harvard ILJ* 464–7.

—— 'Transkei: An Analysis of the Practice of Recognition—Political or Legal?' (1977) 18 *Harvard ILJ* 605–27.

CHAPTER 9. SECESSION

ABI-SAAB, G., 'Wars of National Liberation and the Laws of War' (1972) 3 *Annales d'études Internationales* 93–119.

ADARAMOLA, F., 'The Nigerian Crisis and Foreign Intervention: A Focus on International Law' (1970) 4 *Nigerian LJ* 76–84.

ALEXANDER, C. K., 'Israel in Fieri' (1951) 4 *ILQ* 423–30.

ANGLIN, D. G., 'Britain and the Use of Force in Rhodesia', in M. G. Fry ed., *Freedom and Change. Essays in Honour of Lester B. Pearson* (Toronto, 1975), 43–75.

BAR-YAACOV, N., *The Israel-Syrian Armistice. Problems of Interpretation*, (Jerusalem, 1967).

BAXTER, R. R., 'So-Called "Unprivileged Belligerency"—Spies, Guerillas and Saboteurs' (1951) 28 *BY* 323–45.

BEDJAOUI, M., *Law and the Algerian Revolution* (Brussels, 1961).

BELKHERROUBI, A., *La Naissance et la reconnaissance de la République Algérienne* (Brussels, 1972).

BENNOUNA, M., *Le Consentement à l'ingerence militaire dans les conflits internes* (Paris, 1974).

BIERZANEK, R., 'Le statut juridique des partisans et des mouvements de résistance armée; évolution historique et aspects actuels' *Mélanges Andrassy* (1968), 54–77.

BROSSARD, J., *L'Accession à la souveraineté et le cas du Québec* (Montreal, 1976).

BROWN, P. M., 'The Recognition of Israel' (1948) 42 *AJ* 620–7.

CAREY, T. C., 'Self-Determination in the Post-Colonial Era: The Case of Quebec' (1977) 1 *ASILS ILJ* 47–72.

CARTWRIGHT, H. V., 'Revolutionary Algeria and the United Nations: A Study in Agenda Politics' (Ann Arbor, diss., 1974).

CASTRÉN, E., 'Recognition of Insurgency' (1965) 5 *Indian YIL* 443–54.

CATTAN, H., *Palestine, The Arabs and Israel* (London, 1969).

—— *Palestine and International Law. The Legal Aspects of the Arab-Israeli Conflict* (London, 1973; 2nd edn., 1976).

CHIMANGO, L. J., 'The relevance of humanitarian international law to the liberation struggles in Southern Africa—the case of Moçambique in retrospect' (1975) 8 *CILSA* 287–317.

CRONJE, S., *The World and Nigeria. The Diplomatic History of the Biafran War 1967–1970* (London, 1972).

DAVIDSON, B., *The Liberation of Guiné* (London, 1969).

DE LIMA, F. X., *Intervention in International Law* (Princeton, 1974).

DHOKALIA, R. D., 'Civil Wars and International Law' (1971) 11 *Indian JIL* 219–50.

EAGLETON, C., 'Palestine and the Constitutional Law of the U.N.' (1948) 42 *AJ* 397–9.

ELARABY, N., 'Some Legal Implications of the 1947 Partition Resolution and the 1949 Armistice Agreements' (1968) 33 *Law and Contemporary Problems* 97–108.

EL-FARRA, M. M., 'The Role of the U.N. *vis-à-vis* the Palestine Question' (1968) 33 *Law and Contemporary Problems* 68–77.

ELIAS, T. O., 'The Nigerian Crisis in International Law' (1971) 5 *Nigerian LJ* 1–18.

—— *Africa and the Development of International Law* (Leiden, 1972).

FALK, R. A., *Legal Order in a Violent World* (Princeton, N.J., 1968).

FALK, R. A., ed., *The International Law of Civil War* (Baltimore, 1971).

FEINBERG, N., *On an Arab Jurist's Approach to Zionism and the State of Israel* (Jerusalem, 1971).

FISHER, R. A., 'The Acquisition of International Legal Standing by the Palestine Liberation Organization' (1975) 3 *Syracuse JILC* 221–54.

GERSON, A., 'Trustee-Occupant: The Legal Status of Israel's Presence in the West Bank' (1973) 14 *Harvard ILJ* 1–49.

GINSBURG, G., '"Wars of Liberation" and the Modern Law of Nations—the Soviet Thesis', in H. W. Baade, ed., *The Soviet Impact on International Law* (N.Y., 1965), 66–98.

GORDON, D. C., *The Passing of French Algeria* (London, 1966).

GREENSPAN, M., *The Modern Law of Land Warfare* (California, 1959).

GREENWOOD, F. M., 'The Legal Secession of Quebec . . .' (1978) 12 *UBCLR* 71–84.

HALDERMAN, J. W., 'Some International Constitutional Aspects of the Palestine Case' (1968) 33 *Law and Contemporary Problems* 78–96.

HARCOURT, W., *Letters by Historicus on some Questions of International Law* (London, 1863).

HYDE, C. C., 'The Status of the Republic of Indonesia in International Law' (1949) 49 *Col. LR* 955–66.

IJALAYE, D. A., 'Some Legal Implications of the Nigerian Civil War' *Proceedings of the First Annual Conference of the Nigerian Society of International Law* (Lagos, 1969), 70–114.

IJALAYE, D. A., 'Was "Biafra" at any time a State in International Law?' (1971) 65 *AJ* 551–9.

JAQUET, L. G. M., *Intervention in International Politics* (The Hague, 1971).

JESSUP, P. C., 'The Estrada Doctrine' (1931) 25 *AJ* 719–23.

KAHNG, T. J., *Law, Politics and the Security Council* (The Hague, 1964).

KANE, W. E., *Civil Strife in Latin America: A Legal History of U.S. Involvement* (Baltimore, 1972).

KHAIRALLAH, D. L., *Insurrection under international law* (Beirut, 1973).

KIRK-GREENE, A. H. M., *Crisis and Conflict in Nigeria: A Documentary Sourcebook 1966–1969* (2 vols., Oxford, 1971).

KLEIN, E., 'National Liberation Struggles and Decolonization Policy of the United Nations' (1976) 36 *ZfV* 618–53.

LAUTERPACHT, E., 'Sovereignty over the Gaza Strip' (1952) 6 *ICLQ* 513–16.

—— *Jerusalem and the Holy Places* (London, 1968).

LAUTERPACHT, H., 'Revolutionary Activities against Foreign States' (1928) 22 *AJ* 105 30.

LAZARUS, C., 'Le Statut des Mouvements de Liberation nationale à l'O.N.U.' [1974] *AFDI* 173–200.

LECLERCQ, C., *L'ONU et l'affaire du Congo* (Paris, 1964).

LEMARCHAND, R., 'The Limits of Self-Determination: The Case of the Katanga Secession' (1962) 56 *Am. Pol. Sc. R.* 404–16.

LEVINE, A., 'The status of Sovereignty in East Jerusalem and the West Bank' (1972) 5 *NYUJILP* 485–502.

LUARD, E., ed., *The International Regulation of Civil Wars* (London, 1972).

MARTIN, P. M., *Le Conflit israelo-arab* (Paris, 1973).

MATAS, D., 'Can Quebec Separate?' (1975) 21 *McGill LJ* 387–403.

MAYER, R. A., 'Legal Aspects of Secession' (1968) 3 *Manitoba LR* 61–71.

MEYROWITZ, H., 'La guerilla et le droit de la guerre. Problèmes principaux' (1971) 7 *Rev. belge* 56–72.

MOORE, J. N., ed., *The Arab-Israeli Conflict* (3 vols., Princeton, 1974).

NAYAR, M. C. K., 'Self-determination beyond the colonial context: Biafra in retrospect' (1975) 10 *Texas ILJ* 321–45.

NURICK, I., and BARRETT, R. W., 'Legality of Guerilla Forces and the Laws of War' (1946) 40 *AJ* 563–83.

NWANKWO, A. A., and IFEJIKA, S. U., *The Making of a Nation: Biafra* (London, 1969).

NWOGUGU, E. I., 'The Nigerian Civil War: A Case Study in the Law of War' (1974) 14 *Indian JIL* 13–53.

O'BALLANCE, E., *The Algerian Insurrection 1954–1962* (London, 1967).

O'BRIEN, C. C., *To Katanga and Back: A U.N. Case History* (N.Y., 1962).

OGLESBY, R. A., *Internal War and the Search for Normative Order* (The Hague, 1971).

PANTER-BRICK, S. K., 'The Right to Self-Determination: Its Application to Nigeria' (1968) 44 *Int. Aff.* 254–66.

PAXSON, F. L., *The Independence of the South American Republics. A Study in Recognition and Foreign Policy* (Philadelphia, 1903).

PINTO, R., 'Les Règles du Droit International Concernant la Guerre Civile' (1965) 114 *HR* 455–548.

POST, K. W. J., 'Is there a case for Biafra?' (1968) 44 *Int. Aff.* 26–39.

RONZITTI, N., *Le guerre di liberazione nazionale e il diritto internazionale* (Pisa, 1974).

ROSENAU, J. N., ed., *International Aspects of Civil Strife* (Princeton, 1964).

ROSENNE, S., 'Israel and the International Treaties of Palestine' (1950) 77 *JDI* 1141–73.

—— *Israel's Armistice Agreements with the Arab States* (Tel Aviv, 1951).

—— 'Directions for a Middle East Settlement' (1968) 33 *Law and Contemporary Problems* 44–67.

ROUGIER, A., *Les Guerres civiles et le droit des gens* (Paris, 1903).

RUBIN, A. P., 'The Status of Rebels under the Geneva Conventions of 1949' (1972) 21 *ICLQ* 472–96.

SADOUL, P., *De la guerre civile en droit des gens* (Nancy, 1905).

SANBORN, M. H., 'Standing before the International Court of Justice: The Question of Palestinian Statehood exemplifies the Inconsistencies of the Requirement of Statehood' (1977) 7 *Cal. WILJ* 454–72.

SASTROAMIDJOJO, A., and DELSON, R., 'The Status of the Republic of Indonesia in International Law' (1949) 49 *Col. LR* 344–61.

SHIHATA, I. F. I., 'The Territorial Question and the October War' (1974) 4 *J. Pal. St.* 43–54.

SIMMONDS, R., *Legal Problems arising from the U.N. Military Operations in the Congo* (The Hague, 1968).

SNETSINGER, J., *Truman, the Jewish Vote and the Creation of Israel* (Stanford, 1974).

STANGER, R. J., ed., *Essays on Intervention* (Ohio, 1964).

STEFANESCO, L., *La Guerre civile et les rapports des belligerants* (Paris, 1903).

STEIN, L., *The Balfour Declaration* (London, 1961).

SUZUKI, E., 'Self-Determination and World Public Order: Community Response to Territorial Separation' (1976) 16 *Va. JIL* 779–864.

TAULBEE, J. L., 'Guerilla Insurgency and International Law' (1972) 12 *Indian JIL* 185–99.

TAYLOR, A. M., *Indonesian Independence and the United Nations* (London, 1960).

TEMPERLEY, H. W. V., *The Foreign Policy of Canning 1822–1827* (London, 1925).

Tiewul, S. A., 'Relations between the U.N.O. and the O.A.U. in the Settlement of Secessionist Conflicts' (1975) 16 *Harvard ILJ* 259–302.

Travers, P. J., 'The Legal Effect of United Nations Treatment of the African Liberation Movements and the Palestine Liberation Organization' (1976) 17 *Harvard ILJ* 561–80.

Umozurike, U. O., 'The 1949 Geneva Conventions and Africa' (1971) 11 *Indian JIL* 205–18.

Veuthey, N., 'Règles et principes de droit international humanitaire applicables dans le guerilla' (1971) 7 *Rev. belge* 505–39.

Webster, C. K., *Britain and the Independence of Latin America 1812–1830* (2 vols., Oxford, 1938).

Weisse, C., *Le Droit international appliqué aux guerres civiles* (Lausanne, 1898).

Wright, Q., 'Legal Aspects of the Middle East Situation' (1968) 33 *Law and Contemporary Problems* 5–31.

Yakemtchouk, R., *L'Afrique en droit international* (Paris, 1971).

Zorgbibe, C., *La Guerre civile* (Paris, 1975).

CHAPTER 10. THE DIVIDED STATES

Bathurst, M. E., and Simpson, J. L., *Germany and the North Atlantic Community: A Legal Survey* (London, 1956).

Bathurst, M. E., 'Legal Aspects of the Berlin Problem' (1962) 38 *BY* 255–306.

Bathurst, M. E., Simmons, K. R., et al., *Legal Problems of an Enlarged European Community* (London, 1972).

Battati, H., 'L'admission des deux Allemagnes à l'O.N.U.' [1973] *AFDI* 211–31.

Bishop, J. W., 'The "contractual agreements" with the Federal Republic of Germany' (1955) 49 *AJ* 125–47.

Blanchet, M. T., *La Naissance de l'état associé du Vietnam* (Paris, 1954).

Brownlie, I., *Legal Aspects of the Armed Conflict in Vietnam* (London, 1969).

Cameron, A. W., *Vietnam Crisis. A Documentary History* (2 vols., London, 1971).

Catudal, M., 'The Berlin Agreement of 1971—Has it Worked?' (1976) 25 *ICLQ* 766–800.

—— *The Diplomacy of the Quadripartite Agreement on Berlin* (Berlin, 1976).

Caty, G., *Le Statut juridique des états divisés* (Paris, 1969).

Coret, A., *Le Condominium* (Paris, 1960).

Department of State, 'The legality of United States participation in the defence of Vietnam' (1966) 60 *AJ* 565–85.

Doeker, G., Melsheimer, K., and Shröder, D., 'Berlin and the Quadripartite Agreement of 1971' (1973) 67 *AJ* 44–62.

468   *Bibliography*

FALK, R. A., ed., *The Vietnam War and International Law* (4 vols., Princeton, 1968–76).
FELLER, E., 'The current "Special Status" (*Besonderer Status*) of Berlin— An unresolved problem', (1977) 51 *ALJ* 272–6.
FIRMAGE, E. B., 'Law and the Indochina War: A Retrospective View' [1974] *Utah LR* 1024.
GOODRICH, L. M., *Korea. A Study of United States Policy in the United Nations* (N.Y., 1956).
GORDENKER, L., *The United Nations and the Peaceful Unification of Korea. The Politics of Field Operations 1947–1950* (The Hague, 1959).
GREEN, L. C., 'The Nature of the "War" in Korea' (1951) 4 *ILQ* 462–468.
GREWE, W. G., 'Other Legal Aspects of the Berlin Crisis' (1962) 56 *AJ* 510–13.
HENKIN, L., *The Berlin Crisis and the United Nations* (N.Y., 1959).
HOYT, E. C., 'The United States Reaction to the Korean Attack' (1961) 55 *AJ* 45–76.
HULL, R. H., and NOVOGROD, J. C., *Law and Vietnam* (Dobbs Ferry, N.Y., 1968).
JENNINGS, R. Y., 'Government in Commission' (1946) 23 *BY* 112–41.
JESSUP, P. C., 'The Rights of the U.S. in Berlin' (1949) 43 *AJ* 92–5.
KELSEN, H., 'The Legal Status of Germany according to the Declaration of Berlin' (1945) 39 *AJ* 518–26.
KOENIG, P., 'Le traité fondamental entre les deux Républiques allemandes et son interprétation par le Tribunal constitutional fédéral' [1973] *AFDI* 147–70.
KUNZ, J. L., 'Ending the War with Germany' (1952) 46 *AJ* 114–19.
LEPRETTE, J., 'Le statut de Berlin' [1955] *AFDI* 123–7.
LUSH, C. D., 'The Relationship between Berlin and the F.R.G.' (1965) 14 *ICLQ* 742–87.
MANN, F. A., *Studies in International Law* (Oxford, 1973):
'The Present Legal Status of Germany' (634–59 (1947)).
'Germany's Present Legal Status Revisited' (660–706 (1967)).
MARTINEZ-AGULLO, L. 'Les États Divisés' (1964) 91 *JDI* 265–84.
MOORE, J. N., *Law and the Indochina War* (Princeton, 1972).
MÜNCH, F., 'The German Problem' (1962) 89 *JDI* 5–51.
MURTI, B. N. S., *Divided Vietnam: The Unfinished Struggle* (N.Y., 1964).
NGUYEN-HUU-TRU, *Quelques problèmes de succession d'états concernant le Vietnam* (Brussels, 1970).
OTTENSOOSER, D., 'Termination of War by Unilateral Declaration' (1952) 29 *BY* 435–42.
PINTO, R., 'The International Status of the German Democratic Republic' (1959) 86 *JDI* 313–425.

POTTER, P. B., 'Legal Aspects of the Situation in Korea' (1950) 44 *AJ* 709–13.

SCHICK, F. B., 'Some reflections on the Legal Controversies concerning America's involvement in Vietnam' (1968) 17 *ICLQ* 935–95.

SCHIEDERMAIR, H., 'Le champ d'application territoriale de l'Accord quadripartite sur Berlin' [1973] *AFDI* 171–88.

SHARP, T., *The Wartime Alliance and the Zonal Division of Germany* (Oxford, 1975).

SIMPSON, J. L., 'Berlin—Allied Rights and Responsibilities in the Divided City' (1957) 6 *ICLQ* 83–102.

SKUBISZEWSKI, K., 'The Great Powers and the Settlement in Central Europe' (1975) 18 *Jahrbuch Für Internationales Recht* 92–126.

SONNENFELD, R., 'Succession and continuation. A study of treaty-practice in post-war Germany' (1976) 7 *Netherlands YBIL* 91–130.

STANGER, R. J., ed., *West Berlin: The Legal Context* (Columbus, 1966).

TOMUSCHAT, C., 'The Two Germanies', in Bathurst & ors., *Legal Problems of an Enlarged European Community* (London, 1972), 154–61.

THIERRY, H., 'La Condition Juridique du Nord Vietnam' [1955] *AFDI* 169–78.

VAN LAUN, K., 'The legal status of Germany' (1951) 45 *AJ* 267–85.

WRIGHT, Q., 'The Status of Germany and the Peace Proclamation' (1952) 46 *AJ* 299–308.

—— 'Some Legal Aspects of the Berlin Crisis' (1961) 56 *AJ* 959–65.

—— 'The Legal Aspects of the Vietnamese situation' (1966) 60 *AJ* 750–69.

ZORGBIBE, C., *La question de Berlin* (Paris, 1970).

CHAPTER II. UNIONS AND FEDERATIONS OF STATES

BERNIER, I., *International Legal Aspects of Federalism* (London, 1973).

BROWNLIE, I., 'The United Nations as a Form of Government' in Fawcett and Higgins, eds., *International Organization: Law in Movement* (London, 1974), 26–36.

COHEN, R., 'Legal Problems arising from the dissolution of the Mali Federation' (1960) 36 *BY* 375–84.

CONFORTI, B., 'La personalità internazionale delle unioni di Stati' (1964) 17 *Dir. Int.* 324.

COTRAN, E., 'Some Legal Aspects of the Formation of the U.A.R. and the U.A.S.' (1959) 8 *ICLQ* 346–90.

COWLES, W. B., 'International Law as Applied between Subdivisions of Federations' (1949) 74 *HR* 657–756.

EUROPEAN COMMUNITIES, *Report on European Union*, Bulletin, Supplement 5/75, Luxembourg 1975.

HALAJZUK, 'Les États Fédéraux au droit international' (1963) 13 *OZfOR* 307.

HUBER, M., 'The Intercantonal Law of Switzerland' (1909) 3 *AJ* 62–98.

KASMÉ, B., *La Capacité de l'Organization des Nations Unies de conclure les Traités* (Paris, 1960).

KAUFMANN, W., 'Les Unions Internationales de Nature Economique' (1924) 3 *HR* 181–290.

KUNZ, J. L., *Die Staatenverbindungen* (Stuttgart, 1929).

—— 'Une Nouvelle Théorie de l'État Fédéral' (1930) 11 *RDILC* (3d) 835–77; (1931) 12 *RDILC* (3d) 130–44, 280–302.

LASOK, D., and BRIDGE, J. W., *An Introduction to the Law and Institutions of the European Communities* (London, 1973).

LAUTERPACHT, H., 'Sovereignty and Federation in International Law', in 3 *Collected Papers* 5–25 (1940).

LEOPOLD, P., 'External Relations Power of the EEC in Theory and Practice' (1977) 26 *ICLQ* 54–80.

MANN, F. A., 'The Dyestuffs Case in the Court of Justice of the European Communities' (1973) 22 *ICLQ* 35–50.

NORTON, J. J., 'The Treaty Making Power of the E.E.C. A Constitutional Crisis Facing the E.E.C.?' (1973) 7 *Int. L.* 589–611.

O'CONNELL, D. P., 'State Succession and the effect upon Treaties of entry into a Composite Relationship' (1963) 39 *BY* 54–132.

PARRY, C., 'The Treaty-making power of the U.N.' (1949) 26 *BY* 108–149.

PILOTTI, M., 'Les Unions d'États' (1928) 24 *HR* 447–546.

RAPISARDI-MIRABELLI, A., 'Théorie Générale des Unions Internationales' (1925) 7 *HR* 345–92.

ROBERTSON, A. H., *European Institutions; Co-operation; integration; unification* (3rd edn., London, 1973).

SCHERMERS, H. G., 'Community Law and International Law' (1975) 12 *CMLR* 77–90.

SIMMONDS, K. R., 'External Relations Powers of the E.E.C.—A Recent Ruling of the European Court' (1977) 26 *ICLQ* 208–10.

STEINBERGER, H., 'Constitutional Subdivisions of States or Unions and their Capacity to conclude Treaties' (1967) 27 *ZfV* 411–28.

UDINA, M., *L'estinzione del Impero Austro-Ungarico nel diritto internazionale* (2nd edn., Padua, 1933).

WILDHABER, L., *Treaty-Making Power and Constitution. An International and Comparative Study* (Basel, 1971).

—— 'External Relations of the Swiss Cantons' (1974) 12 *Can. YIL* 211–222.

YOUNG, R., 'The Status of Syria: Old or New' (1962) 56 *AJ* 482–8.

CHAPTER 12. INTERNATIONAL DISPOSITIVE POWERS

ALBRECHT-CARRIÉ, R., *The Concert of Europe* (London, 1968).

AUFRICHT, H. J., 'Principles and Practices of Recognition by International Organizations' (1949) 43 *AJ* 679–704.

BLOCISZEWSKI, J., 'La Restauration de la Pologne et la diplomatie européenne' (1921) 28 *RGDIP* 5–83; (1924) 31 *RGDIP* 89–144.

BLUM, Y. Z., *The Juridical Status of Jerusalem* (Jerusalem, 1974).

BOURQUIN, M., 'La Sainte-Alliance, Un Essai d'Organization Européenne' (1953) 83 *HR* 381–459.

BOVIS, H. E., *The Jerusalem Question 1917–1968* (Stanford, 1971).

BRANDWEINER, H., 'The International Status of Austria', in G. A. Lipsky, ed., *Law and Politics in the World Community* (Berkeley, 1953).

CLEMENS, D. S., *Yalta* (N.Y., 1970).

CLUTE, R. E., *The International Legal Status of Austria 1938–1955* (The Hague, 1962).

COPETTI, M., 'Sulla condizione giuridica internazionale dei principati romeni prima dell'unione (1859) e l'independenza nazionale (1878)', *Studi in Onore di Manlio Udina* (Milan, 1975) I, 231–46.

CRAWFORD, J. R., 'The Polish Question at Yalta and Potsdam', *Studies for a New Central Europe* Ser. 4 No. 1–2 (1977), 89–100.

CRAWLEY, C. W., *The Question of Greek Independence 1821–1833* (Cambridge, 1930).

CZERAPOWICZ, J. V., *International Territorial Authority: Leticia and West New Guinea* (Ann Arbor, 1975).

DE LANNOY, F., *Histoire diplomatique de L'indépendance belge* (Brussels, 1930).

DUPUIS, R., *Le Principe d'équilibre et le concert européen* (Paris, 1909).

DUTKOWSKI, J. S., *L'Occupation de la Crète 1897–1909* (Paris, 1952).

FEIS, H., *Between War and Peace. The Potsdam Conference* (Princeton, 1960).

FROWEIN, J. A., 'Legal Principles of the German *Ostpolitik*' (1974) 23 *ICLQ* 105–26.

GROSS, E. A., 'Expenses of the U.N. for Peace-Keeping Operations' (1963) 17 *Int. Org.* 1–35.

HERZ, H., 'Le problème de la Naissance de l'État et la Décision du Tribunal Arbitral Germano-Polonais du 1er Août 1929' (1936) 17 *RDILC* 564.

HOBZA, A., 'La République tchécoslovaque et le Droit International' (1922) 29 *RGDIP* 385–409.

HOLBRAAD, C., *The Concert of Europe: A Study in German and British International Theory 1815–1914* (London, 1970).

HOLLAND, T. E., *The European Concert in the Eastern Question* (Oxford, 1885).

JONES, S., 'The Status of Jerusalem: Some National and International Aspects' (1968) 33 *Law and Contemporary Problems* 169–82.

KALLAS, M., 'Administration territoriale du Duché de Varsowie (1806–1815)' (1977) 55 *Rev. hist. de droit fr. et etr.* 35–52.

KELSEN, H., *Peace through Law* (Chapel Hill, 1944).

LANDE, A., 'Revindication of the Principle of Legal Equality of States 1871–1914' (1967) 62 *Pol. Sc. Q.* 258–86, 398–417.

LASERSON, H. L., 'The Recognition of Latvia' (1943) 37 *AJ* 233–47.

LAUTERPACHT, H., 'De Facto Recognition, Withdrawal of Recognition, and Conditional Recognition' (1945) 22 *BY* 164–90.

LAWRENCE, T. L., *Essays on Some Disputed Questions in Modern International Law* (Cambridge, 1884).

MAIR, J., 'Austria', in RIAA, *Four Power Control in Germany and Austria* (London, 1956).

MARRIOTT, J. A. R., *The Eastern Question. An Historical Study in European Diplomacy* (4th edn., London, 1940).

NICHOLS, I. C., *The European Pentarchy and the Congress of Vienna, 1822* (The Hague, 1971).

NICHOLSON, H., *The Congress of Vienna* (London, 1946).

NYS, E., 'Le Concert Européen et la notion du Droit International' (1899) 1 *RDILC* (2d) 271–313.

PELT, A., *Libyan Independence and the United Nations. A Case of Planned Decolonization* (Yale, 1970).

PERMAN, D., *The Shaping of the Czechoslovak State* (Leiden, 1962).

PETERSON, G., 'Political Inequality at the Congress of Vienna' (1945) 60 *Pol. Sc. Q.* 522–54.

SATOW, E. M., *International Congresses* (London, 1920).

SEAMAN, L. C. B., *From Vienna to Versailles* (London, 1955).

SPECTOR, S. D., *Rumania at the Paris Peace Conference* (N.Y., 1962).

STEPHEN, W. E., *Revision of the Treaty of Versailles* (Columbia, 1939).

WESTLAKE, J., 'The Political Inequality of States and the Great Powers of Europe', *Collected Papers* (1904), 92–101.

WHEELER-BENNETT, J. W., and NICHOLLS, A., *The Semblance of Peace. The Political Settlement after the Second World War* (London, 1972).

WOODWARD, E. L., *The Congress of Berlin 1878* (London, 1919).

WOOLSEY, L. H., 'The Polish Boundary Question' (1944) 39 *AJ* 441–8.

—— 'Poland at Yalta and Dumbarton Oaks' (1945) 39 *AJ* 295–300.

WRIGHT, H., 'The Legality of the Annexation of Austria by Germany' (1944) 38 *AJ* 621–37.

—— 'Poland and the Crimea Conference' (1945) 39 *AJ* 399–408.

WRIGHT, Q., 'Conflicts between International Law and Treaties' (1917) 11 *AJ* 566–79.

CHAPTER 13. MANDATES AND TRUST TERRITORIES

BARBIER, M., 'L'avenir de la Namibie' (1977) 31 *RJPIC* 43–74.

BENTWICH, N., 'Nationality in the Mandated Territories detached from Turkey' (1926) 7 *BY* 97–109.

—— 'The Sublimation of the Mandate for Iraq' (1930) 10 *BY* 193–5.

—— 'The Status of the Mandatory Power' (1931) 12 *BY* 151.

BERGSMAN, P., 'The Marianas, the United States and the United Nations: the Uncertain Status of the New American Commonwealth' (1976) 6 *Cal. WILJ* 382–411.

BOOYSEN, H., and STEPHAN, G. E. T., 'Decree No. 1 of the United Nations Council for South Africa' (1975) 1 *S. Af. YBIL* 63–86.

BRIERLY, J. L., 'Trusts and Mandates' (1929) 10 *BY* 217–19.

CHENG, BIN, 'The 1966 South West Africa Judgement of the World Court' [1967] *CLP* 181–212.

CHIU, H., 'Succession in International Organization' (1965) 14 *ICLQ* 83–120.

CHOWDHURY, R. N., *International Mandates and Trusteeship System: A Comparative Study* (The Hague, 1955).

CILLIERS, A. C., 'United Nations competence in respect of South West Africa' (1976) 2 *S. Af. YBIL* 128–42.

COCKRAM, G. M., *South West African Mandate* (Capetown, 1976).

DEMPSEY, G., 'Self-Determination and Security in the Pacific: A Study of the Covenant between the United States and the Northern Mariana Islands' (1976) 9 *NYUJILP* 277–302.

DE SMITH, S. A., *Micro-States and Micronesia: Problems of America's Pacific Islands and other Minute Territories* (N.Y., 1970).

DIENA, G., 'Les Mandats Internationaux' (1924) 5 *HR* 214–63.

DUGARD, C. J. R., 'The Revocation of the Mandate for South-West Africa' (1968) 62 *AJ* 78–97.

—— *The South West Africa/Namibia Dispute* (Berkeley, 1973).

ERSTAD, L. R., 'International Law and Dependent Territories: The Case of Micronesia' (1976) 50 *Temple L.Q.* 58–92.

GILCHRIST, H., 'The Japanese Islands: Annexation or Trusteeship' (1944) 22 *For. Aff.* 635–43.

GREEN, D. M., 'Termination of the U.S. Pacific Islands Trusteeship' (1974) 9 *Texas ILJ* 175–204.

HALES, J. C., 'Some Legal Aspects of the Mandate System: Sovereignty-Nationality—Termination and Transfer' (1937) 23 *Grot. ST* 85–126.

HALL, H. DUNCAN, *Mandates, Dependencies and Trusteeship* (Washington, 1948).

HEINE, C., *Micronesia at the Crossroads: A Reappraisal of the Micronesian Political Dilemma* (Canberra, 1974).

HERMAN, L. J., 'The Legal Status of Namibia and of the United Nations Council for Namibia' (1975) 13 *Can. YIL* 306–22.

JAMES, R. E. (*et al.*), *America's Pacific Dependencies* (N.Y., 1949).

LAUTERPACHT, H., 'The Mandate under International Law in the Covenant of the League of Nations', in 3 *Collected Papers* 29–84 (1922).

LEEPER, D. S., 'Sovereignty over Mandates and Trust Territories' (1951) 49 *Michigan LR* 1199–210.

LUCCHINI, L., 'Vers un nouveau statut de la Micronésie on la disparition prochaine de la tutelle' [1975] *AFDI* 155–74.

MANDELSTAM, A-N., *La Société des Nations et les puissances devant le problème Arménien* (Paris, 1925).

MARSTON, G., 'Termination of Trusteeship' (1969) 18 *ICLQ* 1–40.

MCHENRY, D. F., *Micronesia: Trust Betrayed* (Washington, 1975).

METALSKI, J. B., 'Micronesia and Free Association: Can Federalism Save Them?' (1974) 5 *Cal. WILJ* 162–83.

O'CONNELL, D. P., 'Nationality in "C" Class Mandates' (1954) 39 *BY* 458–61.

OLSEN, D. F., 'Piercing Micronesia's Colonial Veil: *Enewetak v. Laird* and *Saipan v. Department of Interior*' (1976) 15 *Col. JTL* 473–95.

PARRY, C., 'The Legal Nature of the Trusteeship Agreements' (1950) 27 *AJ* 164–85.

PÉLICHET, E., *La Personnalité internationale distincte des collectivités sous mandat* (Paris, 1932).

RICHE, J., 'La Souveraineté dans les territoires sous tutelle' (1954) 58 *RGDIP* 399–437.

SCHERMERS, H. G., 'The Namibia Decree in National Courts' (1977) 26 *ICLQ* 81–96.

SHOCKLEY, G. R., 'Enforcement in United States Courts of the United Nations Council for Namibia's Decree on National Resources' (1976) 2 *Yale Studies in World Public Order* 285–342.

SLONIM, S., *South West Africa and the United Nations: An International Mandate in Dispute* (Baltimore, 1973).

SMUTS, GENERAL J., *The League of Nations—A Practical Suggestion* (London, 1919).

STOYANOWSKY, H., *La Théorie Générale des Mandats Internationaux* (Paris, 1925).

THULLEN, G., *Problems of the Trusteeship System. A Study of Political Behaviour in the United Nations* (Geneva, 1964).

TOUSSAINT, C. E., *The Trusteeship System of the United Nations* (N.Y., 1956).

VÉICOPOULOS, N., *Traité des Territoires Dépendants* (Athens, 2 vols., 1960, 1971).

WRIGHT, Q., *Mandates under the League of Nations* (Chicago, 1930).
—— 'Proposed Termination of the Iraq Mandate' (1931) 25 *BY* 436–446.

CHAPTER 14. NON-SELF-GOVERNING TERRITORIES
THE LAW AND PRACTICE OF DECOLONIZATION

AHMAD, S. H., *The United Nations and the Colonies* (N.Y., 1974).
ALLEN, P. II., 'Self-determination in the Western Indian Ocean' *Int. Conc.* No. 560 (November, 1966).
AUSTRALIAN SENATE, STANDING COMMITTEE ON FOREIGN AFFAIRS AND DEFENCE, *United Nations Involvement with Australian Territories* (Canberra, 1975).
BARBIER, M., *Le Comité de décolonization des Nations-Unies* (Paris, 1974).
—— 'L'Avis Consultatif de la Cour de la Haye sur le Sahara Occidental' (1976) 30 *RJPIC* 67–103.
BENOIST, H., *La Condominium des Nouvelles-Hébrides et la Société Mélanesienne* (Paris, 1972).
BLOOMFIELD, L. H., *The British Honduras-Guatemala Dispute* (Toronto, 1973).
BONE, R. C., *The Dynamics of the Western New Guinea (Irian Barat) Problem* (Cornell, 1958, 1962).
BOS, M., 'Surinam's road from self-government to sovereignty' (1976) 7 *Netherlands YBIL* 131–56.
BRIGGS, H. W., 'Recognition and Self-Determination' (1954) 48 *PAS* 23–37.
BRISK, W. J., *The Dilemma of a Ministate: Anguilla* (Studies in International Affairs No. 7, Columbia, 1969).
BRODERICK, M., 'Associated Statehood—A New Form of Decolonization' (1968) 17 *ICLQ* 368–403.
CABRANEZ, J. A., 'The Status of Puerto Rico' (1967) 16 *ICLQ* 531–9.
CARRINGTON, C. E., 'Gibraltar', *Chatham House Memoranda* (1958–1).
CASTEL, A., 'Le statut constitutionel de Hong-Kong' (1977) 31 *RJPIC* 989–1010.
CHAPPEZ, J., 'L'avis consultatif de la C. I. J. du 16 octobre 1975 dans l'affaire du Sahara occidental' (1976) 80 *RGDIP* 1132–87.
CHIROUX, R., 'La Fin d'une "Curiosité Juridique": Le Condominium Franco-Britannique des Nouvelles-Hébrides' (1976) 30 *RJPIC* 309–330.
COHEN, J., 'Les îles Falklands' [1972] *AFDI* 235–62.
DALLIER, P., 'L'administration internationale directe dans le contexte de la décolonization' (1973) 27 *RJPIC* 41–60.
FAVOREU, L., 'La Décision du 30 Décembre 1975 dans l'Affaire des Comores' [1976] *Rev. de Droit Public* 557–81.

FAWCETT, J. E. S., 'Gibraltar: the Legal Issues' (1967) 43 *Int. Aff.* 236–251.

FLORY, M., 'L'avis de la Cour Internationale de Justice sur le Sahara occidental' [1975] *AFDI* 253–77.

FORBES, U., 'The West Indies Associated States. Some Aspects of the Constitutional Arrangements' (1970) 19 *Social & Economic Studies* 57–88.

FRANCK, T. M., 'The Stealing of the Sahara' (1976) 70 *AJ* 694–721.

FRANCK, T. M., and HOFFMAN, P., 'The Right of Self-Determination in Very Small Places' (1976) 8 *NYUJILP* 331–86.

GOEBEL, J., *The Struggle for the Falkland Islands* (New Haven, 1927).

HECTOR, B. J., 'Puerto Rico: Colony or commonwealth' (1973) 6 *NYUJILP* 115–37.

HENDERSON, W., *West New Guinea. The Dispute and its Settlement* (Seton Hall, 1973).

HUMPHREYS, R. A., *The Diplomatic History of British Honduras 1638–1901* (Oxford, 1961).

JACQUIER, B., 'L'Autodétermination du Sahara Espagnol' (1974) 78 *RGDIP* 683–728.

JANIS, M. W., 'The International Court of Justice: Advisory Opinion on the Western Sahara' (1976) 17 *Harvard ILJ* 609–22.

KHOL, D. A., '"The Committee of 24" and the Implementation of the Colonial Declaration' (1970) 3 *Human Rights Journal* 21–50.

KILBRIDE, P. E., 'The Cook Islands Constitution' (1965) 1 *NZULR* 571–6.

KRENZ, F. E., *International Enclaves and Rights of Passage* (Geneva, 1961).

LACHS, M., 'The Law in and of the United Nations' (1960–1) 1 *Indian JIL* 429–42.

LEIBOWITZ, A. H., *Colonial Emancipation in the Pacific and the Caribbean. A Legal and Political Analysis* (N.Y., 1976).

MAESTRE, J-C., 'L'Indivisibilité de la République Française et l'Exercise du Droit d'Auto-détermination' [1976] *Rev. du Droit Public* 431–61.

MATHY, D., 'L'Autodétermination de Petits Territoires Revindiqués par les Etats Tiers' (1974) 10 *Revue belge* 167–205; (1975) 11 *Revue belge* 129–60.

METFORD, J. C. J., 'Falklands or Malvinas? The Background to the Dispute' (1968) 44 *Int. Aff.* 463–81.

MOYNIHAN, D. P., 'Abiotrophy in Turtle Bay: The United Nations in 1975' (1976) 17 *Harvard ILJ* 465–502.

NAWAZ, H. K., 'Colonies, Self-Government and the United Nations' (1962) 11 *Indian YIA* 3–47.

NOGUEIRA, F., *The United Nations and Portugal. A Study of Anti-colonialism* (London, 1963).

O'CONNELL, D. P., 'The Condominium of the New Hebrides' (1968-9) 43 *BY* 71-146.

OSTHEIMER, J. M., *The Politics of the Western Indian Ocean Islands* (N.Y., 1975).

PHILLIPS, SIR FRED, *Freedom in the Caribbean. A Study in Constitutional Change* (N.Y., 1977).

POMERANCE, M., 'Methods of Self-Determination and the Argument of "Primitiveness"' (1974) *Can. YIL* 58-66.

PRÉVOST, J-F., 'Observations sur l'avis consultatif de la Cour Internationale de Justice relatif an Sahara occidental' (1976), 103 *JDI* 831-862.

RABIER, C., and ANGRAND, J., 'Le Territoire Français des Afars et des Issas: Un Avenir Uncertain' (1975) 49 *RGPIC* 473-85.

REISMAN, W. H., *Puerto Rico and the International Process. New Roles in Association* (Washington, 1975).

REISMAN, W. M., 'African Imperialism' (1976) 70 *AJ* 801-2.

REZETTE, R., *The Western Sahara and the Frontiers of Morocco* (Paris, 1975).

RIEDEL, E. H., 'Confrontation in Western Sahara in the Light of the Advisory Opinion of the International Court of Justice of 16 October 1975—A Critical Appraisal' (1976) 19 *German YBIL* 405-42.

RODINSON, G. W. S., 'Exclaves', *Annals of the Association of American Geographers* Vol. 49 (1959), 283-95.

RUZIÉ, D., [Note on the Comoro Case] (1976) 103 *JDI* 392-405.

SIMMONDS, K. R., 'Associated Statehood: A Caribbean Dilemma' in *Mélanges W. J. Ganshof van der Meersch* (Brussels, 1972), 435-47.

—— 'Anguilla—An Interim Settlement' (1972) 21 *ICLQ* 151-7.

SIMPSON, M. D., 'Panama: The Proposed Transfer of the Canal and Canal Zone by Treaty' (1975) 5 *Georgia JICL* 195-215.

SPACKMAN, A., *Constitutional Development in the West Indies 1922-1968* (Barbados, 1975).

STONE, D., 'Self determination in the Cook Islands' (1966) 1 *J. Pac. H.* 168-77.

SUD, U., *The United Nations and Non-Self-Governing Territories* (New Delhi, 1965).

SYMPOSIUM, 'The Applicability of the Principle of Self-Determination to Unintegrated territories of the U.S.' (1973) 67 *PAS* 1-27.

TROUT, F. E., *Morocco's Saharan Frontiers* (Geneva, 1969).

VAN ASBECK, F. M., 'Le Statut actuel des Pays non autonomes d'outre-mer' (1947) 71 *HR* 345-72.

VAN DER KROEF, J. H., 'The West New Guinea Settlement: Its Origins and Implications' (1963) 7 *Orbis* 120-49.

WADELL, D. A. G., 'Developments in the Belize Question 1946-1960' (1961) 55 *AJ* 459-69.

WALDOCK, H. M., 'Disputed Sovereignty in the Falkland Islands Dependency' (1948) 25 *BY* 311–53.

WATT, A., *The United Nations, Confrontation or Consensus* (Canberra, 1974).

WOHLGEMUTH, P., 'The Portuguese Territories and the United Nations' *Int. Conc.* No. 545 (November, 1963).

CHAPTER 15. THE COMMENCEMENT OF STATES

DE BEUS, J. G., *The Jurisprudence of the General Claims Commission, United States and Mexico under the Convention of September 8, 1923* (The Hague, 1938).

JONES, J. M., 'The Retroactive Effect of the Recognition of States and Governments' (1935) 16 *BY* 42–55.

NISOT, J., 'Is the Recognition of a Government Retroactive?' (1943) 21 *Can. B.R.* 627–43.

RALSTON, J. H., *International Arbitral Law and Procedure* (Boston, 1910).

SHOENBORN, W., 'La Nature Juridique du Territoire' (1929) 30 *HR* 85–187.

SILVANIE, HAIG, *Responsibility of States for Acts of Unsuccessful Insurgent Governments* (N.Y., 1939).

—— 'Responsibility of States for Acts of Insurgent Governments' (1939) 33 *AJ* 78–103.

STARKE, J. G., 'The Acquisition of Title to Territory by Newly Emerged States' (1965–6) 41 *BY* 411–16.

CHAPTER 16. PROBLEMS OF IDENTITY, CONTINUITY, AND REVERSION

ALEXANDROWICZ, C. H., 'New and Original States. The Issue of Reversion to Sovereignty' (1969) 45 *Int. Aff.* 465–80.

—— 'The Afro-Asian World and the Law of Nations' (1968) 123 *HR* 117–214.

ANZILOTTI, D., 'La formazione del Regno d'Italia nel riguardi del diritto internazionale' (1912) 6 *Rdi.*

AUFRICHT, H. J., 'State Succession under the Law and Practice of the I.M.F.' (1962) 11 *ICLQ* 154–70.

BLUNTSCHLI, J. C., *The Theory of the State* (3rd Eng. edn., London, 1901).

DABROWA, S., 'The Polish People's Republic and International Treaties Concluded by Poland before World War II' (1968–9) 2 *Pol. YIL* 50–62.

GRZYBOWSKI, K., *Soviet Public International Law. Doctrines and Diplomatic Practice* (Leyden, 1970).

ROMANO, 'I caratteri guiridici della formazione del Regno d'Italia' (1912) 6 *Rdi* 345.

Rozek, T., *Allied Wartime Diplomacy. A Pattern in Poland* (N.Y., 1958).
Taracouzio, T. A., *The Soviet Union and International Law* (N.Y., 1935).

CHAPTER 17. THE EXTINCTION OF STATES

Johnson, D. H. N., 'Acquisitive Prescription in International Law' (1950) 27 *BY* 332–54.
Turack, D. C., 'Passports issued by some Non State Entities' (1968–9) 43 *BY* 209–16.
Grayson, C. T., *Austria's international position 1938–1953; the re-establishment of an independent Austria* (Geneva, 1953).
Green, L. C., 'Dissolution of States and membership of the United Nations', in Schwarzenberger, ed., *Law, Justice and Equity* (1967), 152–67.
Radojkovíc, M., 'La non-reconnaissance des actes contraires au droit', *Mélanges Andrassy* (1968), 225–36.
Raestad, A., 'La cessation d'États d'après le droit des gens' (1939) 20 *RDILC* (3d) 441–9.

Table of Cases

PAGE

Aaland Islands Case (1919) . . 22, 44–5, 85–7, 102, 257, 316, 390, 392
A.B. v. M.B. (1951) 40
Abu Dhabi Arbitration (1951) 183
Ackikian v. Bank of Athens (1923) 418
Administration des Douanes v. Société Cafés Jacques Value (1975) . . 296
Administration of Papua and New Guinea v. Guba & Doriga (1973) . . 184
Administrative Decision No. 1. (1927) 405
Admissions Case See Conditions for Admission. . .
Agency of Canadian Car & Foundry Co. Ltd. v. American Can Co. (1918) . 405
Alabama Arbitration (1872) 254
Al-Fin Corporation's Patent, In re 283
Allen Case (1799) 389
Anon. (1722) 174
Arantzazu Mendi, The (1939) 15
Artukovic v. Boyle (1952) 409
Asylum Case (1950) 33
Attorney General for Canada v. Attorney General for Ontario (1937) . 239, 293
Attorney General v. Ibrahim (1964) 44
Attorney-General v. Cheng (1960) 151
Austrian Citizens (Entitlement to Compensation) Case (1960) . . . 277
Austro-German Customs Union Case (1931) . . 35, 49–51, 54, 186, 316–17

Bank of China v. Wells Fargo Bank & Union Trust Co. (1952–3) . 15, 16
Bank of Ethiopia v. National Bank of England & Liguori (1937) . . 388
Banque de l'Union Parisienne v. Jaudon (1933) 405
Barcelona Traction (Preliminary Objections) (1964) 352
Barcelona Traction (Second Phase) (1970) 13, 81
Baronci v. Ospedale del Bambino Gesu (1957) 155
Bayetto v. Administration d'Enregistrement (1946) 194
Blankard v. Galdy (1692) 174
Blonde, The (1921–2) 166
Boedecker & Ronski, Re (1962) 142
Boguslawski v. Gdynia-Ameryka Linie (1953) 388, 391
Bolivar Railway Co. Claim (1903) 392
Bremen (Hansa City of) v. Prussia (1925) 293
British Coal Corporation v. R. (1935) 242
Buck v. Attorney-General (1965) 216–17, 343

Calder v. Attorney-General of British Columbia (1973) . . . 184
Calvin's case (1608) 174
Campbell v. Hall (1774) 231
Caribtan Corp. v. O.S.H.R.C. (1974) 371

PAGE

Carl Zeiss Stiftung v. *Rayner & Keeler Ltd.* (*No. 2*) (1971) . . 15, 72, 276
Case concerning Acquisition of Polish Nationality (1923) . . . 41–2, 323
Cayuga Indians Claim (1936) 178, 183, 294
C.E.A.T. v. *Società Hungaria* (1951) 162
Chief Tschekedi Khama v. *Ratshosa* (1931) 208
Civil Air Transport Inc. v. *Central Air Transport Corp.* (1953) . . . 388
Clipperton Island Arbitration (1932) 183
Coe v. *Commonwealth* (1978) 180
Competence of the I.L.O. to regulate, incidentally, the work of the Employer
  (1926) 33
Competence of the I.L.O. with respect to Agricultural Labour (1922) . . 33
Concordat (*Germany*) *Case* (1957) 157, 280
Conditions for Admission of a State to Membership in the United Nations
  (1948) 33, 129, 133, 134, 323
Consistency of Certain Danzig Legislative Decrees with the Constitution of the Free
  City (1935) 165
Costa v. *Military Service Commission of Genoa* (1939) 404
Cooper v. *Stuart* (1889) 180
Corfu Channel Case (*Merits*) (1949) 109
Cuculla v. *Mexico* (1868) 21

Dalla Torre, In re (1936) 155
Danzig Pension Case (1929) 166
Danzig Railway Officials (1928) 25
Date of Entry into Force of Versailles Treaty (*Germany*) *Case* (1961) . . 41
Delacher, Re (1962) 277
Delagoa Bay Arbitration (1875) 174
De-Sautels, In re (1974) 419
Deutsche Continental Gas Gesellschaft v. *Polish State* (1929) . 21, 38, 313, 390
Dirk's Patent, In re (1957) 280
Ditzler, Reith & Buess v. *Customs Administration* (1940) . . . 194
Dix Claim (1903) 392
Duff Development Co. v. *Kelantan Government* (1924) . . 15, 56, 61–2
Dupire v. *Dame Dupire-Constantinoff* (1937) 233
Eastern Carelia Advisory Opinion (1923) 33
Eichmann Case (1961) 392, 406
Esposito, Re (1899) 153
European Commission of the Danube (1927) . . . 13, 33, 54, 307–8
European Road Transport Agreement, Re the (1971) . . . 296–7
Exchange of Greek and Turkish Populations (1925) 54
Expenses of the United Nations (1962) . . . 264–5, 326, 327
Ex-Rajah of Coorg v. *East India Co.* (1860) 183

Fijian Land Claims (*Burt Claim*) (1923) 184
Fogarty v. *O'Donague* (1926) 392
Foster v. *Globe Venture Syndicate* (1900) 177
Free City of Danzig and the I.L.O. (1930) . . 164, 165, 239, 318
Free Zones of Upper Savoy and the District of Gex (1930) . . 33, 309

PAGE

G., In re (1945) 65
Gastaldi v. *Lepage Hemery* (1929) 404
German Interests in Polish Upper Silesia (1926) . . 17, 390–1, 394–5, 407
German Inter-Zonal Trade Case (1965) 277
Germany v. *Reparations Commission* (1924) 39, 390, 405
Gold Looted by Germany from Rome in 1943 (1953) 311
Golovitschiner v. *Dori* (1923) 405
Government of Morocco v. *Laurens* (1930) 196, 208
Government of Spain v. *Chancery Lane Safe Deposit Ltd.* (1939) . . . 29
Guaranty Trust Co. of New York v. *United States* (1938) 388

Hamou, Re (1955) 196
Harris v. *Minister of the Interior* (1952) 27
Harshaw Chemical Co.'s Patent, Re (1914) 283
Hartje v. *Yugoslav Military Mission* (1954) 278
Helena, The (1701) 74
Hesperides Hotels Ltd. v. *Aegean Turkish Holidays Ltd.* (1977) . . . 118
Hoani Te Heuheu Tukino v. *Aotea District Maori Land Board* (1941) . 180, 183
Hodgson v. *U.E.S.P.* (1974) 371
Hopkins Claim (1927) 21
Hunt v. *Gordon* (1883) 73–4
Hunt v. *R. (No. 2)* (1882) 74
Hyacinth Pellat Case (1929) 294

Icelandic Fisheries Case (First phase) (1973) 106
Icelandic Fisheries (Second Phase) (1974) 91
I.C.I. Ltd. v. *Commission of the European Communities* (1972) . . . 296
Idler v. *Venezuela* (1885) 389
Internationale Handelsgesellschaft mbH v. *Einfuhr-und Vorratsstelle für Getreide und Futtermittel* (1974) 296
International Fruit Co. NV v. *Produktschap voor Groenten en Fruit (No. 3)* (1975) 296
International Registration of Trade Mark (Germany) Case (1959) . . 276
Interpretation of Peace Treaties (Second Phase) (1950) 33
Interpretation of the Statute of the Memel Territory (Merits) (1932) . . 160
Interpretation of the Treaty of Lausanne (1925) . . . 37, 325, 346, 349
Ionian Ships, The (1855) 208
Irish Free State v. *Guaranty Safe Deposit Co.* (1927) 392
Island of Bulamu Arbitration (1870) 173
Island of Lamu Arbitration (1889) 177
Island of Palmas Case (1928) 36, 48, 173, 174, 178, 183, 188, 198, 199, 233, 293

James, In re (1977) 106
Jani v. *Jani* (1952) 198
Johnson & Graham's Lessee v. *McIntosh* (1823) 174, 184
Jolley v. *Mainka* (1933) 239, 243
Jupiter, The (No. 3) (1927) 388, 389

PAGE

Jurisdiction of the Courts of Danzig (1928)   164

Kanda v. *State of Japan* (1961)   282
Kantrantios v. *Bulgaria* (1926) 208, 237
Katz & Klump v. *Yugoslavia* (1925)   409
Kawasaki Kisen Kabashiki Kaisha of Kobe v. *Bantham Steamship Co. Ltd.*
    (1939)   15
Kruger, In re (1951)   166

L. & JJ. v. *Polish State Railways* (1948)   166
Labrador Boundary, In re (1927)   240
Land Registry of Waldsassen v. *Towns of Eger and Waldsassen* (1965)   .   .   408
Lazard Bros. v. *Midland Bank Ltd.* (1933) 388, 405
Lehigh Valley Railroad Co. v. *State of Russia* (1919, 1927)   .   .   388, 405
Levantesi v. *Governor of Rome* (1940)   155
Levi Claim (1957)   72
Lighthouses Arbitration, Claim No. 11 (1956)   237
Lighthouses in Crete and Samos (1937)   232–7
Lone Wolf v. *Hitchcock* (1903)   183
Lotus, The (1927) 33, 355
Lowinsky v. *Receiver in Bankruptcy* (1936)   405
Luigi Monta of Genoa v. *Cechofracht Co. Ltd.* (1956)   .   .   .   15, 152
Luther v. *Sagor* (1921) 15, 388
Liyanage v. *R.* (1967)   216

M., In re (*Danzig Conviction Case*) (1933)   166
Madonna del Burso, The (1802)   177
Madzimabamuto v. *Lardner-Burke* (1968)   .   .   106, 237, 242, 246
Magellan Pirates, The (1853)   177
Maharaja of Tripura v. *Province of Assam* (1848)   210
Mellenger v. *New Brunswick Development Corporation* (1971)   .   .   293
Ménier v. *P.L.M. Railway Co.* (1938)   196
Metropolitan Chapter in Poznan v. *State Treasury* (1963)   .   .   .   409
Mexican Union Railway Case (1930)   46
Milirrpum v. *Nabalco Pty. Ltd.* (1971) 180, 184
Missouri v. *Holland* (1920)   293
Mizrihi v. *Republic of Cyprus* (1963)   167
Monastery at St Naoum (*Albanian Frontier*)   .   .   .   37, 304, 306–7, 325
Monetary Gold removed from Rome in 1943 (1954)   .   .   .   32, 311
Moriggi, In re (1939)   153
Moore v. *Attorney General* (1935)   242
Muller v. *Roeckling Bros.* (1923)   161
Murray v. *Parkes* (1942)   42
Muscat Dhows Case (1905)   209
Mwenya, Ex parte (1960)   201

PAGE

Namibia Opinion (1971) . 91, 93, 94, 95, 96, 124–8, 221, 327–9, 335, 341,
344, 345, 346, 347, 350–5, 357–8

Nankivel v. *Omsk All Russian Government* (1932) 418
Nanni v. *Pace and the Sovereign Order of Malta* (1935) . . . 34, 160
Naqara v. *Minister of the Interior* (1953) 40
National Bank of Egypt v. *Austria-Hungary Bank* (1924) 208
Nationality Decrees in Tunis & Morocco (1920) . . 142, 186–7, 202, 207
Nationality (Accession of Austria) Case (1954) 42
Ndlwana v. *Hofmeyr* (1934) 231
Nepogodin's Estate, In re (1955) 62
New Jersey v. *Delaware* (1934) 293
Nissan v. *Attorney-General* (1970) 168
Nix, In re (1951) 166
Northern Cameroons Case (1963) 342–4, 366, 395, 406
North Sea Continental Shelf Cases (1969) 38–9
Nottebohm Case (Second Phase) (1955) 40, 190
N.V. Algemeine transport en Expeditie Ondernenning Van Gend en Loos v.
Nederlandse Tarief Commissie (1963) 297

O'Dell & Griffen, Ex parte (1953) 242
OECD Understanding on a Local Cost Standard, Re the (1976) . . . 297
Oetjen v. *Central Leather Co.* (1918) 388
Officier van Justitie v. *Kramer & ors.* (1976) 297
Ol le Ngojo v. *Attorney-General* (1913) 183
Oscar Chinn Case (1934) 317–18
Ottoman Public Debt Arbitration (1925) 390, 404

Padri Benedetti v. *Nunzi* (1957) 153
Panavezys—Saldutiskis Railway Case (1939) 40
Peinitsch v. *Germany* (1923) 72
Phosphates in Morocco (1938) 196, 208
Polish-Czechoslavakian Frontier (Question of Jaworzina) (1923) . 37, 291, 307, 314
Polish Postal Service in Danzig (1925) 166
Polish War Vessels in the Port of Danzig (1931) . . . 33, 165, 166
Ponce v. *Roman Catholic Apostolic Church* (1907) 157
Poznanski v. *Lentz & Hirschfeld* (1925) 40, 390
Princess Paley Olga v. *Weisz* (1929) 388
Principality of Monaco v. *Mississippi* (1934) 293

R. v. *Bottrill, ex parte Keuchenmeister* (1947) 274
R. v. *Burgess, ex parte Henry* (1936) 293
R. v. *Christian* (1924) 345
R. v. *Syliboy* (1929) 182
Railway Pension (Austria) Case (1923) 405
Railway Traffic Between Lithuania and Poland (1931) . . 39, 40
Rann of Kutch Arbitration (1968) 202–3, 210
Rendition of Suspected Criminal (Saar Territory) Case (1955) . . . 161
Reparations for Injuries suffered in the Service of the United Nations (1949) 25–6, 389

PAGE

Republic of Poland v. *Pantol* (1922)   408
Republic of Poland v. *Weisholc* (1919)   408
Republic of Poland v. *Felsenstadt* (1922)   408
Right of Passage over Indian Territory (1960)   .   113, 174, 176, 182, 365, 414
Roselius & Co. v. *Karsten & Turkish Republic* (1926)   .   .   .   404
Russian Roubles (*Attempted Counterfeiting*) *Case* (1919)   .   .   .   405

S., In re petition of (1957)   405
Saar Territory (*Trade Marks*) *Case* (1934)   160
Sabally & N'Jie v. *Attorney General* (1965)   217
Salimoff v. *Standard Oil Co.* (1933)   15
Sapphire, The v. *Napoleon* (1871)   405
Savini, In re (1927)   418
Scarfò v. *Sovereign Order of Malta* (1957)   155
Shehadeh v. *Commissioner of Prisons* (1947)   406
Simon v. *Taylor* (1975)   280
Smith v. *Stewart* (1869)   254
Sobhuza II v. *Miller* (1926) 177, 187
Società Immobiliare Roma—Trieste v. *Stabilimento Tipografico Triestino e Società
    Editrice del 'Piccolo'* (1952)   162
Società Teatro Puccini v. *Commissioner-General of the Government for the Territory
    of Trieste* (1961)   162
Socony Vacuum Oil Co. Claim (1954)   63–4
Solokoff v. *National City Bank* (1924)   15
Southern Rhodesia, In re (1919) 180, 184, 344
South West Africa Cases (*First Phase*) (1962)   345
South West Africa Cases (*Second Phase*) (1966)   91, 227, 238, 314, 345, 352, 354
South West Africa (*Hearing of Petitioners*) *Case* (1956)   .   .   351, 353
South West Africa (*Voting Procedure*) *Case* (1955)   .   .   91, 326–7, 346, 354
Sovereignty over certain Frontier Land (1959)   321
Spanish Zone of Morocco Claims (1928)   .   .   .   201, 203, 208
State v. *Dosso* (1958)   405
State v. *Hynes* (1961)   238
Status of the Saar Territory Case (1930)   161
Status of South West Africa (1950)   .   .   93, 95, 142, 301, 316, 326, 335, 336,
                                                                340–1, 352–5
Statute of Saar Territory Case (1955)   161
Sultan of Johore v. *Abubakar* (1952)   208

Tamasese, In re (1929)   243
Tee-Hit-Ton Indians v. *United States* (1955)   184
Temple Case (1962) 23, 176
Territorial Jurisdiction of the Oder Commission (1929)   .   .   .   33
Thakrar, Ex parte (1977)   201
Thome Guadalupe v. *Assoc. Italiana di S. Cecilia* (1937)   .   .   .   153
Theodore v. *Duncan* (1919)   239
Tinoco Arbitration (1924) 20–1, 24, 266, 405
Treatment of Polish Nationals in the Danzig Territory (1932)   .   .   164–165

PAGE

Trenta v. *Ragonesi* (1938) 153
Trèves Claim (1957) 72

Underhill v. *Hernandez* (1897) 388
Ungarische Kriegsproduckten A.G., In re (1920) 405
United States, ex rel. Zeller v. *Watkins* (1948) 166
United States Nationals in Morocco (1952) . . 195–6, 202, 203, 207, 318
United States v. *Kagama* (1886) 183
United States v. *Pink* (1942) 388
United States v. *Valentine* (1968) 372, 376
United States v. *Vargas* (1974) 371

Valk v. *Kokes* (1950) 418

Wandeweghe v. *B.C.I.* (1973) 296
Warman v. Francis (1958) 183
Weber v. *U.S.S.R.* (1942) 405
Webster Claim (1925) 184
Western Sahara Opinion (1975) . 32, 93, 96–8, 173, 177, 179, 181, 214, 258,
261, 288, 335, 357, 358, 365–6, 367, 378–380, 382–4, 415
White v. *McLean* (1890) 180
Wildormann v. *Stinnes* (1924) 40, 309
Williams v. *Bruffy* (1877) 388
Wimbledon, The (1920) 53-4
Wi Pirata v. *Bishop of Wellington* (1877) 180
Wong Hon, In re (1959) 380
Worcester v. *State of Georgia* (1832) 182
Wulfsohn v. *R.S.F.S.R.* (1923) 15, 21
Wurttemberg & Prussia v. *Baden* (1927) 293

Yrisarri v. *Clement* (1825) 15

Zander Claim (1851) 392

Index

Aaland Islands, 22, 44–5, 85–7, 316
Abyssinia: see Ethiopia
Aden (Protectorate and Colony), 200, 220, 431
   See also South Yemen, People's Republic of
Afars and Isaas, French Territory of, 361, 369, 377, 430
   See also Djibouti
Alaska, 370, 434
Albania, 65, 299, 304, 305, 306–7, 310, 311, 314, 321–2, 325, 415, 418–19
Algeciras, Act of (1906), 194–6, 305
Algeria, 177, 259–60, 262, 378, 415, 430
American Samoa, 434
Andorra, 34, 119, 140, 142, 208
Angola, 111, 136, 260, 435
Anguilla, 374, 432
Anschluss: see Austria
Aragon, 6, 9
Argentina, 133
Armenia, 131, 313, 315, 418, 426
Associated States, 138, 295, 370–7
Australia, 180, 230–46, 292, 293
Austria:
   Continuity of (1918–20), 404–5, 406
   Continuity of (1936–55), 408, 418–19
   Independence of in Customs Union, 49–51, 317
   Non-extinction of (1936), 418–19
   Re-establishment of (1945–55), 299, 310–11
   Responsibility of League of Nations for, 325
   Status of under Dual Monarchy, 54–5, 290–1, 404–5, 406
Austria–Hungary, 54–5, 290–1, 404–6
Autonomous zones, 211–14
Azerbaijan, 69, 108, 313

Bahamas, 431
Bahrain, 38, 191–2, 209, 378
Balfour Declaration (1926), 241, 244–6
Baltic States, 64, 131, 419–20
   See also Estonia; Latvia; Lithuania
Bangladesh, 100, 114, 115–17, 135–6, 138, 247, 260, 262

Bantustans:
   in Namibia, 102, 106, 120, 221
   in South Africa, 120, 222–7
Barbados, 431
Barotse Kingdom, 177
Basutoland, 431
Bechuanaland, 208, 431
Belgian Congo: see Congo (Zaire); Congo, Free State of
Belgium, 247, 248, 255, 256, 302, 303, 320–1
Belize: see British Honduras
Belligerency, recognition of, 252–5, 268–9
Belligerent occupation:
   and continuity of statehood, 57–8, 407
   effects on independence of, 59–60, 281–282
Berlin, 273, 274, 275, 278–80, 287
Berlin Conference (1885), 178–9, 183, 199, 201, 207, 305, 317–18
Berlin, Congress of (1878), 303, 305–6, 307
Bermuda, 431
Bessarabia, 303, 305–6, 309, 315
Bhutan, 189
Biafra, 46, 102, 215, 247, 265–6, 269
Boer Republic, 185
Bophuthatswana, 227
Borneo, 137, 138
Botswana, 431
Boznia–Herzegovina, 303
Brazil, 255, 292
British Cameroons, 221, 342–3, 427
British East India Company, 189
British Guiana, 431
British Honduras, 360, 377, 381, 431
British India, 35, 202–3, 406
   See also India; Indian Native States; Pakistan
British Indian Ocean Territory, 377, 382, 435
British Somaliland, 72, 200, 201, 432
   See also Somali Republic
British Togoland, 427
Brunei, 197–8, 206, 363, 369, 432
Buenos Ayres, 249
Bulgaria, 303
Burma, 218

Burundi, 46, 221
Byelorussia, 132–3, 294

Cambodia, 430
Cameroon, Republic of, 342, 366, 395
    See also British Cameroons; French
        Cameroons
Canada, 53, 230–46, 292, 293
Canadian provinces, 294
Cape Verde Islands, 260–1, 434
Castile, 6, 9
Central African Republic, 424, 430
Chad, 430
Chagos Archipelago, 435
Chanak Incident, 244
China, 59, 62, 135, 144–52, 176, 213, 273,
    286, 287, 380–1, 406, 417
    See also Taiwan
Christmas Island, 434
Civil war, laws of war and, 269–70
Cocos (Keeling) Islands, 374, 434
Colombia, 249
Colonial Declaration (G. A. Res. 1514
    (XV)), 89, 357, 367, 377–9
Colonial enclaves, 112, 117–18, 227–8,
    377–85, 412
Colonial protectorates, 175, 198–201, 202,
    205, 207
Commencement of States:
    and 'illegal entities', 391
    generally, 270, 389–90
    in municipal courts, 387–8
    States '*in statu nascendi*', 391–6
Comoro Archipelago, 361, 434
Concert of Europe, 302–8, 324
Confederate States of America, 256
Confederation of North American States
    (1778–87), 292, 388
Confederations of States, 291–4
Congo (Brazzaville), 430
Congo, Free State of, 185
Congo (Zaire), 42–4, 136, 263–5, 393, 429
Congress of Vienna (1815), 302–3, 321
Cook Islands, 138, 295, 372–4, 375, 431
Cracow, Free City of, 161, 302
Crete, 56, 233–7, 304, 305, 306
Criteria for Statehood:
    and continuity of State personality, 402–
        403, 419–20
    and principle of effectiveness, 77–8
    and principles of legality, 78–84
    and *sui generis* entities, 142–3, 294–5, 296
    and treaty stipulations, 120

and unions of States, 288–9
Apartheid and the Bantustans, 120,
    222–7
Capacity to enter into relations with
    other States, 47–8
Civilization, 73
Defined territory, 36–40, 141, 396–9
Government, 42–7, 73, 417
Illegal use of force and, 106–18, 150–1,
    419–20
Independence, 48–71, 225–6, 255–7,
    277
Legal order, 74–6
Montevideo formula, 36
Nature of, 34–5
Non-recognition and, 120–8
Permanence, 71–2, 396
Permanent population, 40–2
Recognition, 74, 151–2, 421–2
Self-determination, 102–6
Sovereignty, 71, 421
Willingness and ability to observe inter-
    national law, 72–3
Croatia, 63–4
Crown (British), 239
Cuba, 56
Cyprus, 44, 53, 71, 118, 166–9, 271, 287,
    432
Czechoslovakia, 58, 63, 313, 390, 398, 408,
    411, 418–19
    See also Slovakia

Dahomey, 429
Danube, European Commission of, 307–8
Danzig, Free City of, 76, 163–6, 191, 309,
    325, 419
Declaration on Principles of International
    Law (G. A. Res 2625 (XXV)), 90,
    110, 220–1, 271–2, 366, 368
Denmark, 133, 290
Devolution, 55, 215–46
Devolution Agreements, 392–4
Dispositive regimes, 315–19
Divided States, 271–87
Djibouti, 377, 430
    See also Afars and Isaas, French Territory
        of
Dominica, 432
    See also West Indies Associated States
Dominions, 55–6, 69, 131, 133, 230–46,
    290, 392
    See also Australia; Canada; Irish Free

State; New Zealand; Newfoundland; South Africa

East Indonesia, 137, 138
East Timor, 369, 384, 435
Egypt, 187, 294–5, 308
  See also United Arab Republic
Enclaves, 384
  See also Colonial Enclaves
Equatorial Guinea: *see* Guinea
Eritrea, 331–2, 428
Estonia, 39, 64, 131, 313, 419–20
Ethiopia, 200, 310, 311, 331–2, 408, 415, 418–19
European Communities, 193, 289, 292, 295–7
Extinction of States:
  and reversion to sovereignty, 412–16
  and use of force, 107, 115, 407, 408
  generally, 309–10, 417–20
  in League of Nations practice, 131–2
  in period 1935–1945, 309–10, 310–11
  of Papal States, 153
  of pre-1945 Germany, 274–5, 287
  See also Identity and Continuity of States

Falkland Islands, 360, 377, 384, 432
Federations of States, 291–4
Fez, Treaty of (1912), 195–6
Fiji, 220, 432
Finland:
  and Treaty of Paris (1856), 316
  establishment in 1917–1918, 22, 44–5, 85–6, 87, 313, 390
  puppet government in (1939–1940), 65
  status before 1917, 22
Fiume, Free City of, 161, 309
Foreign Jurisdiction Acts (U.K.), 192, 199
Formosa: *see* Taiwan
France, 65, 142
  See also French Union
French Caledonia, 370, 431
French Cameroons, 427
French Equatorial Africa, 430
French Establishments in India, 370, 377, 384, 430
French Guiana, 370, 431
French Indochina, 198, 284–5, 430
French Polynesia, 370, 430
French Somaliland: *see* Afars and Isaas, French Territory of; Djibouti
French Togoland, 427
French Union, 230, 429–31

Gabon, 430
Gambia, 217, 432
Gdansk: *see* Danzig
Georgia, 131
German Confederation (1815–66), 292, 302
German Democratic Republic, 263, 273–281
Germany, Federal Republic of, 273–81, 402
Germany (pre-1945), 274–5, 287, 310, 402, 409
Ghana, 432
Gibraltar, 227, 377, 381, 384, 432
Gilbert & Ellice Islands, 433
Goa, 112–13, 319, 370, 435
Gold Coast, 432
Government:
  as criterion for statehood, 42–7
  distinguished from State, 27–9, 160
  insurgents, liability for, 392
  legality of, 84, 266
  local *de facto* governments, 127, 151
  recognition of, 21, 266
Government, change of and State continuity, 405–6
Governments-in-exile, 65, 407, 409
Great Britain: *see* United Kingdom
Greece, 247, 248, 255, 256, 303, 306, 319–320
Greenland, 370, 429
Grenada, 140, 369, 432
  See also West Indies Associated States
Guam, 434
Guinea, 218, 429, 435
Guinea–Bissau, 77, 102, 106, 111, 114, 136, 215, 247, 260–1, 262, 435
Gulf of Tonkin incident, 285–6

Hanover, 290
Hawaii, 370, 434
Hedjaz: *see* Saudi Arabia
Holy See, 35, 152–60
  See also Vatican City
Hong Kong, 377, 380–1, 432
Hungary, 58, 69, 325, 404–5, 406
  See also Austria–Hungary
Hyderabad, 58, 129, 137, 211, 419

Iceland, 290
Identity and Continuity of States:
  and pre-1945 Germany, 280–1, 402
  and reversion to sovereignty, 412–16

Identity and Continuity of States—*cont.*
  general principles of, 270, 400–4
  multiple change, problem of and, 408–
    412
  Poland (1939–1946), 409–12
  specific rules for, 404–8
Ifni, 370, 377, 383, 384, 435
Independence:
  Actual independence, 56–69
  Formal independence, 52–6
  Relation between formal and actual
    independence, 69–71
India, 112–13, 115–17, 131, 132–3, 189,
    218, 244, 292, 293, 364, 365, 383, 392,
    406, 414–15
  See also British India
Indian Native States, 56, 175, 206, 210–11
Indonesia, 129, 137, 247, 258–9, 332–3,
    382, 431
International Court:
  Associated States and, 138
  Parties to Statute, 138–9
International dispositive powers:
  generally, 299, 301–34
  'Germany as a whole', 277–8, 287
International Law Commission:
  and devolution agreements, 393–4
  and reversion to sovereignty, 415–16
  and secession, 267
  and State succession with respect to
    protectorates, 203–5
  and the dispositive/personal distinction,
    319
  attitude to Statehood questions, 31, 35
International legal personality
  and Non-self-governing Territories,
    366–7
  Concept of, 25–6, 196–7, 422
  continuity of, 392
  of Associated States, 375–7
International protectorates, 188, 194–8
Internationalized territories, 70, 160–9
Inter se doctrine, 239–40, 243
Intervention, 113–14, 114–18, 144, 252–5,
    270
Ionian Islands, 208
Iran, 68–9, 191
  See also Azerbaijan
Iraq, 135, 337, 426
Ireland, 230, 235, 238, 239, 243
Israel, 23, 37–8, 40, 185, 247, 389, 392,
    406, 426
  See also Palestine

Italian Somaliland, 72, 331–2, 336, 428
  See also Somali Republic
Italy:
  and Trieste dispute, 162–3
  colonies in Africa, 315, 330–2, 428
  continuity of with Sardinia–Piedmont,
    404
Ivory Coast, 429

Jamaica, 432
Japanese Peace Treaty (1951), 144–5,
    147–8, 282–3, 348, 428
Jerusalem, 166, 333
Jordan, 338–9, 426
Jus Cogens:
  and extinction of States, 420
  Charter Art. 2(4) as, 106–7, 168, 419–
    420
  generally, 79–83
  racial non-discrimination as, 227
  self-determination as, 81

Kashmir, 211
Katanga, 247, 263–5, 267
Kelantan, 61–2
Kenya, 432
Knights of Malta: *see* Order of St. John of
    Jerusalem
Korea, Democratic People's Republic, 23,
    247, 248, 263, 281–4, 285, 286–7
Korea, Republic of, 281–4, 285, 286–7,
    299
Korean War, 144, 282, 283, 284
Kowloon, 363, 380, 432
Kutch, 202–3
Kuwait, 38, 135, 191–2, 205–6

Laos, 430
Lateran Treaty (1929), 153, 154, 155, 156
Latvia, 39, 64, 131, 313, 419–20
Lausanne, Treaty of (1923), 244–5, 308,
    315, 426
Lauterpacht, theory of recognition, 17–20
Laws of war, 269–70
League of Nations:
  dispositive powers of, 325
  Dominion membership of, 243–4
  Membership practice, 131–2
  revocation of Mandates, 344–8
Lebanon, 66–8, 337–8, 339, 426
Leeward Islands, 432
  See also: Anguilla; West Indies Associ-
    ated States

Lesotho, 431
Liberia, 185
Libya, 299, 325–6, 331–2, 428
Liechtenstein, 131, 139, 140, 190, 208, 422
Lithuania, 39–40, 131, 313, 419–20
Locarno, Treaty of (1925), 244, 245
London, Treaty of (1913), 236, 306–7
Lotus presumption, 33, 165, 166, 350, 355

Macao, 377, 380–1, 435
Madagascar, 415–16, 430
Malawi, 433
Malay States, 198
  See also Brunei; Kelantan
Malaya: *see* Malaysia
Malaysia, 219, 370, 404, 432
Maldives, 140, 198
Mali Federation, 72, 292, 429
Malta, 432
Malvinas: *see* Falkland Islands
Manchukuo: *see* Manchuria
Manchuria, 59–60, 62, 107–8, 114, 115,
  122, 143, 391
Mandate System:
  Albania, proposal for, 304
  and Dominions, 243
  and self-determination, 92, 96, 335
  'C' Mandates, status of, 95
  continuity of personality and, 406
  creation of, 299, 309, 314–15, 335
  effect of termination of League of
    Nations, 316, 340–1
  League of Nations supervision of, 325
  list of, 426–8
  revocation of by League of Nations,
    344–8
  revocation of by United Nations organs,
    350–5
  sovereignty and, 336, 350, 355
  termination of Mandates, 66–7, 337–41
  termination of system, 309, 340–1
  United Nations supervision of, 316,
    326–7
Maratha Empire, 176, 383, 414–15
Mauritania, 38, 378, 380, 382–4, 415, 429
'Mauritanian entity', 288, 378, 382–4, 415
Mauritius, 222, 433, 435
Mayotte, 361, 377, 382, 434
Memel Territory, 160, 163, 309
Mexico, 249
Micronesia: *see* Northern Marianas; Pa-
  cific Islands Strategic Trusteeship
Micro-States, 139–41

Moldavia, 303
Monaco, 36, 56, 140, 193–4, 208, 308, 412
Mongolia, 68, 212
Monroe Doctrine, 251
Montenegro, 303, 418
Morocco, 66, 177, 194–7, 202, 207, 218,
  308, 378, 380, 384, 392, 430
Mozambique, 111, 260, 435
Muscat and Oman, 135, 192, 207, 209,
  213, 369, 433

Namibia:
  as Chapter XI territory, 94, 95
  bantustans in, 102, 106, 120, 221
  continuation of Mandate after 1946,
    316, 340–1
  history of, 336, 428
  non-recognition of South African ad-
    ministration, 124–8, 319
  revocation of Mandate for, 350–5
  United Nations supervision of, 326–7,
    355
National liberation movements, 267, 269
  See also Governments-in-exile; Guinea
    Bissau; Polish National Committee
Nationality, 40–2
Native communities, 176–84
Nauru, 36, 40, 138, 428
Nejd: *see* Saudi Arabia
Nepal, 189–90, 218
Netherlands, 9, 129, 302, 320–1
Netherlands Antilles, 370, 431
Netherlands Union, 230
Neuilly, Treaty of (1919), 308
New Guinea (Trust Territory), 335, 348,
  427
New Hebrides, 434
New Zealand, 180, 372–3
Newfoundland, 238, 239
Niger, 429
Nigeria, 433
Niue, 138, 295, 374, 375, 431
Non-Self-Governing Territories:
  ambit in practice of, 360–1
  and non-colonial territories, 362–3
  and self-determination, 92–3, 96–8,
    357–8
  and 'sovereignty', 363–4, 380–1
  and use of force, 364–6
  criteria for, 93–4
  definition of, 358–60, 362–3
  East Pakistan as, 116–17
  establishment under Chapter XI, 356–7

Non-Self-Governing Territories—*cont.*
   forms of self-government, 369–84
   legal personality, 366–7
   list of, 429–36
   Rhodesia as, 104
   termination of Chapter XI status, 367–384
North Borneo: *see* Sabah
Northern Marianas, 336
   See also Pacific Islands Strategic Trusteeship
Northern Rhodesia, 433
Nyasaland, 433

Oman, *see* Muscat and Oman
Oppenheim, constitutive theory of, 12–15, 88
Order of St. John of Jerusalem, 26, 155, 160
Organization of African Unity, 265
Osimo, Treaty of (1975), 163
Ottoman Empire: *see* Turkey
Outer Mongolia: *see* Mongolia

Pacific Islands Mandate, 340, 347–8, 428
Pacific Islands Strategic Trusteeship, 336, 349–50, 428
Pakistan, 115–17, 406
Palestine, 221, 247, 331, 340, 392, 406, 426
Panama Canal Zone, 360, 363, 377, 381, 434
Papua, 429
Papua New-Guinea, 427, 429
   See also New Guinea (Trust Territory)
Paris Agreements (1973), 285, 287
Paris, Treaty of (1856), 303, 305, 307, 316
Peace Treaties, dispositions anticipatory of, 312–13
Persia: *see* Iran
Personality: *see* International legal personality
Philippines, 131, 132, 393
Pitcairn Islands, 433
Poland:
   and Danzig, 163–6
   and Yalta Conference, 133, 310, 312, 391
   continuity of after 1918, 408, 415
   continuity of after 1945, 407, 409–12
   'extinction' in 1939, 19, 311–12
   in 1918–1919, 17, 312–13, 322–3, 390, 394

   third partition of (1795), 302
Polish National Committee, 312, 390–1, 394
Portugal:
   African colonies, 111–12, 113, 136, 260–261
   Chapter XI territories, 360–1
   Indian enclaves, 112–13, 364, 365, 377, 384
   secession from Spain, 9, 413
   secession of Brazil from, 255
   See also: East Timor
Postliminium, 412–13
Prescription, 78–9
Principal Allied and Associated Powers, 308, 314–15, 345
Protected States, 61–2, 188–94, 311
Protectorates, 61–2, 164, 186–214
   See also Colonial Protectorates; International Protectorates; Protected States
Pueblo incident, 284
Puerto Rico, 295, 361, 371–2, 434
Puppet States and Governments, 62–5, 108, 119, 311, 391, 410–11

Qatar, 191–2

Racial discrimination, 223, 226–7
Rann of Kutch, 202–3
Real Union, 159
Recognition:
   and extinction of States, 420
   and international organizations, 127
   and municipal courts, 15–16, 61–2
   as a subsidiary criterion for statehood, 74, 194, 196
   Collective recognition, 78, 319–23
   conditional recognition, 322–3
   constitutive theory, 17–20, 104–5, 252
   de facto recognition, 21
   de jure recognition, 21
   declaratory theory, 20–3
   early view of, 10–11
   effect of positivist theory on, 12–15
   legal effects of, 23–5, 74, 421–2
   metropolitan recognition of secession, 248–51
   non-recognition, 120–8, 276–7, 337–8
   of belligerency, 252–5, 268–9
   of continuity of pre-1945 Germany, 274–5
   of insurgency, 268–9

relevance to problems of identity and
continuity, 403–4, 406
retrospectivity of, 387–91
third party recognition of secession, 252,
255–7
United Kingdom position, 16
United States position, 67, 218
whether duty to recognize, 16
Representation in international affairs,
190–1, 204, 232, 240, 245
Residual sovereignty, 211–14
Reunion, 370
Reversion of sovereignty, 193, 412–16
Revolution:
distinguished from secession, 215, 247
effect on State continuity, 28, 247, 405–
406
recognition of revolutionary change of
government, 266
Rhodesia:
and non-recognition, 123–4, 319
as Chapter XI territory, 361, 362, 436
effect of non-recognition, 78
grant of independence to, 220, 391
legality of U.D.I., 267
status before U.D.I., 237, 246, 361
whether a State, 77, 103–6, 130, 219
Romania, 301, 303, 305–6, 307–8, 309
Ruanda, 46, 221

Saar Territory, 160–1, 309, 325
Sabah, 370, 433
Salò, Italian Republic of, 72
Samoa, 73, 177
See also American Samoa: Western
Samoa
Samos, 56, 208, 233–7
San Marino, 40, 138, 139, 140, 189–90,
193, 208
São João Batista de Ajudà, 370, 377, 435
São Tomé, Principe and Dependencies,
435
Sarawak, 370, 433
Sardinia–Piedmont, 404
Saudi Arabia, 313
Secession, 9–10, 215, 247–70, 281–4, 284–
285, 309, 361, 374, 390
See also Revolution
Self-determination:
and *jus cogens*, 81
and laws of war, 270
and statehood, 102–6, 219–22, 257–63,
277

and use of force, 108–18
colonial enclaves and, 378–84
conclusion as to, 95–102
consequences of, 94–5
criteria for 'peoples', 91–4
Formosa and, 152
generally, 84–106, 205
Mandate system and, 92, 96, 335
Non-self-governing territories and, 92–
93, 357–8, 363–6, 366–7, 372, 376
Trusteeship system and, 92, 96, 335
Senegal, 218, 429
Serb–Croat–Slovene State:
See Yugoslavia
Serbia, 72, 303, 305, 409
See also Yugoslavia
Sèvres, Treaty of (1920), 308
Seychelles, 433, 435
Shanghai, International Settlement of, 161
Sierra Leone, 216–17, 433
Sikkim, 198, 363
Simla Convention (1914), 213
Sind, 202–3
Singapore, 369, 370, 433
Slovakia, 63
Solomon Islands, 200, 433
Somali Republic, 72, 200, 377
See also Afars and Isaas, French Territory
of; British Somaliland; Italian
Somaliland
South Africa:
and administration of Namibia, 350–5
and Chapter XI of the Charter, 362–3
devolution of, 230–46
bantustans in, 120, 222–7
See also Namibia
South African Republic, 408
South West Africa: *see* Namibia
South Yemen, People's Republic of, 200,
207, 431
Southern Rhodesia: *see* Rhodesia
Sovereign Order of Malta: *see* Order of St.
John of Jerusalem
Sovereignty:
and devolution, 232–7
and international dispositive powers,
314
and Mandated and Trust territories,
336
and Non-self-governing territories,
363–364, 380–1
as criterion for statehood, 71, 196, 421
concept of, 26–7

Sovereignty—*cont.*
  different meanings of distinguished, 26, 27, 32
  reversion to, 412–16
Soviet Union, 15, 85, 132–3, 244, 309, 389, 405, 406
Spain:
  and Chapter XI territories, 360–1
  and South American provinces, 10, 247, 249–52, 253
  Civil War in, 29, 269
Spanish Sahara: *see* Western Sahara
'Special treaty relations', 209
Spheres of influence, 214
St. Germain-en-Laye, Treaty of (1919), 49–51, 308, 318
St. Lucia, 433
  See also West Indies Associated States
St. Vincent, 433
  See also West Indies Associated States
State Succession:
  and dispositive treaties, 319
  and illegal use of force, 107
  and passing of State property, 228
  and reversion to sovereignty, 414
  and socialist revolutions, 406
  devolution agreements, 392–4
  distinguished from State personality, 29–30, 392, 400–4
  Divided States and, 273
  Dominions and, 240
  pre-1945 Germany and, 280–1
  protectorates and, 203–5, 392
  unions of States and, 289
  Vietnam and, 286
  See also Identity and Continuity of States
Statehood:
  and acquisition of territory, 396–9
  and devolution, 215–46
  and functional interpretation, 130, 133
  and government, 27–9
  and illegal use of force, 106–18
  and *Lotus* presumption, 33, 165, 166, 350, 354–5
  and secession, 247–70
  and self-determination, 102–6, 108–18
  and United Nations Charter, 129–30, 137–8, 139
  as a claim of right, 119, 151–2
  as a legal concept, 3–5, 14, 31–4, 422
  Bantustans and, 222–7
  consequences of, 31–4

constituent States of federations, 291–2
'Dependent States', 186–214, 421
distinguished from State succession, 29–30
Divided States, 271–87
  early doctrine of, 5–9
  equality of, 32
  matter of fact, not law, 3–5, 14
  Micro-States, 139–41
  'modes' of creation, 171, 422–3
  non-recognition of, 120–8
  of international protectorates, 196
  See also Commencement of States; Criteria for Statehood; Devolution; Extinction of States; Identity and Continuity of States; Secession; State Succession
Statute of Westminster (1931), 232, 241–2
Sudan, Anglo-Egyptian, 271
Surinam, 369, 370, 431
Suzerainty, 209–11
Swaziland, 176–7, 200, 205, 207, 219, 433
Switzerland, 139, 292, 302
Syria, 66–8, 294–5, 337–8, 339, 402–3, 407–8, 426

Taiwan, 56, 77, 79, 108, 119, 143–52, 286
  See also China
Tanganyika, 427
Tangier, International City of, 161
Tanzania, 433
Terra nullius, 148–9, 173, 174, 178–80
Territory, acquisition by new State, 396–399
  See also Criteria for Statehood
Territory, loss of and State continuity, 404
Thailand, 176
Tibet, 212–13, 261–2
Timor: *see* East Timor
Tokelau Islands, 431
Tonga, 177, 191
Transjordan: *see* Jordan
Transkei, 120, 222–7
  See also Bantustans
Trianon, Treaty of (1920), 308
Trieste, Free City of, 161–3, 309, 329–30
Trinidad and Tobago, 433
Trucial States of Oman, 191–2
Trusteeship system:
  and self-determination, 92, 96, 335
  continuity of personality and, 406
  creation of, 299, 309, 335, 341
  legal effects of termination, 342–4

legal interests in, 366
list of territories, 426–8
revocation of, 348–50
scope of, 93, 426–8
'sovereignty' and, 336, 350, 355
termination of Trusteeship status, 341
Tunisia, 197, 392, 430
Turkey:
and Concert of Europe, 305–6
and Cyprus, 118
continuity with Ottoman Empire, 404
devolution of Empire, 230, 233–7
Treaty of Paris and, 13, 176
Turkish Federated State of Cyprus, 118
Tuvalu, 433

Uganda, 433
Ukraine, 131, 132–3, 294, 313
Unions of States:
and international organizations, 295–7
Associated States as, 295
confederation, 291–4
federation, 291–4
personal union, 9, 290–1
problems of classification of, 288–9, 294–
295
real union, 290–1
United Arab Emirates, 135, 191, 219
United Arab Republic, 294–5, 407
United Kingdom, 9, 16, 103–4, 230–46,
290, 404
United Nations:
admission to membership, 133–7, 319,
322
and Korean conflict, 282–4
and Micro-States, 139–41
and Non-self-governing territories, 356–
384
and principle of self-determination, 89–
91
and sovereignty of Member States, 55
and termination of Chapter XI status,
368–9
and West Irian, 332–3
Articles 32, 35(2) and, 137–8
as Government of Namibia, 355
competence to make territorial dispositions, 323–4, 325–33
General Assembly, status of resolutions,
90–1, 328, 342–4
international responsibility of, 34
Jerusalem and, 333
legal personality of, 25–6

membership of Vatican, 156
original membership, 132–3
peacekeeping, 43–4, 168, 264–5
representation of China in, 145–6
revocation of Mandates by, 350–5
revocation of Trusteeships by, 348–50
Security Council, status of resolutions,
127, 328–9
specialized agencies, membership, 139
Table of membership, 135
Trieste and, 162, 329–30
United States of America:
as a federation, 292, 293
Civil War, 253, 254, 256
War of Independence, 247, 249
Upper Volta, 429
Use of force, rules relating to:
and Cyprus, 168
and extinction of statehood, 107, 115,
407, 408
and Non-self-governing territories, 364–
366
and self-determination, 108–18, 364–6
as criterion for statehood, 106–18, 150–
151
as *jus cogens*, 106–7
in secession conflicts, 266–8

Vassal States, 159, 209–11
Vatican City, 36, 40, 133, 140, 152 60
See also Holy See
Venezuela, 257
Versailles, Treaty of (1919), 54, 243–4,
307, 308, 310, 313, 317, 427
Vienna, Congress of (1815): *see* Congress
of Vienna
Vietnam, Democratic People's Republic,
65, 136, 247, 248, 259, 262, 284–6,
287
Vietnam, Republic of, 65, 134, 136, 284–
286, 287, 430
Vietnam, Socialist Republic of, 136, 284,
286
Virgin Islands, 434

Waitangi, Treaty of (1840), 180, 183
Wallachia, 303
West Indies Associated States, 194, 361,
374–5
West Irian, 332–3, 368, 370, 377, 382, 431
Western Sahara, 181, 288, 358, 369, 370,
378–84, 415, 436

Western Samoa, 141, 190, 295, 428
Wheaton, view of recognition, 8
World War II, termination of, 274

Yalta Conference, 132, 133, 312, 391, 409,
410

Yemen, 72, 218, 262
Yugoslavia, 72, 162–3, 313, 409
    See also Croatia; Serbia

Zambia, 433
Zanzibar, 177, 197, 198, 433